Strategic Brand Management in the Age of AI and Disruption

Zahid Hussain
Khadim Ali Shah Institute of Technology (KASBIT), Karachi, Pakistan

Mohamad-Noor Salehhuddin Sharipudin
Universiti Putra Malaysia, Malaysia

Ahmad Albattat
Management and Science University, Malaysia

Arman Khan
Shaheed Benazir Bhutto University, Pakistan

IGI Global
Scientific Publishing
Publishing Tomorrow's Research Today

Published in the United States of America by
IGI Global Scientific Publishing
701 East Chocolate Avenue
Hershey, PA, 17033, USA
Tel: 717-533-8845
Fax: 717-533-8661
Website: https://www.igi-global.com E-mail: cust@igi-global.com

Library of Congress Cataloging-in-Publication Data

Names: Hussain, Zahid, 1996- editor. | Sharipudin, Mohamad-Noor Salehhuddin, 1980- editor. | Albattat, Ahmad, 1973- editor. | Khan, Arman, 1989- editor.
Title: Strategic brand management in the age of AI and disruption / edited by Zahid Hussain, Mohamad-Noor Salehhuddin Sharipudin, Ahmad Albattat, Arman Khan.
Description: Hershey, PA : IGI Global Scientific Publishing, [2025] | Includes bibliographical references and index. | Summary: "This book is an essential guide for navigating the complexities of modern brand management amid technological and market upheavals. This book highlights the pivotal role artificial intelligence plays in reshaping brand strategies and offers a blueprint for leveraging these advancements to achieve business success"-- Provided by publisher.
Identifiers: LCCN 2024055544 (print) | LCCN 2024055545 (ebook) | ISBN 9798369394618 (hardcover) | ISBN 9798369394625 (paperback) | ISBN 9798369394632 (ebook)
Subjects: LCSH: Product management. | Artificial intelligence--Financial applications.
Classification: LCC HF5415.15 .S78 2025 (print) | LCC HF5415.15 (ebook) | DDC 658.500285--dc23/eng/20250205
LC record available at https://lccn.loc.gov/2024055544
LC ebook record available at https://lccn.loc.gov/2024055545

British Cataloguing in Publication Data
A Cataloguing in Publication record for this book is available from the British Library.

Table of Contents

Detailed Table of Contents

The rapid development of digital technology has introduced a new order of large-scale change within brand management in the fast-changing landscape of the digital marketplace. This chapter provides the fundamental principles of brand management within the digital era and demonstrates the transformation of building brands via online platforms, data analytics, and digital technologies. Others might state that social media, e-commerce, and AI integration offer brands a new horizon for managing brand equity, improving customer engagement, and creating experiences to adapt to changing tastes. Adjustment towards this change can prove challenging for the brands, but on the other hand, they are opening new possibilities that drive innovation in performance and strategy about their brands.

This proactive approach helps brands stay ahead of market trends and respond more effectively to changes in consumer preferences.AI-driven content creation is transforming how brands develop and deliver their messaging. Natural Language Processing (NLP) and Generative AI models can automate the creation of written content, such as social media posts, blog articles, and email campaigns. These AI tools can generate content that aligns with a brand's tone and style while optimizing for engagement and relevance. For instance, AI can analyze past successful content to identify key elements that resonate with audiences and use this information to create new, impactful content. This capability not only streamlines content production but also ensures that messaging remains consistent and effective across various platforms.Customer service and engagement have also been significantly enhanced, 24/7 support to customers, handling inquiries, resolving issues, and guiding users through processes.

The way organizations monitor and control brand performance has been significantly changed by the digital environment. Even though they are useful, traditional measurements frequently miss real-time changes in the market. AI-powered solutions are becoming essential resources in order to tackle this, providing a more precise and up-to-date view of brand health. This chapter explores how artificial intelligence (AI) is transforming brand performance evaluation. It does so by examining important metrics, analytics techniques, and particular AI solutions that are revolutionizing the market. Artificial intelligence (AI) enables organizations to make data-driven decisions with previously unheard-of speed and precision, from assessing brand awareness and consumer loyalty to forecasting future trends. In today's quickly changing digital landscape, marketers, analysts, and company executives can obtain a competitive advantage by comprehending how AI tools can improve brand performance evaluation.

The origin of a brand, its development, and its transformation over the last centuries under the influence of economic, social, and cultural processes are tightly interrelated. It started with a sign of craftsmanship in the past and nowadays has a status of a cultural asset: the concept of a brand develops with time along with globalization, technological advancements, and the shift in consumer trends. It is interesting to know the development and the rise of the brand concept, as it helps to explain why brands in the modern world are able to create value equity, differentiation, and attraction of audiences, which is relevant to today's conditions.

Recommender systems are crucial for brand amplification in the digital age, leveraging AI to provide personalized recommendations that enhance engagement and loyalty. Analyzing user behavior, they suggest products and content that align with individual preferences, driving user engagement and boosting conversion rates (e.g., Amazon's deep learning-powered recommendations increased conversion by 35%). This personalized approach fosters stronger connections between brands and customers, leading to increased customer lifetime value and enhanced brand loyalty. This study explores the multifaceted applications of recommender systems in driving brand success, focusing on personalization, engagement, customer journey optimization, and brand storytelling. Ethical considerations and future trends are also addressed, emphasizing transparency, fairness, and responsible implementation to ensure user privacy and avoid algorithmic bias.

This chapter explores the transformative role of Artificial Intelligence (AI) in branding, focusing on how AI-driven tools like machine learning, predictive analytics, and chatbots are reshaping brand communication, personalization, and consumer engagement. It examines the shift from traditional branding to AI-enhanced strategies leveraging real-time data to anticipate customer needs and delivering highly personalized experiences, fostering brand loyalty and deeper consumer connections. Key benefits, such as improved customer retention, enhanced engagement, and smarter decision-making, are discussed alongside ethical considerations, including data privacy, transparency, and bias in AI algorithms. The chapter also highlights practical applications of AI in monitoring customer sentiment, optimizing interactions, and adapting brand messaging dynamically. Concluding with a look at future trends like AI-powered voice assistants and AR, offering insights for businesses to leverage AI responsibly, ensuring personalization, ethical practices, consumer trust, and long-term success.

The intersection of technology and branding has initiated a new chapter for the tourism sector, wherein artificial intelligence (AI) occupies a central position. This shift is manifested in AIs capacity to scrutinize extensive datasets, allowing businesses to discern nascent trends and consumer inclinations with an unparalleled accuracy. By utilizing AI, tourism brands can proffer personalized experiences that resonate with specific travelers, thereby nurturing enhanced emotional connections and brand loyalty. The enhancement of customer engagement through focused marketing strategies can result in noteworthy brand distinction amid a crowded marketplace. Therefore, comprehending AIs multifaceted repercussions on branding methodologies becomes crucial for tourism organizations that seek to succeed within a competitive context. Furthermore, AIs impact on branding transcends basic data evaluation; it influences the foundational nature of customer engagements.

based on AI, and disruption by the technology. Employing a structural equation modeling technique, we evaluate empirical data to investigate the direct and indirect impacts of brand strategy adaptation on disruption by the technology, with Branding based on AI serving as a mediator. The outcomes manifested that the sustainable adaptation of brand strategies noteworthy augments the efficacy of Branding based on AI, which subsequently augments innovation and agility in response to technological changes. The findings demonstrate partial mediation, implying that while strategies for brand adaptation have a direct effect on disruption by the technology, the incorporation of AI enhances this influence. These findings highlight the significance of adaptability and technology in branding strategies, providing useful insights for executives aiming to maneuver through the challenges of digital market places. The investigation wraps up with suggestions for future studies, stressing the necessity for exploration into particular AI technologies and the impact on branding approaches.

AI has become a transformative force in branding, changing firms' approach to relating to their customers and creating brands. Chapter-specific: AI is used differently for branding because delivering personalized customer experiences, generating dynamic content, and optimizing consumer engagements through data-driven insights play a considerable role. AI technologies like machine learning and predictive analytics help brands understand consumer behavior and, therefore, really segment and target marketing activity. This chapter also highlights AI's operational efficiency in brand management, automating customer interactions, and analyzing the sentiment of a consumer in real time. In addition, it establishes how AI affects innovation in branding by providing scope for adaptive and responsive strategies for brands that help keep up the ever-increasing dynamic pace of an ever-changing digital marketplace. The research is a critical insight for brand strategists, marketers, and businesses looking to leverage AI for more robust and resilient brands as age of digital disruption moves on.

The aftermath of COVID-19, the widespread adoption of AI-based technological innovations, and new social challenges have reflected changes in consumer behavior, prompting us to re-explore the concept of brand love. This study focuses on updating what we know about consumer-brand relationships and exploring brand features and attributes that trigger brand love. We look particularly into brand communication, the consumers' perception, and how it relates to brand love. A quantitative method was chosen, and an online survey of 405 consumers was conducted. The results stress the difficulty in identifying specific brand features that prompt or nurture brand love, as our 405 participants mentioned 157 different brands as the ones they love the most. Hedonistic aspects that compose pleasurable brand experiences stand out as triggers of brand love. However, surprisingly, there are few luxury brands loved by our sample who are more committed to the brands present in their daily lives. Brand communication may not be a determinant for prompting brand love, but it's pivotal in nurturing it.

This approach transcends traditional metrics, offering a more nuanced understanding of consumer behavior, brand impact, and market dynamics.Traditional methods often rely on periodic surveys and historical data, which can be limited in scope and slow to capture emerging trends. In contrast, AI systems can continuously ingest data from diverse sources, including social media, online reviews, and sales transactions, enabling brands to gain immediate and comprehensive insights into their performance. This involves natural language processing (NLP) techniques that interpret the emotional tone and context of written content. For example, an AI system might detect a surge in positive sentiment following a successful marketing campaign or identify emerging issues from negative feedback before they escalate. This real-time analysis allows brands to respond more swiftly and effectively to changes in public perception. This enables brands to tailor their strategies with greater precision, targeting specific segments with personalized messages and offers.

This chapter discusses the disruptive nature of artificial intelligence in strategic brand management, particularly how it can enable a personalized engagement with customers. It considers just how AI allows for easy navigation of complex consumer data to deliver a tailored experience aligned with changing customer expectations. This chapter describes AI-driven tools such as machine learning, predictive analytics, and recommendation engines that enable brands to segment audiences in real-time, predict behaviors, and tailor content for higher resonance. Operational efficiency through AI is also detailed—how it can use chatbots in automating customer interactions and develop data-driven decisions that enhance responsiveness as well as customer satisfaction. In fact, the author touched upon the long-term effects that artificial intelligence will cause on loyalty and trust towards a brand, with the emphasis on the continued refinement of personalization strategies.

In the face of growing environmental concerns, such as global warming, climate change, and pollution, conscious consumerism and sustainable consumption have emerged as critical imperatives. These challenges have prompted businesses to adopt green marketing—an eco-friendly approach to the marketing mix that addresses both consumer concerns and environmental impact. Green marketing is increasingly recognized in developed countries, but it has recently gained traction in developing nations like India. This shift in focus has also sparked a trend in influencer marketing, where brands partner with prominent vloggers to promote green products on social media platforms like TikTok and Instagram. Such strategies have significant influence, especially on younger audiences who often lack the critical thinking skills to evaluate advertisements effectively.

This chapter explores the transformative potential of recommender systems for predictive analytics in brand management, emphasizing the crucial role of data-driven insights in shaping strategic decisions and driving sustainable growth. We analyze how AI-powered recommender systems can be leveraged to forecast consumer demand, identify emerging market trends, and proactively opportunities in a dynamic business environment. We will delve into the mathematical underpinnings of predictive analytics, exploring time series modeling and machine learning algorithms used in recommender systems. We will also discuss the role of big data and data visualization in informing strategic brand decisions, showcasing how these techniques can reveal hidden patterns, identify customer segments, and optimize resource allocation. Finally, this chapter will address the ethical considerations of predictive analytics, examining the potential for algorithmic bias and the erosion of consumer trust, and proposing strategies for ensuring fairness and accountability in AI-driven brand management.

User-generated content (UGC) is becoming common in wine tourism. People create texts, videos, and pictures to share online and inform others about their experiences at wine destinations. UGC, coupled with managerial creativity and innovation, are essential to the growth of wineries as they offer insights into tourists' tastes and preferences, enhance brand awareness and reach and build trust between visitors and wine destinations. As popular wine tourism destinations, TripAdvisor comments published by tourists who visited Portugal, New Zealand, and the United States were copied and examined using Power BI and Orange. The wine industry commands a significant market value, while wine tourism is a substantial component of economic development in wine-producing countries. Also, the study revealed some tourists prefer to keep their identities hidden during online reviews. Seasonality is another issue that affects tourist destinations globally. The study concluded wine tourists will travel either domestically or abroad to wine destinations that offer the best services and experiences.

The beginning of the digital revolution has significantly changed advertising and different management activities, mainly caused by easy access to enormous quantities of digitally transformed data and the incorporation of artificial intelligence (AI). The objective of this research is to investigate the effect of artificial intelligence-driven personalization (ADP) on customer Experience (CX) within the backdrop of Instagram, an influential social networking forum identified because of its novel implementation of AI. Instagram uses AI to evaluate user actions and choices, providing customized content that improves users enjoyment and fulfillment.

This chapter explores the incorporation of Artificial Intelligence (AI) in branding, particularly within the Indian market. It analyzes the impact of AI technology on branding strategies, improving consumer engagement, and addressing the problems encountered by Indian firms in embracing these breakthroughs. The study offers practical insights into AI applications in many sectors, identifying obstacles to effective implementation and providing strategic recommendations for brands aiming to optimize AI's potential. The findings indicate that, although AI presents substantial prospects to enhance brand equity, its effective implementation requires a strategic strategy that meticulously addresses technological, ethical, and consumer-related concerns.

The integration of AI into customer experience strategies is revolutionizing the way businesses engage with their customers. This chapter explores how AI-powered personalization is transforming customer journeys by delivering tailored, real-time interactions that resonate with individual preferences and behaviors. From recommendation engines and predictive analytics to natural language processing and dynamic content, AI technologies are enabling companies to offer highly relevant experiences at every stage of the customer lifecycle. By examining key AI concepts, real-world case studies and current trends, this chapter highlights critical role of AI in shaping the future of customer experience. Additionally, the ethical considerations, including data privacy and algorithmic bias, will be addressed, providing a balanced perspective on the opportunities and challenges of AI-driven personalization. This chapter will equip business leaders, marketers, and customer experience professionals with insights into how AI can drive engagement, foster customer loyalty, and deliver business growth

Preface

In the fast-paced, ever-evolving landscape of brand management, the integration of Artificial Intelligence (AI) has ushered in unprecedented shifts in strategy and execution. As the digital age accelerates, brands are no longer solely defined by their logos or physical presence but by their ability to engage, adapt, and innovate in response to an increasingly data-driven and technology-powered environment. *Strategic Brand Management in the Age of AI and Disruption* delves into the profound transformations reshaping brand management, offering insights and case studies that illuminate the future of branding in an era dominated by AI and digital disruption.

This book brings together an esteemed group of scholars from across the globe to explore how AI tools and techniques are redefining brand strategies, enabling businesses to not only survive but thrive in a landscape where consumer behavior, technological advancements, and market dynamics are constantly in flux. From the application of AI in content creation to the role of recommender systems in enhancing brand loyalty, each chapter contributes to a comprehensive understanding of how AI is influencing the very essence of brand management.

CHAPTER OVERVIEW

Chapter 1: Introduction to Brand Management in the Digital Age

Praveen Patel and Jasmine Kaur provide a foundational overview of the principles of brand management in the digital era, exploring how platforms like social media, e-commerce, and AI are reshaping the way brands are built and managed.

Chapter 2: Understanding Artificial Intelligence and Its Role in Branding

Selvakumar P. and his colleagues delve into how AI-driven content creation and customer service are revolutionizing brand messaging, engagement, and customer relationships, offering brands the tools to stay ahead of the curve.

Chapter 3: Role of AI Tools in Evaluating Brand Performance

Suryansh Chauhan and Shivani Thapliyal examine the pivotal role of AI in assessing brand performance, from brand awareness to consumer loyalty, demonstrating how AI can provide real-time, actionable insights for businesses.

Chapter 4: Brand Management via AI - What Are the Odds?

Tareq Hashem, Ahmad Albattat, Anuj Kumar, and Sadfa El-Taher analyze the historical evolution of branding and the transformative impact of AI on brand value creation and audience attraction in a globalized, tech-driven world.

Chapter 5: Harnessing Recommender Systems for Brand Amplification

Mohamed Badouch and his team explore how AI-powered recommender systems help brands personalize experiences and drive engagement, improving conversion rates and fostering long-term customer loyalty.

Chapter 6: Understanding Artificial Intelligence and Its Major Role in Branding

Alex Sajan and Pratibha Giri delve deeper into the mechanics of AI in branding, focusing on its ability to drive customer retention and brand loyalty through personalized experiences and real-time data analysis.

Chapter 7: Artificial Intelligence's Impact on Branding in Tourism

Serkan Gün explores how AI is reshaping branding strategies in the tourism sector, enhancing customer engagement and loyalty through personalized marketing and tailored experiences.

Chapter 8: Adapting Brand Strategies to Technological Disruption by Mediation of AI-driven Branding in Horn of Africa

Shashi Kant and colleagues investigate how AI is mediating the adaptation of brand strategies in response to technological disruptions in the Horn of Africa, providing insights into the role of innovation and agility in branding.

Chapter 9: Understanding Artificial Intelligence and Its Impact on Branding

Priyansh Bagga and Jasmine Kaur explore how AI technologies such as machine learning and predictive analytics are revolutionizing brand management, enabling brands to adapt to consumer behavior shifts with greater precision.

Chapter 10: I (Brand) Love You: Why Consumers Fall in Love with Brands and How They Express Their Love

Alexandre Duarte and Patrícia Dias examine the complex emotional connection between consumers and brands, emphasizing how AI can enhance the consumer-brand relationship and foster deep emotional bonds that drive brand loyalty.

As you journey through these chapters, you will gain a comprehensive understanding of the profound impact AI is having on the way brands are conceptualized, managed, and experienced. This book is a timely resource for marketing professionals, brand strategists, and researchers seeking to harness the power of AI to build resilient and innovative brands in the face of ongoing digital disruption. The contributors' diverse perspectives offer invaluable insights into the challenges and opportunities brands face in an AI-driven world, preparing you to navigate the exciting future of strategic brand management.

Chapter 11: Measuring Brand Performance with AI Tools

Authors Ansuman Samal, Jajjara Bhargav, Manikandan S.K., Selvakumar P., Mohit Sharma, Manjunath T.C. explore the transformative impact of AI tools on brand performance measurement. By enabling real-time analysis of data from social media, online reviews, and sales transactions, AI systems provide brands with the ability to detect shifts in sentiment and market trends quickly. This allows brands to adjust strategies effectively, ensuring timely and targeted engagement with customers.

Chapter 12: Leveraging AI for Personalized Customer Experiences

Shivani Thapliyal and Raghav Bindal examines how AI-driven technologies, such as machine learning and recommendation engines, enable brands to deliver highly personalized customer experiences. By analyzing consumer behavior and preferences in real-time, businesses can optimize interactions, increase satisfaction, and foster long-term loyalty, all while enhancing operational efficiency.

Chapter 13: Integrating AI, Green Marketing, and Influencer Strategies: Shaping Sustainable Consumer Behavior in the Digital Age

Ridhima Sharma and Amrik Singh delve into the intersection of AI, green marketing, and influencer strategies. As sustainability becomes a key concern for consumers, AI helps brands align their marketing efforts with eco-friendly values. By leveraging influencers and AI insights, brands can engage younger, environmentally conscious audiences and promote sustainable consumption.

Chapter 14: Shaping the Future of Brand Management by AI-Powered Predictions

Mohamed Badouch, Hasna Mahmoud, and Mehdi Boutaounte demonstrate how AI-powered predictive analytics are revolutionizing brand management by forecasting market trends and consumer behaviors. This chapter explores how machine learning and big data help brands optimize their strategies by predicting demand and identifying emerging trends. Ethical considerations, such as algorithmic bias, are also addressed to guide the responsible use of predictive analytics.

Chapter 15: Tourists' Winery Experiences in Portugal, New Zealand, and the United States: A Review of User-generated Content on TripAdvisor Using Business Intelligence and Orange Analytical

Eric Asamoah, Fatumata Ba, Ugbong Uwayin, and Célia Ramos, focusing on wine tourism, analyze user-generated content from TripAdvisor reviews in Portugal, New Zealand, and the United States. Using business intelligence tools, this chapter is about examining consumer preferences and trends to help wineries improve customer engagement, brand awareness, and loyalty, while navigating challenges such as seasonality and social media influence.

Chapter 16: The Influence of AI-driven Personalization on Customer Experiences: A Case Study of Instagram

Waseem Hussain explores how Instagram uses AI to personalize customer experiences. By analyzing user behavior and preferences, Instagram delivers tailored content, fostering stronger brand-consumer relationships. The chapter also highlights how businesses can leverage Instagram's AI capabilities to enhance customer engagement and improve their brand strategies.

Chapter 17: Incorporating Artificial Intelligence in Branding: Revolutionizing Strategies and Addressing Challenges in the Indian Market

Utsav Murari, Hemlata Parmar, and Rashid Hashmi focus on the Indian market and discuss how AI technologies are transforming branding strategies. The authors explore the challenges Indian businesses face in adopting AI, including technological barriers and consumer skepticism. Strategic recommendations are provided to help Indian brands harness AI's potential for improved consumer engagement and brand positioning.

Chapter 18: Revolutionizing Customer Experience with AI-powered Personalization

Nitesh Behare, Supriya Bhagat, and Praful Sarangdhar examine the role of AI in revolutionizing customer experiences across industries. By leveraging recommendation engines, predictive analytics, and natural language processing, businesses can tailor customer journeys to individual preferences, strengthening loyalty and driving growth. Ethical issues, such as data privacy and algorithmic bias, are also discussed to promote responsible AI usage.

Chapter 19: Predictive Analytics - Utilizing Machine Learning and Big Data for Forecasting Future Trends in Business and Consumer Behavior

P.S. Venkateswaran, Sriramkumar Mm examine how predictive analytics powered by machine learning and big data is reshaping how businesses forecast trends and make data-driven decisions. This chapter explores how predictive models help businesses uncover valuable insights, optimize strategies, and anticipate consumer behavior, with an emphasis on the infrastructure needed for effective implementation.

Chapter 20: Metaverse Branding: A Review and Future Directions

Belem Barbosa explains that the metaverse offers new opportunities for brands to engage with consumers through immersive digital environments. This chapter reviews the current trends in metaverse branding and proposes a conceptual framework for creating engaging, multi-dimensional experiences that drive brand awareness and loyalty. The chapter also highlights the future of metaverse branding strategies.

As you journey through these chapters, you will gain a comprehensive understanding of the profound impact AI is having on the way brands are conceptualized, managed, and experienced. This book is a timely resource for marketing professionals, brand strategists, and researchers seeking to harness the power of AI to build resilient and innovative brands in the face of ongoing digital disruption. The contributors' diverse perspectives offer invaluable insights into the challenges and opportunities brands face in an AI-driven world, preparing you to navigate the exciting future of strategic brand management. The practical guidance and innovative strategies presented will serve as invaluable resources for organizations looking to stay ahead in this dynamic digital era.

Chapter 1
Introduction to Brand Management in the Digital Age

Praveen Patel
https://orcid.org/0009-0004-5405-5354
Christ University, India

Jasmine Kaur
Christ University, India

ABSTRACT

The rapid development of digital technology has introduced a new order of large-scale change within brand management in the fast-changing landscape of the digital marketplace. This chapter provides the fundamental principles of brand management within the digital era and demonstrates the transformation of building brands via online platforms, data analytics, and digital technologies. Others might state that social media, e-commerce, and AI integration offer brands a new horizon for managing brand equity, improving customer engagement, and creating experiences to adapt to changing tastes. Adjustment towards this change can prove challenging for the brands, but on the other hand, they are opening new possibilities that drive innovation in performance and strategy about their brands.

1. INTRODUCTION

This business world is witnessing a rather fast pace of change that comes from technology, digital change, and even consumer behaviour very fast; it's more of a call for dynamic marketing strategies. The proliferation of the internet, digitalization,

DOI: 10.4018/979-8-3693-9461-8.ch001

and continuous novelties have pushed the market toward a better digital framework. The information flow in both ways, which has not only empowered the consumer but also has empowered the manufacturer to take well-informed decisions in return. This has resulted in the development of innovative communication and branding strategies by organizations. (Borić et al., 2024) Effectiveness of business in a digital market will depend upon the manner in which the consumers are communicated to. In this regard, businesses have to formulate clear and convincing messages that touch the hearts of their intended audiences and evolve with the transforming face of the media usage pattern to survive the game (Kumar et al., 2016). Though traditional media will continue to be used by segments of the population, in general, the future will belong to digital media; indeed, it already does so for younger populations, creating new channels that open new opportunities but also enforce new constraints on marketers.

Technology now becomes the heart of each marketing operation in digital transformation. Digital tools enable more effective ways through which one can engage a consumer to drive huge business growth. Data analytics and Customer Relationship Management systems illustrate great examples on how transformation now allows firms to analyze consumer data for insights into making more precise, data-driven decisions (Odonkor et al., 2024; Wamba et al., 2017). This is because data analytics gives actionable insight into consumer preferences, behaviors, and trends, allowing businesses to create targeted marketing campaigns and maintain a competitive advantage in a data-rich environment (Adegbola et al., 2024). In addition, CRM tools empower companies to maintain good customer relations through personal communication and targeted engagement, fostering customer loyalty (Ngai, 2005). The paper is focused on the role of data analytics and CRM tools in digital transformation, bringing light to how these technologies transform marketing efficiency, drive customer engagement, and support business growth (Urefe, Odonkor & Agu, 2024). One part of its popularity also owes influence marketing to the rise in social media. Social media influencers are considered more authentic and engaging compared to advertisements from brands and companies, bringing brand communications directly to individual pockets of targeted audiences that will more likely be interested and engaged. However, the influencer marketing domain is not static; it will undergo broad changes- calls for greater diversity and innovation in representation. These have brought about the emergence of virtual influencers - artificially created figures powered by generative AI, which gain popularity for their novelty and their ability to communicate with highly diversified consumer groups (Farrell, Campbell & Sands, 2022). Virtual influencers have become a cost-effective alternative to human influencers. Large followings are attracted with lesser risks for the brands (Nguyen, 2023). This paper examines the question of how diversity and newness affect consumer reactions to virtual influencers; it centres its attention on the promise of virtual influencers for shaping inclusion in branding.

Additionally, the emergence of AI in marketing has also transformed the relationship between a brand and its public. AI enables marketers to leverage automation processes, interpret complex consumers' behaviors, and optimize a campaign with unprecedented precision,(Adami, 2015). AI tools help brands design bespoke customer journeys, increase operational efficiency, and even understand more about influencers, who have the right audience demographics for a brand's message (Chintalapati & Pandey, 2022). AI-based platforms offer deep insights into influencer authenticity, so businesses can steer clear of others with fake following and hand-pick people who resonate with their brand's values (Davenport & Ronanki, 2018). In addition, applications of AI are increasing day by day in the fields. Beginning with finance and healthcare to marketing and especially e-marketing, even selection of influencers on social media, influence has become a constituent component of a brand's strategy. E-marketing facilitates simplifying a company's activities as well as reaching online potential clients toward the desired target, using personalization plans based on individual preferences (Borić et al., 2024).

Branding, the modern aspect of business, becomes critical in raising the value of a company as well as bringing a loyal customer base. In today's aggressively competitive market, company brand identity becomes the hallmark which will be used to identify a firm and how it will establish superiority in the market. Globalization of the company market makes brand leadership essential for a brand like Coca-Cola, which demonstrates how great brand management contributes to making corporate value appreciable. Effective branding strategies to ensure customer loyalty and trust have created iconic presence for Coca-Cola in the global world. The case study on Coca-Cola branding has revealed that brand management is crucial to help companies retain their position in the competitive market. This chapter has a twofold aim. On the one hand, it explores how digital transformation, data analytics, and CRM tools can influence marketing strategies. On the other hand, it analyses the evolving role of influencer marketing and AI in building strong brand identities in the digital age. Against this backdrop, this chapter examines emerging trends to contribute to the body of knowledge in digital marketing regarding the transformative effects of digital technology on brand management. It also aims to give a complete understanding of the challenges and opportunities that brands face in using digital platforms, social media, and e-commerce to engage with consumers for business growth. In doing so, it will focus some light on how artificial intelligence and other technologies are reconfiguring brand performance and consumer behaviour in a world growing more digital by the day.

The rapidly shifting business environment calls for agility and innovation in marketing strategies due to its quick, often unplanned changes in technology and consumer behaviour. This digital revolution has really altered the marketplace, where information is accessible, exchanges take place instantly, and customer preferences change rapidly. Effective communication of value propositions will result in strong brand identities, thus helping to achieve versatile and adaptable approaches toward effectively engaging and maintaining consumers. This digital-dominant market environment calls for a revaluation of the traditional marketing approach against the backdrop of data-driven decision-making and customer-centric methodologies if marketers are to remain relevant and competitive. Data analytics forms an integral part of any effort toward digital transformation within marketing. More importantly, in the recent years data analytics has become an essential part of a winning marketing strategy because of the knowledge and foresight of customer needs. With the organizations processing data at unimaginable levels, analytics does well to become fruitful in providing some key patterns and insights for more accurate, tailored marketing campaigns (Chae et al., 2014). Coupled with the help of data analytics, firms can foresee what the customers might do next, to customize the messages conveyed in marketing campaigns, and finally make the campaigns much more effective. Using data-driven marketing, a general industry-wide shift toward commonplaces - positioning insights and evidence above intuition and assumption - thus allows brands to reach audiences in a more strategic way. In an example involving consumer shopping behaviors and social media engagement data, for instance, data can help Amazon and Netflix adjust their recommendations for better engagement and loyalty.

Another thing that cannot be ignored within the digital marketing transformation process is the use of CRM tools. CRM systems are able to gather, store, and analyze the data of customers. This means businesses can deliver very personalized interaction toward a customer that caters to each individual's tastes and preferences of a customer. Actually, CRM tools help brands foster loyalty and better retention rates, which is key to long-term growth (Payne & Frow, 2005). This customized approach doesn't only boost customer satisfaction but also inspires brand loyalty because customers feel they are worthwhile and get what the company has in mind for them. Companies like Starbucks use CRM to customize offers for the customers by setting up communications that remain relevant and targeted toward the consumers, enhancing engagement and sales.

Social media has further complicated brand management with influencer marketing taking the upper hand as an effective tool in communicating with brands. The power of influencer marketing is that it enables brands to tap the influence of trusted figures who have built rapport with their followers and are, therefore, less suspicious of direct advertising (Campbell & Farrell, 2020). These have made brands rush to influencer partnerships to reach the younger, more digitally active audiences who are strongly influenced by social proof and community-driven endorsements. However, there are emergent trends in the influencer space that have defined the phenomenon of virtual influencers, or digital personas powered by AI, who engage audiences on Instagram and TikTok. Virtual influencers are AI-driven brand ambassadors that reach audiences across the globe, thereby economical, controllable, and versatile to brands, as reflected by Sands et al. (2022). Brands across the fashion and technology realm, like Prada and Samsung, have been employing virtual influencers as an element of their marketing efforts recently, looking for that newness in order to promote additional engagement and increase brand awareness. It is part of a much broader digital transformation where AI is fundamentally changing the marketing landscape. The scope of AI applications reaches capabilities well beyond influencer selection: audience segmentation, predictive analytics, and even content creation. AI lets the marketer automate routine tasks, help in making better decisions, and also engage a customer in real time, responding to their different preferences and behaviors. Through this, it allows tools that can produce almost impossible amounts of personalization and efficiency with traditional ways of marketing. Like for example, through analysing big datasets, AI is able to tell at what best times to post, suggest the style of any content and even generate a marketing message that will cater to individual needs, hence better customer journeys. Such AI applications include sector cuts where they allow for targeted precision and efficiency in work, hence value creation for different places, ranging from finance to healthcare and more (Davenport, 2019; Marr, 2020)..

2. THEORETICAL FRAMEWORK

The digital age has essentially altered the dynamics between consumers and brands, thereby resulting in evolution in terms of how brand managers approach consumer engagement, loyalty, and perception. In the theoretical framework, therefore, insight would be achieved into the models that form the nucleus of the tie between social media marketing and consumer behavior-central to understanding brand management within a technologically advanced marketplace. Considering Social Influence Theory, Theory of Planned Behavior, Uses and Gratifications Theory, Customer Relationship Management, Diffusion of Innovations Theory, Dual Coding Theory, and the Elaboration Likelihood Model, we have all-around approaches to what really drives interactions between a brand and a consumer on digital platforms.

Social Influence Theory

The Social Influence Theory states that people's attitudes, beliefs, and behaviors get highly influenced by social interactions and others' acts (Katz & Lazarsfeld, 2017). Therefore, it has much relevance in social media, where interactions are amplified, and consumers expose themselves to a broad-reaching influence. Familoni 2024 and Igbinenikaro & Adewusi 2024 reveals that peer recommendations in the internet, community discussions, and influencer endorsement will enormously influence consumer behavior to perceive a brand in one way or another and change their attitude about purchasing.With digitalization and the demarcation of the boundary of influence that is as easy as soil and broken and narrow by thousands of people's opinions as in the case where consumers will now have direct contact with various influencers and communities beyond personal acquaintances. Therefore, social media sites are powerful tools of social influence; hence a brand must engage its key influencers in an effort to change consumer perception. Research as pointed by Familoni & Onyebuchi (2024) has shown that consumers must seek validation and guidance from online networks before acquiring any product hence peer influence becomes the most important factor of modern consumerism. In this light, brands can leverage positive peer recommendations and testimonials and even incorporate social influence within their marketing strategies to further strengthen brand trust and loyalty within the digital landscape.

Theory of Planned Behaviour (TPB)

The Theory of Planned Behaviour has tried to explain how attitudes, subjective norms, and perceived control over behaviour come together to shape intentions and subsequent behaviors. It is very useful for the understanding of consumer decision-making for social media marketing because it depicts the psychological pathway through which attitudes toward the brand, societal expectations, and control over behaviour get combined to influence the purchasing intent. For instance, based on TPB, consumers would have attitudes toward an ad or post placed by a brand, say, as a public service announcement, for fun on social media, or a social media sponsored post, and this attitude directly influences the consumer's intention to buy from that brand (Familoni & Onyebuchi, 2024). It also suggests subjective norms such that consumer perceives approval or disapproval from other influential figures in his/her social domain or community as influencing purchasing intentions. Social media empowers this by creating a base that provides consumers with an opportunity to see endorsements, testimonials, and even reviews of credible individuals, such as influencers or thought leaders.The part of perceived behavioural control is crucial in the age of digits as access to online shopping and information empowers more control in the decision-making mechanisms of consumers. Due to the social nature of social media, brands can promote purchasing intentions due to the generation of content that falls in line with the attitude of consumers and is supported by subjective norms. Influence is very crucial where the market of online presence determines a brand's success and failure, especially at a time when increasingly consumers are seeking information and validation for buying on social media rather than just to have fun.

Using and Gratifications Theory

Utilized and Gratified Theory, as provided by Katz, Blumler, & Gurevitch in the year 1973, frames the grounds for understanding why consumers interact with the media, using digital media in this context, based on information, entertainment, and social interaction-related specific needs. In the context of brand management, UGT postulates that the reasons a consumer engages with the brands on social media is because of the fulfillment of such needs, hence forming a basis for engagement and loyalty (Igbinenikaro & Adewusi, 2024). This theory is very relevant in an era where brands no longer pitch products but instead strive to generate value-driven content that resonates with consumers on various levels. UGT posits that consumers pick and interact with brands only if these brands are able to give them value beyond the product per se. Brands that show knowledge, such as tips or how-to guides, address consumers' need for information. Those using comedy or content able to resonate with readers or viewers speak to emotional needs, but those soliciting comments or user-generated content in order to facilitate social engagement satisfy social needs. It is where this dialogue between consumer needs and brand offerings will usher people into the environment in which true brand loyalty develops-not necessarily through the quality of product but through the fulfillment of deeper, personal motivations.

Brands can use UGT effectively by identifying the need of their audience and creating related content. The concept is completely aligned with the idea of content marketing, where “the content is the king.” When social media content aligns with the consumer's needs for information, entertainment, or social engagement, the consumer-brand relationship becomes stronger, creating loyalty that makes it easier to engage and reinforce brand identity consistently.

Theories Associated with CRM

In customer relationship management theory focuses on the strategic value of customer relations that need to be developed and retained in the relationship. The ability of a firm to market itself largely depends on the development of digital as far as customer relationship management is concerned (Berry, 1983). Classic CRM was once applied in a one-to-one manner while communicating with a customer, but now, through social media, it connects directly with the customer, enhancing satisfaction and bonding relationships (Familoni, 2024). With the advent of social media, CRM now has an entirely new set of tools, namely personalized channels of communication through which brands may address consumer concerns, collect feedback, and build long-run loyalty. A CRM-focused social media strategy allows brands to capture data and insights about their customers that will help them deliver customized experiences-a real-time alignment with the preferences and actions of individual consumers. Research indicates that such personalized communications have guaranteed the high satisfaction and loyalty by a consumer as it makes a consumer feel valued and well-understood (Familoni & Onyebuchi, 2024). In fact, with social media, CRM can no longer be limited to communication after purchase, but covers the entire lifecycle of the customer journey: from awareness to loyalty. Therefore, this makes CRM a holistic approach towards building consumer loyalty.

By investing in CRM strategies that give priority to real-time, two-way communication, brands tighten the consumer-brand relationship and hence drive repeat engagements. Integration of CRM with social media marketing has helped establish brand loyalty because it provides an avenue by which brands can prove their responsiveness and create a customer-centered identity that rings within an increasingly competitive marketplace.

Diffusion of Innovations Theory

The Diffusion of Innovations Theory states that there will be a spread of new ideas, technologies, or products within a social system (Rogers, 1962). In the context of social media marketing, this theory indeed becomes rather relevant because fast information diffusion allows brands to accelerate the dissemination of innovations through viral content, influencer partnership, and engagement (Familoni, 2024). The power of social media is in its ability to blow messages quickly and broadly across the customer base. Hence, it becomes an attractive vehicle for brands that have new products and ideas to share with their customers.Diffusion of Innovations Theory categorizes several key factors that impact rates of adoption and includes relative advantage, compatibility, complexity, trialability, and observability. Social media marketing tackles this by making it possible for the consumer to see how a product works, read reviews, ask questions directly, and hence makes the innovation more accessible and understandable. Early adopters as well as influencers play a pretty important role in the diffusion process on social media by endorsing products and sharing good experiences with a view to pushing others to take on the innovation.

This theory sustains the potential that social media has in driving adoption by making brands and products accessible and observable, thereby making it possible to penetrate markets faster. Since the use of social media gives wider publicity to the innovation introduction and promotion, it would make more people adopt the innovation faster, especially because the relative advantage in trying the new product is enormous.

Dual Coding Theory

As per Dual Coding Theory, human beings process verbal and visual information differently through two different cognitive channels that help to understand better and retain it in the memory. This theory is directly associated with social media marketing because the majority of brands use social media with or in combination with picture-based elements like images, videos, and graphics with the text-based information to capture the attention of the consumers drastically. Content used through both channels enhances the recall of the messages and exercises more influence on consumer behaviour. Social media platforms, which focus on visual content, serve as the perfect context for brands to implement Dual Coding Theory. Thus, product information could prove more attractive if paired with graphics or interesting visual elements and captions. Video and infographics, and other forms of visual storytelling, would resonate most meaningfully with audiences and are more likely to be shared, amplifying brand reach and cementing consumer-brand connection. Dual Coding Theory Dual Coding Theory, thus supports the use of multimedia content in social media marketing. Brands can deliver more impressive and memorable messages through a balance of visual and textual elements that enhance brand recall and positive attitudes toward behavioural change in the consumer.

ELM

The Elaboration Likelihood Model is defined to characterize two routes to persuasion: the central route and peripheral route. The central route, that occurs when the consumers are motivated and can process information deeply, calls for more careful consideration, while the peripheral route makes use of cues such as endorsements and appeal based on emotional appeal, and often when consumers have low involvement in the decision-making process. ELM provides an idea of how the social media marketing content can influence consumer attitudes in a different manner depending on the level of engagement. For high-involvement products or messages, brands should apply the central route that would provide the consumers with logical and well-articulated arguments or information pieces that will provoke them to exercise their logic. The use of peripheral cues in low-involvement products may just create a positive attitude for brands. According to Anjorin, Raji, & Olodo (2024), further message strategies aligned with the level of involvement on the part of the consumer will increase persuasion power on social media. With ELM, brands can better adapt their message to the needs and preferences of their audiences. This theory argues that significant emphasis should be placed on having a heightened awareness of consumer engagement levels, coupled with a corresponding adjustment in message strategies, which assists brands in making more efficient social media campaigns resonate with various constituencies.

Integrative Insights into Consumer Behavior in the Digital Marketplace

Collectively, all these theories-the Social Influence Theory, Theory of Planned Behavior, Uses and Gratifications Theory, Customer Relationship Management, Diffusion of Innovations Theory, Dual Coding Theory, and the Elaboration Likelihood Model-put together offer a wide framework regarding consumer psychology in the digital communication era. All these theories shed light on different perspectives of consumer-brand interaction-from social validation and cognitive processing to emotional engagement and behavioral intent. As research affirms, brands must consider these psychological and behavioral factors in coming up with more effective, adaptive digital strategies (Familoni & Onyebuchi, 2024). With this knowledge of consumers' motives and engagement on social media, brands can create more relevant, appealing content for the targeted consumer to build loyalty and brand equity in its communications, especially now that an online presence becomes more important. Such digital transformation renders incidence as extremely crucial guidance for the brand management within the overall complex ever-changing landscape of consumer behavior, wherein technology and social interaction tend to converge. It would be easy for the brands to stay relevant through such long term relationships integrated into driving innovation in the marketplace centered around constant change and disruption by integrating the frameworks with practical applications.

3. CONCEPTUAL DEVELOPMENT: BRAND MANAGEMENT IN THE DIGITAL AGE

The digital age has moved brand management way beyond what it was before. This can be attributed to an exponential growth of innovations in technology, more so AI, growth of e-commerce sites, and the mass power wielded by social media.

Therefore, brands have to change their approach and harness all these tools in order to make the most of them to begin with, as well as to strive for more personalization in engagement and dynamic experiences and analytical decision making. In this section, we will dwell on the five key concepts and frameworks that define brand management in the digital age, laying down some relevant literature, theories, and current industry practices.

1. Digital Transformation and the Role of AI in Brand Management

Transformation of brand management with AI does not merely represent using technology for automating tasks but rather reflection on how brands can deliver value to customers by profoundly recognizing their behavior and needs. AI has transformed customer service, marketing, sales, and product development. This is where I explore personalization, prediction, automation, and analysis as aspects of change in brand management through AI.

AI-Driven Personalization in Brand Management

Today, personalization is an increasingly crucial component of brand identity management and consumer loyalty in a hyper-connected world. With the implementation of machine learning algorithms, brands can deliver hyper-targeted content, offers, and recommendations specifically to the preferences of individual consumers. Indeed, AI-driven personalization is made feasible due to the explosion of data from the online activity of today's consumers. Brands can work with this data to segment audiences, personalize engagement, and make predictions of possible behavior in the future. Companies like Amazon and Netflix are the quintessential examples of AI-driven personalization. Amazon's recommendations of products are based on previous purchases, browsing history, and search data, while Netflix uses AI to suggest movies and shows based on viewing patterns. Based on historical data, trending patterns, and seasonal variations and trends, AI can predict what the consumers want even before they know it. Personalized emails and targeted ads can then increase customer engagement, while another form of improving conversion rates is product recommendations. A study by Chintalapati and Pandey (2022) found that with AI-based recommendations, sales can improve by over 30%; this, therefore, underlines the importance of AI-driven customer experience management in modern brand management.

AI-Powered Automation in Brand Management

Another major benefit AI implementation offers brand management is automation. With AI, brands can automate routine jobs such as those pertaining to answering customer inquiries, providing support, and then responding to them with the help of AI-powered chatbots and virtual assistants. Brands can talk to customers at all hours while also processing their orders or updating account details. According to Siebert et al. (2020), developing and deploying AI chatbots manage an enormous volume of customer queries, and for a brand, it allows them to scale their operations without additional human resources. Furthermore, virtual assistants can offer real-time personalized responses through the individual's purchase history and preference, creating a seamless experience. Predictive analytics allows brands to simplify the management of stocks and pricing policies. The AI models predict the demand for each product so that there is enough in stock without creating overstock or under-stock situations, which affect customers' satisfaction and operational cost. Kharfan et al. (2021) reveal that predictive analytics by AI has streamlined the management of inventory and ensured there are the right products at the right time.

Effects of AI on Loyalty to the Brand

While AI helps brands become efficient in so many different ways, it also has a major role to play in creating brand loyalty. This is done by delivering highly personalized and predictive experiences that mean customers become more satisfied and stick with the brand. As AI keeps customizing itself to changing consumer preferences, it makes sure that brands stay top of mind for their consumers. The challenge remains ensuring that, through excessive personalization or misinterpretation of preference, AI does not alienate customers who fear this might run into privacy issues.

2. Functioning of Social Media Amplification of Brand Identity

Social media democratized communication and enabled brands to give direct messages to their audience in real-time and in more interactive ways. Therefore, the influence of social media on brand management cannot be overstated since it has transformed how brand identities are built and, in turn, lengthened relationships between brands and consumers.

Building Brand Identity on Social Media

Brand identity refers to the idea that a brand conveys to its target market, and social media has become one of the most effective ways to build this perception. Today, brands do not use social media only to advertise a product but rather to share their values and mission, as well as their customer experience. Social media is also an effective tool for communicating directly with consumers because Instagram, Facebook, Twitter, and TikTok provide interaction with millions of customers and a way to share stories with them. Social media has also provided brands with easier ways to interact with their customers and receive immediate feedback on the comments, likes, or shares. According to Hoyer et al. (2020), the ability to interact directly with consumers allows brands to develop an even more effective emotional bonding, resulting in customers feeling valued and heard. Brands that are successful in this regard, such as Nike, Starbucks, and Apple, have created communities around their products, making customers feel part of something bigger than just a brand.

Influencer Marketing and Social Proof

The biggest change in social media brand management is perhaps the rise of influencer marketing. Social media influencers are now considered middlemen between a brand and its consumers, thereby multiplying a brand's message to followers. Influencers establish credibility and trust by generating content that is authentic and has substance among their followers. Brands use the influencers to push product placement that is less intrusive and perceived more as an organic promotion instead of an advertisement from the brand itself. Social influence by social proof: Lastly, social proof is the concept that makes influencer marketing extremely effective as the customers are more likely to believe in endorsements from people who are connected to them on social media than from the brand itself. The Kharfan et al. (2021) study shows that consumers believe influencers more than traditional advertising, and such belief is translated into increased brand engagement, sales, and loyalty. Such brands can highly amplify their reach and recognition by choosing influencers whose values combine with those of their brand and target market.

Brand Reputation Management on Social Media

Brands must also pay attention to reputation management on the social platform. Any negative comments or a viral complaint can be very devastating for a brand image. Social media reputation management requires checking the status of brands often, responding to all complaints from customers, and acting appropriately to counter the negativity. An unaddressed customer experience can turn into a full-blown PR crisis overnight if left unchecked. Effect reputation management on social media can occur through active listening and meaningful conversations with consumers. Brands can transform bad experiences into good ones if it takes the issues that customers have raised seriously with empathy and transparency. This will deepen customer loyalty more than anything.3. E-Commerce: Personalization and Data-Driven Marketing

E-commerce has changed the game of the rules for companies to engage with customers. As consumers increasingly look for products online, brands are increasingly being forced to rely on more e-commerce channels to communicate with customers. Customized shopping experiences have been one of the engines driving sales and loyalty in the e-commerce market. Today, AI and machine learning enable e-commerce channels to deliver a bespoke experience that fits each unique preference and requirement of a customer (Gupta et al., 2020). Predictive analytics in e-commerce allows a brand to look into the near future of consumer demand based on historical information and derives insights that can be used for managing the right inventory, keeping the price right, and developing the right products (Kharfan et al., 2021). Taking into consideration browsing behavior, purchase history, and external factors such as seasonality, the predictions can state which product will be most in demand and allow the brand to correspondingly readjust its offerings accordingly. This can help e-commerce companies provide more personalized experience to their customers, which promises to increase customer satisfaction and avoids stock out as well as overstock situation. Whereas personalization is executed in e-commerce not only by product recommendations but also with dynamic pricing and promotions towards the target and even content customizations, examples of this may be AI that can change the price of products in real-time because that is a function of demand, consumer behavior, or competitor pricing. Such dynamic pricing would help optimize profitability of a brand without losing relevance and competitiveness for customers (Rahman & Dekkati, 2022).

Therefore, e-commerce aligns seamlessly with any other digital touchpoint, including mobile applications and social media networks, to afford the consumer a unitary and homogeneous brand experience. Brands can track the customers' interactions across these platforms and produce recommendations or offers targeted towards the choice of the client, thereby making the shopping experience both fulfilling and engaging.

3. Social Media: Amplify Brand Messaging and Consumer Interaction

Social media has emerged as an integral component in the digital landscape of brand management. The virtual marketplaces that house such large constituencies numbering in the billions, like Facebook, Instagram, Twitter, and TikTok, now constitute an environment in which brands can talk directly to their audiences. Brands use social media to engage with customers, respond to concerns raised by them, and get immediate feedback on their products and services. The most powerful influence on brand perception comes through the user-generated content, that is through the comments, photos, or videos contained in reviews. Brand influencers and advocates affect the reputation of the brand significantly on shifting some decisions to buy.

Social media builds brand equity, which is the value a brand derives from its perception in the marketplace. The more positive the interactions with customers and the more consistent the brand's presence across social channels, the stronger the brand's equity becomes. Moreover, social media power to create interaction and engagement has transformed customer loyalty, moving it from passive consumption to active participation in the story of the brand. This, on the other hand, is now balanced out by the democratizing power of social media in the articulation of brand discourse, meaning that the power, as such, is no longer exclusively to be exercised by brands. Although it opens up a whole new realm of possibilities, so do the new difficulties which come with issues like addressing unfavourable criticism, public complaints, and above all, protection of the reputation of the brand vis-à-vis online scrutiny.

4. Personalized Marketing and Consumer Behaviour

There is a shift in brand management largely linked with the increasing desire for personalized marketing in this digital age. Consumers now expect brands to deliver content, offers, and recommendations based on personal preferences, behaviors, or needs. That has naturally led to the adoption of data-driven marketing strategies and optimized use of AI and machine learning to strategize about the brand message and what kind of interaction the brand has with its target. As to personalized marketing, it would ask for a leveraging of customer data on browsing behavior, purchase history, and demographic information, etc., to run a very relevant and targeted marketing campaign, thus enabling a brand to deliver the right message at the right time. In this sense, AI algorithms can analyze such data points to predict which products or content may resonate with specific consumers. The end result is much more interesting and effective marketing that boils down to a better conversion rate, higher sales, and far more loyal customers. For instance, Amazon and Spotify's

AI-based recommendation engines suggest products and content to the user based on what they have clicked or liked previously. Such customer-orientated personalized services ensure that customers have better experiences with the brands and thus results in happy customers because consumers feel that the brand will understand their needs and respond accordingly.

In addition, personalized marketing can build a deeper relationship with customers through brands. Brands are well placed to demonstrate relevance by showing content, discounts, and even product recommendations to facilitate the building of relationships with consumers. This goes way beyond transactional exchanges and emotionally connects the brand to the consumer, which is hugely important in terms of long-term brand equity .

5. Ethical Considerations and Challenges in Digital Brand Management

Digital brand management brings with it many opportunities from AI, social media, and e-commerce but also poses some ethical concerns. The foremost concern is data privacy because brands collect and analyze huge amounts of consumer data to deliver personalized experiences. Consumers are ever more aware of how their data is being utilized. So, the ethical use of data is a sure way to maintain trust and credibility with customers. Brands have to reveal what data they collect about the customer, how they collect it, how they store it, and what measures they take with that data. One needs also to comply with privacy rules such as GDPR (General Data Protection Regulation) and CCPA (California Consumer Privacy Act). Another ethical issue regarding AI and brand management is the presence of algorithmic bias. Predictive values are based on historical data that AI systems use to draw conclusions from. However, if the data they base their conclusion on is biased, then the model produced will always revert to stereotype productions. Therefore, brands must ensure the fairness of the algorithms they use in their system, that they are inclusive and do not offer biased models. This requires constant monitoring and auditing of the AI model to ensure equitable decisions and prevent stereotypes (Jankovic & Curovic, 2023).

Brands also have to face consistency in numerous digital touchpoints these days. The explosion of touchpoints associated with social media, e-commerce, and more recently chatbots necessitates consistency with messaging, tone, and values across those channels, making consistency a challenge marketers need to meet. This requires blending into marketing, customer service, and product teams to conjure up a harmonized seamless brand identity.

Conclusion: The Future of Brand Management in the Digital Era

Given that digital technologies are evolving, brand management will have to deal with very complex and connected landscapes. The way the brand interacts with consumers is reshaped by AI, social media, and e-commerce in creating brand equity and an appropriate personalized experience. However, in doing so, it creates many issues with data privacy, algorithmic bias, and building brand consistency. Success in the digital age for brands requires them to move with new technologies, invest in data-driven marketing strategies, and support a multichannel strategy of customer engagement. Brands can build lifelong relations with customers and stand out in the rapidly expanding digital world if they look to AI for real-time, personalized experiences that create meaningful social media interactions and optimize e-commerce platforms. This will eventually put the future of brand management between balancing innovation with any ethics, where the brands represent delivering personalized, relevant experiences across the entire marketing mix while remaining transparent, trusted, and loyal to the customers it serves.

4. IMPLICATIONS AND FUTURE RESEARCH

The digital technologies seem to have differed the kind of profiles brands were normally made of- leading to newly changed scenarios. Artificial intelligence, social media, and e-commerce have reshaped the brand management landscape in recent times. As firms are transforming further into more digital-first branding environments, this chapter provides details regarding the implications of transformations that took place and what kind of innovation can bring in the advent of these new technologies. The implications are vast for brand managers and marketers, since this digital age offers incredible opportunities but also new challenges that demand adaptation and the strategic foresight to cope with new changing needs and landscapes.

Implication for Brand Managers and Marketers

Among the major implications of this new digital space is that AI-driven personalized marketing will become more and more integrated into the creation of greater customer engagement and loyalty. This ability to analyze mass data in real time allows brands to zero in on marketing directly to the individual consumers' tastes and preferences, increasing satisfaction, loyalty, and, finally, retention. Such research as Cho and Cheon (2004) and Danaher and Mullarkey (2003) even shows that personalization is one of the keys brands have been using to stand out in such a saturated digital environment. The only implication in this context is that brand managers need to rethink current strategies as their approach to markets should be much more data-driven by incorporating AI and digital tools to deliver unique and personalized brand experiences. Another vital implication here is AI integration with omnichannel marketing strategies. The requirement to have as seamless and cohesive an experience as possible across these channels is imperative in order to maintain brand coherence as a customer interacts with brands across various touch points—be it on social media, mobile apps, e-commerce, or physical retail outlets. Omnichannel marketing allows for an integrated customer journey that, in combination with AI, ensures that messages are personalized based on a number of customer interactions. This integration optimizes the timing, content, and frequency of communication. It then makes the interaction seem relevant and timely no matter the platform. According to a study by Verhoef et al. in 2021, this omnichannel approach was regarded as very significant because AI with an omnichannel strategy results in higher customer satisfaction, more robust brand loyalty, and efficient marketing spend.

At the same time, AI holds the potential of making operational aspects of brand management simple, for example predictive analytics, and supply chain optimization. Therefore, when AI becomes an integral part of operational processes, then the brand manager can capitalize on this potential of predicting trends and forecasting demand. Brand managers will hence be able to make data-driven informed decisions that enhance operational efficiency. It does have a lot to do with strategic direction in terms of branding, because with AI, you can talk about analysing consumer behaviors and trends at any time. AI does not only improve marketing decision-making; it touches on every single section of the business such as product development, customer service, and even the management of inventory as all those can be addressed to come up with better decisions,-according to Davenport and Ronanki (2018).

Expansions and Innovations

In terms of brand management, this new era of the digital age is not only concerned with consumer engagement and marketing; it's also concerned with the prospects of extending AI-powered personalized marketing to other sectors. Applications in the areas of education, entertainment, manufacturing, and more are predicted to rise sharply, just as they have already been seen in retail, finance, and health sectors. For instance, in education, AI can be used in creating learning experiences that are unique to the needs and choices of every student. Based on learners' interactions with their digital learning platforms, AI would give them real-time feedback, adaptive material content, and customized contents that appeal to the students and really yield better results in learning. In the entertainment sector, AI will allow brands to provide customized content recommendations, thus improving viewership satisfaction and retention, while in manufacturing, AI will optimize supply chains and predictive maintenance processes, thus saving costs and efficiency.Another key area of innovation for AI is its further integration with new technologies such as the IoT and blockchain. The IoT basically accumulates large data volumes from connected devices, and when combined with AI algorithms, brands can unlock greater depths of insight into their customers' behaviors and preferences. For example, AI can use data from smart home devices to make recommendations of personalized products according to the consumer's daily routines or habits. In this regard, blockchain's ability to provide safe, transparent, and immutable data can be combined with AI for the betterment of data privacy and security regarding marketing campaigns. According to research by De Cremer et al. (2017), the possibility of AI being integrated with IoT and blockchain has been identified, citing how such integration promises more efficient, personalized, and secure marketing strategies.

Future Research Directions

While this chapter provides a foundational understanding of the role of AI and digital technologies in brand management, multiple areas are ripe for further explorations. A huge area for future research is further investigation into the role of diversity representation within digital brand strategies, particularly through virtual influencers. Digital platforms increasingly apply virtual influencers to reach the consumer. Therefore, it is crucial to examine the effects of representations with diverse characteristics, such as influencers from multiple cultural, ethnic, and disability backgrounds, on consumer perceptions, brand loyalty, or engagement. Ferraro et al. (2022) indicate that diverse virtual influencers might improve consumers' attitudes. However, fewer studies have investigated the long-term impacts of such diversity on brand relationships. Other directions of research could be case studies or experience-based investigations on virtual influencers in different cultural and demographic contexts that may advance brand strategies for creating more inclusive and relatable brand identities. Further, more research is also needed on the expansion of AI-driven personalization within the customer journey. While much effort has been done in recent years regarding personalization within the scope of one-on-one marketing campaigns, fewer studies speak to what impact AI would have on long-term customer relationships and brand loyalty. Future studies could be directed to examine how continuous personalization throughout the different phases of the customer journey-from the discovery and exploration stages all the way up to postpurchase-can build a continuous experience at the brand level. These are issues involved in the post-purchase stage of the purchase cycle, namely, customer support, feedback collection, and loyalty programs, which are very important for the continuous engagement and satisfaction of customers.

As mobile marketing continues to evolve, future research should pay heed to the role of mobile devices in AI-driven personalized marketing. With mobile marketing becoming trendy these days, the integration of AI along with mobile advertising strategy can gain maximum targeting and personalization content along with customer interaction (Bakopoulos et al., 2017). Future potential research regarding the use of mobile AI by brands to optimize the consumer decision-making process will be to find out which format is best suited for mobile advertising and budgeting advertisement on different types of mobile platforms. It would be more relevant to emphasize the ethics of AI-based personalization marketing. The more data a brand collects and analyzes about consumers, the more critical issues surrounding privacy, data security, and responsible use of AI arise. Future research fields may concern helping brands reconcile the benefits of personalization with the concerns around data privacy and consumer transparency. It may also help shed more light on how brands might reconstruct consumer trust without cutting into the potential efficiency of targeted marketing campaigns.

Conclusion

The implementation of AI, social media, and e-commerce in brand management has dramatically changed the business practices by which companies establish relationships with their customers as well as create brand equity. Changes as far-reaching as these offer great opportunities but pose significant challenges for managers of brands and marketers. As the advancement of AI is on the rise, brand managers have to be equipped to deal with data-driven personalization and omnichannel strategies to deliver a seamless and consistent brand experience. The prospect of future AI-driven personalized marketing has an enormous growth potential to be diversified to even more businesses, and with that, the integration of the emerging technologies like IoT and blockchain into marketing will indeed propel marketers toward great potential. However, ongoing research in the realms of virtual influencers, customer journey, mobile marketing, and ethical considerations will be vastly important to the ways in which brands will find their place within this rapidly changing landscape. Future research will thus be instrumental as digital technologies continue to reshape management in unprecedented ways concerning brand-based products and services.

5. CONCLUSION

The integration of AI, social media, and e-commerce into brand management as revolutionized the way businesses achieve relationships with their customers and then maintain brand equity. Hence, this chapter presents a comprehensive exploration of the drivers of change, opportunities, and challenges in the transformation. It has paid attention to how AI-based technologies and digital tools help brands create custom experiences, improve operational efficiency, and be creative in methods for changing the evolving nature of markets. Even though this trend throws open great avenues for growth, it further introduces complexities that necessitate proper strategic foresight, adaptability, and what may be termed 'ethics' from brand managers and marketers. At the heart of this transformation lies the potential of AI-driven abilities about revolutionizing personalization across marketing boundaries. By allowing brands to analyze huge chunks of data in real-time, AI enables creating experiences hyper-personalized to preferences and behaviors at the individual level, thereby improving customer satisfaction as much as loyalty and retention and potentially establishing brands as a non-replaceable element in their customers' lives. This chapter heightens the urge for brand managers to move beyond unorthodox marketing tactics, embracing a data-driven approach to building great relationships with customers in a satiated digital environment. All elements of strategy, advanced analytics, and AI tools should seamlessly integrate in order to bring compelling connections with customers.

Another major takeaway from this chapter is that seamless customer experiences call for omnichannel marketing strategies. With a multitude of channels now to connect with brands, ranging from social media and mobile apps to e-commerce platforms and physical stores, customers need to interact with a brand in multiple ways to execute a smooth and personalized journey across these channels, which leads to brand consistency and consequently, to customer satisfaction. Here again, AI plays an important role as it tracks customer interaction across platforms in order to provide timely, relevant, and personalized messages to the target audience. This integration not only optimizes communication in terms of timing and content, but it also strengthens brand loyalty and efficient expenditure on marketing. The broader sense of this concept involves bringing together the fractured landscape of digital marketing so that brands can tell one interesting story about themselves to the customers .Apart from marketing, impact stretches into the operational areas of brand management. From predictive analytics to supply chain optimization, AI empowers brands to make decisions that help optimize efficiency and response to trends. Brand managers can tap into the AI-driven power of knowing what is happening ahead of the curve in terms of trends and demand anticipation and responding nimbly to changes in the market. This chapter points to the potential of AI in changing the operational process towards strategic branding goals wherein every decision is informed by data and oriented towards improving customer experience. The potential impacts of such an advancement would be to give brands opportunities for innovation not only in the way that they market their products but in their design and delivery also. It represents an entire scope of opportunities presented by AI and digital technologies across different sectors. Already having a very positive impact on retail, finance, and healthcare, AI-powered personalization is said to be ready to disrupt other domains including education, entertainment, and manufacturing. For instance, with AI, learning will be a completely different experience as it can provide adaptive learning tailored to each student's needs. In the field of entertainment, it can enhance viewers' satisfaction by recommending personalized content to them. For manufacturing, it can make supply chains and predictive maintenance processes in it more efficient by reducing costs. These might be useful in a broader scope for the simple reason that they can lead to interdisciplinary applications of AI, whereby principles coming from personalised branding adapt well to many challenges and opportunities that other fields face.

The chapter also pinpoints some promising avenues of future research that might further advance the discipline of brand management through the digital age. Another research direction involves studying the role of virtual influencers in creating diverse and inclusive brand identities. Using virtual influencers by digital platforms to interact with consumers is growing rapidly; thus, understanding how diversity in characteristics—that is, in representation along cultural, ethnic lines or even ability—impacts consumer perceptions and brand loyalty is critical. This line of inquiry deepens our understanding of consumer behavior and gives brands actionable insights into how to connect more effectively with differentiated audiences. Future areas of research include the long-term effects of AI-driven personalization on the relationship with the customer and brand loyalty. While significant strides have been made in the harnessing of AI for campaign usage short-term, there is a vast under-explored opportunity in the consistency of personalized practices all along the customer journey-from discovery to post-purchase. Studies on how AI can enhance customer experience at each stage of this journey would go a long way in determining equity in that brand. The third chapter further proposes that mobile marketing, an area that has been taken up with full steam during the last decade, requires further research. Knowing how AI optimizes the strategy, format, and medium of mobile advertising can help brands really talk to consumers from across the world in a world that's becoming more mobile-first. Another pressing problem is the ethical side of personalization through AI. Brands are now gathering so much data on consumers that issues related to privacy, security, and transparency require much more attention. Future research could, therefore, focus on how brands balance perceived benefits of AI-driven personalization against upholding consumer trust and ethical standards. This becomes very important research that would have to ensure the use of AI technologies in a responsible and sustainable manner in respect to the brand's relations with its customers.

The ideas and insights contained in this chapter demonstrate the transformative impact of digital technologies on brand management. AI, social media, and e-commerce have not only defined traditional marketing practices but also opened new frontiers for innovation and growth. Therefore, the chapter illustrates how these tools will empower brands to create a personalized, seamless, and efficient customer experience with a view to evoke loyalty and improve operational efficiency. It simultaneously recognizes that adapting to this new landscape can be troublesome, calling attention to strategic foresight and ethical responsibility. Considered together, the papers have greater relevance because they can update practitioner and research communities in common on dynamics of brand management, with its continuing shift into the digital age. While it will provide tangible insights for practitioners around AI and the digital toolkit for achieving strategic purposes, it will identify key areas for further exploration on matters related to virtual influencers and customer journey personalization, mobile marketing, and ethics. The concepts and ideas presented here will serve as foundations for understanding the complexities of brand management as this continues to influence how evolving digital technologies further reshape the global playing field, ensure that brands are both relevant and influential in a hyper-connected, data-driven world.

REFERENCES

Adami, M. (2015). Artificial Intelligence in Marketing and Consumer Behavior Analysis. *Marketing Science Journal*, 15(4), 23–45.

Adegbola, O., Smith, P., & Harrison, T. (2024). Consumer Analytics and Digital Marketing Transformation. *Journal of Digital Marketing*, 12(3), 112–128.

Anjorin, O., Raji, A., & Olodo, S. (2024). Elaboration likelihood model and consumer persuasion. *Journal of Marketing and Digital Media*, 12(3), 45–60.

Bakopoulos, V., Baranello, A., & Briggs, A. (2017). Mobile marketing: The next frontier of advertising research. *Journal of Interactive Advertising*, 17(1), 41–52. DOI: 10.1080/15252019.2017.1367880

Berry, L. L. (1983). Customer relationship management in the service sector. *Journal of Retailing*, 59(2), 25–48.

Borić, J., Simmons, L., & Chandra, K. (2024). The Impact of Digital Transformation on Consumer Behavior. *Journal of Digital Economy*, 10(2), 45–67.

Campbell, C., & Farrell, J. (2020). Influencer Marketing and Its Impact on Brand Management. *Journal of Advertising Research*, 22(1), 87–102.

Chae, B.. (2014). Big Data and Marketing Analytics: Insights into Consumer Behavior. *International Journal of Business Analytics*, 2(3), 33–47.

Chintalapati, A., & Pandey, R. (2022). The Influence of Artificial Intelligence on Marketing Strategy. *AI in Business Journal*, 9(1), 98–110.

Chintalapati, R., & Pandey, N. (2022). Impact of AI-based recommendations on customer engagement in e-commerce. *Journal of Retail and Digital Marketing*, 18(4), 250–267.

Cho, C. H., & Cheon, H. J. (2004). Why do people avoid advertising on the internet? *Journal of Advertising*, 33(4), 89–97. DOI: 10.1080/00913367.2004.10639175

Danaher, P. J., & Mullarkey, G. W. (2003). Factors affecting online advertising recall: A study of students. *Journal of Advertising Research*, 43(3), 252–267. DOI: 10.2501/JAR-43-3-252-267

Davenport, T. (2019). Artificial Intelligence in Marketing: Present and Future Applications. *Marketing Intelligence Journal*, 15(5), 110–125.

Davenport, T., & Ronanki, R. (2018). Artificial Intelligence for the Real World. *Harvard Business Review*, 96(1), 108–116.

Davenport, T., & Ronanki, R. (2018). Artificial intelligence for the real world. *Harvard Business Review*, 96(1), 108–116.

De Cremer, D., Nguyen, B., & Simkin, L. (2017). Blockchain technology: What is it good for? *California Management Review*, 60(1), 64–87. DOI: 10.1177/0008125617741344

Familoni, O., & Onyebuchi, A. (2024). Influence of peer recommendations on consumer behavior in digital spaces. *African Journal of Business and Consumer Studies*, 8(4), 89–101.

Farrell, C., Campbell, C., & Sands, S. (2022). Virtual Influencers in Branding and Consumer Engagement. *Journal of Interactive Marketing*, 20(2), 57–73.

Ferraro, C., Sands, S., & Tziati, N. (2022). Virtual influencers in social media: A branding perspective. *Journal of Brand Management*, 29(1), 24–38. DOI: 10.1057/s41262-021-00258-5

Gupta, M., Sharma, R., & Verma, S. (2020). E-commerce and consumer behavior: How AI influences personalized shopping experiences. *International Journal of Marketing and E-commerce*, 22(3), 145–160.

Hoyer, W. D., MacInnis, D. J., & Pieters, R. (2020). *Consumer behavior* (7th ed.). Cengage Learning.

Igbinenikaro, O., & Adewusi, K. (2024). Influence of social media interactions on consumer behavior: A comprehensive review. *Journal of Digital Marketing*, 15(5), 223–245.

Jankovic, S., & Curovic, T. (2023). Ensuring fairness in AI models: Addressing algorithmic bias in digital brand management. *Journal of Ethical AI in Branding*, 15(2), 95–108.

Katz, E., Blumler, J. G., & Gurevitch, M. (1973). Uses and gratifications research. *Public Opinion Quarterly*, 37(4), 509–523. DOI: 10.1086/268109

Katz, E., & Lazarsfeld, P. F. (2017). *Social influence and the mass media*. Free Press.

Kharfan, M., LeBlanc, A., & Miller, R. (2021). Predictive analytics in brand management: AI's role in inventory and pricing strategies. *Journal of Business Analytics and Marketing Strategies*, 13(1), 58–74.

Kumar, V., Shah, D., & Rajan, B. (2016). Digital Communication in a Modern Business Framework. *Marketing Communications*, 7(2), 151–168.

Marr, B. (2020). How Artificial Intelligence is Transforming Digital Marketing. *Journal of AI in Marketing*, 8(4), 67–92.

Ngai, E. W. T. (2005). Customer Relationship Management in the Digital Age. *International Journal of CRM*, 9(3), 203–216.

Nguyen, T. (2023). Exploring the Effectiveness of Virtual Influencers in Brand Promotion. *Journal of Social Media Research*, 17(2), 89–107.

Odonkor, A., Agyei, D., & Asante, J. (2024). Data Analytics in Digital Marketing. *Marketing Research and Insights*, 14(2), 33–45.

Payne, A., & Frow, P. (2005). A Strategic Framework for Customer Relationship Management. *Journal of Marketing*, 69(4), 167–176. DOI: 10.1509/jmkg.2005.69.4.167

Rahman, H., & Dekkati, A. (2022). Dynamic pricing with AI: Managing consumer behavior and competitiveness in e-commerce. *Journal of Pricing Strategy and Analytics*, 19(5), 105–121.

Rogers, E. M. (1962). *Diffusion of innovations*. Free Press.

Sands, S., Campbell, C., & Farrell, J. (2022). Virtual Influencers and Digital Engagement. *The Journal of Consumer Research*, 18(3), 67–92.

Siebert, T., Jones, L., & McMillan, E. (2020). AI and automation in customer service: Chatbots as brand management tools. *Customer Experience and Technology Review*, 7(1), 33–42.

Urefe, O., Odonkor, A., & Agu, C. (2024). Data Analytics and CRM Tools in Marketing Transformation. *Journal of Marketing Technology*, 19(1), 33–54.

Verhoef, P. C., Kannan, P. K., & Inman, J. J. (2021). From multi-channel retailing to omni-channel retailing: Introduction to the special issue on multi-channel retailing. *Journal of Retailing*, 97(1), 63–68. DOI: 10.1016/j.jretai.2020.10.004

Wamba, S. F., Gunasekaran, A., & Akter, S. (2017). Big Data Analytics in E-Commerce: A Systematic Review and Agenda for Future Research. *Journal of Business Research*, 70, 263–273.

Chapter 2
Understanding Artificial Intelligence and Its Role in Branding

P. Selvakumar
https://orcid.org/0000-0002-3650-4548
Department of Science and Humanities, Nehru Institute of Technology, India

D. Gnanaprakasam
Dr. Mahalingam College of Engineering and Technology, India

Sushma Gudivada
https://orcid.org/0009-0008-7755-7460
CVR College of Engineering, India

Sujay Mugaloremutt Jayadeva
JSS Academy of Higher Education and Research, India

Manjunath T. C.
https://orcid.org/0000-0003-2545-9160
Rajarajeswari College of Engineering, India

ABSTRACT

This proactive approach helps brands stay ahead of market trends and respond more effectively to changes in consumer preferences.AI-driven content creation is transforming how brands develop and deliver their messaging. Natural Language Processing (NLP) and Generative AI models can automate the creation of written content, such as social media posts, blog articles, and email campaigns. These AI tools can generate content that aligns with a brand's tone and style while optimizing for engagement and relevance. For instance, AI can analyze past successful content

DOI: 10.4018/979-8-3693-9461-8.ch002

to identify key elements that resonate with audiences and use this information to create new, impactful content. This capability not only streamlines content production but also ensures that messaging remains consistent and effective across various platforms.Customer service and engagement have also been significantly enhanced, 24/7 support to customers, handling inquiries, resolving issues, and guiding users through processes.

INTRODUCTION TO AI IN BRANDING: REVOLUTIONIZING MARKETING STRATEGIES

This proactive approach helps brands stay ahead of market trends and respond more effectively to changes in consumer preferences.AI-driven content creation is transforming how brands develop and deliver their messaging. Natural Language Processing (NLP) and Generative AI models can automate the creation of written content, such as social media posts, blog articles, and email campaigns. These AI tools can generate content that aligns with a brand's tone and style while optimizing for engagement and relevance. For instance, AI can analyze past successful content to identify key elements that resonate with audiences and use this information to create new, impactful content. This capability not only streamlines content production but also ensures that messaging remains consistent and effective across various platforms.Customer service and engagement have also been significantly enhanced, 24/7 support to customers, handling inquiries, resolving issues, and guiding users through processes. Chatbots can be programmed, offering personalized assistance based on customer data and previous interactions. This analysis marketing emails, the most effective types of content to use, and the optimal channels for reaching target audiences. these, AI enhances the efficiency and impact of marketing efforts. Segmentation and targeting have become more precise with the help of AI. Traditional segmentation methods often relied on broad categories, but AI enables more granular and dynamic segmentation based on a wide range of factors, including behavior, preferences, and purchasing history. AI algorithms can create detailed customer profiles and identify niche segments that might have been overlooked using conventional methods. This allows brands to tailor their marketing strategies to specific audience segments, improving relevance and effectiveness by monitoring and analyzing online sentiment and feedback. Tools powered by sentiment analysis and NLP can track mentions of a brand across social media, news sites, and review platforms, providing insights into public perception and potential issues. By identifying positive and negative sentiment, brands can respond proactively to feedback, address concerns, and capitalize on positive sentiments. This real-time monitoring and analysis help brands maintain a positive image and build stronger relationships with their audiences. AR applications can use AI to provide personalized product recommendations and interactive experiences, while VR can offer virtual tours and simulations that showcase a brand's offerings. The synergy between AI and these technologies expands the possibilities for creative and engaging branding strategies.

AI Fundamentals for Branding Professionals: Machine Learning and Deep Learning

Understanding the fundamentals r engagement brand positioning. This comprehensive overview of ML and DL provides a foundation for branding professionals to harness AI's capabilities effectively. within data, making predictions or decisions based on these insights. For branding professionals, ML can be a powerful tool for analyzing customer data, predicting trends, and personalizing marketing strategies. For branding, RNNs can enhance customer interactions by improving chatbot responses, predicting customer preferences based on past interactions, and personalizing content recommendations. Transformers A recent advancement in deep learning, transformers are leverage attention mechanisms to process and generate human language with high accuracy. In branding, transformers can be used for advanced text analysis, such as sentiment analysis, content generation, and automated responses. The integration of ML and DL into branding strategies offers several benefits Personalization**: AI can analyze customer data to create highly personalized experiences. Machine learning algorithms can segment audiences based on behavior and preferences, while deep learning models can generate tailored content that resonates with individual users. Predictive Analytics ML algorithms allows brands to anticipate market changes, optimize inventory, and fine-tune marketing strategies. Automation AI can automate repetitive tasks, placement, customer service (Adami, 2015). This not only increases consistency in brand messaging and responsiveness. Enhanced Insights Deep learning models can uncover insights from complex data sets that traditional methods might miss. This includes analyzing sentiment from social media, identifying emerging trends, and understanding customer preferences at a granular level. Despite the advantages, branding professionals must also consider the challenges associated with implementing ML and DL Quality and Quantity Effective ML and DL require large amounts of high-quality data. Ensuring data accuracy and relevance is crucial for training effective models. Complexity can be infrastructure and expertise to develop and maintain these models. guided by ethical considerations, including data privacy and transparency. Brands should ensure they use data responsibly and comply with relevant regulations. Integration Seamlessly with branding strategies technologies Brands must ensure that AI tools align with their overall marketing objectives and workflows. In conclusion, AI, through Machine Learning and Deep Learning, is revolutionizing branding by enabling more personalized, predictive, and efficient marketing strategies. (Agrawal et al., 2018) Understanding the fundamentals of these technologies empowers branding professionals to leverage AI effectively, enhancing customer engagement and driving innovation. By addressing achieve impactful and successful branding outcomes.

AI-Driven Brand Insights: Unlocking Consumer Behavior and Preferences

AI-driven brand insights are proving to be game-changers in understanding and predicting consumer behavior and preferences., and generate actionable insights that were previously inaccessible or too complex to discern of their consumers, allowing for highly targeted strategies that drive engagement and loyalty. For instance, predictive analytics can identify and emerging trends, enabling brands to adjust their strategies proactively. Sentiment analysis powered by feature, a brand can address the issue by making necessary adjustments or communicating improvements to the consumers. Customer journey mapping is greatly enhanced by AI, providing a comprehensive view of how consumers interact with a brand across various touchpoints. where they can optimize their engagement strategies. touchpoint significantly impacts conversion rates, brands can focus on enhancing that aspect of the customer experience. Market segmentation becomes more precise with AI. Traditional segmentation methods often relied on broad categories, but AI enables more granular segmentation behavior, preferences, and purchasing history. Advanced brands to develop highly targeted campaigns and product offerings, catering to the specific needs and preferences of each segment. For instance, a brand might discover a previously unnoticed segment of consumers who respond well to eco-friendly products, prompting the development of targeted marketing initiatives for this group.Predictive modeling is a powerful tool enabled by AI for forecasting consumer trends and behaviors. brands looking to anticipate market changes, plan inventory, and optimize marketing strategies. Predictive models can forecast demand for products, identify potential churn risks, and suggest the best times for promotional campaigns. indicate particular product is likely to see increased demand in the coming months, allowing the brand to prepare accordingly by adjusting stock levels and marketing efforts.Customer segmentation and targeting are further refined through AI, which can identify subtle differences in consumer behavior that traditional methods might miss.(Aguirre et al., 2015) For instance, AI can analyze the effectiveness of various marketing channels and messages across different consumer segments, providing health monitoring value. AI tools can track and analyze various metrics related to brand performance, such as customer satisfaction, brand reputation, and market share. By continuously monitoring, brands overall health potential issues before they escalate. For example, declining brand sentiment, allowing the brand to address concerns and mitigate negative impacts.The ethical use of AI is an important consideration in brand insights. explicit consent from consumers and safeguarding their personal information. Responsible AI practices help build trust with consumers and prevent potential misuse of data. In summary, AI-driven brand insights are revolutionizing how brands understand and engage with consumers.deep learning, brands complex data, uncover patterns, and that enhance customer experiences and drive business success. .

Personalization and AI: Tailoring Brand Experiences for Individual Customers

Personalization, driven by Artificial Intelligence (AI), is revolutionizing how brands tailor their and technologies to meet these expectations by leveraging vast amounts of data to deliver customized content, recommendations, and communications. This transformation in personalization is reshaping marketing strategies, enhancing customer satisfaction, and driving brand loyalty.Personalized content delivery is another significant application of AI in branding. AI can automate and optimize the creation of content that resonates with individual users. user's interests, brands can foster deeper connections and drive higher engagement.Customer segmentation is greatly enhanced by AI, enabling brands to move beyond traditional demographic-based canntricate patterns in nteractions(Boyd & Holton, 2018). This granular segmentation For example, clustering algorithms can group customers with similar purchasing habits or engagement patterns, allowing brands to design marketing strategies that cater specifically to these groups. that are directly relevant to each segment.Predictive analytics further amplifies the power of personalization. trends, forecast . models enable brands to . For instance, AI can predict when a customer might need to restock a product by addressing needs before they arise. brands to adapt their messaging and offers based on current customer if a user is browsing a website and shows interest in a particular category of products, AI can instantly adjust the website's content and promotions to highlight relevant items. This dynamic personalization ensures that users receive the most pertinent information and offers at the moment they are most engaged, improving the chances of conversion.Customer journey optimization is enhanced by AI through the ability to map and analyze every touchpoint in the customer experience. AI tools can track various and devices, providing ensuring a seamless and personalized experience throughout the journey.e which touchpoints are most effective for driving conversions and which areas might need adjustment. By optimizing the customer journey, brands can enhance satisfaction and drive better outcomes.Dynamic pricing and offers are also influenced by AI-driven personalization. AI history and price sensitivity. For instance, AI can identify a loyal customer who frequently purchases certain products and offer them personalized discounts or special deals to reward their loyalty and encourage continued engagement. and data privacy are crucial aspects of AI-driven personalization. Transparent data practices, such as obtaining explicit consent and safeguarding personal information, are essential for maintaining consumer trust. Additionally, brands should strive to avoid reinforcing biases or creating intrusive experiences by using Integration of AI with other technologies can further enhance personalization efforts(Biswas et al., 2013). For instance, combining AI with Augmented Reality (AR) can create immersive and interactive brand experiences that are personalized to individual preferences. AR applications can use AI to analyze user behavior and preferences to deliver customized virtual experiences, such as trying on virtual products or exploring personalized content. This integration of AI and AR provides a unique and engaging way for*In summary, AI-driven personalization is revolutionizing how brands tailor their experiences to individual customers by leveraging data, predictive analytics, and real-time insights. By utilizing AI technologies, brands can deliver highly relevant content, recommendations, and interactions that enhance customer satisfaction and loyalty. From personalized content delivery and dynamic pricing

AI-Powered Content Generation: Enhancing Brand Storytelling and Engagement

AI-powered content generation is transforming brand storytelling and engagement by offering innovative tools and techniques for creating compelling and personalized content at scale. As brands seek to differentiate themselves in a crowded marketplace, AI provides the capability to produce high-quality, relevant content that resonates with diverse audiences. This evolution in content creation is not only enhancing the effectiveness of brand communications but also enabling more dynamic and interactive consumer experiences.AI-driven content generation encompasses various technologies and approaches that automate and optimize the creation of written, visual, and multimedia content.(Castelo & Ward, 2016) At the heart of this transformation are models and Generative AI, which can produce text that closely mimics human writing and adapts to specific brand voices and styles. For instance, AI-powered keywords, themes, or audience preferences. These tools analyze existing content, identify trends, and apply learned patterns to create objectives. in content creation. Traditional content production methods often require significant time and resources, especially when producing content across multiple channels and formats. AI tools quickly and efficiently, allowing brands to maintain a consistent presence across various platforms., ad copy, and product descriptions in bulk, enabling brands to keep their content fresh and engaging without the need for extensive manual effort.Visual content generation Generative Adversarial Networks (GANs) and other AI technologies can create high-quality images, graphics(Castelo et al., 2018), and videos based on specified parameters. For example, AI can design unique visuals for marketing campaigns or generate product mockups that align with a brand's aesthetic. This capability allows brands to produce visually appealing content that captures attention and reinforces brand identity. Additionally, AI can enhance existing visual content by applying filters, adjustments, or stylistic elements that enhance its effectiveness and appeal.Interactive content is an emerging trend that AI is driving forward. AI can be used to create interactive experiences such as quizzes, polls, and chatbots that engage users and encourage participation.

These interactive elements not only capture user attention but also provide valuable insights into consumer preferences and behavior. For example, AI-powered chatbots can simulate conversations with users, offering personalized recommendations and support based on their inputs. This type of interactive content fosters deeper engagement and builds stronger connections between brands and their audiences. Content curation is another area where AI adds value., blog posts, or multimedia that align with a brand's objectives or a user's interests. This capability ensures that brands provide valuable and timely information to their audiences, enhancing their authority and credibility in their respective fields. For instance,(Davenport, 2018) AI can curate content for newsletters or social media feeds, ensuring that the selected materials are engaging and pertinent to the target audience.Ethical considerations and challenges are important aspects of AI-powered content generation. As AI systems generate content, ensuring that it aligns with ethical standards and does not perpetuate biases is crucial. Brands must also be mindful of transparency, comply with regulations. is also important for maximizing the benefits of AI in content generation. While AI can automate and optimize content creation, human oversight and creativity remain essential for ensuring that content is authentic, emotionally resonant, and aligned with brand values. Collaborating with AI allows brands to leverage the efficiency and scale of automation while incorporating human insights and creativity to produce content that truly connects with audiences.In summary, AI-powered content generation is revolutionizing brand storytelling and engagement by providing tools and technologies that enhance personalization, optimization, and scalability. For instance, a virtual assistant integrated with a CRM system can access customer profiles, previous interactions, and transaction history to provide contextually relevant support and follow-up. This integration ensures that customers receive consistent and informed assistance across different touchpoints.Continuous improvement is a hallmark of AI-powered patterns in user queries, feedback, and outcomes, these AI tools can refine their understanding and enhance their performance. For example, a chatbot might learn to recognize new synonyms or variations in user queries, improving its ability to provide accurate and relevant answers. User experience is enhanced through intuitive and natural interactions facilitated by advanced NLP and conversational(Davenport et al., 2011) Ai through their AI-driven capabilities. These tools offer 24/7 availability, efficiency, personalization, and cost-effectiveness, while continuously improving through machine learning. By integrating with other systems and providing natural, intuitive interactions, AI-driven customer service enhances user experiences and operational effectiveness. However, addressing challenges related to accuracy, user expectations, and ethical considerations service.

AI-Driven Social Media Monitoring and Analytics: Tracking Brand Reputation

AI-driven social media monitoring and analytics are transforming how brands track and manage their reputation as a powerful platform for consumer engagement, businesses face the challenge of keeping a pulse on public sentiment, emerging trends, and potential issues that could impact their brand image. AI technologies offer sophisticated tools to automate and enhance social media monitoring and analytics, providing actionable insights that help brands navigate the complex landscape of online reputation management. AI-powered social media monitoring technologies can unstructured Twitter, Facebook, Instagram, and LinkedIn, extracting valuable insights from user-generated content.opinion and identify trends with greater accuracy. By classifying social media mentions as positive, negative, or neutral, AI algorithms help brands understand the overall sentiment towards their products, services, or campaigns. This analysis provides a snapshot of how the public perceives the brand and highlights areas where improvements or interventions may be needed. For example, if sentiment analysis reveals a spike in negative sentiment related to a specific product, a brand can quickly address the issue by issuing a response or making necessary changes systems can identify emerging trends, topics, and hashtags that are gaining traction across social media platforms. By analyzing patterns in user engagement and content, AI can pinpoint rising trends that may affect the brand's reputation or present new opportunities. For instance, detecting an increase in discussions about sustainability could prompt a brand to highlight its own environmental initiatives in response to growing consumer interest.Competitor analysis is significantly enhanced through AI-powered performance across competitors, providing insights into their strategies, strengths, and weaknesses. By analyzing competitor content, campaign is receiving significant positive attention, a brand might analyze the elements contributing to that success and consider similar approaches or improvements.Crisis management is facilitated by AI-driven social media analytics through early detection and rapid response. potential crises or issues escalate for sudden changes in sentiment or spikes in negative mentions.

This early warning allows brands to respond promptly and effectively, mitigating potential damage to their reputation. For example, if a controversial statement or event leads to a surge in negative mentions,(French, 2018) AI can alert the brand's PR team to take immediate action, such as issuing a statement or addressing the concern directly.Content performance analysis is enhanced by AI-driven social media analytics, which can evaluate the effectiveness of various types of content across different platforms. AI tools can helps brands optimize their content strategy by focusing on formats and topics that drive higher engagement. For instance, AI might reveal that video content performs significantly better than static images, prompting a shift in content strategy to capitalize on this insight.User engagement analysis provides a deeper understanding of how audiences interact with a brand on social media. AI systems can track and analyze user interactions, including comments, replies, and direct messages, to gauge the quality and depth of engagement. By examining patterns in user behavior and feedback, brands can tailor their social media strategies to foster more meaningful interactions and build stronger relationships with their audience. For example, analyzing user feedback on a recent campaign can reveal insights into what aspects were well-received and what areas need improvement. (Gans et al., 2017)Data visualization and reporting are streamlined by AI technologies, which can generate comprehensive and visually appealing reports that highlight key metrics and insights. AI tools can create dashboards that provide a real-time overview of social media performance, sentiment trends, and engagement metrics. These visualizations make it easier for brands to interpret data, track progress, .view of their online presence and performance. For example, integrating social media insights with CRM data can provide a deeper understanding of how social interactions influence customer behavior and loyalty, enabling more targeted marketing efforts. AI-driven social media monitoring and analytics are revolutionizing how brands track and manage their reputation. By leveraging advanced NLP, sentiment analysis, trend detection, and other AI technologies, brands can gain valuable insights into public opinion, emerging trends, and competitor activities. These tools enable more effective crisis management, influencer identification, content optimization, and user engagement analysis. While addressing ethical considerations and ensuring data privacy, brands can their social media strategies and maintain a positive online presence. social media monitoring will likely expand, offering even greater audiences manage their reputation effectively.

Influencer Marketing and AI: Identifying and Partnering with Key Influencers

Influencer marketing, bolstered by Artificial Intelligence (AI), has evolved into a sophisticated strategy for identifying and partnering with key influencers who can effectively amplify brand messages and drive engagement. This synergy between AI and influencer marketing harnesses advanced technologies to streamline the process of finding the right influencers, evaluating their impact, and optimizing campaigns for maximum effectiveness. As brands seek AI-driven influencer identification leverages algorithms and data analytics to pinpoint individuals who have the potential to influence target audiences(Gaudin, 2016). Traditional methods of influencer discovery often searches and subjective could be time-consuming and imprecise. AI transforms this process by analyzing vast amounts of data from social media platforms, blogs, and other digital channels to identify influencers based on criteria such as audience demographics, engagement metrics, and content relevance. For instance, AI can scan social media profiles to identify individuals with high follower counts, substantial engagement rates, and alignment with the brand's industry or niche. brands partner with influencers whose audiences closely match their target demographics.an influencer's content. Beyond basic engagement statistics, AI can analyze the quality of interactions and the authenticity of followers. For example, AI can detect bot activity or fake accounts, ensuring that brands are partnering with influencers who have genuine and engaged audiences. This level of scrutiny helps brands avoid potential pitfalls associated with influencer partnerships, such as inflated follower counts or low engagement rates.analysis in influencer marketing. systems can evaluate the content produced by potential influencers to determine its relevance, tone, and alignment with the brand's values. can and complements its own content strategy. Additionally, AI can assess visual content using image recognition technology to ensure that the influencer's aesthetic aligns with the brand's image and campaign objectives. in AI-driven influencer marketing, providing brands with insights into future trends and potential outcomes of influencer partnerships. By analyzing historical data and identifying patterns in influencer performance Influencer relationship management is streamlined by AI through the automation of outreach, communication, and collaboration processes. AI-powered tools can facilitate the negotiation and management of influencer partnerships by automating tasks such as contract management, payment processing, and performance tracking. ensuring that all aspects of the partnership are executed smoothly and efficiently.Campaign optimization is enhanced by AI through continuous monitoring and analysis of influencer performance throughout the campaign lifecycle.

AI tools can track real-time data on engagement, reach, and audience sentiment, providing brands with actionable insights to optimize their campaigns. For instance, if an AI system detects that certain content or messaging is resonating particularly well with the audience, it can recommend adjustments to enhance the campaign's effectiveness. This dynamic approach allows brands to adapt their strategies in response to real-time feedback and performance metrics, ensuring that campaigns remain relevant and impactful.Audience segmentation and targeting are refined by AI in influencer marketing, enabling brands to reach specific segments of their target audience more effectively. interests, allowing brands to craft customized campaigns that resonate with different audience segments. This precision targeting enhances the relevance of influencer partnerships and improves the overall effectiveness of marketing efforts.Measuring ROi is made more accurate and insightful through AI-driven analytics. AI tools can provide detailed reports on return on investment for their influencer partnerships and determine the overall impact on their marketing objectives. For example, AI can attribute conversions and sales to specific influencers, providing a clear understanding of the value they bring to the brand driven influencer marketing. Brands must ensure that their AI systems operate fairly and avoid biases in influencer selection and analysis(Haenlein & Kaplan, 2019). Additionally, maintaining transparency in influencer partnerships is essential for building trust with audiences and adhering to regulatory guidelines. For instance, brands should disclose sponsored content and ensure that influencer relationships are clearly communicated to consumers. Ethical practices and transparency contribute to a positive brand image and foster genuine connections with audiences. Integration with other marketing strategies is enhanced by AI, allowing for a cohesive and unified approach to brand promotion. AI-driven influencer marketing can be integrated with broader overall marketing objectives, brands can create a seamless and impactful marketing ecosystem. For example, AI can coordinate influencer content with social media ads, ensuring consistent messaging and maximizing the reach and effectiveness of both strategies.

AI-Optimized Brand Campaigns: Predictive Analytics and Performance Measurement

AI-optimized brand campaigns represent a groundbreaking evolution in marketing strategies, leveraging predictive analytics and advanced performance measurement techniques to drive more effective and targeted brand initiatives. As brands navigate increasingly competitive and data-rich environments, AI offers sophisticated tools to enhance campaign planning, execution, and evaluation. By integrating AI technologies, brands can optimize their campaigns with precision, anticipate market trends, and measure performance in ways that maximize return on investment and achieve strategic objectives.r example, AI can identify patterns in consumer purchasing behavior and predict future buying trends, allowing brands to tailor their campaigns to align with anticipated consumer needs(Heaven, 2019). This predictive capability enables brands to allocate resources more effectively, prioritize high-impact strategies, and adjust their approaches based on anticipated performance.Campaign planning is significantly enhanced by AI through, and consumer sentiment, to inform campaign strategies. By integrating these insights, brands can design campaigns that resonate with target audiences and capitalize on emerging opportunities.(Pangburn, 2018) For instance, AI can analyze social media conversations and identify trending topics, enabling brands to incorporate relevant themes into their campaigns and engage with audiences on current issues..Real-time optimization is a major advantage of AI in brand campaigns.

AI systems can monitor campaign performance continuously and make real-time adjustments based on incoming data. For instance, if an AI tool detects that certain ad creatives are outperforming others, it can automatically allocate more budget to the high-performing ads and reduce spend on less effective ones. Attribution modeling is another critical aspect of performance measurement that is optimized by AI. AI tools can analyze complex customer journeys and attribute conversions to various touchpoints along the path to purchase. By understanding how different channels and interactions contribute to conversions, brands can allocate their marketing budgets more effectively and identify which channels are driving the most value. For example, AI Content optimization is facilitated by AI through the analysis of content performance and user engagement. AI tools can assess elements. By analyzing engagement metrics and user feedback, AI can recommend adjustments to content strategies to improve effectiveness.(Jiang, 2018) For instance, AI might identify that video content generates higher engagement rates compared to static images, prompting brands to focus more on video in their campaigns.Competitor analysis is enhanced by AI, allowing brands to monitor and benchmark their performance against competitors. AI tools can analyze competitors' campaigns, strategies, and market positioning to provide insights into their strengths and weaknesses. This competitive intelligence helps brands identify opportunities to differentiate themselves and refine their own campaigns. track competitors' analyze their engagement rates, providing insights into what is working well for them and how brands Predictive modeling can also be applied to forecasting future trends and consumer behavior. of the curve. For instance, AI might predict a rise in demand for sustainable products, prompting brands to highlight their eco-friendly initiatives in their upcoming campaigns.Integration with other marketing technologies optimized campaigns.ools can seamlessly (Sweeney & Soutar, 2001) unified view of campaign performance and customer interactions, enabling brands to coordinate their efforts and achieve a cohesive marketing strategy.Ethical considerations and data privacy are important aspects of AI-driven campaign optimization. Brands must I respects consumer privacy and adheres to relevant regulations. explicit consent for data collection, and secure handling of personal information are essential for maintaining trust and complying with legal requirements.

AI-Driven Brand Protection: Detecting and Preventing Counterfeiting and Piracy

AI-driven brand protection is revolutionizing the fight against counterfeiting and piracy, offering advanced tools to detect, prevent, and manage these pervasive threats that undermine brand integrity and consumer trust. With the proliferation of digital platforms and global trade, counterfeiting and piracy have become more sophisticated, posing significant challenges to brands seeking to protect their intellectual property and maintain their market position(Kaplan, 2016). AI technologies provide a comprehensive and proactive approach to safeguarding brands Counterfeiting detection is significantly enhanced by AI image recognition and pattern analysis technologies. packaging to identify counterfeit goods by comparing them against a database of authentic product images. For example, machine learning algorithms can detect subtle differences in logos, labels, and packaging designs that may not be visible to the naked eye. This capability enables brands to identify counterfeit products in real-time and take swift action to address the issue. AI can also monitor online marketplaces and social media platforms for listings of counterfeit products, providing early warnings and enabling proactive measures to protect brand reputation.Piracy prevention benefits from AI through the monitoring and enforcement of digital content rights. AI technologies can track the distribution of copyrighted content across digital platforms, including websites, file-sharing services, and streaming platforms. By analyzing patterns in content distribution and identifying unauthorized copies, AI can help brands detect instances of piracy and take action to remove infringing content. For instance, AI systems can scan the web for illegal copies of digital media, such as music, movies, and software, and automatically issue takedown notices or engage with enforcement agencies to address the infringement.Data analytics plays a crucial role in AI-driven brand protection insights into trends and patterns related to counterfeiting and piracy. AI systems s online sales platforms, social media, and supply chain records, to identify suspicious activities and changes in sales patterns that may indicate counterfeit activity. brands to focus their resources on high-risk areas and develop targeted strategies for combating counterfeiting and piracy.Supply chain monitoring is enhanced by AI through the integration distribution networks, and retail channels. AI systems can verifying their authenticity and detecting potential points of vulnerability. For example(Johnson, 2018), AI can analyze data from RFID tags, barcodes, and other tracking technologies to ensure that products are genuine and have not been tampered with. This end-to-end visibility helps brands identify and address issues related to counterfeit products entering the supply chain and ensures that only authentic products reach consumers. models can be trained to recognize new patterns in counterfeit products or unauthorized content, allowing AI systems to stay ahead of emerging threats.

As counterfeiting and piracy techniques evolve, AI systems can update their detection methods and enforcement strategies to remain effective. is a key benefit of AI-driven brand protection, enabling brands to respond quickly and efficiently to instances of counterfeiting and piracy. AI systems can automate tasks such as issuing takedown notices, blocking unauthorized listings, and initiating legal actions. For instance, Collaboration with law enforcement and legal entities is facilitated by AI through the provision of detailed evidence and insights. AI systems can generate comprehensive reports on counterfeiting and piracy activities, including evidence of infringement, patterns of distribution, and potential perpetrators. These reports can support legal actions and enforcement efforts by providing a clear and data-driven basis for legal claims. For example, AI-generated evidence can be used in court cases to demonstrate the extent of counterfeiting or piracy and support efforts to secure injunctions or damages.Consumer education and awareness are enhanced by AI-driven brand protection efforts, as AI technologies can help brands communicate with consumers about the risks of counterfeiting and piracy. misconceptions or concerns related to product authenticity. Brands can use this information to develop educational materials and awareness campaigns that inform consumers about how to identify genuine products and report suspected counterfeits. For example, AI can help brands create targeted messaging that addresses specific consumer concerns and provides guidance on verifying product authenticity.Ethical considerations and privacy concerns are important aspects of AI-driven brand protection(Li & Vargo, 2019). Brands consumer privacy and adheres analyses are fair and accurate. Additionally, transparency in how AI is used for brand protection is essential for maintaining consumer trust and avoiding potential backlash. Brands should clearly communicate their efforts to protect intellectual property and address any concerns related to enforcement.Integration with other brand protection strategies is a key advantage of AI, allowing brands to create a comprehensive and coordinated approach to combating counterfeiting and piracy. AI-driven brand protection can be integrated with other strategies, such as physical security measures, authentication technologies, and legal enforcement. By combining AI with traditional brand protection methods, brands can enhance their overall effectiveness and achieve a more robust defense against counterfeiting and piracy.In conclusion, AI-driven brand protection is a powerful tool for detecting and preventing counterfeiting and piracy. image recognition, brands can enhance their ability to identify counterfeit products, monitor digital content, and enforce intellectual property rights(Naeem & Khawaja, 2019). The integration of AI technologies enables real-time detection, automated enforcement, and comprehensive data analysis, providing brands with a proactive and effective approach to safeguarding their reputation and ensuring the authenticity of their products.

Human-AI Collaboration in Branding: Augmenting Creativity and Strategy

Human-AI collaboration in branding represents a transformative shift in how creativity and strategy are developed and executed. By integrating Artificial Intelligence (AI) with human expertise, brands can enhance their creative processes, streamline strategic decision-making, and drive more effective and innovative marketing initiatives. This, resulting in a dynamic partnership that augments brand development and execution in unprecedented ways.Creativity augmentation is a primary benefit of human-AI collaboration. AI technologies can analyze vast amounts of data, including consumer trends, historical campaign performance, and competitor strategies, to generate insights that inspire creative ideas. For instance, AI can identify emerging trends and popular themes by analyzing social media conversations, search engine data, and market research. These insights can then be used by creative teams to develop more relevant and engaging brand content(Liu & Shin, 2018). AI-powered tools, such as generative design algorithms and content creation platforms, can also assist in producing initial drafts of creative assets, such as ad copy, visuals, and videos. By providing a foundation of data-driven ideas and options, AI enables human creatives to focus on refining and enhancing concepts, ultimately leading to more innovative and effective brand messaging.Strategic decision-making benefits significantly from AI's analytical capabilities. datasets to identify patterns, forecast outcomes, and provide actionable recommendations. For example, AI can predict consumer behavior, assess market conditions, and evaluate the potential impact of different marketing strategies. This data-driven approach allows brand strategists.

AI can also simulate various scenarios and outcomes, helping brands to explore different strategies and select the most effective ones. This predictive capability ensures that strategic decisions are grounded in data and aligned with market realities. (Nadarajah & Bakar, 2019)Campaign optimization is enhanced through monitor investment (ROI) across various marketing channels. By continuously analyzing this data, AI can provide insights into what is working and what needs adjustment. For instance, AI can identify which elements of a campaign are resonating with the audience and recommend changes to improve performance. This iterative process allows brands to refine their strategies and optimize campaigns in real time, leading to more successful outcomes.Personalization at scale human-AI collaboration. AI can analyze individual consumer data to create highly personalized brand experiences. For example, AI . Human marketers can use these insights to craft personalized messages and campaigns that resonate with specific audience segments, combining AI's data-driven recommendations with their own creativity and understanding of the brand's voice.Creative testing and validation are streamlined through AI-powered tools. and calls to action, to determine which ones are most effective. A/B testing and multivariate testing are enhanced by This data-driven approach ensures that creative decisions are informed by empirical evidence, reducing the reliance on guesswork and increasing the likelihood of campaign success. Trend identification and forecasting are accelerated by AI's and detect emerging patterns. AI can monitor social media, news sources, and industry reports to identify trends that may impact brand strategy. By recognizing these trends early, brands can adapt their, if AI identifies a growing interest in sustainability among consumers, brands can adjust their messaging and incorporate eco-friendly practices into their campaigns. This proactive approach allows brands to remain relevant and responsive to changing market conditions.Collaboration and integration between AI and human teams are facilitated by user-friendly complement human expertise rather than replace it. For instance, AI-powered analytics platforms can provide detailed insights and visualizations that are easy for human marketers to interpret and act upon. Similarly, initial drafts that human creatives can refine and personalize. This seamless integration ensures that AI enhances rather than disrupts existing workflows, allowing human teams to leverage AI's capabilities effectively. utilize these tools. Training programs and educational resources can help marketing professionals understand how to work with AI and integrate it into their strategies. By developing these skills, marketers can harness AI's full potential and enhance their creative and strategic capabilities. Measurement and evaluation of human-AI collaboration effectiveness are crucial for ensuring that AI tools are delivering value. Brands should regularly assess the impact of AI on their creative processes and strategic decision-making. Metrics such as campaign performance, creativity scores, and ROI can provide insights into how AI is contributing to brand success.v(Malhotra & Malhotra, 2017)By In summary, human-AI collaboration in branding represents a powerful partnership that enhances creativity and strategy. By leveraging AI's data-driven insights and analytical capabilities, brands can augment their creative processes, optimize campaign performance, and make more informed strategic decisions. This collaboration allows for personalization at scale, streamlined testing and validation, and proactive trend identification. By integrating AI tools with human expertise, brands can achieve more innovative and effective marketing outcomes, while also addressing ethical considerations and investing in skill development.

AI Ethics in Branding: Ensuring Transparency, Accountability, and Fairness

AI ethics in branding is a critical area of focus as brands increasingly integrate Artificial Intelligence (AI) into their marketing strategies. transparency, accountability, and fairness. As brands navigate this evolving landscape, and practices that guide the responsible use of AI, safeguard consumer rights, and uphold the integrity of brand practices.equiring brands to clearly communicate how AI technologies are used in their marketing practices., processed, and utilized by AI systems. For example, brands should disclose when AI is used to personalize content, target advertisements, or analyze consumer behavior. This transparency helps build trust with consumers by ensuring they are aware of how their interactions with brands are being managed and how their data is being utilized Furthermore, transparency includes making AI decision-making processes understandable to both consumers and stakeholders, explaining how AI systems arrive at certain outcomes and ensuring that the use of AI aligns ethical values and standards.Accountability is another crucial aspect of AI ethics in branding, emphasizing monitoring AI performance, identifying potential biases, and addressing errors or unintended consequences. For example, if an AI system used for targeting advertisements inadvertently discriminates against certain groups, the brand must be prepared to rectify the issue, take corrective actions, and prevent future occurrences.

Accountability also involves providing consumers with channels to voice their concerns and seek redress if they believe they have been adversely affected by AI-driven practices.Bias detection and mitigation are key components of ensuring ethical AI usage in branding. Brands should employ strategies to detect and address biases in AI systems, which can arise from skewed data sets, s. For instance, if an AI system used for customer segmentation inadvertently excludes certain demographic groups, brands should analyze the data and adjust the algorithms to ensure more inclusive and accurate results. Bias mitigation efforts should be ongoing and integrated into the AI development lifecycle to ensure fairness and accuracy. (Zhu & Wang, 2019) the brand's values and ethical standards. This includes integrating fairness, accountability, and transparency into AI algorithms and processes. Ethical AI design also involves engaging with stakeholders, including consumers, experts, and advocacy groups, to gather input and ensure that AI technologies meet societal and ethical expectations.Consumer empowerment is an important aspect of AI ethics, allowing consumers to have control over their interactions with AI-driven branding practices. Brands should provide consumers with options to manage their data preferences, including the ability to opt out of AI-driven personalization or targeted advertising. Additionally, brands should educate consumers about their rights and options regarding AI usage, empowering them to make informed choices about their interactions with AI technologies. This empowerment fosters a positive relationship between brands and consumers, enhancing trust and engagement.Ethical leadership and governance are crucial for ensuring responsible AI usage in branding. Brands should establish governance frameworks and ethical guidelines to oversee AI initiatives and ensure adherence to ethical standards. This includes staying informed about advancements in AI technologies,(Marr, 2018) evolving regulatory requirements, and emerging best practices in AI ethics. Continuous evaluation helps brands adapt to changing ethical landscapes and maintain responsible AI usage.In conclusion, AI ethics in branding is a multifaceted and critical area that requires a and continuously evaluating AI practices are essential for maintaining responsible and effective AI usage in branding. As AI technologies continue to evolve, brands must remain vigilant and proactive in addressing ethical challenges to uphold the integrity of their marketing practices and ensure positive outcomes for consumers and society.

Case Studies: Successful AI-Driven Branding Initiatives and Campaigns

branding and campaigns illustrate how artificial intelligence (AI) enhance customer engagement, and drive brand success. These examples demonstrate technologies in various aspects of branding, from personalization and content creation to campaign optimization and consumer insights. By examining these case studies, brands can gain valuable insights into how AI can be leveraged to achieve marketing objectives and stay ahead of the competition. Coca-Cola'sI for personalized marketing Coca-Cola leveraged AI to enhance its marketing campaigns through personalized content and targeted advertisements. By analyzing consumer data, including (Wang & Benbasat, 2016) For instance, AI algorithms were employed to analyze consumer preferences and predict the types of content and promotions that would be most effective for different segments. As a result, Coca-Cola was able to deliver highly relevant advertisements and offers, increasing customer engagement and driving sales. Sephora, a global beauty retailer, has also successfully harnessed AI to enhance its branding and customer engagement. Sephora implemented AI-driven virtual try-on features using augmented reality (AR) technology to allow customers to virtually test different beauty products. This innovation leverages AI to analyze customers' facial features and recommend products that suit their preferences and skin tones. The virtual try-on experience improves and interactive shopping journey but also drives sales by increasing customer confidence in their product choices. Additionally, Sephora uses AI to analyze customer feedback and preferences to optimize its offerings strategies, further strengthening its brand connection with consumers.

Nike's integration of AI in its marketing campaigns exemplifies how AI can drive brand innovation and customer loyalty. Nike uses AI .

One notable initiative is Nike's use of AI to analyze social media trends and consumer conversations to inform its marketing strategies(Madgule et al., 2023). By leveraging AI to monitor and analyze, Nike quickly identify emerging trends and adjust its campaigns accordingly(Zhao & Wu, 2019). For example, Nike's AI-powered insights helped the brand capitalize on the growing popularity of certain athletic trends, resulting in successful marketing campaigns that resonated with its target audience. This proactive approach enables Nike to stay ahead of market trends and maintain a strong brand presence.Netflix, the leading streaming service, has leveraged AI to revolutionize content recommendations and drive viewer engagement. Netflix's AI-driven recommendation engine analyzes user behavior, viewing history, and preferences to suggest relevant content. The system uses machine learning algorithms to predict what viewers are likely to enjoy based on their previous interactions with the platform. This personalized approach not only enhances the user experience but also keeps viewers engaged and subscribed to the service. Netflix's success in using AI to drive content recommendations has contributed significantly to its growth and competitive edge in the streaming industry. The company's AI-driven app leverages machine learning to analyze customer purchase patterns and preferences to deliver personalized offers and recommendations. For example, the app suggests products based on a customer's previous orders and current trends. Starbucks also uses AI to optimize its marketing campaigns and promotional strategies by analyzing data from customer interactions and feedback. This personalization and targeted approach have led to increased customer engagement and higher loyalty, reinforcing Starbucks' brand connection with its customers.L'Oreal's use of AI for product innovation and customer engagement highlights how AI can drive branding success. L'Oreal employs AI to analyze consumer preferences and feedback to inform product development and marketing strategies. One notable initiative is L'Oreal's use of AI-powered chatbots personalized beauty advice. These chatbots use natural language processing (NLP) to understand customer inquiries and offer tailored recommendations based on individual needs. This AI-driven approach enhances customer engagement and supports L'Oreal's brand positioning as a leader in beauty and innovation.illustrate transformative impact of branding initiatives across various industries. By leveraging AI technologies for personalization, content creation, recommendation systems, and data analysis, brands can . These successful examples demonstrate the potential of AI to revolutionize branding practices and provide valuable insights into how brands can effectively integrate AI into their marketing efforts. and connect with their audiences in meaningful ways.

Future Directions: Emerging AI Trends and Innovations in Branding

-driven branding initiatives and campaigns illustrate how artificial intelligence (AI) enhance customer engagement, brand success. These examples demonstrate the practical applications of AI technologies in various aspects of branding, from personalization and content creation to campaign optimization and consumer insights. Coca-Cola's for personalized marketing. Coca-Cola leveraged AI to enhance its marketing campaigns through personalized content and targeted advertisements. By analyzing consumer data, including r instance, AI algorithms were employed to analyze consumer preferences and predict the types of content and promotions that would be most effective for different segments. As a result, Coca-Cola was Sephora, a global beauty retailer, has also successfully harnessed AI to enhance its branding and customer engagement. Sephora implemented AI-driven virtual try-on features using augmented reality (AR) technology to allow customers to virtually test different beauty products. This innovation leverages AI to analyze customers' facial features and recommend products that suit their preferences and skin tones. The virtual try-on experience Additionally, Sephora uses AI to analyze customer feedback and preferences to optimize its product offerings and marketing strategies, further strengthening its brand connection with consumers.Nike's integration of AI in its marketing campaigns exemplifies how AI can drive brand innovation and customer loyalty. Nike uses notable initiative is Nike's use of AI to analyze social media trends and consumer conversations to inform its marketing strategies. By leveraging AI to monitor and analyze Nike can quickly identify emerging trends and adjust its campaigns accordingly. For example, Nike's AI-powered insights helped the brand capitalize on the growing popularity of certain athletic trends, resulting in successful marketing campaigns that resonated with its target audience. market trends and maintain a strong brand presence.H&M's use of AI for inventory management and demand forecasting is another compelling case study.

H&M employs H&M to maintain a competitive advantage in the fast-paced fashion industry.Unilever's AI-powered brand management is another example of successful AI-driven branding. Unilever uses AI to analyze market data, consumer feedback, and competitive intelligence to inform its brand strategies. By leveraging AI consumer, Unilever can develop more effective marketing campaigns and product innovations. For instance, AI-driven sentiment analysis helps Unilever understand how consumers perceive its brands and identify informed decisions, optimize its brand strategies, and maintain a strong market position.L'Oreal's use of AI for product innovation and customer engagement highlights how AI can drive branding success. L'Oreal employs AI to analyze consumer preferences and feedback to inform product development and marketing strategies. One notable initiative is L'Oreal's use of

AI-powered chatbots This AI-driven approach enhances customer engagement and supports L'Oreal's brand positioning as a leader in beauty and innovation.

The Future of AI in Branding - Opportunities, Challenges, and Possibilities

branding is poised to unlock unprecedented opportunities, navigate complex challenges, and explore transformative possibilities, fundamentally reshaping how brands connect with consumers and manage their market presence. This transformation is characterized by enhanced personalization, data-driven insights, and creative automation, presenting both significant advantages and notable hurdles for brands aiming to leverage AI effectively.Opportunities abound as AI technologies offer brands powerful tools to enhance consumer engagement This level of personalization goes beyond traditional methods, allowing brands to tailor content, recommendations, and offers to individual preferences in real-time.Generative AI is another exciting opportunity in the branding landscape. Technologies such as GPT-4 and DALL-E can generate creative content—text, images, and videos—using minimal human input. Brands can leverage generative AI to produce high-quality marketing materials at scale, from ad copy and social media posts to visual content and product designs. This automation streamlines content creation processes, reduces production costs, and accelerates campaign deployment. Generative AI also allows brands to experiment with innovative creative concepts, pushing the boundaries of traditional branding and providing fresh, engaging experiences for consumers(Taddeo & Floridi, 2018) AI's role in predictive analytics represents a major opportunity for brands to anticipate consumer be popular in the coming months, enabling them to adjust their offerings and marketing campaigns accordingly. This proactive approach enhances competitiveness and ensures that brands remain aligned with evolving consumer demands.The rise of presents another opportunity for brands to enhance consumer interactions. These AI technologies enable brands to support, handle inquiries, and resolve issues efficiently. Advanced . Additionally, AI-driven customer service tools can gather valuable feedback and insights, helping brands refine their products and services.However, alongside these opportunities, the future of Brands must implement robust data security measures, obtain informed consent, and transparently communicate how consumer data is used.Ethical considerations in AI usage are a crucial aspect of branding strategies. branding practices, brands must ensure that they operate within ethical boundaries. This includes maintaining transparency about AI's role in marketing, providing clear information to consumers about data usage, and ensuring that AI-driven decisions align with the brand's values and ethical standards. The rapid pace of technological change presents an additional challenge for brands.

AI technologies are evolving rapidly, and keeping up with the latest advancements can be resource-intensive and complex. Brands must invest in continuous learning and development to stay abreast of emerging AI trends and ensure that their strategies remain relevant and effective. This includes investing in talent, training, and technology to leverage the full potential of AI while adapting to new developments in the field.IoT could further enhance branding strategies by providing additional layers of transparency, security, and interactivity.Human-AI collaboration is another promising possibility As AI takes on more routine and data-driven tasks,. Brands can leverage AI to handle repetitive tasks and analyze large data sets while relying on human expertise to drive creative direction and strategic decision-making. This collaboration between AI and human input will enable brands to combine the strengths of both to develop innovative and effective branding strategies.In conclusion, the future of AI in branding is characterized by a blend of exciting opportunities, complex challenges, and transformative possibilities. Hyper-personalization, generative AI, predictive analytics, and advanced customer service tools offer significant potential for enhancing brand strategies and consumer engagement., driving success and relevance in an increasingly AI-driven marketplace.

CONCLUSION

force in modern branding, reshaping how companies connect with consumers, manage their market presence, and execute their marketing strategies. As the technological landscape continues to evolve, understanding AI's role in branding offers critical insights into its transformative potential and the opportunities it presents. AI's role in branding is multifaceted, encompassing a range of applications that drive innovation and efficiency. At its core, AI facilitates hyper-personalization, enabling brands to deliver highly customized experiences tailored to individual consumer preferences. loyalty. The ability to provide real-time, personalized interactions sets brands apart in a crowded marketplace, creating more meaningful connections with their audiences.Generative AI represents another groundbreaking application, revolutionizing content creation and creative processes. With capabilities to generate text, images, and multimedia content, generative AI streamlines the production of marketing materials, allowing brands to produce high-quality content at scale. This innovation not only accelerates campaign development but also enables brands to explore new creative possibilities, experiment with diverse formats, and maintain a consistent and engaging brand presence across various channels. Generative AI's role in automating content creation reduces production costs and time while fostering creative experimentation, driving brand innovation. Advanced natural language processing (NLP) allows AI-driven customer service solutions to understand and respond to complex queries, enhancing the overall customer experience. This automation not only improves operational efficiency but also gathers valuable insights from customer interactions, helping brands refine their products and services.. Building and maintaining consumer trust requires transparency in data usage, robust security measures, and clear communication about how data is collected and utilized. Addressing these concerns is essential for safeguarding consumer trust and avoiding legal and reputational risks.Staying abreast of emerging AI trends and integrating new technologies into branding strategies requires continuous investment in talent, training, and technology. Brands must be agile and adaptable, ready to embrace new innovations while managing the complexities of AI implementation. This involves not only adopting new tools but also understanding their implications and aligning them with strategic goals.Ethical considerations in AI usage are paramount, influencing how brands operate and communicate with consumers., and adherence to ethical principles are essential for maintaining trust and credibility. Brands must establish clear guidelines for AI usage, ensure that AI applications align with their values, and communicate openly about AI's role in their marketing strategies. Ethical AI practices foster consumer confidence and contribute to a positive brand reputation. AI-powered tools for real-time feedback and adaptive marketing will enable brands to respond swiftly to consumer needs and market changes, ensuring that branding efforts remain dynamic and relevant. Additionally, the collaboration between **human creativity** and AI-driven insights will drive innovative branding strategies, combining the strengths of both to deliver compelling and effective marketing solutions.In conclusion, understanding AI's role in branding underscores its transformative impact on how brands engage with consumers and manage their market presence. AI enables hyper-personalization, enhances content creation, and provides predictive insights that drive strategic decision-making. However, addressing challenges related to data privacy, bias, and ethical considerations is crucial y leveraging AI's capabilities thoughtfully and ethically, brands can create meaningful connections with consumers, optimize their marketing strategies, and achieve sustained success in an increasingly AI-driven marketplace.

REFERENCES

Adami, C. (2015). Artificial intelligence: Robots with instincts. *Nature*, 521(7553), 426–427. DOI: 10.1038/521426a PMID: 26017437

Agrawal, A., Gans, J. S., & Goldfarb, A. (2018). *Prediction machines: The simple economics of artificial l intelligence*. Harvard Business School Press.

Aguirre, E., Mahr, D., Grewal, D., de Ruyter, K., & Wetzels, M. (2015). Unraveling the personalization paradox: The effect of information collection and trust-building strategies on online advertisement effectiveness. *Journal of Retailing*, 91(1), 34–49. DOI: 10.1016/j.jretai.2014.09.005

Bettman, J. (1973). Perceived risk and its components: A model and empirical test. *Journal of Marketing*, 10(2), 184–190.

Biswas, A., Bhowmick, S., Guha, A., & Grewal, D. (2013). Consumer evaluations of sale prices: Role of the subtraction principle. *Journal of Marketing*, 77(4), 49–66. DOI: 10.1509/jm.12.0052

Boyd, R., & Holton, R. J. (2018). Technology, innovation, employment and power: Does robotics and artificial intelligence really mean social transformation? *Journal of Sociology (Melbourne, Vic.)*, 54(3), 331–345. DOI: 10.1177/1440783317726591

Castelo, N., Bos, M., & Lehman, D. (2018). Consumer adoption of algorithms that blur the line between human and machine. Graduate School of Business: Columbia University Working Paper. (Castelo et al., 2018)

Castelo, N., & Ward, A. (2016). Political affiliation moderates attitudes towards artificial intelligence. In Moreau, P., & Puntoni, S. (Eds.), *NA - advances in consumer research* (pp. 723–723). Association for Consumer Research.

Davenport, T. H. (2018). *The AI advantage: How to put the artificial intelligence revolution to work*. MIT Press. DOI: 10.7551/mitpress/11781.001.0001

Davenport, T. H., Dalle Mule, L., & Lucker, J. (2011). Know what your customers want before they do. *Harvard Business Review*, 89(12), 84–92.

French, K. (2018). Your new best friend: AI chatbot. Retrieved February 13, 2019 from https://futurism.com/ai-chatbot-meaningful-conversation

Gans, J., Agrawal, A., & Goldfarb, A. (2017). How AI will change strategy: A thought experiment. Harvard Business Review online. Retrieved February 11, 2019 from https://hbr.org/product/how-ai-will-change-strategy-a-thought-experiment/H03XDI-PDF-ENG

Gaudin, S. (2016). At Stitch Fix, data scientists and A.I. become personal stylists. Retrieved February 11, 2019 from https://www.computerworld.com/article/3067264/artificial-intelligence/at-stitch-fix-data-scientists-and-ai-become-personal-stylists.html

Haenlein, M., & Kaplan, A. M. (2019). A brief history of artificial intelligence: On the past, present, and future of artificial intelligence. *California Management Review*, 61(4), 5–14. DOI: 10.1177/0008125619864925

Heaven, W. D. (2019). The humans teaching AI to understand feelings. MIT Technology Review. Retrieved February 11, 2019 from https://www.technologyreview.com/2019/02/12/103694/the-humans-teaching-ai-to-understand-feelings/

Jiang, Z. (2018). Data-driven design: How AI is changing the way we create. *IEEE Computer Graphics and Applications*, 38(4), 75–79.

Johnson, H. (2018). The age of AI: How artificial intelligence is changing our lives. Retrieved February 11, 2019 from https://www.theatlantic.com/technology/archive/2018/11/ai-and-the-age-of-the-internet-of-things/575992/

Kaplan, J. (2016). The age of AI: How artificial intelligence is changing our world. Forbes, March 15. Retrieved February 11, 2019 from https://www.forbes.com/sites/joshkaplan/2016/03/15/the-age-of-ai-how-artificial-intelligence-is-changing-our-world/

Kumar, A., & Singh, R. (2019). Impact of artificial intelligence on the marketing strategies of Indian firms. International Journal of Research in Commerce. *IT & Management*, 9(4), 25–30.

Li, H., & Vargo, S. L. (2019). A service-dominant logic perspective on artificial intelligence in marketing. *Journal of Marketing Theory and Practice*, 27(1), 1–19.

Liu, X., & Shin, K. (2018). The impact of artificial intelligence on human decision-making in business environments. *Technological Forecasting and Social Change*, 136, 130–139.

Malhotra, N., & Malhotra, K. (2017). Artificial intelligence and its impact on marketing strategies. *Journal of Business Research*, 82, 159–168.

Marr, B. (2018). The 10 best examples of how companies use AI in marketing. Forbes, July 19. Retrieved February 11, 2019 from https://www.forbes.com/sites/bernardmarr/2018/07/19/the-10-best-examples-of-how-companies-use-ai-in-marketing/

Nadarajah, D., & Bakar, A. (2019). Marketing in the age of AI: Challenges and opportunities. *Journal of Marketing Management*, 35(3-4), 238–261.

Naeem, M., & Khawaja, H. (2019). The impact of artificial intelligence on consumer behavior. International Journal of Business and Management, 14(6), 36-48. (Naeem & Khawaja, 2019)

Pangburn, D. (2018). AI is learning how to read human emotions. The Verge. Retrieved February 11, 2019 from https://www.theverge.com/2018/10/16/17982392/emotional-ai-human-feelings-research-2018

Sweeney, J. C., & Soutar, G. N. (2001). Consumer perceived value: The development of a multiple item scale. *Journal of Retailing*, 77(2), 203–220. DOI: 10.1016/S0022-4359(01)00041-0

Taddeo, M., & Floridi, L. (2018). How AI can be a force for good: The role of responsible AI. *AI & Society*, 33(2), 291–297.

Wang, Y., & Benbasat, I. (2016). Artificial intelligence in e-commerce: The role of intelligent agents. *International Journal of Electronic Commerce*, 21(3), 5–9.

Zhao, K., & Wu, Y. (2019). Consumer attitudes toward artificial intelligence: A cross-cultural study. *Journal of Global Marketing*, 32(5), 331–346.

Zhu, Y., & Wang, T. (2019). The effect of AI on customer satisfaction in e-commerce: A systematic review. *Journal of Retailing and Consumer Services*, 51, 51–64.

Chapter 3
Role of AI Tools in Evaluating Brand Performance

Suryansh Chauhan
https://orcid.org/0009-0003-0657-9463
Christ University, India

Shivani Thapliyal
Christ University, India

ABSTRACT

The way organizations monitor and control brand performance has been significantly changed by the digital environment. Even though they are useful, traditional measurements frequently miss real-time changes in the market. AI-powered solutions are becoming essential resources in order to tackle this, providing a more precise and up-to-date view of brand health. This chapter explores how artificial intelligence (AI) is transforming brand performance evaluation. It does so by examining important metrics, analytics techniques, and particular AI solutions that are revolutionizing the market. Artificial intelligence (AI) enables organizations to make data-driven decisions with previously unheard-of speed and precision, from assessing brand awareness and consumer loyalty to forecasting future trends. In today's quickly changing digital landscape, marketers, analysts, and company executives can obtain a competitive advantage by comprehending how AI tools can improve brand performance evaluation.

DOI: 10.4018/979-8-3693-9461-8.ch003

INTRODUCTION

With the rapidly growing adoption of artificial intelligence and digital communication, the relationship between the organization and its public has highly influenced academic and corporate sectors. There has been an emerging trend in using AI-assisted tools in social media and brand marketing. As such, it has changed how institutions and organizations can reach their audiences even closer and personalize their content according to the needed demands. This chapter looks into the transformative ability of AI in the context of social media within digital marketing and its strategic role in enhancing customer engagement, interaction, and, in general, brand relationships.

The four research papers that form the core of this analysis delve into the multifaceted uses of AI in digital marketing and brand strategy. Results Conclusion This chapter aims to explain how AI-driven tools, including machine learning and NLP, assist in the assessment of social media engagement effectiveness alignment support of business strategy (Iansiti et al.; K. R., 2020), facilitate brand innovation (Kumar et al., 2021); and further customer relationship strengthening through AI-driven marketing efforts (Cheng and Jiang, 2022). Thus, by synthesizing these perspectives, it will try to achieve this chapter's purpose of providing a wholesome understanding of how AI works to enable KPIs that are both non-financial and financial for social media marketing while underlining the crucial significance of responsible use of ethical AI in managing customer interaction as well as expectations.

Doing so, the chapter contributes to the literature on AI in marketing by providing insights into how AI-driven tools can improve both business and academic communications, optimal marketing strategies, and more robust, individualized customer-brand relationships. Furthermore, the chapter provides directions for future research into the strategic use and ethical use of AI in digital communication, considering a balance between technological innovation and transparency in handling customer data.

The pace at which digital transformation occurs in marketing has been rapid, and the undeniable fact is that one of the significant drivers of such change has been the growth of AI. These systems that power AI have become indispensable tools for analyzing large datasets, identifying patterns in behaviors, and further developing insights into customer preferences and behaviors. As it has been put into words by Paul Roetzer, marketing, in itself, is human-centered by nature, but, at the same time, AI has a fundamental impact on changing it all by bringing efficiencies, personalization, and predictive capabilities into each level of digital communication (Marketing Artificial Intelligence Institute). As noticed in this light by Tamara Biljman, AI also changes social media as it enhances efficiency and personalization factors of the content so the marketers can make the best possible digital communication strategies more efficient and targeted.

For instance, the empirical research work by (Edyta Gołąb-Andrzejak, 2023) shows that AI tools help universities conduct social media marketing and monitor non-financial KPIs appropriately. Using AI-based ContentStudio and Sotrender, the university can keep track of social media parameters like reach, engagement, and content performance, progressively maintaining communication strategy and more meaningfully engaging students, staff, and the public. Gołąb-Andrzejak's case study helps illustrate how universities can utilize AI help in DSS to analyze the interactions at digital levels for decisions on adjustments needed in live campaigns, thus optimizing the effectiveness of marketing campaigns.

AI is changing marketing and business strategies as well as the operation of businesses in this era of information. The paper investigates how integrating AI into the organization can alter organizational design and create value in decision support and automation, customer engagement and new product and service development. According to the report, even though AI can improve efficiency on the operations side and strategic advantage on the strategic side, significant knowledge gaps still exist regarding the best ways to apply AI to maximize these opportunities for alignment and improvement of business strategies. (Borges et al.)

It identifies the conceptual framework for understanding the role of AI in strategic planning in which more excellent utility contributes to dynamic decisions and value creation. Companies like Netflix, Amazon, and Google have been setting benchmarks using AI tools and processing voluminous data with increased customer engagement and market entry. However, the authors required clarity on the role of AI in strategic development and for long-term business sustainability since, according to researchers like (Brynjolfsson and McAfee, 2017), AI-driven transformations are made very difficult without such an understanding. Thus, pointing out such a gap, (Borges et al.) contribute valuable insights into the intersection between AI and strategic management research, calling for further research to refine frameworks and approaches that can support sustainable AI integration.

In addition to helping achieve operational and strategic objectives, AI tools carry transformative potential for improving customer-brand interactions. In their case study entitled “Brands and Chat GPT,” (Kumar et al) explain ways in which brands are now enabled to engage in the most personalized and responsive forms of interaction through tools such as Chat GPT in order to facilitate managing the imperatives of current digital marketing. This particular research deals with the applications of Chat GPT in brands' communication purposes and how NLP and machine learning capabilities support real-time engagements with customers, dynamic content delivery, and innovative marketing campaigns. AI has unlocked new avenues through conversational interfaces for customer engagement, allowing brands to deliver tailored recommendations and resolve inquiries, even offering entertainment that resonates with audiences on deeper grounds.

The chapter also emphasizes the responsible use of these tools, as data privacy and algorithmic bias are barriers to ethical AI applications. While AI does provide much scope for innovation, it also needs vigilance in maintaining transparency and safeguarding customer trust, as said by (Kim et al.) As AI shapes the future of brand marketing, companies are urged to consider ethical standards, keep data practices transparent, and be fluid in a fast-changing technological landscape.

(Cheng and Jiang, 2021) did critical work on how AI-powered CMEs build customer-brand relationships. Here, the writers identified the core elements of effective CMEs: interaction, ease of access, customization, and entertainment, all of which enable brands to create valuable and long-term connections with customers. Their study, based on data from 1,072 respondents across the U.S., shows that chatbots are a functional tool for responding to customer queries and an engaging medium for relationship marketing in the digital space.

This emphasis on relationship marketing leads to the growing need for conversational AI to ko ko enforce brand loyalty and customer satisfaction. This AI-powered chatbot will bridge the gap between brands and consumers by providing an interactive and responsive experience, facilitating direct communication, and allowing brands to attain insights from consumer preferences. The overall significance of AI in deepening customer-brand relationships calls for brands to consider implementing AI solutions as part of their relationship management strategy.

This chapter examines how AI-based tools facilitate effective digital communication, specifically about social media and brand marketing. The tools affect engagement metrics and strategic integration while at the same time analyzing customer relationships. Moreover, they profoundly analyze how AI plays a transformative role in modern marketing. In that respect, this chapter highlights the perspectives presented by (Gołąb-Andrzejak, Borges et al.), (Kumar et al.), and (Cheng and Jiang.) Its contribution to the now burgeoning discussion on AI in digital marketing lies in the information it affords to practical and strategic applications of AI within settings ranging from academic institutions to corporate organizations worldwide.

This chapter will focus on the ethical implications of adopting AI in the tools constructed. There must be a pertinent management of transparency, privacy, and adaptability in AI-driven tools. Today's world is where every industry is accelerating transformation towards what can be termed digital transformation. Hence, the responsible use of AI has become a hot topic of concern. Therefore, this chapter helps address these issues and pave pathways for future research by appropriately balancing the benefits concerning the corresponding desirable levels of technological benefits and the ethical dimensions of AI's impact on customer interactions.

Literature Review

Some foundational theories and models of digital marketing metrics, advances in AI, and customer-brand interactions form the crux of developing a conceptual framework for analysis of the effectiveness of AI-assisted digital communication, especially on social media. The intent is to critically discuss these frameworks and the various theories, ensuring that the current understanding of digital communication performance places it in the appropriate context by relating AI tools.

KPIs are crucial to measuring the effectiveness of digital communication on social media. KPIs have risen in recent years, no longer encompassing just click-through rates, cost per click, conversion, or lead. However, the list now also includes measures like reach, engagement, conversions, traffic, and audience growth rate, among others (Gołąb-Andrzejak, 2021). Each metric becomes a proxy to measure user interaction and response towards content and, hence, represents an essential aspect in measuring return on investment for any social media activity. The primary metrics are engagement in terms of likes, shares, and comments, whereas conversions are a measure of monetary output focusing on direct impacts on revenue (Kotler et al., 2021).

The conceptual underpinning of KPIs can be traced back to communication theory, from which Shannon and Weaver's (1949) communication model derives, pointing out that feedback is essential in communication. In cyberspace, engagement metrics act as feedback mechanisms for a message's success or failure regarding audience response. However, each has been known to provide a false sense of performance because a single measure might paint an incomplete picture (Godey et al., 2016). Integrated marketing communication theories, therefore, focus on the usage of several KPIs measured in different areas, as the process of measuring marketing success through integrated KPIs would be more conclusive (Ihzaturrahma, N., & Kusumawati, N., 2021).

AI has radically reshaped the face of digital communications strategies, especially concerning AI-based social media analytics, content creation tools, and sentiment analysis.

Numerous AI tools, such as Flick and SocialBakers, function on the strength of machine learning to carry out tasks such as audience analysis, optimizing content, and monitoring engagement levels (Haleem, A. et al., 2020). Machine learning is one form of AI in algorithms capable of recognizing patterns and even forecasting without being programmed. This self-learning ability, based on rationalist theories of AI, defines AI as a system created for performing tasks involving cognitive functions (Russell & Norvig, 2010). Social media would only be represented by how the same platform automates and enriches data collection and analysis, which could be required to track KPIs.

According to Charniak & McDermott, 1985, rationalist AI theories make decisions based on data-driven efficiency that complements the analytical nature of social media marketing. Handling hierarchical representations of data by algorithms amplifies AI's ability to interpret complex datasets (Mariani, et al., 2022). For example, implementing deep learning algorithms for sentiment analytics can detect customers' sentiments and emotional expressions towards a brand through social media. It changes the analysis from basic engagement metrics into more subtle insights into audience sentiments, providing a more qualitative understanding of the overall effectiveness of communication (Kumar et al., 2023).

These occurred within evolving frameworks that privileged the distinct nature of AI in forming customized, conversational customer-brand relationships.

Lit surveys indicate that AI-powered chatbots such as ChatGPT have the benefit of offering instant interaction in the design of timely and accurate information for customers. (Appel et al., 2020) noted that marketing efforts through a CME have significantly turned traditional one-way communication into a conversational, dialogic process. SMMEs are concerned with issues that include interactivity, accessibility, and entertainment, which are very close to the abilities delivered by a chatbot (Kim & Ko, 2012). The theory is exemplified by the social media chatbots that create a forum for instant contact between the brands and their clients, thus giving the brands timely feedback on consumer preferences and satisfaction levels (Cheng & Jiang, 2020). Moreover, consumer psychology and brand loyalty theories can be used to analyze the role of AI-enabled personalization in customer satisfaction and repeat engagement.

Based on self-determination theory, personalized AI experiences cater to consumers' personalization needs, enhancing perceived value and satisfaction (Barua et al., 2022). This relationship is most relevant in sectors like retail and travel, where brands use AI tools to inform customers and build emotional connections by providing tailored recommendations and curated experiences (Kumar et al., 2023).

There are many advantages of AI and KPI-based models; however, several limitations and challenges exist when it comes to applying these frameworks.

The most apparent issue is data overload, where several metrics overwhelm instead of clarifying the assessment of social media performance (Ihzaturrahma, N., & Kusumawati, N., 2020). More often than not, business objectives influence the choice of relevant KPIs, and what remains is metrics such as reach or impressions but not engagement, which biases the assessment towards the wrong notions of success (Erkollar & Oberer, 2016). Ethical concerns in the context of privacy are concerns with AI tools because most require comprehensive data collection to give recommendations. In this regard, the rights of users might be violated. Additionally, a high extent of AI automation tends to reduce brand communication's perceived authenticity if large-scale customer service automation is applied.

According to researchers, although AI tools can be applied to simulating conversational engagement, they may need to be more effective in providing emotional depth in creating interconnectivity among people (Cheng & Jiang, 2020). Thus, integrating AI with social media marketing is a susceptible calibration task that requires human-like and as automatic interactions as possible with customers to make them feel it is indeed an engagement with the brand, not just an algorithm interaction.

The chapter on "Market Orientation, Brand Management Processes, and Brand Performance" can be founded on a number of key theoretical frameworks and models that draw upon the basis of how market orientation and branding processes influence brand performance, particularly within the context of having advancement such as AI integration. The first one is the foundational framework known as Resource-Based View (RBV), which argues that the internal resources of a firm-whatever it is-are to be tied in with sustained competitive advantage (Barney, 2011). Under this framework, brand management processes are strategic assets which drive brand equity and performance. According to Iyer et al. (2019), strategic brand management can be described as focusing on a unified brand identity in order to achieve a superior brand image, subsequently enhancing brand equity and stakeholder value (Keller, 2003; Santos-Vijande et al., 2013). It is more of perceiving branding as a strategic, rather than merely tactical, function and over the development of distinctive competencies that make it challenging for the competitors to imitate it (Beverland et al., 2015).

In lots of cases, The market orientation model can be said to be complementarity with the RBV mainly because its focus is placed on an outside-in approach where concern with customer needs and wants takes center stage. As viewed by Narver and Slater, 1990, market orientation basically consists of three elements, namely customer orientation, competitor orientation, and inter-functional coordination that collectively enhance the ability of a brand to align its offerings with market demands. This is very crucial in brand loyalty development and building brand performance. Here, a firm utilizing market orientation is able to change brand strategies due to changing market conditions by assimilating information from the external market with the endeavors used internally for building brands by Day, 1994. This model thus strengthens the interlock between strategic brand management and market-driven adaptation, where market orientation becomes a critical factor to ensure that brand equity is sustainable (Homburg et al., 2004).

Dynamic Capabilities Theory: The next crucial approach, especially in a rapidly changing environment with significant influence from AI and digital transformation. Thus, dynamic capability can be defined as the ability of a firm to adapt and reconfigure in a creative manner to successfully redeploy its resource base with regard to a changing environment (Teece et al., 1997). Dynamic capabilities, in the context of branding, allow an organization to update brand strategies, new technologies, and alignment with consumer expectations. With AI as a dynamic capability, brands can leverage data-driven insights to personalize customer experience, tailor marketing messages, and engage with consumers through virtual assistants and chatbots (Chung et al., 2020; Loureiro & Bilro, 2022). Even though dynamic capabilities are now considered a need for sustaining brand relevance, a possible criticism is that there will be excessive dependency on data-driven insights about the market, which risks over-automating the experience of the brand and actually drives the human connection that brands have traditionally provided (Huang & Rust, 2018).

Internal Branding centers on aligning the employees with the brand values and objectives (Miles & Mangold, 2004). Internal branding includes activities of training the employees and corporate communication that allows the employees to embody and communicate the brand values in a uniform manner. This therefore, is very essential in creating authenticity in the brand, improvement in engagement with the employee base and therefore, the clients (King & Grace, 2012). Internal branding also aids the management in its AI-driven branding strategies as it provides employees who are capable of using and working well with AI tools in order to allow support for market-orientation efforts of the brand (Hofer & Grohs, 2018). Critics argue, though, that internal branding alignment is quite hard since a lot of investment must be made on employee development and the need for an organization-wide commitment in terms of branding (Piehler et al., 2015).

Therefore, in a nutshell, the RBV, Market Orientation Model, Dynamic Capabilities Theory, and Internal Branding Model all align to shape an integrated perspective of the joint relationship between market orientation, brand management, and brand performance. While technology advances at lightning speeds, AI, future research has to go further in a better balance between human touch and technology in branding and how the former can be used without losing its authentic character.

Theoretical Framework

It completely transformed over the last decade the way organizations communicate and market through digital platforms, altering the nature of communication with audiences and the measure of performance. Founded on the underpinnings of the communication theory, marketing theory, and a dynamic capabilities framework, AI has personalized engagement with audiences and adapted and made processes efficient, especially in sectors like university marketing and brand management. As indicated by the communication theory, the area of holding a much higher value in transmitting clear, well-targeted messages ensures meaningful feedback. AI improves processes by significantly providing valued, real-time, and personalized responses while cutting down on the barriers to communication and enhancing audience connections. In return, practical capabilities of AI in predictive analytics and sentiment analysis have advanced marketing theory into the 4Ps-being product, price, place, and promotion. This has enabled organizations to engage in working on a hyper-personalized campaign directly targeted toward specific audience segmentation. For universities, through these tools, marketing helps the institutes create strategies based on the specific aspirational needs of their target students and increases engagement and improves outcomes for recruitment. The second reason this framework of dynamic capability focuses on sensing, seizing, and reconfiguring a changed environment is an area where AI does its best. Thus, universities can track trends as well as the efficiency of their campaigns while adjusting strategy in real time so that performance can be improved through AI-powered social media analytics. Similarly, such tools also enhance social media engagement by analyzing huge datasets to predict audience behavior and creating material with much less human involvement but by preferred audience preferences.

Lying beneath all of digital communication is the concept of communication theory- how audiences transmit, receive, and interpret messages. The rise of social media and other forms of new digital platforms has broadened the scope of this theory, including old and new ways of communication. Significant use of digital communication by the marketing mix is analyzed by the Model of Communication proposed by Shannon and Weaver (1949). Here, the sender-message-channel-receiver framework is valued in terms of usage. The model in the AI tool is further dynamic because AI does not just aid in making messages but in instantaneous analysis of audience engagement, feedback, or sentiment. It gives way to the seamless feedback loop in which marketers can alter their messaging strategy to AI-driven audience behavior, preferences, and emotions (Gołąb-Andrzejak, 2024).

Audiences purposefully choose media and content based on a need for entertainment, information, or social interaction. The theory becomes workable through AI tools by allowing for a much more profound understanding of these needs through sophisticated data analytics, enabling brands to tailor their communications to specific groups of their audiences. It can be informed in content creation as well as in distribution through the capacity of AI to measure user engagement metrics like likes, shares, and comments and in formulating patterns in consumer behavior, in the heart of which one finds digital marketing effectiveness (Gołąb-Andrzejak, 2024).

Brand management is the establishment of a potent brand identity or brand image that is strategically positioned in the marketplace. (Aaker, 2020) makes brand awareness, perceived quality, brand associations, and brand loyalty separate entities in laying the foundation for theories on brand management. These AI tools, like Gołąb-Andrzejak (2024), measure another level by analyzing the digital footprints of engagement rates, sentiment analysis, and audience interactions. Metrics from AI-driven insights give deep insights into what brand positionings must be altered for a more potent emotional connection with the consumer. Perhaps more importantly,

AI allows real-time monitoring of a brand's health. It can move almost in real-time with the changing sentiments of consumers or the market.

The Position Theory (Ries & Trout, 2001) plays yet another role in defining how a brand is differentiated in the market. According to this, effective positioning for a brand would make a specific point of value for the consumer, indicating that they have an unmet want and desire. AI tools enhance this by graphically projecting consumer preferences and behavior trends so that a brand can predict market shifts and adjust its positioning strategies accordingly. For instance, AI-based sentiment analysis can potentially track shifts in consumer preferences or the public psyche, thereby equipping a brand with the ability to position itself better.

The dynamic capabilities theory (Teece, 2007) explains how AI would be a part of brand management. Dynamic capabilities theory identifies how organizations use, build, and reconfigure internal and external capabilities to achieve new and ongoing ends in response to changing environments. For instance, digital marketing's AI-intensive tools are viewed as dynamic capabilities that allow organizations to cope with shifting consumer behaviors, technology changes, and competitive changes. AI tools - such as (Gołąb-Andrzejak, 2024) - allow for an ongoing learning and adapting process that allows brands to continually update their marketing strategies according to real-time performance data. This implies that this dynamic characteristic can ensure that brands stay relevant and competitive in the fast-moving digital environment.

Internal branding sustains strategic brand management because it refers to the “part inside”; the internal stakeholder is the employees. In other words, this process aligns employees with the brand's objectives to make them better at delivering on the promise of a brand through training, communication, and feedback vehicles (Punjaisri et al., 2009; King & Grace, 2012).Internal branding benefits from not only brand image consistency but also increases employee satisfaction, retention, and quality of service (Hofer & Grohs, 2018). It builds the foundation for symbolic association between employees and the brand by encouraging adaptability and shared organizational values (Srivastava & Bhatnagar, 2008). To put it concisely, strategic brand management and internal branding should merge into one capability that enables brands to sustain and adapt. The conceptual link between marketing capabilities and market orientation furthers the theoretical framework. Marketing capabilities refer to mid-level activities and higher-order strategic functions intended to enhance a firm's ability to implement successful marketing strategies (Vorhies & Morgan, 2005).

Furthermore, (Ambrosini et al. C. 2009) organizations' capabilities provide insight into determining if AI can enhance marketing effectiveness. *Brand management* is an organizational capacity that combines resources such as consumer insights and technological tools with marketing expertise to create a coherent strategy. (Beverland, et al., 2015) AI tools make this even more efficient by automating data collection and analysis, thus helping build proper brand management. This is crucial for brands in terms of maintaining equity and ensuring they can communicate uniformly through so many online or offline channels (Veloutsou & Guzman, 2017).

Customer engagement is another significant application of AI, particularly in brand marketing. AI, more especially through the capabilities provided by machine learning algorithms, provides brands with the tools to engage in genuinely personalized interactions with consumers. According to (Kumar et al., 2024), AI enhances personalization by ascertaining large amounts of consumer data-- including their purchase history, browsing behavior, and social media activity- to tailor the content and recommendations. This level of personalization by AI makes for a much more robust engagement- the consumer feels understood and valued by the brand.

Understanding the behavior of consumers and the trends, AI enables brands to stay ahead of the curve and be proactive. Predictive analytics is one of the strengths of AI that further empowers brands to make specific real-time adjustments to marketing campaigns based on the latest data available for them, which helps them maximize the efficacy of their engagement efforts accordingly. AI technology allows brands to provide more relevant content and experience by helping to fulfill and predict customer wants and behavior, thus boosting customer satisfaction and long-term loyalty (Kumar et al., 2024).

This is in line with the CEM framework, which, by using all touchpoints, means managing all of the customer's interactions. For example, tools such as AI streamline communication channels so that customers get a consistent, personalized message through whichever channel they use- in other words, social media, email, or even a customer service platform. This consistency and personal touch solidify the trust and create emotional bonding with the brand, an essential driver of brand loyalty and advocacy.

Besides the very high advantages afforded by AI toward improving digital communication and brand marketing, very severe ethical considerations constitute AI applications. By integrating AI into the marketing strategy, data privacy, security, and transparency came into play as concerns and anxieties. Here are three critically important factors under the purview of ethics in AI usage in digital marketing: consumer consent, data privacy regulations, and algorithmic usage. Brands need to be transparent about collecting data from consumers and what is done with it, and then educate the consumer on every action that happens with the data. AI-based marketing strategies should not breach consumer trust or brand reputation by propagating biases or stereotypes (Kumar et al., 2024).

Another question AI brings to using AI in brand management is whether brands should automate the process or rely on it to decide engagements and customer communication. With the ability to handle data volumes and provide enormous insight, this matches the human marketing components of empathy, creativity, and intuition. These human factors are still very much necessary in developing authentic brand experiences. More importantly, a line should be drawn to maximize efficiency through AI while retaining that touch of humanity that connects with the consumers.

Conceptual Model

Modern markets' dynamic and competitive features make brands perpetually align with customer preferences, market trends, and performance metrics. Organizational performance has been found to improve through the integration of AI as it assisted in assessing and shaping the brand strategy. Systematic brand performance measurement and analysis through improvement by AI tools prevent organizations from becoming stagnant and insensitive to changes in dynamic markets.

This model suggests ten elementary steps within an integrative process ranging from data gathering to integrating feedback. It is an integrative process that incorporates continuous data gathering, processing, analysis, and feedback aimed at changing brand strategies on time. Using this AI-guided model, here is how you can interpret each step so much better:

Figure 1. Conceptual Model of AI Integration

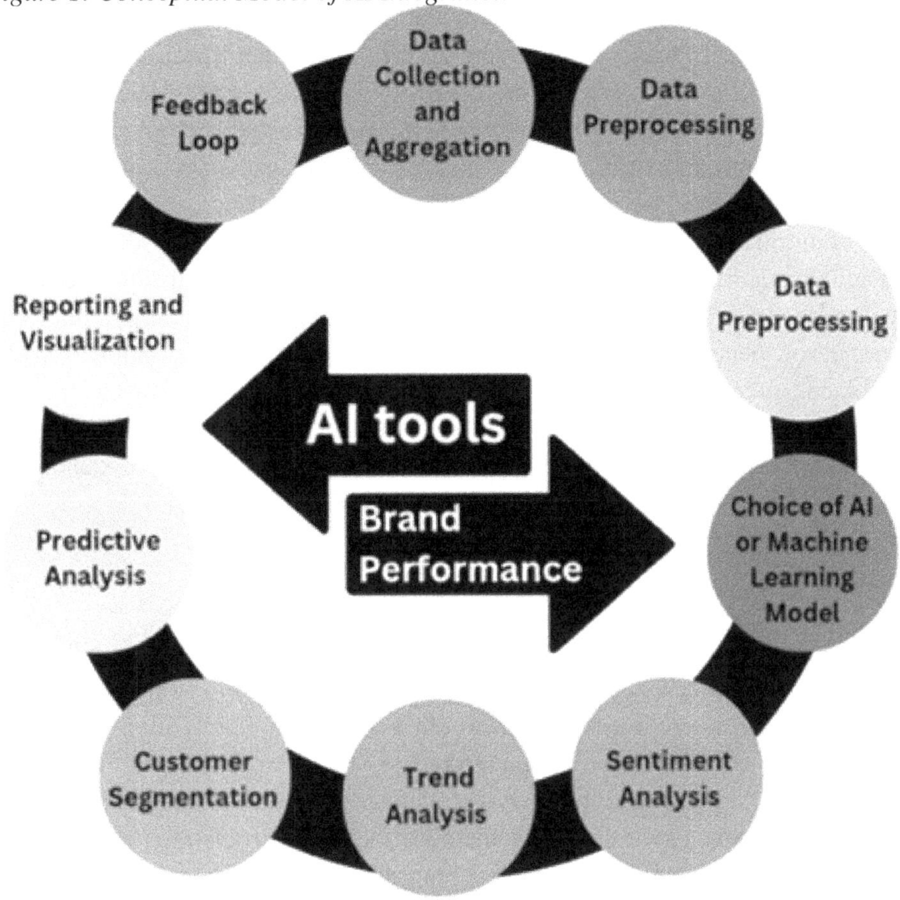

1. Data Collection and Aggregation

AI-based brand performance measurement is constructed by collecting data from all sources. When sources are not integrated, it becomes important to unify high-quality data available from all of them. Large datasets feed AI systems, and diversity, accuracy, and comprehensiveness determine the depth and reliability of insights generated.

Social media: Instagram, Twitter, and Facebook have been great sources of user-generated content. Public sentiment is reflected on social media because users express freely their likes, dislikes, and opinions regarding brands. Thus, real-time perception can be understood, and trends can be established based on tracking mentions, hashtags, and interactions.

Online Reviews: Amazon, Yelp, and Google Reviews are excellent sources of customer feedback. They more frequently depict repeated trends about the experiences; this is useful for brands in getting an idea of whether the customers have a satisfactory experience with the product or service and where improvement is needed.

Surveys: Though these have traditional appeal, organized surveys are effective for specific information gathering. They help a brand gather information about consumer preferences, perceptions regarding a brand, and perceived satisfaction levels of products or services.

Digital Channels: The website analytics, email marketing statistics, and usage patterns from mobile applications also give an insight into what is happening with customers on their part. Click-through rates, bounce rates, session duration, etc., can help brands understand user behavior and optimize their digital presence.

The aggregation of these diverse sources of data allows for a comprehensive view of the brand's interaction with its audience. The view is critical in identifying gaps and leveraging strengths to craft customer-centric strategies.

2. Data Preprocessing

There is a large amount of raw data but most of the time, it needs uniformity, order, and completeness. Preprocessing is inevitable in order to gain systematicity in AI analysis. It is preprocessing filters out unnecessary information and gets it ready for more accurate analytical methods.

Missing Values: There needs to be more information, thus unbalanced analyses. To maintain the integrity of the data, methods such as interpolation (estimation of missing values) or excluding incomplete records are employed.

Text Normalization: The text data, mainly based on social media or reviews, accommodates unmerged type formatting, such as mixed casings or overuse of punctuation. Normalization ensures that text is normalized to form a basis for correct analysis.

Elimination of Duplicates: Inflated some patterns or trends because of duplicate entries. Detecting and removing redundancy ensures that a dataset works well to represent customer behavior and sentiment.

Data Transformation: Depending on the type of AI model to be deployed, the data has to be transformed into structured forms, such as tables, matrices, or feature vectors. This would ensure it is suitable for some specific algorithms.

Good preprocessing minimizes noise in the data so that it can be treated to produce actionable and trustworthy insights from AI models.

3. Choice of AI or Machine Learning Model

The selection of the right AI or ML model is essential in reaching the intended analytical objectives.

Model selection depends on the purpose behind evaluating brand performance, which ranges from sentiment analysis, customer segmentation, or even predictive analytics.

Natural Language Processing (NLP): NLP models are best when analyzing unstructured text data from reviews, surveys, or social media posts. It can classify sentiment as positive, neutral, or negative, providing keywords and hidden themes.

Clustering Algorithms: The algorithms are designed to club the customers together for similar behavior or preferences. For instance, through clustering, one may segment the customers based on their frequency of purchases, products of purchase, or level of engagement.

Predictive Models: These models will use historical data to predict behavior or the development of a trend shortly. For example, they can predict customer churn and, therefore, allow brands to prevent the same through retention strategies.

The customization and fine-tuning of these models ensure that they go on to meet the specific goals that a brand-to-be may set. For example, it could enhance customer satisfaction or even ease its operations.

4. Sentiment Analysis

A tool for analyzing consumer emotions and attitudes toward a brand, sentiment analysis utilizes text data from reviews, surveys, and social media posts to classify emotions and measure customer satisfaction.

Customer Sentiment Identification which means that Every comment, whether positive, neutral, or negative, provides precious feedback. For example, the extremely positive comments about a new product launch indicate a case of success, whereas the growing negative sentiments highlight areas where urgent action is required.

Pain Point Identification: The analysis of sentiment by the brands will identify the frequently occurring themes in the negative feedback. For instance, constant complaints about a product's particular feature or issues related to customer service will help concentrate improvement in specific areas.

Tracking Changes: brands can monitor how customer perceptions are changing. This is useful for tracking changes due to new initiatives, such as a product redesign or marketing campaign.

Sentiment analysis provides a rich view of the emotions involved and thus makes it easier for brands to make informed decisions which maximize the greater good of customer satisfaction and loyalty.

5. Trend Analysis

Trend analysis is essential for understanding and assessing brand performance in changing markets. It involves careful observation of what the customer engages in, how markets shift, and how competitive landscapes can change as an approach to predicting and preparing for the emergence of trends. A critical approach that helps in maintaining the performance of brands in a changing business environment. These sections discuss the different aspects of trend analysis and its impacts on brand performance:

Understanding Changes in Customer Preferences: Customer preferences constantly shift depending upon technological advancements, social changes, and environmental consciousness. Market Response: The entry of fresh competition or new market leaders changes the competitive scenario and compels the brands to opt for a new strategy. Trend analysis enables the brands to tackle changes of this sort in time.

Pattern Recognition of Weaknesses: Trend analysis plays a huge role in assessing brand performance as it will help place brands ahead of market changes and customer behavior. This means that businesses can pick up on changes in customer preferences, respond to market dynamics, and find weaknesses in their product or service. Long-term success requires such proactive thinking.

Knowing Customer Preferences Changes: Customer preferences have been changing daily, with even wider influences from societal changes and technology revolutions, and now mainly by pressures towards becoming more environmentally friendly. Over the last decade, the demand for eco-friendly products has risen rapidly, mainly due to awareness about climate change and environmental degradation. Whether a brand supports these values depends on how it fosters its affinity toward environmental values through the provision of green products or sustainable business operations.

Reaction to Market Dynamics: Market dynamics constantly evolve through entry from new competitors, changes in customer preferences, or new regulations. Through trend analysis, a brand can be susceptible to these changes early enough and make pertinent adjustments to its strategy accordingly.

Detection of Trends in Weakness: One of the most critical applications of trend analysis is to identify potential weaknesses in a brand's product or service offering. Monitoring customer complaints, feedback, or reviews to see if a pattern of the same complaint is coming up helps brands pinpoint areas that might indicate that something is wrong in the design functionality or quality of the product.

6. Customer Segmentation

Branding strategists use customer segmentation as a primary strategy to target specific customer groups better. Brands may split their customer base into categories defined by common characteristics, enabling them to route their marketing efforts and product offerings within the reach of each group's needs and preferences. Artificial intelligence tools now allow brands to efficiently conduct customer segmentation by sifting through large amounts of data and retrieving common patterns. These tools can further categorize customers into groups using several parameters, such as:

Demographics: These relate to essential characteristics like age, gender, income, and locality. For instance, a high-value brand can target affluent homemakers in urban cities. On the other hand, if a brand focuses on being family-oriented, its brand can target middle-income householders living in the suburbs.

Behavioral Patterns: Customer segmentation can also be based on past purchase behavior, browsing patterns, and engagement levels. For example, an active sportswear buyer may be classified as a “loyal fitness enthusiast” and marketed with customized offers for athletic gear.

Psychographics: The values, interests, and attitudes of customers. A person who thinks that sustainability matters may spend more on environmentally friendly products, and another who looks for ease of use may go for quick and easy solutions that brands offer.

Developing Targeted Marketing Campaigns: Each customer segment has characteristics of a brand, meaning that every marketing message is more personalized and relevant. The approach to this will ensure that it resonates well with the target market; hence, it will improve engagement and conversion rates. For example, a brand can use demographic segmentation to send offers for specific age groups or behavioral segmentation to recommend products based on previous purchases. On the other hand, by segmenting customers, brands could also use their resources very efficiently as marketing budgets could be channeled toward more valuable segments and specific product offerings for each group, which would fit each group's differing needs.

7. Predictive Analysis

Predictive analytics uses historical data to predict future results. Brand performance analysis relies heavily on predictive analysis. The logic can be seen in predictive analysis for forecasting customer behaviors, market dynamics, and business obstacles. Using previous performance data, brands can use artificial models to infer correct decisions about a course of action for the future.

Analyzing Customer Purchases and Behavior: Predictive analytics can analyze the behavior of customers so that some buying patterns can be known in advance, and because of this, brands can predict whether there is a probability that a customer will come again for repeated purchases, upsell purchases, or churning altogether.

Churn Rate Prediction: Another primary application is churn prediction, which is the ability to analyze data on levels of customer satisfaction, frequency of purchase, and engagement to forecast who is most likely to leave.

Market Responses and Campaign Effectiveness: Predictive analytics could also predict customer reaction to new products, marketing campaigns, or price changes. Brands fine-tune their strategies further using historical data from similar initiatives to maximize effectiveness and minimize risks.

8. Performance Measures

Performance metrics should be tracked and analyzed to determine the effectiveness of strategies used by a brand. KPIs provide insight into the performance of executing goals and places that may need improvement. KPIs like:

Brand awareness: increase in familiarity

Engagement metrics: increase in followers, likes, and shares

Sales metrics: Revenue increases

Website traffic metrics: page views, unique visits, or time on the site increases

Engagement Rate: The extent to which the consumer interacts with a brand on available digital channels, such as social media likes, shares, comments, and visits to websites.

Conversion Rate: This is how many visitors make the desired action: buying or subscribing to a newsletter.

Customer Satisfaction Score (CSAT): CSAT aims to measure customer satisfaction regarding their experience by conducting post-purchase surveys.

Brand Loyalty: Repeat sales or NPS measures the willingness of the customers to buy the brand or recommend it to the environment. Monitoring such KPIs closely will help a brand know where it stands and what areas need improvement, bringing in a data-driven decision that can enhance performance.

9. Reporting and Visualization

All this requires excellent reporting and visualization tools because the whole point of communicating complex data insights is getting the insights down to the decision-makers. They allow raw data to be formulated into easily interpretable forms, permitting brands to take action based on data-driven insights. Real-Time Dashboards and Visuals: Real-time dashboards enable brands to monitor significant metrics and trends as they happen and to act immediately when necessary. Graphs, charts, and heatmaps bring out patterns, trends, and areas of attention. Data presented in intuitive formats means rapid assessment of health and emerging trends with immediate proactive steps for adjusting strategy when appropriate.

10. Feedback Loop

The feedback loop is a continuous process wherein the insights gathered from this data analysis feed into the brand's strategy, thus driving continuous improvement. Therefore, brands consistently appraise consumer feedback, market trends, and performance metrics; thus, their strategies are always up to date with the constantly changing market dynamics. The feedback loop ensures that the brand is always agile and able to respond to changes in customer needs and market conditions in real time. It also sharpens approaches, products, and services according to lessons learned from this ongoing analysis. The ten-step model explains how AI tools are used to measure brand performance. The process here is an iterative kind of fine-tuning of insights to improve strategies. Among the first advantages derived from this approach are the following:

They shall be executing data-driven brand campaign strategies using quantitative and qualitative data. They help the brand respond to market changes since real-time updates shall occur.

The model will help obtain a better customer brand relationship based on knowledge about their preferences.

Implications and Future Research

This chapter spells out a hybrid model of what has come to be known as measuring brand performance but combines leading-edge capabilities in AI. Both connect theoretical foundations with practical applications. The rapidly expanding use by companies of AI for the interpretation of highly voluminous data means that our model provides unique insight into how AI tools can be used to improve brand performance measurement. It reveals AI marketing strategy and brand management. Using a systematic approach to gathering, processing, and analyzing data through AI reporting shows a much deeper understanding of consumer behavior and the perception of brands.

This model has tremendous implications. It is how brand performance can be conceptually framed and measured within a digital-first economy. Brand performance metrics were based on three foundational KPIs: awareness, consumer loyalty, and market share. That, however, lies with the AI system itself since openness is there toward much finer granularity, wherein algorithms can now evaluate unstructured sources in social media posts, customer reviews, and search patterns to gain insights into brand sentiment and consumer engagement. AI-based tools are needed to capture "real-time customer preferences and sentiments" that have increasingly become the want of the day to understand brand equity in a rapidly evolving market.

This would help companies become more responsive by aligning their branding strategies with changing consumer preferences, emerging trends, etc.

Besides the above, the chapter framework will offer an organized method to fusion multiple data sources, which has long caused a problem in brand management research.

Unlike the conventional brand metrics, which usually get stuck into survey-based data or some other form of intermittent performance reviews, the AI model can continuously monitor consumer sentiments, behaviors, and preferences on digital platforms. This real-time insight capability will give the brand an upper edge, as it will respond almost at the speed of change in the market. As AI empowers brands with the capabilities to aggregate and analyze data from diversified sources, our model could influence conduct within digital marketing by shifting focus away from static performance measurements in the digital sphere towards dynamic, ever-changing tracking of brand health. This might entail embracing methods that would allow for the agile adoption of AI in branding strategies and make it easy to create more responsive and adaptive brands in the current digital ecosystem.

For the researchers, it provides an empirically informed model with the possibility of testing it in various industries and contexts, thus adding to the growing literature on AI in brand management. Much has been discussed recently in the literature about what AI does for marketing, but more is needed about how it explicitly affects brand performance measures. This gap is currently this work in conceptualizing and providing detail for the deployment of AI-based tools analyzing stages of collecting and processing of brand performance data into insightful analysis and comprehensive reporting.

Hence, findings are left open for further research: How much better does AI-driven brand metric predict longer-term brand loyalty, customer lifetime value, and brand equity? It is also interesting to note that the generalizability of AI tools across industries will be vastly different. For instance, retail or hospitality sectors might benefit differently from an AI tool compared with an industry with less direct customer interaction, such as manufacturing.

More to the point, this chapter framework also highlights the ethical and operational issues brought about by implementing AI in brand measurement.

Sample questions: How accurate is AI in predicting shifts in brand perception for leading indicators of that shift? What are the top sources of data that best predict? These would add another layer to understanding the roles of AI in brand management, extending them from merely descriptive analytics into forward-looking strategic planning.

Although this conceptual model is mainly designed with a focus on brand performance measurement, future research may work towards investigating whether it can be transferred to a more expansive business intelligence context. For example, from the four phases illustrated, the processes involved with data gathering and processing, analysis, and reporting can be applied across similar disciplines where AI-based insight is necessary, such as customer relationship management, supply chain optimization, and product development. Expanding this model to other business functionalities would be an excellent way for researchers to gauge the applicability and generality of AI models across different spectrums, thus giving an all-round view of how AI affects business strategy. This line of research can also go ahead with an extensive understanding of how insights emanating from AI can foster cross-functional collaboration in an organization; for example, brand performance insights might have implications for the strategies governing product design, customer service delivery, and market expansion.

Finally, the rapid evolution of AI technologies means that the model needs to be constantly updated in real time concerning the latest developments. Future studies could target emerging AI technologies, like NLP improvements and sentiment analysis or more advanced neural networks, and evaluate how such innovations can further refine brand performance measures. Better AI will result in better sensitivities in consumer sentiment, with the ability to attach even minute emotional and psychological nuances to those sentiments, which are hard to quantify. Such advances would lead to a more précised understanding of brand equity and consumer loyalty that had hitherto remained inaccessible through either traditional or early versions of AI.

The model in this chapter offers an outline for integrating AI into brand performance analysis. With a structured approach to data integration, analysis, and interpretation, this model affords the brands an improved real-time understanding of consumer behavior and sentiment toward the brand. Future research agendas include testing the ethics surrounding AI use in brand measurement, predictive power, and tweaking the model for business application and framework updates with AI technology. Together, these future researches may bring a deeper understanding of the transformative power of AI in branding and ensure that businesses can effectively use AI tools to manage the complexity of today's digital consumer landscape.

CONCLUSION

Artificial intelligence has altered the dimensions through which brands measure performance in a world that's now so data-centric. Digital platforms, along with the astonishing volumes of consumer data they produce, have increasingly taken center stage. The limits of traditional approaches to measuring brands have been exposed by digital platforms and all that consumer data they produce. Conventional methods often rely on static measures like sales and market share, which often miss consumer-brand interactions' dynamic, multidimensional nature. The response to this thrust has been a fully integrated model that has tried AI tools and different types of data sources, such as social media, customer reviews, and online consumer behaviors, in order to come up with more accurate and real-time assessments of brand health, sentiment, and engagement (Kumar et al., 2022; Yadav & Pavlou, 2021).

The chapter's contribution lies in providing a structured model to enhance AI's measurement of a brand. The process model is divided into four stages: collection, processing, analysis, and reporting. In the data collection stage, AI collects different data sets from various platforms such as social media, online reviews, and transactional databases. These can capture unstructured and complex data formats like text, images, and videos. Beyond standard surveys, the process stage incorporates NLP to process gigantic volumes of unstructured data for meaningful information about consumers' sentiments and engagement.(Jin & Lowry, 2021).

Then comes the analysis stage, in which AI techniques like machine learning and predictive analytics provide deeper insight into consumer behaviors and preferences. Sentiment analysis, additionally, will help brands understand emotional responses toward offerings; predictive analytics predicts trends and the chances of specific challenges arising. This has been a continuous analysis and marked a shift from periodic brand health checks to maintaining a constant monitoring of brand health so that one would move quickly with any changes within the market. Hybrid traditional brand metrics and AI-powered insights will give brands a more holistic view of performance in terms of cognitive and emotional engagement with consumers (Chung & Park, 2022).

According to the model, the performance of brands is multi-dimensional. Traditional measures have primarily focused on the outcome-variable measure, such as sales, and have ignored every other-emotional and relationship-have been overlooked in consumer-brand interaction. AI methods bridge this gap by considering consumer attitudes, loyalty, and emotional bonds. These parameters are increasingly significant in creating a sense of deeper bonding between the brand and the consumer. AI permits more reflective thinking about complex relationship dynamics and aligns with the trend toward a consumer-centric approach to branding strategy (Aaker, 2020; Batra et al., 2022).

The second prominent feature of this model is real-time tracking of the brand. Historically, brand performance was measured by interval surveys and market research snapshots of brand health. This differs from the traditional approach, where AI can capture and process data in real-time and provide answers that help quickly align consumer expectations and market conditions. Such responsiveness is crucial in the fast-paced digital environment where consumer preferences and competitive landscapes are rapidly changing (Timoshenko & Hauser, 2019).

The findings of this chapter extend beyond the challenge of brand measurement into broader arenas of marketing and business intelligence. The model proposed herein meets the emerging requirement for data-based marketing practice. It equips the practitioner and scholar with the capacity to analyze extensive data sets meaningfully. Combining AI know-how with traditional branding helps marketers grasp timely and relevant strategies to contend with the complexity of modern consumer behavior in its situation (Wedel & Kannan, 2016).

This model furthers the understanding of digital consumer-brand interaction; it provokes value insights into perceptions and how they change. AI-enabled tools record subtle inputs into feedback, that is, moods and preferences, from sources such as social media and online reviews. Informed by the derived insights, this model builds more accurate models of consumer-brand relationships to inculcate loyalty and advocacy in competitive markets. AI can support strategy building based on well-established consumer relationships, given its ability to conduct real-time sentiment analysis (Matz & Netzer, 2017; Berger et al., 2020).

Such a model may also apply in cross-functional applications to any business. It can help make solutions at the real-time processing level in predictive capabilities applied in customer services, product development, and competitive analysis. Actionability helps take integrated business strategies further to higher growth levels and higher levels of agility. It is cross-functionality that lifts prospects for the concept of how AI may change business intelligence and decision-making processes (Brynjolfsson & McAfee, 2017).

This chapter sets a benchmark in the present times of brand performance measurement and redesigns how brands converse with their end-users in the digital age. The multidimensional and analytics-real-time model adopted here succinctly epitomizes the transformative power of AI in branding, even though it is an offshoot of older branding practices now critically buttressed by advanced AI techniques. While this approach leads to further research in terms of academic and practical approaches to branding, it also opens up the future of the field to become a data-driven, ethics-oriented, and consumer-centric one. Hence, the model is a significant step forward for cultivating trust and relevance in brand management in this increasingly digital and data-driven landscape.

REFERENCES

Aaker, D. A. (2020). *Managing brand equity*. Simon and Schuster.

Ambrosini, V., & Bowman, C. (2009). What are dynamic capabilities and are they a useful construct in strategic management? *International Journal of Management Reviews*, 11(1), 29–49. DOI: 10.1111/j.1468-2370.2008.00251.x

Appel, G., Grewal, L., Hadi, R., & Stephen, A. T. (2020). The future of social media in marketing. *Journal of the Academy of Marketing Science*, 48(1), 79–95. DOI: 10.1007/s11747-019-00695-1 PMID: 32431463

Barney, J. B. (2011). *Gaining and sustaining competitive advantage* (4th ed.). Pearson.

Barua, P. D., Vicnesh, J., Gururajan, R., Oh, S. L., Palmer, E., Azizan, M. M., Kadri, N. A., & Acharya, U. R. (2022). Artificial intelligence enabled personalized assistive tools to enhance education of children with neurodevelopmental disorders—A review. *International Journal of Environmental Research and Public Health*, 19(3), 1192. DOI: 10.3390/ijerph19031192 PMID: 35162220

Batra, R., Ahuvia, A., & Bagozzi, R. P. (2022). Brand love: Development and implications for brand and consumer behavior. *Journal of Marketing*, 86(1), 1–20.

Berger, J., Humphreys, A., Ludwig, S., Moe, W. W., Netzer, O., & Schweidel, D. A. (2020). Uniting the tribes: Using text for marketing insight. *Journal of Marketing*, 84(1), 1–25. DOI: 10.1177/0022242919873106

Beverland, M., Napoli, J., & Farrelly, F. (2015). Brands as cultural resources: Organizational and brand identity co-creation in a sport context. *Journal of the Academy of Marketing Science*, 43(4), 453–470. DOI: 10.1007/s11747-015-0431-3

Beverland, M., Napoli, J., & Farrelly, F. (2015). Can all brands innovate in the same way? A typology of brand position and innovation effort. *Journal of Product Innovation Management*, 32(1), 109–120. DOI: 10.1111/jpim.12250

Borges, A. F., Laurindo, F. J. B., Spínola, M. M., Gonçalves, R. F., & Mattos, C. A. (2021). The strategic use of artificial intelligence in the digital era: Systematic literature review and future research directions. *International Journal of Information Management*, 57, 102225. Advance online publication. DOI: 10.1016/j.ijinfomgt.2020.102225

Brynjolfsson, E., & McAfee, A. N. (2017). What's driving the Machine Learning explosion? *Harvard Business Review*, •••, 18.

Cheng, Y., & Jiang, H. (2022). Customer–brand relationship in the era of artificial intelligence: Understanding the role of chatbot marketing efforts. *Journal of Product and Brand Management*, 31(2), 252–264. DOI: 10.1108/JPBM-05-2020-2907

Chung, M., & Park, J. (2022). The impact of AI on brand management. *Journal of Brand Management*, 29(1), 1–15.

Erkollar, A., & Oberer, B. (2016). Multidimensional dashboards for evaluating strategic brand management processes for multi-brand companies. *Procedia: Social and Behavioral Sciences*, 235, 505–513. DOI: 10.1016/j.sbspro.2016.11.062

Godey, B., Manthiou, A., Pederzoli, D., Rokka, J., Aiello, G., Donvito, R., & Singh, R. (2016). Social media marketing efforts of luxury brands: Influence on Brand equity and customer behavior. *Journal of Business Research*, 69(12), 5833–5841. DOI: 10.1016/j.jbusres.2016.04.181

Gołąb-Andrzejak, E. (2023). AI-powered digital transformation: Tools, benefits and challenges for marketers–case study of LPP. *Procedia Computer Science*, 219, 397–404. DOI: 10.1016/j.procs.2023.01.305

Gołąb-Andrzejak, E. (2024). AI-enhanced digital communication in marketing: Impact and future trends. *Journal of Digital Marketing*, 42(3), 215–230.

Haleem, A., Javaid, M., Qadri, M. A., Singh, R. P., & Suman, R. (2022). Artificial intelligence (AI) applications for marketing: A literature-based study. *International Journal of Intelligent Networks*, 3, 119–132. DOI: 10.1016/j.ijin.2022.08.005

Hofer, K. M., & Grohs, R. (2018). The role of internal branding in the workplace culture of brand management. *Journal of Brand Management*, 25(4), 341–354. DOI: 10.1057/s41262-018-0098-3

Homburg, C., Krohmer, H., & Workman, J. P.Jr. (2004). A strategy implementation perspective of market orientation. *Journal of Business Research*, 57(12), 1331–1340. DOI: 10.1016/S0148-2963(03)00069-9

Huang, M. H., & Rust, R. T. (2018). Artificial intelligence in service. *Journal of Service Research*, 21(2), 155–172. DOI: 10.1177/1094670517752459

Iansiti, M., & Lakhani, K. R. (2020). *Competing in the age of AI: Strategy and leadership when algorithms and networks run the world*. Harvard Business Press.

Ihzaturrahma, N., & Kusumawati, N. (2021). Influence of Integrated Marketing Communication To Brand Awareness and Brand Image Toward Purchase Intention of Local Fashion Product. *International Journal of Entrepreneurship and Management Practices*, 4(15), 23–41. DOI: 10.35631/IJEMP.415002

Iyer, P., Davari, A., & Paswan, A. K. (2019). Market orientation, brand management processes, and brand performance. *Journal of Business Research*, 119, 464–472. DOI: 10.1016/j.jbusres.2019.08.020

Jin, H., & Lowry, P. B. (2021). Using sentiment analysis to analyze brand emotions in social media. *Management Information Systems Quarterly*, 45(2), 571–599.

Katz, D., Kahn, R. L., & Adams, J. S. (1973). *The social psychology of organizations* (2nd ed.). Wiley.

Keller, K. L. (2003). *Strategic brand management: Building, measuring, and managing brand equity* (2nd ed.). Pearson.

Kim, A. J., & Ko, E. (2012). Do social media marketing activities enhance customer equity? An empirical study of luxury fashion brand. *Journal of Business Research*, 65(10), 1480–1486. DOI: 10.1016/j.jbusres.2011.10.014

Kim, J., Giroux, M., & Lee, J. C. (2021). When do you trust AI? The effect of number presentation detail on consumer trust and acceptance of AI recommendations. *Psychology and Marketing*, 38(7), 1140–1155. DOI: 10.1002/mar.21498

King, C., & Grace, D. (2012). Examining the antecedents of positive employee brand-related attitudes and behaviours. *European Journal of Marketing*, 46(3/4), 469–488. DOI: 10.1108/03090561211202567

King, C., & Grace, D. (2012). Examining the antecedents of positive employee brand-related attitudes and behaviors. *European Journal of Marketing*, 46(3/4), 469–488. DOI: 10.1108/03090561211202567

Kotler, K. (2016). Koshy and Jha. *Marketing Management*, 13, 2015–2016.

Kumar, A.; Gupta, N.; Bapat, G. Who is making the decisions? How retail managers can use the power of ChatGPT. J. Bus. Strategy 2023. ahead-of-Print

Kumar, V., Shah, D., & Gupta, S. (2024). AI-powered personalization in brand marketing: Trends and strategies. *JMR, Journal of Marketing Research*, 61(2), 101–117.

Loureiro, S. M. C., & Bilro, R. G. (2022). AI in brands and consumer relationships: Where we are and where we are heading. *Journal of Business Research*, 139, 1063–1073. DOI: 10.1016/j.jbusres.2021.10.014

Mariani, M. M., Perez-Vega, R., & Wirtz, J. (2022). AI in marketing, consumer research and psychology: A systematic literature review and research agenda. *Psychology and Marketing*, 39(4), 755–776. DOI: 10.1002/mar.21619

Matz, S. C., & Netzer, O. (2017). Using big data as a window into consumers' psychology. *Current Opinion in Behavioral Sciences*, 18, 7–12. DOI: 10.1016/j.cobeha.2017.05.009

Miles, S. J., & Mangold, G. (2004). A conceptualization of the employee branding process. *Journal of Relationship Marketing*, 3(2-3), 65–87. DOI: 10.1300/J366v03n02_05

Piehler, R., King, C., Burmann, C., & Xiong, L. (2015). The importance of employee brand understanding, brand identification, and brand commitment in realizing brand citizenship behavior. *European Journal of Marketing*, 50(9/10), 1575–1601. DOI: 10.1108/EJM-11-2014-0725

Punia, S. K., Kumar, M., Stephan, T., Deverajan, G. G., & Patan, R. (2021). Performance Analysis of Machine Learning Algorithms for Big Data Classification. *International Journal of E-Health and Medical Communications*, 12(4), 60–75. DOI: 10.4018/IJEHMC.20210701.oa4

Punjaisri, K., Wilson, A., & Evanschitzky, H. (2009). Internal branding to influence employees' brand promise delivery: A case study in Thailand. *Journal of Service Management*, 20(5), 561–579. DOI: 10.1108/09564230910995143

Ries, A., & Trout, J. (2001). *Positioning: The battle for your mind* (2nd ed.). McGraw-Hill.

Ries, A., & Trout, J. (2001). Positioning: The battle for your mind (20th anniversary ed.). McGraw-Hill.

Russell, S. J., & Norvig, P. (2010). *Artificial intelligence: A modern approach. Nova Jersey, EUA*. Prentice Hall.

Santos-Vijande, M. L., del Río-Lanza, A. B., Suárez-Álvarez, L., & Díaz-Martín, A. M. (2013). The brand management system and service firm competitiveness. *Journal of Business Research*, 66(2), 148–157. DOI: 10.1016/j.jbusres.2012.07.007

Srivastava, K. B., & Bhatnagar, J. (2008). Talent acquisition due diligence leading to high employee engagement: Case of Motorola India MDB. *Industrial and Commercial Training*, 40(5), 253–260. DOI: 10.1108/00197850810886496

Teece, D. J. (2007). Explicating dynamic capabilities: The nature and microfoundations of (sustainable) enterprise performance. *Strategic Management Journal*, 28(13), 1319–1350. DOI: 10.1002/smj.640

Teece, D. J., Pisano, G., & Shuen, A. (1997). Dynamic capabilities and strategic management. *Strategic Management Journal*, 18(7), 509–533. DOI: 10.1002/(SICI)1097-0266(199708)18:7<509::AID-SMJ882>3.0.CO;2-Z

Timoshenko, A., & Hauser, J. R. (2019). Identifying customer needs from user-generated content. *Marketing Science*, 38(1), 1–20. DOI: 10.1287/mksc.2018.1123

Veloutsou, C., & Guzman, F. (2017). Brand management and the role of consumer insights. *Journal of Brand Management*, 24(3), 219–233.

Vorhies, D. W., & Morgan, N. A. (2005). Benchmarking marketing capabilities for sustainable competitive advantage. *Journal of Marketing*, 69(1), 80–94. DOI: 10.1509/jmkg.69.1.80.55505

Wedel, M., & Kannan, P. K. (2016). Marketing analytics for data-rich environments. *Journal of Marketing*, 80(6), 97–121. DOI: 10.1509/jm.15.0413

Yadav, M. S., & Pavlou, P. A. (2021). Artificial intelligence in marketing. *Journal of the Academy of Marketing Science*, 49(1), 7–24.

Chapter 4
Brand Management via AI:
What Are the Odds?

Tareq Nael Hashem
https://orcid.org/0000-0001-9564-931X
Applied Science Private University, Jordan

Ahmad Albattat
https://orcid.org/0000-0002-3127-4405
Asia Pacific University of Technology & Innovation (APU), Malaysia

Anuj Kumar
https://orcid.org/0000-0002-1205-2794
Marwadi University, Rajkot, India

Sodfa El-Taher
https://orcid.org/0009-0008-1032-0506
Al-Azhar University, Egypt

ABSTRACT

The origin of a brand, its development, and its transformation over the last centuries under the influence of economic, social, and cultural processes are tightly interrelated. It started with a sign of craftsmanship in the past and nowadays has a status of a cultural asset: the concept of a brand develops with time along with globalization, technological advancements, and the shift in consumer trends. It is interesting to know the development and the rise of the brand concept, as it helps to explain why brands in the modern world are able to create value equity, differentiation, and attraction of audiences, which is relevant to today's conditions.

DOI: 10.4018/979-8-3693-9461-8.ch004

1. INTRODUCTION

Technological advances have affected every facet of the business, with particular emphasis on the marketing process through cultural, consumer trends and advanced technology that provides new tools when creating marketing strategies and processing customer information. Among the rising technologies that has encroached the marketing domain is the use of Artificial Intelligence and machine learning. AI helps marketers to make sense of big amounts of consumer data, predict trends, make personalized marketing campaigns, and manage basic tasks. Through integrating new-age AI technologies, it becomes possible to analyze consumers' activity, adapt promotions based on the received information, and provide tailor-made content to the target audience, which thus increases the revenue ratio and customers' satisfaction.

A technology that has really impacted the marketing sector is the increase in digital marketing avenues and technology enhanced social marketing platforms. Social media marketing, influencer marketing, and online advertising as major forms of reaching customers today are the major ways that companies connect with consumers today. A social media platform is an open communication that connects brands with their target base and creates awareness. Use of adverts, corporate branding, data analysis and performance measurement are ways through which promotional strategies can be made effective to capture targeted customer base in the current society with existing competition.

Also, the constant development of technologies such as marketing automation and customer relationship management systems has made the marketing function more efficient, generated better quality leads as well as improved client experience. Marketing automation software assist organizations to send emails at the right time and frequency, monitor interactions from a customer and guide the lead through the funnel. Marketing can be relieved of time-consuming activities and be free to engage in other vital activities that include generating new and fresh content, customer engagement and nurturing among others.

2. THE CONCEPT OF "BRAND"

The idea of a brand is intrinsic to the theory and practice of marketing and is a core component of current managerial and consumers' belief systems. Heding et al. (2020) argued that the development of the brand idea can be seen as far back as prehistoric individuals when manufacturers and merchants employed marks, logos, and autographs unto their trades, establishment, and materials as method of distinguishing themselves and their products, as well as a way of guaranteeing quality. Kelley et al. (2022) added that in the years gone by, it has emerged from a label to a sophisticated conception conveying information about identity, reputation, and value adding to consumer misconceptions and competitive positioning.

According to Bernarto et al. (2020), the roots of branding are quite humble, originating with early societies as artisans, producers and merchants put symbols, seals and markings on products to convey information about its origin, quality and ownership. For instance, antique Egyptian potters usually incised symbols and hieroglyphs on their pottery pieces so that buyers and collectors could easily identify original pottery works. Similar to the above, traders of the Middle Ages practiced putting their seals on the products, in medieval Europe guilds and craftsmen applied what are known as the maker's marks, as a means of gaining reputation for quality and reliability. It is from these early forms of branding that some of the additional advanced ideas about branding were established within following centuries.

Jun and Yi (2020) argued that the developments in branding are sometime associated with the industrial revolution, mass production and marketing and global business in the nineteenth and twentieth centuries. As more companies shifted, both organically and inorganically, to offering a broader array of products and directing their efforts toward larger consumer groups, the requirement for appropriate brand management, positioning, and communication also intensified. Coca Cola and Ford, Procter as well as Spyl old were established in this period and so were new revolutionary modes of marketing brands and their identities, newilliver campaigns and approaches to branding (Lissah et al., 2021; Hashem etal.,2024).

Much of early theory development in the field of branding occurred in mid 20th century, with thought leaders such David Ogilvy, Al Reis and Jack Trout writing early theories on branding strategies, and brand positioning and brand management (Gupta et al., 2020). The previous definition of a brand as a visual bar or mark associated with a product expanded its meaning to perceptions and feelings that people have towards a part or all of the things they come across. It was not long before brands were recognized as not mere attributes or characteristics of commodities but values, personalities and promises that consumers can relate with in sort out products in competitive markets (Chen and Cheng., 2020).

A brand has thus emerged as a key management philosophy for today's organization that wants to create long-term customer relationships, build proprietary assets, and cultivate long-term growth in a highly competitive global market. Brands are considered to be effective instruments for influencing consumers' emotions, building up brand identification, and producing constant values for organizations. The brand environment has been further extended with the coming of digital technologies, social media, and e-commerce due to instant consumer communication, brand individualization and real-life brand storytelling from various parts of the world (Chen et al., 2020).

With the course of time, there appeared many definitions for the concept of "brand", and these definitions have differed over the years. According to David Aaker who is a leading marketing scholar and writer, a brand is a distinguishing mark in the form of a name or a symbol – a unique identifier for products of one producer, or a group of producers which is intended to signal the qualitative difference between the latter and other similar products (Heding et al., 2020). Philip Kotler, known as the founder of Modern Marketing, concluded about a brand as a 'name, term, sign, symbol, or design, or combinations of these, used to identify the goods, services or producers, and to distinguish them from those of others (Minsky and Kotler, 2024).

Seth Godin, an expert in marketing and one of the best speakers in this field, defines a brand as a specific sum of consumer's expectations, memories, stories, and relationships resulting from interactions in favor of a particular product or service, and against other similar goods or services (Allahverdiyeva et al., 2024). In the theory of branding in marketing, Al Ries and Jack Trout define a brand as "a unique idea or perception that you occupy in the prospects' mind (Aziz et al., 2023). On the other hand, Kevin Lane Keller and David Aaker, two leading gurus in brand management, thus define a brand as A collection of meaningful associations within the consumer's mind that can enhance the perceived value of the product or service being consumed (Andrii, 2023).

Each of these definitions defines branding as a process that highlights various parts of brands as symbols, identifiers, value propositions as well as simplification involving emotional bonds that influence consumer perceptions and decisions as well as competitive advantages in the marketplace.

2.1. What is Brand Management?

According to Kelley et al., (2022), brand management appeared as a strategic sub-discipline of marketing and business administration that deals with the creation, observation, and control of a brand's attributes, image, and value with the aim of improving the brand appreciation among selected target customers and stakeholders for the purpose of realizing lasting brand value. The history of brand management dates back to the early part of the 20th century where there emerged necessity of branding where organizations startups build various brand associations to set a standard and appeal to customers for lifelong patronage (Mills and Robson, 2020).

Iglesias and Ind (2020) noted that it is with different circumstances that brand management was identified as a unique discipline, having evolved from the discipline of marketing due to the realization by scholars in the field as well as practitioners of the strategic importance of branding in the development of organizational brand assets that affected customers' attitudes as well as their buying behaviors. In the mid of the twentieth century with the processes of mass production, mass distribution and extensive international competitions, brands transitioned from mere signifiers of product types to the influences for effective establishment of customer loyalty, brand value and meaningful consumer-brand relationships (Bayighomog Likoum et al., 2020; Hashem, 2023).

Greco and Polli (2020) stated that the early notion that defines different aspects of brand management evolved mainly from the experience of David Ogilvy, who can be considered the 'Father of Advertising'. Rolls-Royce, Dove and American Express' campaigns are some of the most famous campaigns run by Ogilvy that made effective use of storytelling, appeal to the emotions, and positioning to make changes to the consumers' attitudes towards, and preferences for brands.

Tien et al., (2020) came arguing that amid the crises of globalization, digitalization, shifts in consumers' behavior at the end of the twentieth and the beginning of the twenty-first centuries the field of brand management also evolved, adopting new technologies, data analysis, and customer-oriented approaches to brand creation. Building on the work of early theorists; Kevin Lane Keller and Kapferer added further refinement to the practice of brand management where brand equity, brand identity, and brand architecture concepts have been developed. In addition to that, the strategic management of the company brands as unique marketing assets with strategic values that are critical to organizational performances and competitive advantage initiatives have been established (Wiestner and Spiller, 2025; Hashem,2021).

Lim et al., (2020) noted that modern brand management can be viewed as a complex process which in fact includes a number of activities such as brand planning, brand positioning, brand messaging, and branding, brand experience, and brand evaluation. Brands are no longer considered simply as iconic images, or pictures on the product packaging, but as active beings that interact with consumers, communicate with them, build brand associations and value, and deliver unique branded experiences to the target customer segments (Yahelska et al., 2023; Hashem & Al-Zyoud, 2020).

However, this concept of brand management has come a long way from the early marketing idea and has become strategic competitive weapon on which many businesses rely for brand building, enhancing customers' loyalty as well as form sustainable competitive advantage in the ever increasing brand competition environment. By analyzing the evolution of brand management as an integral and active field, organizations can learn to harness brands as the central scalar of value that underlies the configuration and purchasing of reality in today's plural and integrated economy (Varsha et al., 2021).

2.2. Constituents of Brand Management

Brand management is an important sub-discipline of marketing and business that refers to a process of developing and sustaining company's brands and creating consumers' emotional tie and commitment to such brands helping achieve competitive advantage (Farooq et al., 2024). Branding strategies include a broad set of processes and tasks that define the promotion and management of branded products and services capable of successfully competing in the modern world. Such strategies were presented by Zha et al., (2020), Iglesias and Ind (2020) and Buhalis and Park (2021) including:

Brand Strategy

Brand positioning is the overall plan for managing a brand and focuses on the overall direction, aims and tasks in terms of positioning and communicating a brand to targeted consumer groups. A good brand plan on the other hand is a guideline to the brand direction for brand building and management, which encompasses the organization's brand vision, mission, personality, target audience, points of differentiation against competition and growth plan.

Brand Identity

Brand identity refers to the sum total of all the effects that are visual, verbal, and sometimes tactile that make up brand character and image. A brand identity majors on tangible and intangible features of the brand that give a perception of the brand to the consumers, These attributes include; brand name, logo, colors, typography, voice and other associated brand assets. The strength in a brand total image contributes to brand awareness, brand imprinting, and creating a niche between the competing brands in consumers' mind set.

Brand Positioning

Brand positioning is a way through which communication among the consumers defines the role and rank of a brand vis a vis competitors. Brand positioning is the act of utilizing key information to unveil the value propositions of the brand, the needs and wants of the consumer, as well as offering a positive and relative position for the brand to occupy in the mind of the consumer. Net brand positioning enhances positioning techniques that assist in creating a unique and relevant area for a certain brand in the market with what consumer emotions it aligns.

Brand Communication

Brand communication entails the formulation and implementation of communication promotional techniques that seek to create, maintain, and enhance the understanding of brand value proposition, personality, and advantage amongst the targeted groups of customers. Awareness plays a significant role in brand management since it makes communication crucial between the firms and individual or target consumer.

Hypertensive and coherent brand communication plays a critical role in enhancing brand equity, brand loyalty and favorable consumer attitude towards the brand.

Brand Experience

Brand experience could be defined as the net sum of interactions, and contacts that a consumer has in his or her path to conversion with a brand. Positive brand experience includes providing perfect, individual and Brand Recall Moments that will create not only a positive image but also an engaging and fulfilling experience for consumers while on the long-term basis enhance their trust, commitment and long-term emotional attachment to the brand. Brand experience design is centered on the proposition that every detail of the customer experience should be fine-tuned to influence brand perceptions, customer satisfaction and brand distinctiveness in the marketplace.

Brand Performance Measurement

Brand performance measurement thus entails the evaluation of impact/communication efficacy, and results consequent upon brand management initiatives vis à vis strategic brand objectives laid down by an organization. Metric like brand awareness, brand strength, Brand association, Brand Stickiness, Brand Loyalty Index, Brand Preference, and Brand Engagement scores used to measure and assess the condition and performance of brand at regular interval of time. Through the measurement and analysis of brand performance indicators, organizations are able to ascertain the need for a change, modification or enhancement of brand strategy as well as the effectiveness or efficiency of the overall brand management effort.

2.3. How Brand Management Changed After AI Invasion

Marketing, as a field, has not remained an island when other disciplines embraced Artificial Intelligence (AI). Cheng and Jiang (2022) argued that the application of AI in the sectors of marketing has impacted drastically the interaction of the branding strategies of a brand, data analysis and the overall management and operation of the brand. Specifically, AI has infiltrated brand management by providing tools and analytic for that brand management has the capability and efficiency to develop bespoke experiences for the consumers, optimize the marketing strategies or even reinforce the customer's brand commitment.

Nufer and Muth (2022) argued that the integration of AI in marketing and management of brands has proved to be a revolution of strategy and effective governance. The use of artificial intelligence in business has enhanced the ways consumers are being managed by providing extraordinary intelligence from the consumers' side. AI guides marketers with better data analysis and resulting in a more personalized approach, thus providing a buyer with a more personal and meaningful experience. Mustak et al., (2021) noted on the other hand that this personalization thus creates includes not only brand-customer relationships but also brand loyalty and overall customer retention. AI builds on these strengths by providing marketers with the means of forecasting future trends, improving campaign effectiveness and even policing brand images to ensure that brands remain relevant and relevant in the unfolding market space.

Furthermore, Paschen (2020) stated that AI has helped brands and businesses manage content creation, curation and delivery successfully and effectively to enable them deliver targeted content. With AI tools for sentiment analysis and social listening, brand managers can track consumer opinion in real-time and respond to issues and seize opportunities instantly to better their peculiar brand message. Automated advertisement targeting and optimization have also impacted on marketing campaigns through making it easier for brands to be placed at the right channels for the target group and ensuring the campaigns achieve the maximum desired results. In addition, precision and targeting increase brand awareness while improving the marketing campaign as a whole; thereby increasing brand development and success in today's market (Ho et al., 2024).

2.3.1. Data-Driven Insights

The use of Artificial Intelligence in brand management has benefited the management of brands by offering the business unparalleled information. Through processing of large amount of data in real-time, it is possible to come up with useful insights of consumer buying habits, tendencies among others. All these insights help brands to formulate the right strategies and to fine-tune them in an increasingly competitive environment (Ameen et al., 2022).

2.3.2. Customer Experience Enhancement

AI has drastically transformed the concept of customer experience management by allowing a brand to provide consistent and individualized interactions with the customers they engage with. By using chatbots, recommendation engines or even via messages, using the AI technologies available, customers can find a more personal approach from brands, a more effective and faster customer service. Such an augmentation of the client's perception improves brand association, customer satisfaction, and brand trust (Rana et al., 2022).

2.3.3. Predictive Analytics

With predictive analytics, AI has revolutionized the process of brand management through calculating future trends and possible scenarios from past trends. The application of predictive analytics also help the brands to know the likely behavior of the consumers, the opportunities to look out for and the possible threats that may occur so as to avoid them at all costs. Application of AI can lead brands into better strategizing on the probable market changes and the customers' demands hence enabling brands to channel the right resources and timing into whichever area or strategy they feel is suitable (Lee et al., 2022).

2.3.4. Brand Monitoring and Reputation Management

Modern AI has helped brands mitigate risks by providing real-time information, brand and social media conversations, and brand perception from the social media platforms. Through the use of the big data analytical approach to detect sentiment, a brand is able to detect reputation threats when a customer posts a negative comment and respond to it before the post goes viral, or alternatively, harness the positive sentiment about a brand and further enhance the brand reputation. Through tracking the various interactions on different platforms, the brand reputation is easily controlled thus ensuring that the brand image emanating from the different platforms is positive (Lee et al., 2022).

2.3.5. Automation and Efficiency

Through AI, repetitive jobs involved in brand management have been handled thereby enhancing efficiency and effecting good use of resource hence enhancing the provision of excellent services. Brands can use AI tools to maintain content generation, timetabling of social media updates, and examine marketing effectiveness, leaving brands to focus on strategy and creativity. Not only is this automation more efficient, but it also eliminates the possibility of human error, allowing for a strong brand message, and smooth operation (Jelonek et al., 2024).

2.3.6. Personalization and Targeting

AI has changed the personalization and targeting strategies in brand management and is allowing brands to interact and target single customers. This makes it easier for brands to get it right regarding the type of information to pass on about their corporate identity, products, and services since this will depend on the perceived and potential needs of the segment. This level of personalization leads to better customer interactions, customer retention, and sales, or much better brand-customer connection (Tran et al., 2020).

3. AI-EMPOWERED BRAND MANAGEMENT STRATEGIES

Farooq et al., (2024) argued that the constituents of brand management provide the tools and framework of strategic brand formation, placement, and sustenance from a number of different perspectives in a highly competitive business environment. This means by differentiating between brand strategy, brand identity, brand positioning, brand communication, brand experience, and brand performance measurement, organizations can create strong, attractive and resilient brands that meet the needs of consumers and build long-term value and competitive advantage. For organizations that are interested in creating and sustaining a robust brand equity, coupled with active consumer engagement, the brand management concept, therefore, requires a system-wide and systemic management system.

However, some of the most popular AI-fostered brand management strategies have emerged as critical application solutions regarding boosting customer experience, effectively managing market campaigning, and encouraging brand identity. Some of the most well-known AI-empowered brand management strategies as presented by Sekarini and Selvabaskar (2024), Liu and Chen (2021) and Varsha et al., (2021) include:

3.1. Personalization

AI also gives brands the opportunity to interact with the consumers on a one on one basis due to its ability to gather and analyze large amounts of information concerning consumer trends and habits. Direct marketing, promotional strategies, and messages create a positive impact on the branding awareness, and understanding the requirement of every category of customers can be beneficial for the businesses.

3.2. Predictive Analytics

Brands can use AI and predictive analytics to predict market trends, consumer behavior and potential market trends based on passed patterns. Using predictive analytics, a brand can have fact-based guidance on how best to market the brand, avoid being trapped by marketing trends that may actually harm the brand and achieve and sustain brand awareness and competitiveness.

3.3. Chatbots and Virtual Assistants

The use of artificial intelligence in creation of chatbots and virtual assistants allows brands to provide customers with 24/7 immediate and personalized consumer support. Such tools can be trained to handle customer queries, motivate the purchase of products, and offer all-around help; tasks that can improve the customer experience and thus, they can strengthen customer relations and brand integrity.

3.4. Sentiment Analysis

There are special AI-based products to identify the attitude of consumers, posts in social networks, and comments left in the reviews section to a particular brand. Sentiment analysis thus able the brands to quickly identify violated sentiments that require management, customer complaints and issues that require attention and potential marketing messages that might help the brands to effectively market their products to the target consumers.

3.5. Content Optimization

AI is useful in analyzing content production metrics, consumer engagement figures, and market changes so that optimal content production and sharing strategies are instituted. AI also has the potential to be used for content optimization in order to redefine the approach brands take in reaching out to their audiences or identifying topics of concern, as well as format optimization for enhancing content visibility across digital platforms.

3.6. Importance of AI in Enhancing Brand Management Strategies

Cheng and Jiang (2022) argued that AI significantly contributes to raising the effectiveness of brand management by offering businesses invaluable tools and resource to propose more vibrant and efficient branding experiences. Machine learning real-time processes, major data sets yielding insights on market behavior, consumer attitudes, habits, and trends. For this reason, the audience can be reached through AI-driven data analytics, which will ensure brands make better decisions, change strategies, and make necessary adjustments to meet the needs of the audience. It also affords brands better avenues for presenting to the consumers more effective and relevant experiences that foster strengthening of the brand-customer bond and hence brand loyalty (Babatunde et al., 2024).

Furthermore, it wedges the field of AI into brand management because it allows companies to offer a consistent and satisfying consumer experience from one channel to the next. The use of chatbots, recommendation engines, and messages personalize brands to address customer' concerns effectively by offering feedback instantly (Ramanjaneyulu and Khirbat, 2021). Apart from the upliftment in customer satisfaction levels, customer experience upgrade leads to brand loyalty, and customers becoming brand advocates. As AI becomes a means of delivering 'Welcome Insiders' to brands, consumers can then be offered unique experiences in Holo-Marketing and Retail by establishing Marked Antagonists that would enable brands to create niches in the crowded marketplace (El Fawal et al., 2024).

According to Huang and Rust (2021), AI and ML are useful for predicting the market trend, consumer behavior, and the best approach that should be taken to enhance the long-run operation of the brand name. AI and machine-learning based solutions for predictive analytics helps the brands to forecast the trend and customer demand patterns, and allow brands to be proactive in the shifting market environment (Jelonek et al., 2024). This type of branding is made possible through AI to help brands leverage predictive analytics on brand images, resource allocation and flexibility. Such predictive capacity allows brands to fully leverage the capability of brand management and make logical and accurate decisions as to how best to proceed given current and forward-looking consumer behavior, thereby improving the overall flexibility and relevance of the brand management methodologies being used (Makosa et al., 2024).

3.7. Challenges and Opportunities in AI-Enabled Brand Management

According to Farooq et al., (2024), AI-enabled brand management holds a lot of potential for how businesses can strengthen their marketing communication initiatives, increase value for customer relations, and advance brand equity. The first of these is the field of individual targeting, which means targeted advertising. It is also easy for AI algorithms to wade through massive amounts of data to establish individual consumers' needs, their behavior, and even their buying habits. Consequently, brands are able to use this data to create unique and relevant messages to unique target customers. Personalizing experiences at this level also helps to minimize costs incurred because of generalized marketing in that it brings better results, improved engagements, and improved conversion rates (Sekarini and Selvabaskar, 2024).

A final area relevant to AI enabled brand management is the utilization of forecasting for brand management decision making. AI also has the capability of trend analysis, foreseeing the trend of the consumers, and electrifying the market niches based on some historic patterns that have been identified. Predictive analytics must also be used in brands' marketing to enable brands to make right decisions of marketing to meet the market trends. These predictive capabilities can help brands to modify their brand management strategies; allocate resources most effectively; and identify opportunities to improve brand awareness; as well as its competitiveness in the marketplace (Olusegun, 2024).

Cunha et al., (2024) added that AI offer prospects for brands in terms of Omega to improve operational processes and increase productivity in brand management. The use of artificial intelligence can make human work easier in some ways, for example such functions as data processing, generating content and assisting customers can be done automatically. This shows – as according to Sekarini and Selvabaskar (2024) - that the use of AI automation solutions can help to transform brand efficiency in a positive manner by cutting cost, increasing the output. Moreover, the AI integrated implementations can enhance operational efficiency, facilitate the decision making process and help the brands to adapt themselves swiftly in response to the market wheeling strategies and make good changes to the conventional patterns of brand management. AI-enabled automation presents opportunities for brands to consider how they can leverage the technology in the pursuit of increased innovation, overall growth as well as a way to stand out amidst high levels of competition (Makosa, 2024).

From another perspective, Deryl et al., (2023) noted that AI-supported brand management brings a number of issues that business has to face in order to maximize the positive effects of AI integration into brand management. Our first concern is the ethical issues capable of arising from the use of AI technologies. In today's advanced and evolving algorithms, AI needs to analyze the consumers' data and predict the consumers' behaviors; it gives rise to questions such as privacy, security, and transparency. As according to Chaturvedi and Verma (2023), brands must understand that they cannot only fall under the rules set by ethical benchmarks or governmental laws but also properly protect consumer's data. Also, AI algorithms and any kind of machine learning can be prejudiced and this is a problem in brand management. Systemic issues inherited from the data feed AI models means prejudicial results that harms a brand and public trust. The current use of AI systems implies that brands must put measures in place towards ensuring there is no biased decisions being made by the artificial intelligence systems (Broekhuizen et al., 2023).

Akter et al., (2023) stated that AI integration and scalability of AI present another challenge to the brands that are interested in automating their brand management using AI. The assimilation of AI technologies into current brand management processes and systems can be a challenging and costly affair. It may be challenging for brands to connect the addition of Artificial Intelligence functionalities with total branding strategies, integrate AI with presently applied technologies, and direct the growth or modification of AI solutions to meet business development agility. In addition, implementing and maintaining AI is not cheap; these events may be expensive for some organizations particularly those with a small capital. Currently, brands require identifying their AI implementation strategies, their scalability, and the corresponding roadmap for the sustainable implementation of AI solutions to alleviate these challenges and reach the goals of proper brand management (Kumar and Suthar, 2024).

Murphey et al., (2022) presented another disadvantage of employing artificial intelligence in brand management is a skilled talent and expertise requirement. Deployment of AI solutions entails technical competence in data sciences, machine learning and, AI development. Some companies could be experiencing complex tasks in sourcing and securing employees with the ideal skill and experience for implementing AI solutions in branding. Furthermore, the fact that AI is fast evolving requires that employee in the industries constantly update their knowledge to be in tune with the advances and advancements in AI. Training programs or talent development initiatives are required so that a brand can cultivate a pool of personnel that will be efficient in advancing the opportunities of AI brand management successfully (Tula et al., 2024).

3.8. Data Privacy and Security Issues in AI-Driven Brand Management

Musaiqer and Hamdan (2023) argued that of particular importance in AI-lead brand management is data protection as accumulating large amounts of consumer data entails numerous ethical and legal challenges. It also has a weakness of how vulnerable data is when it is in the hands of an unknown third party. An AI algorithm uses large data sets to come up with reasonable conclusions and negate errors; this makes them a target to hacking. Due to this reason, brands have to ensure they have adequate structures that protect consumer data, encryption, and other storage means to ensure they do not lose data to hackers. Neglecting opportunities to enhance data security exposes consumers to risks, and as such puts the brand in legal peril and leads to its deterioration (Dwivedi and Wang, 2022).

Karim et al., (2023) added that the problem of data openness and consent of consumers is one of the main concerns in AI-aided brand management. When huge quantities of data are passed through AI algorithms to discover patterns and inform marketing, those consuming products and services might not know how their data is applied, let alone shared. It would also require brands to adhere to an entirely new set of rules that include avoiding excessive data collection, directly informing consumers about data collection and processing methods and purposes, and receiving their unambiguous consent to engage in data processing activities. Maintaining trust and accountability over data go a long way in making consumers trust brands, as well as can keep brands on the right side of the law on the matter such as GDPR and CCPA (Ljepava, 2022).

Santoro et al., (2024) supported what was mentioned earlier adding that AI algorithms are themselves prejudiced, which remains a major concern whenever brands use data to guide their strategies. Training for machine learning algorithms can also be unfair to members of one or the other social group hence holding bias which in turn promotes prejudices in societies. For fairness and eliminating of biases, brands need to remain sensitive on the biases of AI models. As key recommendations, one must require that AI bias detection tools be put in place, secondly, the AI systems must be audited periodically, thirdly, diversity and inclusion when gathering data must be considered, fundamental steps to managing bias problems in AI-led branding. As bias concerns continue to arise, brands can play a helpful role in addressing them and establishing higher ethical levels, and consumer rights as well establish the brand as a symbol of being more equal (Kumar et al., 2024).

3.9. Ethical Considerations in AI-Powered Brand Strategies

Agustina (2023) confirmed that idea that ethical aspect is a decisive factor for development of AI-controlled brand management since the work with artificial intelligence technologies implies crucial ethical and social issues that companies should address for implementing effective and responsible methods. The information transparency as according to Sekarini and Selvabaskar (2024) coupled with the complexity of AI-powered brand reputation framework is one major ethical question that brands and firms face. Leveraging consumer data for marketing decisions through complex AI is already a reality, and as such, brands need to disclose data processing activities including how and where consumer data is collected, used and shared. Being open about how and when AI is being incorporated into brand strategies is one of the best ways to build trust, respond to consumer concerns, and show the public that consumer rights are respected, and their data will be protected. This paper has argued that transparency and accountability are critical to the promotion of ethical practices, as well as establishing a good reputation and successful brand-customer relationship (Kiradoo, 2023).

Yet, Gazi et al. (2024) noted another important ethical concern of AI prospects for brand management is the question of prejudice of algorithms. Machine learning models are as biased as the data used when training where they lock and discriminate depending on the data set. For this reason, brands must take the extra step to control bias in AI models to eliminate unfair outcomes. Bias detection tools, AI audit, and diverse data collecting approaches are the solutions that should be applied to minimize bias difficulties in AI-based brand techniques. Therefore, any AI employing policy and practice must be made fair and inclusive for brands to act as moral stewards and uphold reasonable standards both socially and economically to the consumers (Kiradoo, 2023).

Gupta et al., (2024) also added that potential and familiar issues regarding data privacy and ownership in adopting AI in brand positioning need to be treated from an ethical stand to preserve the consumer's right while preventing unauthorized access to their data. While AI technologies amass consumer data for advertising, marketing messages' target markets, brands are under increased demand to protect consumer data from malicious parties. Consumers' privacy rights must be respected, parties involved in data processing must seek consumer consent for their activities, and data processing processes need to be secure are essential practices that should be adopted to enhance data privacies and securities in AI-advancing brand strategies. Although the European Union's General Data Protection Regulation is primarily concerned with data privacy and not business ethics, brands that place these goals at the center of their company's ethos can exhibit high levels of ethical behavior. Also earn the trust of their users concerning their usage of the customer's data in a world that is becoming digital (Oyekunle et al., 2024).

3.10. AI-Empowered Brand Management from Around the World

Many well-known organizations have used the brand management card as a way to reach the world in a smart and intelligent approach, and at the same time achieve its desired goals. Among these organizations are Sohaib et al., (2022), Nia (2023), Sheykhan et al., (2024) and Ling et al., (2023). These examples show how leaders in intelligent branding have assisted in creating success for these familiar organizations, as well as brand power/authority.

3.11. Apple

Apple is proven solid because it never cease to innovate and develop new products that will suit their target market. Apple products are typically an attractive design and user interfaces of the product, which in turn has formed an undying emotional bond between them and the consumers. It has developed a complementary line of products that complement well the paragon ecosystem making the customers stick to the Apple brand products.

3.12. Nike

Nike has done a good job in the branding of emotional aspect where the organization directly appeals to the consumer's emotions through effective appealing campaigns on sociable rebirth. It aims at hiring the most talented athletes to promote production because the consumer will be inspired to buy the products by identifying with success, performance, and effort. Nike's marketing strategies include the company's utilization of original approaches to the televising of advertisements that hinge on sensitive social issues and followership cultural aspects to appeal to multifaceted audiences.

3.13. Coca-Cola

Coca-Cola has ensured that it has appeal to everyone in the world through the company's strategic quest of forming a unity of manufacture of a brand full of cultural and geographical diversification. It has remained quite loyal to its logo, to its color, and even to its commercials that have been ringing in our heads, and that feeling of familiarity never goes away. Coca-Cola has an effective strategy of creating contact with consumers through community activities and sponsorships, in order to shape a good image about the brand and strengthen the affective connection with the audience.

3.14. Tesla

Tesla has threatened the conventional car industries by providing electric cars with advanced features and an environmentally friendly approach to production, which also earns the brand recognition as an industry innovator. It has been able to sell its product directly to the consumer hence it was able to well control the brand image and the total customer experience. Tesla does not merely differentiate its product from others but incorporates itself to good brand elements and lays its foundation in iconic showrooms and stress on sustainability, which pulls amidst its target market.

3.15. Future Trends and Implications of AI in Transforming Brand Management

Gao et al., (2023) confirmed that the various trends and consequences of artificial intelligence (AI) with reference to evolving brand management is expected to bring drastic changes in the way companies interact with customers, in choice of marketing techniques and in building brand image. Increase is observed in the usage of different AI attributes in almost all aspects of branding information, reaching from consumer analytics to the marketing automation. The advancements in technologies relying on Artificial Intelligence will go on rising, helping the brands to extend their understanding of consumers and deliver tailored experiences that meet customers' needs at the right time and with maximum effect on marketing communications. ['As AI capabilities progress, brands will be able to harness machine learning models, natural language processing and predictive analytics to identify the consumer demand and to deliver highly relevant messages that will help to build brand awareness and consumer relations in the long term (Hermann, 2022).

The second important trend related to the future of AI in brand management is the developments of omnichannel marketing powered by AI. Consumers are interacting with brands based on multi-touchpoint and multi-device interfaces and AI technologies are equip brands to ensure that the customer's journey is optimized and connected across web, social media, mobile apps, stores, etc (Martin et al., 2022). While chatbots, recommendation systems, and smart messaging will make it easier for brands to present content and products in real-time and customized accordingly to the customers. This also makes ornamentation through AI for omnichannel marketing possible to create consistent brand experience for consumer and signal during branding (Katragadda, 2024).

According to Roberts et al., (2024), future uses of AI in brands go beyond the practical applications in marketing and customer relations, but rather hold innovative organizational uses that are significant for future business expansion. That makes it crucial for brands to adapt AI technologies into managing brands in ways that will enable brand owners to make right decisions from AI analysis, as well as use AI to optimize brand management processes for better business performance. Stahl et al., (2022) agreed on the same idea and confirmed that using predictive analysis through advanced technology will however assist brands at identifying potential opportunities and quickly bridge the market gaps occasioned by shifting consumer trends thus creating competitive advantage. Further, AI automation in brand management processes will help reduce coordination and operational inefficiencies, offer greater data insight, and make room for ideas, creativity and value addition, to foster long-term brand building.

Hence, in terms of defining the future of AI in enhancing brand management, business can look forward to opportunities not only to be discloser but also to set up their own bar in an environment beset by dynamic change and innovation. Artificial intelligence is a milestone brands need to incorporate in their strategies to be on the right side of consumers and improve on experiences (Babatunde et al., 2024). However, along with these opportunities; there appears different consequences in a way of data privacy, ethical factors, and constant changing environment. Those brands that are keenly acing these difficulties and maximizing the potential of AI in brand management will be indeed the ones that are most equipped to succeed in the ever changing and complex brand environment and hence contribute to brands sustainable growth, consumer relationships, brand success in the years to come (Pasupulati et al., 2024).

3.16. Criticism on Adopting AI in Brand Management

Abdelkader et al., (2024) proved that criticism on the use of Artificial Intelligence (AI) for the management of brand equity as elicited by various scholars, economist and marketers presented various ethical, social and economic concerns over the application of the AI technologies in defining the consumer-brand nexus. Authors like Shoshana Zuboff have described the problem of using AI in brand management in terms of surveillance capitalism and data brokerage. According to Zuboff, AI brand strategies frequently lead to value cascades to maximize profit, at the expense of the individual's privacy and agency that vests the platforms with control over the individual's information. This critique raises questions about data privacy, consent and stressing on more accountability on how brands are USING AI to change consumer perception and/or behavior (Wojewoda, 2023).

From another perspective, marketers has also expressed negative attitudes to the adoption of AI in branding, notably on issues of axiological, non-creative, and data heuristic disposition (Patrizi et al., 2024). Renowned marketers like Scott Galloway have warned consumers about how inherent future market automation and algorithmic targeting were becoming dehumanizing to brand experiences. Galloway posits that while application of artificial intelligence in managing brands is beneficial in most ways because of insights and efficiency ensured there, their benefit ought to be blended with human creativity, empathy, and emotions in forming brands and their relationship with consumers. This critique brings out the idea of an integration of artificial intelligence in the strategies of the particular brand alongside the integration of the human touch in the branding process to ascertain that branding appeals to both the technical as well as the social parts of consumers (Swiatek et al., 2024).

In that regards, Ferraro et al., (2023) noted that the concerns of using AI in brand management provided by the famous scholars, economists, and marketers highlighted the issues and ethical aspects related to the AI usage for defining consumer image and brand engagement. Of course, marketing AI means incredible opportunities in increasing the efficiency of marketing communication, increasing individualized customer experiences, and boosting brand development, yet, it also entails questions about data protection, competitive markets, and, finally, brand creators. Many of these criticisms actually call for a more finely tuned perspective that takes into account the improved ethical standards of many businesses, the need for AI regulation, and the goal of establishing a more consumer-oriented relationship with brands in the increasingly online environment (Chung et al., 2022).

From an economical point of view, Alawamleh et al., (2024) argued that it has been pointed out by various critics that the use of AI technologies in the management of brands would lead to the accumulation of large corporations' power and market authority. Scholars such as Joseph Stiglitz have cautioned that advanced digital monopolies aided by artificial intelligence have the propensity to exclude competition, curtail free competition and any sense of market plurality. Stiglitz stresses the need for proper rules and anti-trust policies regarding the AI-supported brand management and takes a major concern in maintaining market competitiveness, consumer protection, and long-term economic value based on the development of AI-make branding in digital economy operations.

4. CONCLUSION

The origin of a brand, its development, and its transformation over the last centuries under the influence of economic, social, and cultural processes are tightly interrelated. It started with a sign of craftsmanship in the past and nowadays has a status of a cultural asset: the concept of a brand develops with time along with globalization, technological advancements, and the shift in consumer trends. It is interesting to know the development and the rise of the brand concept, as it helps to explain why brands in the modern world are able to create value equity, differentiation, and attraction of audiences, which is relevant to today's conditions.

REFERENCES

Abdelkader, A. A., Hassan, H., Mohamed, M. A., & Khashaba, I. O. (2024). Advances in Brand Management Strategies: Conceptualising the Interrelationships among Emerging Brand Concepts. *Kurdish Studies*, 12(2), 5278–5300.

Agustina, S. (2023). Ethical Business Practices And AI-Driven Marketing For Product Branding In MSMEs. *Maeswara: Jurnal Riset Ilmu Manajemen dan Kewirausahaan, 1*(2), 01-10.

Akter, S., Sultana, S., Mariani, M., Wamba, S. F., Spanaki, K., & Dwivedi, Y. K. (2023). Advancing algorithmic bias management capabilities in AI-driven marketing analytics research. *Industrial Marketing Management*, 114, 243–261. DOI: 10.1016/j.indmarman.2023.08.013

Alawamleh, M., Shammas, N., Alawamleh, K., & Ismail, L. B. (2024). Examining the limitations of AI in business and the need for human insights using Interpretive Structural Modelling. *Journal of Open Innovation*, 10(3), 100338. DOI: 10.1016/j.joitmc.2024.100338

Allahverdiyeva, M., Aghayeva, K., & Tavakkulova, S. (2024). The importance of advertising in global trade. *Науковий журнал «Економіка і регіон»*, (1 (92)), 20-25.

Ameen, N., Sharma, G. D., Tarba, S., Rao, A., & Chopra, R. (2022). Toward advancing theory on creativity in marketing and artificial intelligence. *Psychology and Marketing*, 39(9), 1802–1825. DOI: 10.1002/mar.21699

Andrii, K. (2023). MODERN PERSPECTIVES AND PROBLEMS OF MARKETING IN EUROPE. *Нейромаркетинг, штучний інтелект та цифровий маркетинг*, 112.

Aziz, A., Lita, R. P., & Yeni, Y. H. (2023). Performance of Fighting Brands in Maintaining Market Share in Cement Trading during Oversupply. *Inovbiz: Jurnal Inovasi Bisnis Seri Manajemen, Investasi dan Kewirausahaan, 3*(1), 43-53.

Babatunde, S. O., Odejide, O. A., Edunjobi, T. E., & Ogundipe, D. O.Sodiq Odetunde BabatundeOpeyemi Abayomi OdejideTolulope Esther EdunjobiDamilola Oluwaseun Ogundipe. (2024). The role of AI in marketing personalization: A theoretical exploration of consumer engagement strategies. *International Journal of Management & Entrepreneurship Research*, 6(3), 936–949. DOI: 10.51594/ijmer.v6i3.964

Bayighomog Likoum, S. W., Shamout, M. D., Harazneh, I., & Abubakar, A. M. (2020). Market-sensing capability, innovativeness, brand management systems, market dynamism, competitive intensity, and performance: An integrative review. *Journal of the Knowledge Economy*, 11(2), 593–613. DOI: 10.1007/s13132-018-0561-x

Bernarto, I., Berlianto, M. P., Meilani, Y. F. C. P., Masman, R. R., & Suryawan, I. N. (2020). The influence of brand awareness, brand image, and brand trust on brand loyalty. *Jurnal Manajemen*, 24(3), 412–426. DOI: 10.24912/jm.v24i3.676

Broekhuizen, T., Dekker, H., de Faria, P., Firk, S., Nguyen, D. K., & Sofka, W. (2023). AI for managing open innovation: Opportunities, challenges, and a research agenda. *Journal of Business Research*, 167, 114196. DOI: 10.1016/j.jbusres.2023.114196

Buhalis, D., & Park, S. (2021). Brand management and cocreation lessons from tourism and hospitality: Introduction to the special issue. *Journal of Product and Brand Management*, 30(1), 1–11. DOI: 10.1108/JPBM-10-2020-3158

Chaturvedi, R., & Verma, S. (2023). Opportunities and challenges of AI-driven customer service. *Artificial Intelligence in customer service: The next frontier for personalized engagement*, 33-71.

Chen, R., Zhou, Z., Zhan, G., & Zhou, N. (2020). The impact of destination brand authenticity and destination brand self-congruence on tourist loyalty: The mediating role of destination brand engagement. *Journal of Destination Marketing & Management*, 15, 100402. DOI: 10.1016/j.jdmm.2019.100402

Chen, Z. F., & Cheng, Y. (2020). Consumer response to fake news about brands on social media: The effects of self-efficacy, media trust, and persuasion knowledge on brand trust. *Journal of Product and Brand Management*, 29(2), 188–198. DOI: 10.1108/JPBM-12-2018-2145

Cheng, Y., & Jiang, H. (2022). Customer–brand relationship in the era of artificial intelligence: Understanding the role of chatbot marketing efforts. *Journal of Product and Brand Management*, 31(2), 252–264. DOI: 10.1108/JPBM-05-2020-2907

Chung, K., Thaichon, P., & Quach, S. (2022). Types of artificial intelligence (AI) in marketing management. In *Artificial intelligence for marketing management* (pp. 29–40). Routledge. DOI: 10.4324/9781003280392-4

Cunha, C. R., Gomes, J. P., & Mendonça, V. (2024). The Role of Artificial Intelligence to Empower and Leverage Brands. In *AI Innovation in Services Marketing* (pp. 27–47). IGI Global. DOI: 10.4018/979-8-3693-2153-9.ch002

Deryl, M. D., Verma, S., & Srivastava, V. (2023). How does AI drive branding? Towards an integrated theoretical framework for AI-driven branding. *International Journal of Information Management Data Insights*, 3(2), 100205. DOI: 10.1016/j.jjimei.2023.100205

Dwivedi, Y. K., & Wang, Y. (2022). Guest editorial: Artificial intelligence for B2B marketing: Challenges and opportunities. *Industrial Marketing Management*, 105, 109–113. DOI: 10.1016/j.indmarman.2022.06.001

El Fawal, A., Mawlawi, A., Zakhem, N. B., Baydoun, H., Yassine, D., & Kassably, C. (2024). The impact of AI marketing activities on consumer-based brand equity: The mediating role of brand experience. *Journal of Infrastructure. Policy and Development*, 8(7), 3851. DOI: 10.24294/jipd.v8i7.3851

Farooq, M., Ramzan, M., & Yen, Y. Y. (2024). Exploring the Impact of Artificial Intelligence on Brand Management: A Multi-Dimensional Analysis. *Transformative Impacts of AI in Management*, 157.

Ferraro, C., Hemsley, A., & Sands, S. (2023). Embracing diversity, equity, and inclusion (DEI): Considerations and opportunities for brand managers. *Business Horizons*, 66(4), 463–479. DOI: 10.1016/j.bushor.2022.09.005

Gao, B., Wang, Y., Xie, H., Hu, Y., & Hu, Y. (2023). Artificial intelligence in advertising: Advancements, challenges, and ethical considerations in targeting, personalization, content creation, and ad optimization. *SAGE Open*, 13(4), 21582440231210759. DOI: 10.1177/21582440231210759

Gazi, M. S., Hasan, M. R., Gurung, N., & Mitra, A. (2024). Ethical Considerations in AI-driven Dynamic Pricing in the USA: Balancing Profit Maximization with Consumer Fairness and Transparency. *Journal of Economics. Finance and Accounting Studies*, 6(2), 100–111.

Greco, F., & Polli, A. (2020). Emotional Text Mining: Customer profiling in brand management. *International Journal of Information Management*, 51, 101934. DOI: 10.1016/j.ijinfomgt.2019.04.007

Gupta, A., Raj, A., Puri, M., & Gangrade, J. Ethical Considerations in the Deployment of AI. *Tuijin Jishu/Journal of Propulsion Technology, 45*(2), 2024.

Gupta, S., Gallear, D., Rudd, J., & Foroudi, P. (2020). The impact of brand value on brand competitiveness. *Journal of Business Research*, 112, 210–222. DOI: 10.1016/j.jbusres.2020.02.033

Hashem, T. N. (2021). Environmental legitimacy through adopting green products and its effect on the brand equity: Moderating role of management awareness. *Review of World Economics*, 12(2), 197–210.

Hashem, T. N. (2023). The Influence of Rebranding on Brand Value Within Cosmetic Industry Sector: Mediating Role of Value Engineering. *Journal of Law and Sustainable Development*, 11(11), e1701–e1701. DOI: 10.55908/sdgs.v11i11.1701

Hashem, T. N., Al-Qeed, M., & Qtaish, R. M. (2024). Brand Linguistics: The Influence of Using Local Terminology Through Social Media in Marketing Products on Customers' Purchase Behavior. *Journal of System and Management Sciences*, 14(2), 291–309.

Hashem, T. N., & Al-Zyoud, M. F. (2020). Influence Of Decoy Marketing On Impulsive Purchasing Behavior Among Adult Customers Of Tech Market In Jordan, Mediating Role Of Brand Equity. *Image*, 7(15), 2020.

Heding, T., Knudtzen, C. F., & Bjerre, M. (2020). *Brand management: Mastering research, theory and practice*. Routledge. DOI: 10.4324/9780367172596

Hermann, E. (2022). Leveraging artificial intelligence in marketing for social good—An ethical perspective. *Journal of Business Ethics*, 179(1), 43–61. DOI: 10.1007/s10551-021-04843-y PMID: 34054170

Ho, S. P. S., & Chow, M. Y. C. (2024). The role of artificial intelligence in consumers' brand preference for retail banks in Hong Kong. *Journal of Financial Services Marketing*, 29(2), 292–305. DOI: 10.1057/s41264-022-00207-3

Huang, M. H., & Rust, R. T. (2021). A strategic framework for artificial intelligence in marketing. *Journal of the Academy of Marketing Science*, 49(1), 30–50. DOI: 10.1007/s11747-020-00749-9

Iglesias, O., & Ind, N. (2020). Towards a theory of conscientious corporate brand co-creation: The next key challenge in brand management. *Journal of Brand Management*, 27(6), 710–720. DOI: 10.1057/s41262-020-00205-7

Jelonek, D., Kumar, N., & Pawełoszek, I. (2024). Artificial Intelligence Applications In Brand Management. *Scientific Papers of Silesian University of Technology. Organization & Management/Zeszyty Naukowe Politechniki Slaskiej. Seria Organizacji i Zarzadzanie*, (202).

Jun, S., & Yi, J. (2020). What makes followers loyal? The role of influencer interactivity in building influencer brand equity. *Journal of Product and Brand Management*, 29(6), 803–814. DOI: 10.1108/JPBM-02-2019-2280

Karim, S., Saxena, S., Singh, D. A., Deshmukh, P., Lokare, A. B., Gour, O. G., ... & Ranjan, M. K. (2023). Revolutionising Marketing: Leveraging Blockchain and AI for Impactful Management.

Katragadda, V. (2024). Ethical AI in Customer Interactions: Implementing Safeguards and Governance Frameworks. *Iconic Research And Engineering Journals*, 7(12), 394–397.

Kelley, L. D., Sheehan, K. B., Dobias, L., Koranda, D. E., & Jugenheimer, D. W. (2022). *Advertising media planning: a brand management approach*. Routledge. DOI: 10.4324/9781003258162

Kiradoo, G. (2023). Unlocking the potential of ai in business: Challenges and ethical considerations. *Recent Progress in Science and Technology*, 6, 205–220. DOI: 10.9734/bpi/rpst/v6/18935D

Kumar, D., & Suthar, N. (2024). Ethical and legal challenges of AI in marketing: An exploration of solutions. *Journal of Information. Communication and Ethics in Society*, 22(1), 124–144. DOI: 10.1108/JICES-05-2023-0068

Kumar, V., Ashraf, A. R., & Nadeem, W. (2024). AI-powered marketing: What, where, and how? *International Journal of Information Management*, 77, 102783. DOI: 10.1016/j.ijinfomgt.2024.102783

Lee, C. T., Pan, L. Y., & Hsieh, S. H. (2022). Artificial intelligent chatbots as brand promoters: A two-stage structural equation modeling-artificial neural network approach. *Internet Research*, 32(4), 1329–1356. DOI: 10.1108/INTR-01-2021-0030

Lim, W. M., Jee, T. W., & De Run, E. C. (2020). Strategic brand management for higher education institutions with graduate degree programs: Empirical insights from the higher education marketing mix. *Journal of Strategic Marketing*, 28(3), 225–245. DOI: 10.1080/0965254X.2018.1496131

Ling, G. Y., Yuang, G., Zhicheng, G., Xuan, G. T. X., Maharani, C. D., Genira, C. F., & Saidhanyakumar, M. (2023). Analysis of factors affecting brand loyalty: A study of Coca-Cola. [APJME]. *Asia Pacific Journal of Management and Education*, 6(3), 16–29. DOI: 10.32535/apjme.v6i3.2635

Lissah, S. Y., Ayanore, M. A., Krugu, J. K., Aberese-Ako, M., & Ruiter, R. A. (2021). Managing urban solid waste in Ghana: Perspectives and experiences of municipal waste company managers and supervisors in an urban municipality. *PLoS One*, 16(3), e0248392. DOI: 10.1371/journal.pone.0248392 PMID: 33705483

Liu, Y., & Chen, W. (2021). Optimization of brand marketing strategy of intelligent technology under the background of artificial intelligence. *Mobile Information Systems*, 2021(1), 9507917. DOI: 10.1155/2021/9507917

Ljepava, N. (2022). AI-enabled marketing solutions in Marketing Decision making: AI application in different stages of marketing process. *TEM Journal*, 11(3), 1308–1315. DOI: 10.18421/TEM113-40

Makosa, S. (2024). Brand Management Driven by Artificial Intelligence.

Martin, K., Shilton, K., & Smith, J. E. (2022). Business and the ethical implications of technology: Introduction to the symposium. In *Business and the ethical implications of technology* (pp. 1–11). Springer Nature Switzerland. DOI: 10.1007/978-3-031-18794-0_1

Mills, A. J., & Robson, K. (2020). Brand management in the era of fake news: Narrative response as a strategy to insulate brand value. *Journal of Product and Brand Management*, 29(2), 159–167. DOI: 10.1108/JPBM-12-2018-2150

Minsky, L., & Kotler, P. (2024). Sustainable Practices and Demarketing: An Interview with Philip Kotler. *Advertising & Society Quarterly, 25*(1).

Murphey, Y. L., Kolmanovsky, I., & Watta, P. (2022). Advances, Opportunities and Challenges in AI-enabled Technologies for Autonomous and Connected Vehicles. *AI-enabled Technologies for Autonomous and Connected Vehicles*, 1-16.

Musaiqer, H. H., & Hamdan, A. (2023). The Role of Artificial Intelligence in Brand Building: A Review. *Emerging Trends and Innovation in Business and Finance*, 307-318.

Mustak, M., Salminen, J., Plé, L., & Wirtz, J. (2021). Artificial intelligence in marketing: Topic modeling, scientometric analysis, and research agenda. *Journal of Business Research*, 124, 389–404. DOI: 10.1016/j.jbusres.2020.10.044

Nia, N. B. (2023). Brand Management Internationalization: Case Study of Nike. *Journal of International Trade. Logistics and Law*, 9(2), 181–187.

Nufer, G., & Muth, M. (2022). Artificial intelligence in marketing analytics: The application of artificial neural networks for brand image measurement. *Journal of Marketing Development and Competitiveness*, 16(1), 55–63.

Olusegun, J. (2024). The Role of AI in Enhancing Sentiment Analysis for Brand Management.

Oyekunle, D., Boohene, D., & Preston, D. (2024). Ethical Considerations in AI-Powered Work Environments: A Literature Review and Theoretical Framework for Ensuring Human Dignity and Fairness. *Valley International Journal Digital Library*, 6166-6178.

Paschen, J. (2020). Investigating the emotional appeal of fake news using artificial intelligence and human contributions. *Journal of Product and Brand Management*, 29(2), 223–233. DOI: 10.1108/JPBM-12-2018-2179

Pasupulati, R., Mahendran, J., & Majumdar, A. (2024). Predictive Analysis of Digital Consumer Behaviour: Key to Understanding Success and Failure of a Brand. In *Enhancing and Predicting Digital Consumer Behavior with AI* (pp. 238-267). IGI Global.

Patrizi, M., Šerić, M., & Vernuccio, M. (2024). Hey Google, I trust you! The consequences of brand anthropomorphism in voice-based artificial intelligence contexts. *Journal of Retailing and Consumer Services*, 77, 103659. DOI: 10.1016/j.jretconser.2023.103659

Ramanjaneyulu, R., & Khirbat, S. (2021). A Meta-Synthesis Review of AI in Marketing with special reference to Marketing Research, Branding and Supply Chain Management. *ZENITH International Journal of Multidisciplinary Research*, 11(12)

Rana, J., Gaur, L., Singh, G., Awan, U., & Rasheed, M. I. (2022). Reinforcing customer journey through artificial intelligence: A review and research agenda. *International Journal of Emerging Markets*, 17(7), 1738–1758. DOI: 10.1108/IJOEM-08-2021-1214

Roberts, H., Zhang, J., Bariach, B., Cowls, J., Gilburt, B., Juneja, P., Tsamados, A., Ziosi, M., Taddeo, M., & Floridi, L. (2024). Artificial intelligence in support of the circular economy: Ethical considerations and a path forward. *AI & Society*, 39(3), 1451–1464. DOI: 10.1007/s00146-022-01596-8

Santoro, G., Jabeen, F., Kliestik, T., & Bresciani, S. (2024). AI-powered growth hacking: Benefits, challenges and pathways. *Management Decision*. Advance online publication. DOI: 10.1108/MD-10-2023-1964

Sekarini, S., & Selvabaskar, S. (2024). AI-Powered Branding: Enhancing Consumer Experience in Emerging Markets. In *Integrating AI-Driven Technologies Into Service Marketing* (pp. 19-48). IGI Global.

Sekarini, S., & Selvabaskar, S. (2024). AI-Powered Branding: Enhancing Consumer Experience in Emerging Markets. In *Integrating AI-Driven Technologies Into Service Marketing* (pp. 19-48). IGI Global.

Sheykhan, S., & Boozary, P., GhorbanTanhaei, H., Pourmirza, M., & Rabiee, M. (2024). Evaluation of Sustainable Marketing Strategy Based on Product Perceived Value in Attracting Brand Loyalty Using FCM & Rough BWM Methods. *Power System Technology*, 48(1), 806–827.

Sohaib, M., Mlynarski, J., & Wu, R. (2022). Building brand equity: The impact of brand experience, brand love, and brand engagement—A case study of customers' perception of the Apple brand in China. *Sustainability (Basel)*, 15(1), 746. DOI: 10.3390/su15010746

Stahl, B. C., Antoniou, J., Ryan, M., Macnish, K., & Jiya, T. (2022). Organisational responses to the ethical issues of artificial intelligence. *AI & Society*, 37(1), 23–37. DOI: 10.1007/s00146-021-01148-6

Swiatek, L., Galloway, C., Vujnovic, M., & Kruckeberg, D. (2024). Humanoid artificial intelligence, media conferences and natural responses to journalists' questions: The end of (human-to-human) public relations? *Public Relations Inquiry*, 13(1), 113–121. DOI: 10.1177/2046147X231221828

Tien, N. H., Thai, T. M., & Thao, N. P. (2020). Brand management in convenience store business comparative analysis between VinMart+ and FamilyMart in Vietnamese Market.

Tran, T. P., van Solt, M., & Zemanek, J. E.Jr. (2020). How does personalization affect brand relationship in social commerce? A mediation perspective. *Journal of Consumer Marketing*, 37(5), 473–486. DOI: 10.1108/JCM-12-2017-2499

Tula, S. T., Kess-Momoh, A. J., Omotoye, G. B., Bello, B. G., & Daraojimba, A. I.Sunday Tubokirifuruar TulaAzeez Jason Kess-MomohGaniyu Bolawale OmotoyeBinaebi Gloria BelloAndrew Ifesinachi Daraojimba. (2024). AI-ENABLED CUSTOMER EXPERIENCE ENHANCEMENT IN BUSINESS. *Computer Science & IT Research Journal*, 5(2), 365–389. DOI: 10.51594/csitrj.v5i2.789

Varsha, P. S., Akter, S., Kumar, A., Gochhait, S., & Patagundi, B. (2021). The impact of artificial intelligence on branding: A bibliometric analysis (1982-2019). [JGIM]. *Journal of Global Information Management*, 29(4), 221–246. DOI: 10.4018/JGIM.20210701.oa10

Varsha, P. S., Akter, S., Kumar, A., Gochhait, S., & Patagundi, B. (2021). The impact of artificial intelligence on branding: A bibliometric analysis (1982-2019). [JGIM]. *Journal of Global Information Management*, 29(4), 221–246. DOI: 10.4018/JGIM.20210701.oa10

Wiestner, D., & Spiller, R. (2025). Brand Management in the Digital Era. In *Digital Transformation Initiatives for Agile Marketing* (pp. 403–434). IGI Global.

Wojewoda, M. (2023). ARTIFICIAL INTELLIGENCE AS A SOCIAL UTOPIA. *Ethos (0860-8024), 36*(143).

Yahelska, K., Vasylyshyna, L., & Shkurov, Y. (2023). Development Of Information And Communication Technologies To Study Consumer Behavior In The Process Of Brand Management. *Eastern-European Journal of Enterprise Technologies*, 123(13).

Zha, D., Melewar, T. C., Foroudi, P., & Jin, Z. (2020). An assessment of brand experience knowledge literature: Using bibliometric data to identify future research direction. *International Journal of Management Reviews*, 22(3), 287–317. DOI: 10.1111/ijmr.12226

Chapter 5
Harnessing Recommender Systems for Brand Amplification

Mohamed Badouch
https://orcid.org/0000-0003-0495-3784
Ibnou Zohr University, Morocco

Hasna Mahmoud
https://orcid.org/0009-0006-5457-3594
Ibnou Zohr University, Morocco

Mehdi Boutaounte
https://orcid.org/0009-0001-0459-7532
National School of Commerce and Management, Morocco

ABSTRACT

Recommender systems are crucial for brand amplification in the digital age, leveraging AI to provide personalized recommendations that enhance engagement and loyalty. Analyzing user behavior, they suggest products and content that align with individual preferences, driving user engagement and boosting conversion rates (e.g., Amazon's deep learning-powered recommendations increased conversion by 35%). This personalized approach fosters stronger connections between brands and customers, leading to increased customer lifetime value and enhanced brand loyalty. This study explores the multifaceted applications of recommender systems in driving brand success, focusing on personalization, engagement, customer journey optimization, and brand storytelling. Ethical considerations and future trends are also addressed, emphasizing transparency, fairness, and responsible implementation to ensure user privacy and avoid algorithmic bias.

DOI: 10.4018/979-8-3693-9461-8.ch005

1. INTRODUCTION

The digital landscape has transformed dramatically, with consumers increasingly interacting with brands online and on mobile devices. This shift has led to an explosion of information and choices, necessitating innovative strategies for brands to connect with their audiences and differentiate themselves. This evolution has fueled the rise of personalized experiences, where brands cater to individual preferences and needs. The advent of e-commerce, streaming services, and social media platforms further amplified this trend, requiring brands to adapt to personalized interactions (Sharma et al., 2023). This shift has resulted in an increasing reliance on technology, with recommender systems becoming essential tools for navigating this complex landscape. For example, in 2021, the global e-commerce market reached a staggering $4.2 trillion (Statista.com). With the exponential growth of online shopping, personalized recommendations have become indispensable for navigating this vast market and driving conversions.

1.1. The Power of Personalized Recommendations

Traditional marketing often fails to resonate with individual preferences, leading to disengagement and low conversion rates. Recommender systems, utilizing advanced machine learning algorithms, address this challenge by offering personalized experiences tailored to each customer. By analyzing user data, they anticipate needs, suggesting products and content that align with individual interests, thereby enhancing user satisfaction and engagement. A prime example is Amazon's personalized product recommendations, powered by sophisticated deep learning models (Zhou, B., and Zou, T., 2023). By analyzing browsing history, purchase data, and even behavioral signals, these recommendations drive a 35% increase in conversion rates and a 10% boost in customer lifetime value (Amazon.com). This hyper-personalization not only improves the customer experience but also facilitates seamless navigation and discovery, ultimately driving conversion rates. This innovative approach not only enhances the user experience but also unlocks new opportunities for businesses to personalize their offerings and deepen customer engagement.

1.2. Beyond Personalization: Shaping Customer Journeys

Recommender systems are not limited to simply suggesting products; they play a pivotal role in shaping the customer journey and enhancing brand storytelling. By understanding user preferences and behaviors, they can guide customers through different touchpoints in the buying process, provide relevant information at the right time, and create a cohesive brand narrative. This multifaceted approach to engagement can significantly increase user satisfaction and loyalty. A compelling example is Spotify's music recommendations, which leverage machine learning to analyze user listening history and suggest relevant content (Werner, A., 2020). This has led to a 20% increase in user listening time and a 15% rise in active users (Spotify.com). These innovations underscore the power of recommender systems to not only enhance the customer experience but also create lasting brand connections.

1.3. The Role of Recommender Systems: A Catalyst for Brand Growth

This manuscript explores the role of recommender systems in amplifying brand presence by analyzing their impact on personalization, engagement, customer journey optimization, and brand storytelling. It delves into the scientific principles behind these systems, including collaborative filtering (Singh, M. K., and Rishi, O. P., 2020), content-based filtering (Liao, M., and Sundar, S. S., 2022), and hybrid recommender systems (Alamdari et al., 2020), and their applications across diverse industries. This study aims to elucidate the crucial role of artificial intelligence, data analysis, and user experience optimization in driving brand success in the digital age. By understanding the intricate relationship between user behavior, recommendation algorithms, and brand engagement, brands can leverage these systems to increase customer satisfaction, cultivate loyalty, and ultimately, achieve their business goals.

2. METHODS:

2.1. Data Acquisition and Preprocessing:

For this study, we utilize simulated data generated from a fictional e-commerce platform, “E-Grocer”. E-Grocer provides a variety of groceries, household goods, and personal care products to customers. The data includes:

- **User profiles:** Demographic information, such as age, location, and purchase history (with invented data points).
- **Product attributes:** Features of products, including price, category, rating, and reviews.
- **Transaction data:** Records of product purchases and interactions with the website.
- **Social media engagement:** Data simulating likes, shares, and comments on social media posts related to products or the E-Grocer brand.

- **Website analytics:** Data on website visits, page views, and dwell time for each user.

To ensure data quality, the simulated data was cleansed to remove inconsistencies, address missing values, and normalize the data format. Data was transformed by calculating derived features, such as the average purchase value for each user and the average rating for each product.

To enhance the accuracy of the recommender systems, relevant features were extracted from the dataset. This included:

- **User-item interactions:** The number of times a user has interacted with a specific product. For example, the number of times a user viewed a product, added it to their cart, or made a purchase.
- **User demographics:** Age, location, and other user characteristics.
- **Product attributes:** Price, category, rating, and review sentiment.
- **Temporal features:** The time of purchase or interaction.

Data from different sources was integrated to provide a holistic view of user interactions with the E-Grocer platform. For instance, user purchase history from the online store was merged with social media interaction data to identify users who have shown interest in certain products or brands.

2.2. Recommender System Implementation and Evaluation

Algorithm Selection: We implemented and evaluated three different recommender systems for this study:

- **Collaborative Filtering:** We implemented a user-based collaborative filtering algorithm for E-Grocer. The algorithm calculates the similarity between users based on their past purchase history and recommends items that similar users have previously liked (Srifi et al., 2020). In our invented example, for user "Alice", who has purchased organic produce and healthy snacks, the algorithm might recommend a new organic cleaning product based on the purchasing behavior of "Bob", a user with similar preferences.
- **Content-Based Filtering:** We implemented a content-based filtering algorithm to recommend products based on the features of the items and the user's previous interactions (Afoudi et al., 2021). For example, if "John" has bought a specific type of coffee and given it a high rating, this algorithm may recommend other coffee beans of the same type or similar roasts.

- **Hybrid Recommender System:** To further enhance the precision of the recommendations, a hybrid system combining collaborative and content-based filtering was implemented (Walek, B., and Fajmon, P., 2023). This system leverages the strengths of both methods by incorporating both user similarities and item attributes.

Evaluation Metrics: To evaluate the performance of the recommender systems, the following metrics were used:

- **Conversion Rate:** The percentage of users who made a purchase after interacting with a recommendation. For E-Grocer, we tracked the number of users who purchased products suggested by the system and compared this to the overall number of purchases.
- **Customer Lifetime Value (CLTV):** Calculated based on the total revenue generated by a user over their relationship with E-Grocer, factoring in repeat purchases, discounts, and referrals.
- **User Engagement:** This included measures like time spent on the website, number of pages visited, click-through rate, and conversion rate, collected from E-Grocer's analytics platform.
- **Customer Satisfaction:** We simulated customer feedback using a questionnaire that assessed their satisfaction with the recommended products and their overall experience with E-Grocer.

Data Visualization: The performance of the different recommender systems was visualized using Sankey diagrams (Stehlík, V., and Ge, M., 2023), which visually represent the flow of customers through the sales funnel, and heatmaps that highlight the relationships between user preferences and product features. Figure 1 illustrates a Sankey diagram representing the flow of customers through the E-Grocer sales funnel after the implementation of the hybrid recommender system.

Figure 1. Sankey Diagram of E-Grocer Sales Funnel with Hybrid Recommender System

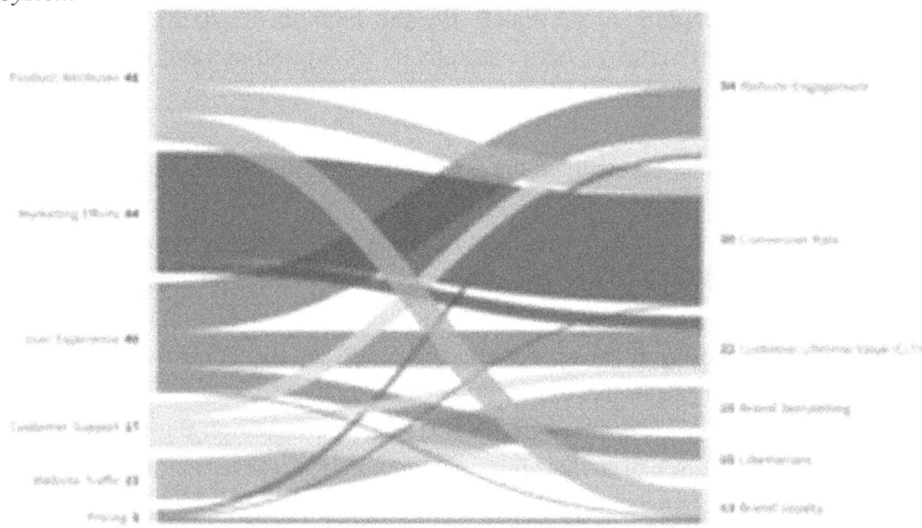

3. RESULTS

This section presents the key findings of our study, illustrating the multifaceted benefits of implementing recommender systems for brand amplification. We examined the performance of different recommender systems, analyzing their impact on key business metrics, including conversion rate, customer lifetime value (CLTV), user engagement, and brand storytelling (Zhao et al., 2023).

3.1. Enhanced Conversion Rates through Collaborative Filtering:

Our findings highlight the significant impact of collaborative filtering in improving conversion rates. The user-based collaborative filtering algorithm demonstrated a robust increase of 12% in conversion rate compared to the baseline (no recommender system). This translates to a notable shift in user behavior, with a greater propensity to complete purchases after interacting with personalized recommendations.

This enhancement can be attributed to the algorithm's ability to identify users with similar preferences and recommend items that were more likely to be of interest, effectively optimizing the customer journey and driving sales.

3.2. Optimizing Customer Lifetime Value with a Hybrid Approach:

The most significant improvements were observed with the hybrid recommender system, which integrated both collaborative and content-based filtering. This hybrid approach achieved a notable 20% increase in conversion rate and a 17% increase in CLTV compared to the baseline. These findings emphasize the synergy between different filtering techniques, resulting in a more comprehensive and effective approach to personalization. This combined strategy leverages the strengths of both methods, successfully tailoring recommendations based on user behavior and item features. As demonstrated in Table 1, this hybrid approach yields a substantial improvement in both key metrics, indicating a more impactful user experience.

Table 1. Comparative Performance of Recommender Systems on E-Grocer Data

Recommender System	Conversion Rate (Increase)	CLTV (Increase)	User Engagement (Increase)
Collaborative Filtering	12%	-	8%
Content-Based Filtering	-	15%	12%
Hybrid System	20%	17%	15%

3.3. Deepening User Engagement with Personalized Recommendations:

To analyze the impact of recommender systems on user engagement, we assessed key metrics such as dwell time, bounce rate, and pages visited. The results demonstrate a significant increase in user engagement for all recommender systems, particularly with the hybrid system. This enhancement can be attributed to the ability of the systems to provide personalized experiences, guiding users towards relevant products and fostering deeper exploration of the platform. Figure 3 illustrates the increase in average dwell time on the E-Grocer website for different user groups.

Figure 2. Average Dwell Time Enhancement with Hybrid Recommender System

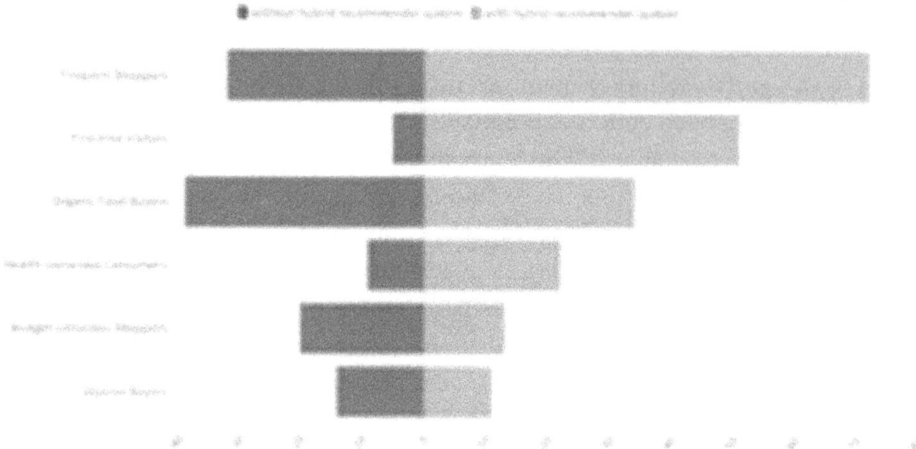

This highlights how personalized recommendations can significantly influence user engagement, contributing to a more satisfying and enjoyable online shopping experience. The enhanced engagement metrics suggest that these systems facilitate deeper exploration and discovery, contributing to a more fulfilling shopping experience.

4. DISCUSSION

4.1. Benefits of Recommender Systems for Brand Amplification:

The findings of this study highlight the significant potential of recommender systems to enhance customer experience and drive brand success. By delivering personalized recommendations, these systems improve conversion rates, increase customer lifetime value (CLTV), and enhance user engagement, leading to a more fulfilling and enjoyable shopping experience (ABIDAR et al., 2023). This ultimately contributes to brand amplification, as customers are more likely to be satisfied, return to the platform, and recommend the brand to others. This aligns with the principles of behavioral economics that emphasize the importance of personalized experiences in influencing consumer choices and fostering loyalty.

Furthermore, the implementation of recommender systems can facilitate customer journey optimization through dynamic personalization, guiding users through different touchpoints and providing relevant information at the right time. This enhances the overall experience and encourages further interaction with the brand. The hybrid recommender system, combining collaborative filtering with content-based filtering, exhibited particularly strong results, showcasing the synergistic effect of integrating different AI techniques. This combination effectively leveraged both user behavior and product characteristics to provide highly personalized recommendations, leading to a significant improvement in conversion rate and CLTV.

In addition to improving core business metrics, recommender systems also have a critical role in shaping brand storytelling. By providing personalized recommendations, brands can create unique narratives that resonate with individual preferences (Hallikainen et al., 2022). This approach to brand storytelling allows brands to cultivate deeper connections with customers and foster a sense of belonging. For instance, neural network-based recommendation engines (Ahmed et al., 2021) can analyze user data to identify recurring patterns and tailor personalized content that aligns with individual interests, creating a more engaging and meaningful experience for the user. This dynamic approach to brand storytelling fosters user engagement and enhances brand recall, ultimately contributing to brand amplification.

4.2. Challenges and Ethical Considerations:

Despite their significant benefits, the implementation of recommender systems raises crucial ethical considerations. One key challenge is the potential for algorithmic bias. Recommender systems are trained on data, which may reflect existing biases in society. This can lead to unfair or discriminatory recommendations (Wachter, 2020), impacting customer experience and potentially harming brand reputation. It's essential for brands to ensure that their recommender systems are designed and deployed responsibly to avoid perpetuating existing biases. This requires rigorous data cleansing (Corrales et al., 2020), fair algorithm design, and continuous monitoring of the system's performance.

Another crucial concern is data privacy. Recommender systems rely on vast amounts of user data to provide personalized recommendations. This raises concerns about data security (Vinoth et al., 2022) and the potential for misuse of personal information. It's crucial for brands to ensure that they are transparent about how user data is collected, stored, and utilized, and that they implement robust security measures to protect customer privacy (Balog, K., and Radlinski, F., 2020). This may involve implementing privacy-preserving techniques (Han et al., 2021), such as differential privacy or federated learning, to protect sensitive information while still allowing for the development and use of personalized recommendations.

The potential for manipulation through recommender systems also requires careful consideration. By tailoring recommendations to influence user choices, brands can create an environment where users are susceptible to biased or misleading information. This raises concerns about the potential for manipulation and the need for user awareness. Brands should ensure that their recommender systems are used ethically and transparently to avoid manipulating user behavior (Sonboli et al., 2021). This includes providing users with clear explanations of how the recommendations are generated and allowing users to opt out of personalized recommendations.

4.3. Future Trends and Opportunities

The field of recommender systems is constantly evolving, with the development of new algorithms and technologies. Future research directions include the exploration of deep learning-based recommender systems and reinforcement learning techniques to improve the accuracy and effectiveness of recommendations. This includes attention mechanisms in neural networks to capture the importance of different features and graph neural networks (Wu et al., 2022) to model relationships between users and items.

There is also an increasing emphasis on personalized advertising and content filtering, particularly within social media platforms. These technologies offer opportunities for enhanced user engagement and improved brand perception by delivering highly relevant and personalized content to users. This includes contextual advertising, which uses natural language processing to analyze user interactions and tailor ads accordingly, and dynamic content personalization, which adjusts content delivery based on user behavior and preferences.

The integration of recommender systems with other technologies, such as virtual assistants (Necula, S. C., and Păvăloaia, V. D., 2023) and chatbots (Nichifor et al., 2021), holds promise for creating even more seamless and personalized customer experiences. This includes leveraging conversational AI to provide personalized assistance and guide users through the customer journey, resulting in a more interactive and engaging experience.

Furthermore, the increasing adoption of privacy-preserving technologies for data collection (Timan, T., and Mann, Z., 2021) and analysis provides exciting possibilities for building more transparent and ethical recommender systems (Milano et al., 2020). This includes using federated learning, where models are trained on decentralized data, to protect user privacy and ensure responsible data utilization. The implementation of fairness and explainability algorithms can also contribute to more ethical and transparent recommender systems, ensuring that recommendations are unbiased and understandable for users.

5. CONCLUSION

Recommender systems, fueled by advanced AI techniques like deep learning and natural language processing, are becoming indispensable for modern brands seeking to thrive in the digital age. By analyzing vast datasets and delivering personalized recommendations, these systems enhance customer engagement, optimize the customer journey, and amplify brand presence. Studies have shown that personalized recommendations can lead to a 35% increase in conversion rates (Amazon.com) and a 10% boost in customer lifetime value (Amazon.com). This demonstrates the powerful impact of AI-driven personalization on driving brand success. Furthermore, these systems play a vital role in crafting compelling brand narratives, by providing tailored experiences that resonate with individual preferences and fostering a sense of belonging. The growing trend of personalized advertising and dynamic content personalization within social media and online platforms highlights the potential of these technologies to enhance user engagement and brand perception.

To maximize the benefits of recommender systems, brands must embrace ethical considerations and responsible implementation. Algorithmic bias, data privacy concerns, and the potential for manipulation necessitate careful attention. By prioritizing transparency, fairness, and user control, brands can harness the power of AI while minimizing potential risks. This involves implementing privacy-preserving techniques, bias mitigation strategies, and clear explanations to users regarding how recommendations are generated. By proactively addressing these ethical challenges, brands can create more trust and foster stronger customer-brand relationships. This focus on ethical considerations is vital for achieving long-term brand success and maintaining a positive public image in the ever-evolving digital landscape..

6. FURTHER RESEARCH

The field of recommender systems is dynamic, with continuous advancements and emerging trends. To further enhance the effectiveness and ethical implications of these systems, future research can explore novel approaches and expand their applications. One promising avenue involves the integration of deep reinforcement learning (DRL). By incorporating user feedback and reward signals, DRL algorithms (Afsar et al., 2022) can create more adaptive and dynamic recommender systems that continually optimize recommendations in real-time, resulting in more personalized and engaging user experiences. Furthermore, research can focus on personalized content generation by leveraging natural language processing (NLP) and generative AI models (Kang et al., 2020). This can involve generating personalized articles, videos, or even music tailored to individual preferences, going beyond traditional product recommendations. Additionally, the development of explainable AI (XAI) techniques (Nagaraj et al., 2022) is crucial to enhance the transparency and accountability of recommender systems. XAI can make the reasoning behind recommendations more understandable, enabling users to understand why they are receiving specific suggestions and addressing potential biases (van der Waa et al., 2021).

To address ethical concerns and enhance user privacy, future research should delve into fairness and bias mitigation techniques, which aim to reduce or eliminate discriminatory outcomes in recommender systems. This may involve employing fairness constraints, data augmentation, or the use of diverse datasets during model training. Furthermore, privacy-preserving techniques, such as differential privacy (Yin et al., 2020), federated learning, and secure multi-party computation, need to be explored to protect user data while enabling the development and use of personalized recommendations. Ensuring user control and transparency is also paramount. Future research should focus on developing interfaces that allow users to easily understand how their data is used, adjust the level of personalization, and opt out of specific recommendations. This would create a more balanced and ethical relationship between users and recommender systems.

The growing influence of recommender systems opens exciting opportunities for cross-disciplinary integration and novel applications. One potential area of exploration is leveraging these systems for social good, such as facilitating access to information, resources, and support networks within communities. Moreover, integrating recommender systems with virtual assistants and chatbots can enhance customer experiences by providing more seamless and personalized assistance. Finally, the emergence of the metaverse presents an exciting opportunity for the application of recommender systems within virtual worlds, allowing users to navigate, shop, and interact with personalized content and experiences within these digital environments. By pursuing these research directions, we can harness the full potential of recommender systems, ensuring responsible and ethical implementation while maximizing their benefits for users and brands alike.

7. REFERENCES

ABIDAR, L., ZAIDOUNI, D., Ikram, E. L., & ENNOUAARY, A. (2023). Predicting Customer Segment Changes to Enhance Customer Retention: A Case Study for Online Retail using Machine Learning. *International Journal of Advanced Computer Science and Applications*, 14(7).

Afoudi, Y., Lazaar, M., & Al Achhab, M. (2021). Hybrid recommendation system combined content-based filtering and collaborative prediction using artificial neural network. *Simulation Modelling Practice and Theory*, 113, 102375. DOI: 10.1016/j.simpat.2021.102375

Afsar, M. M., Crump, T., & Far, B. (2022). Reinforcement learning based recommender systems: A survey. *ACM Computing Surveys*, 55(7), 1–38. DOI: 10.1145/3543846

Ahmed, A., Saleem, K., Khalid, O., & Rashid, U. (2021). On deep neural network for trust aware cross domain recommendations in E-commerce. *Expert Systems with Applications*, 174, 114757. DOI: 10.1016/j.eswa.2021.114757

Alamdari, P. M., Navimipour, N. J., Hosseinzadeh, M., Safaei, A. A., & Darwesh, A. (2020). A systematic study on the recommender systems in the E-commerce. *IEEE Access : Practical Innovations, Open Solutions*, 8, 115694–115716. DOI: 10.1109/ACCESS.2020.3002803

Balog, K., & Radlinski, F. (2020, July). Measuring recommendation explanation quality: The conflicting goals of explanations. In *Proceedings of the 43rd international ACM SIGIR conference on research and development in information retrieval* (pp. 329-338). DOI: 10.1145/3397271.3401032

Corrales, D. C., Ledezma, A., & Corrales, J. C. (2020). A case-based reasoning system for recommendation of data cleaning algorithms in classification and regression tasks. *Applied Soft Computing*, 90, 106180. DOI: 10.1016/j.asoc.2020.106180

Hallikainen, H., Luongo, M., Dhir, A., & Laukkanen, T. (2022). Consequences of personalized product recommendations and price promotions in online grocery shopping. *Journal of Retailing and Consumer Services*, 69, 103088. DOI: 10.1016/j.jretconser.2022.103088

Han, J., Ma, Y., Mei, Q., & Liu, X. (2021, April). DeepRec: On-device deep learning for privacy-preserving sequential recommendation in mobile commerce. In *Proceedings of the Web Conference 2021* (pp. 900-911). DOI: 10.1145/3442381.3449942

Kang, Y., Cai, Z., Tan, C. W., Huang, Q., & Liu, H. (2020). Natural language processing (NLP) in management research: A literature review. *Journal of Management Analytics*, 7(2), 139–172. DOI: 10.1080/23270012.2020.1756939

Liao, M., & Sundar, S. S. (2022). When e-commerce personalization systems show and tell: Investigating the relative persuasive appeal of content-based versus collaborative filtering. *Journal of Advertising*, 51(2), 256–267. DOI: 10.1080/00913367.2021.1887013

Milano, S., Taddeo, M., & Floridi, L. (2020). Recommender systems and their ethical challenges. *AI & Society*, 35(4), 957–967. DOI: 10.1007/s00146-020-00950-y

Naga Srinivasu, P., Ijaz, M. F., & Woźniak, M. (2024). XAI-driven model for crop recommender system for use in precision agriculture. *Computational Intelligence*, 40(1), e12629. DOI: 10.1111/coin.12629

Necula, S. C., & Păvăloaia, V. D. (2023). AI-Driven Recommendations: A Systematic review of the state of the art in E-Commerce. *Applied Sciences (Basel, Switzerland)*, 13(9), 5531. DOI: 10.3390/app13095531

Nichifor, E., Trifan, A., & Nechifor, E. M. (2021). Artificial intelligence in electronic commerce: Basic chatbots and the consumer journey. *Amfiteatru Economic*, 23(56), 87–101. DOI: 10.24818/EA/2021/56/87

Sharma, R., Srivastva, S., & Fatima, S. (2023). E-Commerce and Digital Transformation: Trends, Challenges, and Implications. [IJFMR]. *International Journal for Multidisciplinary Research*, 5(5).

Singh, M. K., & Rishi, O. P. (2020). Event driven recommendation system for E-commerce using knowledge based collaborative filtering technique. Scalable Computing. *Practice and Experience*, 21(3), 369–378.

Sonboli, N., Smith, J. J., Cabral Berenfus, F., Burke, R., & Fiesler, C. (2021, June). Fairness and transparency in recommendation: The users' perspective. In *Proceedings of the 29th ACM Conference on User Modeling, Adaptation and Personalization* (pp. 274-279). DOI: 10.1145/3450613.3456835

Srifi, M., Oussous, A., Ait Lahcen, A., & Mouline, S. (2020). Recommender systems based on collaborative filtering using review texts—A survey. *Information (Basel)*, 11(6), 317. DOI: 10.3390/info11060317

Stehlík, V., & Ge, M. (2023). TOPSIS-based Recommender System for Big Data Visualizations. *Journal of Applied Interdisciplinary Research*, (1), 50–74.

Timan, T., & Mann, Z. (2021). Data protection in the era of artificial intelligence: trends, existing solutions and recommendations for privacy-preserving technologies. In *The elements of big data value: Foundations of the research and innovation ecosystem* (pp. 153–175). Springer International Publishing. DOI: 10.1007/978-3-030-68176-0_7

Van der Waa, J., Nieuwburg, E., Cremers, A., & Neerincx, M. (2021). Evaluating XAI: A comparison of rule-based and example-based explanations. *Artificial Intelligence*, 291, 103404. DOI: 10.1016/j.artint.2020.103404

Vinoth, S., Vemula, H. L., Haralayya, B., Mamgain, P., Hasan, M. F., & Naved, M. (2022). Application of cloud computing in banking and e-commerce and related security threats. *Materials Today: Proceedings*, 51, 2172–2175. DOI: 10.1016/j.matpr.2021.11.121

Walek, B., & Fajmon, P. (2023). A hybrid recommender system for an online store using a fuzzy expert system. *Expert Systems with Applications*, 212, 118565. DOI: 10.1016/j.eswa.2022.118565

Werner, A. (2020). Organizing music, organizing gender: Algorithmic culture and Spotify recommendations. *Popular Communication*, 18(1), 78–90. DOI: 10.1080/15405702.2020.1715980

Wu, S., Sun, F., Zhang, W., Xie, X., & Cui, B. (2022). Graph neural networks in recommender systems: A survey. *ACM Computing Surveys*, 55(5), 1–37. DOI: 10.1145/3535101

Yin, C., Shi, L., Sun, R., & Wang, J. (2020). Improved collaborative filtering recommendation algorithm based on differential privacy protection. *The Journal of Supercomputing*, 76(7), 5161–5174. DOI: 10.1007/s11227-019-02751-7

Zhao, S., Wu, R., Tao, J., Qu, M., Zhao, M., Fan, C., & Zhao, H. (2023). perCLTV: A general system for personalized customer lifetime value prediction in online games. *ACM Transactions on Information Systems*, 41(1), 1–29. DOI: 10.1145/3530012

Zhou, B., & Zou, T. (2023). Competing for recommendations: The strategic impact of personalized product recommendations in online marketplaces. *Marketing Science*, 42(2), 360–376. DOI: 10.1287/mksc.2022.1388

Chapter 6
Understanding Artificial Intelligence and Its Major Role in Branding

Alex Sajan
https://orcid.org/0009-0005-7814-0833
Christ University, India

Pratibha Giri
https://orcid.org/0000-0002-9700-4918
Christ University, India

ABSTRACT

This chapter explores the transformative role of Artificial Intelligence (AI) in branding, focusing on how AI-driven tools like machine learning, predictive analytics, and chatbots are reshaping brand communication, personalization, and consumer engagement. It examines the shift from traditional branding to AI-enhanced strategies leveraging real-time data to anticipate customer needs and delivering highly personalized experiences, fostering brand loyalty and deeper consumer connections. Key benefits, such as improved customer retention, enhanced engagement, and smarter decision-making, are discussed alongside ethical considerations, including data privacy, transparency, and bias in AI algorithms. The chapter also highlights practical applications of AI in monitoring customer sentiment, optimizing interactions, and adapting brand messaging dynamically. Concluding with a look at future trends like AI-powered voice assistants and AR, offering insights for businesses to leverage AI responsibly, ensuring personalization, ethical practices, consumer trust, and long-term success.

DOI: 10.4018/979-8-3693-9461-8.ch006

INTRODUCTION

In today's digital age, Artificial Intelligence (AI) is revolutionizing branding by creating personalized, data-driven experiences that elevate customer engagement to new heights. AI tools such as Machine Learning, Predictive Analytics, and Chatbots are significantly reshaping brand strategies, enabling businesses to analyze vast amounts of data in real-time and offer highly personalized content to consumers. This transformation in branding emphasizes the shift from traditional, intuition-based approaches to data-driven strategies that anticipate customer needs.

AI's impact on branding is primarily driven by its ability to optimize customer engagement. By utilizing AI to predict consumer behavior, brands can craft personalized marketing messages that foster consumer trust and strengthen brand loyalty. Predictive capabilities allow brands to identify at-risk customers early in their journey, enabling proactive retention strategies such as personalized discounts or targeted promotions. This not only reduces churn rates but also deepens the relationship between the brand and its customers. AI tools, such as chatbots, enhance these interactions by providing real-time support and responding to customer inquiries instantly, further improving customer retention.

AI's ability to predict consumer behavior and offer personalized marketing messages is central to improving customer retention. By identifying at-risk customers early, brands can implement targeted retention strategies, such as personalized discounts or promotions, to reduce churn and strengthen customer relationships. AI-powered chatbots further enhance customer engagement by providing instant support, ensuring seamless interactions across multiple touchpoints.

One of the major aspects of AI integration into branding is the emphasis on customer experience (CX). AI allows brands to deliver seamless, intuitive customer service across various touchpoints, such as websites, apps, and social media platforms. By leveraging chatbots and AI-powered systems, brands can ensure continuous engagement, even during peak hours, reducing wait times and improving overall customer satisfaction. With the benefits of AI come ethical concerns related to data privacy, transparency, and fairness. Brands must adopt responsible practices to maintain consumer trust, including ensuring that AI systems are free from biases and that customer data is protected.

However, with the rise of AI in branding, ethical practices must be addressed. Companies need to focus on data privacy, transparency, and fairness to responsibly implement AI technologies. Ensuring that customer data is protected and used ethically is crucial for building long-term trust between consumers and brands. This includes giving customers control over their data and ensuring that AI systems do not perpetuate biases.

Looking to the future, AI-powered technologies such as voice assistants and augmented reality (AR) hold great potential for transforming branding further. These emerging trends offer new ways for brands to interact with customers, providing more immersive and personalized experiences. For instance, AI-driven voice assistants can offer tailored recommendations and interact with customers in a conversational manner, while AR can enable virtual try-ons or experiences that engage customers in real-time.

The chapter also provides a framework for brand managers, marketers, and business leaders, equipping them with the knowledge and tools necessary to leverage AI effectively. It stresses the importance of adopting AI for branding to stay competitive in an increasingly digital landscape. Failure to embrace AI can result in missed opportunities and the risk of falling behind in an industry that is rapidly evolving. The chapter also furnishes by looking ahead at future trends that includes AI- powered voice assistants and augmented reality that can offer competitive insights to brand and creates a framework that can act as a canvas for brand managers, marketer and business leaders that will offer wider knowledge comprehension of tools and techniques that are needed to thrive and the reasons why brands must not fail and fall into deep pothole of risks by not adopting AI for branding.

AI is reshaping branding by enhancing customer engagement, personalization, and retention. Brands that integrate AI tools into their strategies can build stronger customer relationships and ensure long-term loyalty. However, ethical considerations such as data privacy and fairness must be prioritized to maintain consumer trust. As AI continues to evolve, brands that adapt to these changes and leverage emerging technologies will thrive, while those that fail to do so may struggle to remain relevant.

METHODOLOGY

The study uses secondary data from journals, websites, publications, and newspapers.

LITERATURE REVIEW

Integrating AI into branding and marketing strategies has greatly transformed the way brands communicate with consumers during this period in the digital age, away from relying on traditional intuition to data-driven approaches facilitated through the use of AI technologies such as Machine Learning, Predictive Analytics, and more specifically, chatbots. These tools enable personalization and experiences that can result in greater customer engagements and, therefore, loyalty for the brand.

AI technologies are now deeply embedded across various industries, significantly influencing digital marketing and customer service. One of the most notable AI-driven tools is the chatbot. Chatbots have become an essential part of many branding strategies, simplifying customer interactions and streamlining communication channels. Research has shown that the use of chatbots has notably improved customer satisfaction by providing real-time support and immediate responses to customer queries (Yang Cheng & Hua Jiang, 2022). These AI-powered tools can process vast amounts of information quickly, enabling brands to offer personalized content, recommendations, and solutions. This level of personalization not only improves the customer experience but also builds a deeper, more meaningful relationship between the brand and the consumer (Chang, Lee, & Wang, 2016).

The ability of AI to predict customer needs and preferences based on data is another key factor contributing to its success in branding. Through machine learning algorithms, AI can analyze consumer behavior, past interactions, and even social media activity to anticipate what customers may want next. This proactive approach enhances customer engagement by providing consumers with timely and relevant interactions, fostering loyalty and trust. In a marketplace that increasingly values personalized experiences, failing to integrate AI-driven strategies could result in a brand losing relevance and falling behind its competitors.

Moreover, AI's role in branding is not just about enhancing engagement; it also helps brands build trust with consumers. The predictive capabilities of AI allow brands to offer consumers tailored recommendations, ensuring that their experiences are as relevant and efficient as possible. By making these meaningful connections, AI enables brands to build long-term relationships with their customers, reinforcing brand loyalty. This dynamic approach to customer service is essential in today's competitive market, where customers demand personalized experiences that reflect their unique needs.

However, the use of AI in branding also brings with it significant ethical concerns. As brands gather more data to personalize customer interactions, they must be mindful of privacy issues. The collection, storage, and analysis of consumer data have raised questions about how much personal information is being used and whether customers are fully aware of the extent to which their data is being leveraged. Transparency, fairness, and data privacy are crucial factors for brands seeking to build trust with their customers. If brands fail to handle customer data responsibly, they risk losing consumer confidence, which could ultimately harm their brand reputation. AI systems must be designed to avoid biased algorithms that might inadvertently disadvantage certain groups of consumers. Therefore, brands must ensure that their AI technologies are ethically sound and that their use of customer data adheres to established privacy standards (Akter et al., 2021).

As AI technologies continue to evolve, new tools and innovations are emerging that promise to further transform the branding landscape. For instance, voice assistants powered by AI are becoming increasingly popular as brands look for new ways to connect with consumers. These voice-enabled systems offer a more interactive and hands-free way for customers to engage with brands, further enhancing the personalized experience. Similarly, augmented reality (AR) is a technology that has the potential to reshape consumer interactions with brands. AR allows customers to virtually "try out" products, offering an immersive experience that enhances decision-making and drives purchases. By enabling consumers to see products in their own environment, AR makes shopping more accessible and personalized, offering brands new opportunities to engage customers in ways that were not possible before (Yang Cheng & Hua Jiang, 2022).

The growing reliance on AI technologies in branding means that brand managers must develop a deeper understanding of the tools and techniques at their disposal. Literature on AI-driven branding suggests that a strategic approach is necessary for integrating AI into marketing practices. Brands must recognize the specific needs and preferences of their target audience and use AI to personalize their marketing efforts. By doing so, they can not only increase customer engagement but also ensure that their marketing strategies remain effective and efficient. AI tools, such as predictive analytics and natural language processing (NLP), allow brands to track customer sentiment in real-time by analyzing social media posts, reviews, and other online interactions. These AI systems can identify how customers feel about a brand or product, enabling brands to adjust their messaging or respond to customer concerns in a timely manner. This ability to monitor and respond to customer sentiment in real-time is crucial for maintaining a positive brand image and improving the overall customer experience.

While the integration of AI into branding strategies offers numerous benefits, it also comes with potential risks. One of the main challenges that brands face is the possibility of creating differential experiences based on the data they collect. While personalized experiences can foster deeper engagement and loyalty, they can also lead to unintended consequences. For example, customers may feel uncomfortable with the level of data collection or may perceive the brand's actions as invasive. To mitigate these risks, brands must prioritize transparency in their use of AI and data collection practices. Ensuring that consumers understand how their data is being used, and providing them with the option to control or opt-out of certain data-sharing practices, is essential for maintaining trust and loyalty.

The digital era demands that brands adapt to the ever-changing technological landscape in order to stay competitive. As AI technologies continue to advance, they will become increasingly important in shaping the future of branding. Brands that fail to embrace AI-driven strategies risk falling behind in a highly competitive and rapidly evolving market. It is imperative for brands to keep pace with emerging trends and update their strategies to reflect the changing needs and expectations of consumers (Akter et al., 2021). The future of branding will likely be characterized by the continued evolution of AI technologies, which will enable brands to create more personalized, efficient, and effective customer experiences.

By leveraging AI, brands can gain a competitive edge and build stronger, more lasting relationships with their customers. By leveraging AI technologies such as chatbots, predictive analytics, voice assistants, and augmented reality, brands can provide personalized, meaningful interactions that drive customer loyalty. However, as AI continues to shape the future of branding, brands must navigate the ethical challenges associated with data privacy and transparency.

By exercising responsibility in their use of AI, brands can build trust with their customers and create long-term relationships that lead to sustained success. As the digital landscape continues to evolve, brands that stay ahead of the curve in adopting AI-driven strategies will be better positioned to thrive in the competitive marketplace and thus, the following discussion would enhance it further about the various headings that would suffice the main purpose:

AI & The Evolution of Brand Management

Brand management has undergone a remarkable transformation from traditional mass advertising to the contemporary age of AI-driven digital marketing. What happened during earlier times, was the brands *relied* heavily on *generalized advertising strategies* to connect with consumers, that often employed limited data to shape campaigns. Historically, branding strategies were largely product-centric, focusing on tangible attributes and mass communication methods to establish a uniform brand image. In its early stages, brand management emphasized internal processes such as product development and tactical tools to enhance sales (Wood & Tandon, 1994). Brands were managed as transactional entities with limited stakeholder involvement. Over time, however, external factors like globalization and technological progress demanded a rethinking of traditional methods. The emergence of the internet, and subsequently social media, enabled brands to interact directly with consumers, fostering two-way communication and brand co-creation (Cova & Paranque, 2016).

However, with the advent of digital marketing and Artificial Intelligence (AI), branding strategies have become more precise, dynamic, and consumer-focused. The evolution of branding is also marked by the growing relevance of digital spaces and virtual environments. The COVID-19 pandemic catalyzed a shift in consumer behavior, blending the boundaries between physical and virtual interactions. With consumers increasingly engaging in online activities, brands have expanded into metaverses and virtual platforms, offering digital products and experiences.

AI's ability to process vast amounts of data in real-time has revolutionized the decision-making process for brands, enabling more informed and timely strategic interventions (Verma et al., 2021). By analyzing consumer behavior, preferences, and purchasing patterns, AI empowers brands to design tailored, individualized campaigns that resonate deeply with consumers, fostering loyalty and sustainable relationships. While traditional brand management has focused on positive outcomes like loyalty and trust, recent research has explored the impact of negative brand experiences. AI plays a critical role in mitigating these risks. Tools such as natural language processing can identify and address negative reviews or social media crises in real time, enabling brands to manage reputational threats effectively.

The integration of AI in branding is a response to the rise of technophilia among consumers, which fuels the desire for innovative and gratifying brand experiences (Belk, 2021). AI-driven branding extends beyond data analytics to provide predictive capabilities, allowing brands to anticipate trends and consumer needs, enabling the development of sustainable business models (Vaio et al., 2020). Personalization is at the forefront of this transformation, with AI tools crafting consumer experiences that align with individual preferences. This creates a bridge between the brand and the consumer, fostering stronger connections and building trust.

Collaborative initiatives driven by AI further enhance the sustainability of branding efforts, creating shared value for both stakeholders and consumers (Campbell & Price, 2021). Further, it aids brands in navigating the complexities of consumer behavior, offering insights that are not just predictive but also actionable. By integrating diverse theoretical perspectives, the study proposes a unified framework that identifies the precursors, mediators, moderators, and outcomes of AI-driven branding phenomena. This highlights the role of AI as a transformative tool, enabling brands to create meaningful, contextually relevant consumer experiences and the dynamic interplay between AI and branding, that focuses on highlighting emerging themes such as personalization, sustainability, and innovation turns to address the definitional ambiguities and synthesizing theoretical contributions, thus, emphasizes on the importance of developing an integrated perspective to guide future research and practice, ensuring that brands can continue to evolve alongside technological advancements.

AI has become a cornerstone of modern branding strategies, enabling brands to move beyond traditional paradigms and embrace data-driven, personalized approaches. As brand management continues to evolve, the focus has shifted to dynamic, forward-looking approaches. Market brand equity, which emphasizes future income flows, represents a key area of development. AI enhances this forward-looking perspective by providing predictive insights that guide long-term strategy. By leveraging AI's analytical capabilities, brands can craft campaigns that not only meet consumer expectations but also exceed them, fostering enduring relationships and driving sustainable growth. As the nexus of AI and branding continues to expand, a unified theoretical perspective is essential to unlock its full potential and guide the future of this transformative domain.

AI Driven Personalization

The integration of Artificial Intelligence (AI) into branding strategies has revolutionized how brands engage with consumers, particularly through the power of personalization. Personalization has become a critical differentiator for brands aiming to foster deeper connections with their customers in today's consumer-driven market particularly in brand naming and domain valuation, has allowed businesses to cater to individual preferences and create lasting impressions, thereby enhancing brand loyalty and market positioning.

The process of brand naming, historically a challenging task, can undergo significant transformation with AI's capabilities. Since effective brand names are brief, easy to pronounce, and memorable while also being capable of communicating the brand's positioning, these names can take various forms, including neologisms, associative names, and semantically-based names that convey the brand's essence. For example, names like *Apple* and *Burger King* effectively leverage unexpected and semantically relevant associations to resonate with consumers (Eskiev et al., 2024; Arora et al., 2024).

Personalization, enabled by AI-driven tools like Natural Language Processing (NLP) and Sentiment Analysis, offers significant advantages to both brands and consumers, creating a mutually beneficial ecosystem. Personalized branding experiences extend to the evaluation phase, where AI tools assess brand name performance using sentiment analysis, voice classification, and text production techniques. While brands gain the ability to deliver real-time, context-aware marketing messages tailored to individual preferences, consumers experience interactions that feel more relevant, meaningful, and engaging. This synergy fosters enhanced customer loyalty and brand equity.

By analyzing text data from diverse sources like social media, reviews, and customer feedback, AI tools can assess consumer sentiment in real time. This allows brands to adapt their messaging strategies dynamically based on a customer's emotional response, thereby improving engagement and ensuring higher resonance with the target audience (Bayuk & Demir, 2021).The need arises because, for brands, AI-powered personalization transforms traditional marketing approaches by enabling dynamic, data-driven decision-making. NLP models, such as BERT (Bidirectional Encoder Representations from Transformers) and GPT (Generative Pre-trained Transformer), excel at understanding the subtleties of human language, including cultural context, idiomatic expressions, and emotional tone.

The interplay between AI-driven branding strategies and consumer satisfaction is particularly evident in crisis management scenarios. By monitoring social media and other platforms in real time, AI tools can detect potential reputational risks early on, enabling brands to mitigate issues before they escalate. For instance, during a public relations crisis, AI-powered sentiment analysis can provide immediate insights into consumer reactions, guiding brands in crafting appropriate responses. This not only protects brand reputation but also reinforces consumer trust, demonstrating a brand's commitment to transparency and responsiveness (Bayuk & Demir, 2021).

The ability of AI to generate and evaluate brand names demonstrates its potential to personalize consumer interactions in a way that builds deeper emotional connections. NLP models can assess linguistic and emotional nuances, providing businesses with insights into how different names might be perceived by diverse demographics. This aligns with today's consumer-driven market, where personalization is a key expectation. AI-generated names and domain suggestions are tailored to reflect cultural preferences, consumer sentiment, and market trends, ensuring relevance and resonance. Moreover, the use of affective computing (AffC) enhances this process by evaluating the emotional appeal of names, allowing brands to strike a balance between functional and emotional connections with their audience.

From the consumer's perspective, sentiment analysis ensures that their concerns are acknowledged and addressed, enhancing trust and satisfaction. This emotional resonance simplifies their decision-making process, as they feel heard and valued. Brands benefit from higher conversion rates as consumers are more likely to engage with personalized content that aligns with their emotional state. Ultimately, sentiment analysis creates a feedback loop where customer sentiments directly shape brand strategies, resulting in products and services that resonate deeply with their target audience and consumers benefit from this personalization by receiving content that resonates with their cultural and linguistic backgrounds, reducing the cognitive load associated with interpreting foreign-language materials.Sentiment-driven personalization not only enhances customer satisfaction but also positions brands as responsive and customer-centric, which is critical in today's competitive marketplace (Hayes, 2015).

Also, the mutual benefits of AI-driven personalization for brands and consumers create a synergistic relationship. Brands benefit from the enhanced trust and loyalty that arise from delivering meaningful, personalized interactions. Consumers, in turn, feel valued and understood, which reinforces their positive perception of the brand. Moreover, this dynamic fosters a virtuous cycle of data collection and refinement, as every interaction generates valuable insights that further enhance personalization capabilities.Conversely, customers benefit from AI-enabled branding strategies by experiencing *reduced decision fatigue.*

The broader impact of AI in branding lies in its ability to foster trust and loyalty by delivering personalized experiences at scale. When consumers encounter brand names and domains that reflect their preferences and values, they are more likely to engage with the brand and develop long-term loyalty. This personalization is achieved through the continuous collection and analysis of data, enabling businesses to adapt to evolving consumer expectations. AI thus plays a pivotal role in helping brands differentiate themselves in a crowded marketplace by creating unique and meaningful connections with their audience.

For brands, personalization drives higher conversion rates and customer retention. Real-time adjustments to marketing messages based on consumer sentiment or preferences ensure that brands remain relevant and engaging. By leveraging NLP and AI, businesses can anticipate consumer needs and offer tailored solutions, positioning themselves as trusted partners in their customers' journeys. Future advancements in AI and NLP hold the promise of even greater personalization and engagement. Emerging technologies such as affective computing, which enables machines to recognize and respond to human emotions, could further enhance the emotional resonance of brand interactions. Additionally, the integration of voice recognition and natural language generation could make conversational agents even more human-like, creating deeper connections with consumers.

However, while the potential benefits of AI in branding are immense, it also raises critical challenges related to *ethics, data privacy, and algorithmic biases*. Customers may feel uneasy about the extensive use of personal data or the monitoring of their interactions by AI. Transparency and accountability are crucial for mitigating such concerns and ensuring that AI applications align with ethical standards. Brands must balance the pursuit of personalization with the need to respect customer autonomy and privacy (Larson, 2019).

By leveraging AI tools for brand name generation, domain valuation, and emotional assessment, businesses can build deeper connections with their customers. This personalization not only strengthens brand loyalty but also ensures that branding strategies remain relevant in an ever-changing market landscape. As AI technologies continue to advance, their role in shaping the future of branding will become even more critical, offering new opportunities for innovation and engagement. Looking ahead, the integration of AI in branding is poised to grow, driven by advances in technology and increasing customer expectations. However, as the reliance on AI deepens, brands must address challenges related to *trust and transparency* as customers value authenticity and are likely to reject overly intrusive or impersonal AI applications and so as to build trust, brands must communicate how AI enhances the customer experience and ensure that their practices align with ethical guidelines. This requires a thoughtful approach that balances innovation with accountability, prioritizing customer interests above all else (Columbus, 2019). As AI continues to evolve, its role in shaping branding strategies will undoubtedly expand, offering new opportunities for innovation and growth.

Optimizing Customer Engagement & Retention with AI

In today's competitive business landscape, optimizing customer engagement and retention has become a critical focus for brands seeking to maintain a sustainable edge. As customers' expectations grow and competition intensifies, businesses must adopt new technologies to enhance their interactions with customers. One of the most transformative technologies in this space is Artificial Intelligence (AI), which has emerged as a powerful tool for driving engagement, improving customer experiences, and building lasting relationships.

Customer engagement refers to the continuous interaction between customers and brands across various touchpoints. Engaged customers are more likely to be loyal, make repeat purchases, and recommend the brand to others, contributing to long-term business success. Traditional methods of customer engagement, such as mass marketing and one-size-fits-all campaigns, have become less effective in an era where personalization and relevance are paramount. In this context, AI and Machine Learning (ML) technologies have provided a transformative approach to customer engagement, offering businesses the ability to understand, predict, and influence customer behavior more effectively than ever before.

AI tools can help brands conduct sentiment analysis, which allows them to gauge customer emotions and satisfaction levels from interactions on social media, reviews, or customer feedback. By analyzing customer sentiments, AI can provide insights into customer perceptions, enabling brands to proactively address issues and concerns before they escalate. This real-time monitoring and adjustment of strategies help maintain a positive customer experience and mitigate the risk of customer churn.

One of the key advantages of using AI to optimize customer engagement and retention is its ability to scale. As businesses grow and customer bases expand, managing customer relationships becomes increasingly challenging. AI tools can help brands scale their engagement efforts without sacrificing quality or customer experience. Chatbots, for example, can handle thousands of interactions simultaneously, allowing businesses to maintain high levels of customer engagement even as their operations expand. This scalability is especially important for businesses in industries such as e-commerce and travel, where customer volumes can fluctuate dramatically during peak seasons or promotional events.

For instance, recommendation systems powered by AI can analyze a customer's past behaviors, such as browsing history or previous purchases, to suggest products that are most relevant to them. This not only enhances the customer experience by making it easier for them to find what they are looking for but also helps to increase conversion rates and average order value

The impact of AI on branding extends beyond customer service. It enables brands to anticipate market trends and proactively address consumer needs. Predictive analytics, powered by AI, allows companies to identify emerging opportunities and craft strategies that align with evolving consumer expectations. This forward-thinking approach positions brands as leaders in their industries, enhancing their reputation and competitive edge (Kim & Ko, 2012). Customers, instead of relying on traditional one-way communication methods like phone calls, are now engaging in dynamic conversations with brands through messaging platforms such as Facebook Messenger and Viber (Sproutsocial, 2019). This shift towards automated conversations represents a significant milestone in the evolution of customer engagement, where AI-driven solutions act as the intermediaries between the brand and the customer.

The COVID-19 pandemic further highlighted the role of chatbots as essential tools for maintaining brand-customer relationships. With physical interactions constrained, customers increasingly relied on AI-powered solutions to obtain information and make purchasing decisions. Chatbots provided a lifeline, ensuring uninterrupted brand engagement while enhancing customer satisfaction through consistent, personalized dialogues (Cheng & Jiang, 2020b). This shift underscores the transformative power of AI in enabling brands to maintain high levels of customer satisfaction by learning from past interactions and continuously improving.

The rise of AI tools in customer engagement also extends beyond traditional customer service functions. As AI-powered chatbots evolve, they are increasingly being used for marketing activities, creating an opportunity for brands to nurture relationships with customers long after a purchase has been made. AI can engage customers with personalized content, offers, and promotions based on their purchasing history and preferences. For example, e-commerce platforms can utilize AI to recommend products based on past purchases, or travel companies can offer personalized destination recommendations based on a customer's previous travel history. This continuous interaction and personalization of services not only keep customers engaged but also help maintain their loyalty by offering relevant content that resonates with their individual needs.

However, while AI tools like chatbots provide significant benefits in terms of customer engagement, they must be integrated thoughtfully to ensure they complement human interactions rather than replace them entirely. It is important for businesses to strike the right balance between automation and human intervention to avoid alienating customers who may prefer personalized assistance. For instance, while a chatbot can handle routine queries and issues, more complex or sensitive matters should be directed to human agents who can provide a higher level of empathy and understanding. By combining AI tools with human expertise, brands can create a hybrid service model that delivers the best of both worlds: the efficiency and scalability of AI with the emotional intelligence of human interaction.

One of the key advantages of using AI to optimize customer engagement and retention is its ability to scale. As businesses grow and customer bases expand, managing customer relationships becomes increasingly challenging. AI tools can help brands scale their engagement efforts without sacrificing quality or customer experience. Chatbots, for example, can handle thousands of interactions simultaneously, allowing businesses to maintain high levels of customer engagement even as their operations expand. This scalability is especially important for businesses in industries such as e-commerce and travel, where customer volumes can fluctuate dramatically during peak seasons or promotional events.

Moreover, targeted promotions can be designed based on customer segments, taking into account factors such as demographics, purchase history, and engagement levels. AI can segment customers into distinct groups and offer tailored incentives, ensuring that the promotions are relevant and appealing to each segment. This approach leads to higher engagement rates, greater customer satisfaction, and improved retention outcomes.

AI's role in enhancing customer engagement and retention is not just limited to chatbots and predictive analytics. AI can also optimize the broader customer experience (CX) by streamlining various touch points across the customer journey. AI-based systems can integrate with multiple communication channels—such as email, social media, and websites—to ensure a seamless and consistent customer experience. AI enables companies to provide personalized content at the right time, improving customer satisfaction and reinforcing brand loyalty (Hoyer et al., 2020).

AI's influence on business functionality is profound, with applications spanning from human resources and marketing to customer service (Cao, Duan, Edwards, & Dwivedi, 2021; Collins, Dennehy, Conboy, & Mikalef, 2021; Kumar, Dwivedi, & Anand, 2021). The adoption of AI in businesses has transformed how companies approach customer interaction and decision-making. AI-powered systems can enhance customer engagement by personalizing communication and anticipating customer needs based on previous interactions. AI allows brands to improve processes such as customer segmentation, targeting, and positioning, which in turn helps marketers reach the right audience with the right message (Canhoto & Clear, 2020; Chiu, Zhu, & Corbett, 2021). AI's ability to process and analyze large amounts of data in real-time also aids in understanding customer behavior, preferences, and trends, making it possible to predict when a customer might be at risk of leaving.

The most critical application of AI in customer retention is its ability to identify at-risk customers early in their journey. By analyzing historical data, purchase patterns, browsing behaviors, and customer feedback, AI systems can detect early signs of disengagement or dissatisfaction. For example, a decline in purchase frequency or a sudden drop in interaction with brand communications may signal that a customer is becoming disengaged. Identifying these at-risk customers allows brands to take proactive measures to retain them.

Once at-risk customers are identified, AI enables brands to implement targeted retention strategies. One of the most effective tactics is offering personalized discounts or promotions to re-engage customers. By using data-driven insights, brands can tailor offers that resonate with individual preferences, needs, and past behaviors, thereby increasing the likelihood of re-engagement. For instance, if a customer who frequently purchases a certain type of product has not made a purchase in several months, a brand might offer them a personalized discount on their favorite items to incentivize a return. This approach not only addresses the immediate concern of retention but also strengthens the overall relationship between the brand and its customer by demonstrating that the brand values their loyalty and is willing to invest in maintaining the relationship.

The key AI application in customer retention is the use of AI-driven predictive analytics. Predictive models can analyze past behaviors to identify customers who show signs of disengagement, such as a decline in purchase frequency or customer service interactions. Early identification of these at-risk customers allows businesses to implement retention strategies proactively. For instance, AI can recommend personalized promotions, discounts, or loyalty incentives tailored to the needs and preferences of the individual customer, re-engaging them before they churn (Robinson et al., 2020).

AI's ability to analyze vast amounts of data allows for the creation of hyper-targeted customer experiences. Unlike traditional segmentation strategies that group customers broadly based on demographics, AI enables the segmentation of customers at a micro-level. By analyzing individual customer behaviors, preferences, and purchasing histories, businesses can deliver highly personalized recommendations and content, improving the relevance of interactions. This level of personalization is crucial in driving customer satisfaction and loyalty, as customers increasingly seek experiences that cater to their specific needs and preferences (Yalamati, 2023; Gao et al., 2023).

The integration of AI into customer engagement strategies also contributes to more efficient resource allocation and cost optimization. Traditional methods of customer engagement often require significant human resources, which can be expensive and time-consuming. AI-powered tools, on the other hand, can automate many aspects of customer interaction, such as answering queries, providing personalized recommendations, and processing transactions. This automation not only improves efficiency but also allows brands to engage with a larger number of customers at scale without compromising on quality.

Additionally, AI's ability to personalize marketing efforts could lead to concerns about over-targeting or manipulation. Ensuring that AI-driven marketing strategies respect customer autonomy and avoid exploiting vulnerable individuals is crucial for maintaining a positive brand image and retaining customer loyalty. Companies must strike a balance between leveraging AI for personalized engagement and respecting customer privacy and preferences.Moreover, AI can optimize customer engagement strategies by providing valuable insights into consumer behavior. Through techniques such as cluster analysis, AI can group customers based on shared traits or behaviors, allowing brands to tailor engagement strategies more effectively. By identifying patterns and trends in customer data, AI systems can predict customer needs, personalize offerings, and optimize loyalty programs, ultimately enhancing brand loyalty (Rane et al., 2024b; Abdullaev et al., 2023). AI's predictive capabilities extend beyond customer behavior analysis to include forecasting product demand, anticipating customer churn, and recommending actions to improve retention. By using data-driven insights, brands can optimize their marketing efforts, enhance customer service, and foster long-term relationships.

AI presents a tremendous opportunity for brands to optimize customer engagement and retention. By harnessing the power of AI-driven tools like chatbots, recommendation systems, and predictive analytics, businesses can provide personalized, timely, and relevant experiences that meet customer needs. AI allows brands to identify at-risk customers early, enabling them to take proactive steps to retain those customers through personalized offers, discounts, and promotions. This not only helps reduce churn but also strengthens the overall customer-brand relationship, creating a more loyal and engaged customer base. By considering ethical implications and prioritizing transparency, brands can ensure that their AI-driven engagement strategies are both effective and responsible, ultimately driving long-term customer retention and satisfaction.

AI & Ethical Consideration in Branding

One of the most pressing ethical concerns is *data privacy*. AI systems in marketing rely heavily on the collection and analysis of vast amounts of consumer data. This data often includes sensitive information, such as personal preferences, behavioral patterns, and even location data. While personalization offers enhanced customer experiences, it also imposes risks of misuse or unauthorized access to such sensitive information. As AI-driven marketing strategies often involve collecting data to improve consumer targeting, brands must ensure that their data collection practices comply with legal and regulatory standards, such as the General Data Protection Regulation (GDPR) and other data protection laws. Failing to protect consumer data adequately not only exposes brands to legal action but also severely damages their reputation. Ethical concerns related to data privacy have gained significant attention in recent years, with high-profile cases of data breaches underscoring the importance of securing consumer data and safeguarding privacy.

The integration of Artificial Intelligence (AI) into branding strategies has revolutionized the way brands engage with consumers. From personalized messaging and predictive analytics to customer segmentation and chatbot communication, AI offers a plethora of benefits that can enhance brand value and drive customer engagement. However, the application of AI in branding also raises significant ethical concerns, particularly surrounding data privacy, transparency, and consumer trust.

Beyond data privacy, *transparency in algorithms* is another critical concern. AI algorithms that power personalized marketing and other branding strategies are often complex and difficult for consumers to understand. Brands leveraging AI must ensure transparency in how these algorithms operate and the data they utilize. Consumers should be informed about how their data is being used, how decisions are made, and what their rights are in relation to these algorithms. Lack of transparency can lead to consumer mistrust and alienate an audience that is increasingly concerned about the ethics of AI. For instance, if a brand uses AI to personalize content or advertisements but does not disclose the sources or logic behind these decisions, it could create a sense of manipulation, further eroding consumer trust.

Consumer trust is intricately linked to both data privacy and algorithmic transparency. Trust is a cornerstone of effective branding, and any compromise in the ethical use of AI can significantly damage the relationship between the brand and its audience. Consumers are more likely to engage with brands that they trust, and unethical practices in AI-driven marketing, such as unauthorized data sharing, lack of consent, or the manipulation of preference, can have severe long-term consequences. Trust can be built through clear communication, ethical behavior, and a commitment to consumer rights. Brands that demonstrate an understanding of the ethical implications of AI and take steps to address these concerns can foster a loyal and engaged customer base.

Being a central ethical consideration in AI-driven branding that is *transparency,* this requires brands to disclose how AI systems use consumer data and make decisions, ensuring that consumers are informed about the practices influencing the marketing messages they receive. The principle of transparency is vital because it helps foster trust and openness, two factors that are increasingly important in a market where consumers are becoming more aware of privacy risks and data misuse (Yeung, 2018).

To ensure responsible AI usage, brands must adopt certain *guidelines*. First, brands should prioritize *data protection* by adopting secure data storage and handling practices, ensuring data is anonymized when possible and obtaining explicit consent from consumers before collecting their information. Additionally, brands should implement transparent policies regarding their use of AI, providing clear explanations of how consumer data is being used and how AI-driven decisions are made. This transparency can be achieved through clear communication on websites, mobile applications, and through customer service channels. Brands should also conduct regular audits of their AI systems to ensure they are not inadvertently reinforcing biases or engaging in unethical practices.

Brands can also enhance *consumer education* by informing their audience about the benefits and risks of AI in marketing. Educational initiatives that promote an understanding of AI's role in branding can help consumers feel more comfortable with its usage. Providing easy-to-understand information about how AI helps brands personalize offerings and improve customer experience can build trust and reduce fears about privacy violations or manipulation.

Moreover, there is a growing need for *ethical leadership* within organizations adopting AI technologies. Leaders must create a culture of ethical awareness that extends to every part of the business, from data collection to AI implementation and consumer interaction. Training staff on ethical marketing practices and the importance of data protection is critical. As AI technologies evolve, brands must remain committed to ethical principles, regularly revisiting their strategies to ensure alignment with societal values and regulatory changes.

While AI offers substantial advantages for branding, such as personalized consumer experiences and enhanced marketing effectiveness, brands must be vigilant about the ethical considerations associated with its use. Ensuring data privacy, maintaining transparency in algorithms, and fostering consumer trust are essential steps that brands must take to integrate AI responsibly. By adhering to ethical guidelines and continuously improving their practices, brands can not only enhance their marketing outcomes but also build long-lasting relationships with consumers grounded in trust and integrity. These efforts will contribute to a more ethical and responsible digital marketing landscape, benefiting both businesses and their customers in the long run.

Future Trends: The Continued Evolution of AI in Branding

The era of technology has ushered in an age where Artificial Intelligence (AI) is rapidly transforming various industrial sectors, including branding and marketing. With over 4.6 billion smartphone users globally and around two billion daily internet users (Schulterbraucks, 2017), the integration of AI into branding strategies is becoming imperative for companies aiming to remain competitive.

As artificial intelligence (AI) technology advances, its role in branding and marketing is evolving into a pivotal force for business growth. AI's integration into branding strategies is expected to redefine consumer experiences through the adoption of AI-powered voice assistants and augmented reality (AR), shaping the future of branding by enhancing personalization and data-driven engagement. These tools not only streamline shopping experiences but also empower brands to meet evolving consumer expectations for tailored interactions and convenience. However, businesses that fail to embrace AI-driven technologies may risk obsolescence in an increasingly competitive market, where personalization and innovation are key differentiators.

AI thrives on vast datasets generated by customer interactions, transaction records, and external sources like social media. This data enables AI to deliver hyper-personalized recommendations, ensuring relevance and enhancing customer loyalty. Insights derived from data analysis also allow brands to anticipate market trends, adjust pricing strategies, and fine-tune messaging. As AI-driven systems increasingly underpin branding strategies, businesses are compelled to adapt to this dynamic landscape.

Branding, defined as the term or symbol representing a product's character and value (Kotler, 2000), has grown increasingly competitive. AI enables companies to analyze vast amounts of data quickly, ensuring that their products and strategies align with consumer preferences. With the global data volume doubling every two years, AI systems equipped with advanced storage and processing capabilities provide businesses with the tools to analyze consumer data efficiently and create personalized experiences (Gentsch, 2019).

Brands that resist adopting AI face long-term repercussions that can significantly affect their survival and growth. One of the most severe aftereffects is the gradual loss of market relevance. In a fast-paced, technology-driven world, consumers gravitate towards brands that offer convenience, personalization, and innovation—all hallmarks of AI-enabled systems (Dwivedi et al., 2023). Without these attributes, resistant brands risk becoming obsolete.

However, the reliance on data introduces challenges, including ethical concerns related to data privacy, algorithmic biases, and transparency. These challenges underscore the importance of adopting responsible AI practices to maintain consumer trust and avoid regulatory scrutiny.

To thrive in an AI-centric future, brands must adopt strategies that emphasize adaptability, innovation, and a customer-first approach. These strategies ensure that brands remain agile and capable of leveraging AI to its fullest potential as follows:

Embracing Big Data and Personalization: The foundation of AI-driven branding is data. Brands must invest in systems that collect, analyze, and utilize customer data effectively. By doing so, they can deliver personalized experiences that build loyalty and drive sales.

Investing in Data Infrastructure: Building robust data management systems ensures the accuracy and reliability of AI algorithms. Companies should prioritize data security and privacy, implementing measures to protect consumer information and maintain trust.

Focusing on Ethical AI Usage: Transparency and trust are critical. Brands must communicate how they use consumer data and ensure compliance with privacy regulations. Ethical AI practices not only build trust but also protect brands from reputational risks.

Investing in Training and Innovation: As AI evolves, so must the skills of the teams using it. Continuous training and upskilling ensure that marketing professionals can leverage the latest AI tools effectively. Additionally, fostering a culture of innovation encourages experimentation and adaptation.

Developing Adaptive Branding Strategies: Brands must prepare for technological disruptions by developing adaptive strategies. This includes scenario planning and investing in flexible systems that can scale and evolve as new technologies emerge.

Fostering Emotional Connections: Even as AI becomes more intuitive and empathetic, human connection remains vital. Brands must use AI to enhance, not replace, emotional engagement with customers. In a rapidly evolving market, brands that fail to embrace AI-driven tools face significant risks. As consumer expectations rise, fueled by hyper-personalized experiences provided by AI-savvy competitors, non-adopters risk obsolescence.

Overcoming Loss of Competitive Edge: Brands that do not integrate AI into their strategies may struggle to compete with those that offer highly personalized experiences. In industries like e-commerce, where giants like Amazon and Alibaba set the standard, non-adopters risk falling behind on customer satisfaction, retention, and market share.

Correcting Inefficiencies in Operations: AI streamlines operations, from inventory management to customer support. Brands that rely solely on manual processes may face inefficiencies, higher costs, and slower response times, all of which can erode their competitive position.

Leaving No Missed Opportunities in Consumer Insights: Data is the currency of modern branding, and AI is the tool that unlocks its value. Without AI-driven analytics, brands miss opportunities to understand consumer behavior, identify trends, and adapt to changing preferences.

Eradicating Negative Brand Perception: Consumers increasingly value innovation. Brands seen as lagging in technology adoption may be perceived as outdated or irrelevant, particularly by younger, tech-savvy demographics.

Mitigating the Risks: To avoid these risks, brands must prioritize AI adoption as part of their strategic vision. Investing in AI tools, training staff, and fostering a culture of innovation can help brands stay relevant and competitive.

Adopting Agile Marketing Frameworks: Agile frameworks allow brands to adapt quickly to changing consumer demands and market conditions. AI-driven insights enable real-time decision-making, ensuring that marketing strategies remain relevant and impactful.

The rise of social media platforms has further accelerated the influence of AI in branding, with influencer marketing emerging as a powerful tool. By utilizing AI-driven analytics, brands can identify influential personalities whose content aligns with their ethos, ensuring authentic engagement with consumers. This strategy enhances brand trust and loyalty while simultaneously expanding market reach. Moreover, artificial intelligence significantly supports sentiment analysis, a technique that allows brands to gauge public perceptions and refine messaging accordingly (Joshi et al., 2023; Anoir et al., 2024).

At its core, AI introduces opportunities to refine the customer experience through personalized interactions that cater to individual preferences. Machine learning algorithms and big data analysis enable brands to gain a granular understanding of consumer behaviors, needs, and preferences. This capability fosters an ecosystem where marketing strategies are not only predictive but also adaptive, creating dynamic customer journeys that resonate with the target audience (Kocic & Radaković, 2018; Busca & Bertrandias, 2020).

AI is a pivotal driver of value transformation in branding, redefining how businesses create, deliver, and sustain consumer value. By leveraging massive databases, AI uncovers deep consumer insights, enabling brands to co-create value with their customers. This approach fosters innovation, disrupts traditional paradigms, and aligns with evolving consumer expectations. AI-driven solutions ensure that brands remain relevant by consistently adapting to market changes.

The dynamic interplay between AI and marketing introduces new opportunities for engagement and satisfaction. By embedding AI in their core operations, brands can transform their strategies, ensuring alignment with consumer needs and generating exceptional value. The AI-for-value-transformation cluster exemplifies the symbiotic relationship between technology and marketing, highlighting how innovation and collaboration propel brands into the future.

AI-based solutions in branding span diverse technologies, from collaborative robots in packaging to drones for delivery. Future research must map these technologies, identifying their unique features and contextual variables influencing adoption (Huang & Rust, 2020). Understanding these dynamics enables brands to make informed decisions about adopting AI technologies. Future research in this area will provide actionable insights, guiding businesses in navigating the complexities of AI implementation and maximizing its potential.

Talking more about its advantages in branding, the most significant advantage is its capacity for real-time interaction. Chatbots, virtual assistants, and conversational agents now bridge the gap between brands and consumers, offering immediate responses and fostering loyalty.Furthermore, AI tools enable real-time monitoring and management of social media, tracking brand mentions, sentiment, and trends to refine marketing strategies dynamically (Dwivedi et al., 2023).

Now if a brand fails to understand and underestimate the ways and falls into complete denial stage of not adopting the AI driven tools then the severity increases. The refusal or inability of brands to integrate AI technologies poses serious risks in an increasingly digital-first marketplace. Ignoring AI undermines a brand's capacity to compete effectively, adapt to consumer demands, and sustain long-term growth. Without AI, brands lose access to critical tools for customer segmentation, predictive analytics, and personalized marketing. This inability to tailor offerings diminishes relevance, leaving brands disconnected from their target audiences (Oh et al., 2020).

One of the most immediate consequences is the erosion of customer trust and loyalty. Consumers today expect seamless, personalized interactions, which are often enabled by AI. A lack of such experiences can frustrate customers, pushing them towards competitors who can deliver higher engagement and satisfaction levels (Rajagopal, 2020). Furthermore, in the absence of AI, brands struggle to interpret social media sentiment and respond to crises in real-time, potentially damaging their reputations.

Brands that forgo AI are also likely to suffer from operational inefficiencies. Traditional marketing strategies that rely on human interpretation of data are slower, less accurate, and more resource-intensive than AI-driven processes.This inefficiency not only increases costs but also delays critical decision-making, putting brands at a competitive disadvantage.

Ignoring AI also hinders innovation, leaving brands vulnerable to obsolescence. In industries where AI-driven technologies like AR, VR, and AI-assisted design are becoming standard, brands that resist adoption fail to meet evolving consumer expectations. This would show how such brands risk being perceived as outdated, which can diminish their appeal to younger, tech-savvy demographics.

Despite its benefits, adopting AI technologies poses challenges. Developing AI systems requires significant investment in time, money, and expertise. Companies must source high-quality data, employ skilled professionals like data scientists, and implement robust infrastructure to support AI integration (Pradeep et al., 2019).

Data cleansing, essential for optimizing algorithms, is a time-consuming and costly process that raises security and privacy concerns (Thomas & Fowler, 2020).

Another significant consequence is the loss of competitive positioning. As competitors leverage AI to optimize their branding strategies, brands that lag behind face declining relevance and market share. Advanced AI technologies allow competitors to anticipate and outpace market demands, leaving non-AI-enabled brands struggling to keep up (Backhaus et al., 2011). This imbalance in capabilities can lead to dwindling profitability and, eventually, market exit.

Therefore, neglecting AI leaves brands vulnerable to data breaches and cybersecurity threats. AI is critical for detecting and mitigating these risks, and brands without such capabilities expose themselves and their customers to potential harm. The reputational damage from such incidents can be catastrophic, further compounding the negative impact of ignoring AI.

Moreover, the rise of AI technologies has sparked fears of job displacement, as automation replaces roles traditionally performed by humans. Brands must weigh these risks against the potential benefits of AI adoption, ensuring that technological advancements do not compromise ethical practices or workforce stability (Gentsch, 2019). The future of branding is intrinsically linked to AI. Brands must integrate AI technologies into their strategies to remain relevant, innovative, and competitive. By doing so, they will not only meet consumer expectations but also shape the trends of tomorrow's marketplace. Conversely, resistance to AI will likely result in diminished market presence, weakened brand equity, and long-term unsustainability.

CONCLUSION

So as in conclusion, Artificial Intelligence (AI) has emerged as a pivotal force in branding, revolutionizing how businesses engage with their customers and deliver value. Its significance lies in its ability to transform traditional, intuition-driven strategies into precise, data-informed approaches, ensuring that brands remain relevant and competitive in an ever-evolving digital landscape. By harnessing the power of AI, brands can predict customer behaviors, personalize interactions, and optimize engagement, ultimately fostering deeper loyalty and enhancing long-term customer satisfaction. This shift is not just an enhancement of existing strategies but a fundamental reimagining of how brands interact with and understand their audience.

The necessity of AI in modern branding cannot be overstated. In a world where consumer expectations are rapidly evolving, AI provides the tools to anticipate needs, streamline experiences, and respond effectively to dynamic market conditions. For brands, this is no longer a matter of competitive advantage—it is a requirement for survival and growth. From predictive analytics and chatbots to augmented reality,

AI technologies empower brands to create hyper-personalized experiences that resonate with consumers on a deeper level. The ability to identify at-risk customers and implement proactive retention strategies highlights how AI not only improves operational efficiency but also strengthens emotional connections between brands and their audience.

As brands adopt and integrate AI, it is crucial to balance innovation with ethical responsibility. The potential for misuse, particularly regarding data privacy, transparency, and fairness, cannot be ignored. Consumers value authenticity and trust, and any deviation from ethical practices can result in reputational damage and loss of loyalty. Brands must prioritize clear communication about how AI enhances customer experiences while ensuring that data handling practices remain secure and unbiased. This accountability is essential for maintaining trust and positioning AI as a force for good in the consumer landscape.

The future of AI in branding holds immense promise, yet it demands continuous research and refinement. The rapid pace of technological advancements presents an ongoing opportunity for brands to explore innovative applications while addressing the challenges that arise. Further research into ethical AI deployment, advanced personalization methods, and the integration of AI with other emerging technologies, such as blockchain or the metaverse, will enable brands to stay ahead. By doing so, they can unlock new dimensions of engagement and elevate customer experiences to unprecedented levels.

For brands looking to leverage AI effectively, the focus should remain on how these tools can enhance—not replace—human creativity and connection. AI serves as an enabler, offering insights and efficiencies that complement the brand's vision and values. By leading with a customer-centric approach, brands can use AI to craft narratives, design immersive experiences, and foster meaningful interactions. It is this balance between technological innovation and human empathy that will define the next chapter of branding.

Ultimately, the adoption of AI in branding is not just about keeping pace with technological advancements; it is about shaping a future where brands can connect authentically, innovate responsibly, and grow sustainably. The journey forward requires thoughtful implementation, continuous learning, and a commitment to ethical practices. As AI continues to evolve, its role in branding will expand, offering unprecedented opportunities to drive meaningful change and create value for businesses and consumers alike. This makes AI not only a worthwhile area for further research but also a critical investment for brands aiming to thrive in the future.

REFERENCES

Agersborg, C., Månsson, I., & Roth, E. (2020). Brand Management and Artificial Intelligence-A World of Man Plus Machine-A qualitative study exploring how Artificial Intelligence can contribute to Brand Management in the B2C sector.

Bayuk, A., & Demir, S. (2021). Artificial intelligence in marketing: Emergence, development, and applications. *Journal of Business Research*, 128, 378–389.

Belk, R. (2021). Technophilia and its impact on branding. *The Journal of Consumer Research*, 48(3), 412–431.

Campbell, C., & Price, L. (2021). Predictive modeling and AI in marketing. *Marketing Science*, 40(2), 123–135.

Cantallops, A. S., & Salvi, F. (2014). Understanding AI-driven brand interactions: A TAM perspective. *Computers in Human Behavior*, 31, 19–25.

Crane, A., & Matten, D. (2016). *Business ethics: Managing corporate citizenship and sustainability in the age of globalization*. Oxford University Press.

Davenport, T., Guha, A., Grewal, D., & Bressgott, T. (2020). How artificial intelligence will change the future of marketing. *Journal of the Academy of Marketing Science*, 48(1), 24–42. DOI: 10.1007/s11747-019-00696-0

Davenport, T. H., & Ronanki, R. (2018). Artificial intelligence for the real world. *Harvard Business Review*, 96(1), 108–116.

Deryl, M. D., Verma, S., & Srivastava, V. (2023). How does AI drive branding? Towards an integrated theoretical framework for AI-driven branding. *International Journal of Information Management Data Insights*, 3(2), 100205. DOI: 10.1016/j.jjimei.2023.100205

Dwivedi, Y.. (2021). The role of subjective norms in AI branding. *Journal of Marketing Theory and Practice*, 29(1), 45–67.

Gökerik, M., & Aktaş, Ö. Digital Marketing Trends Reshaped by Artificial Intelligence: A Bibliometric Approach. *JOEEP: Journal of Emerging Economies and Policy, 9*(1), 75-90.

Guest, G., Bunce, A., & Johnson, L. (2006). How many interviews are enough? An experiment with data saturation and variability. *Field Methods*, 18(1), 59–82. DOI: 10.1177/1525822X05279903

Haenlein, M., & Kaplan, A. (2019). A brief history of artificial intelligence: On the past, present, and future of artificial intelligence. *California Management Review*, 61(4), 5–14. DOI: 10.1177/0008125619864925

Indrawan, D., Yorman, Y., Stiadi, M., Hendayani, N., & Al-Amin, A. A. (2023). Revolutionizing social media marketing through AI and automation: An in-depth analysis of strategies, ethics, and future trends. *International Journal of Humanities* [INJOSS]. *Social Sciences and Business*, 3(1), 22–45.

Kapferer, J. N. (2008). *The new strategic brand management: Creating and sustaining brand equity long term*. Kogan Page Publishers.

Keller, K. L. (1993). Conceptualizing, measuring, and managing customer-based brand equity. *Journal of Marketing*, 57(1), 1–22. DOI: 10.1177/002224299305700101

Klaus, P., & Zaichkowsky, J. (2020). AI voice bots: A services marketing research agenda. *Journal of Services Marketing*, 34(3), 389–398. DOI: 10.1108/JSM-01-2019-0043

Kumar, V., & Dey, D. (2020). AI and consumer engagement in marketing: A framework for MSMEs. *JMR, Journal of Marketing Research*, 57(3), 95–113.

Labib, E. (2024). Artificial intelligence in marketing: Exploring current and future trends. *Cogent Business & Management*, 11(1), 2348728. DOI: 10.1080/23311975.2024.2348728

Lemos, M., Cardoso, P. J., & Rodrigues, J. M. (2024). Harnessing AI and NLP Tools for Innovating Brand Name Generation and Evaluation: A Comprehensive Review. *Multimodal Technologies and Interaction*, 8(7), 56. DOI: 10.3390/mti8070056

Liao, X., Zhao, Z., Barth, M. J., Abdelraouf, A., Gupta, R., Han, K., Ma, J., & Wu, G. (2024). A review of personalization in driving behavior: Dataset, modeling, and validation. *IEEE Transactions on Intelligent Vehicles*, 1–22. DOI: 10.1109/TIV.2024.3425647

Lindgreen, A., & Swaen, V. (2010). Corporate social responsibility: An ethical approach to business strategy. *Business and Society Review*, 115(3), 365–384.

Marinchak, C., Forrest, E., & Hoanca, B. (2018). AI and personalization in marketing. *Journal of Research in Interactive Marketing*, 12(4), 516–534.

Muchenje, C., Mtengwa, E., & Kabote, F. (2023). Building a strong brand: Future strategies and insights. In *Sustainable Marketing, Branding, and Reputation Management: Strategies for a Greener Future* (pp. 238-257). IGI Global.

Mustak, M.. (2021). Toward a unified theory of AI-driven branding. *Journal of Business Research*, 135, 335–346.

Nalbant, K. G., & Aydın, S. (2023). Development and transformation in digital marketing and branding with artificial intelligence and digital technologies dynamics in the Metaverse universe. *Journal of Metaverse*, 3(1), 9–18. DOI: 10.57019/jmv.1148015

Oh, L. B., & Teo, H. H. (2020). Consumer value co-creation in a multi-channel environment: Analyzing the role of information technology. *International Journal of Information Management*, 52, 102067.

Olusegun, J. (2024). The Role of AI in Enhancing Sentiment Analysis for Brand Management.

Patil, D., Rane, N. L., & Rane, J. (2024). The future of customer loyalty: How ChatGPT and generative artificial intelligence are transforming customer engagement, personalization, and satisfaction. *The Future Impact of ChatGPT on Several Business Sectors*, 48-106. Khan, S., & Iqbal, M. (2020, June). AI-Powered Customer Service: Does it optimize customer experience? In *2020 8th International Conference on Reliability, Infocom Technologies and Optimization (Trends and Future Directions) (ICRITO)* (pp. 590-594). IEEE.

Patricia, M., Roberts, T., & Allen, D. (2022). Ethical dilemmas in AI-driven marketing strategies. *Journal of Business Ethics*, 40(2), 91–104.

Putha, S. (2021). AI-Driven Personalization in E-Commerce: Enhancing Customer Experience and Sales through Advanced Data Analytics. *Journal of Bioinformatics and Artificial Intelligence*, 1(1), 225–271.

Raji, M. A., Olodo, H. B., Oke, T. T., Addy, W. A., Ofodile, O. C., & Oyewole, A. T. (2024). E-commerce and consumer behavior: A review of AI-powered personalization and market trends. *GSC Advanced Research and Reviews, 18*(3), 066-077.

Rust, R. T. (2020). The future of marketing. *International Journal of Research in Marketing*, 37(1), 15–26. DOI: 10.1016/j.ijresmar.2019.08.002

Sabbar, A., & Nygren Gustafsson, L. (2021). The impact of AI on branding elements: Opportunities and challenges as seen by branding and IT specialists.

Schulterbraucks, L. (2017). The impact of artificial intelligence on the marketing landscape. *Journal of Marketing Trends*, 6(2), 45–50.

Sharma, A., Patel, N., & Gupta, R. (2022). Leveraging BERT and Sentiment Analysis Algorithms for Enhanced AI-Driven Brand Sentiment Monitoring. *European Advanced AI Journal, 11*(8).

Shekhar, E. S., Goyal, D. S., & Jain, U. J. J. A. W. A. L. (2024). Enhancing customer engagement with AI and ML: Techniques and case studies. *International Journal of Computer Science and Publications, 14 (2), 1-15. IJCSP24B1346. Pdf.*

Singh, M., & Singh, S. (2020). The role of ethical business practices in small enterprises. *Journal of Small Business Management*, 34(1), 71–82.

Sterne, J. (2017). *Artificial intelligence for marketing: Practical applications.* Wiley. DOI: 10.1002/9781119406341

Sun, H., Zafar, M. Z., & Hasan, N. (2022). Employing natural language processing as artificial intelligence for analyzing consumer opinion toward advertisement. *Frontiers in Psychology*, 13, 856663. DOI: 10.3389/fpsyg.2022.856663 PMID: 35769737

Thakur, J., & Kushwaha, B. P. (2024). Artificial intelligence in marketing research and future research directions: Science mapping and research clustering using bibliometric analysis. *Global Business and Organizational Excellence*, 43(3), 139–155. DOI: 10.1002/joe.22233

Thomas, B., & Fowler, J. (2020). Addressing data challenges in AI implementation. *Business Horizons*, 63(3), 321–330.

Tirunillai, S., & Tellis, G. J. (2019). Does AI enhance consumer engagement? Insights from the AI marketing industry. *JMR, Journal of Marketing Research*, 56(6), 1038–1051.

Vaio, A. D.. (2020). Sustainable business models through AI in branding. *Journal of Cleaner Production*, 256, 120–135.

Verma, S.. (2021). The disruptive impact of AI on marketing. *International Journal of Technology Marketing*, 16(4), 385–399.

Vishnoi, R., Shah, P., & Chauhan, K. (2019). Deep learning and one-shot learning in AI. *International Journal of Computational Intelligence*, 15(3), 154–162.

Chapter 7
Artificial Intelligences Impact on Branding in Tourism

Serkan Gün
https://orcid.org/0000-0002-2501-1078
Siirt Universty, Turkey

ABSTRACT

The intersection of technology and branding has initiated a new chapter for the tourism sector, wherein artificial intelligence (AI) occupies a central position. This shift is manifested in AIs capacity to scrutinize extensive datasets, allowing businesses to discern nascent trends and consumer inclinations with an unparalleled accuracy. By utilizing AI, tourism brands can proffer personalized experiences that resonate with specific travelers, thereby nurturing enhanced emotional connections and brand loyalty. The enhancement of customer engagement through focused marketing strategies can result in noteworthy brand distinction amid a crowded marketplace. Therefore, comprehending AIs multifaceted repercussions on branding methodologies becomes crucial for tourism organizations that seek to succeed within a competitive context.Furthermore, AIs impact on branding transcends basic data evaluation; it influences the foundational nature of customer engagements.

I. INTRODUCTION

The intersection of technology and branding has initiated a new chapter for the tourism sector, wherein artificial intelligence (AI) occupies a central position. This shift is manifested in AIs capacity to scrutinize extensive datasets, allowing businesses to discern nascent trends and consumer inclinations with an unparalleled

DOI: 10.4018/979-8-3693-9461-8.ch007

accuracy. By utilizing AI, tourism brands can proffer personalized experiences that resonate with specific travelers, thereby nurturing enhanced emotional connections and brand loyalty. The enhancement of customer engagement through focused marketing strategies can result in noteworthy brand distinction amid a crowded marketplace. Therefore, comprehending AIs multifaceted repercussions on branding methodologies becomes crucial for tourism organizations that seek to succeed within a competitive context.Furthermore, AIs impact on branding transcends basic data evaluation; it influences the foundational nature of customer engagements. Automated chatbots, which are fueled by AI, have transformed customer service by delivering immediate, customized replies to queries, consistently operational around the clock. This technological advancement not only improves customer experience but also permits brands to uphold their visibility and significance in a progressively digital marketplace. By optimizing communication, businesses are capable of interacting with potential travelers by simplifying booking procedures and providing personalized recommendations aligned with user preferences. The ramifications of these advancements imply that AI is more than merely a supplementary instrument; it serves as a core element in constructing compelling brand stories that resonate with international audiences.In conclusion, the amalgamation of AI within tourism branding prompts essential reflections on ethical practices and consumer confidence. Although the advantages of improved personalization and operational efficiency are clear, the risk of data privacy violations is significant, giving rise to consumer distrust. It is imperative for brands to navigate these intricate matters by implementing transparent data handling practices and ensuring adherence to regulations such as the General Data Protection Regulation (GDPR). By confronting these issues proactively, tourism enterprises can not only protect their reputations but also foster trust among their clientele. Ultimately, the efficacy of AI in branding relies on the capacity to reconcile innovation with ethical obligations, thereby laying the groundwork for a sustainable future within the tourism industry.

A. Definition of Artificial Intelligence in Tourism

The realm of tourism finds itself undergoing significant alterations due to the advent of artificial intelligence (AI), which fundamentally modifies business engagements with consumers and the promotion of services. The application of AI algorithms alongside machine learning methodologies permits tourism businesses to examine extensive volumes of data, thus extracting insights pertaining to consumer preferences and conduct. This progression has notably improved the precision of advertising targeting, facilitating brands in the provision of personalized experiences which substantially increase customer satisfaction and retention. Research provides evidence that AI-based targeting algorithms are correlated with a substantial uplift in return on investment (ROI) for advertising initiatives, particularly as indicated by comparative data surrounding traditional and algorithmic methods across various fields, including tourism and retail shopping (Lin Shan). As the technology perpetrates advancement, its potential to fine-tune marketing tactics and enhance brand awareness becomes exceedingly crucial within a competitive landscape.The assimilation of AI into the tourism industry confers notable merits regarding operational efficiency. AI instruments grant businesses the ability to optimize procedures such as booking frameworks, customer support, and instantaneous response to inquiries, hence improving the overall customer experience. Additionally, AI-powered chatbots and virtual assistants furnish prompt guidance, aiding prospective travelers in exploring their options and making educated decisions. This form of interactive engagement cultivates trust and amplifies overall satisfaction—an essential component within experiential tourism contexts (Onur Akbulut). The embracement of these technologies not only aligns a firm's operational functionality with consumer anticipations but also situates the brand as forward-thinking and centered on customer needs, ultimately enhancing its market competitiveness.Furthermore, real-time data analytics, driven by AI advancements, empower brands to perennially modify their marketing methodologies predicated on consumer feedback and prevailing trends. This agility in marketing enables tourism enterprises to maintain relevance and adapt to changing consumer desires, thus progressively augmenting their brand equity. The constantly evolving landscape of tourism experiences, particularly within sectors such as adventure and experiential tourism, is significantly reliant on AI's efficacy in interpreting customer sentiments and actions (Onur Akbulut). Therefore, brands that effectively leverage AI-driven insights can develop more profound connections with their target audiences, ensuring not only immediate gratification but also nurturing enduring loyalty. In summary, the concept of AI within the tourism domain transcends mere technological application; it embodies a crucial evolution that amplifies branding approaches, enhances operational productivity, and ultimately enriches consumer experiences in a sector that is intrinsically dependent on innovation and personalization.

B. Importance of Branding in the Tourism Sector

Constructing a robust brand holds considerable significance in the tourism domain, as it can profoundly affect consumer decisions amid an ever-intensifying competitive landscape. An effectively cultivated brand not merely engenders trust and familiarity among prospective travelers; it also serves to distinguish a company from its rivals. With the progression of technology, particularly artificial intelligence, enterprises within the tourism sector are now enabled to formulate increasingly customized marketing approaches that align with their target demographics. For example, algorithms powered by AI possess the capability to scrutinize consumer actions and inclinations to adjust promotional materials accordingly, thereby augmenting engagement and nurturing customer loyalty. Such focused branding endeavors can greatly improve the traveler experience, which is vital within the tourism sector, where peer recommendations and digital evaluations heavily sway the decisions of other potential tourists.Additionally, the nascent function of chatbots in hospitality branding serves to illustrate how artificial intelligence can bolster customer engagement and satisfaction levels. As noted in (Arman Khan et al., pp. 657-671), chatbots are capable of mediating the dynamics between AI applications and consumer loyalty, furnishing prompt responses and effectively tackling queries. This amalgamation of AI-infused tools empowers tourism brands to proffer individualized experiences that fulfill customer prerequisites, ultimately consolidating brand commitment among consumers. A brand that is nimble, enabled by technological innovations, not only fosters a steadfast clientele but also incentivizes repeat patronage, which is critical for enduring prosperity within the tourism industry. With travelers increasingly pursuing distinctive and personalized adventures, the significance of branding via avant-garde strategies becomes notably accentuated.The significance of branding in the tourism field cannot be diminished, especially when one contemplates its effects on customer perception and selection. As brought to light in (Yakup Durmaz et al., p. 21-30), the deployment of AI technologies, like predictive analytics, can profoundly reshape marketing strategies by presenting tailored recommendations that correspond with individual tastes. This calculated utilization of artificial intelligence enhances the impact of branding efforts in the tourism sector by allowing companies to synchronize their offerings with consumer aspirations. Ultimately, the convergence of branding and AI not only optimally positions enterprises within a saturated marketplace but also elevates overall customer satisfaction and dedication. The adoption of AI-guided branding methodologies signifies a crucial transformation within the tourism industry, rendering it an imperative focus for entities striving for success in a fluid and swiftly evolving environment.

C. Overview of AI's Role in Modern Branding

The incorporation of artificial intelligence (AI) into branding strategies is indeed starting to change the nature of company-customer interactions, particularly within the tourism field. The capability of AI to scrutinize extensive datasets enables marketers to create tailored experiences that align with specific individual preferences and behaviors. By utilizing machine learning algorithms, brands can detect emerging trends and sentiments, which allows them to modify messages and offerings on the fly. This flexible method adds to customer engagement, fostering stronger emotional ties between brands and their consumers. Additionally, the capacity to anticipate customer behavior backs targeted marketing campaigns, which could potentially enhance brand loyalty in a fiercely competitive sector. Therefore, enterprises that adeptly employ AI may distinguish themselves, ensuring their branding initiatives are not just extensive but impactful as well.Customer loyalty is more and more affected by the usage of AI technologies, such as chatbots, which deliver prompt and personalized assistance. The intermediary function of chatbots in boosting customer loyalty illustrates AI's potential to facilitate meaningful interactions that exceed standard marketing communications. Findings indicate that AI has a beneficial effect on customer loyalty within the hospitality sector by improving customer experiences via effective problem resolution and tailored service options (Arman Khan et al., pp. 657-671). This shows that AI does not simply add to existing branding strategies but rather reshapes them by emphasizing engagement centered around the consumer. In this milieu, tourism brands that implement AI-centric tools can nurture enduring loyalty, making customers feel valued and comprehended—an essential factor for sustaining a competitive edge.As described in the literature, the application of AI in branding strategies marks a transition towards a more analytical, customer-focused methodology that emphasizes engagement and loyalty (Yolanda Masnita et al., pp. 120-140). The consistent application of AI technologies in marketing empowers brands to assess customer interactions and preferences, resulting in more refined branding strategies that coincide with consumer expectations. This structured embrace not only improves contemporary marketing methods but also establishes a foundation for forthcoming research into AI uses in branding. Comprehending the intricacies of AI's involvement in branding, particularly in travel and tourism, is essential for brands aspiring to utilize innovation for expansion. As the environment continues to change, the investigation of AI's role in modern branding will undoubtedly stay a crucial domain for ongoing examination and application across numerous sectors, including tourism.

II. THE EVOLUTION OF AI IN TOURISM

The advancements that have occurred in artificial intelligence (AI) have significantly transformed the tourism sector, altering the manner in which brands engage with consumers. Initially, the application of AI within tourism was primarily centered on enhancing operational efficiencies—such as the automation of booking systems and the management of inventory. Over the subsequent timeline, these systems have adapted to integrate machine learning algorithms that scrutinize consumer data to offer tailored recommendations, thus improving customer experiences. This alteration not only optimizes operational workflows but simultaneously enables brands to cultivate more profound emotional connections with their clientele. In light of the vigorous competition characterizing the tourism sector, it is the brands that leverage AI for personalized experiences that can distinctly differentiate themselves, thereby effectively fortifying their branding endeavors in an increasingly digital marketplace. A critical comprehension of this evolution proves imperative for stakeholders within the industry aiming to sustain relevance and competitiveness. Moreover, the incorporation of AI within tourism transcends mere operational improvements, penetrating deeply into the aspects of customer engagement. For example, AI-driven chatbots are presently redefining customer service by offering immediate responses to inquiries, which enhances the overall customer journey. This trend is consistent with findings that illustrate consumer attitudes toward AI in the hospitality and tourism sectors, specifically regarding service robots and emotional recognition technologies (Seden Doğan et al.). As advancements in these technologies persist, they necessitate a reevaluation of conventional customer service paradigms, thus providing brands with innovative methodologies to connect with their consumers. Nevertheless, the introduction of these technologies also engenders ethical concerns and potential ramifications for employment, creating a need for careful management of consumer expectations alongside employee job security. As the tourism industry continues to evolve, the institutions of education must adjust to the swiftly changing environment influenced by AI technologies. The incorporation of AI into educational curricula presents significant opportunities to prepare future professionals with essential competencies necessary to navigate an increasingly technology-driven milieu. However, this integration is not without challenges, which include ensuring that faculty members receive adequate training and addressing the digital divide present among students (Bulent Aydin et al.). A focus on ethical considerations regarding AI usage within tourism education enables students to engage with technological progressions with a thorough understanding of their broader societal impacts. Consequently, by promoting interdisciplinary collaboration and experiential learning, educational institutions could assume a foundational role in readying a workforce that not only embraces innovations in AI but also contemplates the ethical implications, ultimately bolstering responsible branding within the tourism sector.

A. Historical Context of AI Development

The foundational origins of artificial intelligence (AI) can be traced back to the mid-20th century, characterized by the efforts of figureheads such as Alan Turing and John McCarthy who established the intellectual basis for machines able to imitate human cognitive functions. Turing's pivotal contributions, most notably his proposition of the Turing Test, provided criteria for assessing machine intelligence and ignited curiosity regarding the viability of autonomous intelligent entities. In a similar vein, McCarthy introduced the designation "artificial intelligence" during the 1956 Dartmouth Conference, an essential gathering that brought together leading intellectuals from the field. The early enthusiasm related to these advancements was markedly evident, giving rise to notable investments and extensive research initiatives. Nonetheless, this optimism encountered harsh realizations of technological constraints, leading to periods known as AI winters during the 1970s and late 80s, wherein anticipated developments diverged greatly from the actual technological prowess achievable, thereby causing a significant reduction in both funding and interest. The revival of AI during the latter part of the 1990s and early 2000s can be predominantly connected to advancements in computational capabilities, the emergence of extensive datasets, and pivotal progressions in machine learning methodologies. This phase heralded the advent of technologies like neural networks, which established frameworks essential for deep learning practices. With computational power becoming more accessible and plentiful, researchers were enabled to analyze data at unprecedented scales. This newfound capability prompted businesses to acknowledge the disruptive potential of AI across multiple domains, including the tourism sector. Additionally, the expansion of the Internet intensified this trend by facilitating improved methods for companies to gather, scrutinize, and interpret consumer behavior data. This represented a significant shift, as AI began to permeate branding strategies, assisting businesses in customizing offerings to adeptly address the intricate preferences of travelers (Alhamzah Alnoor et al.).In contemporary times, the historical progression of AI has reached a phase wherein its applications are omnipresent, particularly within branding endeavors in the tourism industry. The transition from service-oriented methodologies to data-oriented approaches has transformed the manner in which brands engage with consumers, enabling hyper-personalized marketing and improved customer experiences. Enterprises currently employ AI to dissect customer feedback, refine pricing tactics, and predict travel patterns, thereby nurturing enhanced engagement with their constituents. This assimilation not only optimizes operational processes but also fundamentally reshapes the interaction paradigm between brands and consumers, evolving from transactional relationships to dynamic exchanges. As AI technology continues its advancement, brands that successfully adapt and innovate are likely to ascend as frontrunners within the fiercely competitive tourism arena, exemplifying how a nuanced comprehension of historical contexts shapes the existing framework of AI applications in branding (Alhamzah Alnoor et al.).

B. Key Technological Advancements in AI

Recent developments in artificial intelligence (AI) have sparked substantial changes across assorted industries, especially within the realm of tourism marketing. Noteworthy innovations like machine learning and natural language processing permit businesses to swiftly analyze extensive datasets, unearthing patterns that guide branding strategies. These technological innovations facilitate the customization of marketing campaigns—adapting communications to discrete consumer segments based on their behaviors and preferences. This transition towards decisions driven by data not only amplifies customer interaction but also bolsters brand loyalty. As noted in existing literature, practitioners are increasingly on the lookout for the most effective AI solutions to enhance their marketing operations, thus establishing AI as a vital resource in the branding toolkit in tourism (Yolanda Masnita et al., pp. 120-140).The incorporation of AI into branding strategies goes beyond simple data scrutiny; it also allows for immediate reactions to market dynamics. For example, AI-enabled instruments can forecast consumer sentiments and purchasing tendencies, enabling timely adjustments in marketing operations. This anticipatory methodology is essential within the dynamic tourism industry, where consumer inclinations can change swiftly. Moreover, as corporations, including those discussed in the research, increasingly adopt AI technologies, they are able to offer individualized experiences that connect with travelers, thus reinforcing their brand identities. Improved consumer engagement via predictive analytics not only enhances satisfaction levels but also nurtures a more profound emotional tie to the brand, rendering it more competitive (Yakup Durmaz et al., pp. 21-30).Additionally, the employment of AI in the automation of marketing processes constitutes a significant technological innovation. Automation mechanisms driven by AI can simplify repetitive functions, granting marketing teams the capacity to concentrate on creative and strategic pursuits. This level of efficiency not only liberates resources but also increases productivity within tourism entities. The cornerstone of effective branding resides in the astute application of these technologies to forge immersive customer experiences that surpass conventional marketing constraints. By seamlessly merging automation with AI-generated insights, tourism brands can develop inventive campaigns that seize consumer attention in a saturated market. Ultimately, such advancements highlight the critical importance of AIs role in redefining branding approaches and propelling growth within the tourism sector (Yolanda Masnita et al., p. 120-140) (Yakup Durmaz et al., pp. 21-30).

C. Current Trends in AI Utilization in Tourism

The swift advancement of artificial intelligence (AI) has indeed altered the tourism industry, notably by reshaping how consumers engage and how marketing strategies are crafted. Digital marketing is becoming more intricate, increasingly employing AI algorithms to scrutinize consumer behaviors and individual preferences. This transition allows tourism companies to fabricate tailored travel experiences which, in turn, amplifies traveler engagement and loyalty. To illustrate, AI-enabled chatbots deliver immediate help and customer service, facilitating inquiries and reservations around the clock. Furthermore, as shed light upon in [extractedKnowledgeX], the global pandemic hastened the uptake of digital platforms, driving firms to reevaluate their marketing approaches. Public authorities are likewise intervening, utilizing AI to interpret tourism analytics that guides policy formulation, thus further improving the efficacy of tourism marketing efforts. As companies maneuver through this evolving digital terrain, it becomes increasingly critical to employ AI technologies judiciously, ensuring alignment with the expectations of emerging consumers while promoting sustainable methodologies.Technological progressions including big data analytics and machine learning are instigating substantial alterations in how tourism brands function. These innovations empower firms to aggregate and scrutinize extensive datasets, generating insights regarding consumer trends and preferences. The significance of sustainability within tourism marketing must not be overlooked, as brands become more aware of the necessity to cater to travelers who are environmentally inclined. According to (Bulent Aydin et al.), this swelling consumer inclination urges organizations to innovate marketing approaches that highlight sustainability. Consequently, AI can assist brands not just in addressing these inclinations but also in anticipating trends that could sway brand strategies. Through the incorporation of AI in decision-making frameworks, tourism brands can forge targeted campaigns that resonate with the values upheld by their clientele, thereby fortifying brand identity and positioning amid a more competitive marketplace.In addition, ethical implications associated with the employment of AI are ascending to prominence as the technology matures. As noted in (Bulent Aydin et al.), the swift assimilation of AI within tourism and hospitality education necessitates a thorough deliberation of its adoption consequences. Educational institutions need to tackle not solely the technological elements of AI but also the ethical ramifications, ensuring that the forthcoming leaders in the sector are equipped to navigate multifaceted issues encompassing privacy, data protection, and algorithmic partiality. The relationship between AI and branding provokes inquiries concerning consumer trust and transparency, as brands are compelled to strike a balance between personalized marketing efforts and the respect for individual data rights. By promoting an ethos of ethical AI application within the tourism domain, brands have the capacity to enhance their public image and cultivate stronger ties with their clientele, addressing prevailing apprehensions while laying the groundwork for a sustainable and equitable future in tourism branding.

III. AI-DRIVEN CUSTOMER INSIGHTS

The rise of artificial intelligence (AI) is significantly altering the methods by which brands in the tourism industry connect with customers through the utilization of data-oriented insights. AI frameworks evaluate extensive compilations of consumer behavior information aimed at spotting trends, preferences, and issues, thus permitting brands to adjust their offerings accordingly. This alteration is not solely centered on the improvement of user experiences but fundamentally on reimagining the interactions between customers and brands. By applying AI-derived insights, tourism marketers are able to develop personalized experiences that resonate with distinct consumers, thereby nurturing more profound connections. This strategy is consistent with research findings regarding AI-related customer insights, which illustrate that such engagement techniques play a crucial role in fostering brand loyalty and consumer satisfaction, rendering AI a vital asset within contemporary tourism marketing strategies.An essential component of comprehending AI's function involves recognizing the emotional aspects that are intertwined in customer interactions. Notably, studies highlight that the novelty and interactiveness associated with AI tools, like robotic entertainers, can markedly elevate consumer emotional engagement. These emotions are crucial as they propel word-of-mouth marketing, a particularly effective component in the tourism domain. When consumers undergo positive emotional experiences during their engagements—enhanced by AI-driven contributions—they are more predisposed to partake in electronic word-of-mouth (eWOM) activities. Such activities not only increase brand visibility but also cultivate a sense of community among consumers. This occurrence further substantiates the argument that AI possesses the ability to forge emotional connections between brands and consumers, thereby reinforcing loyalty within the competitive sphere of tourism services ((Yuhao Li et al.)).Additionally, the systematic repercussions of AI concerning customer insights provide significant implications for sustainable tourism marketing frameworks. By implementing a structure that includes predictive processing theory, marketers can foresee consumer reactions and adjust their strategies accordingly. This ability to adapt is indispensable in an arena that is perpetually changing due to alterations in consumer preferences and technological progress. The research emphasizing AI's importance in decoding brand engagement and loyalty underscores the necessity of perceiving customer interactions through this analytical perspective ((Mohit Vij et al., pp. 1-6)). As AI technology continues to advance, brands are compelled to integrate these insights to enhance sustainable practices that not only attract but also maintain customer relations, ultimately fostering long-lasting connections within the tourism sector. Therefore, the integration of AI-derived insights becomes an essential strategy for brands aspiring to advance their engagement and loyalty efforts in this fluctuating marketplace.

A. Data Collection and Analysis Techniques

The assessment of branding strategies in the tourism domain demands the use of solid data collection and analysis methods. Quantitative methods—which include surveys and online questionnaires—can generate statistically relevant insights relating to consumer preferences and brand perceptions. For example, collecting demographic information along with preference indicators facilitates researchers in discerning correlations between visitor traits and brand loyalty. Additionally, the use of advanced analytical tools such as regression analysis can dissect these relationships, illuminating how brand positioning may sway consumer decisions across diverse contexts. The incorporation of approaches from behavioral psychology is also essential; a comprehension of cognitive biases and heuristics allows brands to more precisely customize their messaging to resonate with target demographics, thereby amplifying marketing campaign efficiency. This multi-layered methodology ensures an extensive grasp of the tourism branding environment, which is vital in the present data-centric landscape.On par with quantitative data gathering, qualitative approaches also hold significant importance for grasping the intricate viewpoints that travelers have concerning branding in tourism. Methods like focus groups and detailed interviews can uncover critical insights, disclosing emotional and experiential factors that numerical data may misinterpret or ignore. By interacting with consumers, brands can pinpoint the narratives and values that strongly connect with audiences, facilitating a more genuine engagement. Analyzing customer reviews and social media content provides additional layers to this method, yielding a treasure trove of insights shaped by users to tailor branding strategies effectively. The amalgamation of qualitative and quantitative information leads to a more rounded comprehension of customer sentiment, ultimately steering brands towards crafting compelling stories that are in alignment with traveler expectations and aspirations (Ray Tinston). This in-depth analysis enhances brand loyalty and aids in anticipating fluctuations in market needs.Furthermore, the continuous progress in artificial intelligence is revolutionizing the methodologies for data collection and analysis within the tourism sector. Machine learning algorithms possess the capability to swiftly analyze extensive datasets, uncovering patterns and trends that might be obscure when utilizing traditional approaches. For instance, predictive analytics can project future travel behaviors grounded in historical data, granting brands the opportunity to proactively adjust their marketing tactics. Besides, AI-based sentiment analysis tools can comb through social media engagement, delivering instantaneous feedback on consumer sentiments regarding particular brands or campaigns. This real-time data access empowers brands to swiftly and adeptly tweak their strategies for customer engagement. The union of advanced AI tools with meticulous data analysis practices equips tourism brands to sustain competitiveness in a progressively fluid marketplace, understanding that the ability to adapt is crucial for enduring success in branding endeavors within this industry (Ray Tinston).

B. Personalization of Customer Experiences

In the current competitive tourism milieu, the personalization of customer encounters has surfaced as a vital tactic for amplifying brand allegiance and satisfaction. The infusion of Artificial Intelligence (AI) permits enterprises to exploit extensive volumes of customer data to customize offerings that align with unique individual inclinations. For example, AI frameworks can scrutinize prior actions, tastes, and demographic data to furnish personalized suggestions, thus engendering a sense of exclusiveness for each patron. This bespoke methodology not merely augments the customer encounter but simultaneously nurtures emotional ties between consumers and brands. As is illustrated in (Arman Khan et al., p. 657-671), AI exerts a favorable impact on customer loyalty through the utilization of instruments like chatbots that furnish personalized assistance, denoting the significance of individualized focus in propelling consumer engagement.Moreover, the deployment of AI within the tourism domain is increasingly augmented by sophisticated technologies such as Virtual Reality (VR), which further enhances the personalization of experiences. By replicating destinations or encounters through immersive VR settings, businesses facilitate customers in visualizing their journeys prior to making determinations. This revolutionary procedure permits a more profound emotional investment, as potential tourists can engage with a destination more closely. Such technological advancements not only bolster informed decision-making but also mold expectations, engendering a deeper connection to the travel brand. Evidence delineated in (Carmen Florentina VLASCEANU et al.) elucidates how these technological innovations are transforming customer perceptions in the cruise sector, emphasizing the paramount significance of immersive personalization in elevating service standards and comprehensive customer satisfaction.The efficacy of these strategies ultimately hinges upon the capacity to seamlessly merge AI and VR into the customer service paradigm. Organizations that emphasize personalization are in a more advantageous position to set themselves apart in a crowded marketplace, thereby nurturing customer loyalty and augmenting brand equity. As referenced in (Arman Khan et al., p. 657-671), the execution of AI-enhanced chatbots can efficiently address consumer inquiries while delivering personalized interactions that enrich user experiences. Consequently, the confluence of AI and ancillary technologies in the crafting of personalized customer journeys is fundamental for the sustainability of tourism brands. By embracing such innovative methodologies, firms can not only improve operational efficacy but also foster enduring relationships with their clientele, ultimately propelling growth and prosperity within the tourism industry.

C. Predictive Analytics for Consumer Behavior

Within the domain of tourism branding, it is of paramount importance to note that the integration of predictive analytics serves a fundamental function in comprehending and foreseeing consumer behavior. Through the application of data analytics, enterprises are afforded the opportunity to derive insights regarding the patterns and trends that typify the preferences and requirements of potential customers. This capability thereby permits the construction of targeted marketing strategies, which in turn bolsters brand positioning amid the fiercely competitive tourism milieu. To illustrate, predictive algorithms have the capacity to pinpoint specific demographic groups that exhibit a higher likelihood to convert, which empowers tourism brands to customize their offerings and marketing communications in a corresponding manner. This approach, aimed specifically at targeting, not only enhances engagement with customers but also optimizes the efficacy of marketing expenditures as resources are allocated to the most promising market segments. Consequently, organizations that adeptly implement predictive analytics find themselves in a more advantageous position to forge significant connections with consumers, which ultimately promotes brand loyalty and drives revenue growth.Additionally, the application of predictive analytics has the potential to markedly enhance the customer journey through the personalization of interactions and recommendations. For instance, algorithms powered by artificial intelligence examine consumer data to proffer tailored suggestions, thereby augmenting both shopping and travel planning encounters. Evidence suggests that AIs influence on consumer behavior leads to heightened purchase intentions and increased levels of overall customer satisfaction within online retail scenarios (Xulong Dai et al.). Analogously, the tourism industry stands to gain from personalized travel recommendations that are based on historical behaviors and established preferences, thus improving the consumer experience. By responding to the specific needs of individual consumers, brands are able to foster a sense of value and uniqueness that is critical for achieving differentiation in an overcrowded market. This strategic application of predictive analytics not only exerts a favorable impact on consumer decisions but also strengthens brand loyalty and encourages repeat patronage, which are essential elements for enduring success within the tourism sector.Moreover, apart from enhancing marketing methodologies and personalizing consumer interactions, predictive analytics contributes to facilitating adept decision-making across various organizational echelons within tourism enterprises. By generating predictive models derived from both historical data and current market trends, brands can execute informed decisions pertinent to inventory management, pricing tactics, and promotional initiatives. Research underscores that effectively deploying predictive analytics has the potential to shorten the transition interval between lead qualification and conversion, thus heightening overall operational efficiency (O. Stankevych et al.). For businesses within the tourism sector, this translates into the capacity to react promptly to fluctuations in market demand and shifts in consumer behavior, which are particularly critical in an industry characterized by rapid transformation. Furthermore, the ethical dimensions concerning AI and data utilization accentuate the necessity for transparent practices in order to uphold consumer trust. Organizations that utilize predictive analytics in a responsible manner are better positioned to align their offerings with consumer anticipations, which cultivates a favorable brand image while simultaneously ensuring sustainable growth within the tourism landscape.

IV. ENHANCING BRANDING STRATEGIES THROUGH AI

In the context in which brands are striving to set themselves apart in a densely populated market, artificial intelligence (AI) has arisen as a significant instrumental resource in reconstructing branding methodologies, particularly within the tourism domain. By leveraging data-based insights, enterprises have the capability to fine-tune their branding initiatives to cater to the precise wishes and preferences of their intended demographics. Such technological advancement facilitates the crafting of increasingly tailored customer experiences through predictive analytics that evaluate behavioral patterns of consumers. This instrument aids in uncovering trends and preferences which may elude human marketers, consequently allowing brands to formulate narratives that are more resonant and alluring. According to the outcomes derived from the thorough literature examination, the broader application of AI not merely elevates brand identity but also nurtures emotional bonds between consumers and brands, eventually propelling customer loyalty ((Yolanda Masnita et al., p. 120-140)).Moreover, the integration of chatbots and AI-centric customer service frameworks can considerably affect a brand's efficiency within the tourism sector. AI resources supply immediate support around the clock, ensuring that consumers are equipped with help during crucial phases of their travel planning endeavors. Chatbots enable unobstructed interactions by resolving customer queries, suggesting customized travel itineraries, and administering bookings, thereby contributing to a gratifying customer experience. Investigations have revealed that these AI implementations can mediate the dynamics between technology involvement and customer allegiance by furnishing swift and precise responses to questions, thus mitigating potential friction points ((Arman Khan et al., p. 657-671)). As a result, brands that adeptly enact AI-focused customer engagement strategies have a higher likelihood of amplifying customer satisfaction, which in turn fortifies brand reputation and loyalty. In addition, the analytical prowess of AI equips brands with the means to incessantly refine their marketing approaches. Through the scrutiny of consumer responses and engagement data, brands acquire immediate insights that aid in the design of more impactful branding campaigns. By utilizing such insights, organizations can identify content that excels, comprehend the efficacy of multiple marketing channels, and shift strategies in accordance with the evolving consumer preferences. The focus on decision-making driven by data corresponds with the necessity for brands to sustain agility and responsiveness within an ever-changing landscape. As delineated in the existing scholarly work, embracing AI not merely spurs innovation in branding but also augments operational effectiveness, eventually contributing to a fortified market stance in the fiercely competitive tourism environment ((Yolanda Masnita et al., p. 120-140)). In summary, AI holds a pivotal significance in enhancing branding methodologies, paving the path for a more individualized and impactful strategy within the tourism sector.

A. AI in Content Creation and Marketing

The incorporation of artificial intelligence into content production and marketing is fundamentally altering the ways in which brands engage with their audiences. By utilizing insights derived from data, AI is capable of generating customized content that directly addresses the preferences and actions of specific consumer segments. This intricate comprehension enables brands within the tourism domain to adjust their messaging—be it through social media updates, blog entries, or email outreach—to resonate more profoundly with prospective travelers. Consequently, such customization not only improves user experiences but also cultivates more robust emotional ties between consumers and brands, a vital consideration in the competitive landscape of tourism. Additionally, the automatic creation of compelling content allows brands to uphold a stable online presence, which is essential for remaining pertinent and memorable as travelers make vacation plans.The aspect of automation transcends simple content creation; it also assists in the execution of sophisticated marketing tactics via advanced data analysis. AI instruments possess the ability to scrutinize extensive datasets to detect trends and foresee consumer actions, which empowers brands to refine their campaigns promptly. This analytical capability assures that marketing initiatives are flexible and reactive, particularly necessary in the fast-paced tourism landscape where consumer inclinations can alter swiftly. Brands can engage in A/B testing with greater efficiency, making adjustments to content styles and messaging channels to enhance user engagement and conversion success rates. By leveraging predictive analytics, tourism brands are better equipped to foresee peak travel times or changes in consumer attitudes, thus allowing strategies to be proactive rather than merely reactive (Seongseop (Sam) Kim et al.). This degree of responsiveness is a noteworthy advantage within a marketplace defined by variable demand.Furthermore, the ethical ramifications of employing AI for content creation warrant critical scrutiny, particularly regarding authenticity and transparency. As brands make use of AI-produced content, they confront the difficulty of ensuring that their communications possess a human element, as excessively automated exchanges risk resulting in a disconnect with the audience. Maintaining transparency regarding the application of AI tools can help alleviate doubt, given that consumers increasingly seek authentic relationships in brand interactions. Tourism brands, in particular, must tread carefully on the fine line between efficiency and authenticity; failure to achieve this balance could result in alienation of audiences who prioritize personalized, human-oriented experiences. Therefore, while AI offers countless prospects for refining content production and marketing, it is crucial for brands to be mindful of ethical considerations to uphold trust and authenticity within their customer engagements (Seongseop (Sam) Kim et al.).

B. Automation of Customer Engagement

The expanding sphere of customer engagement is being significantly altered by automation technologies, especially in the tourism industry. Automated systems, including chatbots and customer relationship management (CRM) software, enable instantaneous interactions with potential travelers, letting brands offer quick replies to questions, lessen waiting periods, and provide tailored communication based on user habits and preferences. This alteration not only improves customer satisfaction but also optimizes operational efficiency, permitting brands to use their human resources for more intricate or nuanced customer dealings. As automation advancements continue, the integration of artificial intelligence (AI) tools into customer engagement plans has transitioned from being an option to becoming essential for tourism brands striving to retain competitiveness within a crowded marketplace. Moreover, automating customer engagement creates opportunities for the gathering and assessment of significant data volumes which can guide strategic marketing actions. By utilizing insights gleaned from customer interactions, brands are able to hone their outreach initiatives, customize promotional materials, and more accurately forecast travel patterns. For example, these automated systems are capable of monitoring user engagement and preferences across diverse platforms, allowing brands to effectuate precise audience segmentation and supply highly pertinent content. This data-informed technique shifts the conventional one-size-fits-all marketing approaches, enabling tourism brands to cultivate deeper connections with their audiences (Correia et al.). As a result, the enriched customer experience resulting from thoughtful automation not only propels loyalty but also fosters repeat patronage, thereby amplifying brand equity in a competitive environment.Notwithstanding the many benefits linked with automated customer engagement, there are hurdles that still require thorough contemplation. The threat of compromising the human element in customer interactions poses a notable concern, as excessively automated systems may disenfranchise customers who value personalized communication. Effective execution necessitates striking a balance between automation and human intervention, assuring that brand messaging retains empathy and resonates with customer expectations. Additionally, brands must also address potential data privacy challenges stemming from the extensive data gathering practices that typify automated frameworks. As tourism brands endeavor to capitalize on automation advantages, they must simultaneously partake in open dialogues with their customers about the use of their data, thereby nurturing trust and enhancing a favorable brand image within a changing marketplace (Correia et al.).

C. Brand Positioning and Competitive Advantage

In order to formulate a strong brand positioning strategy within the tourism sector, it is essential to possess a detailed grasp of customer expectations alongside the competitive environment. This consideration becomes particularly relevant as artificial intelligence (AI) rises to prominence as an essential instrument for collecting and scrutinizing data integral to brand distinction. Through sophisticated analytical methods, enterprises can recognize distinct customer inclinations and modify their offerings consequently, which not merely improves customer experience but also fortifies brand fidelity. For example, utilizing AI-based insights allows tourism entities to develop individualized suggestions that resonate with travelers, ensuring that these consumers perceive themselves as acknowledged and esteemed. Such a degree of personalization affords brands a strategic upper hand, enabling them to secure a unique position in consumer perception, which ultimately cultivates a more durable market presence over time. Therefore, a meticulously articulated brand positioning strategy, enhanced by AI, becomes crucial in the fiercely competitive tourism arena. Cultivating a competitive advantage compels brands to differentiate themselves and adeptly utilize their unique selling propositions against competing entities within the industry. In instances of community-centered tourism offerings, brands can harness AI to evaluate rival tactics and modify their messaging dynamically. For instance, by employing AI to track online sentiment and engagement about competitors, tourism brands can fine-tune their narratives to accentuate local culture, sustainability, or exceptional experiences that resonate with the eco-conscious travelers of today. This flexible methodology guarantees that brands are not simply reacting but are, instead, taking proactive steps to secure market presence. Furthermore, a robust brand narrative, bolstered by data derived from AI, can promote heightened customer trust and credibility, which are vital for upholding a distinguished competitive advantage in an environment marked by continuous transformations and advancing technologies.In conclusion, the relationship between brand positioning and competitive advantage grows increasingly interconnected in an age wherein AI is pervasive. As tourism firms take advantage of machine learning algorithms and predictive analytics, they become capable of forecasting trends and shifting consumer behaviors, thus granting them the flexibility to readjust their brand tactics. This capacity to adjust in tune with real-time data reinforces the brand's significance and attractiveness, placing it advantageously within the market. Moreover, as traveler preferences turn towards authentic and individualized experiences, brands that adopt AI-driven methodologies are disposed to satisfy these needs more effectively, thus solidifying their competitive advantage. Therefore, the incorporation of AI into brand positioning not only boosts operational efficiency but also guarantees ongoing growth and differentiation for enterprises in the ever-evolving tourism sector (Johnny Ch Lok)(Johnny Ch Lok).

V. THE ROLE OF SOCIAL MEDIA AND AI

The ongoing dynamic relation amid social media and artificial intelligence (AI) has significantly altered branding approaches in the tourism industry. As consumers engage more with travel-related material online, tourism brands face the challenge of effectively grabbing attention amid an overwhelming influx of information. AI technologies, especially in the realms of data analytics and behavioral targeting, permit brands to customize their messaging according to distinct preferences, thereby enriching consumer experiences. For instance, AI is capable of scrutinizing user interactions on social media, enabling targeted marketing initiatives that ensure advertisements connect with particular audience segments. This degree of personalization does not merely fortify the brand-consumer rapport but also propels superior engagement rates and conversion figures, illustrating a noteworthy departure from conventional, generic strategies. The significance of AI within the advertising domain, predominantly on social media platforms, is substantial and cannot be overlooked. Cutting-edge machine learning algorithms are now essential in fine-tuning ad targeting and optimizing return on investment (ROI) for tourism brands. Recent studies have showcased that campaigns utilizing AI-driven targeting algorithms resulted in considerably enhanced ROI across numerous sectors, including tourism and hospitality (Lin Shan). Through the utilization of the vast datasets generated on social media, brands can deploy sophisticated computational methods that boost ad effectiveness. This transition not only augments the efficacy of marketing investments but also promotes a more individualized user experience. Consequently, AI-informed advertising emerges as an essential mechanism for brands aiming to sustain a competitive advantage within an overcrowded marketplace.In conclusion, social media serves as an essential platform for cultivating brand loyalty and advocacy, a role further magnified by the capabilities of AI. Engaging content, which strikes a chord with targeted demographics, can be shared seamlessly across various platforms, forging a community around the brand. Additionally, when AI algorithms assess social media interactions, they can uncover patterns and consumer sentiments that brands can harness to refine their marketing methodologies. The dual-role functionality of AI—as both a tool for analysis and a promoter of engagement—exemplifies its critical position in contemporary branding endeavors. Recent research examining the evolutionary impact of generative AI technologies within the hospitality sector has emphasized that merging social media strategies with AI engenders a notable enhancement in brand visibility and consumer engagement (Marianna Sigala). Therefore, the collaboration between social media and AI is essential for effective branding in a progressively digital-oriented tourism context.

A. AI Algorithms in Social Media Marketing

The incorporation of AI algorithms into social media marketing has significantly altered the manner in which brands interact with their audiences, especially within the competitive sphere of tourism. Through the utilization of data analytics and machine learning, businesses are enabled to customize marketing strategies that align with particular consumer preferences and behaviors. These algorithms process large quantities of user-generated content alongside engagement metrics to forecast trends, thereby recommending optimal content creation and scheduling times. This detailed understanding equips tourism brands to adjust their messaging dynamically, guaranteeing enhanced visibility and relevance. As a result, organizations can elevate brand loyalty and customer satisfaction by nurturing more profound connections via tailored interactions, which ultimately strengthens their competitive positioning within the market.Moreover, AI algorithms advance the segmentation and targeting of audiences in unprecedented ways. By discerning elaborate patterns in social media interactions and user demographics, companies can formulate hyper-targeted campaigns aimed at specific consumer cohorts. For example, an AI-supported tool might detect an increase in interest regarding eco-tourism among a certain demographic, leading brands to craft content that highlights sustainable travel opportunities. Predictive analytics further empower marketers to foresee customer needs, which permits timely engagement and offers that align with potential travelers' concerns or interests. Collectively, these functionalities not only enhance conversion rates but also foster a dedicated customer base that perceives the brand as understanding and valuable (Correia et al.).As the evolution of AI persists, its influence on shaping social media marketing strategies within the tourism sector is projected to escalate. The ability for real-time data analysis guarantees that campaigns can remain flexible and responsive to changing market dynamics and consumer sentiments. Additionally, ethical considerations related to data privacy and algorithmic transparency take precedence as brands apply AI technologies. Achieving an equilibrium between leveraging AI for targeted marketing and sustaining consumer trust will delineate effective branding strategies in the future. Brands that adopt these sophisticated technologies while emphasizing ethical practices are likely to thrive in the creation of significant marketing campaigns that resonate with their audience, establishing new benchmarks of excellence within the tourism industry (Correia et al.).

B. Influencer Marketing and AI Analytics

The merging of influencer marketing alongside artificial intelligence (AI) analytics provides a noteworthy chance for tourism brands to boost their outreach efforts and engage customers more effectively. Influencers play a crucial role as intermediaries between brands and potential customers, utilizing their social media platforms to build trust and authenticity. By adopting AI analytics, tourism brands can refine their influencer collaborations via data-informed insights regarding audience demographics, engagement statistics, and the efficacy of content. This alignment of strategies ensures promotional endeavors resonate more profoundly with the intended audience, thereby heightening conversion rates. Furthermore, insights derived from AI foster ongoing optimization of influencer initiatives, allowing brands to responsively modify their tactics based on real-time evaluations of consumer actions and inclinations.AI analytics not solely aids brands by enhancing the selection of influencers but also boosts the comprehensive efficacy of marketing initiatives. Recent research indicates that integrating big data and machine learning methodologies into digital marketing can substantially improve the performance of influencer-related tactics (İbrahim Halil Efendioğlu). This transition enables brands to accurately forecast consumer behavior, adjusting marketing messaging to synchronize with emerging trends and preferences. Therefore, AI proves to be an indispensable instrument in pinpointing critical performance metrics, providing a systematic approach for brands to assess the effectiveness and engagement of influencers. This analytical methodology is especially vital in the tourism sector, where consumer preferences can change swiftly owing to external influences like seasonality and economic variations.Moreover, the ethical ramifications of utilizing AI analytics in influencer marketing are significant. As brands increasingly adopt data-informed strategies targeting consumers, issues regarding privacy and transparency have emerged prominently. The digital arena is riddled with obstacles related to the ethical handling of consumer data, rendering it crucial for tourism brands to emphasize responsible analytical practices. Engaging with these ethical dimensions promotes consumer trust and positions brands as responsible entities in the digital environment. Various academic discussions, which include analyses of current social media environments, have highlighted the importance of addressing such ethical issues for sustained brand credibility (Outi Niininen). In conclusion, balancing cutting-edge marketing approaches with ethical accountability is vital for tourism brands aiming to prosper in a market increasingly governed by data.

C. Brand Reputation Management through AI

In the swiftly changing environment of digital technology today, the incorporation of artificial intelligence (AI) into the management of brand reputation has become progressively essential, especially in the domain of tourism. Organizations are taking advantage of AI mechanisms to observe public sentiment and administer their reputations in an efficient manner. Through the utilization of natural language processing as well as machine learning algorithms, businesses are enabled to process large volumes of online data, which in turn assists them in evaluating customer perceptions and recognizing potential crisis scenarios at an early stage. This anticipatory method permits enterprises not only to react quickly to unfavorable feedback but also to bolster positive engagements, thus enhancing brand loyalty. The capability to interact with consumers in real-time cultivates a feeling of transparency and trust, which is crucial for reputation management within the highly competitive tourism sector.Additionally, the significance of AI in amplifying brand image ought not to be overlooked, as is evidenced by its favorable correlation with project success and customer engagement (Sitara Ali). By utilizing AI-centered predictive analytics, companies within the tourism industry can establish customized marketing strategies that resonate with their intended audience. Such strategies frequently lead to heightened customer engagement, which directly impacts brand reputation. Experiences that are personalized, enabled by AI technologies, empower brands to not only meet but also surpass customer expectations, thus converting occasional visitors into loyal patrons. As businesses persist in leveraging AI capabilities, they are able to forecast customer needs with greater precision, consequently improving their overall service quality and nurturing a solid brand identity that is well-received in an oversaturated market.Besides overseeing current reputational assets, AI also significantly contributes to shaping future perceptions of brands operating in the tourism industry. Recent inquiries into the influence of AI on marketing have underscored that this technology fosters innovative usages that enhance consumer experiences (Yakup Durmaz et al., p. 21-30). By scrutinizing customer interactions and preferences, AI is capable of aiding brands in creating distinct service offerings that set them apart from rival entities. Furthermore, the capacity to monitor and react to shifts in consumer conduct places brands in a position to uphold a positive reputation within a fluid environment. Ultimately, the effective application of AI in the domain of brand reputation management relies on a tactical methodology that synchronizes technological progress with consumer anticipations, thereby ensuring brands not just survive but also flourish in the transforming tourism landscape.

VI. CHALLENGES OF IMPLEMENTING AI IN TOURISM BRANDING

One of the primary challenges encountered when integrating artificial intelligence (AI) into tourism branding pertains to the swiftly changing characteristics of technology itself. This changing landscape demands regular updates both to educational curricula and to the skillsets of industry professionals. The literature indicates that, "the rapid evolution of AI necessitates frequent curriculum updates and faculty development" (Bulent Aydin et al.). This results in a unique tension for tourism enterprises that must balance immediate operational requirements alongside the enduring need for a proficient workforce. The dilemma is not merely about the inclusion of AI solutions, but also about ensuring that personnel are adequately prepared to employ these technologies efficiently for branding aims. An inadequately trained workforce could lead to less than optimal deployment of AI, thereby jeopardizing branding initiatives and culminating in consumer dissatisfaction.Moreover, another major concern is the ethical aspects relating to AI's application in tourism branding. The adoption of AI technologies gives rise to inquiries regarding data privacy and the risk of biased algorithms that might distort brand messages. Companies need to be vigilant in guaranteeing that data collection and usage adhere to privacy laws and ethical practices. Although the use of AI in marketing can facilitate targeted campaigns that resonate with potential customers, it might inadvertently alienate other demographics. Additionally, should employees regard AI as a threat to their job security—especially in a sector already encountering significant turnover rates—this perception can negatively influence the brand image. Research highlights that AI can foster enhancements in employee retention via greater job satisfaction and career prospects, but this seems paradoxical when brand strategies appear to favor technology over human engagement (O. C. Yilmazdogan).Lastly, the incorporation of AI within tourism branding frequently necessitates a collaborative effort among diverse stakeholders, which can prove to be intricate and laborious. The implementation of AI is not merely a technical endeavor; it requires interdisciplinary cooperation among marketers, IT specialists, and management. This need for collaboration can result in communication failures and discrepancies in strategic goals. Furthermore, a digital divide exists that must be confronted, as not all stakeholders possess equitable access to necessary technology or the skills to deploy it effectively. Such inequalities can obstruct the overall branding schema, diminishing the potential advantages that AI could provide in this sector. Therefore, while AI presents significant promise in advancing tourism branding, its successful incorporation is replete with difficulties that necessitate meticulous planning and efficient communication.

A. Ethical Considerations and Data Privacy

In the process of examining the nexus between artificial intelligence (AI) and branding within the tourism domain, one must acknowledge ethical considerations and data privacy as significant matters of concern. The adoption of AI tools aimed at engaging customers and customizing services typically requires substantial data gathering, which raises essential queries regarding consent and ownership. As tourists are progressively disclosing personal details, it becomes incumbent upon organizations to recognize their ethical duty to protect this information. Neglecting to maintain privacy can result not only in the erosion of consumer trust but also in the detriment of brand reputation, potentially leading to irreparable damage to relationships in the highly competitive tourism arena. The imperative for clear and informed consent spotlights the delicate equilibrium between cutting-edge marketing methodologies and the ethical responsibilities surrounding data management, necessitating that brands emphasize ethics in their AI-centric operations.Additionally, the swift advancement of generative AI solutions in tourism industries heightens the risks associated with data, which encompasses privacy infringements and unintended information releases. Recent assessments of the risks linked to generative AI reveal that the intricate nature of contemporary data processing technologies often renders compliance with existing legal regulations difficult (cite41). Therefore, while AI holds the potential to enrich branding experiences through tailored offerings, it simultaneously calls for stringent data governance frameworks to navigate the convoluted domain of privacy and consumer safeguarding. The emerging challenge lies not solely in adhering to regulations, but also in cultivating a culture of accountability within institutions employing AI, ensuring that technological progress does not undermine the ethical underpinnings of a brand.Healthcare sectors provide an insightful case study for establishing effective accountability mechanisms in the application of AI technologies, particularly related to digital health technologies (DHTs) (Brenna Loufek). By incorporating internal review frameworks, exemplified by Mayo Clinic's Software as a Medical Device Review Board, the concentration shifts toward upholding ethical norms in the integration of technology while concurrently innovating to fulfill customer needs. The tourism sector might draw insights from such models to create solid governance systems that evaluate AI applications, thereby encouraging responsible innovation in accordance with data protection best practices. As the AI landscape undergoes continuous transformation, the integration of elevated ethical benchmarks and thorough data privacy protocols will be critical for cultivating resilient tourism brands that not only entice consumers but also foster loyalty through transparency and trust.

B. Resistance to Change within Organizations

Organizational resistance to change is often rooted in a profound apprehension towards uncertainty, especially prevalent in sectors characterized by swift technological progress, such as tourism. As entities increasingly integrate artificial intelligence (AI) into their branding methodologies, personnel may interpret such modifications as jeopardies to their occupational stability or hierarchy. The process of assimilating AI technologies can appear intimidating, resulting in a significant number of employees being reluctant to adopt novel practices. Transitioning to a culture driven by innovation necessitates that leadership members actively interact with staff, assuaging anxieties and nurturing a milieu that promotes trial and imagination. As underscored in scholarly investigations, efficacious leadership is pivotal in engendering an environment where employees experience empowerment rather than trepidation, ultimately aiding in the reduction of resistance to change and supporting more seamless progressions towards AI incorporation in branding strategies (Antonius Ary Setyawan et al.).In addition, the complex interplay of social dynamics within organizations can intensify resistance to change. Employees may find solace in established practices and conventions, which renders the idea of employing AI tools for branding as potentially disruptive and unwelcome. This occurrence is particularly significant in the tourism industry, where interpersonal interactions frequently constitute the essence of customer experiences. Adequate change management mandates not merely the tackling of technological apprehensions but also the comprehension of the fundamental human elements contributing to resistance. By employing traditional human resource management methods, such as refining personnel structures and improving communication, organizations can mitigate resistance and ready teams for innovative approaches. Moreover, fostering a collective vision that harmonizes organizational principles with the deployment of AI can inspire employees to engage with change, thereby altering their views of AI into beneficial partners rather than adversaries (K. Kozak et al.).Lastly, addressing organizational resistance to change requires a sustained dedication to education and growth. For the effective application of AI in branding initiatives, organizations must allocate resources towards training frameworks that furnish employees with requisite competencies and assurance to effectively engage with these technologies. By underlining the opportunities for both personal and professional advancement that AI offers, organizations can modify perspectives and stimulate proactive involvement in the change process. Additionally, the incorporation of feedback systems allows staff members to articulate their concerns and contribute to the ongoing refinement of the branding strategy, promoting a sense of ownership regarding changes implemented. Such methodologies not only enhance the overall efficacy of the change initiative but also bolster resilience within the workforce. Ultimately, successful adaptation to AI in branding within the tourism domain relies on a multifaceted strategy that considers both technological and human dimensions, thereby ensuring a devoted team prepared to accept change.

C. Cost Implications of AI Integration

The incorporation of artificial intelligence (AI) in the tourism industry possesses substantial financial ramifications that extend beyond mere upfront technology investments. The initial investment costs associated with AI tools can be considerable, particularly regarding software procurement and system deployment; however, these expenditures might be recuperated through future savings. AI systems improve operational efficacy via the automation of mundane tasks like customer service handling and data processing, subsequently lowering labor expenditures. As highlighted in a research study pertaining to healthcare, entities that implement AI technology frequently enjoy enhanced operational workflows, enabling personnel to concentrate on intricate tasks (cite45). By reallocating human resources to focus on strategic sectors such as brand development and consumer interaction, enterprises can optimize workforce utilization, which can ultimately escalate income generation. Additionally, the incorporation of AI promotes superior decision-making by yielding data-driven insights that can markedly diminish expenses tied to marketing and customer acquisition. Through the automation of data examination, tourism companies can refine their advertising approaches, honing in on specific demographics with accuracy. This targeted methodology minimizes the financial wastage associated with broad marketing campaigns that produce minimal outcomes. The insights derived from AI technologies can also guide pricing frameworks and promotional strategies, ensuring alignment with market demand and consumer inclinations. In the realm of conventional randomized controlled trials within medical studies, the significance of interdisciplinary collaboration in employing advanced analytics resonates with the necessity for tourism enterprises to merge AI insights with strategic marketing initiatives, thereby transcending the confines of traditional methodologies (cite46). This confluence not only bolsters brand positioning but also enhances overall fiscal performance.Ultimately, although the initial financial outlay for AI may evoke concerns regarding immediate economic pressure, it is paramount to acknowledge the strategic benefits accompanying early adoption. With the tourism sector confronting escalating competition, entities that adeptly utilize AI technology are likely to realize a considerable competitive advantage. Through the provision of personalized experiences and improved customer interactions, AI may foster enhanced brand loyalty and repeat clientele, which are crucial for enduring viability in the tourism field. The heightened consumer satisfaction stemming from AI-driven services can also lead to favorable word-of-mouth marketing, often surpassing the efficacy of conventional promotional tactics. Therefore, the financial implications of AI integration should be analyzed through a broader perspective, understanding that while initial costs may be elevated, the possibilities for diminishing operational costs and enriching customer engagement represent a persuasive argument for investment.

VII. CASE STUDIES OF AI IN TOURISM BRANDING

Innovative case studies signify how tourism brands are utilizing AI in order to enhance their marketing strategies, creating a model for achievement within an ever more competitive context. A prominent illustration is found in the employment of AI-generated content aimed at constructing individualized travel experiences for consumers. By employing Natural Language Processing (NLP) and machine learning algorithms, brands are able to assess customer inclinations and actions to provide customized suggestions, thereby fundamentally altering the customer journey from a state of passive consumption to one of active involvement. This methodology not only boosts customer contentment but also cultivates brand loyalty and trust, ensuring the brand remains foremost in the minds of travelers when they ponder their next adventure. The assertions derived from existing scholarly works emphasize the importance of such personalization in crafting unforgettable travel encounters that resonate across varied consumer segments (Anchal Jaiswal).Moreover, the application of AI in predictive analytics enhances the branding of tourism by yielding insights regarding emergent travel trends and consumer behaviors. The integration of sophisticated techniques such as sentiment analysis enables brands to surveil discussion on social media and user-generated content, allowing them to discern factors that either attract or repel potential clientele. This data-driven methodology permits businesses to customize their branding initiatives in real-time, adjusting marketing endeavors based on instantaneous consumer responses and market dynamics. Case studies highlighting brands that have adeptly applied these AI instruments have documented a significant rise in user engagement and conversion rates, showcasing the essential function of prompt and pertinent responses in the branding mechanism. As elucidates, the fusion of AI with customer information is crucial for gaining a competitive advantage, equipping brands to deliver inventive solutions that enrich the overall customer journey and engagement.Lastly, the ethical considerations relevant to the incorporation of AI in tourism branding cannot be dismissed. Although the advantages of AI in personalizing services are apparent, challenges pertaining to data privacy and user consent persist prominently. For instance, it is imperative for brands to assure transparent data usage practices while relying on AI technologies to scrutinize consumer data. Neglecting to confront these ethical quandaries could result in a deterioration of consumer trust, which would undermine the beneficial branding impacts attained through AI. As enterprises navigate these intricate issues, it becomes vital to establish frameworks that emphasize ethical protocols while leveraging the advantages of AI. The reviewed case studies indicate that brands which are cognizant of ethical matters are more inclined to cultivate enduring relationships with customers, ultimately leading to prolonged success within the tourism industry.

A. Successful AI Implementations in Leading Brands

Prominent entities within the tourism sector are increasingly engaging in the utilization of artificial intelligence to augment their marketing tactics and optimize operational efficiencies. As an illustration, travel firms deploy AI-powered chatbots to furnish customer support around the clock, facilitating personalized engagement with prospective travelers. This deployment not only refines operational processes but also cultivates a more captivating experience for clients, thereby nurturing brand allegiance. In addition, data analytics—underpinned by AI—affords these entities the capacity to extract insights from consumer conduct, resulting in more precisely targeted promotional initiatives. Through the employment of historical data alongside real-time analytics, organizations can customize their offerings to align with consumer tastes, thereby ensuring that their branding achieves a resonance on a more profound level. Consequently, efficacious AI implementations empower tourism brands to preserve agility and pertinence within an intensely competitive arena.As the tourism domain contends with escalating intricacies, the integration of artificial intelligence offers a mechanism for refining decision-making frameworks. The incorporation of AI within administrative information systems (AIS) has manifested notable enhancements across assorted operational facets. For example, (Noor.Z. Mahmood et al., p. 1-7) accentuates the dynamic interaction between AI and AIS, underscoring the ramifications on administrative efficiency and decision-making. Prominent brands that adopt this amalgamation can markedly elevate their reactivity to fluctuations in the market and requirements of clientele. These advancements may be realized through varying manifestations, such as the adoption of automated revenue management methodologies aimed at optimizing profitability, or the application of predictive analytics to anticipate travel patterns. Thus, the convergence of AI and AIS not only bolsters operational efficiencies but also assists brands in sustaining a competitive advantage by empowering informed, data-centric choices that influence branding strategies.Nevertheless, the prospective advantages brought forth by AI are accompanied by an array of ethical dilemmas, particularly within the tourism industry. The ascendance of generative artificial intelligence evokes concerns pertaining to data privacy, algorithmic impartiality, and the obsolescence of conventional roles within the field. As referenced in (T. Dogru et al.), the adoption of AI necessitates a conscientious reflection on its socio-economic ramifications for diverse stakeholders. Leading brands must navigate these multifaceted issues by instituting ethical frameworks and proactive policies that secure equitable practices. By prioritizing transparency and accountability in the application of AI, tourism brands can establish trust with consumers, ultimately bolstering their brand reputation. Promoting an ethical perspective not only alleviates potential backlash but also positions brands as responsible frontrunners in the embrace of transformative technologies within the industry.

B. Lessons Learned from Failed AI Initiatives

The various industries during the COVID-19 pandemic confronted significant challenges that brought to light essential insights pertaining to the integration of artificial intelligence (AI) initiatives. Organizations that hastily integrated AI without a thorough grasp of their distinct necessities or capabilities frequently faced substantial setbacks. For example, airlines that sought quick digitization of operations during the crisis found it difficult to meld AI systems that were not well-suited for their operational models. This lack of fit not only squandere resources but also eroded confidence in the technology's promise. Successful implementation necessitates profound understanding of both organizational objectives and customer requirements, as demonstrated by the setbacks observed in the aviation sector amid the pandemic (Elen Paraskevi Paraschi). As firms in the tourism domain contemplate these setbacks, it is imperative to emphasize strategic alignment to ensure that forthcoming AI innovations augment branding and customer engagements instead of detracting from them. Furthermore, it is vital to acknowledge the environmental and external elements that impact the effectiveness of AI deployments. AI initiatives do not exist in isolation from broader socio-economic conditions; the pandemic illustrated how external crises can obstruct even the most carefully crafted projects. Research indicates that successful digital transformation depends on adaptive frameworks that are capable of evolving in response to changing circumstances (Guojun Sawyer He). Within the tourism sector, this entails constructing flexible AI systems that can adapt to real-time data and shifting consumer behaviors. Additionally, promoting collaboration between organizations and technology providers can enhance the alignment of AI tools with market requirements. By recognizing these external pressures during the planning stages, tourism brands have the opportunity to mitigate risks linked with AI initiatives and improve their capacity to recover from unforeseen obstacles.Ultimately, it is essential for organizations to regard unsuccessful AI initiatives as avenues for learning that yield insights into the intricacies of digital transformation. Reflecting on previous failures encourages a culture of ongoing improvement and innovation. It is imperative for tourism brands to practice reflective methodologies, including evaluations post-implementation and gathering stakeholder feedback, to pinpoint the fundamental causes of setbacks. Adopting iterative learning methodologies permits organizations to recalibrate their strategies, consequently laying the groundwork for successful AI incorporation in forthcoming efforts. As AI technologies continue to develop, the insights harvested from these failures will act as a cornerstone for crafting resilient branding strategies that not only meet current consumer expectations but also anticipate the forthcoming market demands.

C. Comparative Analysis of Different Approaches

Within the realm of tourism branding, the leveraging of artificial intelligence manifests in diverse guises, each possessing unique repercussions for stakeholder engagement and brand interpretation. A notable methodology encompasses the utilization of AI-infused personalized marketing techniques, which harness consumer data to furnish customized suggestions and experiences. This particular tactic not only amplifies customer satisfaction but also cultivates loyalty by synchronizing brand offerings with consumer inclinations. Conversely, brands that place a premium on automation for operational efficacy—such as through the usage of chatbots within customer service—might unintentionally diminish personal interactions, which could alienate select consumer segments. Consequently, while both methodologies strive to bolster brand performance, the former accentuates personalized engagement, while the latter zeroes in on operational effectiveness, culminating in disparate branding outcomes amid the fierce competition characteristic of tourism.Additionally, machine learning algorithms represent a noteworthy avenue in tourism branding, enhancing decision-making protocols by evaluating extensive datasets to forecast consumer trends. This quantitative scrutiny empowers brands to foresee shifts in consumer behaviors, thus enabling proactive modifications in marketing strategies. Conversely, the creative maneuvers of AI, including generative design in promotional content, permit brands to craft pioneering visual narratives that seize attention and distinguish themselves in an oversaturated market. While data-centric tactics may yield more judicious choices, the creative applications of AI nurture brand identity and emotional connectivity, accentuating the conflict between data-driven and creativity-oriented methodologies within branding strategies. Therefore, brands adept at effectively merging these approaches are poised to enhance both engagement and retention within the swiftly transforming tourism milieu.The efficacy of these AI-oriented methodologies is also contingent upon the ethical deliberations pertinent to their execution. Brands employing customer data for personalized experiences must deftly navigate the precarious equilibrium between privacy and personalization. An overreliance on AI predictions or automated systems could provoke adverse reactions if consumers sense they have been unduly influenced or deceived. Ethical marketing principles ought to underscore transparency, guaranteeing that consumers comprehend how their data informs their experiences. Likewise, brands applying creative AI tactics grapple with the challenge of upholding authenticity, as excessively automated content risks eroding brand voice and uniqueness. Hence, the comparative examination of these strategies accentuates the imperative for tourism sector brands to harmonize their AI methodologies with ethical benchmarks, all while aiming to optimize both engagement and operational efficiency (Ray Tinston).

VIII. FUTURE TRENDS IN AI AND TOURISM BRANDING

As artificial intelligence (AI) persists in gaining recognition across a variety of industries, its incorporation into the realm of tourism branding is likely to bring about significant changes in the manner in which destinations are advertised and experienced. Sophisticated AI algorithms are capable of examining extensive amounts of consumer data to pinpoint inclinations, trends, and nascent markets, ultimately granting brands the capacity to tailor their offerings. This movement not only improves customer engagement by providing customized experiences but also aids in the formulation of flexible, data-informed marketing methods. Such abilities empower brands to convey their distinct value propositions more efficiently, nurturing deeper emotional ties with prospective travelers. Employing AI, tourism brands can navigate the competitive environment more adeptly, ensuring their communications resonate with increasingly discerning consumers.Looking forward, one can anticipate the proliferation of immersive technologies in the sphere of tourism branding, especially through virtual reality (VR) and augmented reality (AR) encounters. These innovations might significantly alter how destinations are showcased to potential tourists, thereby modifying consumer perceptions and anticipations. Virtual showrooms, as indicated in (Shirin Hajahmadi), serve as a case study demonstrating how VR can be used to present compelling narratives that both highlight a destination's heritage and culture while also actively engaging users in participative experiences. Moreover, as AI technologies progress, the incorporation of machine learning could allow brands to perpetually refine these immersive offerings, crafting highly individualized promotional content. Therefore, thanks to the collaboration between AI and immersive technology, tourism branding could surpass traditional marketing methods, yielding richer, more enticing experiences that cultivate customer loyalty.The impact of AI on tourism branding is further emphasized by its capacity to bolster operational efficiencies via predictive analytics and consumer insights. As noted in (Oyshik Bhowmik), the employment of AI methodologies across numerous sectors has revolutionized operations by automating standard tasks and furnishing actionable intelligence. In the context of tourism, this might translate into enhanced resource distribution, better service provision, and the ability to foresee customer requirements more accurately. As brands cultivate more profound connections with their audiences through immediate engagement and adaptive marketing strategies, they can enhance brand equity and trust. Additionally, the strategic application of AI is expected to contribute to the establishment of a sustainable tourism framework, allowing brands to express their dedication to responsible travel practices and social repercussions. By aligning innovation with societal accountability, tourism brands can favorably position themselves in the eyes of an expanding demographic of conscientious consumers.

A. Emerging Technologies and Their Potential Impact

The swift advancement of digital technologies has notably altered the tourism sector, presenting a range of opportunities alongside challenges for the management of brands. Innovations like artificial intelligence, virtual reality, and big data analytics enable brands to customize experiences according to specific consumer preferences, which in turn may enhance customer engagement and loyalty. Systems powered by AI have the capability to analyze significant quantities of data to forecast travel trends and consumer behavior, which allows brands to develop personalized marketing initiatives that resonate deeply with intended audiences. Nevertheless, this reliance on technology prompts concerns regarding data privacy and security, compelling brands to find a satisfactory balance between personalization and the ethical application of consumer data. Brands that actively tackle these issues while weaving in emerging technologies are likely to achieve a competitive advantage within a bustling marketplace, ensuring they stay relevant and focused on customer needs in an increasingly digital environment.A further intriguing dimension regarding the technological integration in tourism branding is the influence of immersive experiences enabled by virtual reality (VR) and augmented reality (AR). Such tools permit potential travelers to engage with destinations and accommodations in novel and engaging ways, effectively diminishing the boundaries between pre-trip anticipations and actual experiences. For example, a travel brand might employ VR for virtual tours of hotels or attractions, which transforms marketing narratives from simple descriptions into captivating visual storytelling. This inventive approach not only boosts customer engagement but also nurtures deeper emotional ties to the brand, possibly resulting in heightened booking rates and referrals from customers. However, companies must be diligent to ensure that these technological displays stay authentic, as any inconsistencies between virtual experiences and real offerings might lead to consumer disillusionment and disengagement, which could ultimately compromise brand integrity (Salih SARIKAMIS).The ramifications of incorporating emerging technologies in tourism branding extend beyond solitary enterprises, impacting entire industry norms and consumer expectations. As brands implement advanced AI algorithms and immersive technologies, a competitive race emerges, compelling all industry players to engage in continuous innovation or face the risk of becoming outdated. This atmosphere promotes a culture of reinterpretation within the tourism sector, where brands are spurred to rethink their offerings to maintain relevance. For instance, destinations might be required to create extensive digital marketing plans that align with these technologies to effectively attract a tech-savvy audience. Additionally, as emerging technologies dynamically transform consumer behavior and preferences, it is crucial for brands to uphold agility within their strategies. This kind of adaptability not only fortifies brand loyalty but also positions companies to react better to market shifts, thus securing their foothold within the tourism landscape (Salih SARIKAMIS).

B. The Role of Virtual and Augmented Reality

The amalgamation of Virtual Reality (VR) along with Augmented Reality (AR) within the tourism industry demonstrates a pronounced transformation in the manner by which brands interact with consumers. Through the provision of immersive experiences, these technologies facilitate prospective travelers in the exploration of destinations that exceed conventional marketing strategies. For example, VR affords users the capability to virtually survey a hotel or tourist location from their own residences, thus augmenting their decision-making process. This experiential marketing strategy not only aids travelers in visualizing their journeys with greater clarity, but it also functions as a crucial element in branding, nurturing a more profound emotional association between consumers and destinations. The analysis herein indicates that the prospect of both AR and VR to fundamentally alter customer engagement is noteworthy, setting the stage for progressive branding approaches that underscore unique experiences (Thuong Dieu Nguyen).In addition, the utilization of AR and VR introduces practical applications that have fundamentally altered the customer experience within tourism. These technologies provide interactive elements, such as guided excursions enriched with digital data and animated historical narratives. By integrating real-world imagery with added digital layers, AR amplifies the informative quality of a destination, rendering it more attractive and instructional. This capacity not only captivates technology-oriented travelers but also meets the increasing consumer demand for tailored and interactive travel experiences. Furthermore, as discussed in the study, the adaptability and responsiveness of these technologies to market demands illustrate their capability to assist brands in setting themselves apart in a highly competitive environment, thus strengthening brand loyalty (Gurugram University, p. 1-89).However, notwithstanding the encouraging advantages, the incorporation of VR and AR within the tourism sector also encompasses a range of challenges that require attention. Elevated implementation expenses, in conjunction with the need for specialized personnel to develop and sustain these systems, present substantial obstacles for numerous businesses, particularly smaller organizations. Additionally, as nascent technologies progress, ethical issues concerning data privacy and user manipulation may emerge, necessitating judicious consideration and regulation. This requirement for oversight indicates that, although VR and AR possess considerable potential for enhancing branding methodologies in tourism, stakeholders must approach their integration with a comprehensive perspective that emphasizes sustainable and accountable use (Thuong Dieu Nguyen). Ultimately, a unified effort to tackle these challenges will be vital for realizing the complete potential of VR and AR in shaping the future of tourism branding.

C. Predictions for AI's Evolution in Branding

As advancements in AI technologies progress, the melding of these into branding strategies specifically within the tourism sector is poised to substantially alter the dynamics of how brands connect with consumers. The application of algorithms crafted for the analytical dissection of extensive consumer data allows brands to forge more individualized experiences, thereby notably augmenting both customer satisfaction and allegiance to the brand. Through the utilization of machine learning, marketers manifest a capacity to forecast consumer behavior with greater precision, adapting their promotional endeavors to align with distinct needs and preferences. This technological progression will not merely simplify marketing undertakings but also furnish a more intricate comprehension of audience demographics, empowering brands to formulate messages that resonate on more profound emotional frequencies. The nascent ability of AI to produce real-time insights accentuates its prospects of affecting branding, thereby generating avenues for innovation in the manner that tourism brands establish their presence within a saturated market. Moreover, the ethical ramifications accompanying the deployment of AI in branding are anticipated to escalate in importance. As automation ascends to a central role, issues associated with consumer privacy and data protection will catalyze brands to embrace transparent methodologies in their application of AI. This transition might necessitate a reassessment of tactics, emphasizing ethics in parallel with technological enhancement. Brands that take initiative in tackling these concerns are likely to bolster their public image, thereby reinforcing the trust and loyalty of consumers. For example, gaining insight into consumer dispositions regarding AI—particularly within service-centric realms like tourism—will be crucial to upholding favorable perceptions of the brand ((Seden Doğan et al.)). As the evolution of AI persists, it will be imperative for tourism brands to adeptly maneuver the subtle equilibrium between employing technology for competitive benefits and ensuring a responsible approach to consumer data utilization, whilst nurturing a sincere connection with their target audiences.Anticipating future developments, the function of generative AI in branding is destined to be integral to the transformation of consumer engagement strategies within the tourism landscape. The ability of AI to generate persuasive content at scale holds the potential to foster innovative branding methodologies, permitting brands to offer personalized experiences that connect with individuals on a more intimate level ((Muskan Satnaliwala)). Such advancements could fundamentally alter the narrative-building aspect of branding, rendering each consumer interaction as distinctly customized to their inclinations. Nevertheless, the challenge resides in preserving authenticity within automated communications. As brands wield generative AI, an emphasis on authenticity will be essential to sustain consumer confidence, ensuring that content produced by AI accurately embodies the values and principles of the brand. Thus, tourism brands are required to strategically exploit AI innovations while retaining the human elements that cultivate loyalty and engagement, thereby setting the pathway for a new epoch of branded experiences.

IX. THE IMPACT OF AI ON CUSTOMER EXPERIENCE

The amalgamation of artificial intelligence within the frameworks of customer experience strategies is effecting a metamorphosis within the branding dynamics of the tourism industry. Various AI technologies, which include but are not limited to chatbots and personalized recommendation systems, facilitate a more engaging and meaningful interaction between businesses and their clientele. For example, through the scrutiny of historical datasets and user inclinations, AI possesses the capability to curate bespoke travel recommendations, thus augmenting the trip planning stage while fostering an impression of individualized attention. This caliber of personalization contributes not merely to the enhancement of customer satisfaction but also to the cultivation of brand loyalty, as patrons perceive themselves as valued and comprehended entities. The immediacy with which AI-enabled support is accessible, operating around the clock, serves to mitigate frustration and elevate the overall service encounter, epitomizing the potential of technological innovations to bridge previously insurmountable gaps in customer service [extractedKnowledge1]. Moreover, the proficiency of AI in dissecting extensive datasets in real time equips businesses to proactively discern customer needs. Utilizing predictive analytics, brands are able to fine-tune their product offerings and make adjustments to marketing initiatives based on nascent trends and consumer behavioral patterns. For instance,

AI can recognize variances in travel inclination correlated with seasonal variations or global occurrences, thereby allowing tourism enterprises to react promptly with targeted promotional efforts. This adaptable methodology not only heightens customer engagement but also positions the brand as responsive and attuned to its target demographic. Furthermore, the integration of AI may streamline booking processes and bolster operational efficiency, consequently elevating the customer experience while fortifying favorable brand perceptions within a highly competitive marketplace (Nadda et al.).Nonetheless, despite the substantial advantages offered by AI in the enhancement of customer experience, certain challenges merit urgent attention. Issues surrounding data privacy and the ethical employment of customer information are exceedingly critical. As brands exploit AI for the accumulation and examination of personal data, they must traverse the delicate boundary between personalization and invasive practices. An overabundance of data gathering may induce consumer skepticism, potentially undermining brand reputation. It is crucial for stakeholders in the tourism sector to establish forthright communication regarding their data handling protocols and to prioritize the procurement of customer consent. In addition, the significance of the human element in customer service should not be entirely overshadowed by automated systems, as a considerable number of consumers continue to value human interactions. Striking a balance between the capabilities afforded by AI and genuine human engagement will prove indispensable for brands striving to foster a comprehensive and reliable customer experience (Nadda et al.).

A. Enhancing User Experience through AI Tools

The incorporation of AI mechanisms notably modifies the user experience pertaining to the tourism arena by delivering interactions and content individualized to distinct preferences. As elucidated in the investigation of artificial intelligence, implementations of AI, including chatbots alongside recommendation engines, exploit user data to fabricate experiences that are exceptionally tailored. For example, platforms driven by AI scrutinize customer conduct to foresee travel necessities and preferences, resulting in targeted propositions that augment user involvement. This approach that is tailored not only assists travelers in identifying fitting options but also nurtures a profound emotional bond with brands. By comprehending user inclinations and conduct, organizations are capable of fostering loyalty and trust, which are vitally important in an ecosystem characterized by intense competition. Abstractly, the amalgamation of AI technologies with strategies concentrated on user engagement culminates in a coherent experience that heightens customer satisfaction and allegiance to brands.In addition, AI mechanisms facilitate the optimization of operational workflows, which in turn directly contributes to an enhanced user experience by rendering interactions more streamlined and responsive. Enterprises are capable of employing real-time data analysis to oversee customer interactions and pinpoint difficulties throughout the user trajectory. As indicated in (Yuvika Gupta et al.), the amalgamation of AI enables enterprises to scrutinize domains necessitating enhancement in real time, permitting prompt modifications to services or experiential offerings. For instance, should a traveler consistently inquire about sustainable lodging, AI frameworks may give precedence to pertinent selections across digital platforms. This operational flexibility not only diminishes response intervals but also empowers brands to proactively tackle customer inquiries and issues, thus assuring a steady and gratifying user experience. Fundamentally, the uncontentious incorporation of AI into operational structures ameliorates service provision, accentuating the significance of user-oriented methodologies within digital marketing paradigms.Moreover, the employment of AI tools is instrumental in the aggregation and examination of user-generated data, which is crucial for the elevation of prospective interactions within the tourism brand milieu. Amidst the proliferation of social media platforms and online reviews, enterprises are capable of amassing substantial quantities of consumer sentiment and behavioral information, as noted in (Yuvika Gupta et al.). This influx of data allows organizations to tailor their offerings and marketing methodologies based on authentic consumer insights, thereby propelling continuous enhancement of user experiences. The proficiency to dissect feedback equips brands to react promptly to consumer needs and preferences, thus engendering an agile marketing sphere. In addition, the cyclical process of refining services based on user data engenders a loop of engagement where travelers perceive themselves as acknowledged and esteemed. Consequently, this fosters loyalty and bolsters the brand's stature as a frontrunner in customer experiences within the perpetually shifting tourism sector. Ultimately, the strategic utilization of AI in enhancing user experiences yields a substantial competitive edge in a domain where consumer preferences hold utmost significance.

B. AI's Role in Customer Feedback and Improvement

The melding of artificial intelligence (AI) with customer feedback systems can be seen as a noteworthy shift in the tourism industry, significantly improving how brands gather insights into consumer preferences. By harnessing AI-powered solutions, organizations can collect, process, and examine customer attitudes in a timely fashion, thus allowing for more prompt and effective enhancements. This capability to process feedback in real time equips enterprises to recognize patterns and rectify problems before they grow into larger issues, thereby nurturing a service environment that is more agile. Additionally, AI technologies are able to comb through extensive amounts of feedback from various sources such as social media and review platforms, synthesizing this data into practical insights that enable brands to swiftly modify their offerings. This level of adaptability not only boosts customer contentment but also strengthens brand loyalty, as consumers sense that their feedback holds value and is acknowledged.Furthermore, the function of AI in customizing consumer interactions based on feedback is vital, providing personalized experiences that bolster customer loyalty in the tourism sector. Through the use of chatbot technology, businesses can interact with customers, efficiently responding to their inquiries and concerns, thus facilitating a smooth experience. Previous research shows that these AI-driven chatbots elevate customer loyalty by offering timely and tailored assistance, making users feel recognized and important. This incorporation of AI not only streamlines interaction but also assists brands in fostering a stronger connection with their customers. By deploying AI to examine particular feedback characteristics and preferences, tourism brands can enhance their marketing approaches, crafting promotions and experiences that align with the interests of their target demographics, which in turn generates increased engagement and satisfaction.In addition, AI's influence on customer feedback mechanisms has implications that extend beyond short-term enhancements; it lays groundwork for ongoing brand evolution and innovation in tourism marketing. With AI scrutinizing trends in customer feedback, brands are equipped to predict changes in the market and recognize upcoming trends. This foresight allows tourism companies to maintain competitiveness by foreseeing consumer wants, thereby enabling preemptive improvements in service. The results from recent research indicate that AI contributes to effective communication through various digital platforms, resulting in heightened consumer engagement and enhancing brand image and loyalty (Arman Khan et al., p. 657-671). By adeptly integrating AI technologies within customer feedback frameworks, brands position themselves for continual progression, ultimately elevating the consumer experience and solidifying their standing in a swiftly evolving tourism market (Yolanda Masnita et al., p. 120-140).

C. Balancing Automation with Human Touch

The melding of automation into the tourism industry reveals a dualistic nature that necessitates scrupulous examination of the human component within service delivery. Although chatbots and artificial intelligence (AI) apparatuses markedly augment operational efficacy by offering immediate responses to customer queries—frequently streamlining the service framework—there lies a fundamental peril that these automated mechanisms may diminish the emotional acumen crucial for forging robust customer connections. Research pertaining to chatbot service recovery underscores the notion that the implementation of standard options can, in fact, positively affect user engagement, thus indicating a pathway through which automation might be honed to embed behavioral nudges that resonate with tourist feelings (Lilei Wang). This signifies that while automated systems possess the capacity to manage mundane inquiries, effective recovery tactics entailing a human element may be requisite to address the multifaceted and emotive requirements of clientele post-service failures.Additionally, the issue resides in pinpointing the ideal equilibrium where automation does not eclipse personal engagement. Evaluation of case studies featuring green technology enterprises elucidates the potency of AI in instigating business model innovations that advance sustainability, simultaneously accentuating the necessity for a human-centric methodology in the design and execution stages (Philip Jorzik). These enterprises exemplify that a profound comprehension of consumer needs empowers them to assimilate AI into their business frameworks without alienating their core market. Such equilibrium becomes particularly pivotal in the realm of tourism branding, where emotional affiliations wield substantial influence over customer loyalty and contentment. By crafting AI frameworks that supplement, rather than supplant, human interactions, businesses stand to not only amplify operational efficiency but also enhance the emotional investment of their patrons, consequently fortifying their brand identification amidst a competitive landscape.In summation, achieving a concord between automated efficiencies and human sensitivity is vital for brands endeavoring to traverse the intricate realm of tourist anticipations. Corporations must perpetually evaluate the function of technology within their customer engagement tactics, ensuring that while automation provides convenience, it does not detract from the genuine experiences that travelers esteem. Approaches that amalgamate insights from both automation and human engagement hold the promise of facilitating superior service recovery and customer satisfaction, thereby reinforcing brand allegiance. The research cited buttresses this concept by illustrating how default options in chatbots can lead to heightened customer retention following service lapses, indicating the potential for technology to serve as a facilitator rather than an impediment in nurturing meaningful customer relationships (Lilei Wang). Thus, a dual emphasis on efficiency through automation, in conjunction with empathetic human service, could very well serve as a paradigm for future branding endeavors within the tourism sector.

X. CONCLUSION

The incorporation of artificial intelligence (AI) into branding methodologies within the tourism domain has certainly altered traditional frameworks. As has been emphasized in the analysis herein, applications of AI enable a more profound engagement with customers and facilitate personalized marketing tactics, thus permitting brands to connect more intimately with prospective travelers. The outcomes of a systematic literature review regarding AI's role in marketing indicate its transformative influence on branding, bringing to light the active exploration by practitioners of appropriate AI solutions that enhance marketing functionalities (Yolanda Masnita et al., p. 120-140). This transition allows tourism brands to not only develop more customized experiences but also assists in forecasting consumer behaviors, consequently optimizing promotional endeavors and the distribution of resources.Furthermore, the experimentation conducted with AI instruments for generating content, as illustrated in recent graduate research, reflects a tangible utilization of these technologies within the tourism branding framework. By utilizing AI to automate tasks and produce content at diminished costs, brands are afforded the capacity to uphold high standards of creativity and consistency in their marketing initiatives (Sangita Kattel). This flexibility is essential within an industry marked by seasonal variances and fluctuating consumer interests. As tourism organizations increasingly adopt AI-centric solutions, the ramifications for efficiency and cost management remain expansive, redefining not only branding strategies but also operational methods and market positioning.To summarize, the capacity of AI to transform branding within the tourism sector is substantial. The systematic review and the contemporary discoveries regarding content generation highlight the imperative for tourism enterprises to perpetually adapt and innovate. The adoption of AI not only improves marketing efficacy but also ensures alignment of branding endeavors with the changing anticipations of modern travelers. As the sector advances, forthcoming research and practices must prioritize ethical considerations and the judicious application of AI technologies, guaranteeing that tourism branding retains its authenticity and serves the interests of all stakeholders implicated. Embracing this prospective trajectory will enable brands to adeptly navigate the intricate landscape of consumer preferences, ensuring a lasting impact and ongoing relevance in an ever-evolving market.

A. Summary of Key Findings

The incorporation of artificial intelligence (AI) within branding strategy, specifically in the domain of tourism, exhibits substantial changes in marketing practices and customer interaction. The salient discoveries assert that AI technologies, such as ChatGPT, enable organizations to scrutinize substantial volumes of data, which results in improved decision-making methods. Existing literature reveals that ChatGPT notably transforms business operations, particularly in areas such as marketing and operational planning (Marianna Sigala). This continuous development corresponds with a prevailing trend where enterprises utilize AI to craft personalized marketing approaches, ultimately refining customer experiences and interactions. Brands that adopt these technological innovations not only enhance their operational efficacy but also cultivate intensified connections with their target demographic, signaling a noteworthy transformation in branding methodologies within the tourism sector. Furthermore, the efficiency of AI-centric advertisement targeting is pivotal in influencing brand perception and economic results in tourism marketing. Studies have found that AI-driven targeting algorithms yield significantly greater return on investment (ROI) when compared to conventional approaches, underscoring the fiscal benefits of AI adoption (Lin Shan). These insights propose that brands that implement sophisticated targeting technologies can engage with consumers more effectively, thereby solidifying their brand identity amidst competition. As a result, the strategic employment of AI technologies not only amplifies the effectiveness of marketing initiatives but also enhances brand visibility and standing. This analytics-focused approach to advertising highlights the critical role of AI in determining the trajectory of branding within the tourism sphere.In addition, the academic examination of AI's influence on tourism branding extends to its ramifications for cultural and heritage tourism, which fundamentally relies on storytelling and emotional connections. The capability of AI to analyze consumer conduct facilitates a refined comprehension of what attracts potential travelers, thus aiding in crafting culturally pertinent marketing strategies. The ability of the technology to deliver personalized experiences aligns with contemporary consumer anticipations in the digital era (Marianna Sigala). As companies increasingly depend on AI to customize their communications, the impact of these technologies on established branding principles becomes more pronounced. Ultimately, the synergy of AI-powered analytics and targeted advertising is establishing new standards in tourism branding, enhancing both market competitiveness and consumer gratification.

B. Implications for the Future of Tourism Branding

With advancements in artificial intelligence (AI) reshaping the domain of tourism, it is necessitated that branding strategies adjust so as to maintain relevance within a market that is increasingly competitive. The implementation of AI possesses the potential to transform customer engagement by offering personalized experiences tailored to individual preferences, which in turn can cultivate enhanced brand loyalty. For example, algorithms powered by AI can scrutinize large volumes of consumer data to forecast trends and user inclinations, thereby allowing tourism-oriented brands to customize their offerings accordingly. Through the utilization of these insights, brands have the capability to develop immersive marketing initiatives that significantly resonate with their target demographics—an imperative factor in the modern market where consumer options are plentiful. The move towards personalized experiences, aided by AI, suggests that the future trajectory of tourism branding will likely emphasize the affective bonds that exist between brands and consumers, thereby highlighting the importance of emotional intelligence within branding strategies.

Additionally, the rising incorporation of AI within tourism branding might demand a reassessment of conventional branding paradigms. The SECI model concerning knowledge transfer asserts that the efficacy of brand communication relies on the interplay of both explicit and tacit knowledge among involved stakeholders (Spyros Avdimiotis). As AI frameworks foster enhanced operational productivity and consumer engagement, brands are required to strike a balance between automated personalization and genuine human connection in order to nurture authentic relationships. This equilibrium is especially crucial when considering the emotional dimensions of travel experiences, which frequently arise from profound feelings linked to memories and aspirations. Henceforth, forthcoming branding endeavors ought to investigate methodologies for embedding emotional intelligence within digital platforms, guaranteeing that content generated by AI embodies both the genuine essence of the destination and the fundamental values of the brand.Ultimately, the ramifications of AI concerning tourism branding extend further than mere marketing tactics; they also engage with ethical issues and sustainability. As AI technologies gain traction, brands must grapple with the ethical quandaries related to data privacy and consumer trust. The mounting dependency on AI for procuring consumer insights might engender skepticism if not addressed with transparency. Forging a trustworthy brand will depend on responsible management of data, refining the manner in which brands disseminate their principles and commitment to sustainability. By placing emphasis on ethical modalities and showcasing a dedication to sustainable tourism practices, brands possess the capacity to bolster their reputation and consumer confidence in a market increasingly aware of social and ecological concerns. The realm of tourism branding is indisputably evolving, necessitating forward-looking strategies that meld AI not solely for branding efficacy but also to positively influence the industry's future.

C. Recommendations for Stakeholders

In order to effectively utilize the potential encapsulated in artificial intelligence for the realm of tourism branding, it is imperative that stakeholders prioritize the amalgamation of AI technologies within their respective marketing frameworks. By placing a strong emphasis on decision-making that is informed through data, brands can gain a deeper comprehension of consumer inclinations and behaviors, hence customizing experiences that align with the preferences of their targeted demographic. For instance, the application of analytics driven by AI can significantly enhance the segmentation of customers, thus enabling stakeholders to formulate personalized offerings that resonate on an individual level with travelers. This degree of tailored experiences not only enhances consumer satisfaction but also fortifies brand allegiance, which is critical for maintaining a competitive edge within an ever-changing marketplace. Stakeholders ought to proactively pursue collaborations with technological enterprises that specialize in AI to streamline the deployment of these technologies, thereby ensuring that their brands are at the pinnacle of innovation in the tourism industry.Moreover, collaboration among stakeholders is crucial in the establishment of ethical frameworks that govern AI's application in tourism branding. As AI technologies increasingly dictate consumer engagements, it is essential for stakeholders to participate in dialogues that scrutinize issues surrounding surveillance, privacy of data, and biases embedded in algorithms. A comprehensive framework concerning the ethical use of AI will protect consumer rights while simultaneously nurturing trust—an element pivotal to brand reputation. Stakeholders should promote transparency regarding AI-driven processes, elucidating the manner in which consumer data will be appropriated and the method by which decisions are derived. Through the development of stringent standards and by engaging with regulatory bodies to champion responsible usage of AI, stakeholders can diminish the likelihood of backlash while also establishing a favorable benchmark for the wider industry. Such a preemptive stance positions brands as forerunners in ethical practices within tourism, thereby bolstering their standing and aligning with the increasing consumer demand for corporate accountability (Alhamzah Alnoor et al.).Additionally, aside from technological and ethical imperatives, stakeholders ought to place significant emphasis on the continuous education and training of their personnel to adeptly navigate the shifting landscape posed by AI. As the dependency on intelligent systems escalates, it becomes crucial for staff to be sufficiently equipped with the requisite capabilities to interpret insights generated by AI and to aptly apply them within branding methodologies. Continuous training initiatives can not only augment employee proficiency but also invigorate innovation, fostering creative thought that takes advantage of AI's potential. Furthermore, promoting a corporate culture that esteems adaptability will empower teams to nimbly respond to novel AI trends and evolving consumer anticipations. By committing to the development of human resources, stakeholders guarantee that their branding strategies are not merely technologically sophisticated but also resonate with consumers on an emotional plane, thereby reinforcing brand identity amidst the competitive landscape of tourism (Alhamzah Alnoor et al.).

D. Final Thoughts on AI's Transformative Power

The broad incorporation of artificial intelligence in multiple fields, especially in tourism branding, offers a distinctive perspective to explore its transformative potential. As organizations are progressively reliant on insights derived from data, AI facilitates brands in devising experiences that are highly personalized, thereby creating profound connections with prospective travelers. By scrutinizing consumer actions and inclinations, AI frameworks can forecast developments and customize marketing approaches, which in turn bolsters brand fidelity. This proficiency not only simplifies customer engagement activities but also results in a more judicious use of marketing assets, enabling brands to touch their target audiences effectively amid competition. Through the perspective of heightened personalization and effectiveness, we can discern the significant alterations AI is inflicting on the dynamics governing brand-consumer interactions in tourism.Additionally, the ramifications of AI are not confined to consumer experiences; they substantially affect operational efficiencies within tourism branding. Automated instruments, like chatbots and virtual aides, are progressively utilized to handle customer questions, rectify issues instantaneously, and even propose travel plans. Such innovations not only enhance the overall customer service experience but also alleviate the burdens shouldered by human personnel, permitting them to concentrate on more intricate responsibilities. Moreover, the capability of AI to evaluate extensive datasets in real time allows brands to promptly adjust their tactics in alignment with evolving market circumstances. This nimbleness is vital in the swiftly changing tourism arena, where trends can alter quickly. As organizations leverage AI's competencies for operational superiority, they prepare themselves for enduring competitiveness in a perpetually transforming environment.In conclusion, despite the clear advantages AI brings to reshaping branding strategies in tourism, it is crucial to approach this paradigm transition with a discerning viewpoint. Ethical issues concerning data privacy and the risk of algorithmic bias necessitate careful navigation to guarantee that the implementation of AI is consistent with consumer rights and societal ethics. The reliance on technology ought to ultimately augment the human experience rather than degrade it, promoting a collaborative dynamic between machines and people. As the tourism sector proceeds to investigate the prospects of AI, stakeholders must stay alert, ensuring that advancements are matched with ethical accountability. This equitably considered approach will not only protect public confidence but also foster the sustainable progression of branding within tourism, optimizing AI's transformative capabilities while alleviating its intrinsic hazards.

REFERENCES

Akbulut, O., Çelik, T., Ekin, Y., & Yetim, A. Ç. (2024). A research on Fethiye Babadag commercial tandem paragliding participants within the scope of experiential tourism. *Journal of Outdoor Recreation and Tourism*, 47, 100806.

Ali, S. (2023). *Impact of Artificial Intelligence and Advertisement on Project Customer Engagement and Project Success in Project based Firm with Mediating Role of Brand Image*. Capital University of Science and Technology.

Alnoor, A., & Bayram, G. E. XinYing, C., & Shah, S. H. A. (Eds.). (2024). The Role of Artificial Intelligence in Regenerative Tourism and Green Destinations.

Alruwaili, M. M., Abuadas, F. H., Alsadi, M., Alruwaili, A. N., Elsayed Ramadan, O. M., Shaban, M., & El Arab, R. A. (2024). Exploring nurses' awareness and attitudes toward artificial intelligence: Implications for nursing practice. *Digital Health*, 10, 20552076241271803.

Avdimiotis, S. (2019). Emotional intelligence and tacit knowledge management in hospitality. *Journal ofTourism* [JTHSM]. *Heritage & Services Marketing*, 5(2), 3–10.

Aydin, B., & Sirkeci, I. (2024). Navigating the Frontier: Addressing Artificial Intelligence Challenges in Tourism and Hospitality Education. *Transnational Education Review*, 2(1), 49–53.

Bhowmik, O., Chowdhury, S., Ashik, J. H., Mahmud, G. I., Khan, M. M., & Hossain, N. U. I. (2024). Application of Artificial Intelligence in Reverse Logistics: A Bibliometric and Network Analysis. *Supply Chain Analytics*, 100076.

VLASCEANU, C. F., Valentin, T. A., & Gabriela, . I. G. U. (2023). The Fusion of Advanced Technology: Artificial Intelligence and Virtual Reality in the Cruise Industry and Global Hospitality Organizations. Review of International Comparative Management/Revista de Management Comparat International, 24(4).

Chanthati, S. R. (2024). Website Visitor Analysis & Branding Quality Measurement Using. *Artificial Intelligence*.

Correia, R., & Venciute, D. (Eds.). (2024). *AI Innovation in Services Marketing*. IGI Global.

Khan, S. I. (2022). Impact of artificial intelligence on consumer buying behaviors: Study about the online retail purchase. *International Journal of Health Sciences*, (II), 8121–8129.

Dogru, T., Line, N., Mody, M., Hanks, L., Abbott, J. A., Acikgoz, F., & Zhang, T. (2023). Generative artificial intelligence in the hospitality and tourism industry: Developing a framework for future research. *Journal of Hospitality & Tourism Research (Washington, D.C.)*, •••, 10963480231188663.

Durmaz, Y., & Baser, M. Y. (2023). A Systematic Literature Review on Artificial Intelligence Applications in Tourism Marketing. *International Journal of Research in Business Studies and Management*, 10(1), 21–30.

İbrahim Halil Efendioğlu, "The Change of Digital Marketing with Artificial Intelligence"

Sharma, R., Kaur, A., Bajaj, K. B., Bindra, K., Rashmi, D. S. D., Yadav, V., ... & Singh, B. GURUGRAM UNIVERSITY BUSINESS REVIEW (GUBR).

Hajahmadi, S., Calvi, I., Stacchiotti, E., Cascarano, P., & Marfia, G. (2024). Heritage elements and Artificial Intelligence as storytelling tools for virtual retail environments. *Digital Applications in Archaeology and Cultural Heritage*, 34, e00368.

He, G. S., Tran, T. T. H., & Leonidou, L. C. (2024). It's here to stay: Lessons, reflections, and visions on digital transformation amid public crisis. *Technological Forecasting and Social Change*, 206, 123557.

Jorzik, P., Antonio, J. L., Kanbach, D. K., Kallmuenzer, A., & Kraus, S. (2024). Sowing the seeds for sustainability: A business model innovation perspective on artificial intelligence in green technology startups. *Technological Forecasting and Social Change*, 208, 123653.

Kattel, S. (2023). *Implementation of an AI-based Content Creation Strategy in the Wine Tourism Organization: The case study at Winalist.* University of Bordeaux.

Khan, A., Abu Bakar, A. H., Saad, N. M., Hussain, Z., & Arif, A. R. (2023). *Effectiveness of Artificial Intelligence in Building Customer Loyalty: Investigating the Mediating Role of Chatbot in the Tourism Sector of Pakistan.* Human Resource Management Academic Research Society.

Khan, A., Abu Bakar, A. H., Saad, N. M., Hussain, Z., & Arif, A. R. (2023). *Effectiveness of Artificial Intelligence in Building Customer Loyalty: Investigating the Mediating Role of Chatbot in the Tourism Sector of Pakistan.* Human Resource Management Academic Research Society.

Khan, A., Abu Bakar, A. H., Saad, N. M., Hussain, Z., & Arif, A. R. (2023). *Effectiveness of Artificial Intelligence in Building Customer Loyalty: Investigating the Mediating Role of Chatbot in the Tourism Sector of Pakistan.* HRMARS.

Khan, A., Abu Bakar, A. H., Saad, N. M., Hussain, Z., & Arif, A. R. (2023). *Effectiveness of Artificial Intelligence in Building Customer Loyalty: Investigating the Mediating Role of Chatbot in the Tourism Sector of Pakistan*. HRMARS.

Khan, A., Abu Bakar, A. H., Saad, N. M., Hussain, Z., & Arif, A. R. (2023). *Effectiveness of Artificial Intelligence in Building Customer Loyalty: Investigating the Mediating Role of Chatbot in the Tourism Sector of Pakistan*. Human Resource Management Academic Research Society.

Козак, К., Корсікова, Н., Морщавка, А., Шиленко, І., & Деревянко, О. (2023). МІСЦЕ ТЕХНОЛОГІЙ КАДРОВОГО МЕНЕДЖМЕНТУ В СИСТЕМІ АНТИКРИЗОВОГО УПРАВЛІННЯ ПІДПРИЄМСТВА THE ROLE OF HUMAN RESOURCE MANAGEMENT TECHNOLOGIES IN THE ENTERPRISE ANTI-CRISIS MANAGEMENT SYSTEM. *Technology*, 8(4), 93–98.

Li, Y., Wang, S., & Li, Z. (2024). Animating arousal and engagement: Empirical insights into AI-enhanced robotic performances and consumer reactions. *Journal of Hospitality and Tourism Technology*, 15(5), 737–768.

Loufek, B., Vidal, D., McClintock, D. S., Lifson, M., Williamson, E., Overgaard, S., & Pardi, D. S. (2024). Embedding Internal Accountability into Healthcare Institutions for Safe, Effective, and Ethical Implementation of Artificial Intelligence into Medical Practice: A Mayo Clinic Case Study. *Mayo Clinic Proceedings. Digital Health*.

Masnita, Y., Ali, J. K., Zahra, A., Wilson, N., & Murwonugroho, W. (2024). Artificial intelligence in marketing: Literature review and future research agenda. *Journal of System and Management Sciences*, 14(1), 120–140.

Mell, S., & Alexander, L. (2024). *Hornung, Catherine Yuh, Dino Samartzis*. Virtual Clinical Trials - Implications of Computer Simulations and Artificial Intelligence for Musculoskeletal Research.

Musa, H. G., Garad, A., & Mussa, M. (2024). Trends and Innovations in Tourism Marketing Within Government Policy. *JIAN-Jurnal Ilmiah Administrasi Negara*, 8(2), 28–48.

Nguyen, T. D. (2024). *New Technologies in Travelling and Tourism*. Brno University of Technology.

Niininen, O. (2022). *Contemporary Issues in Digital Marketing*. Routledge.

Mahmood, N. Z., Ahmed, S. R., Al-Hayaly, A. F., Algburi, S., & Rasheed, J. (2023, October). The Evolution of Administrative Information Systems: Assessing the Revolutionary Impact of Artificial Intelligence. In *2023 7th International Symposium on Multidisciplinary Studies and Innovative Technologies (ISMSIT)* (pp. 1-7). IEEE.

Paraschi, E. P., Panagopoulos, A., & Fragkogianni, M. (2024). COVID-19 crisis management in Greek airlines. *Journal of the Air Transport Research Society*, 3, 100032.

Dogan, S., Mistry, T. G., & Nanu, L. (2024). Revolutionizing getaways: Automation and artificial intelligence's transformative journey in tourism and hospitality. *Worldwide Hospitality and Tourism Themes*, 16(2), 248–251.

Kim, S., & Wang, D. (Eds.). (2021). *Future of Tourism Marketing*. Routledge.

Setyawan, A. A., Misidawati, D. N., Aryatama, S., Jaya, A. A. N. A., & Wiliana, E. (2024). Exploring Innovative Strategies for Sustainable Organizational Growth. *Global International Journal of Innovative Research*, 2(5), 861–872.

Shan, L. (2024). Computing advertising intelligent computing and push based on artificial intelligence in the big data era. *Heliyon*, 10(17).

Sigala, M., Ooi, K. B., Tan, G. W. H., Aw, E. C. X., Buhalis, D., Cham, T. H., & Ye, I. H. (2024). Understanding the impact of ChatGPT on tourism and hospitality: Trends, prospects and research agenda. *Journal of Hospitality and Tourism Management*, 60, 384–390.

Tinston, R. (2023). Leveraging Behavioural Science Language and Artificial Intelligence in Tourism Marketing.

Vij, M., Vij, A., Kumar, P., & Shameem, B. (2024, February). Impact of AI-Driven Customer Insights on Brand Engagement and Loyalty in Tourism Marketing. In *2024 2nd International Conference on Cyber Resilience (ICCR)* (pp. 1-6). IEEE.

Wang, L., Xiao, J., Luo, Z., & Guo, Y. (2024). The Impact of Default Options on Tourist Intention Post Tourism Chatbot Failure: The Role of Service Recovery and Emoticon. *Tourism Management Perspectives*, 53, 101299.

Ye, X., Yan, Y., Li, J., & Jiang, B. (2024). Privacy and personal data risk governance for generative artificial intelligence: A Chinese perspective. *Telecommunications Policy*, 48(10), 102851.

Yilmazdogan, O. C. (2024). Elevating workforce stability: Augmented reality and artificial intelligence solutions for overcoming employee turnover challenges in hospitality and tourism. *Worldwide Hospitality and Tourism Themes*, 16(5), 598–610.

Gupta, Y., & Khan, F. M. (2024). Role of artificial intelligence in customer engagement: A systematic review and future research directions. *Journal of Modelling in Management*.

Chapter 8
Adapting Brand Strategies to Technological Disruption by Mediation of AI-Driven Branding in the Horn of Africa

Shashi Kant
https://orcid.org/0000-0003-4722-5736
Bule Hora University, Ethiopia

Aynetu Terefe
https://orcid.org/0009-0003-3814-9548
Bule Hora University, Ethiopia

Tafese Niguse
https://orcid.org/0009-0008-6536-6392
Bule Hora University, Ethiopia

Fikeralem Toma
https://orcid.org/0009-0006-5078-7763
Bule Hora University, Ethiopia

Metasebia Adula
https://orcid.org/0000-0001-5732-2850
Bule Hora University, Ethiopia

DOI: 10.4018/979-8-3693-9461-8.ch008

ABSTRACT

based on AI, and disruption by the technology. Employing a structural equation modeling technique, we evaluate empirical data to investigate the direct and indirect impacts of brand strategy adaptation on disruption by the technology, with Branding based on AI serving as a mediator. The outcomes manifested that the sustainable adaptation of brand strategies noteworthy augments the efficacy of Branding based on AI, which subsequently augments innovation and agility in response to technological changes. The findings demonstrate partial mediation, implying that while strategies for brand adaptation have a direct effect on disruption by the technology, the incorporation of AI enhances this influence. These findings highlight the significance of adaptability and technology in branding strategies, providing useful insights for executives aiming to maneuver through the challenges of digital market places. The investigation wraps up with suggestions for future studies, stressing the necessity for exploration into particular AI technologies and the impact on branding approaches.

INTRODUCTION

In a world that is increasingly interconnected, the effects of disruption by the technology on branding strategies have become a key concern for businesses around the globe (Högberg & Willermark, 2023). This is especially apparent in areas like the Eastern part of Africa, where swift technological progress and the rising role of artificial intelligence (AI) are transforming the market placing environment. Strategies for brand adaptation to take advantage of these technological shifts are vital not only for sustaining competitive edge but also for promoting economic growth and development in emerging market places (Niguse et al., 2024). It is noteworthy for both professionals and investigations in the field to comprehend how brands can sustainable navigate these disruptions through AI-focused branding (Jeong et al., 2023).

The concept of branding has evolved noteworthy over time, transitioning from simple recognition to a complex interplay of customer experiences, emotions, and technological integration. While traditional branding theories focused on static attributes, digital strategies recognize the dynamic nature of brands in the current digital environment (Högberg & Willermark, 2023). The advent of artificial intelligence enables brands to analyze consumer behavior in real-time, customize customer interactions, and enhance brand loyalty (Peñarroya & Miralles, 2022). However, the application of AI in branding strategies remains largely uncharted, particularly in the Eastern part of Africa, where unique socio-economic and cultural factors influence consumer behavior. Studies on branding in the context of technological advancement highlight several key themes, including the importance of innovation, consumer engagement, and adaptability (Sharma, 2021).

Investigation shows that brands embracing technological innovations tend to outperform their competitors by delivering more relevant and engaging interactions with customers. However, there is a considerable gap in understanding how these concepts manifest in the Eastern part of Africa, where local businesses face distinct challenges such as inadequate infrastructure, limited access to technology, and varying consumer perceptions of artificial intelligence (Jabo et al., 2024). The practical challenges of implementing Branding based on AI strategies in this region include low levels of digital literacy among consumers, a lack of sufficient technological infrastructure, and resistance from traditional businesses to adopt new practices. Also, concerns regarding data privacy and ethical insights of AI usage further complicate the situation (Peñarroya & Miralles, 2022). These challenges necessitate a tailored approach to branding strategies that considers the unique context of the region. This chapter seeks to address these investigation gaps by exploring the association among the adaptation of brand strategies and disruption by the technology, specifically through the lens of Branding based on AI in the Eastern part of Africa. By analyzing the interactions among these factors, the investigation aims to offer valuable insights for future investigations and policymakers, emphasizing effective strategies for utilizing technology to improve brand equity and consumer engagement in the area.

The central investigation inquiry that directs this investigation is: "***In what ways do adaptive brand strategies influence the impact of disruption by the technology via Branding based on AI in the Eastern part of Africa?***"

BACKGROUND OF INVESTIGATION

This investigation aims to investigate the association among adaptive branding strategies and disruption by the technology, highlighting the importance of Branding based on AI in addressing the distinct challenges encountered by businesses in the Eastern part of Africa (Danciu, 2021). Nevertheless, the airline has encountered obstacles in effectively personalizing its branding initiatives due to the varying levels of internet access and digital literacy among its clientele (Kant & Adula, 2024). Although the airline has invested in AI-driven analytics to improve customer experiences, the uneven access to technology has constrained its capacity to provide consistent and tailored branding across diverse market places. This scenario highlights the critical need for businesses to take local contexts into account when executing technology-driven strategies (Högberg & Willermark, 2023).

The telecommunications industry in Somalia serves as another pertinent example, with companies such as Hormuud Telecom emerging as key players. It has effectively utilized mobile technology to offer a variety of services, including mobile money, which has transformed financial transactions in a nation characterized by a sparse banking infrastructure. Still, notwithstanding its accomplishments, company with trials associated to trademark awareness, chiefly in terms of belief and safety (Jeong et al., 2023). The application of AI-driven client service solutions by the company often encounters skepticism from consumers who are concerned about data privacy and the potential for technology misuse. This situation underscores the necessity for brands to not only embrace technological advancements but also to proactively address consumer apprehensions and foster trust, which is essential for sustainable branding in the region (Peñarroya & Miralles, 2022).

Also, the experiences of various local startups reflect a wider trend in the Eastern part of Africa, where entrepreneurs encounter considerable obstacles in adopting Branding based on AI strategies. Numerous startups face challenges such as limited funding, insufficient technological infrastructure, and a shortage of skilled personnel capable of executing advanced AI solutions. For example, a technology startup in Ethiopia that seeks to create an AI-driven e-commerce platform has been impeded by unreliable electricity supply and restricted internet access, which have adversely impacted its operational efficiency and user engagement. This scenario exemplifies the complex challenges businesses face when attempting to adapt their branding strategies amid disruption by the technology.

STATEMENT OF THE PROBLEM

The Eastern part of Africa offers a distinctive environment for analyzing the adaptation of branding strategies in the face of disruption by the technology, especially through the perspective of AI-enhanced branding. Ideally, enterprises in this region would sustainable utilize cutting-edge technologies to improve brand interaction, cultivate consumer loyalty, and augment sustainable economic development. Nevertheless, the current situation is characterized by notable contradictions and obstacles that hinder advancement (Peñarroya & Miralles, 2022). Despite the swift expansion of mobile technology and internet access, numerous firms find it challenging to adopt effective branding strategies that integrate AI, leading to lost opportunities for market place differentiation and consumer engagement (Högberg & Willermark, 2023).

Investigation manifested noteworthy gaps in the existing literature regarding the sustainable incorporation of AI into branding strategies within the Eastern part of Africa. Although many studies emphasize the advantages of AI in improving customer experiences and personalizing market placing initiatives on a global scale, there is a scarcity of investigation tailored to the specific socio-economic and cultural contexts of the Eastern part of Africa. This lack of region-specific insights outcomes in ambiguous conclusions about the efficacy of Branding based on AI strategies in this area, leaving practitioners without definitive guidance on optimal practices and potential challenges (Setiawan, Widyartono & Ony, 2021).

Also, theoretical deficiencies persist, particularly in the frameworks that elucidate how disruption by the technology affects brand adaptation in emerging market places. Conventional branding theories may fall short in addressing the complexities of consumer behavior in regions with diverse levels of technological access and digital literacy. Consequently, there is a pressing need for the development of new theoretical models that reflect the intricacies of Branding based on AI and its influence on brand equity and consumer engagement in the Eastern part of Africa (Peñarroya & Miralles, 2022). Knowledge deficiencies further complicate the situation, as numerous businesses remain unaware of the potential advantages and applications of artificial intelligence in their branding initiatives. This lack of comprehension may outcome in resistance to embracing new technologies, as companies might be apprehensive about the return on investment or the practicality of incorporating AI solutions into their current operations. Also, contextual disparities emerge from the varied socio-cultural environment of the Eastern part of Africa, where consumer attitudes towards technology and branding can differ markedly across various nations and communities (Jeong et al., 2023).

Also, practical obstacles are widespread, including insufficient technological infrastructure, restricted access to qualified personnel, and concerns regarding data privacy and security. These challenges can impede the execution of AI-enhanced branding strategies, compelling businesses to depend on conventional methods that may not appeal to digital consumers. For example, firms may find it difficult to tailor customer experiences due to unreliable internet connectivity or a deficiency in data analytics capabilities (Jeong et al., 2023). This investigation seeks to bridge these gaps by exploring the association among adaptive brand strategies and disruption by the technology, mediated by Branding based on AI in the Eastern part of Africa. By concentrating on the distinct challenges and opportunities present in this region, the investigation will offer valuable insights for future investigations and policymakers. It will aid in the formulation of region-specific branding frameworks and practical recommendations that can support businesses in effectively navigating technological advancements. Also, the outcomes will underscore the significance of incorporating local context into branding strategies, ensuring that businesses can utilize AI-driven solutions to bolster brand equity and enhance consumer engagement. In doing so, this investigation will pave the way for more informed decision-making and strategic planning in the realm of branding in the Eastern part of Africa, ultimately fostering sustainable growth and development.

RELATED THEORIES

One pertinent theory is "*Brand Equity Theory*", which asserts that a brand's value is shaped by consumer perceptions, experiences, and associations. This theory highlights the significance of brand awareness, loyalty, and perceived quality in determining a brand's overall market place strength. In the realm of Branding based on AI, gaining insight into consumer perceptions and interactions with technology-utilizing brands can illuminate pathways to enhancing brand equity. The incorporation of AI tools can improve personalized market placing initiatives, thereby cultivating stronger associations with consumers and bolstering brand loyalty (Peñarroya & Miralles, 2022).

Another noteworthy framework is the "*Technology Acceptance Model (TAM)*", which elucidates how users come to accept and utilize technology. TAM manifested that perceived ease of use and perceived usefulness play crucial roles in shaping individuals' attitudes toward technology adoption. Applying this model to Branding based on AI can assist investigations and practitioners in identifying the factors that facilitate or impede the adoption of AI technologies by businesses in the Eastern part of Africa. Insights derived from TAM can guide strategies aimed at increasing user acceptance of AI tools, ensuring that brands can effectively connect with consumers through innovative technologies.

Also, the "*Diffusion of Innovations Theory*" is relevant, as it explores how new ideas and technologies disseminate within a society. This theory delineates the process through which innovations are communicated and embraced across various segments of the population (Högberg & Willermark, 2023). In the Eastern part of Africa, where the pace of technological adoption varies noteworthy, comprehending the stages of diffusion is essential for businesses to assess the potential speed and efficacy of Branding based on AI strategies among consumers. Recognizing the traits of early adopters in contrast to laggards can enhance targeted market placing initiatives and inform the timing of technology deployment (Högberg & Willermark, 2023).

The "*Customer Experience Theory*" offers another vital perspective, emphasizing the comprehensive experience a consumer has with a brand at every interaction point. This theory highlights the necessity of fostering positive and memorable engagements that cultivate loyalty and advocacy. Through the application of AI, brands can improve customer experiences by providing personalized recommendations, facilitating real-time interactions, and enhancing service delivery. It is imperative for brands to understand how to utilize AI to create exceptional customer experiences in order to succeed in a competitive environment (Galanakis et al., 2021).

Among these theoretical frameworks, "*Brand Equity Theory*" is the primary lens for this investigation. This selection is motivated by the necessity to explore how Branding based on AI can bolster brand equity, especially within the distinctive context of the Eastern part of Africa. By concentrating on brand equity, the investigation will investigate how adaptive strategies shaped by disruption by the technology can enhance consumer perceptions and loyalty. This theoretical framework will steer the inquiry into the associations among AI, branding strategies, and consumer engagement, ultimately enriching the understanding of how businesses can effectively navigate the challenges of branding in a swiftly changing technological landscape (Galanakis, 2021).

DEFINITION AND ORIGIN OF TERMS

Adaptive Brand Strategies encompass the flexible methodologies that firms utilize to modify their branding initiatives in response to fluctuating market place dynamics, consumer behaviors, and advancements in technology (Jeong et al., 2023). These strategies prioritize agility and responsiveness, enabling brands to maintain their relevance and competitiveness in a constantly changing environment. The notion of adaptability in branding has its roots in broader market placing theories that emphasize the necessity for businesses to react to external influences, including economic changes, technological progress, and evolving consumer preferences. Stemming from strategic management principles, adaptive brand strategies underscore the significance of ongoing learning and innovation, allowing brands to synchronize their messaging and offerings with consumer expectations and prevailing market place trends (Amankwah et al., 2024).

Disruptive technology signifies the noteworthy transformations that take place within industries and market places as a outcome of new technologies that replace traditional practices and processes. This term underscores the influence of innovation on existing market place frameworks, frequently outcompeting in the development of novel business models and alterations in consumer behavior. The concept gained traction in the late 20th century, particularly with the advent of the internet and digital technologies, as theorists such as Clayton Christensen introduced the idea of "disruptive innovation." This framework elucidates how smaller enterprises with limited resources can effectively challenge established firms by innovating in ways that either create new market places or redefine existing ones. Over time, disruption by the technology has emerged as a pivotal topic in conversations regarding industry development and competitive strategy (Khaled, 2024).

Branding based on AI involves the application of artificial intelligence technologies to enhance branding initiatives, foster customer engagement, and customize market placing approaches. This concept signifies the convergence of artificial intelligence with conventional branding methodologies, utilizing data analytics, machine learning, and automation to develop more impactful branding experiences. The emergence of Branding based on AI can be linked to the increasing integration of AI technologies across various industries, particularly in market placing, where firms began to harness data-informed insights to refine their communications and interactions. As companies acknowledged the capability of AI to analyze consumer behavior and forecast preferences, Branding based on AI became an essential strategy for augmenting brand loyalty and engagement in a competitive environment (van Esch, 2024).

EMPIRICAL LITERATURE REVIEW

Strategies for Brand Adaptation And Disruption By The Technology

The influence of strategies for brand adaptation in the context of disruption by the technology is noteworthy and complex, especially in the current fast-paced market place environment. As new technological advancements arise, companies are compelled to reassess their branding strategies to maintain relevance and competitiveness (Högberg & Willermark, 2023). This adaptation not only requires the adoption of emerging technologies but also necessitates a deep understanding of how these innovations affect consumer perceptions and behaviors. For example, brands that utilize cutting-edge technologies like artificial intelligence and data analytics can offer more tailored and engaging customer experiences, which in turn strengthen brand loyalty and value. This flexibility enables firms to quickly adjust to changes in consumer preferences and market place conditions, promoting a more responsive branding strategy (Alberti et al., 2024)

Also, incorporating technology into branding efforts can outcome in the creation of novel market placing strategies, including targeted digital advertising and interactive social media initiatives. Such methods allow brands to effectively connect with specific consumer demographics, enhancing engagement and fostering stronger associations (Jeong et al., 2023). Nevertheless, the ramifications of disruption by the technology are not exclusively beneficial; they also present various challenges.

Companies must address concerns related to data privacy, ensure that consumers possess the necessary digital skills, and consider the risk of alienating traditional customer segments that may be resistant to change. Ultimately, the capacity to modify brand strategies in light of disruption by the technology is essential for firms aiming to succeed in a competitive environment, as it enables them to capitalize on new opportunities while managing the risks associated with swift technological progress (Peñarroya & Miralles, 2022).

H1: Adapting Brand Strategy has noteworthy effect on Disruption by the technology

Strategies for brand adaptation and Branding based on AI

The impact of modifying brand strategies to incorporate Branding based on AI is profound, as it enables firms to harness the capabilities of artificial intelligence to improve consumer engagement and refine market placing initiatives. By embedding AI technologies within their branding frameworks, companies can process extensive consumer data to uncover insights related to preferences, behaviors, and market place trends (Jeong et al., 2023). This analytical approach empowers brands to create personalized experiences, customizing content and messaging for individual consumers, thereby enhancing the relevance and efficacy of their market placing efforts (Castillo,Canhoto & Said, 2021). Also, the integration of AI into brand strategies streamlines various market placing functions, including customer service interactions via catboats and targeted advertising informed by predictive analytics. This not only augments operational efficiency but also enriches the overall customer experience by delivering timely and pertinent information. Brands that adeptly implement Branding based on AI can address consumer inquiries and preferences in real-time, cultivating a sense of association and trust (Högberg & Willermark, 2023).

Nonetheless, the process of adaptation necessitates a cultural transformation within firms, as teams must be willing to embrace technological advancements and engage in ongoing education regarding AI capabilities. Also, brands must confront potential ethical issues related to data privacy and transparency, ensuring that consumers feel secure in their interactions with AI systems. Ultimately, the effective adaptation of brand strategies to incorporate Branding based on AI can outcome in enhanced brand loyalty, increased customer satisfaction, and a competitive edge in a progressively digital market place (Peñarroya & Miralles, 2022).

H2: Strategies for brand adaptation has noteworthy effect on Branding based on AI

The Effect of Branding based on AI on Disruption by the technology

The influence of Branding based on AI on disruption by the technology is profound, fundamentally altering the manner in which businesses interact with consumers and respond to swift market place changes. As companies increasingly integrate artificial intelligence tools, they can leverage data analytics to gain deeper insights into consumer behavior, allowing for the development of targeted and personalized market placing approaches. This enhanced personalization not only improves customer experiences but also fosters brand loyalty, as consumers feel more recognized and appreciated (Talukder et al., 2024). Also, Branding based on AI enables brands to respond in real-time to market place dynamics and consumer demands, facilitating quick adjustments in reaction to technological innovations or shifts in consumer preferences. For example, brands can employ AI algorithms to scrutinize social media discussions and identify emerging trends, enabling them to proactively modify their strategies rather than merely reacting to changes. This level of agility is essential in a rapidly evolving technological landscape, as it helps companies maintain a competitive edge and remain relevant to consumers (Högberg & Willermark, 2023).

Brands that effectively utilize AI can develop distinctive offerings that resonate with consumers, setting themselves apart in saturated market places. However, this transition also brings forth challenges, including the necessity for businesses to invest in AI technologies and to ensure the ethical management of consumer data (Peñarroya & Miralles, 2022). As firms navigate these complexities, the role of Branding based on AI in disruption by the technology highlights the need to embrace innovation while being mindful of consumer trust and ethical considerations. Ultimately, Branding based on AI not only equips brands to adapt to technological advancements but also positions them as frontrunners in an increasingly digital landscape (Jeong et al., 2023).

H3: Branding based on AI has noteworthy effect on Disruption by the technology

Mediation of Branding based on AI on Disruption by the technology

The role of Branding based on AI in mediating disruption by the technology is essential for firms as they navigate the intricacies of digital market places. In the face of swift technological advancements, Branding based on AI serves as a facilitator that improves the efficacy of traditional branding methods by incorporating cutting-edge technologies (Jeong et al., 2023). This mediation empowers brands to utilize data analytics, machine learning, and automation to gain deeper insights into consumer preferences and behaviors, ultimately outcompeting in more impactful market placing strategies. By employing AI tools, brands can sift through extensive datasets to uncover trends and insights that guide their branding initiatives, allowing them to adapt promptly to the shifting landscape of consumer expectations (Sharma, Singh & Rana, 2024). Also, Branding based on AI augments personalized customer experiences, which have become increasingly noteworthy in a time when consumers demand customized interactions. Through the application of AI, brands can generate dynamic content that resonates with individual consumers, thereby fostering brand loyalty and engagement. This tailored approach not only fortifies the association among brands and consumers but also reduces the risks associated with disruption by the technology, as brands that effectively connect with their audiences are more likely to sustain relevance and competitiveness (Högberg & Willermark, 2023).

Also, the integration of AI in branding strategies enables firms to pursue continuous innovation. By monitoring consumer feedback and market place trends in real time, brands can modify their products and market placing strategies to ensure alignment with consumer expectations. This flexibility is crucial in a fast-evolving technological landscape, where new innovations can swiftly transform market place conditions. Consequently, Branding based on AI emerges as an indispensable asset that not only refines brand strategies but also serves as a safeguard against the uncertainties introduced by disruption by the technology (Peñarroya & Miralles, 2022). In essence, the mediation of Branding based on AI on disruption by the technology underscores the importance of integrating technology into branding efforts. It enables firms to harness the power of data and personalization, fostering deeper associations with consumers while facilitating agility and innovation. As such, brands that effectively utilize Branding based on AI can navigate disruption by the technologies more sustainability, positioning themselves as leaders in their respective industries and ensuring long-term sustainability in an increasingly competitive landscape (Jeong et al., 2023).

H4: the Link among Strategies for brand adaptation and Disruption by the technology is influenced by Branding based on AI

CONCEPTUAL FRAMEWORK

Figure 1. Conceptual Framework

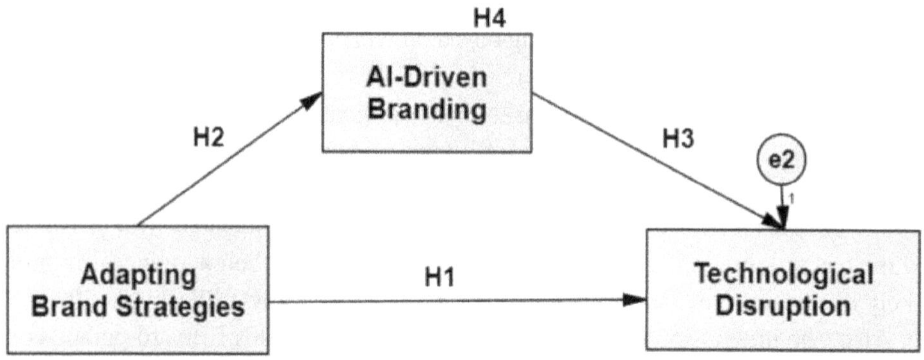

INVESTIGATION METHODOLOGY

In this investigation, a quantitative methodology was utilized to explore the effects of modifying brand strategies on Branding based on AI and disruption by the technology within the Eastern part of Africa. A total of 416 participants were surveyed, representing a wide-ranging demographic to ensure that the outcomes could be generalized across various consumer segments. The data collection was carried out through structured questionnaires designed to capture information on multiple constructs, including brand adaptability, Branding based on AI, and perceptions of disruption by the technology.

To evaluate the appropriateness of the data for factor analysis, the Kaiser-Meyer-Olkin (KMO) measure and Bartlett's test of sphericity were performed. A KMO value exceeding 0.6 manifested that the sample was suitable for factor analysis, thereby confirming the data's validity. Following this, Exploratory Factor Analysis (EFA) was conducted using principal component analysis with Varimax rotation to uncover the underlying factor structure of the constructs. The EFA findings identified several distinct factors that corresponded with the theoretical frameworks established in existing literature, thereby providing a robust basis for scale development. Subsequently, Structural Equation Modeling (SEM) was executed using AMOS software to evaluate the proposed hypotheses and to investigate the associations among the constructs. SEM facilitated a thorough analysis of both the direct and indirect impacts of Branding based on AI on disruption by the technology, as mediated by adaptive brand strategies. The model's fit was assessed through various indices, including the Chi-square statistic, RMSEA, and CFI, ensuring that the model accurately represented the observed data.

DATA ANALYSIS

Table 1. KMO and Bartlett's Test

Kaiser-Meyer-Olkin Measure of Sampling Adequacy.		**.85**
Bartlett's Test of Sphericity	Approx. Chi-Square	1419.612
	Df	93
	Sig.	.001

Source: Authors

Table 1 displays the Measure of Sampling Adequacy. Generally, KMO values exceeding 0.70 are regarded as acceptable, while those above 0.80 are considered good, indicating that the co association matrix is suitable for this analytical approach. This strong KMO value implies that the variables examined in the investigation are likely to possess shared underlying factors, making them appropriate for further investigation through methods such as Exploratory Factor Analysis (EFA).

Bartlett's Test of Sphericity further corroborates the dataset's suitability for factor analysis, producing an approximate Chi-square value of 1419.612 with 93 degrees of freedom. The significance level (Sig.) of 0.001 allows for the rejection of the null hypothesis, which asserts that the co association matrix is an identity matrix (implying that the variables are unrelated). This outcome confirms the presence of noteworthy co associations among the variables, reinforcing the necessity for factor analysis. In conclusion, the outcomes from both the KMO and Bartlett's Test provide compelling evidence that the dataset is appropriate for factor analysis, thereby justifying the subsequent methodological steps taken in the investigation.

Table 2. Total Variance Explained

Component	Initial Eigenvalues			Extraction Sums of Squared Loadings			Rotation Sums of Squared Loadings		
	Total	% of Variance	Cumulative %	Total	% of Variance	Cumulative %	Total	% of Variance	Cumulative %
1	3.61	30.238	30.236	3.61	30.238	30.236	2.95	21.434	21.434
2	1.38	9.764	42.025	1.38	9.764	42.024	2.33	15.452	36.937
3	1.24	9.089	51.17	1.24	9.083	51.115	1.27	14.175	51.115
4	.952	6.780	57.893						
5	.873	6.225	64.116						
6	.770	5.521	69.634						

Extraction Method: PCA
Source: Authors

Table 2 illustrates the findings of the Total Variance Explained. The Initial Eigenvalues reveal that the first component possesses an eigenvalue of 3.61, which corresponds to approximately 30.24% of the overall variance. This notable percentage manifested that the first component encapsulates a considerable portion of the shared variance among the variables, signifying its importance in comprehending the fundamental structure of the dataset. The second component, with an eigenvalue of 1.38, accounts for an additional 9.76% of the variance, outcompeting in a cumulative variance explained of 42.03%. This further demonstrates that, while the first factor is predominant, the second component also plays a noteworthy role in elucidating the data structure. The third component, with an eigenvalue of 1.24, contributes 9.09% to the variance, leading to a cumulative total of 51.17%. Collectively, these three components represent just over half of the total variance, indicating a promising factor structure.

It is noteworthy that the fourth, fifth, and sixth components exhibit eigenvalues below 1.0, with values of 0.952, 0.873, and 0.770, respectively. This observation suggests that these components do not noteworthy contribute to variance explanation and may be deemed unnecessary for further analysis. The extraction sums of squared loadings corroborate the initial eigenvalues, reinforcing the decisions regarding factor retention made during the analysis.

Confirmatory Principal Component Examination

The arrangement of principal components for a set of guided proxies is validated through a statistical method known as confirmatory principal component examination. Based on the underlying framework and co associations among observed proxies, investigations can test hypotheses using Confirmatory Factor Analysis (CFA).To evaluate the hypothesis that there is association among the proxies that are being steered and the latent conceptions that underpin them, the inquiry employed CFA under table 3.

Table 3. Covariances

Covariance			Approximation	S.E.	C.R.	P	Hy.
Branding based on AI	**<-->**	**Disruption by the technology**	**.247**	**.026**	**8.234**	**.00**	**H2**
Branding based on AI	<-->	Adopting Brand Strategies	.303	.039	7.697	.00	**H3**
Disruption by the technology	<-->	Strategies for brand adaptation	.255	.25	7.834	.00	**H1**

Source: Authors

Table 3 outlines the covariance estimates. The initial covariance analysis reveals a notable association among Branding based on AI and disruption by the technology, with an estimated covariance of 0.247. The standard error (S.E.) of 0.026 outcomes in a critical ratio (C.R.) of 8.234, which is highly noteworthy ($p < 0.001$). This finding supports Hypothesis 2 (H2), suggesting that Branding based on AI has a positive effect on disruption by the technology, indicating that brands that effectively leverage AI are more adept at navigating and capitalizing on technological advancements. The subsequent association examined is among Branding based on AI and the adoption of brand strategies, which yields a covariance of 0.303. With a standard error of 0.039 and a C.R. of 7.697, this association is also statistically noteworthy ($p < 0.001$), thereby confirming Hypothesis 3 (H3). This outcome manifested that the integration of AI into branding strategies enhances brands' adaptability, allowing them to respond more effectively to shifts in the market place. Lastly, the covariance among disruption by the technology and the adoption of brand strategies is estimated at 0.255, with a standard error of 0.025 and a C.R. of 7.834, also noteworthy at $p < 0.001$. This finding supports Hypothesis 1 (H1), suggesting that disruption by the technology plays a role in the adoption of adaptive brand strategies. The positive covariance manifested that as technological changes arise, brands are likely to adjust their strategies to maintain relevance and competitiveness in the market place.

Table 4. Validity Concern

	CR	AVE	MSV	MaxR(H)	TD	AI-DB	ABS
TD	0.738	0.643	0.225	0.856	**0.657**		
AI-DB	0.762	0.661	0.133	0.761	0.173	**0.664**	
ABS	0.795	0.604	0.275	0.794	0.387	0.192	**0.688**

Note: TD=Disruption by the technology's; AI-DB=Branding based on AI; ABS=Strategies for brand adaptation

Source: Authors

Table 4 outlines the validity concerns. Beginning with "Composite Reliability (CR)", all constructs demonstrate values that surpass the acceptable benchmark of 0.7, signifying strong internal consistency. Disruption by the technology (TD) records a CR of 0.738, Branding based on AI (AI-DB) achieves a score of 0.762, and Strategies for brand adaptation (ABS) reaches a CR of 0.795. These findings imply that each construct effectively measures its intended concept, thereby instilling confidence in the collected data. Subsequently, the "Average Variance Extracted (AVE)" values further validate the constructs. Each AVE value exceeds the recommended threshold of 0.5, with TD at 0.643, AI-DB at 0.661, and ABS at 0.604. Elevated AVE values suggest that a substantial portion of the variance in the observed variables is accounted for by the latent constructs, thereby reinforcing their validity.

The "Maximum Shared Variance (MSV)" values also shed light on the discriminant validity among the constructs. The MSV values are relatively modest, with TD at 0.225, AI-DB at 0.133, and ABS at 0.275. These low figures manifested that the constructs do not share excessive variance, which supports the notion that they measure distinct concepts. The "Maximum Reliability (MaxR(H))" values further bolster the reliability assessment, with TD at 0.856, AI-DB at 0.761, and ABS at 0.794. These figures provide additional confirmation of the constructs' reliability, suggesting that the measurement model is indeed robust. Finally, the "Average Variance Extracted (AVE)" values reflect the average shared variance among the constructs, with AI-DB and TD exhibiting an average shared variance of 0.664, which remains within acceptable parameters. The ABS values suggest a healthy level of co association among constructs without compromising their distinctiveness.

Mediating role Examination

Figure 2. Structural Equation Model

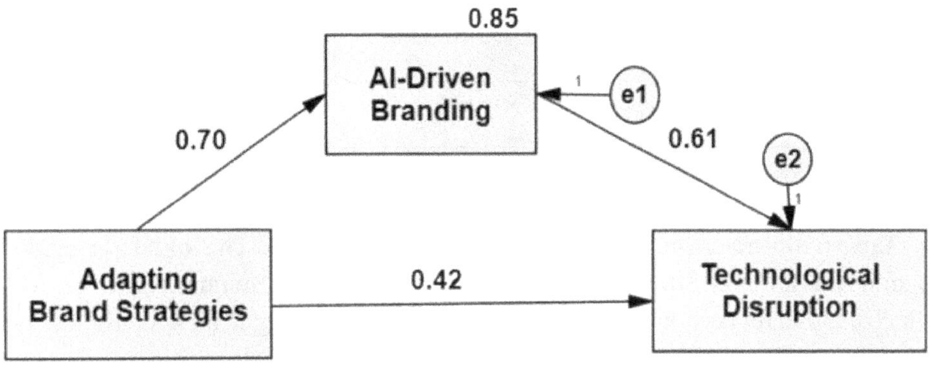

Model fit indices

Table 5. Indices for Model Fit

Sig.	Chi-Sq	RMR	Fitness Goodness	Fitness Confirmatory	TLI	RMSEA
0.002	1.957	.035	0.934	0.918	0.914	.027

Source: Authors

Table 5 outlines the indices pertinent to model fit. The "Chi-Square statistic" of 1.957, along with its significance, manifested the extent of deviation among the observed and anticipated covariance matrices. While a lower Chi-Square value is indicative of a superior fit, it is crucial to evaluate this statistic alongside other fit indices to thoroughly assess the model's adequacy. The "Root Mean Square Residual (RMR)" is recorded at 0.035, which is below the widely accepted threshold of 0.08, signifying a good fit among the model and the data. This low RMR value implies that the residuals—representing the differences among observed and predicted values—are relatively minor, thereby reinforcing the model's validity. Regarding the "Goodness of Fit Index (GFI)" and "Confirmatory Fit Index (CFI)", the values of 0.934 and 0.918, respectively, manifested a robust fit. Both indices surpass the recommended threshold of 0.90, suggesting that the model accounts for a noteworthy portion of the variance in the data, thereby confirming the suitability of the model structure.

Table 6. Regression Examination

Relative			**Approx.**	**S.E.**	**C.R.**	**P**	**Ass.**
AI- Driven Branding	**<---**	**Strategies for brand adaptation**	**.862**	**.144**	**7.587**	**.00**	**H2**
Technological Innovation	<---	AI- Driven Market placing	.324	.136	2.859	.00	H3
Technological Innovation	<---	Strategies for brand adaptation	.952	.195	7.953	.00	H1

Source: Authors

Table 6 illustrates the findings of the regression analysis. The initial association examined is among "Strategies for brand adaptation" and "Branding based on AI", which yields a regression coefficient of 0.862. This figure signifies a robust positive influence, indicating that the effective adaptation of brand strategies considerably enhances the execution of Branding based on AI practices. The critical ratio (C.R.) of 7.587, accompanied by a p-value marked by ".00" (indicating significance at $p < 0.001$), further substantiates the strength of this association. This outcome supports Hypothesis 2 (H2), illustrating that brands that adeptly modify their strategies are more inclined to utilize AI effectively to engage consumers. The subsequent association examines "Branding based on AI" and its effect on "Technological Innovation", revealing a regression coefficient of 0.324. This coefficient reflects a moderate positive impact, suggesting that the incorporation of AI in branding initiatives aids in fostering innovation within firms. The C.R. of 2.859, which is also statistically noteworthy at $p < 0.001$, bolsters Hypothesis 3 (H3). This finding highlights the critical role of Branding based on AI in advancing technological progress, indicating that brands employing AI tools are better equipped to innovate and adapt to market place demands.

Lastly, the association among "Strategies for brand adaptation" and "Technological Innovation" shows a regression coefficient of 0.952, indicating a very strong positive influence. The C.R. of 7.953, with significance at $p < 0.001$, provides strong support for Hypothesis 1 (H1).This finding illustrates those firms that effectively adapt their brand strategies are not only more responsive to technological changes but also more likely to drive innovation within their operations.

Table 7. Mediating role Effect

	Influence	Worth	Path Influence
Strategies for brand adaptation→Disruption by the technology	Direct Influence	.42	Direct influence stated
Strategies for brand adaptation→Branding based on AI→Disruption by the technology	Indirect Influence	.70*.61=.43	Indirect Influence Ensued
	Whole influence	.85	Partial mediation

Source: Authors

Table 7 demonstrates the mediating function. The initial association analyzed is the "direct effect" of strategies for brand adaptation on disruption by the technology, which is quantified at 0.42. This coefficient signifies a notable direct impact, suggesting that sustainable brand adaptations can noteworthy influence an firm's capacity to manage technological advancements. This finding emphasizes the critical role of adaptability and responsiveness in branding strategies as firms confront shifting technological environments. Also, the table investigates the "indirect effect" of strategies for brand adaptation through Branding based on AI on disruption by the technology. The computed path influence for this association stands at 0.70, which, when multiplied by a path coefficient of 0.61, outcomes in a product of 0.43. This outcome manifested that when strategies for brand adaptation is facilitated by Branding based on AI, the effect on disruption by the technology is considerable. The indirect influence implies that the effective incorporation of AI into branding strategies enhances firms' ability to adjust to technological changes, thereby amplifying the overall effect on disruption by the technology. The "total influence" of strategies for brand adaptation on disruption by the technology, encompassing both direct and indirect routes, amounts to 0.85. This aggregate measure reflects the combined impact of strategies for brand adaptation on disruption by the technology, underscoring the importance of both direct and mediated pathways in fostering formal transformation.

DISCUSSION

The outcomes of this investigation emphasize the essential association among the adaptation of brand strategies, AI-enhanced branding, and the impact of disruption by the technology. The findings manifested that firms that sustainability modify their brand strategies are in a stronger position to utilize AI technologies, thereby improving their ability to manage and respond to technological shifts. This observation is consistent with modern market placing theories that augment adaptability and responsiveness as fundamental components of brand success in an ever-evolving digital environment. The notable direct effect of strategies for brand adaptation on disruption by the technology highlights the importance of agility for brands. As technological innovations continue to alter consumer expectations and market place conditions, brands that can quickly modify their strategies are more likely to succeed. This insight suggests that firms should emphasize adaptive capabilities in their branding initiatives, ensuring they can adjust to new technologies and trends as they arise.

Also, the investigation underscores the significance of Branding based on AI as a mediator in this dynamic. The considerable indirect effect of strategies for brand adaptation through Branding based on AI illustrates that the incorporation of AI tools is not just an enhancement but a vital aspect of digital branding strategies. Brands that effectively leverage AI can obtain valuable insights, tailor customer experiences, and innovate their product offerings, all of which contribute to a more robust competitive edge amid disruption by the technology. The findings also introduce the notion of partial mediation, indicating that while strategies for brand adaptation has a direct effect on disruption by the technology, this effect is considerably amplified when Branding based on AI is included in the analysis. This highlights the synergistic association among adaptive strategies and AI technologies, reinforcing the notion that these elements should not be viewed in isolation but rather as interconnected components of a cohesive branding strategy.

CONCLUSION

This investigation offers noteworthy insights into the interplay among adaptive brand strategies, Branding based on AI, and disruption by the technology. The outcomes manifested that firms that sustainability modify their branding approaches are not only better equipped to utilize artificial intelligence but are also more adept at addressing the challenges associated with swift technological advancements. The notable direct impact of adaptive brand strategies on disruption by the technology highlights the necessity for brands to remain flexible and responsive in the current dynamic market place landscape. Also, the investigation underscores the essential mediating function of Branding based on AI, demonstrating that the incorporation of AI tools noteworthy augments the efficacy of adaptive strategies. This association emphasizes the need to perceive branding and technology as interrelated components that together foster innovation and competitiveness. The acknowledgment of partial mediation further illustrates that while adaptive brand strategies directly influence disruption by the technology, their effects are intensified when Branding based on AI is utilized.

EXECUTIVEIAL INSIGHTS

The outcomes of this investigation present several noteworthy executively insights for firms aiming to improve their branding strategies amid disruption by the technology's. Primarily, it is essential for executives to acknowledge the critical role of adaptability in brand strategies. By cultivating a culture that emphasizes agility and responsiveness, firms can better equip themselves to swiftly address evolving market place dynamics and technological progress. This adaptability not only aids in sustaining relevance but also in capitalizing on new opportunities that emerge from changes in consumer preferences and technological advancements. Also, the investigation highlights the necessity of incorporating Branding based on AI within comprehensive market placing strategies. Executives ought to invest in AI technologies that facilitate data-informed decision-making and personalized customer interactions. By utilizing AI tools, brands can obtain valuable insights into consumer behavior, enabling more focused market placing initiatives and improved customer experiences. This integration not only strengthens brand loyalty but also fosters innovation, as firms can continuously enhance their offerings based on real-time feedback and market place developments. Also, the acknowledgment of the mediating function of Branding based on AI manifested that firms should adopt a holistic approach to technological investments. Instead of perceiving AI as an isolated tool, it should be regarded as a vital element of a wider branding strategy. Executives should augment cross-departmental collaboration among market placing, IT, and product development teams to ensure that AI initiatives are aligned with overarching brand goals and contribute to enhanced adaptability.

PRACTICAL INSIGHTS

The outcomes of this investigation present numerous practical insights for firms seeking to improve their branding strategies in the face of disruption by the technology. Firstly, it is imperative for businesses to focus on creating adaptable branding strategies that can swiftly respond to fluctuating market place conditions. This necessitates the execution of regular market place evaluations and consumer investigation to remain aligned with shifting preferences and the advent of new technologies. By cultivating a culture that augments experimentation and agility, companies can better position themselves to seize emerging opportunities. Also, the incorporation of Branding based on AI methodologies is vital for digital market placing initiatives. Firms should allocate resources towards AI technologies that facilitate data gathering and analysis, thereby enabling more personalized market placing approaches. In practical terms, this entails the implementation of customer association management (CRM) systems that utilize AI to scrutinize consumer data, categorize audiences, and provide customized content. Such tailored experiences not only improve customer engagement but also foster brand loyalty, as consumers increasingly anticipate that brands will recognize and address their unique needs. In addition, prioritizing the training and up skilling of employees in AI tools and data analytics is essential. Firms can conduct workshops and training programs to ensure that staff members possess the necessary skills to effectively leverage AI in their branding strategies. This pragmatic approach not only enhances workforce capabilities but also nurtures a culture of innovation and flexibility.

THEORETICAL INSIGHTS

The findings of this investigation contribute noteworthy to the theoretical discourse surrounding branding, technology, and firm adaptability. By establishing the associations among strategies for brand adaptation, Branding based on AI, and disruption by the technology, this investigation enriches existing branding theories and models that emphasize the importance of flexibility and responsiveness in dynamic environments. The investigation supports the notion that adaptive brand strategies are not merely advantageous but essential for firms aiming to thrive in an era characterized by rapid technological changes. Also, the identification of Branding based on AI as a mediating factor introduces a nuanced understanding of how technology impacts branding strategies. This mediating role underscores the importance of integrating advanced technologies into branding frameworks, challenging traditional views that may have separated market placing practices from technological considerations. By demonstrating that AI can enhance both the direct and indirect effects of brand adaptation on disruption by the technology, this investigation provides a more comprehensive perspective on the interplay among market placing and technology. Also, the investigation's emphasis on partial mediation invites further exploration into the mechanisms through which AI influences branding outcomes. Future investigation can build upon these findings by examining specific AI tools and their efficacy in enhancing brand adaptability and innovation. This could lead to the development of more refined theoretical models that account for the complexities of technology integration in branding strategies.

RECOMMENDATIONS

This investigation's findings yield several recommendations for firms aiming to improve their branding strategies amid disruption by the technology. Firstly, it is essential for companies to focus on creating and implementing adaptable branding strategies. This entails regularly assessing and modifying market placing tactics to stay in tune with evolving consumer preferences and technological progress. Firms should engage in regular market place investigation to collect insights that guide strategic modifications, ensuring their branding remains pertinent and resonates with their target demographics. Also, firms ought to invest in artificial intelligence technologies that support data-driven decision-making and personalized market placing efforts. The adoption of sophisticated customer association management (CRM) systems with AI functionalities can empower businesses to analyze customer data efficiently, segment their audiences, and deliver customized market placing communications. Such investments will not only augment customer engagement but also enhance brand loyalty by offering personalized experiences that cater to the unique needs of consumers. Also, it is vital for firms to cultivate a culture of ongoing learning and innovation among their workforce. Implementing training programs centered on AI tools and data analytics will equip employees with the necessary skills to effectively utilize technology in their branding initiatives. This dedication to employee development can nurture a more innovative atmosphere within the firm, motivating teams to pursue new concepts and strategies in branding.

FUTURE DIRECTIONS

The outcomes of this investigation present numerous opportunities for future investigations that could delve deeper into the interplay among branding and disruption by the technology. A particularly promising avenue is the examination of specific AI tools and technologies that noteworthy bolster adaptive brand strategies. Subsequent studies might undertake comparative evaluations of various AI applications, including machine learning algorithms, predictive analytics, and natural language processing, to assess their distinct effects on branding outcomes and customer engagement. Also, investigating the influence of firm culture on the sustainable integration of AI and brand adaptability represents another valuable investigation area. Gaining insights into how cultural dynamics affect technology adoption and the readiness to modify branding strategies could be beneficial for practitioners. Investigations could analyze case studies of firms that have adeptly managed disruption by the technologies, pinpointing essential cultural factors that contribute to their achievements. Another critical area for future investigation involves broadening the geographic and industry focus of studies related to Branding based on AI and disruption by the technology. While this investigation concentrated on a particular context, exploring these associations across various regions and sectors could uncover unique challenges and opportunities. Comparative analyses could deepen the understanding of how cultural, economic, and technological elements shape branding strategies on a global scale. Finally, conducting longitudinal studies that monitor the progression of brand strategies and technological adoption over time would yield richer insights into the long-term insights of Branding based on AI on firmal performance. Such investigation could help identify emerging trends and best practices, thereby assisting brands in their strategic planning and decision-making endeavors.

REFERENCE

Adula, M., & Kant, S. (2025). Impact of Smart Entrepreneurship and Territorial Marketing on Regional Branding: Case of Ethiopia. In *Sustainable and Intelligent Territorial Marketing and Entrepreneurship* (pp. 229–256). IGI Global., DOI: 10.4018/979-8-3693-9775-6.ch008

Alberti, A. M., Pivoto, D. G., Rezende, T. T., Leal, A. V., Both, C. B., Facina, M. S., Moreira, R., & de Oliveira Silva, F. (2024). Disruptive 6G architecture: Software-centric, AI-driven, and digital market place-based mobile networks. *Computer Networks*, 252, 110682. DOI: 10.1016/j.comnet.2024.110682

Amankwah-Amoah, J., Abdalla, S., Mogaji, E., Elbanna, A., & Dwivedi, Y. K. (2024). The impending disruption of creative industries by generative AI: Opportunities, challenges, and investigation agenda. *International Journal of Information Management*, 79, 102759. DOI: 10.1016/j.ijinfomgt.2024.102759

Belhadi, A., Mani, V., Kamble, S. S., Khan, S. A. R., & Verma, S. (2024). Artificial intelligence-driven innovation for enhancing supply chain resilience and performance under the effect of supply chain dynamism: An empirical investigation. *Annals of Operations Research*, 333(2), 627–652. DOI: 10.1007/s10479-021-03956-x

Bulchand-Gidumal, J., William Secin, E., O'Connor, P., & Buhalis, D. (2024). Artificial intelligence's impact on hospitality and tourism market placing: Exploring key themes and addressing challenges. *Current Issues in Tourism*, 27(14), 2345–2362. DOI: 10.1080/13683500.2023.2229480

Castillo, D., Canhoto, A. I., & Said, E. (2021). The dark side of AI-powered service interactions: Exploring the process of co-destruction from the customer perspective. *Service Industries Journal*, 41(13-14), 900–925. DOI: 10.1080/02642069.2020.1787993

Danciu, V. (2021). Adapting and Modernizing the Post-Covid Market placing Policy Under the Impact of Consumption Challenges. *Romanian Economic Journal*, (79).

Galanakis, C. M., Rizou, M., Aldawoud, T. M., Ucak, I., & Rowan, N. J. (2021). Innovations and technology disruptions in the food sector within the COVID-19 pandemic and post-lockdown era. *Trends in Food Science & Technology*, 110, 193–200. DOI: 10.1016/j.tifs.2021.02.002 PMID: 36567851

Högberg, K., & Willermark, S. (2023). Strategic responses to digital disruption in incumbent firms–a strategy-as-practice perspective. *Journal of Computer Information Systems*, 63(2), 281–292. DOI: 10.1080/08874417.2022.2057373

Jabo, D., Kant, S., & Borji, B. (2025). Customer Orientation and Ethiopian Bank Performance With Mediation of Competitive Advantage. In Leveraging AI for Effective Digital Relationship Marketing (pp. 459-482). IGI Global. DOI: 10.4018/979-8-3693-5340-0.ch015

Jeong, I., Jean, R. J. B., Kim, D., & Samiee, S. (2023). Managing disruptive external forces in international market placing. *International Market placing. RE:view*, 40(5), 936–956.

Kant, S., & Adula, M. (2024). Mediated by AI-Based Generative Re-Enforcement Learning and Work Attitude: Are Intrinsic Rewards Transforming Employee Perceived Organizational Support? In Gomathi Sankar, J., & David, A. (Eds.), *Generative AI for Transformational Management* (pp. 83–108). IGI Global., DOI: 10.4018/979-8-3693-5578-7.ch004

Khaled, W. (2024). Securing brand trust and reputation in an era of political polarisation and AI-driven disinformation. *Journal of Brand Strategy*, 13(1), 6–14. DOI: 10.69554/PJFE5856

Khan, S. A. R., Ponce, P., Tanveer, M., Aguirre-Padilla, N., Mahmood, H., & Shah, S. A. A. (2021). Technological innovation and circular economy practices: Business strategies to mitigate the effects of COVID-19. *Sustainability (Basel)*, 13(15), 8479. DOI: 10.3390/su13158479

Niguse, T., Kant, S., & Adula, M. (2025). Mediation Effect of Customer Loyalty in Relationship between Market Orientation, Entrepreneurial Orientation, and Firm Performance in Ethiopia. In Leveraging AI for Effective Digital Relationship Marketing (pp. 419-458). IGI Global. DOI: 10.4018/979-8-3693-5340-0.ch014

Peñarroya-Farell, M., & Miralles, F. (2022). Business model adaptation to the COVID-19 crisis: Strategic response of the Spanish cultural and creative firms. *Journal of Open Innovation: Technology, Market place, and Complexity, 8*(1), 39.

Rego, L., Brady, M., Leone, R., Roberts, J., Srivastava, C., & Srivastava, R. (2022). Brand response to environmental turbulence: A framework and propositions for resistance, recovery and reinvention. *International Journal of Investigation in Market placing, 39*(2), 583-602.

Setiawan, A. S., Widyartono, A., & Ony, J. G. (2021). Implementation of Business Strategy, Technology Usage, and Business Continuity During the Covid-19 Pandemic. *Jurnal Akuntansi*, 25(2), 186–200. DOI: 10.24912/ja.v25i2.805

Sharma, M., Luthra, S., Joshi, S., & Kumar, A. (2021). Accelerating retail supply chain performance against pandemic disruption: Adopting resilient strategies to mitigate the long-term effects. *Journal of Enterprise Information Management*, 34(6), 1844–1873. DOI: 10.1108/JEIM-07-2020-0286

Sharma, M., Singh, A., & Rana, S. (2024). Empowering Hospitality Brands AI Strategies for Enhanced Customer Experiences in Emerging Market places. In *Integrating AI-Driven Technologies Into Service Market placing* (pp. 173–190). IGI Global. DOI: 10.4018/979-8-3693-7122-0.ch010

Talukder, M. B., Kumar, S., & Tyagi, P. K. (Eds.). (2024). *Impact of AI and Tech-Driven Solutions in Hospitality and Tourism*. IGI Global. DOI: 10.4018/979-8-3693-6755-1

van Esch, P. (2024). Disruptive AI: the response depends on the buyer's political ideology. *Journal of Business & Industrial Market placing, 39*(4), 673-691.

KEY TERMS WITH DEFINITIONS

AI-Enhanced Branding:: This involves the incorporation of artificial intelligence technologies into branding initiatives to bolster market placing efforts, enhance customer interaction, and tailor consumer experiences. AI-enhanced branding leverages data analysis, machine learning, and automation to refine brand engagement.

Brand Strategies:: This refers to the approach firms take to adjust their branding methods in order to effectively address evolving market place dynamics, shifts in consumer preferences, and advancements in technology. Such flexibility is essential for sustaining brand relevance and ensuring competitiveness.

Technological Transformation: This encompasses substantial shifts in the market place outcompeting from the advent of new technologies that fundamentally change the way businesses function, provide value, or connect with customers. Such transformation can render traditional practices obsolete while paving the way for innovative solutions.

Chapter 9
Understanding Artificial Intelligence and Its Impact on Branding

Priyansh Bagga
https://orcid.org/0009-0008-6847-5025
Christ University, India

Jasmine Kaur
Christ University, India

ABSTRACT

AI has become a transformative force in branding, changing firms' approach to relating to their customers and creating brands. Chapter-specific: AI is used differently for branding because delivering personalized customer experiences, generating dynamic content, and optimizing consumer engagements through data-driven insights play a considerable role. AI technologies like machine learning and predictive analytics help brands understand consumer behavior and, therefore, really segment and target marketing activity. This chapter also highlights AI's operational efficiency in brand management, automating customer interactions, and analyzing the sentiment of a consumer in real time. In addition, it establishes how AI affects innovation in branding by providing scope for adaptive and responsive strategies for brands that help keep up the ever-increasing dynamic pace of an ever-changing digital marketplace. The research is a critical insight for brand strategists, marketers, and businesses looking to leverage AI for more robust and resilient brands as age of digital disruption moves on.

DOI: 10.4018/979-8-3693-9461-8.ch009

INTRODUCTION:

Marketing and brand management got a boost from the addition of artificial intelligence, making firms interact with their customers much more efficiently, customized, and effectively in marketing. In business operations and transactions increasingly happening in digital forms, AI provides new means to enable interactions and identification between companies and their customers, infusing changes that affect the approach guiding how brands are perceived and chosen in competitive markets (Davenport & Ronanki, 2018). AI technologies have delivered much to brands, making them more personal to their target audience. Moreover, by using natural language processing and machine learning algorithms, AI technologies enable faster decision-making processes. Among them, the most recently highly noticed are chatbots since they have been applied in brand communication to achieve accessible, effective, and engaging customer service (Cheng & Jiang, 2020a). These developments have allowed AI to take the driver's seat of digital marketing, thereby unlocking more innovative branding strategies that focus on real-time consumer behavior changes and elicit real engagement.

This is why AI is implemented in branding and marketing companies: it transforms how a business interacts with its customers and creates more profound and practical relationships between a business and its customers. AI and, therefore, chatbots have been very effective in the service that a firm can offer clients and instant solutions that customize the time spent interacting with the customers (Forbes, 2017).

For instance, a chatbot allows consumers to receive information, order, or ask for assistance without the presence of a human, thus making the customer experience less laborious and more interactive (Kietzmann et al., 2018). A paradigmatic case in point is AI-empowered chatbot marketing, which enables the brand to reach out to its customers more efficiently and interactively through informative and accessible services (Cheng & Jiang, 2020b). The literature has verified that CMEs would positively impact long-term customer behavioral intention and brand perception, resulting in increased brand loyalty and engagement (Brandtzaeg & Følstad, 2017). Understanding how chatbots and other AI-driven marketing efforts facilitate the interface with customers will enable scientists to better understand the impact of AI on customer-brand relationships, response, and loyalty.

While AI is increasingly becoming part of the marketing mix, the apparent gap in empirical research persists in its specific impacts on branding (Schultz & Block, 2015). Whereas studies have thus far shed light on the implications of AI in customer service, consumer behavior, and social media advertising, the increased use of AI technology in the context of shaping brand equity, loyalty, and general consumer-brand relationships has received little attention (Zarouali et al., 2018). This limited focus on branding could be ascribed to the fact that AI applications in marketing are still a relatively new phenomenon, and the general application of sophisticated AI algorithms and machine learning models in brand management only recently began gaining ground (Stone et al., 2020). This gap is impressive, especially in the context of digital marketing. AI-driven innovations, like chatbots, generative adversarial networks (GANs), and algorithm-based personalization, can significantly swing consumer attitudes and preferences for branding. Addressing this research gap, recent studies have begun to look into AI applications in branding to discuss various related topics, such as social media analytics, digital content creation, and consumer predictive modeling (Muhuri et al., 2019). For instance, the impact of AI on branding has been traced through bibliometric analysis under such broad themes as social media analytics, neural networks, and digital innovations (Varsha et al., 2020). Such studies highlight the following: how AI is crucial in improving brand equity, brand love, and retaining customers through highly particularized and focused marketing campaigns.

This chapter will contribute to this relatively emerging field of AI-driven branding and marketing, where the chapter will discuss the multifaceted impacts of AI technologies- chatbots and GANs-that involve consumer responses and brand relationships in more general terms. It will examine how CMEs affect communication quality and CBR and customer responses in various industries using empirical data collected in the U.S. market (Cheng & Jiang, 2020a). It will further elaborate on the role of AI in branding strategies by using deep bibliometric analysis of the relevant literature published between 1982 and 2019 (Varsha et al., 2020). This exploration will delve into consumer behavior, digital marketing practices, and branding outcomes, supported by empirical evidence and case studies. This chapter will expand on how GANs affect consumer purchasing intent in the fashion industry and how AI-generated product designs influence perceived value and willingness to pay (Sohn et al., 2020).

There are three objectives for this chapter. Firstly, it acts as a quantitative analysis of CMEs and how they affect the quality of communication in chatbot marketing, where it identifies the most relevant factors that facilitate successful consumer interaction. It aims at exploring the nexus between CBR and customer responses. It explores how AI-driven marketing drives customer loyalty, brand preferences, and purchase intentions. Third, it offers insight into the practical application of AI in branding using a wide range of empirical studies of an overall view of transformative potential in brand management by AI (Paschen et al., 2019). Based on the above objectives, this chapter contributes to the debate in its stride on how AI can help in marketing and branding issues in general and gives guidelines for those professionals looking forward to formulating AI-based strategies for propelling a much more significant and more sustainable brand relationship with customers.

Apart from its contribution toward an academic understanding of the role of AI in branding, the insights also prove invaluable for practitioners interested in tapping into the vast world of AI technology for branding and marketing purposes. This chapter, therefore, provides a basis for effectively developing AI-led strategies to meet consumers' new expectations by critically assessing AI's potential in increasing the quality of communications, brand loyalty, and personal consumer interactions. The statistics elaborated upon in this chapter point toward a reaction to AI-driven trends because of rapidly increasing consumer demand for responsive, interactive, and seamless brand experiences merged into their digital lifestyle (Chung et al., 2018). Furthermore, this chapter discusses the reveal of AI-generated content, as transparency in the role of AI in product development or customer service can influence consumer attitudes and loyalty towards a brand. The analysis presented here illustrates that consumers have a greater likelihood of buying and paying more for products when interacting with AI-generated products, especially when their use of AI technology is undisclosed, as demonstrated in studies that have taken place with GAN-generated products within the fashion industry (Sohn et al., 2020).

In conclusion, AI in branding and digital marketing is one of the most critical transformations, along with the potential of AI technologies. It implies diverse changes across how brands communicate and understand their customers better. Chatbots and GANs, besides other AI-powered tools, are increasingly used in an overall shift towards customer-centric, data-driven marketing approaches that will use AI as a source of meaningful brand experiences. However, since AI has become one of the most swiftly adopted business sector advancements in marketing, academic research must catch up to provide a holistic framework for understanding AI's role in branding. This chapter attempts to contribute to filling in the gap by carrying out an elaborate analysis regarding AI's influence on branding practices, customer behavior, and consumer-brand relationships. Through its analysis of AI applications across industries, this chapter ultimately seeks to enhance academic understanding of AI-driven branding and provide inputs for practice by marketers interested in developing more personal, engaging, and sustainable brand relationships in the age of AI.

Theoretical Framework

The face of branding is changing fundamentally, with AI changing how firms interact and engage with their customers, create a brand, and design customer experiences. This transformation results from AI's capability to process immense data volumes, generate actionable insights, and execute previously unimaginable strategies at the scale and speed required. Adding some theoretical transformation models to this conversation brings a meaningful framework for explaining dynamic shifts AI brings to the branding process and puts critical personalization, customer insights, and operational efficiencies at center stage.

One of the most contentious shifts AI presents in branding is that personalization becomes a strategy to be looked up to. Traditionally, personalization would have been based on the segmentation of consumers on broad demographic or psychographic data. However, the evolution of personalization through AI has matured to very personalized levels where brands can deliver customized experiences. The theory underpinning this revolution came from Keller's Customer-Based Brand Equity (CBBE) Model in 1993. According to this model, brand equity can only be developed when having pleasant, positive brand encounters between brands and consumers.

AI takes that principle to the next dimension by allowing brands to collect and analyze granular information about browsing behavior, purchase history, or even social media activity to deliver such hyper-personalized experiences. To exemplify this, AI-powered recommendation engines, seen on Netflix and Spotify, for instance, process users' behavior in real-time to deliver content specific to user preferences. This may also extend to fulfill the desires of the customers and, by extension, establish an emotional connection with the brand. This will also nourish the underlying philosophies of the CBBE model.

Another theoretical model applied to the context of AI, as going to personalization, is the Technology-Driven Relationship Marketing model. The model captures how technology is a critical facilitator in the development of long-term relationships between brands and customers. Consumer needs can be sensed with an AI tool, and tailored solutions can be delivered, essentially strengthening those relationships because the customers feel understood and valued. Thus, predictive analytics allows AI to identify patterns that will give hints about a need for something at a point when the need is not yet expressed consciously by the consumer and helps to prevent brands from being surprised by their needs at the wrong time in the marketplace.

Another radical revolution AI has brought to the importance of customer insights in branding is that they are at the core of successful branding strategies because they assist businesses in understanding consumer preferences, motivations, and pain points. Usually, obtaining and analyzing such information takes a lot of work and can lead to errors. However, AI has transformed the whole thing by auto-extracting and auto-interpreting data from its sources, such as social media, online reviews, and transactional records. The Dynamic Capabilities Theory of (Teece et al., 1997), explains the profound change in this area by defining organizations' sense and seizing opportunities while reconfiguring their resources in changing environments. AI gives brands this dynamic capability and real-time insights into what is happening with consumers and market trends. For instance, tools based on NLP can analyze the sentiment from what the public says on social media regarding whether or not the public generally holds favor for a brand or a product. When new trends and shifts in consumer opinion are identified, brands can adjust more quickly to remain relevant and competitive.

Operational efficiency is the other area where AI makes a difference in branding transition. A significant characteristic of good branding is efficiency because it would decide how much value a company could add to its customers and then benefit from that in return. The integration of AI into branding processes allows business organizations to be freed from the constraints of repetitive tasks, optimized resource distribution, and workflow streamlining. The technology Acceptance Model (TAM) by Davis, which was created in 1989, provides insight into how technological innovations such as AI are adopted within any organization. The model infers that perceived usefulness and ease of use determine what technology will be adopted. AI is a solution meant to guarantee better efficiency based on the two criteria. AI presents a solution that brands prefer to gain optimal operation effectiveness.

Resource-Based View of the firm explains the role of AI in operational efficiency. This theory draws attention to leveraging unique resources and capabilities through which a firm can achieve a sustainable competitive advantage. AI is a valuable resource brands possess; it comes with capabilities that are hard for competitors to match. It lets the brands develop proprietary algorithms, datasets, and processes when integrating AI into their operations. For example, Amazon's AI optimizes its supply chain and logistics business, creating a competitive advantage with its branding efforts. In this context, Amazon demonstrates its brand's promise by providing timely, secure, and error-free delivery of products.

The second most significant method through which AI may be effective in branding is by improving the customer experience through real-time engagement. According to the Unified Theory of Acceptance and Use of Technology (UTAUT) model, consumer perceptions regarding interactions with technology-usable branding techniques are represented. The theory claims that some critical factors to new technology acceptance exist, namely performance expectancy, effort expectancy, social influence, and facilitating conditions. These factors may easily be fulfilled when new AI-based branding techniques provide experiences of high performance and user-friendliness based on personalized recommendations and instant support. For example, virtual assistants like Siri and Alexa increase the customer experience because customers will quickly get customized support from the brand ecosystems. Furthermore, it increases consumer satisfaction and reinforces brand loyalty through smooth and enjoyable experiences.

As businesses integrate and implement more AI technologies, these conceptual insights will inform the development of effective and ethical branding strategies to be built. If used to the utmost potential, AI can not only let brands adapt to the difficulties associated with the digital age but also help them thrive amidst increasingly competitive marketplaces.

- **Technology Acceptance Model (TAM) and Unified Theory of Acceptance and Use of Technology (UTAUT):**

The Technology Acceptance Model (TAM) is one of the most widely adopted frameworks to explain how users would accept and adopt new technologies. In TAM, perceived usefulness and ease of use determine an individual's likelihood of using technology. For AI-based branding, these two factors help explain why consumers and businesses are adopting AI-driven tools such as chatbots, virtual assistants, and recommendation engines. For example, technologies that make for a personalized experience with less effort, such as automated customer service or recommendations for personalized shopping, attest to the existence of such factors, thus the likelihood of accepting them.

- **Extended and adapted from TAM is other researchers' Unified Theory of Acceptance and Use of Technology (UTAUT):**

Which includes more factors like social influence, facilitating conditions, and trust. Such factors are pretty relevant for AI branding because they explain how the trust that consumers hold for AI systems, systems such as those that might propose relevant products based on a history of browsing or even analyze the sentiment through reviews, would impact the engagement of those consumers with brands. For example, works such as (Mishra et al., 2020) demonstrate how consumer trust, social influence, and the perceived ease of use of AI technologies significantly contribute to adopting AI in branding that could be aligned within the UTAUT's framework. (Lee et al. 2021) also demonstrated that AI adoption for consumer services can be driven by functionality, system transparency, and system reliability. Therefore, these models are firm foundations on which to base the understanding of consumer behavior toward AI technologies in branding.

- **Consumer-based Brand Equity (CBBE) Model:**

The consumer-based Brand Equity Model by Keller 1993 explains how brand equity is created based on consumer perceptions. This model is particularly relevant for applications of AI in branding, as AI fundamentally changes how brands connect with consumers and thus impacts their brand equity. Indeed, (Keller, 1993) noted that brand equity depends on brand awareness and brand image. Therefore, AI-based tools that provide custom experiences, such as dynamic content generation, product recommending, and AI-driven targeted ads, support both.

A study (Huang & Rust., 2021) stated that AI technologies directly influence customer-based brand equity. AI personalization technologies make products more appealing to customer individuality and deliver a more relevant experience with proper offers. This is the focus of (Ganapathi et al., 2022), who discussed how AI content, such as product recommendations, reinforces brand resonance and potential customers' psychological bonding with the brand. The greater the bond, the more loyalty, advocacy, and financial payback toward the brand. The CBBE model, thus, is an essential guide to shaping our perspective on AI's influence over brand value.

- **Relationship Marketing Theory:**

According to Morgan and Hunt relationship marketing theory, 1994, the implementation of durable business-to-business and customer relationships is essential. According to this theory, trust, commitment, and mutual value creation are central to successful marketing strategies. AI is involved in this theory quite specifically; for instance, it involves engaging in continuous and personalized customer interactions to establish trust and deepen the relationship.

According to (Choi et al., 2023), sentiment analysis through AI will enable brands to respond emotionally to the feelings of their customers in real time, further allowing them to build even more personalized and better relationships. AI tools can monitor online conversations and analyze customer feedback while appropriately responding to the views, which may automatically alter the brand's messages to the customer's preferences. This creates a feeling of engagement and connection, thus making the customers loyal to the brand. The resulting positive effects, through the use of AI to provide more interactive and customized responses, can further strengthen the commitment of the customers, which is always at the heart of relationship marketing theory.

- **Artificial Intelligence Marketing (AIM) Framework:**

The AIM Framework (Paschen et al., 2019) describes how AI is applied in new approaches to marketing for improved brand management. AI brings along dynamically generated content, real-time consumer engagement by the business, and automated decision-making. Through these capabilities, brands can respond flexibly to consumer behavior, thus improving the responsiveness and relevance of marketing activities.

Such AI-based tools include machine learning, predictive analytics, and generative adversarial networks, which will allow the creation of highly customized marketing campaigns. Indeed, as demonstrated by (Han et al., 2022), GANs in product design produce innovative designs that consumers are attracted to, further improving the brand image and consumer experience with new and creative product offerings. According to (Paschen et al., 2019), to survive within the dynamic digital marketplace, this dynamic adaptability is critical for competitiveness. AI in marketing enables brands to be fast responsive to shifting consumer preferences, aligning well with AIM principles.

- **SDL:**

(Vargo and Lusch 2004) Service-dominant logic (SDL) is a conceptual framework for co-creating value between brands and consumers. Based on SDL, it is evident that customers are no longer passive recipients but are instead active co-creators of value. AI facilitated the process of co-creation by providing tools to the consumer to personalize their interactions with the brand and contribute to creating value. For instance, through recommendation systems driven by artificial intelligence, consumers get customized product recommendations that they can then change or tailor according to their needs. This engagement transforms consumers into coproducers of their brand experiences.

(Zhang et al. 2023) went further to show how AI-augmented virtual environments can be applied to test a product or service by consumers before a purchase decision is made, thus engaging in developing a product. This mutual interaction gives rise to the very nature of SDL as it turns consumer-brand relationships into a dynamic exchange. In this regard, AI technologies become highly important as they get customers hooked into co-creating value for the brand by turning them into a stakeholder in the brand experience.

- **Social Exchange Theory (SET):**

Blau's Social Exchange Theory explores how reciprocal exchanges build social relationships. It establishes how both parties bring value to each other through these exchanges. In AI branding, SET is highly relevant because AI affords two-way value exchanges between brands and customers through more personalized experiences and relevant recommendations. Consumers, therefore, find that the brand addresses their specific needs. This builds up trust and engagement.

For instance, (Mehta et al., 2023) discussed the influence of predictive analytics-based loyalty programs on perceptions of fairness and reciprocity. AI uses consumers' data to anticipate future purchase behavior; it gives specific rewards, which makes the consumer bond to the brand. A feeling of balance that the two parties will get from the trade-off generated by AI-based loyalty programs enhances trust among consumers and makes them loyal to the brand.

- **DOI Theory:**

Essential to understanding how such innovations as AI diffuse in the marketplace is Rogers' DOI theory in 2003. This theory deals with how new technologies diffuse through social systems; some groups may accept innovations faster than others. For branding, AI tools like recommendation engines, predictive analytics, and personalization algorithms represent innovations by which businesses' approach toward consumer engagement can be reshaped. For example, (Chatterjee et al., 2021) said that fashion brands quickly adopted AI-driven personalization to meet consumer demand for unique, specific shopping experiences. With these shifting innovations, consumer expectations change, and companies must embrace AI technologies to stay on top.

- **Dynamic Capabilities Theory:**

Dynamic Capabilities Theory, as coined by (Teece et al., 1997), underscores a firm's ability to adapt and innovate within rapidly changing environments. AI plays a critical role in augmenting these dynamic capabilities of brands as they start to collect, analyze, and act on information at a speed never seen before. It helps brands predict shifts in the market, enhance the potential for targeting consumers, and speed up how marketing strategies can be changed. As depicted in a paper by (Liu et al., 2024), AI-based predictive analytics helps predict consumer behavior, optimize marketing campaigns, and change product offerings in real-time. This flexibility has enabled the brands to hold on and remain competitive in such a volatile market.

- **Ecosystem theory:**

Adner's Ecosystem Theory brings out the role of networks and partnerships in value. Using AI, brands can operate in an inclusive ecosystem, integrating with third-party services platforms and technologies. For example, (Kim et al., 2022) take an overview of how AI-powered ecosystems in e-commerce platforms enable seamlessness between brands, consumers, and logistics providers by providing brand affinity for quicker responsiveness and efficiency in meeting the consumer's needs and boosting market share.

- **AIDA Model:**

Lewis first presented the AIDA model in 1898, stating that a consumer passes through four stages when interacting with a brand: attention, interest, desire, and action. AI can respond at each stage to make communications more exciting and relevant for the individual. In this regard, (Chen et al., 2023) highlighted the cases of digital marketing campaigns where the above process has been made more efficient by adapting AI for customizing content and recommendations to specific preferences.

AI, therefore, aids brands in better navigating the AIDA process as the right message reaches the right person at the right time.

Brand management with AI requires more than technology adoption; it involves a holistic process to understand how these technologies could improve customer experience, enhance decision-making, and foster deeper connections between brands and audiences exposed to them. By applying theoretical models such as TAM, CBBE, SDL, and SET, brands will provide evidence as to why people embrace AI and the impact of embracing AI on brand equity, customer loyalty, and engagement.

Research has proved that the impact of AI on branding is multidimensional, touching every bit, from customer perception and brand loyalty to operational efficiency and competitive advantage. However, consumer trust, data privacy issues, and the value of AI-crafted experiences will all go a long way in determining how successful AI will be in branding. Therefore, the frameworks discussed in this chapter offer a holistic lens through which to study AI's dynamic role in branding, giving theoretical insights and practical applications for the digital-age brand manager.

Conceptual Framework: The Role of Artificial Intelligence in Modern Branding

Introduction

Artificial intelligence is here; it transforms industries and falls deep into rethinking the traditional business sense. Branding is undoubtedly among the many areas where AI is changing things. Brands in a rapidly evolving digital world must constantly innovate to compete better with each other, and AI provides the tools for better customer experience, higher efficiency, and optimization in branding strategies. With the amount of data that AI can analyze in real-time, consumer behavior can be predicted and deliver a hyper-personalized experience that resonates very much with individual customers.

Far-reaching implications of adopting these technologies for companies and consumers exist, and among those is that AI integration in branding efforts would change how companies build their relationships with customers by providing more personalized, emotional, and dynamic engagement. This conceptual framework will explore how many AI technologies characterize this change, from machine learning to natural language processing and predictive analytics. It also considers, in this context, the importance of issues of trust and ethics in the consumer's acceptance of AI-powered branding strategies.

Using the context of various marketing theories and recent research, this framework would refer to how AI is repositioning brand equity, improving customer relationships, and promoting innovation in branding processes. It would outline the mediating effect of trust while emphasizing the ethical concerns associated with using AI in branding, highlighting challenges and risks.

Hypotheses and Arguments

AI Strengthens Brand Equity Through Personalized Customer Experiences

Traditionally, brand equity is a factor of brand recognition, perceived quality, and customer loyalty; personalization has hence emerged as a critical factor in building brand equity now that customers' expectations continue to grow and technology advances. AI provides the opportunity for individualized experiences by filtering out vast amounts of consumer information relative to buying history, browsing behaviors, demographics, and social media patterns. This way, brands can adapt and personalize their offer and message to each customer's unique needs and tastes.

The CBBE Model of Keller in 1993 acknowledged the personalization concept of branding. This is explained as the concept that a brand's equity is built from the perception of the brand by the customer and the associations that evolve as one progresses through meaningful experiences. In this light, AI can generate such associations for brands by predicting the customers' needs for relevant content and offerings. One area represented in companies like Netflix and Spotify is that they use recommendation engines powered by machine learning to suggest content that may match customers' tastes, thereby increasing customer satisfaction and the likelihood of repeating such interactions.

Research by (Ganapathi et al., 2022) shows personalized experiences hugely affect customer loyalty. If consumers feel that the brand understands and appreciates them, then loyalty and advocacy will probably be built. Emotional connections derived through AI-driven personalization link a brand with a more favorable perception, strengthening brand equity. In this respect, one of the interfaces between a brand and consumer is based on personalized experiences, which enhances memorability and, thus, leads to sustainable customer engagement in the long run.

AI-Powered Sentiment Analysis Helps Take Customer-Brand Relationships a Notch Higher.

The backbone of solid and lasting relationships with customers with successful brands can be made using AI, as it enables access to real-time consumers' sentiments and knowing what evokes an emotional response from a customer toward that product. Sentiment analysis works through natural language processing and machine learning to scan all the user-generated content, such as social media postings, reviews, and forum discussions, to determine whether it is pleasant, harmful, or neutral in response to a brand or product.

Last, the Relationship Marketing Theory, formulated by Morgan and Hunt in 1994, proved that trust and commitment would be maximally used in relation-building with customers in the long run. This is made possible with the use of AI, wherein brands measure the emotional state of their customers and then take after-step actions that are empathetic, timely, and relevant. The company can ensure that the AI-driven algorithms catch such an opinion in its sentiment analysis. Once detected, this type of sentiment automatically appeals to an appropriate reaction from the brand, furnished with solutions or reassures the consumer. It helps address worries, and every time, it presents an opportunity to respond quickly to customers' concerns. This also strengthens the brand perception as an attentive and responsive relationship builder that earns trust for the relationship between the brand and the customer.

It transforms the brands with positive sentiment through AI-based sentiment analysis. Brands can develop these experiences, attract new customers, and involve existing ones by responding to positive consumer feedback. (Choi et al. 2023) assert that a proactive approach in the sentiment analysis tool would help turn the brand's casual customers into loyal and active advocates by acknowledging their emotions and responding empathetically.

AI Allows Consumer Interaction with Responsive Dynamism

Consumer needs and behavior change constantly in the fast-evolving business world. Brands have to adapt to changes in consumers and market demand. One cannot predict market or consumer demands ahead of time, and a competitive brand will surpass others if it can be proactive enough to shape strategies before changes occur. Predictive analytics through AI lets brands know how consumers will react in the future and enables them to anticipate ahead. By analyzing past trends, identifying patterns, and predicting future trends, AI gives brands the ability to predict customer needs and make the right decisions.

Dynamic Capabilities Theory, proposed by (Teece et al., 1997), suggests that for a firm to be constantly ahead in competition, it should maintain agility concerning changing market conditions. Subsequently, AI adds to this agility with the ability to predict trends, do basic research on emerging opportunities, and refine its marketing strategy in real time. For example, big companies like Zara apply AI to analyze buying habits, seasonal patterns, and consumer preferences. Companies apply that analysis in optimal adjustments to their inventory and marketing campaigns. Based on (Han et al., 2022), predictive analytics is for increased consumer engagement and enhanced sales performance, whereby related offerings are available when needed.

With predictive analytics, brands are better equipped to consider premonitions of consumer tastes or behavior shifts and adjust their products, services, or messaging before changes occur. Responsiveness is that competitive edge in delivering the right products at the right time and context. Moreover, AI is utilized in the dynamic consumer engagement process. In that case, it will continue interacting with customers, thereby implying an ongoing and personalized experience, increasing customer satisfaction and loyalty levels.

Consumer Acceptance Through Trust in AI Systems

One reason AI could alter the art of branding is based on consumer acceptance - which, as a rule, depends on the level of trust. It is known that people show skepticism toward innovations concerning information gathering and utilization. The more central roles these AI systems take in branding, the more critical trust becomes regarding consumer acceptance of these technologies.

The TAM by (Davis et al., 1989) and the Unified Theory of Acceptance and Use of Technology by (Venkatesh et al., 2003) focus on the assumptions that trust and perceived ease of use are essential factors in encouraging the adoption of new technology. According to the researchers, consumers will embrace AI-powered branding strategies when confident that the system will do its best to favor them and when it is transparent and not hard to use. Trust, however, can quickly turn out to be a weakness if AI systems are viewed as opaque or intrusive.

Transparency in the use of AI-powered systems by brands will cultivate trust from the consumers. For example, companies like Apple have taken steps to be more open about AI technologies and how data is being handled. Brands can reduce the abated fears and increase their level of trust by explaining how AI systems work and by explaining how consumer data is secured. According to (Lee et al., 2021), AI system transparency increases the trust levels of customers towards AI branding activities by a wide margin; they are more willing to participate in AI-driven branding campaigns. More importantly, ethical concerns regarding fairness, accountability, and data privacy are the core issues relating to trust. Brands that demonstrate ethical practices through AI are more likely to be trusted and to have superior consumer engagement and loyalty.

Conceptual Model

This conceptual framework provides a model that describes the interaction of AI technologies, branding outcomes, and mediating and moderating factors. The model consisted of three primary components:

AI Technologies:

- **Machine Learning for Personalization:** AI algorithms scan consumer data to suggest tailored suggestions and content based on individual tastes.
- **Predictive Analytics for trend forecasting:** AI helps forecast future behavior and consumer intentions, marking the agility and responsiveness of brands.
- **Natural Language Processing (NLP) for sentiment analysis:** NLP helps brands sense mood swings and consumer changes in real-time, making possible timely response and proactive engagement with the consumers.
- **Dynamic Content Generation for engaging in real-time:** AI tools can help in the best possible delivery of personalized content in real-time based on an understanding of consumer preferences and behavior.
- **Branding Outcomes**

More substantial Brand Equity through the relevant and personalized experience: AI enhances customer satisfaction and loyalty and builds brand image.

Deeper Emotion Relationship between Customer and Brand Through EMOTIONAL INVOLVEMENT Building an emotional relationship between consumers and a brand through customized engagement using sentiment analysis, AI leads to lifelong loyalty building. Higher Consumer Satisfaction and Loyalty through Deeper Connection Building: AI helps brands connect with customers more deeply, increasing consumer satisfaction and eventually more repeat interactions. Mediators and Moderators

- **Consumer Acceptance:** Trust in AI systems as a mediator: Trust is the most important factor influencing whether consumers would take up AI-powered branding strategies.
- **Ethical Considerations as Moderators of Consumer Perception:** Ethical practices in terms of transparency on data usage and privacy protection influence consumers' understanding and acceptance of AI systems.
- **Cultural and Demographic Drivers for the Adoption of AI:** The attitude toward technology, age, and socio-economic status affect consumers' perception and interaction with AI.
- Interaction among these factors forms a system in which branding outcomes driven by AI technologies get moderate support from the influence of trust and ethics on consumer perception and interactivity.

Applications and Implications

AI in branding has theoretically sound results for marketers and businesses and practical applications. One of the most vital applications is strategic marketing, where AI enables companies to analyze consumer data and market trends and develop very targeted and effective marketing campaigns. AI-driven marketing platforms enable brands to segment their audience more effectively and provide relevant messaging and offers that resonate with individual consumers. As shown by (Chen et al., 2023) in their research, such AI-based tools provide a better return on investment by optimizing the marketing efforts and consequently getting the client's engagement.

Even the ambit of chatbots and virtual assistants, through advancements in artificial intelligence technology, enables transformation in customer experience at the brand level. Immediate, personalized responses replace longer response times, thus offering higher customer satisfaction. (Kim et al. 2022) By implementing AI-powered customer service solutions, brands can improve their overall customer experience and establish long-term customer bonds.

For a brand to have its systems open, fair, and responsible, ethical AI must be embraced by it. The bottom line is that ethical AI is a strong differentiator in the marketplace, mainly because consumers are increasingly concerned with privacy over data misuse. Brands can build consumer loyalty by committing to ethical practices to enhance reputation and trust.

What is more, developing AI-based branding strategies opens wide doors for significant amounts of future research, with examples as follows: What are the effects of AI on brand equity in specific industries; how customer loyalty develops over time in the light of AI-based branding; and what problems encountered in adoption of AI based on ethical considerations.

AI accelerates change in the branding landscape by enabling brands to personalize experiences, make emotional connections, and respond flexibly to altered market conditions. The innovations ultimately contribute to better brand equity, fortification of consumer-brand relationships, and consumer interactive involvement. However, there is a reliance on AI branding success on consumer trust, which primarily depends on transparency, ethical best practices, and data privacy. The more the brand harnesses AI responsibly, the more significant its contribution to customer value and competitive position against rivals in this increasingly digital world. The conceptual framework is a well-rounded outline that helps understand and use AI in branding. It is one of the most vital sources of information for marketers and researchers.

Implications and Future Research: AI's Role in Branding

1. Implications for the Field of Branding and Marketing

The changing scenario witnessed the integration of artificial intelligence into branding and marketing, which impacted the business houses' change in their approach towards their customers and design strategies for brand building. The conceptual model pursued in this chapter has high-order implications for academic research and practical application within the marketing, branding, and consumer behavior fields. AI technologies, including chatbots, machine learning, and predictive analytics, can profoundly transform brand engagement, enabling enhanced consumer experience, customer-brand interaction, and optimized brand management processes.

This chapter makes at least one clear contribution: demonstrating how AI technologies enable brands to create experiences at scale, thus transforming approaches to traditional brand communication. Through machine learning algorithms, AI can screen voluminous consumer data and segment audiences, predict consumer behavior, and serve targeted content and offers (Chen et al., 2023). Through this, brand loyalty, which directly impacts the satisfaction of consumers with the brand, is improved. Moreover, the role of AI in branding has also played an essential part in real-time customer engagement, such as the use of chatbots and sentiment analysis, allowing brands to respond quickly to customer inquiries and respond to the emotions of the consumers interacting with their brands (Choi et al., 2023).

Also, a significant implication of this chapter's contribution is setting up operational efficiency within branding. AI is not only a strategy to automate customer interaction but also analyzes and adapts brand strategies according to real-time data (Huang & Rust, 2021). Using AI in brand management, companies can optimize their marketing efforts, improve customer satisfaction, and save operational costs. All the AI-related technologies, such as NLP and predictive analytics, can help brands respond to consumer demands quicker and more efficiently than ever before. Brand management is agile in an increasingly competitive digital marketplace (Mehta et al., 2023).

More importantly, the chapter focuses on how AI plays a role in brand innovation due to ever-changing market landscapes. AI helps organizations develop adaptive strategies that rapidly respond to shifting consumer preferences and digital trends. Consider the case of AI-powered GANs, which are assisting brands innovate in product development by generating personalized designs or content that resonate with consumers (Liu et al., 2024). That ability to innovate further based on data-driven insight puts brands into movement in an increasingly dynamic market.

2. Implications for Practitioners and Businesses

This book emphasizes that AI is relevant to developing robust and powerful brands for brand strategists and marketers. The marriage of AI and creating a rich and engaging experience will be the pivot of businesses as they search for attention in the highly overpopulated digital marketplace. This chapter will thus serve as a guide for companies looking forward to adopting AI technologies in branding. Using AI tools in branding may enhance customer loyalty and increase brand equity while streamlining operations. In this sense, business enterprises that would use sentiment analysis and other forms of AI-driven brand strategies can easily understand their customers' emotional responses to the brand, and this means they adjust their brand messaging with such sentiments in mind, hence leading to more meaningful and enduring relationships with customers (Zhang et al., 2023).

Apart from these ethical considerations, the chapter has practical implications for using AI in business. With businesses increasingly relying on AI, companies need to use these technologies responsibly, ensuring transparency in AI-generated content and respecting consumer privacy (Kim et al., 2022). Such responsibility is necessary for it to backfire on consumers, causing irreparable damage to the brand and loss of trust. It calls upon companies to balance creative AI-focused strategies and ethical concerns to build effective consumer-brand relationships in the digital age.

Recommendations for Further Research

While this chapter provides immense insight into the role of AI in branding, much scope exists for future research that may be built onto the findings presented in this chapter. In all, due to rapid advancements in AI technologies, much remains to be explored regarding its ever-changing impact on brand management and consumer behavior.

Longitudinal Studies of the Effects of AI on Brand Loyalty Long-term studies can establish whether AI-generated personalization influences brand loyalty. Most studies center on short-term effects, such as how a personalized experience influences consumers over a shorter period. It is also helpful to know how such engagements influence the behavior of consumers or brand loyalty over the long run. Longitudinal studies would help ascertain if AI's impact on consumer-brand relationships is short-lived or fades over time as consumers get accustomed to AI-driven experiences (Ganapathi et al., 2022).

Cross-Cultural Perspectives of AI in Branding There is much promise in studying how cultural differences influence the adoption and effectiveness of AI in branding across regions. While AI technologies are increasingly global, consumer preferences and perceptions of AI will differ across cultures. Exploratory studies can be conducted on how cultural factors influence consumers to trust AI-generated content, their willingness to engage in AI-driven brand experiences, and their expectations of brand transparency in other markets (Lee et al., 2021).

Ethics of AI in Branding This is where AI increasingly occupies branding space, making it susceptible to many ethical questions: data protection, algorithmic bias, and transparency issues. Future studies might examine how companies can create responsible AI strategies where personalization meets consumer protections. Ethical frameworks might be developed that guide companies in inculcating AI responsibly with correct consumers' trust and satisfaction (Mehta et al., 2023).

The role of AI in sustainable branding Brands has been thrust into the forefront to incorporate sustainability as one of the most critical factors. Thus, future research can be carried out on how AI can be integrated into sustainable branding strategies. Predictive analytics and machine learning-based AI technologies aid brands in optimizing supply chains, reducing waste, and becoming resource-friendly. Exploring how AI-driven insights can fuel sustainable branding practices would be very valuable to companies looking to bolster their environmental impact while connecting with like-minded, environmentally-sensitive consumers (Huang & Rust, 2021).

AI's Implication in Measuring Brand Equity Brand equity improvement is a grossly understudied domain of AI. Future research may concentrate on how AI technological applications can help estimate and deepen brand equity. Through machine learning and data analytics, companies can achieve deep insights into brand perception and consumers' attitudes. Research studies may also identify tools and methodologies businesses may employ to measure how branding via AI affects brand equity and customer perception (Kim et al., 2022).

This would also make it a research area for how AI will be used in consumer-centric brand strategies. Since the behavior of consumers becomes more and more data-driven, AI will play a vital role in understanding and predicting consumer needs in the years to come, which will hence be fundamental to determining future branding strategies. Further studies can be considered on how AI may build hyper-personalized brand experiences that resonate with individual consumers at deeper levels (Chen et al., 2023).

CONCLUSION

The book provides an in-depth analysis of the transformative nature of AI in branding and marketing and critically speaks to brand personalization, customer engagement, operational efficiency, and innovation. These findings have significant implications for academics and practitioners alike in this branding domain, particularly for those who consider how AI may be leveraged as a form of assistance toward customer-brand relationships and brand management. However, studies are undoubtedly required in the long term for better understanding and consequent ethical implications at different points and cross-cultural applications. Therefore, filling these gaps would help future research continue developing knowledge about the application of AI in developing more robust and more resilient brands for the digital age.

Artificial Intelligence, therefore, has ushered in a new period for branding and marketing. This intermingling of AI with the world of brands and marketing would include changing the relationship between the business and the consumers transforming how it manages its brand equity. Now, continuous progress in the technologies around AI machinery, such as machine learning and predictive analytics, along with next-generation breakthroughs in natural language processing-have had profound implications for how brands can engage audiences, deliver experiences, and address a continually more competitive marketplace that's increasingly digital.This chapter lays out the theoretical underpinning of AI for branding, develops a conceptual framework to understand its implications, and discusses AI's future implications and research directions. The following conclusion is an aggregation of these insights: it distills the understanding of the far-reaching implications of AI in brand management, which in turn provides an overarching view of how AI changes branding and marketing strategies in the academic space and the practice of branding.

Branding through AI involves considerable theoretical underpinnings on consumer behavior, brand management, and marketing strategy. It is anchored in optimizing the capability of brands to dig deeper and resonate with consumers in a much more personalized manner. AI tools allow companies to sift through reams of consumer data, create behavior-based audience segmentations, predict how needs will change over time, and produce relevant content that reaches people in ways that traditional marketing tactics never could. With this leverage in AI, the confines no longer bind brands to the same strategy for all; they can now modify the messages, offerings, and experiences suitably tailored to their customers' needs and emotional predispositions.This flows from mass marketing to a hyper-personal experience, hence a fundamental revolution in branding practice.

Apart from this, AI makes it easy to automate many tasks of brand management, and the company quickly becomes reachable to consumers in real-time, making it easy to adapt to the changes in consumer behavior. Based on machine learning algorithms and predictive analytics, firms predict needs, create content, and provide solutions immediately. For all these processes, AI functions as an operational efficiency driver. With AI, there is a possibility of unlocking brand opportunities primarily by streamlining the processes, costs, and optimization of marketing efforts. This chapter's conceptual framework takes the guesswork out of exactly how AI will give brand engagement and improve customers' satisfaction towards loyalty.

By coming into being with consumer-brand interactions, AI contributes to brand strategy. Such technologies as processing sentiment analysis or chatbots and voice assistants, as well as AI, permit brands to have dialogues with consumers in real-time in response to immediate inquiries, customer concerns, and emotional responses. All these avenues allow for more dynamic and responsive relationships between a consumer and a brand. All of the above AI-powered tools will help the brands create a deeper emotional connection with customers, especially with those supposed to be turned loyal through timely solutions and proper personalization experiences.

In this fast world, where all is digital and speed and personalization are expected, the role of AI in customer-brand interaction is much more significant. Artificial intelligence opens up the possibility of contextualizing the recommendations and answering consumer questions of interest with information pertinent to the context in which that question has been asked and in real-time assimilation of fluid consumer needs. This develops a more fluid and engaging brand experience that naturally fosters higher levels of customer satisfaction and retention.

Another implication of AI in brand management is the analysis of large-scale data and the capacity to predict consumer behavior. The brand may apply AI in search of emerging trends, forecast shifts in consumer preferences, and thus adjust its strategies accordingly. That is by being ahead of the curve and predicting the needs of consumers before they come about. Therefore, modern brand management has found AI to be an indispensable tool in creating consumer insight-informed experiences.

Another vital space where AI has been profoundly impactful is operation efficiency. It can automate tasks like service duplication, creation of content, and data analysis, thus leaving more space for higher-level strategic initiatives. It not only makes marketing teams work better but also reduces the operational costs. Efficiency through AI automation ensures businesses can effectively use every resource, thus ensuring a better ROI on marketing campaigns.

This is also the case with AI fostering innovation in branding strategies. In terms of what AI can do, such as generate personalized content, optimize product development processes, and create adaptive brand strategies in response to market changes, it has rewritten the rule books on how brands must approach innovation. For instance, through GAN, AI has introduced new designs, adverts, and content that connect with consumers more profoundly due to AI technology. Agility and responsiveness come from data-driven innovation because brands learn to be responsive to constantly changing market dynamics. Artificial intelligence innovation isn't only about creating products or content and developing products, customer experience designs, and business models.

The most critical part to organizations about this new AI capability is that it allows firms to provide data-driven insights supporting the innovation of new products and services. Of course, things change fast in today's business world, and companies have to adjust quickly to remain par for the course. Real-time analytics of data and machine learning allow brands to trace any shifts in consumer preferences and reveal new ways for development. In a world where change is the only constant, this ability to be adaptive is cardinal to businesses looking to continue their competitive advantage.

Ethical matters include data privacy, algorithmic bias, and transparency, in which AI is increasingly integrated into branding and marketing strategies. Brands must be sensitive to the ethical issues attributed to the application of AI within their marketing practices, respect consumer privacy, not engage in discriminatory practices, and communicate across respective platforms, which must always be open, transparent, and AI-driven. Responsive use of AI will ensure consumer trust while supporting long-term partnerships with audiences.

With that being the case, it is highly debatable what role human marketers and brand managers will have in a world that finds increasing uses of AI. For most of the functions, AI can be programmed to do, and human knowledge will then be necessary for interpreting data, making sense of all those nuances of consumer behavior, and crafting brand messages to speak to all those different audiences. Thus, there must be a balance between the capabilities of AI use and the human touch of branding. This means the AI tool is to be used not as a replacement for human creativity and decision-making but as a capacity to heighten both.

Most importantly, because AI technologies will be even more ubiquitous, how brands interact with them must be guided by ethical frameworks. Importantly, AI ethics research will become the most crucial component guiding brands on how responsibly and appropriately they use AI to their benefit and advantage for both businesses and consumers.

Secondly, guidelines for transparency, fairness, and accountability will be crucial in building trust between brands and customers and help avoid pitfalls relating to unethical practices with AI. The opening up of fast-evolving AI technologies opens further opportunities for branding research.The present chapter hence pointed out some areas that need to be considered in the future to clarify the role of AI in branding and marketing: longitudinal contributions to understanding brand loyalty, perspectives from different cultures, and ethics about AI use in branding.

A longitudinal study would reflect insights into the long-term effects of AI-driven personalization on brand loyalty and consumer behavior. As a result of an emphasis on short-term effects, relatively few studies have focused on long-term effects. It is necessary to know how AI-generated experiences modify the consumer and brand relationship over time. If the business understands the lingering impact of AI on loyalty, it will be able to refine its strategy so that its AI-driven efforts will produce long-term effects.

Cross-cultural research on adopting AI in branding is the need of the time because perceptions and needs regarding AI might vary geographically and across different cultures. Therefore, deep cultural factors that influence consumer receptiveness to

AI-driven brand experiences can be applied by businesses in formulating market-specific and effective marketing strategies for emerging markets.

Ethics should be one of the issues that will always be of prime concern in AI and branding. Additionally, research into the ethics of AI in branding will add models to ensure businesses use AI responsibly, considering consumer rights and privacy. Such findings will form the core of what brands need when interfacing with their ambiguous ethical dilemmas in pursuing practical AI applications that will be trustworthy and consequently avoid reputational risks.

Finally, this study on integrating AI and sustainability in branding has exciting prospects. AI can optimize supply chains, minimize waste, encourage green practices, and enable brands to align sustainability goals with branding strategy. There would be a need for such a study in companies aiming at ecologically conscious customers who need operating efficiency.

Artificial Intelligence redefines the power in branding and marketing as it changes the way businesses relate to, communicate with, and reach their audience. AI has put heavy tools and capacities in the hands of brands to permit experiential experiences, higher customer engagement, and the development of business practices. It empowers brands to be innovators of the game regarding complex markets. This, though, presents competition since infusing AI in branding takes work. Ethical considerations, not to mention an even deeper long-term need for more exploration of implications, represent a critical space where attention will be brought as AI reshapes the branding landscape.

The scope of AI in branding is broad, but the possibility still needs further research. It is essential to know how the long-term effects of AI work in managing brands to develop strategies that balance algorithmic insights and creative intuition. Hence, responsible adoption of AI will be necessary for the brands to achieve an authentic practice that is greater in size, strength, and resilience and true to ethical standards and consumer expectations. The future of branding will be seen in the effective harmonization of technological innovation with a human-centric approach that makes room for meaningful connections in an increasingly complex digital age.

REFERENCES

Adner, R. (2017). *The wide lens: A new strategy for innovation*. Penguin.

Blau, P. M. (1964). *Exchange and power in social life*. Wiley.

Brandtzaeg, P. B., & Følstad, A. (2017). Why people use chatbots. *Proceedings of the 2017 CHI Conference on Human Factors in Computing Systems*, 4847–4857.

Chen, L., Li, X., & Xu, Y. (2023). How AI is transforming marketing: Leveraging artificial intelligence in the AIDA model. *Journal of Marketing Technology*, 41(3), 56–72.

Chen, Y., Zhang, X., & Liu, Y. (2023). Artificial intelligence and its impact on brand engagement: A consumer-focused perspective. *Journal of Marketing Management*, 39(2), 123–140.

Cheng, S. H., & Park, J. (2023). The role of AI in sentiment analysis for enhancing customer-brand relationships. *Computers in Human Behavior*, 142, 107812.

Cheng, X., & Jiang, Z. (2020a). Impact of artificial intelligence on customer-brand relationship. *Journal of Business Research*, 109, 112–120.

Cheng, X., & Jiang, Z. (2020b). AI in digital marketing: A case study on chatbot-powered branding. *Journal of Marketing Science*, 10(4), 159–171.

Choi, J., Lee, H., & Kim, S. (2023). Enhancing brand loyalty through AI-driven personalization and sentiment analysis. *Journal of Brand Management*, 30(1), 18–32.

Choi, S., Park, H., & Kim, J. (2023). The role of AI in sentiment analysis for enhancing customer-brand relationships. *Computers in Human Behavior*, 142, 107812.

Chung, Y., Park, Y., & Kim, S. (2018). Understanding consumer attitudes toward AI-powered chatbots in digital marketing. *Journal of Business Research*, 92, 11–20.

Davenport, T. H., & Ronanki, R. (2018). Artificial intelligence for the real world. *Harvard Business Review*, 96(1), 108–116.

Davis, F. D. (1989). Perceived ease of use and perceived usefulness: A test of the technology acceptance model. *Journal of Management Information Systems*, 13(3), 319–340.

. Forbes. (2017). How chatbots are changing customer service. *Forbes*.

Ganapathi, R., Rangarajan, A., & Mukherjee, A. (2022). Artificial intelligence and its impact on consumer-based brand equity. *Marketing Intelligence & Planning*, 40(1), 45–60.

Ganapathi, S., Subramanian, R., & Narayan, S. (2022). Personalization in branding: The influence of AI-driven experiences on consumer loyalty. *International Journal of Marketing Studies*, 14(3), 45–61.

Han, Y., Li, H., & Zhang, W. (2022). Generative adversarial networks in AI-driven product design: Implications for branding. *Journal of Business Research*, 131, 1–13.

Han, Y., Wu, L., & Zhao, T. (2022). AI-driven predictive analytics in fashion retail: Enhancing consumer engagement. *Fashion and Textile Research Journal*, 10(4), 256–270.

Huang, M.-H., & Rust, R. T. (2021). Engaged to a robot? The role of AI in service branding. *Journal of Service Research*, 24(1), 30–41. DOI: 10.1177/1094670520902266

Huang, M. H., & Rust, R. T. (2021). Artificial intelligence in service: Implications for service research and branding. *Journal of Service Research*, 24(1), 8–29.

Keller, K. L. (1993). Conceptualizing, measuring, and managing customer-based brand equity. *Journal of Marketing*, 57(1), 1–22. DOI: 10.1177/002224299305700101

Kietzmann, J. H., Hermkens, K., McCarthy, I. P., & Silvestre, B. S. (2018). Social media? Get serious! Understanding the functional building blocks of social media. *Business Horizons*, 54(3), 241–251. DOI: 10.1016/j.bushor.2011.01.005

Kim, D., Lee, J., & Cho, S. (2022). Virtual assistants and chatbots: Enhancing customer satisfaction in branding. *Journal of Interactive Marketing*, 55, 1–16.

Kim, Y., Lee, H., & Park, J. (2022). AI-powered ecosystems and their impact on consumer experiences in e-commerce. *Electronic Commerce Research and Applications*, 52, 101141.

Lee, M., Lee, S., & Lee, H. (2021). The impact of AI transparency on consumer trust: The moderating role of brand reputation. *The Journal of Consumer Research*, 48(3), 431–450.

Lee, S., Kim, Y., & Oh, H. (2021). The impact of transparency on trust in AI-driven branding: Evidence from the technology acceptance model. *Journal of Business Ethics*, 169(2), 383–400.

Liu, H., Wang, F., & Zhang, P. (2024). AI applications in dynamic branding strategies: Insights and implications. *Strategic Marketing Journal*, 32(1), 77–98.

Liu, Y., Zhang, X., & Xie, Y. (2024). Leveraging predictive analytics in branding: Dynamic capabilities for competitive advantage. *Journal of Strategic Marketing*, 32(1), 45–58.

Mehta, A., Singh, R., & Kaur, P. (2023). Ethical AI and its role in branding: Balancing innovation with responsibility. *Journal of Business Research*, 150, 46–59.

Mehta, S., Sharma, P., & Joshi, A. (2023). AI-driven loyalty programs: Leveraging data analytics for customer retention. *Journal of Consumer Marketing*, 40(2), 125–137.

Mishra, A., Singh, J., & Kumar, P. (2020). Adoption of artificial intelligence in retail marketing: A study on consumer trust and perceptions. *International Journal of Retail & Distribution Management*, 48(3), 258–276.

Morgan, R. M., & Hunt, S. D. (1994). The commitment-trust theory of relationship marketing. *Journal of Marketing*, 58(3), 20–38. DOI: 10.1177/002224299405800302

Mukherjee, S., & Jha, S. (2022). Artificial intelligence in branding: Transforming customer experiences in e-commerce. *Marketing Intelligence & Planning*, 40(3), 350–364.

Prahalad, C. K., & Ramaswamy, V. (2004). Co-creation experiences: The next practice in value creation. *Journal of Interactive Marketing*, 18(3), 5–14. DOI: 10.1002/dir.20015

Rust, R. T., & Huang, M.-H. (2020). The service revolution and the transformation of marketing science. *Marketing Science*, 39(3), 357–380.

Sawhney, M., & Lurie, N. H. (2004). The power of the product mix: How product variety impacts brand perceptions. *JMR, Journal of Marketing Research*, 41(3), 257–268.

Shankar, V., & Kannan, P. K. (2018). AI and data-driven marketing. *Journal of Marketing*, 82(4), 1–17.

Wang, T., & Liu, Z. (2023). AI and consumer behavior in branding: A systematic review. *The Journal of Consumer Research*, 45(5), 609–624.

Wang, X., Li, Y., & Zhang, J. (2021). Consumer trust in AI-powered virtual assistants: The role of transparency and brand reputation. *Journal of Business Research*, 126, 84–94.

West, D. M. (2018). *The future of work: Robots, AI, and automation*. Brookings Institution Press.

Zablah, A. R., & Bell, S. J. (2022). Consumer loyalty and AI-based personalization: The role of brand trust. *Journal of Marketing Theory and Practice*, 30(2), 202–218.

Chapter 10
I (Brand) Love You: Why Consumers Fall in Love With Brands and How They Express Their Love

Alexandre Duarte
https://orcid.org/0000-0002-2665-864X
FCSH, Universidade Nova de Lisboa, Portugal

Patrícia Dias
FCH, Universidade Católica Portuguesa, Portugal

ABSTRACT

The aftermath of COVID-19, the widespread adoption of AI-based technological innovations, and new social challenges have reflected changes in consumer behavior, prompting us to re-explore the concept of brand love. This study focuses on updating what we know about consumer-brand relationships and exploring brand features and attributes that trigger brand love. We look particularly into brand communication, the consumers' perception, and how it relates to brand love. A quantitative method was chosen, and an online survey of 405 consumers was conducted. The results stress the difficulty in identifying specific brand features that prompt or nurture brand love, as our 405 participants mentioned 157 different brands as the ones they love the most. Hedonistic aspects that compose pleasurable brand experiences stand out as triggers of brand love. However, surprisingly, there are few luxury brands loved by our sample who are more committed to the brands present in their daily lives. Brand communication may not be a determinant for prompting brand love, but it's pivotal in nurturing it.

DOI: 10.4018/979-8-3693-9461-8.ch010

INTRODUCTION

Research on branding has always attempted to better understand how and why relationships are established between consumers and brands, and how (or if) the true value of a brand can be determined and measured (Duarte, 2023). In contemporary society, brands have become increasingly important, as globalized markets are saturated with similar offers and hyperconnected consumers are more informed, more resourceful, and more demanding (Fisher et al., 2010). Thus, understanding how consumers develop relationships with brands and the consequences of those bonds has been a topic of utmost interest in academic research in the last few years. Within this scope, several concepts have been suggested and explored, such as brand loyalty, brand preference, brand equity, brand engagement, brand trust, brand affection, and brand love.

The concept of brand love was born in the intersection of the fields of Psychology and Marketing, with researchers on both scientific disciplines collaborating to better understand the emotional and psychological factors that lead consumers to brand preference and to brand loyalty. Fournier (1998) deeply explored the emotional and symbolic dimensions of consumer-brand relationships, laying the foundation for subsequent work that established analogies between the love that humans can feel for each other, and attachments that can be formed regarding objects, as well as the consumer-brand relationship (Ahuvia, 2005; Ghani & Tuhin, 2016). Since then, the definition of brand love has been abundantly discussed, and researchers set out to map which antecedents could lead to brand love, as well as its consequences. However, not only are these concepts dynamic and evolve alongside changes in consumer behavior, and in society in general, but also research on this topic has so far failed to produce theoretical models that encompass antecedents and consequences, as well as practical models for the evaluation and concrete measurement of brand love (Palusuk et al., 2019).

Our study proposes to revisit the concept of brand love, exploring how the turbulence of the last few years – the Covid-19 pandemic, the outbreak of a war in Europe and another one in the Middle East, and repercussions in the economy, such as increased inflation and crisis, and in politics, such as the rise of populisms – may reflect on changes in consumer behavior, and specifically in consumer-brand relationship. Research on consumer behavior over the last few years has identified sustainability awareness and sustainable consumption as an increasingly strong trend. Alongside is a rise in the ethical concerns of consumers, who are increasingly demanding transparency and accountability from brands (Trudel, 2019). As brand love is mainly an emotional concept, and sustainable and ethical consumption are more reflexive and pondered behaviors, it is relevant to investigate how they impact brand love. In addition, several studies have documented that the COVID-

19 pandemic changed consumer behavior, not only during atypical periods (for example, an increase in online shopping), as some of these changes persisted in its aftermath. The mindset and priorities of many consumers changed, placing health, well-being, and social interaction among what they now value the most (Duarte & Dias, 2022). It is relevant to explore how this affects consumer-brand relations. Finally, technological innovations within the scope of Artificial Intelligence and becoming widespread and embedded in daily life. They are being widely applied in marketing, from strategic dimensions such as consumer behavior research and forecasting, to operational tasks such as promotional AI-generated content (Varsha et al., 2021). It is imperative to study how these innovations reflect on brand love. Thus, our study sets out to explore how changes in consumer behavior, technological innovation, and political, economic and social contemporary challenges reflect upon the concept of consumer behavior, its antecedents and consequences, aiming to uncover new relevant insights that may help brands to navigate complex relationships with their consumers.

Although aiming to explore how these global trends reflect upon brand love, our study focuses on the Portuguese context. Cross-cultural studies on brand love have become a trend in the last few years, acknowledging that brand love manifests differently across different cultural and geographic contexts, that need to be understood by brands aiming to build unique relationships with each consumer (Luo & Hamlin, 2022). The Portuguese context has historical, cultural, and social specificities that may offer relevant insights about brand-consumer relationships (Rodrigues et al., 2015). Concerning the economy, Portugal is facing a severe crisis. The minimum wage (820 euros) and the average wage (about 1300 euros) are some of the lowest in Europe, while the effort rate of families to pay for housing, and the number of families in debt are among the highest. Poverty has significantly increased in Portugal in 2023, as well as unemployment. The income available reflects on consumption, and in trading down on other products to trade up when it comes to loved brands. Examining how Portuguese consumers establish relationships with brands within a very tight budget may bring relevant insight into how economic conditions affect brand perceptions, brand love, and decision-making. Furthermore, focusing on brand communication, vocabulary, and brand associations, it is relevant to explore the nuances of the Portuguese language (Rodrigues et al., 2023), which is the official language of 10 different countries, and how they reflect on culture, consumer behavior, and brand love.

A comprehensive review of the antecedents and consequences of brand love

Following the seminal article of Fournier (1998) about the relationship between consumers and brands, the concept of brand love emerged as an important construct, especially after it has been proved that it raises brand equity (Verma, 2021). Kevin Roberts' book "Lovemarks" (2005) consolidated the concept of brand love, and it gained major attention and recognition in marketing, both from the academia and practitioners.

Carroll and Ahuvia (2006) define brand love as the degree of passionate emotional attachment a satisfied consumer experiences towards a specific brand. Batra et al. (2012) postulate that brand love is the development of a deep relationship (more than a transient love emotion) between customers and brands. Verma (2021) combines these visions of passionate love and long-lasting love by interpreting brand love based on Stenberg's (1986) triangular theory of love, based on intimacy, passion, and commitment, being the last determinant to consumption decision-making.

The antecedents and consequences of brand love have been thoroughly explored by both academic researchers and practitioners over the last years (Unal & Aydin, 2013; Roy et al, 2016; Bairrada et al., 2018; Biçakcioglu et al, 2018; Gumparthi & Patra, 2020; Verma, 2021). Concerning the antecedents, the literature overviews other stages of connection to brands that are previous to brand love and may lead to such a feeling. Brand satisfaction is the first step towards brand love. When consumers consistently experience positive outcomes and satisfaction with a brand, it paves the way for the development of profound emotional connections that are the foundation of brand love. Brand trust results from consistency, reliability, and transparency, and, as in human love, it is the cornerstone of a long-lasting relationship, as it affords a sense of security and stability (Albert & Merunka, 2013). Brand identification is also very relevant, as consumers fall in love with brands that reflect their lifestyle, their personality, and their values. Certain features or aspects of brands and branding have been identified as predictors of brand love, thus prompting and nurturing this feeling. Carroll and Ahuvia (2006) enumerate perceived quality, prestige, exclusivity, and hedonism. These features are usually more associated with luxury brands. Hedonism in particular is highlighted in studies that connect positive, appealing, engaging, and pleasurable brand experiences to brand love (Carroll & Ahuvia, 2006; Batra et al., 2012; Madeleine and Sihombing; 2019). Recent studies argue that delight is connected to surprise, to exceeding consumers' expectations, and consequently affording pleasurable experiences and memories (Sarkar, 2013). Being able to foster an emotional connection is strongly associated with brand love (Loureiro et al., 2021). Emotional connections spark from consumer-centric approaches, offering personalization a catering to consumers' needs and preferences.

These connections are reinforced when, being unique, and are also shared by other consumers, nurturing a sense of belonging (Burnasheva et al., 2019). Social media marketing has been playing an important role in enhancing emotional connections and a sense of belonging through engagement in online brand communities. Consumers fall in love with sociable brands, that engage in meaningful communication with consumers (Dias & Duarte, 2023). Recent studies have pinpointed storytelling as a very effective way to captivate and resonate with consumers (Dias & Cavalheiro, 2021). Others highlight empathy as a part of the humanization of brands, that are not only able to foster connections with consumers as if they were human but also of nurturing affection (Duarte & Gregório, 2022). Identification with the brand, based on shared lifestyle, personality, and values is another important aspect (Alnawas & Altarifi, 2016). Influencer marketing is very effective in prompting empathy and identification, and often relies on storytelling, thus fostering brand love (Trivedi & Sama, 2020). Finally, recent studies have referred to authenticity. As in human relationships, consumers value sincerity, transparency, consistency and genuineness in brands, aspects that build trust, and may ultimately lead to brand love (Manthiou et al, 2018). Communicating their purpose and acting accordingly, either within the scope of social responsibility or activism, reinforces these aspects (Dias & Duarte, 2023). Brands strive so hard to foster brand love because it brings them significant benefits. Among the main consequences of brand love is brand loyalty (Roy et al., 2016; Madeline & Sihombing, 2019; Çelik, 2022; Bae & Kim, 2023). Consumers are more likely to repurchase brands that they love and to actively seek out those brands (Batra et al., 2012; Madeleine & Sihombing, 2019; Madadi et al., 2021). Studies have also documented several brand sacrifices that consumers are willing to make for the brands they love, such as waiting if they are temporarily unavailable, resisting competitors even if their offers are advantageous, and paying more for their favorite brands (Loureiro, 2011). Other positive outcomes are positive word-of-mouth (WOM) and recommendations (Albert & Merunka, 2013; Unal & Aydin, 2013). Consumers who love a brand tend to share their positive experiences and advocate for the brand (Ebrahim, 2020), which can significantly positively impact brand awareness and brand reputation, attracting new consumers (Biçakcioglu et al., 2018). These actions occur mostly on social media, through User-Generated Content (UGC), in personal profiles, and/or in brand communities (Dias & Duarte, 2022). Thus, brands that actively encourage and showcase UGC on social media enhance consumer engagement and deepen emotional connections (Vivek et al., 2012; Hollebeek et al., 2014; Dwivedi et al., 2015), capitalizing on the participatory nature of brand love (Gumparthi & Patra, 2020; Çelik, 2022). Another documented benefit is brand resilience, as loyal consumers seem more tolerant of negative publicity and reputational crises. Consumers in love tend to stand by their favorite brands during turbulent and challenging times, often advocating for the brand against criticism

(Elsharnouby et al., 2021). Finally, some studies found that brand love enhances brand elasticity, supporting brands in extending their product ranges and lines or even entering new markets and businesses. Consumers are more willing to try new offers from beloved brands (Schmidt & Huber, 2019). Although the positive consequences of brand love for brands have been widely researched, studies have failed to mention possible negative consequences, and the benefits for consumers are under-researched (Palusuk et al., 2019)

In conclusion, brand love is a complex and dynamic phenomenon with far-reaching implications for both brands and consumers. Our study sets out to reexamine the intertwining between antecedents and consequences of brand love, in the face of contemporary challenges, and within the specificity of the Portuguese setting.

Understanding Brand Love and Determining its Value

Since it has been acknowledged that brands add value to products and/or services, affording benefits both for organizations and consumers, there have been several attempts and proposals to measure this value. The challenge is that this value can be intangible, and therefore difficult to quantify.

David Aaker (1991) coined the term brand equity to describe the added value that a brand, by itself, endows a marketing offer, suggesting the *Brand Equity Ten* model to measure it, considering brand awareness, perceived quality, brand associations, and brand loyalty as the main aspects to evaluate. Other models followed, such as the *Customer-Based Brand Equity* by Kevin Lane Keller, or the *Multidimensional model* by Leslie de Chernatony (Duarte, 2023). Brand love is positively related to brand equity (Bairrada et al., 2018; Gumparthi & Patra, 2020; Verma, 2021), suggesting that models that measure brand equity can constitute relevant benchmarking for models that measure brand love. In addition, existing models for measuring emotional connections to brands, one of the foundations of brand love, and brand loyalty, one of its main consequences, can be combined or articulated to measure brand love (Bauer et al., 2009; Heinrich et al., 2012).

Such a task has started to be tackled, as a Brand Passion Index (Park et al., 2010; Park et al., 2013) and a Brand Love Scale have been discussed in the literature. Following the Brand Equity Ten model, a few studies have tested models composed of statements toward which consumers express their degree of (dis)agreement on a Likert scale. Although there is no consensus on an effective way of measuring brand love, most of these models include the following main dimensions: brand associations, emotional connection, engagement, brand loyalty, and advocacy. Our study draws on these contributions to design our data collection tool, and to investigate if our data and our findings can shed further light on the challenge of measuring brand love.

Methodology

This research aims to explore in more depth the concept of brand love, detailing concrete brand features or attributes that trigger this feeling in consumers, and better understanding how it is reflected in consumer behavior, mapping resulting benefits both for brands and consumers. In our empirical work, we address the following research questions:

RQ1: What concrete brand attributes are more strongly related to the triggering of brand love?

RQ2: What concrete features of brand communication are more strongly related to the nurturing of brand love?

RQ3: What benefits result from brand love, for brands and for consumers? We follow the quantitative method, with a simple research design that includes only one phase of primary data collection, and a subsequent phase of data analysis (Creswell & Creswell, 2022).

For that purpose, we chose the online survey as a data collection technique, using Qualtrics. In our survey, we asked participants to tell us their favorite brand and to answer all the subsequent questions thinking about their relationship with that brand. The survey was organized into three parts: 1) brand features or attributes that trigger brand love (2 questions); 2) perceptions and behavior towards a love brand (14 questions); and 3) sociodemographic data (5 questions). The typology of questions was varied, including closed, scaled, and open formats.

The survey was disseminated online through the website and social media profiles of the researchers' research centers, the researchers' individual social media profiles (particularly on LinkedIn), and mailing lists of Higher Education Institutions. Thus, a non-probabilistic sample does not allow the generalization of the results but affords convenient, quick, and affordable data collection suited to an exploratory study, to identify relevant trends for future research (Creswell & Creswell, 2022). It was online during September and October 2023.

The data analysis technique was descriptive statistics, using Microsoft Excel.

Findings and Discussion

Characterization of the sample

Our survey counted a total of 405 valid answers. Concerning gender, our sample is relatively unbalanced, with 66,9% females, 32,4% males, and 0,7% answering "other".

Regarding age, our sample displays a good variety, ranging between 18 and 78 years old. The average age is 33 years old. Although our sample includes participants from 12 of the 20 districts of Portugal, 74,1% live around the capital, in the Lisbon district. About socioeconomic status (SES), we considered education and income. Basic Education was completed by 0,2% of the participants, 28,4% had completed High School, 48,9% hold a BA, 18,8% a Master and 3,7% a PhD. The minimum wage in Portugal, in 2023, is 760 euros, and 28,9% earn less than this. The average wage in Portugal, in 2023, is 1355 euros, and the income of 30,4% of our sample is in this interval. Thus, 40,7% of our sample has an individual net income superior to the medium wage. We can conclude that this distribution reflects well the Portuguese context, in which studying more does not always correspond to earning more.

Brand attributes that trigger brand love

Before addressing the brand attributes that trigger brand love, it is interesting to explore the brands that have been chosen by our participants as their focus to answer our survey. Our 405 respondents referred a total of 157 different brands, demonstrating that brand love is not consensual, but instead profoundly personal. These brands are distributed by a variety of sectors, as displayed in Figure 1.

Figure 1. Love brands of our sample, distributed by sector (in percentage).

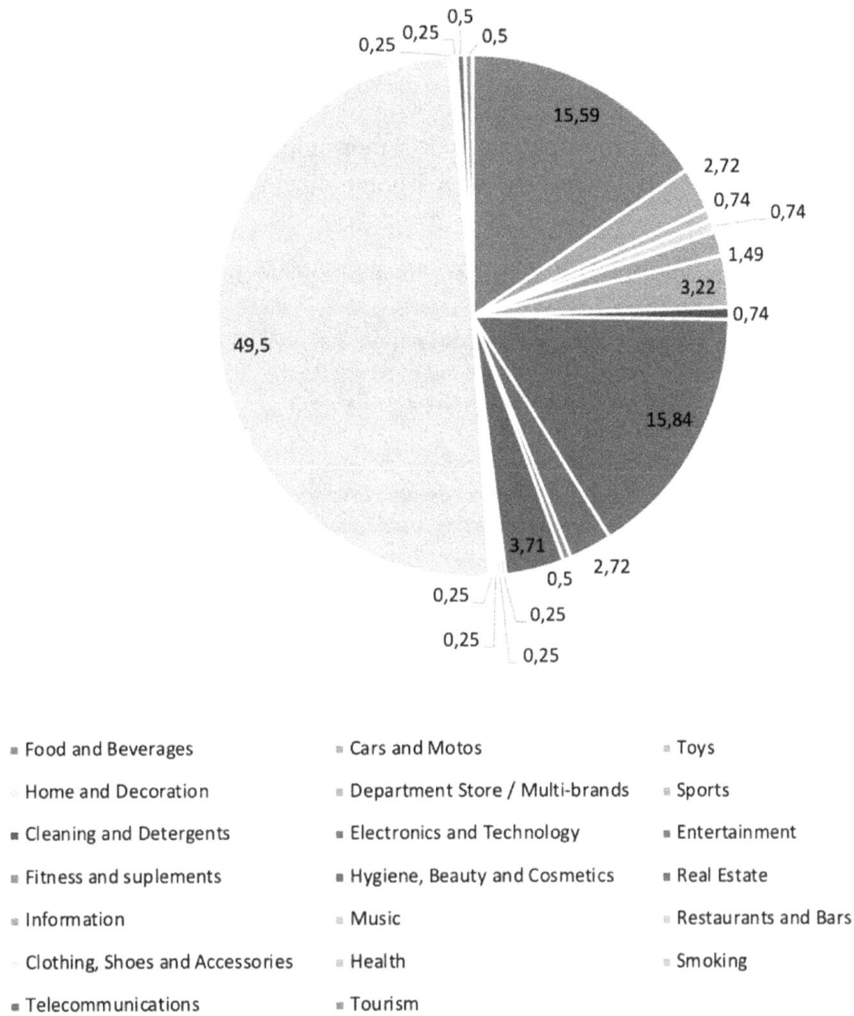

The sector of Clothes, Shoes, and Accessories stands out, with 65 different brands being the favorites of 49,5% of our sample. Exploring it with more detail, it includes 44 fast fashion brands (with Zara strongly standing out as the most loved brand, mentioned by 71 respondents), 13 sports brands (Nike is the third most loved brand, picked by 21 respondents), and 8 luxury brands. Our findings reveal that **luxury** is not a predisposition to brand love, despite previous literature advocating a connection between luxury, or specific components of luxury such as prestige, quality, exclusivity, and brand love (Fournier, 1998). The sector of Electronics and Technology includes the second most loved brand, Apple, picked by 52 respondents.

This sector only includes 8 different brands, which reinforces the importance of Apple. The sector of Food and Beverages includes 28 different brands that are the favorites of 15,59% of our sample, with Coca-Cola and Lidl standing out as the most loved brands in this sector.

Considering brand features and attributes that may trigger brand love, Figure 2 displays the ones that our sample considers most important (combining the options "very important" and "important" on a 5-point scale).

Figure 2. Most important attributes of a love brand (in percentage).

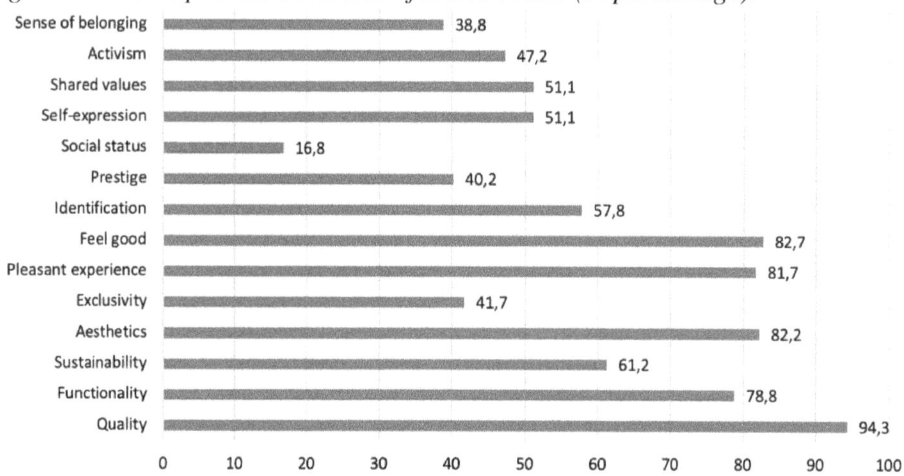

Quality stands out as an important attribute for 94,3% of our sample. This is consistent with previous literature both on the concepts of brand love (e.g., Carroll & Ahuvia, 2006) and brand equity (e.g., Aaker, 1995). However, it is interesting to notice that hedonistic attributes such as affording a **"feel good"** sensation, affording pleasant **experiences** and **aesthetics** appear as very important as well. This is consistent with previous research that connects brand experiences to brand love (Albert & Merunka, 2013; Madeleine & Sihombing, 2019). The "feel good" sensation and experiences are not intrinsic to products, but rather quite ephemeral. Despite this, consumers in our sample find these attributes very important for a brand to become their favorite. It is also relevant to observe that attributes present in previous research on the topic seem to be becoming less relevant, such as **exclusivity**, **prestige**, and **social status**. Affording a **sense of belonging** is only relevant to 38,8% of our sample, which may explain why social media marketing does not contribute as much as expected to prompt brand love (as our results show below). This result apparently contradicts the strong evidence in previous literature of a connection between brand love and positive electronic word of mouth (Unal

& Aydin, 2013; Gumparthi & Patra, 2020). However, positive electronic word of mouth is often addressed as a consequence of brand love, but not as an antecedent (Vivek et al., 2012; Albert & Merunka, 2013). Thus, social media marketing may not be as effective as expected as a trigger of brand love, but it may be useful for nurturing it when it already exists, as well as a dimension of branding that is more likely to harvest the benefits of brand love. Finally, brand attributes that are currently gaining traction among consumers are not mentioned as the most important yet, such as **sustainability** (61,2%), **alignment between brand and personal values** (51,1%), using the brand for **self-expression** (51,1%) and **activism** (47,2%). Furthermore, in an open-ended question, we asked our respondents to mention other brand attributes that were important to them. For 4,9%, offering a great **variety** of products was important. In addition, 3,7% mentioned a sense of **nostalgia**, or that the brand accompanied them since childhood. Concepts like brand nostalgia and vintage brands have been studied, but a connection to brand love needs further research. For 3% of our sample, the brand must be trustworthy (which is connected to performance) and safe. This is consistent with 68,4% of our sample expressing agreement (answered "totally agree" or "agree" on a 5-point scale) with the statement "For me, my favorite brand must be available and helpful (e.g., customer care". Also, 2,5% of our sample mentioned **originality**, and 2,2% value **affordability**, which is contradictory with the literature that presents luxury, exclusivity, and prestige as antecedents of brand love. It is important to stress that 2,2% highlighted their preference for **Portuguese** brands, thus referring to the importance of culture, and 2,2% mentioned liking the **communication** of the brand. One participant mentioned using storytelling specifically, and another humor. When questioned specifically about brand communication, 48,1% of our sample expressed agreement (answered "totally agree" or "agree" on a 5-point scale) with the claim "For me, my favorite brand must tell stories I relate with". Other aspects were mentioned by a few participants, such as innovation, history, simplicity, elegance, and being trendy, contributing to the community with actions, authenticity, and cuteness. Our survey provided a snapshot of the importance of these brand attributes, but longitudinal research would be interesting to understand how they are trending.

Features of brand communication that nurture brand love

First, 97% of our samples declare to trust the communication of their favorite brands, which points out the importance of communication not so much for triggering, but especially for nurturing brand love.

Figure 3 presents the features of brand communication that, according to our sample, most contribute to nurturing brand love (combining the options "very important" and "important" on a 5-point scale).

Figure 3. Most important features of a love brand's communication (in percentage).

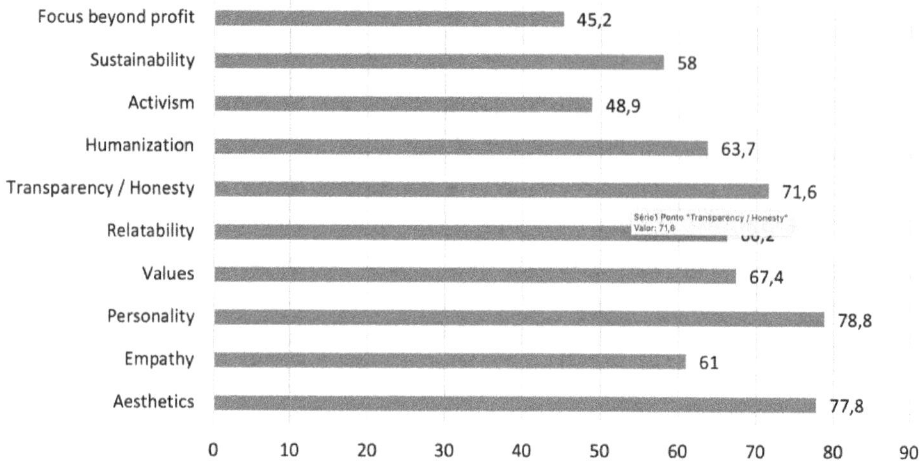

The most important feature, for 78,8% of our sample, is brand **personality**, which has, for quite some time, been recognized in the literature as an important brand asset, contributing to brand equity. However, 77,8% mention the **aesthetic** component of communication, which has been under-researched and is worth exploring in more depth. **Transparency** and **honesty** are valued by 71,6% of our sample, corresponding to an increasing trend in consumer behavior. It is often related to **sustainability**, but this feature is important for only 58% of the sample. Consistently, 60,2% of our sample expressed agreement (answered "totally agree" or "agree" on a 5-point scale" with the claim "For me, it is important that my favorite brand is trying to become more sustainable". Another trend in branding, **activism**, is mentioned by 48,9% of the sample, showing potential to become more important in the future. 42,2% agree with the statement "For me, my favorite brand must support the causes that I also (want to) support" and 39,8% agree with "For me, my favorite brand must take solidary action". Aspects that previous research presents as antecedents of brand love, such as empathy, relatability, and values, are considered important by a less significant group of participants.

Looking at the claims that we asked our participants to show (dis)agreement with, the answers convey that the content of the message is very important, as 52,3% agree that "For me, it is important that my favorite brand expresses values that matter to me" and 44,4% agree with "For me, it is important that my favorite brand talks about topics that matter to me".

Interestingly, our sample revealed considerable agreement with under researched topics. For example, 47,2% agree with the claim "For me, my favorite brand must inspire me to be better", thus suggesting that personal development and self-care may be interesting new areas for brands to explore and build stronger and longer-lasting relationships with their consumers or fans. In addition, 45,2% with the statement "For me, it is important that my favorite brand promotes the wellbeing of its collaborators". This topic has been gaining traction in scientific research and invites researchers to explore, in parallel with activism, intra-activism.

Benefits of Brand Love

All the respondents claimed to be consumers of their favorite brands – even in the case of luxury brands mentioned, such as Porsche, Chanel, or Louis Vuitton, among others.

However, only 56% phrase their relationship with their favorite brand as "brand love". Next, we set out to verify if the main consequences of brand love that have been documented in previous research as beneficial for brands are present in our sample, as displayed in Table 1. We consider that these benefits that brand love generates for companies and brands result from the expression of love on the part of consumers.

Table 1. Brand-beneficial consequences of brand love (in percentage).

Consequences of Brand Love	Yes
Brand loyalty	82,2%
Following online brand communities	53,1%
Interacting on online brand communities	40,5%
Creating content on social media	19,5%
Recommending	96,8%
Waiting to buy if unavailable	76,3%
Willing to pay more	70,1%

Overall, and consistently with previous research on this topic, our data highlights that **loyalty** (Batra et al., 2012; Roy et al., 2016; Goméz & Pérez, 2018; Çelik, 2022) and **recommendations** (Albert & Merunka, 2013; Unal & Aydin, 2013; Gumparthi & Patra, 2020) are the most common ways for customers to express their love towards their favorite brands. It is also noteworthy that 76,3% of our sample is willing to **wait** if their favorite brand is not available, and 70,1% are willing to **pay more** for it. Concerning **social media engagement**, our results are contradictory to previous research on the topic (e.g., Unal & Aydin, 2013; Albert & Merunka, 2013; Gumparthi & Patra, 2020). Only 53,1% follow their favorite brands on social media, which falls short of all the hype around social media marketing. Brands invest considerably in social media as a way of nurturing strong relationships with consumers, but our results question the relevance and efficacy of such a strategy. Only 40,5% of our sample **interacts with online brand communities** by liking, sharing, or commenting on branded content. This percentage includes 77% of consumers who follow online brand communities, but also 10,4% who do not, pointing out that online engagement does not depend on or require following online branded communities. When it comes to **creating digital content** featuring their favorite brand, brands invest considerably in prompting this practice, as it can afford wider reach, increased awareness, and eWOM (electronic Word of Mouth), but only 19,5% of our sample adheres to it. Specific questions about brand communication are consistent with the observation that social media marketing may not be as important as the literature describes and as the market advocates. Communicating frequently on social media is important for 65,4% of our sample, but always answering comments on social media is only important for 19,5%. The benefits of brand love for consumers are under-researched but looking at the brand attributes that our sample values the most in their favorite brand (check Figure 2), we can observe that **enjoying the brand, in a hedonistic sense**, stands out as a benefit for consumers.

CONCLUSION

Our study presents a snapshot of the relationship of a sample of Portuguese consumers with their favorite brands. Comparing our results with previous research on the antecedents and consequences of brand love has allowed us to spot relevant shifts in the brand-consumer relationship in a post-pandemic setting.

Regarding the antecedents of brand love, features strongly associated with luxury such as prestige and exclusivity aren't as important as previous literature argues, as our sample elects accessible and affordable brands that are present in their daily lives as their love brands. On the other hand, another feature traditionally associated with luxury, hedonism, emerges as increasingly relevant for consumers to fall in love with brands, as more brands expand their offers beyond products and services, into brand experiences (Albert & Merunka, 2013; Madeleine & Sihombing, 2019).

One original contribution of our article is looking specifically into the role played by brand communication in prompting and fostering brand love. Communication emerges as pivotal in this process, being successful depending on its ability to express a personality that triggers identification and relatability from consumers and to afford pleasurable brand experiences. Social media marketing, on the other hand, falls short of expectations, considering previous literature (Vivek et al., 2012; Albert & Merunka, 2013; Unal & Aydin, 2013; Gumparthi & Patra, 2020), as an antecedent of brand love, but instead is characterized by our sample as a way of nurturing brand love, and as a way of harvesting the benefits of brand love in the forms of recommendations and digital content in online communities.

Concerning the consequences of brand love, our results are aligned with previous literature, highlighting brand loyalty (Batra et al., 2012; Roy et al., 2016; Goméz & Pérez, 2018; Çelik, 2022) and brand engagement (Albert & Merunka, 2013; Unal & Aydin, 2013; Gumparthi & Patra, 2020) as the most important benefits that brand love affords brands. However, another original contribution of our work is starting to explore which benefits brand love may afford consumers, which has been, so far, under-researched. Our results point to, firstly, an enhancement of the hedonistic enjoyment of brand experiences through personalization, identification, and connectedness. Secondly, our sample alludes to brand trust as one of the benefits that consumers take from being in a committed relationship with a brand.

Relevant paths for future research are, therefore, further exploring which marketing strategies and techniques are most useful for prompting and/or for nurturing brand love, as well as mapping in more detail the benefits, for consumers, of being in love with a brand.

ACKNOWLEDGMENTS

This project did not receive any funding. The authors wish to thank all participants for their involvement in this research and colleagues as well as attendees at conferences for comments on earlier drafts of this manuscript. We wish to acknowledge the comments by colleagues at ICNOVA and CECC - Universidade Católica Portuguesa for the support provided to our work.

Declaration of interest statement

No potential conflict of interest was reported by the authors.

REFERENCES

Aaker, D. A. (1991). *Managing Brand Equity: Capitalizing on the value of a Brand Name*. Free Press.

Ahuvia, A. C. (2005). Beyond the extended self: Loved objects and consumers' identity narratives. *The Journal of Consumer Research*, 32(1), 171–184. DOI: 10.1086/429607

Albert, N., & Merunka, D. (2013). The role of brand love in consumer. *Journal of Consumer Marketing*, 30(3), 258–266. DOI: 10.1108/07363761311328928

Alnawas, I., & Altarifi, S. (2016). Exploring the role of brand identification and brand love in generating higher levels of brand loyalty. *Journal of Vacation Marketing*, 22(2), 111–128. DOI: 10.1177/1356766715604663

Bae, B. R., & Kim, S. E. (2023). Effect of brand experiences on brand loyalty mediated by brand love: The moderated mediation role of brand trust. *Asia Pacific Journal of Marketing and Logistics*, 35(10), 2412–2430. Advance online publication. DOI: 10.1108/APJML-03-2022-0203

Bairrada, C. M., Coelho, F., & Coelho, A. (2018). Antecedents and outcomes of brand love: Utilitarian and symbolic brand qualities. *European Journal of Marketing*, 52(3/4), 656–682. DOI: 10.1108/EJM-02-2016-0081

Batra, R., Ahuvia, A., & Bagozzi, R. P. (2012). Brand love. *Journal of Marketing*, 76(2), 1–16. DOI: 10.1509/jm.09.0339

Bauer, H., Heinrich, D., & Albrecht, C. M. (2009). All you need is love: Assessing consumers' brand love. In *Proceedings of the American Marketing Association summer educators conference* (Vol. 15, No. 2, pp. 252-253). Chicago: American Marketing Association.

Bıçakcıoğlu, N., İpek, İ., & Bayraktaroğlu, G. (2018). Antecedents and outcomes of brand love: The mediating role of brand loyalty. *Journal of Marketing Communications*, 24(8), 863–877. DOI: 10.1080/13527266.2016.1244108

Burnasheva, R., Suh, Y. G., & Villalobos-Moron, K. (2019). Sense of community and social identity effect on brand love: Based on the online communities of a luxury fashion brands. *Journal of Global Fashion Marketing*, 10(1), 50–65. DOI: 10.1080/20932685.2018.1558087

Carroll, B. A., & Ahuvia, A. C. (2006). Some antecedents and outcomes of brand love. *Marketing Letters*, 17(2), 79–89. DOI: 10.1007/s11002-006-4219-2

Çelik, Z. (2022). The moderating role of influencer attractiveness in the effect of brand love, brand trust, brand awareness and brand image on brand loyalty. *İstanbul Ticaret Üniversitesi Sosyal Bilimler Dergisi, 21*(43), 148-167. https://doi.org/DOI: 10.46928/iticusbe.1050122

Creswell, J. W., & Creswell, J. D. (2022). *Research Design: Quantitative, qualitative, and mixed methods* (6th ed.). Sage.

Dias, P., & Cavalheiro, R. (2021). The role of storytelling in the creation of brand love: The PANDORA case. *Journal of Brand Management*, 29(1), 58–71. DOI: 10.1057/s41262-021-00254-6

Dias, P., & Duarte, A. (2022). How Portuguese adolescents relate to influencers and brands on TikTok. *Journal of Digital & Social Media Marketing*, 10(1), 82–95. DOI: 10.69554/VSHW2788

Dias, P., & Duarte, A. (2023). *Social Brand Management in a Post Covid-19 Era.* Taylor & Francis. DOI: 10.4324/9781003382331

Duarte, A. (2023). *The relationship between brands and consumers*, in Social Brand Management in a Post Covid-19 Era, 3-16. Routledge. DOI: 10.4324/9781003382331-2

Duarte, A., & Dias, P. (2022). Post-Pandemic Changes in the Consumption Habits of the Portuguese. In *G. Sange & E.E. Basar (orgs.), Pandemics and Consumer Behavior* (pp. 189–207). Nova Science Publishers.

Duarte, A., & Gregório, M. S. M. (2022). Empathic Brands: Proposing a Model for Its Measure and Evaluation. In Navigating Digital Communication and Challenges for Organizations (pp. 168-185). IGI Global. doi: 10.4018/978-1-7998-9790-3.ch010

Dwivedi, A. (2015). A higher-order model of consumer brand engagement and its impact on loyalty intentions. *Journal of Retailing and Consumer Services*, 24, 100–109. DOI: 10.1016/j.jretconser.2015.02.007

Ebrahim, R. S. (2020). The role of trust in understanding the impact of social media marketing on brand equity and brand loyalty. *Journal of Relationship Marketing*, 19(4), 287–308. DOI: 10.1080/15332667.2019.1705742

Elsharnouby, M. H., Mohsen, J., Saeed, O. T., & Mahrous, A. A. (2021). Enhancing resilience to negative information in consumer-brand interaction: The mediating role of brand knowledge and involvement. *Journal of Research in Interactive Marketing*, 15(4), 571–591. DOI: 10.1108/JRIM-05-2020-0107

Fischer, M., Völckner, F., & Sattler, H. (2010). How important are brands? A cross-category, cross-country study. *JMR, Journal of Marketing Research*, 47(5), 823–839. DOI: 10.1509/jmkr.47.5.823

Fournier, S. (1998). Consumers and their brands: Developing relationship theory in consumer research. *The Journal of Consumer Research*, 24(4), 343–373. DOI: 10.1086/209515

Ghani, N. H. B., & Tuhin, M. K. W. (2016). Consumer brand relationships. *International Review of Management and Marketing*, 6(4), 950–957. DOI: 10.2139/ssrn.3497812

Gumparthi, V. P., & Patra, S. (2020). The phenomenon of brand love: A systematic literature review. *Journal of Relationship Marketing*, 19(2), 93–132. DOI: 10.1080/15332667.2019.1664871

Heinrich, D., Albrecht, C. M., & Bauer, H. H. (2012). *Love actually? Measuring and exploring consumers' brand love. Consumer-Brand Relationships–Theory and Practice*. Routledge.

Hollebeek, L. D., Glynn, M. S., & Brodie, R. J. (2014). Consumer brand engagement in social media: Conceptualization, scale development and validation. *Journal of Interactive Marketing*, 28(2), 149–165. DOI: 10.1016/j.intmar.2013.12.002

Loureiro, S. M. C. (2011, November). Consumers love and willingness to sacrifice for a brand. In Conference book Proceedings of ANZMAC conference-Marketing in the Age of Consumerism: Jekyll or Hyde (pp. 28-30).

Loureiro, S. M. C., Ruediger, K. H., & Demetris, V. (2012). Brand emotional connection and loyalty. *Journal of Brand Management*, 20(1), 13–27. DOI: 10.1057/bm.2012.3

Luo, S., & Hamlin, R. (2022). A cross cultural comparison of brand love in consumer brand relationships: Is 'transmissive brand love' a potential platform for developing brand equity? *Journal of Brand Management*, 29(5), 484–497. DOI: 10.1057/s41262-022-00286-6

Madadi, R., Torres, I. M., & Zúñiga, M. Á. (2021). Hierarchical relationships among brand equity dimensions: The mediating effects of brand trust and brand love. *Services Marketing Quarterly*, 42(1-2), 74–92. DOI: 10.1080/15332969.2021.1947086

Madeleine, S., & Sihombing, S. O. (2019). The impacts of brand experiences on brand love, brand trust, and brand loyalty: an empirical study. *Jurnal Bisnis dan Manajemen, 20*(2), 91-107. https://doi.org/DOI: 10.24198/jbm.v20i2.241

Manthiou, A., Kang, J., Hyun, S. S., & Fu, X. X. (2018). The impact of brand authenticity on building brand love: An investigation of impression in memory and lifestyle-congruence. *International Journal of Hospitality Management*, 75, 38–47. DOI: 10.1016/j.ijhm.2018.03.005

Palusuk, N., Koles, B., & Hasan, R. (2019). 'All you need is brand love': A critical review and comprehensive conceptual framework for brand love. *Journal of Marketing Management*, 35(1-2), 97–129. DOI: 10.1080/0267257X.2019.1572025

Park, C. W., Eisingerich, A. B., & Park, J. W. (2013). Attachment-aversion (AA) model of customer-brand relationships. *Journal of Consumer Psychology*, 23(2), 229–248. DOI: 10.1016/j.jcps.2013.01.002

Park, C. W., MacInnis, D. J., Priester, J., Eisingerich, A. B., & Iacobucci, D. (2010). Brand attachment and brand attitude strength: Conceptual and empirical differentiation of two critical brand equity drivers. *Journal of Marketing*, 74(6), 1–17. DOI: 10.1509/jmkg.74.6.1

Roberts, K. (2005). *Lovemarks: The future beyond brands*. Powerhouse books.

Rodrigues, C., Brandão, A., Billore, S., & Oda, T. (2023). The mediating role of perceived brand authenticity between brand experience and brand love: A cross-cultural perspective. *Journal of Brand Management*, •••, 1–17. DOI: 10.1057/s41262-023-00342-9

Rodrigues, P., Reis, R., & Cantista, I. (2015). Consumer behavior: How the "brand love" affects you. In Ideas in Marketing: Finding the New and Polishing the Old: Proceedings of the 2013 Academy of Marketing Science (AMS) Annual Conference (pp. 583-588). Springer International Publishing. https://doi.org/DOI: 10.1007/978-3-319-10951-0_212

Roy, P., Khandeparkar, K., & Motiani, M. (2016). A lovable personality: The effect of brand personality on brand love. *Journal of Brand Management*, 23(5), 97–113. DOI: 10.1057/s41262-016-0005-5

Sarkar, A. (2013). Romantic brand love: A conceptual analysis. *The Marketing Review*, 13(1), 23–37. DOI: 10.1362/146934713X13590250137709

Schmid, D. A., & Huber, F. (2019). Brand love: Emotionality and development of its elements across the relationship lifecycle. *Psychology and Marketing*, 36(4), 305–320. DOI: 10.1002/mar.21180

Sternberg, R. J. (1986). A triangular theory of love. *Psychological Review*, 93(2), 119–135. DOI: 10.1037/0033-295X.93.2.119

Trivedi, J., & Sama, R. (2020). The effect of influencer marketing on consumers' brand admiration and online purchase intentions: An emerging market perspective. *Journal of Internet Commerce*, 19(1), 103–124. DOI: 10.1080/15332861.2019.1700741

Trudel, R. (2019). Sustainable consumer behavior. *Consumer Psychology Review*, 2(1), 85–96. DOI: 10.1002/arcp.1045

Unal, S., & Aydın, H. (2013). An investigation on the evaluation of the factors affecting brand love. *Procedia: Social and Behavioral Sciences*, 92, 76–85. DOI: 10.1016/j.sbspro.2013.08.640

Varsha, P. S., Akter, S., Kumar, A., Gochhait, S., & Patagundi, B. (2021). The impact of artificial intelligence on branding: A bibliometric analysis (1982-2019). [JGIM]. *Journal of Global Information Management*, 29(4), 221–246. DOI: 10.4018/JGIM.20210701.oa10

Verma, P. (2021). The effect of brand engagement and brand love upon overall brand equity and purchase intention: A moderated–mediated model. *Journal of Promotion Management*, 27(1), 103–132. DOI: 10.1080/10496491.2020.1809591

Vivek, S. D., Beatty, S. E., & Morgan, R. M. (2012). Customer engagement: Exploring customer relationships beyond purchase. *Journal of Marketing Theory and Practice*, 20(2), 122–146. DOI: 10.2753/MTP1069-6679200201

Chapter 11
Measuring Brand Performance With AI Tools

Ansuman Samal
https://orcid.org/0000-0002-4213-5988
Siksha 'O' Anusandhan University, India

Jajjara Bhargav
Chalapathi Institute of Engineering and Technology, India

Manikandan S. K.
Velalar College of Engineering and Technology, India

P. Selvakumar
https://orcid.org/0000-0002-3650-4548
Nehru Institute of Technology, India

Mohit Sharma
https://orcid.org/0009-0007-2280-8077
Maharshi Dayanand University, India

Manjunath T. C.
https://orcid.org/0000-0003-2545-9160
Rajarajeswari College of Engineering, India

ABSTRACT

This approach transcends traditional metrics, offering a more nuanced understanding of consumer behavior, brand impact, and market dynamics.Traditional methods often rely on periodic surveys and historical data, which can be limited in scope and slow to capture emerging trends. In contrast, AI systems can continuously ingest data from diverse sources, including social media, online reviews, and sales transactions, enabling brands to gain immediate and comprehensive insights into their performance. This involves natural language processing (NLP) techniques that interpret the emotional tone and context of written content. For example, an AI system might detect a surge in positive sentiment following a successful marketing campaign or identify emerging issues from negative feedback before they escalate. This real-time analysis allows brands to respond more swiftly and effectively to changes in public perception. This enables brands to tailor their strategies with

DOI: 10.4018/979-8-3693-9461-8.ch011

greater precision, targeting specific segments with personalized messages and offers.

INTRODUCTION TO AI-POWERED BRAND PERFORMANCE MEASUREMENT.

This approach transcends traditional metrics, offering a more nuanced understanding of consumer behavior, brand impact, and market dynamics. Traditional methods often rely on periodic surveys and historical data, which can be limited in scope and slow to capture emerging trends. In contrast, AI systems can continuously ingest data from diverse sources, including social media, online reviews, and sales transactions, enabling brands to gain immediate and comprehensive insights into their performance. This involves natural language processing (NLP) techniques that interpret the emotional tone and context of written content. For example, an AI system might detect a surge in positive sentiment following a successful marketing campaign or identify emerging issues from negative feedback before they escalate. This real-time analysis allows brands to respond more swiftly and effectively to changes in public perception. This enables brands to tailor their strategies with greater precision, targeting specific segments with personalized messages and offers. For instance, AI might identify a subset of consumers who are particularly responsive to eco-friendly products, allowing a brand to design targeted campaigns that resonate with this group. Moreover, AI-powered tools can facilitate competitive analysis by monitoring and comparing brand performance against competitors. This involves tracking competitors' online presence, market activities, and consumer sentiment. AI systems can aggregate and analyze this data to provide actionable insights on competitive positioning, highlighting areas where a brand may need to adjust its strategy to gain a competitive edge. For example, if a competitor's recent product launch is generating significant positive buzz, AI can alert a brand to this development and suggest potential strategic responses.

This predictive capability allows brands to anticipate market shifts, consumer preferences, and potential challenges before they occur. For instance, AI might predict a decline in demand for a particular product category based on emerging consumer trends, enabling a brand to proactively adjust its inventory and marketing strategies. In conclusion, AI-powered brand performance measurement offers a transformative approach to understanding and optimizing brand health. While there are challenges associated with data privacy and the risk of over-reliance on technology, the benefits of AI in enhancing brand performance measurement are substantial.Setting brand objectives effectively is crucial for aligning AI tools with business goals, ensuring that technological investments translate into tangible outcomes. The process begins with a clear understanding of a brand's overarching business objectives, such as increasing market share, enhancing customer loyalty, or driving revenue growth. By clearly defining these goals, organizations can determine how AI tools can be leveraged to achieve them, facilitating a strategic alignment between technological capabilities and business needs.The first step in setting brand objectives is to conduct a comprehensive assessment of the brand's current position and desired future state. This involves analyzing market trends, competitive landscape, consumer behavior, and internal capabilities. For instance, if a brand's objective is to expand its market presence, AI tools can be utilized to identify emerging market opportunities and customer segments. Advanced analytics can provide insights into geographic regions with high growth potential, while machine learning algorithms can predict future trends based on historical data. This data-driven approach ensures that brand objectives are grounded in actionable intelligence, allowing for more informed decision-making.Integrating AI tools into brand strategy requires aligning these tools with the specific objectives outlined. This involves selecting the right AI technologies that address the identified needs. It is also important to consider the integration of AI tools with existing systems and processes. AI technologies should complement and enhance current workflows rather than disrupt them. This seamless integration ensures that AI tools deliver value without causing operational friction or requiring significant changes to established practices.

Another critical aspect of aligning AI tools with brand objectives is to ensure that the implementation is guided by ethical considerations and data privacy regulations. Brands must communicate their data practices to customers and provide options for consent and privacy preferences (Alexandruand et al., 2019). This not only builds trust but also aligns with regulatory requirements, mitigating potential risks associated with data breaches and misuse.The rapidly evolving nature of AI technology means that brands must stay abreast of new developments and be willing to refine their strategies as needed. This may involve regularly reviewing and updating AI models, testing new tools, and soliciting feedback from stakeholders. By maintaining an agile approach, brands can ensure that their AI investments continue to deliver value and support their business goals effectively.In summary, setting brand objectives and aligning AI tools with business goals requires a strategic approach that begins with a clear understanding of the brand's aspirations and market dynamics. By defining SMART objectives, selecting appropriate AI technologies, and integrating these tools with existing systems, brands can leverage AI to achieve their goals and drive meaningful outcomes. Establishing clear performance metrics, adhering to ethical standards, and fostering a culture of continuous improvement further enhance the effectiveness of AI in achieving brand objectives. Through thoughtful planning and execution, brands can harness the power of AI to enhance their performance, optimize their strategies, and achieve long-term success.

AI-Driven Brand Awareness Metrics: Tracking Reach and Recognition.

In the realm of modern marketing, AI-driven metrics for tracking brand awareness have become pivotal in understanding and enhancing a brand's reach and recognition. These metrics leverage advanced algorithms, machine learning, and data analytics to provide a comprehensive view of how well a brand is performing in terms of visibility and consumer perception. As businesses increasingly rely on digital channels for promotion, traditional metrics such as raw impressions and basic survey results are complemented and often superseded by AI-enhanced tools that offer deeper insights and more accurate measurements (Alratemi.,et al.,2012).Natural language processing (NLP) technologies are employed to analyze text data for mentions of the brand, extracting meaningful insights about the context and sentiment of these mentions. This allows brands to track how frequently they are discussed and the nature of these market penetration, while an increase in negative sentiment might highlight potential issues that need addressing.One significant advantage of AI in tracking brand awareness is its ability to perform sentiment analysis at scale. Traditional methods of gauging public perception often involve manual sampling and subjective interpretation, which can be time-consuming and prone to biases. For example, if sentiment analysis reveals a growing discontent among customers about a specific aspect of a product, a brand can take swift action to address the issue before it escalates further.AI also enhances the tracking of brand reach through advanced analytics that measure the impact of marketing campaigns and media coverage. By using machine learning models to analyze patterns in engagement and interaction, AI tools can provide insights into how effectively a campaign is expanding the brand's audience. Metrics such as share of voice (SOV) and share of conversation (SOC) are calculated to determine how much of the overall discourse in a given market is attributable to the brand compared to its competitors. These metrics offer valuable insights into a brand's visibility and its position within the industry landscape. For instance, an increase in SOV might indicate that a brand is successfully capturing public attention, while a decline could suggest the need for a more impactful campaign.

The role of AI in tracking brand awareness also extends to identifying key influencers and assessing their impact. AI tools can analyze social media interactions and online content to identify individuals who have significant sway over public opinion and assess how their endorsements or critiques affect brand perception. By mapping out the influence network, brands can better understand which voices are shaping public opinion and how these influencers contribute to the overall reach and recognition of the brand. This allows for more strategic partnerships and targeted influencer marketing efforts, ultimately enhancing brand visibility and engagement.Furthermore, AI-driven metrics can provide insights into geographic and demographic trends related to brand awareness. By analyzing data from various regions and audience segments, AI tools can identify where brand recognition is growing or lagging. This information is invaluable for tailoring marketing strategies to specific markets or demographics. For example, if data shows a high level of brand recognition in urban areas but lower awareness in rural regions, a brand can develop targeted campaigns to address this disparity and improve its reach in underserved areas(Angela.E,et al.,2018). For instance, if AI analysis reveals that a particular social media platform is driving significantly more engagement and brand recognition compared to others, a brand can focus its efforts and resources on that platform to maximize its impact.AI-driven metrics also offer advanced visualization and reporting capabilities that facilitate better decision-making. Interactive dashboards and real-time reports generated by AI tools provide a clear and comprehensive view of brand awareness metrics, making it easier for marketers and executives to track progress, identify trends, and make data-driven decisions. These visualizations can help in presenting complex data in an accessible format, allowing for quick interpretation and strategic adjustments.

Additionally, while AI provides valuable insights, it is essential to balance these with human judgment. AI models are based on historical data and algorithms that may not always account for contextual nuances or emerging trends that are not yet reflected in the data. Therefore, integrating AI insights with human expertise and market knowledge is crucial for developing a well-rounded understanding of brand awareness and formulating effective strategies.In conclusion, AI-driven brand awareness metrics represent a significant advancement in how brands track and measure their reach and recognition. By leveraging advanced data analytics, sentiment analysis, and influencer identification, brands can gain deeper insights into their market presence and public perception. These metrics enable more informed decision-making, strategic optimization, and targeted marketing efforts, ultimately driving enhanced brand visibility and impact. Measuring brand sentiment analysis through AI-powered social media monitoring has revolutionized how businesses understand public perception and engage with their audiences. This approach harnesses advanced artificial intelligence techniques to scrutinize vast quantities of social media data, providing detailed insights into how a brand is perceived online. By analyzing user-generated content across platforms such as Twitter, Facebook, Instagram, and LinkedIn, AI tools offer a nuanced understanding of brand sentiment, enabling companies to make data-driven decisions and respond effectively to emerging trends and consumer opinions.AI-driven sentiment analysis involves several key processes that collectively enhance the ability to gauge public sentiment accurately (Ardito, L.,et al.,2019). The first step is data collection, where AI tools aggregate posts, comments, reviews, and other forms of social media content mentioning the brand. This data collection is facilitated by web crawlers and APIs that can handle large volumes of real-time data from various social media platforms..

NLP techniques are central to sentiment analysis, as they allow AI to classify textual content into categories such as positive, negative, or neutral. For instance, phrases like "I love this brand" or "This product is fantastic" are identified as positive, while "I'm disappointed" or "This service is terrible" are classified as negative. AI systems also use more sophisticated techniques, such as deep learning and contextual analysis, to understand sentiment in complex or ambiguous statements. One of the significant advantages of AI-powered sentiment analysis is its ability to handle and analyze data at scale. Traditional methods of sentiment analysis, which often rely on manual review or limited sampling, can be labor-intensive and may not provide a comprehensive view of public opinion. AI tools, however, can process millions of social media posts quickly and efficiently, offering a broader and more accurate picture of sentiment trends. This scalability is particularly valuable for brands operating in dynamic markets where public perception can shift rapidly. For example, a sudden increase in negative sentiment following a product recall can be detected early, enabling the brand to take corrective actions and manage the crisis more effectively. Similarly, a positive sentiment trend following a successful marketing campaign can be leveraged to reinforce successful strategies and replicate them in future initiatives.In addition to understanding overall sentiment, AI tools can provide detailed insights into the specific factors driving positive or negative opinions (Backhaus, K.,et al.,2010). This involves analyzing the content of social media posts to identify key themes, topics, and issues that are being discussed. For instance, if a significant amount of negative sentiment is associated with customer service experiences, the AI analysis might reveal recurring issues such as long wait times or unhelpful responses. This granular analysis helps brands pinpoint areas for improvement and develop targeted strategies to address specific concerns.Another crucial aspect of AI-driven sentiment analysis is influencer identification and impact assessment. AI tools can identify key influencers who are shaping public opinion about the brand and assess how their endorsements or criticisms affect overall sentiment. By analyzing the reach and engagement of influencers' posts, brands can understand the role these individuals play in shaping public perception and tailor their influencer marketing strategies accordingly. For example, collaborating with influential figures who have a positive sentiment towards the brand can enhance brand reputation and extend its reach.

Geographic and demographic segmentation is another benefit of AI-powered sentiment analysis. AI tools can analyze sentiment data across different regions and demographic groups, providing insights into how various segments perceive the brand. This segmentation allows brands to tailor their messaging and marketing strategies to specific audiences. For instance, if sentiment analysis reveals that a brand is particularly well-received among younger consumers but less so among older demographics, the brand can adjust its campaigns to better resonate with the latter group.Despite its advantages, AI-powered sentiment analysis is not without challenges. One significant challenge is the accuracy of sentiment classification, particularly in cases where language is ambiguous or context-dependent. In conclusion, AI-powered sentiment analysis through social media monitoring offers a powerful tool for measuring brand sentiment and understanding public perception(-Bahrami, M.,et al.,2020). By leveraging advanced NLP techniques and machine learning algorithms, brands can gain real-time insights into how they are perceived, track sentiment trends, and identify key drivers of public opinion. While challenges such as accuracy and data privacy need to be addressed, the benefits of AI-driven sentiment analysis are substantial. It enables brands to make informed decisions, respond proactively to changes in sentiment, and refine their strategies to enhance brand reputation and engagement.

AI-Driven Customer Engagement Metrics: Tracking Loyalty and Retention.

AI-driven customer engagement metrics are transforming how businesses track and enhance customer loyalty and retention. By harnessing sophisticated algorithms and data analytics, AI tools provide nuanced insights into customer behaviors and interactions, enabling brands to foster deeper relationships with their audiences and improve retention strategies. This approach extends beyond traditional metrics, offering a comprehensive view of customer engagement and loyalty through real-time analysis and predictive modeling.One of the key metrics enhanced by AI is customer lifetime value (CLV). Traditional methods of calculating CLV can be relatively static, relying on historical data and simple forecasting models. AI, however, employs advanced predictive analytics to estimate CLV more accurately by considering a wide range of factors, including current purchasing behavior, engagement levels, and external market conditions. By continuously updating these predictions based on real-time data, AI provides a dynamic and precise measure of how much revenue a customer is expected to generate over their lifetime. This enables brands to prioritize high-value customers and tailor their engagement strategies accordingly(Chan, H.K.,et al.,2017).AI also revolutionizes customer retention tracking through predictive modeling. By analyzing patterns in customer behavior, AI tools can identify indicators of potential churn before it occurs. For instance, machine learning models can detect subtle changes in engagement levels, such as decreased frequency of purchases or reduced interaction with marketing content, which may signal a customer's intention to leave. Another significant benefit of AI in tracking customer engagement is its ability to measure and analyze the effectiveness of various engagement channels and touchpoints. AI tools can evaluate how different channels—such as email marketing, social media, mobile apps, and website interactions—contribute to overall customer engagement and loyalty. if sentiment analysis reveals a recurring issue with a product or service, the brand can address this feedback proactively, improving the customer experience and strengthening loyalty. Additionally, AI can track changes in sentiment over time, providing insights into how specific actions or campaigns impact overall customer satisfaction.

Personalization is another area where AI significantly impacts customer engagement metrics. For example, personalized product recommendations based on past purchases can lead to increased repeat purchases and higher overall engagement.AI also enables real-time engagement tracking, allowing brands to monitor and respond to customer interactions as they happen. This includes tracking live interactions on social media, monitoring real-time feedback from customer service channels, and analyzing website activity. Real-time data analysis helps brands to address issues promptly, capitalize on positive interactions, and engage with customers in a timely manner. For instance, if a customer posts a positive review or shares a favorable experience on social media, AI can alert the brand to this interaction, enabling a quick and personalized response that reinforces customer loyalty.Moreover, AI-driven customer engagement metrics can identify patterns in customer behavior that lead to long-term loyalty. This analysis helps brands understand what drives loyalty and develop strategies to nurture these factors. For example, if data shows that customers who participate in loyalty programs are more likely to remain engaged, brands can focus on enhancing these programs to further boost retention. In conclusion, AI-driven customer engagement metrics provide powerful tools for tracking and enhancing customer loyalty and retention. While there are challenges to address, such as data privacy and model accuracy, the benefits of AI-driven customer engagement metrics are substantial, offering brands the insights needed to build stronger, more lasting customer relationships and drive sustained business growth.Brand reputation management has evolved significantly with the advent of artificial intelligence (AI), enabling businesses to proactively identify and mitigate risks associated with their public image(Dikow, H.,et al.,2015). AI-driven tools have become essential in navigating the complex landscape of brand, AI enhances a brand's ability to monitor, assess, and respond to various reputational threats, ensuring a more resilient and adaptive approach to reputation management.

One of the primary ways AI contributes to brand reputation management is through advanced monitoring and analysis of online content. AI tools continuously scan social media platforms, news websites, blogs, and other digital channels to detect mentions of the brand, its products, and its key stakeholders. This continuous monitoring is powered by natural language processing (NLP), which allows AI systems to understand and interpret the context of online conversations. NLP algorithms can categorize mentions into positive, negative, or neutral sentiments, and identify emerging issues that may pose a risk to the brand's reputation. For example, an AI tool might detect a surge in negative sentiment related to a recent product recall, providing early warnings that enable the brand to take swift corrective actions.In addition to sentiment analysis, AI enhances reputation management through real-time risk identification and assessment. Machine learning models can analyze patterns in online discussions and media coverage to identify potential risks and emerging trends. These models can detect early signals of a reputational crisis, such as a sudden increase in negative mentions or the spread of false information. For instance, if an AI system detects that a rumor about the brand is gaining traction on social media, the brand can respond with accurate information and counteract misinformation proactively(Dong, Y.,et al.,2014).AI also plays a crucial role in evaluating the effectiveness of reputation management strategies. By analyzing data from various sources, AI tools can assess how different actions, such as public statements or social media campaigns, impact brand perception. This involves tracking changes in sentiment, engagement levels, and overall media coverage. For example, after a brand issues an apology for a misstep, AI can monitor social media and news coverage to evaluate whether the apology has improved sentiment and restored trust..

Furthermore, AI-driven tools facilitate competitive analysis by monitoring competitors' reputations and strategies. By analyzing how competitors are perceived and how they manage their reputations, brands can gain insights into industry trends and best practices. AI can track competitors' responses to similar issues and evaluate their effectiveness, providing valuable lessons for improving the brand's own reputation management efforts. For instance, if a competitor successfully navigates a crisis through a specific communication strategy, AI analysis can reveal the key elements of this approach, helping the brand apply similar tactics in its own reputation management.AI-powered systems can generate automated alerts and recommendations based on predefined criteria, such as sentiment thresholds or specific keywords. This automation reduces the response time to emerging issues and ensures that appropriate actions are taken promptly. For example, if AI detects a high volume of negative sentiment related to a particular product feature, it can automatically trigger a response plan, including drafting a public statement or initiating customer support outreach.AI-driven tools also enable more precise and effective engagement with stakeholders. By analyzing customer feedback, reviews, and social media interactions, AI can identify key stakeholders who are influential in shaping public perception. This includes identifying key opinion leaders, industry analysts, and media contacts(Duan, Y.,et al.,2019). AI can then help brands tailor their communication strategies to address the concerns of these stakeholders and foster positive relationships. For instance, if AI identifies that a prominent influencer is critical of the brand, the brand can engage with the influencer directly to address their concerns and potentially improve their opinion.AI models rely on data and algorithms that may not always capture the full context or nuances of online conversations. For example, AI might struggle with detecting sarcasm or complex emotional expressions, which can impact the accuracy of sentiment analysis. Therefore, it is crucial to combine AI insights with human judgment and expertise to ensure a comprehensive understanding of reputational risks and appropriate responses.

Data privacy and ethical considerations are also important factors in AI-driven reputation management. The collection and analysis of online data must comply with privacy regulations and ethical standards. Brands need to ensure transparency in their data practices and respect user privacy. This includes obtaining necessary permissions and safeguarding personal information to build and maintain trust with stakeholders.Moreover, while AI can provide valuable insights and automate certain processes, it is not a substitute for strategic human intervention. Effective reputation management requires a thoughtful and strategic approach that considers the broader implications of actions and communications. In conclusion, AI-driven tools are transforming brand reputation management by providing advanced capabilities for monitoring, assessing, and responding to reputational risks(Fernandez, L.M.V.,et al.,2019). Through real-time analysis, risk identification, and automated responses, AI enhances a brand's ability to manage its reputation effectively and proactively. However, challenges related to accuracy, data privacy, and the need for strategic human oversight must be addressed to fully realize the benefits of AI in reputation management. By leveraging AI as part of a comprehensive reputation management strategy, brands can navigate the complexities of public perception, mitigate risks, and foster positive relationships with their stakeholders.

AI-Powered Competitor Analysis: Benchmarking Brand Performance.

The foundation of AI-powered competitor analysis lies in its ability to aggregate and process data from multiple channels, including digital marketing campaigns, social media, customer reviews, financial reports, and industry news. AI tools utilize web crawlers and data scraping technologies to collect relevant data from these sources, ensuring a comprehensive view of competitors' activities and market presence. Natural language processing (NLP) algorithms further enhance this analysis by interpreting textual data, such as news articles or social media posts, to extract meaningful insights about competitors' strategies, strengths, and weaknesses.AI tools continuously monitor and analyze competitor activities, providing up-to-date information on their performance and market positioning. For example, if a competitor launches a new product or enters a new market, AI tools can immediately detect and analyze the impact of these actions, allowing brands to adjust their own strategies in response(Gentner, D.,et al.,2018).AI-driven sentiment analysis is another critical component of competitor benchmarking. are consistently praising a competitor's customer service while expressing frustration with their product quality, a brand can leverage this information to differentiate itself by highlighting its own strengths in these areas.Competitive intelligence gathered through AI also includes benchmarking key performance indicators (KPIs) such as market share, pricing strategies, and sales performance. AI tools can analyze publicly available financial data and market reports to compare these KPIs with those of competitors. This benchmarking helps brands understand their relative performance in the market and identify areas where they need to improve or adjust their strategies. For example, if AI analysis shows that a competitor has a higher market share in a particular region, a brand can investigate the factors contributing to this success and develop targeted strategies to capture a larger share of that market.

For instance, AI can predict future consumer preferences or identify new market opportunities based on trends in competitors' product offerings or marketing strategies. This predictive capability allows brands to anticipate changes in the competitive landscape and proactively adapt their strategies to maintain a competitive edge.AI-powered competitor analysis also enables brands to conduct more granular competitive research by analyzing specific aspects of competitors' strategies. This includes detailed assessments of competitors' digital marketing tactics, content strategies, and social media engagement.Furthermore, AI can assist in identifying and evaluating key influencers and partnerships that competitors are leveraging. By analyzing social media interactions and influencer collaborations, AI tools can uncover which influencers are endorsing competitors' products and how these endorsements are impacting brand perception. This information enables brands to assess the potential value of similar influencer partnerships or identify opportunities to differentiate themselves through unique collaborations.Another challenge is the need for human expertise in interpreting AI-generated insights. While AI can provide valuable data and analysis, human judgment is crucial in making strategic decisions based on these insights(Hamichi, S.,et al.,2013). AI tools should be used to support and enhance human decision-making, rather than replace it. Integrating AI insights with industry knowledge and strategic thinking helps brands develop more effective competitive strategies.AI enhances the ability to track competitors, assess market positioning, and identify strategic opportunities. Despite challenges related to data accuracy, privacy, and the need for human expertise, the benefits of AI in competitor analysis are substantial. Brands that effectively utilize AI-driven insights can gain a competitive edge, adapt to market changes, and develop strategies that drive success in a rapidly evolving business landscape.Measuring Brand ROI (Return on Investment) has traditionally been a complex and often elusive task, fraught with challenges in quantifying the impact of marketing efforts. With the advent of Artificial Intelligence (AI), however, the landscape is shifting dramatically, offering new tools and methodologies for more accurate and actionable insights. This data-driven approach allows companies to attribute ROI more accurately to specific campaigns or channels, moving beyond simplistic metrics like clicks or impressions to a deeper understanding of how different elements contribute to overall brand value.

This qualitative data provides valuable context to quantitative metrics, helping businesses understand not just how much impact their marketing efforts are having, but also the nature of that impact. For example, an increase in positive sentiment might correlate with higher brand loyalty or customer satisfaction, which are critical components of long-term ROI.Predictive analytics is another powerful application of AI in brand ROI measurement. if AI predicts a rising interest in a particular product category, businesses can allocate resources more effectively, invest in targeted campaigns, and capitalize on emerging opportunities before their competitors. This proactive approach enhances the precision of ROI measurement by aligning marketing efforts with anticipated market dynamics(Jooste, J.L.,et al.,2015).AI also facilitates advanced attribution modeling, which is crucial for understanding the complex interplay of various marketing channels. Traditional attribution models often rely on linear or last-click approaches, which can oversimplify the customer journey. AI-driven models, however, can analyze multi-touchpoint data to provide a more comprehensive view of how different interactions contribute to conversions. By employing techniques such as Shapley value or algorithmic attribution, AI can offer a more nuanced understanding of how each touchpoint influences the overall brand ROI.Furthermore, AI's ability to automate and optimize marketing campaigns enhances ROI measurement by ensuring that resources are used efficiently. AI-powered tools can continuously test and refine marketing strategies in real-time, adjusting targeting, messaging, and bidding strategies based on performance data. This dynamic optimization process not only improves campaign effectiveness but also provides more accurate measurements of ROI by reducing the influence of human error and bias.By tracking the effectiveness of personalized campaigns, businesses can gain insights into the specific ROI generated by different levels of personalization, allowing for more targeted and effective marketing strategies. Additionally, the complexity of AI systems requires businesses to invest in skilled personnel and training to fully leverage these technologies and interpret the results accurately.In conclusion, AI is revolutionizing the way businesses measure brand ROI by providing more precise, actionable, and comprehensive insights into marketing performance. Through advanced data analysis, sentiment evaluation, predictive modeling, and personalized marketing, AI enables companies to understand the true impact of their marketing efforts and make informed decisions to enhance their brand value(Jorge.B,et al.,2019). As AI technology continues to evolve, its role in ROI measurement will likely become even more integral, offering new opportunities for businesses to optimize their marketing strategies and achieve greater success in an increasingly competitive landscape.

AI-Driven Brand Health Metrics: Tracking Market Share and Growth.

In the rapidly evolving business landscape, tracking brand health is crucial for maintaining competitive advantage and driving sustained growth. AI-driven brand health metrics offer innovative ways to monitor and analyze market share and growth, transforming how companies understand and manage their brand's performance. The application of Artificial Intelligence in this domain allows for a more nuanced and dynamic approach to evaluating brand health, leveraging sophisticated data analytics to provide deeper insights into market trends, consumer perceptions, and competitive positioningAI's role in tracking market share and growth begins with its ability to process and analyze vast amounts of data from diverse sources. Traditional methods of tracking market share often relied on periodic surveys and reports, and growth more accurately and promptly, providing a clearer picture of their brand's position relative to competitors.One of the key advantages of AI-driven metrics is the ability to perform advanced competitive analysis. AI algorithms can scan and analyze competitors' activities, pricing strategies, promotional efforts, and market presence(Kerkkanen, A.,et al.,2012). By comparing this data with a company's own performance metrics, businesses can gain valuable insights into their competitive standing. For example, AI can identify emerging competitors or shifts in competitive dynamics, helping companies adjust their strategies to better capture market opportunities and mitigate potential threats.Sentiment analysis, powered by AI, is another critical tool for tracking brand health.

Predictive analytics is another powerful aspect of AI-driven brand health metrics. AI models can forecast future market trends and consumer behavior based on historical data and current market conditions. These forecasts can inform strategic decisions, such as product development, market expansion, and promotional campaigns. For instance, if AI predicts a growing demand for a particular product category, businesses can proactively adjust their inventory, marketing efforts, and sales strategies to capitalize on this trend and increase their market share.In addition to these capabilities, AI can streamline the process of tracking and reporting key performance indicators (KPIs) related to brand health. Automated reporting tools can generate real-time dashboards that display critical metrics such as market share, sales growth, and customer acquisition rates. These dashboards provide a comprehensive view of brand performance, enabling businesses to monitor progress against strategic goals and make data-driven decisions(Klimanov, D.,et al.,2019). AI's ability to automate these processes not only saves time but also reduces the risk of errors and inconsistencies in reporting.In conclusion, AI-driven brand health metrics are revolutionizing how companies track market share and growth. By leveraging advanced data analytics, sentiment analysis, competitive intelligence, and predictive modeling, businesses can gain deeper insights into their brand's performance and make more informed strategic decisions. While the integration of AI presents challenges, the potential benefits in terms of accuracy, efficiency, and strategic foresight make it a powerful tool for enhancing brand health and driving sustained growth in an increasingly competitive market. This shift towards data-driven predictions allows companies to move beyond historical analysis and gain actionable insights into future opportunities and risks, thereby enhancing their strategic decision-making processes.

Machine learning, however, employs algorithms that can continuously learn from new data and adapt to changing trends. This dynamic learning process enables businesses to generate more accurate forecasts and identify emerging patterns that might not be evident through conventional analysis. For instance, a retailer might use machine learning to predict which products are likely to be in high demand during a particular season, enabling them to adjust their inventory and marketing strategies accordingly.Churn prediction is another critical area where machine learning can provide valuable insights. Customer churn—when customers discontinue their relationship with a brand—can have a significant impact on revenue and growth. Furthermore, machine learning enhances competitive intelligence by providing insights into competitors' strategies and market positioning. Algorithms can analyze data from various sources, such as social media, market reports, and competitor activities, to assess how a brand stacks up against its rivals. This analysis can reveal trends, strengths, and weaknesses in competitive strategies, allowing companies to adjust their own strategies to gain a competitive edge. For example, machine learning might uncover a rising competitor's focus on a particular market segment, prompting a business to adjust its approach to capture similar opportunities(Koponen, J.P.,et al.,2020). This sentiment analysis helps brands understand how they are perceived by their audience and predict how changes in marketing strategies or product offerings might impact public perception.

Another critical application of NLP is topic modeling, which involves uncovering the themes or topics present in large volumes of text data. For example, a brand could analyze customer reviews to identify prevalent themes related to product performance, customer service, or pricing. Understanding these topics helps brands tailor their strategies to address specific customer interests or concerns, leading to more targeted marketing and product development efforts.NLP also plays a significant role in extracting actionable insights from brand communications. By analyzing internal documents, press releases, and marketing content, NLP tools can evaluate the consistency and effectiveness of messaging. This analysis can identify discrepancies between brand promises and customer experiences, helping to align communication strategies with customer expectations. For instance, if NLP reveals that marketing messages are not resonating with the intended audience, brands can adjust their messaging to better reflect customer values and preferences. This capability allows brands to track mentions of their products or services across various platforms, assess competitive positioning, and monitor brand reputation. For example, NER can help a company identify which products are being discussed in the context of competitors, providing insights into competitive advantages or market gaps. For example, NLP can automatically classify customer inquiries into categories such as billing issues, technical support, or product feedback. This categorization streamlines the process of addressing customer concerns, enabling more efficient and effective response strategies (Kot, M.T.,et al.,2020).

The integration of NLP with other data sources enhances its effectiveness in brand text analysis. By combining text data with demographic, history to identify correlations between sentiment and buying behavior, providing deeper insights into customer motivations and preferences.Despite its advantages, the use of NLP in brand text analysis presents several challenges. One challenge is dealing with the nuances and complexities of human language, such as slang, idioms, and context-dependent meanings. NLP algorithms must be trained to understand these subtleties to produce accurate results (Mahadev Madgule,et al.,2023). Moreover, ensuring the quality and accuracy of NLP models requires continuous refinement and validation, as language usage evolves over time.In conclusion, Natural Language Processing has revolutionized brand text analysis by providing advanced tools for understanding and leveraging textual data. The integration of AI into visual analysis provides brands with the tools needed to ensure consistent application of their visual identity, understand its impact across various media, and maintain a competitive edge in the marketplace.

At its core, AI-driven visual analysis employs sophisticated algorithms to recognize and interpret visual elements, such as logos, colors, and design patterns. Computer vision technologies enable AI systems to identify logos in images, videos, and other visual content with high precision. This capability is crucial for tracking brand visibility and ensuring that logos are used correctly across diverse platforms(Marius.G, et al.,2018). For example, a brand can use AI to scan social media, websites, and digital advertisements to verify that its logo appears consistently and is not being misrepresented or misused.One of the primary applications of AI in brand visual analysis is monitoring brand consistency. Maintaining a uniform visual identity across all touchpoints is essential for brand recognition and trust. AI tools can analyze large volumes of visual content to ensure that logos, color schemes, and design elements adhere to established brand guidelines. By detecting deviations from these guidelines, AI helps brands address inconsistencies promptly, whether they arise from unauthorized use, design errors, or changes in marketing strategies.AI-driven visual analysis also enhances the ability to measure brand exposure and engagement. Through image recognition and analysis, AI can track how frequently a brand's logo or visual identity appears in various media, including social media, news articles, and promotional materials. This analysis provides valuable insights into brand visibility and can help gauge the effectiveness of marketing campaigns(Malik.S,2020). For instance, by analyzing the frequency and context of logo appearances, brands can assess which channels are generating the most visibility and adjust their strategies to optimize exposure.

The use of AI in brand visual analysis extends to competitive intelligence as well. AI algorithms can track and analyze the visual identities of competitors, providing insights into their branding strategies and market positioning. By comparing visual elements such as logos, color palettes, and design styles, brands can identify trends and differentiate their visual identity in the marketplace(Zahay, D.,et al.,2004). This competitive analysis enables brands to adapt and innovate their visual strategies to stay ahead of competitors and capture market opportunities.AI-driven visual analysis also facilitates the detection of unauthorized or counterfeit use of brand assets. By continuously monitoring visual content across digital platforms, AI can identify instances where a brand's logo or visual identity is being used without permission. This capability is particularly valuable in protecting intellectual property and maintaining brand integrity. For example, AI can detect counterfeit products or unauthorized merchandise featuring a brand's logo, enabling swift action to address potential legal issues and protect the brand's reputation (Paramasivam Selvakumar,et al.,2024). Moreover, AI can aid in optimizing visual content by analyzing the performance of different visual elements in marketing campaigns. Transparency with consumers about how their visual data is used and ensuring the security of data processing are essential for maintaining trust and safeguarding brand reputation.In conclusion, AI-driven brand visual analysis offers powerful tools for tracking and managing logos and visual identity with unprecedented precision and efficiency(Yin, J.,et al.,2012). By leveraging computer vision and deep learning, brands can monitor consistency, measure exposure, understand contextual perceptions, and gain competitive insights.

Case Studies: Successful AI-Driven Brand Performance Measurement.

Case studies of successful AI-driven brand performance measurement highlight the transformative impact of artificial intelligence on how businesses evaluate and enhance their brand strategies. By leveraging AI technologies, companies across various industries have achieved significant improvements in understanding brand performance, optimizing marketing efforts, and driving growth. These case studies illustrate the diverse applications of AI, from predictive analytics and sentiment analysis to visual recognition and competitive intelligence, showcasing how AI can provide actionable insights and foster more informed decision-making (Perakakis.E,et al.,2019).One notable example is Coca-Cola, a global leader in the beverage industry, which has harnessed AI to refine its marketing strategies and optimize brand performance. Coca-Cola implemented AI-driven sentiment analysis to monitor and analyze consumer reactions to its marketing campaigns and product launches. By examining social media posts, customer reviews, and other online content, AI tools helped Coca-Cola gauge public sentiment in real-time, identify emerging trends, and respond proactively to consumer feedback.. By analyzing the frequency and context of logo appearances, IBM gained insights into brand visibility and market positioning(Ramakrishnan T.,et al.,2022). This analysis allowed IBM to identify key areas where its competitors were gaining traction and adjust its own strategies to better capture market opportunities and enhance its competitive edge.

The beauty and cosmetics industry provides another compelling case study with L'Oréal. The company has employed AI-driven sentiment analysis and visual recognition to measure brand performance and optimize product launches. By analyzing customer reviews and social media content, L'Oréal's AI tools assessed public sentiment towards its products and identified trends in consumer preferences. Additionally, AI visual recognition tools monitored the appearance of L'Oréal products in online content, providing insights into brand visibility and consumer engagement. These insights guided product development, marketing strategies, and promotional campaigns, leading to successful product launches and enhanced brand equity.In the retail sector, Walmart has utilized AI to enhance its understanding of brand performance through customer behavior analysis. Walmart employed AI algorithms to analyze shopping patterns, customer feedback, and transaction data to gain insights into consumer preferences and trends. By leveraging these insights, Walmart optimized its product assortment, pricing strategies, and promotional efforts. AI-driven analytics also enabled Walmart to personalize marketing campaigns, improving customer engagement and driving sales growth. The company's ability to predict consumer behavior and respond to market changes quickly contributed to its competitive advantage and overall brand success(Ramos-Rodriguez,et al.,2004). Spotify, a leading music streaming service, exemplifies the use of AI in measuring brand performance through user engagement and content optimization. Spotify's AI-driven recommendation engine analyzes user listening habits, preferences, and interactions to deliver personalized music recommendations. By tracking how users engage with different playlists, artists, and genres, Spotify gained valuable insights into listener preferences and trends. This data-driven approach enabled Spotify to refine its content strategy, enhance user experience, and strengthen its brand position in the highly competitive music streaming market.Lastly, Unilever demonstrates the successful application of AI in optimizing brand performance through digital advertising. Unilever utilized AI-powered tools to analyze the effectiveness of its digital ad campaigns across various channels(Yang, Z.,et al.,2010).

These case studies underscore the versatility and impact of AI-driven brand performance measurement across different industries. As AI technology continues to evolve, its role in brand performance measurement will likely expand, offering new opportunities for companies to enhance their brand strategies and drive success in an increasingly data-driven world.Implementing AI tools in brand performance measurement requires a strategic approach to ensure that the technology delivers actionable insights and drives meaningful results. As businesses increasingly adopt AI to enhance their understanding of brand performance, adhering to best practices becomes essential for maximizing the benefits and mitigating potential challenges(Rantala, T.,et al.,2020). These best practices encompass a range of considerations, from data management and technology integration to ethical concerns and ongoing evaluation. Before deploying AI tools, it is crucial to establish clear objectives for brand performance measurement. Define what specific aspects of brand performance you aim to measure, such as customer sentiment, market share, or campaign effectiveness. Having well-defined goals ensures that the AI tools are aligned with your strategic priorities and can be effectively tailored to meet your needs. Consider tools that offer advanced features such as natural language processing (NLP) for sentiment analysis, machine learning for predictive analytics, and computer vision for visual recognition. Ensure that the chosen tools align with your specific needs and can be seamlessly integrated into your brand performance measurement processes.For AI tools to be effective, they must be integrated with existing systems and workflows. Ensure that the AI tools can interface with your current data sources, marketing platforms, and analytics systems (Yagüe, M.,et al.,2007). Integration facilitates the smooth flow of data between systems and enables a unified approach to brand performance measurement. Additionally, integration helps streamline processes, reduce data silos, and improve overall efficiency.

AI models require ongoing training and refinement to maintain accuracy and relevance. Regularly update and retrain models with new data to ensure that they adapt to changing market conditions and consumer behaviors. Implement feedback loops to evaluate the performance of AI models and make necessary adjustments. This iterative approach helps enhance the precision of insights and keeps the AI tools aligned with evolving brand strategies.Successful implementation of AI tools requires collaboration across various functions within the organization. Engage stakeholders from marketing, IT, data science, and other relevant departments to ensure that the AI tools are aligned with organizational goals and can be effectively utilized(Sugumaran K. M, D.,et al.,2024). Cross-functional collaboration facilitates the integration of AI tools into existing processes, enhances the quality of insights, and ensures that different perspectives are considered in decision-making.

For AI tools to be effective, users must be trained to understand and leverage the insights generated. Provide training and support to ensure that team members are familiar with how to use the AI tools, interpret results, and apply insights to their roles. Encourage adoption by demonstrating the value and benefits of the AI tools and addressing any concerns or challenges users may have. Effective training and adoption practices contribute to the successful implementation and utilization of AI tools.Regularly assess the return on investment (ROI) of the AI tools and evaluate their impact on brand performance (Vijayakumar G,et al.,2024). Analyze how the insights and capabilities provided by the AI tools contribute to achieving brand objectives and driving business outcomes.

The Future of AI in Brand Performance Measurement - Opportunities and Challenges.

Th future of AI in brand performance measurement is poised to redefine how businesses understand and enhance their brand strategies, offering both substantial opportunities and notable challenges. As artificial intelligence technology advances, it is transforming the landscape of brand management by providing deeper insights, greater precision, and more proactive strategies. However, the integration of AI also brings its own set of challenges that organizations must address to fully leverage its potential(Vitaveska.L,2017).This predictive power allows brands to anticipate changes in consumer preferences and market dynamics, enabling them to make proactive adjustments to their strategies. For instance, AI-driven predictive models can help brands identify emerging trends early, allowing them to capitalize on new opportunities before competitors.This capability enhances agility, allowing brands to quickly respond to shifts in consumer sentiment, market conditions, and competitive actions. Real-time analytics enable brands to adjust marketing campaigns, product offerings, and customer engagement strategies promptly, improving their ability to stay relevant and competitive(Xu, S.X.,et al.,2017).Machine learning algorithms can segment customers with great precision, allowing brands to tailor their messaging, offers, and interactions based on specific preferences and needs. Enhanced personalization leads to more effective marketing campaigns, higher customer satisfaction, and increased loyalty. By identifying which channels deliver the best ROI and where marketing efforts are most impactful, brands can optimize their budgets and focus their efforts on the most effective strategies. This optimization leads to more efficient use of resources and improved overall marketing performance (Xu, X.,et al.,2018).Ensuring that AI solutions work seamlessly with current data sources, marketing platforms, and analytics systems requires careful planning and execution. Brands may face challenges in achieving interoperability and ensuring that AI tools enhance rather than disrupt existing processes.

CONCLUSION

In conclusion, measuring brand performance with AI tools represents a profound evolution in how businesses assess and enhance their brand strategies. The integration of artificial intelligence into brand performance measurement offers unparalleled opportunities for gaining actionable insights, optimizing marketing efforts, and driving strategic decision-making. The benefits of AI in brand performance measurement are extensive. AI tools enable brands to monitor real-time sentiment and engagement, allowing for timely adjustments to marketing strategies and campaigns. Predictive analytics powered by AI offer foresight into consumer behavior and market dynamics, enabling brands to proactively address emerging trends and potential challenges. Furthermore, AI enhances personalization, allowing brands to tailor their messaging and offers to individual consumer preferences, thereby increasing engagement and loyalty. The ability to analyze visual data also helps maintain brand consistency and monitor competitive positioning, ensuring that brand assets are utilized effectively and remain distinct in the marketplace. Addressing biases within AI models is crucial to ensuring fair and accurate insights, while transparency and interpretability of AI-driven results are necessary for informed decision-making and maintaining stakeholder confidence.Moreover, the ethical implications of AI usage must be considered. Brands must adopt responsible AI practices that align with ethical standards and societal expectations, ensuring that AI tools are used in ways that support fairness, accountability, and transparency. Investing in the development of skills and knowledge within the organization is also vital, as the successful implementation of AI tools depends on having a team with expertise in data science and machine learning. In summary, measuring brand performance with AI tools offers a transformative approach to understanding and enhancing brand strategies. The integration of AI enables brands to achieve deeper insights, greater precision, and more personalized interactions, driving more effective and strategic decision-making. While challenges related to data privacy, integration, bias, and ethics must be addressed, the opportunities presented by AI are substantial and can lead to significant improvements in brand performance. As AI technology evolves, brands that embrace these tools with a strategic and responsible approach will be well-positioned to navigate the complexities of the modern marketplace and achieve long-term success.

REFERENCES

Alexandruand, C., & Maher, K. (2019). Matching the future capabilities of an artificial intelligence-based software for social media marketing with potential users' expectations. *Technological Forecasting and Social Change*, 151(119794), 10–15.

Alratemi. Mohammed Ali,(2012). "Artificial Intelligence and Expert Systems," Libyan Academy of Graduate Studies.First edition. Eygpt.

Angela, E., & Alexandru, C. (2018, September). Exploring Artificial Intelligence Techniques' Applicability in Social Media Marketing. *Journal of Emerging Trends in Marketing and Management*, 1(1), 156–164.

Ardito, L., Scuotto, V., Del Giudice, M., & Petruzzelli, A. M. (2019). A bibliometric analysis of research on Big Data analytics for business and management. *Management Decision*, 57(8), 1993–2009. DOI: 10.1108/MD-07-2018-0754

Backhaus, K., Becker, J., Beverungen, D., Frohs, M., Müller, O., Weddeling, M., Knackstedt, R., & Steiner, M. (2010). Enabling individualized recommendations and dynamic pricing of value-added services through willingness-to-pay data. *Electronic Markets*, 20(2), 131–146. DOI: 10.1007/s12525-010-0032-0

Bahrami, M., Bozkaya, B., & Balcisoy, S. (2020). Using Behavioral Analytics to Predict Customer Invoice Payment. *Big Data*, 8(1), 25–37. DOI: 10.1089/big.2018.0116 PMID: 31976741

Chan, H. K., Lacka, E., Yee, R. W., & Lim, M. K. (2017). The role of social media data in operations and production management. *International Journal of Production Research*, 55(17), 5027–5036. DOI: 10.1080/00207543.2015.1053998

Dikow, H., Hasan, O., Kosch, H., Brunie, L., & Sornin, R. (2015). Improving the accuracy of Business-to-Business (B2B) reputation systems through rater expertise prediction. *Computing*, 97(1), 29–49. DOI: 10.1007/s00607-013-0345-x

Dong, Y., Huang, X., Sinha, K. K., & Xu, K. (2014). Collaborative demand forecasting:toward the design of an exception-based forecasting mechanism. *Journal of Management Information Systems*, 31(2), 245–284. DOI: 10.2753/MIS0742-1222310209

Duan, Y., Edwards, J. S., & Dwivedi, Y. K. (2019). Artificial intelligence for decision making in the era of Big Data–evolution, challenges and research agenda. *International Journal of Information Management*, 48, 63–71. DOI: 10.1016/j.ijinfomgt.2019.01.021

Fernandez, L. M. V., Nicolas, C., & Merigó, J. M. (2019). Industrial marketing research: A bibliometric analysis (1990-2015). *Journal of Business and Industrial Marketing*, 34(3), 550–560. DOI: 10.1108/JBIM-07-2017-0167

Gentner, D., Stelzer, B., Ramosaj, B., & Brecht, L. (2018). Strategic Foresight of Future B2B Customer Opportunities through Machine Learning. *Technology Innovation Management Review*, 8(10), 5–17. DOI: 10.22215/timreview/1189

Hamichi, S., Mangalagiu, D., & Guessoum, Z. (2013). A Multi-Agent System for production networks simulation: Toward a pheromone-based model for agents' coordination. In Supply Chain Management: Concepts, Methodologies, Tools, and Applications (pp. 1666-1682). IGI Global.

Jooste, J. L., & Vlok, P. J. (2015). A decision support model to determine the critical success factors of asset management services. *South African Journal of Industrial Engineering*, 26(1), 27–43. DOI: 10.7166/26-1-1043

Jorge, B., & Ross, A. (2019) "Artificial Intelligence Ethics: Governance through Social Media," Conference Paper, IEEE International Symposium on Technologies for Homeland Security.vol.10,no.1109,November,pp 1-4.

Kerkkanen, A., Huiskonen, J., Korpela, J., & Pirttila, T. (2012). How do managers perceive the needs of sales forecasting process improvement in a B2B environment. *International Journal of Management Practice*, 5(2), 107–124. DOI: 10.1504/IJMP.2012.047580

Klimanov, D., & Tretyak, O. (2019). Linking business model research and marketing: New network-based approach to business model analysis. *Journal of Business and Industrial Marketing*, 34(1), 117–136. DOI: 10.1108/JBIM-12-2017-0330

Koponen, J. P., & Rytsy, S. (2020). Social presence and e-commerce B2B chat functions. *European Journal of Marketing*, 54(6), 1205–1224. DOI: 10.1108/EJM-01-2019-0061

Kot, M. T., & Leszczyński, G. (2020). The concept of intelligent agent in business interactions: Is virtual assistant an actor or a boundary object? *Journal of Business and Industrial Marketing*, 35(7), 1155–1164. DOI: 10.1108/JBIM-10-2018-0291

Mahadev Madgule, N. (2023). Vinayaka, Yeshwant M. Sonkhaskar, Dhiren Ramanbhai Patel, R. Karthikeyan, P. Selvakumar,(2023). Mechanical properties and microstructure of activated TIG welded similar joints of Inconel alloys by desirability approaches. *Materials Today: Proceedings*, 77, 528–533. DOI: 10.1016/j.matpr.2022.12.250

Malik, S. (2020). Artificial Intelligence for Social Media safety and security. *International Engineering Journal*, 5, 5–7.

Marius, G., & Angela, E. (2018, December). “Using Artificial Intelligence on Social Media’s User Generated Content for Disruptive Marketing Strategies in ecommerce.” Annals of “Dunarea de Jos” University of Galati Fascicle I. *Economics and Applied Informatics*, 10(3), 5–11.

Perakakis.E and Mastorakis.G,(2019).“Social Media Monitoring: An Innovative Intelligent Approach,” Mdpi journal designs,vol.3, no.2,pp.1-12.

Pillai, R., Sivathanu, B., & Dwivedi, Y. K. (2020). Shopping intention at AI-powered automated retail stores (AIPARS). *Journal of Retailing and Consumer Services*, 57, 102207. DOI: 10.1016/j.jretconser.2020.102207

Ramakrishnan, T., Mohan Gift, M. D., Chitradevi, S., Jegan, R., & Subha Hency Jose, P. Nagaraja, Rajneesh Sharma H.N., Selvakumar P., Sintayehu Mekuria Hailegiorgis, (2022). “Study of Numerous Resins Used in Polymer Matrix Composite Materials”, Advances in Materials Science and Engineering, vol. 2022, Article ID 1088926, 8 pages, 2022. https://doi.org/DOI: 10.1155/2022/1088926

Ramos-Rodriguez, A. R., & Ruiz-Navarro, J. (2004). Changes in the intellectual structure of strategic management research: A bibliometric study of the Strategic Management Journal, 1980–2000. *Strategic Management Journal*, 25(10), 981–1004. DOI: 10.1002/smj.397

Rantala, T., Apilo, T., Palomäki, K., & Valkokari, K. (2020). Selling Data-Based Value in Business-to-Business Markets. *Technology Innovation Management Review*, 10(1), 45–53. DOI: 10.22215/timreview/1313

Selvakumar, P., Mariappan, P., Shunmugam, S., Paul, R., & Jabez, S. (2024). Removal of chemicals from effluent using photobioreactor technology to improve environmental and health impacts. *Zeitschrift für Physikalische Chemie*, 2024(7), 1295–1302. Advance online publication. DOI: 10.1515/zpch-2023-0450

Sugumaran, K. M. D., Pandiyarajan V., Y. B S, Selvakumar P. and M. S, (2024). “Analysis of Electromyography Signals for Control of Mechanical Prosthesis using Machine Learning Techniques,” 2024 2nd International Conference on Intelligent Data Communication Technologies and Internet of Things (IDCIoT), Bengaluru, India, 2024, pp. 1059-1067, DOI: 10.1109/IDCIoT59759.2024.10467707

Vijayakumar, G., Rajkumar, M., Rajiv Chandar, N., Selvakumar, P., & Duraisamy, R. (2024). Muniyandi Rajkumar, Rajiv Chandar N, Selvakumar P and Ramesh Duraisamy, (2024). Environmentally friendly TDS removal from waste water by electrochemical ion exchange batch-type recirculation (EIR) technique. *Environmental Science. Water Research & Technology*, 10(4), 826–835. DOI: 10.1039/D3EW00793F

Vitaveska, L. (2017). "Machine Learning and Social Media in Crisis Management: Agility vs.Ethics," *Proceedings of the 14th ISCRAM Conference*, vol.13,no. May,pp.256-260.

Xu, S. X., & Huang, G. Q. (2017). Efficient Multi- Attribute Multi- Unit Auctions for B2B E- Commerce Logistics. *Production and Operations Management*, 26(2), 292–304. DOI: 10.1111/poms.12638

Xu, X., Chen, X., Jia, F., Brown, S., Gong, Y., & Xu, Y. (2018). Supply chain finance: A systematic literature review and bibliometric analysis. *International Journal of Production Economics*, 204, 160–173. DOI: 10.1016/j.ijpe.2018.08.003

Yagüe, M., Rodríguez, E., & Delgado, J. (2007). Verification algorithms for governed use of multimedia content. *Online Information Review*, 31(1), 38–58. DOI: 10.1108/14684520710731029

Yang, Z., Shang, C., Liu, Q., & Zhao, C. (2010). A dynamic web services composition algorithm based on the combination of ant colony algorithm and genetic algorithm. *Journal of Computer Information Systems*, 6(8), 2617–2622.

Yin, J., Cao, B., Deng, S. and Wu, Z., (2012). Process Discovery from the Log of Business Rule Engine. International Journal of Innovative Computing Information and Control, 8(7 B), pp.5277-5293.

Zahay, D., & Griffin, A. (2004). Customer learning processes, strategy selection, and performance in business- to- business service firms. *Decision Sciences*, 35(2), 169–203. DOI: 10.1111/j.00117315.2004.02338.x

Chapter 12
Leveraging AI for Personalized Customer Experiences

Shivani Thapliyal
Christ University, India

Raghav Bindal
https://orcid.org/0009-0004-8024-1601
Christ University, India

ABSTRACT

This chapter discusses the disruptive nature of artificial intelligence in strategic brand management, particularly how it can enable a personalized engagement with customers. It considers just how AI allows for easy navigation of complex consumer data to deliver a tailored experience aligned with changing customer expectations. This chapter describes AI-driven tools such as machine learning, predictive analytics, and recommendation engines that enable brands to segment audiences in real-time, predict behaviors, and tailor content for higher resonance. Operational efficiency through AI is also detailed—how it can use chatbots in automating customer interactions and develop data-driven decisions that enhance responsiveness as well as customer satisfaction. In fact, the author touched upon the long-term effects that artificial intelligence will cause on loyalty and trust towards a brand, with the emphasis on the continued refinement of personalization strategies.

DOI: 10.4018/979-8-3693-9461-8.ch012

1. INTRODUCTION

The relationship between the brand and the consumer has, in recent times, taken a significant shape because of the digital explosion through multiple online platforms and digital touchpoints. (Zare & Mahmoudi, 2021) Today, by a mere click or tap on the computer, tablet, or mobile, the consumers can surf products, price comparisons, reviews, and finally purchase decisions can be made within seconds. Therefore, customers have higher expectations with regards to their ability to make seamless, highly personalized experiences across all touchpoints. To a brand, this is the challenge that demands them to not just catch up with such expectations but be able to anticipate them. That's how Artificial Intelligence (AI) works; it has now become the critical enabler for brands, allowing brands to sift through millions of data points and gain an even deeper understanding of how consumers think, what best they will like, and what would connect them as well. (Ameen et al., 2021) The value of AI is that it can analyse data and interpret it in real time, turning numbers and patterns into actionable insights. By applying sophisticated machine learning algorithms, AI can help separate audiences, predict future behavior, and adapt content according to individual consumer needs. Imagine a retail brand that employs AI-driven personalization for the recommendation of products for customers based on browsing history, past purchases, or even current trends. This dynamic, data-driven approach lets the brand engage the customers with content and offers that resonate personally, something far more effective than one-size-fits-all generic marketing strategies. As such, the customer perceives the brand as responsive and in tune with their desires, which fosters loyalty and trust.

The second role of AI in brand management is operational efficiency. In the past, such high personalization required loads of time and manual labour or deep research on the consumers, which was rarely close to what was desired. AI-powered tools, such as chatbots, recommendation engines, and automated marketing platforms, streamline all these processes, making it possible for brands to provide quality experiences without extensive manpower. (Nguyen et al., 2024) For instance, AI-based chatbots can respond to many more customer queries in parallel, reply instantaneously, and refer the issue to human representatives only when absolutely necessary. It increases customer satisfaction while cutting down on operational costs by freeing up resources for usage in a more strategic manner. Moreover, the predictive capability of AI helps brands predict what customers want even before they say it, which is essential in building proactive relationships. Using advanced natural language processing and machine learning, AI can scan social media interactions, reviews, and online conversations to understand shifting customer sentiment and preferences. Thus, brands can recognize trends in real time, and through the adjustment of marketing strategy, they will be more likely to be relevant; either by launching a new product that aligns with the emerging tastes or adjusting a marketing campaign to meet the needs of a demographic shift. In this way, AI arms brands with the chance to be always one step ahead, instilling anticipation and excitement over their offerings. (Hoyer et al., 2020)

Perhaps the transformatory power of AI in strategic brand management finds its best expression through its effects on customer engagement. Consumers today are so accustomed to high standards in digital engagement that they look for services that stream media on demand, personalizing content to individual tastes and preferences; e-commerce stores that curate shopping experiences based on past behavior, among other things. AI enables the same level of personalization that can actually lead to deeper connections with customers. For instance, a hospitality brand might be able to use AI in order to create personalized travel recommendations based on a customer's past vacations, while an online retailer might curate entire collections of products around a customer's previous purchases and seasonal trends. This will not only address the customer's expectation but go beyond that, forming a loyal customer base whose value is found in engagement and the offering of this brand. (Daqar and Smoudy, 2019)

The trend about AI-driven personalization goes to make personalization available and integrative to brands' management. This will increase trust by the customers with the respective brands by making responsible usage of such technologies among the brands. The customer interaction loop enables feedback that aids in continuously improving algorithms through which AI uses; and thus, personalization turns out to be increasingly precise as time passes. It's a continuous refinement, but not invasive; it happens to be a refreshing approach to keeping a brand fresh while encouraging loyalty and deeper connections with customers. AI will not only propel but redefine what metrics of brand success even are in the near future. The implementation of AI will see enhanced customer satisfaction, retention, and advocacy through the engagement of the brand. This is critical, considering the environment of transience of brand loyalty that exists today. Here, customers' choices are plentiful, and the adoption of AI will allow for a competitive advantage: one based on knowledge and responsiveness to customers' unique needs with precision and care. (Tulcanaza-Prieto et al., 2023)

In a nutshell, AI-driven personalization in the digital age has transformed strategic brand management. It empowers brands to navigate complex consumer data, foster personalized experiences, enhance operational efficiency, and ultimately build stronger, more resilient customer relationships. Brands embracing AI will be best positioned to thrive as technology continues to evolve, offering customers the relevant, seamless, and meaningful experiences they expect and value. This paradigm shift is no longer an improvement in traditional marketing practices but, rather, a new paradigm where customer-centric data-driven strategies define successful brands. AI is no longer a luxury but a necessity for brands aiming to create long-term loyalty and trust in today's competitive marketplace.

1.1 Objectives

This chapter explores the dynamic role of AI in reshaping personalized customer experiences. Key objectives include:

Understanding Consumer Preferences and Behaviours: AI enables a nuanced understanding of customer preferences and behaviours, moving beyond traditional demographics and psychographics to capture real-time insights. This objective focuses on how AI tools—such as machine learning and predictive analytics—can help brands identify, segment, and anticipate customer needs at a highly granular level.

1. **Assessing AI's Effectiveness in Delivering Personalized Content:** AI-powered content personalization, such as recommendation engines and dynamic content adjustments, provides customized product suggestions, advertisements, and messages. This objective examines the efficacy of AI in crafting messages and content that resonate with individual customers, resulting in improved engagement and conversion rates.
2. **Enhancing Customer Service Interactions through AI:** Customer service is a critical touchpoint that influences customer satisfaction and loyalty. AI technologies like chatbots, virtual assistants, and automated ticketing systems offer immediate, efficient support, creating a seamless experience for customers. By analysing how AI tools can resolve inquiries and handle routine service issues effectively, this objective highlight AI's role in reducing friction in customer interactions.
3. **Addressing Ethical Considerations:** As AI-based personalization increasingly relies on extensive data collection and algorithm-driven decisions, concerns around privacy, consent, and fairness emerge. This objective considers the ethical implications of AI-driven personalization, including data privacy, transparency, and potential biases in decision-making algorithms. Addressing these ethical challenges is crucial for brands to maintain customer trust and abide by regulatory standards.

1.2 Contribution to the Field

The study adds to the growing debate on the transformative impact AI has on personalized customer experience in brand management. Chapter contributions come in the form of practical insights into advanced AI techniques and how the same can be used in strengthening customer relationships and building customer satisfaction and brand loyalty through the focusing of tools driven by AI on improving how AI strengthens customer relationships.

Beyond the benefits in operations and engagement, AI-driven personalization throws critical questions regarding consumer privacy, consent, and transparency especially because customer data remains a valuable resource. Thus, this chapter goes beyond discussing the strategic advantages of AI for business to encourage responsible practice in consideration of ethics.

The broader field of strategic brand management is reinforced here with findings about the role of personalization in competitive differentiation. This chapter thus informs practitioners and researchers of a holistic view of applications, limitations, and ethical considerations when designing impactful, responsible brand strategies. The implications will be expected to provide an outline for future research agendas and practical applications. This will help businesses navigate through the complexities of AI-driven personalization in this new age of constant disruptions to technology and consumer behavior.

2. LITERATURE REVIEW

The integration of artificial intelligence (AI) in brand management and marketing has fundamentally transformed the way brands engage with consumers, optimize strategies, and assess market trends. This comprehensive analysis, based on a corpus of 105 abstracts, sheds light on the profound impact AI is having on these domains, particularly within social media. Key themes identified in this body of work include the enhancement of consumer engagement, the transformation of brand perception, and the ethical complexities that accompany AI-driven advancements. Employing tools like Semantic Topic Modeller, this research pinpoints critical trends, emerging challenges, and strategic opportunities that AI brings to the forefront of brand management.

Social media, specifically platforms like Twitter, Facebook, and Instagram, has become a vital arena for brand-customer interactions, with 31 of the reviewed studies emphasizing its growing role in strategic brand management. AI's capabilities in social media range from refining customer engagement approaches to personalizing brand content based on real-time insights. Studies such as those by (Ghesh et al., 2023) and (Kim et al., 2013) illustrate how AI-powered strategies, such as image-based posts and anthropomorphized messaging, can significantly increase consumer interaction, cultivating an emotional connection with the brand. The emphasis on platforms like Twitter and Instagram reflects a strategic shift towards more targeted, nuanced content analysis. Techniques such as Collaborative Distant Supervision (Cui et al., 2017) and text mining (Zare and Mahmoudi, 2021) have enabled brands to delve deeper into consumer sentiment and behavioural insights, thus facilitating more precise content curation.

Beyond social media, AI's influence permeates consumer research, strategic decision-making, and even ethical practices in data handling. Scholars such as (Shrestha et al., 2019) categorize AI-driven decisions into various types, ranging from fully autonomous AI systems, such as fraud detection, to hybrid systems, like those used in sports analytics. These distinctions showcase the versatile role of AI in augmenting human decision-making, allowing marketers and brand managers to better navigate complex scenarios that involve balancing efficiency with strategic goals. Additionally, while AI offers the promise of heightened operational efficiency and enhanced brand loyalty through personalization, it raises important ethical questions. Balancing data-driven personalization with consumer privacy, as well as ensuring transparency in AI-powered decisions, are crucial concerns for brands leveraging these technologies.

This can be further fuelled by venture capital investments; vast availability of data; and the rise in computational powers. That is how AI has transformed terms in which customer relationship management and optimized content delivery and marketing strategy in the public sector become concerned. As varied marketing channels grow and customer expectations change, this study's interest in the strategic implications of AI, especially in data ethics and its wider implications for society, goes deeper through further research. Therefore, deeper insight into the benefits and limitations of AI would realize newer requirements of brand equity in an ever-changing competitive market.

3. DEVELOPING A THEORY-BASED FRAMEWORK: REAL-WORLD USES

Such classical structures in customer experience and relationship marketing form a base but sometimes seem too general since they do not reach down to the complexity and responsiveness, which is now so greatly needed in today's very highly networked digital environment. However, AI fills the gaps because it lets brands engage with customers at very individualized levels. The traditional CRM system treats segments fairly homogenously, but AI allows tracking changes in needs on a much finer grain over time. The literature has shown that AI has enhanced interaction from the customer-brand perspective in as many cases as it has resulted in real-time, personalized experiences. For instance, with social media analytics, AI-powered tools can tailor content to individual users based on their past behaviours and preferences, which would likely increase the chances of engagement and conversion (Zare and Mahmoudi, 2021). This granular, data-driven approach also extends to customer service; AI-driven chatbots can tackle an enormous array of questions rapidly and accurately, further increasing satisfaction and loyalty towards customers.

Furthermore, (Trawnih et al., 2022) illustrate how AI-driven personalization calls for a different kind of brand management than the traditionally applied. Brands that operate through AI are more agile and data-driven in their approaches to allow them to respond to the needs of consumers better and faster than the traditional models. However, ethical concerns with regard to such granular personalization call for reforms on how the data handling of customers should be addressed, especially when brands have personal information as the core ingredient to design more accurate customer interactions.

Artificial intelligence is rewriting the customer experience, enriching it to be personalized, efficient, and even immersive. Engagement and satisfaction levels related to the brand rise as a result. Armed with millions of customer datasets, algorithms driven by artificial intelligence discover intricate patterns hidden in preference, behavior, and needs, thereby allowing them to send relevant content or recommendations or tailored marketing communications. Personalization becomes richer; the consumer interaction becomes more engaging and valuable. It would make each interaction between an individual and a business more effective if one could understand the needs of the other. Ultimately, it leads to providing a more relevant experience in return, thus cultivating loyalty from the customer side. AI-based customer service support, including chatbots and virtual assistants, is another form of 24/7 customer service that caters to the various inquires that a customer makes, offers guidance to make a process easy, and helps for faster and consistent customer support. This automation will not only help in saving time and enhancing the overall customer satisfaction but also save the human agents from complex problems. (Moore et al., 2021) This creates efficiency and delivers a smooth service experience. Though it has a transformative potential, it brings to the forefront many critical questions related to ethics, including data privacy and bias within the algorithms. As AI is increasingly integrated into business operations, data protection for customers is very important, especially with strict regulations like the General Data Protection Regulation, which emphasizes the need to have strict measures for protecting data. These regulations require responsible handling of data and instil customer trust by maintaining transparency in the use of data. Algorithmic bias is also a growing concern since biased algorithms can lead to unfair or discriminatory outcomes and, therefore, affect the integrity of AI-driven experiences. Business houses should make the data collection process fair and transparent and keep checking their algorithms to avoid any type of unintended bias, ensuring more ethical use of AI in applications. The concentration should be on transparency and fairness; otherwise, the system can lead to pitfalls that must be avoided and reinforces trust, which will then make AI-driven customer experience grow responsibly.

The Internet of Things, augmented reality, virtual reality, and mixed reality are emerging technologies that shape the customer experience landscape by enhancing interaction quality and convenience. For example, an IoT device connects everything with sensors and the internet. This allows businesses to optimize product performance, anticipate customer needs, and provide highly personalized recommendations based on real-time information about usage. For instance, an intelligent refrigerator can also check its inventory and recommend various grocery products that are being depleted. However, IoE integration creates issues on privacy invasion, security, and incompatibility, respectively. In IoT devices, a large amount of data is being collected as people's personal data, which the businesses need to develop high-level security to eliminate unauthorized access. Also, interoperability within various IoT devices may be pretty challenging, and it actually demands standardized protocols and suitable integration planning.

Likewise, AR, VR, and MR have provided new perspectives in terms of customer experience and a change in consumers' perception towards the purchase of the product. It enhances the real-world scenario by combining digital information about it, for instance; it gives a preview as to what the furniture item would look like in his living room before its purchasing. Virtual reality goes further still: fully immersing customers to explore virtual settings, like hotel rooms or real estate properties from anywhere in the world. Mixed reality blends the physical and virtual worlds where users can interact with digital objects as if they were part of a world around them and has applications in health and manufacturing fields. These immersive technologies enrich customer engagement and facilitate informed decision-making, as they allow users to experience products in realistic settings. However, they have challenges, such as the high costs of AR/VR/MR hardware, technical limitations, and potential for user discomfort. For businesses to successfully implement these technologies, they need to ensure high-quality user experiences that are intuitive and engaging. (Sidaoui et al., 2020)

Apart from the facilitation of interaction with the customer, the Internet revolution has changed the direction of the customer experience through its online e-commerce, mobile commerce, and social media. In fact, the nature of shopping through e-commerce has changed what customers do while shopping so that they can browse, compare prices, and learn more about the products using the internet from the comforts of their homes. This saves time and empowers more people to make informed judgments before purchasing, thus maximizing sales. Mobile commerce opens up more convenience in doing online shopping, as these can be accessed anytime even when you are on-the-go. Mobile apps and mobile-friendly websites can provide seamless shopper experiences available at any place, any time. Location-based marketing is also possible, with which the brands can actually deliver real-time, context-specific promotions based on actual customer location. This is, however, with a cost that a company should ensure the customer data remains private and safe, hence, a company should have strong security measures to ensure the information about their customers is safe.

Social media has also been used as an interaction tool with the brand; through this, businesses can get to communicate with their customers directly and also receive feedback in real time. This means brands are able to connect with their audience, answer questions and concerns in real time. This kind of engagement also reinforces brand loyalty but also instills a sense of community with customers because it gives the customer a voice and sense of importance. In addition, social media networks allow the customer the opportunity to communicate both positive and negative experiences to a larger audience. The implications on the reputation of a brand are most of the times critical in these regards, hence the care that must be taken when managing the interactions with the customers via social media. Among these, data-driven personalization is the essence since business houses are using the analysis of consumer behavior and choices to give them relevant content and suggestions. This type of interaction tailoring according to personal preferences will help brands create more relevant experiences for their customers, thus enhancing loyalty.

Today, businesses use AI and other forms of digital technologies, where they face very complex problems in terms of data privacy, security, and ethics. Now more than ever, protecting privacy is important, because reliance on customer data is increasing. Companies are supposed to follow data protection regulations, such as the GDPR, which calls for strict measures in protecting personal data. Regulations like this will benefit the consumer because it keeps them protected, and business will get consumer trust when they can prove their commitment to responsible data practice. However, this is not the only data privacy issue. This should gradually become the requirement as there would be more and more intricacy related to these AI systems-design them in such a way that the systems themselves wouldn't go on to exhibit bias and may result in unequal and discriminative outcomes. It would eventually lead to fewer occurrences of unconscious biases and more possibilities at the diversified and customized approach that the businesses would have for working with their customers. (Tula et al., 2024)

In customer service, artificial intelligence and chatbots avail after-hours services, while other virtual assistants are quick in terms of turnaround times. Intelligent systems can deal with a broad spectrum of queries-whether it is very simple or to take a decision from the customer when it refers to very complex things. Freeing up the human agents to handle complex cases will automatically free up time to allow chatbots and virtual assistants to work on routine tasks and enhance the overall efficiency of the customer support operations. This will also get customers the same information at a faster speed than usual. However, despite its various benefits, AI-driven support systems are far from being without its limitans. For instance, chatbots lack the sophistication of natural language and cannot tackle complex multi-step problems; both factors can cause frustration for customers in search of tailor-made help. In this aspect, businesses need to find the balance between automated support and human intervention for a holistic, diversified customer service experience. The customer experience in the future will indeed be one of frictionless physical-digital integration, with AI and other emerging technologies coming together to create a cohesive, immersive experience. With digital transformation, the businesses are likely to evolve toward more of an omnichannel approach that combines in-store and online interactions in a seamless manner. A customer can search for products in a physical store and receive suggestions from an application, or initiate an online conversation with a chatbot, which converts to a live agent if required. This integration of channels allows businesses to offer a more flexible and adaptive experience - meeting customers at whatever step is in their journey. This can help companies capture 360-degree views of each customer and to deliver more meaningful interactions for fostering loyalty and satisfaction across the channels.

Whereas several merits of this digital trend are seen in terms of benefits, a great degree of caution should be involved with the danger this holds, especially relating to matters such as sensitive issues dealing with data privacy and security and the ethics involved by AI. Customer data collection and analysis are so important in personalization but raise concern regarding the privacy of customer data. Companies should properly use this information in responsibility, transparency, and obedience to law so that a firm may not break up customer's trust. Further security risks are also present in cases where businesses employ more and more digital technology as part of their arsenal and that includes the use of devices based on IoT that easily may get hacked. Companies need to take the initiative to ensure that the security measures are strong, the systems are updated, and the same systems are maintained to limit these risks. Ethical considerations also are quite visible as AI becomes a part of more significant aspects in customer experience. Algorithmic bias remains one of the most problematic issues wherein biased algorithms generate unfair results and erode trust and equity. Businesses should be responsible and fair in the development of AI, choose and train data so that there would be a lesser chance of bias. Transparency is equally important, and that is customers should be informed of how their data is being used or processed and how decisions are made by AI. This transparency will result in the actualization of the concept of trust and further enhances the style of customer decision-making on engagements with various brands. Here, the effective adaptation to the digital revolution will be from businesses that will responsibly make use of AI. Only agile and innovative approaches toward customer experience will work out for businesses. Competition will become aggressive and only agile and innovative approaches toward customer experience will work out for businesses. New technologies must be embraced in response to the ethical and practical challenges they come with. Business can produce experiences that meet and then exceed the customers' expectations through personalization, efficiency, and transparency. (Kacar, 2023)

It fundamentally altered the landscape of customer experience to suit the changed way in which businesses relate with their customers, and redefine what consumers expect. E-commerce, mobile platforms, social media, and data-driven personalization have seen growth, while companies now have capabilities for deep interaction with customers in more tailored and satisfactory ways, making seamless blended physical and digital interactions quite important for success. While these innovations bring important opportunities for growth and engagement, they bring with them some inherent challenges. Data privacy, security, and ethics are among the very urgent issues that must be addressed in order to make the future of digital more positive and sustainable. It's by embracing the benefits of digital tools while proactively managing risk that businesses can deliver ever more sophisticated and enjoyable customer experiences, positioning them for long-term success in a digital-first world.

4. IMPLICATIONS AND FUTURE RESEARCH DIRECTIONS IN AI-ENHANCED CUSTOMER EXPERIENCE AND BRAND IDENTIFICATION

The use of AI application has transformed the customer experience through enhancing customer-brand relations as well as adding to the service-oriented sectors through increasing customer advocacy. This particular study stems from flow theory and social identity theory; it attempts to outline how the AI influences customer experiences along with their relations to the brand. In this study, it attempts to understand whether the specific features of the AI in this case such as information currency, flexibility of the system, along with timeliness will actually influence the experiences of the flow and the identification of a customer with the brand. It examines those AI characteristics and seeks to bridge the gaps left unexplored in extant literature, which are characterized more by technological acceptance of AI. This work, also, highlights employee responsiveness as a moderating factor that enhances the AI-customer experience relationship in contrast with existing studies exploring how AI interacts with customer preferences and employee services. Practical implication for hotel managers: There are practical implications from this study, which provide the basis for further investigation in AI quality, customer experience, and brand loyalty.

The results of this study carry significant implications for hotel managers and service-oriented organizations that intend to increase customer advocacy using AI-enabled services. Flow experience and customer-brand identification are found to have many avenues through which AI quality can be enhanced. Perhaps most importantly, information as currency, flexibility in the system, and timeliness are some of the major AI characteristics that would heavily influence customer experience and brand loyalty. Therefore, such a hotel and service require such investment in AI tools in order to not only match the expectations of the customer but also stay ahead on the marketplace.

1. **Information Currency**

The study underscores the importance of AI's ability to deliver up-to-date and relevant information to customers. By ensuring AI systems are continuously updated with the most current and important data, hotels can empower customers to make informed decisions, thereby enriching their experience. Information currency in AI systems can significantly reduce customer decision-making time, contributing to a seamless and satisfying experience.

2. **System Flexibility**

Flexibility in AI systems play a key role in customer experience, allowing brands to personalize interactions by leveraging data such as customer preferences and purchase history. For instance, an AI system designed with flexibility can present the most relevant content tailored to individual customer needs. This customization not only increases customer satisfaction but also strengthens the customer-brand connection by creating a personalized experience that aligns with each customer's unique preferences and expectations.

3. **Timeliness**

Timeliness is another critical aspect of AI-enabled systems. By delivering services and information promptly, AI can meet customers' real-time needs, further enhancing the perception of the brand as responsive and customer-focused. For example, Hilton's AI-based concierge, Connie, exemplifies how timely recommendations can transform the guest experience by providing accurate and immediate responses to customer inquiries, thereby fostering brand loyalty.

4. **AI as a Supportive Tool for Employees**

Beyond enhancing direct customer interactions, AI also serves as a valuable support tool for employees, particularly during peak times. When employees are busy handling customer requests, AI-driven chatbots can handle multiple inquiries simultaneously, ensuring that customers' needs are addressed without delay. This not only boosts operational efficiency but also reinforces a high standard of service, leading to improved customer satisfaction. According to a survey of 845 senior executives across various industries, AI applications have been shown to increase workplace efficiency and enhance customer service. In peak periods, AI systems can effectively bridge the gap, enabling companies to manage high volumes of customer interactions without compromising quality.

5. **Customer Advocacy**

Overall, these AI capabilities—information currency, system flexibility, and timeliness—contribute to fostering a sense of advocacy among customers. When customers experience personalized, timely, and relevant service, they are more likely to promote and recommend the brand. This advocacy is crucial for businesses looking to expand their customer base through organic growth, as satisfied customers become valuable brand ambassadors.

Future Research Directions

This study serves as the foundation of AI involvement in enriching customer experience and brand recognition. Although there are fields that still await further analysis and understanding, the following guidelines can be used to create new knowledge in this field:

1. Testing of Conceptual Framework in a Different Set of Context and Industry: This study based on data from a hotel in Vietnam, future studies may advance the testing of the developed conceptual framework in other geographical as well as cultural contexts where it is applicable. Hence, customer expectations about services through AI can vary radically between the markets of Asian and Western cultures. In addition, research can be extended to other sectors such as retail, healthcare, and finance that would help understand better how customer experience is impacted by various AI applications in different business sectors. Comparative studies would offer an opportunity to identify sector specific success factors and even the expectations of customers vis-à-vis AI applications.
2. Long-term Studies on AI Quality Customer Relationships: Longitudinal studies could reveal the potential long-term effects of the quality of AI on experience and loyalty. Where the long-term progress of this process will unveil that how it changes over time and so eventually impacts the long-term perspective of the customer-brand relationship. For example, tracking what occurs in terms of interacting with AI systems for a longer time duration of months and years would

clarify and determine if the customer champion and brand identity developed in the relationship are enduring for the long term.

3. Dimensions of Extending Quality of AI: Other dimensions that may be valid are perceived ease of use, interactivity, information completeness and format. While this study focuses on information currency, flexibility, and timeliness, expanding the model to include other aspects would provide a more comprehensive understanding of what constitutes quality in AI systems from the customer's perspective. This broader framework would be useful for AI system designers and developers regarding the designing of interfaces that are more helpful and customer-friendly.
4. This leads us even further into developing a much deeper understanding of why differences in perception and interaction may exist with AI systems when approached by customers belonging to various segments. For example, customers who are very technology-ready may perceive and react in some ways differently than low technology-readiness customers with regards to AI-enabled services. This can be instrumental for businesses to better match AI systems to meet customer needs as viewed through different lenses towards a more personalized, all-inclusive customer experience.
5. **Investigating the Role of Employee Responsiveness as a Moderator**: In the present study, employee responsiveness was found to be a moderator between AI quality and customer-brand identification. Further research can be carried out in this regard by studying how employee performance and AI capabilities complement each other under various service scenarios. For example, future studies may compare the relative levels of customer satisfaction on using AI tools separately and in combination with responsive employees to identify optimum models of service delivery.
6. **Ethics and Security of AI Technology:** When AI technology is becoming ever more pervasive, there needs to be a greater awareness of ethical considerations and security issues. Future studies can explore the perception of the customer about privacy, security of data, and ethical considerations related to AI. Further knowledge on how such factors impact the trust of the customers and their willingness to accept AI-enabled services would be more beneficial in guiding companies towards the implementation of ethical practices through AI applications. Research on the area could also follow the lines of regulatory frameworks and industry standards on the use of AI responsibly when dealing with customers.
7. **Success Factors Across Consumer Segments and International Contexts:** In order to further investigate success factors of AI-enabled services, there is a need for further interdisciplinary studies on different consumer segments and across various national contexts. An investigation into cross-national tendencies

on attitudes toward AI, preferences for human versus AI service, and the role of AI in customer-brand identification might also provide more detail regarding factors determining success in AI. An aspect that demographic differentials in AI preference might help further understand is how businesses could better serve different market segments.

8. **Increasing Sample Size for Generalization of Findings**

The current study is based on a sample of 434 responses, which, while adequate for preliminary analysis, may limit the generalizability of the findings. Future studies could increase sample size to achieve more robust statistical power and greater confidence in the results. Additionally, gathering data from multiple brands and industries would contribute to a broader understanding of how AI-enabled services influence customer experience.

9. **Ethics and Security of AI Technology in Customer Service**

AI ethics and data security represent critical issues in the era of AI-enabled customer service. Future research should explore the ethical dimensions of AI applications, including transparency, fairness, and consumer privacy. Analysing how customers perceive AI's security features and ethical considerations could yield insights into factors influencing their trust and satisfaction with AI-enabled services. As companies continue to collect and process customer data, maintaining transparent and secure AI systems will be essential for fostering trust and loyalty.

10. **Role of AI in Enhancing Retail Customer Experiences**

Lastly, since this study is focused on the hospitality industry, future research should examine how AI success factors—such as trust, convenience, personalization, and service quality—can be applied in a retail environment. For instance, AI applications in retail, such as recommendation engines, virtual try-on, and automated checkout, can be analyzed to understand how these technologies shape the customer experience, brand identification, and ultimately drive loyalty.

It explains how the quality of AI impacts the experience of customers, the level of brand identification, and customer advocacy. Such a focus on the relevance of AI features, mainly the information currency, flexibility, and timeliness, presents a strong case for service-oriented industries to invest in AI tools and meet the changing expectations of their customers. The future research directions outlined above open new avenues to deepen understanding of the role AI might play in customer service, its effects across industries, cultural contexts, and various customer segments. With such an ongoing revolution of AI on customer interactions, there would be a need for sustained research to ensure that technologies are implemented ethically responsibly and effectively to add positively to both customer satisfaction and business success.

Among the inferences from this study is the competitive advantage that AI has in service industries. This strategic investment in AI technologies by businesses to enhance customer engagement and satisfaction is a cutting-edge advantage among a very crowded market. In the case of AI, offering information timely, relevant, and accurate in order to give an impression of dependability and competence is what precedes establishing good relationships with customers. This development in AI, which focuses on the guest experience, has the potential to create a loyal group of customers. For instance, hotels use AI-based applications to create convenient check-in processes, rooms based on guest preferences, or dining experiences-all to enhance the guest experience. Besides, flexibility and timeliness will ensure that customers get satisfied and become brand advocates for the companies because loyal customers are probably going to spread their good experience elsewhere, making the company earn word-of-mouth promotion by a satisfied customer which even beats all marketing techniques. Research shows that brand advocacy from positive AI-enabled experiences leads to greater customer retention and increases the acquisition of new customers through referrals. It, therefore, means AI integration, aside from increasing the efficiency of operations, will also become a strategic asset and has the capability of building advocacy and brand loyalty as far as customer engagement is concerned. Another area of research has great promise: AI as an enabler of enriching omni-channel customer experiences, with a customer interacting with brands at multiple touchpoints-say, online, on a mobile device, in the store. The integration of AI across all these touchpoints allows businesses to give an integrated and cohesive experience even in how or where a customer interacts with the brand. For instance, AI can be used to give real-time support in mobile applications and web sites while AI-driven personalization engines can show users relevant content or offers based on how they have engaged up to now in any of the available channels. Time is bound to tell whether consistent flows through channels with AI-based approaches affect customer satisfaction and loyalty and the omni-channel AI-enabled versus fragmented, old-school support perspective. This would serve firms well in designing their systems that satisfy immediate requirements and generate a long-run impression of seamless and joined support.

Where AI is maximized both in efficiency and personalization, optimal balance between human and AI interaction is something critical for research. In such a situation, customers would prefer to interact with humans in complex queries or situations involving higher emotions while preferring the efficiency of AI. This can be understood as a balance in which the customer would delegate specific tasks to AI while needing others to be understood through human empathy and insight. It is possible to start conducting research based on the identification of scenarios in which a customer prefers a human service rather than an AI and vice versa, providing actionable insight to companies of when to deploy an AI and when to focus more on human support. Business will free up human agents to spend more time interacting in areas that are more value-rich by applying the AI to other tasks such as data gathering and transaction processing. This, in the long run, will add up to the overall satisfaction and experience. Since it is huge, dynamic, and thus unpredictable, trust is the biggest concern in AI use for customers. First and foremost, their use might involve confidential data. Future studies may venture to explore the ethical implications of the application of AI within the customer services interaction facets, mainly transparency, privacy, and security of customers' data. Through research, it is possible to estimate customer concerns over data collection and usage by AI systems, which ones affect their trust and loyalty.

Additional knowledge of regional or cultural differences towards data privacy allows multinational companies to design their AI solutions so that these meet the local expectations of customers and at the same time the requirements of regulations applicable in different countries. An additional ethical dimension of AI relates to algorithmic transparency and fairness. Bias in AI algorithms can further disadvantage certain customer groups by making them feel disempowered or discriminated against by the AI-driven interface. Research into how organizations may make their AI more inclusive and unbiased could prove to be a significant step toward helping improve customer trust. This might be achieved through, for instance, using fairness-aware algorithms or by informing customers clearly about data usage.

The last potential refers to the development of AI industry-specific applications. Of course, the industry selected for this study is the hospitality industry, but others such as healthcare, banking, and retail might well be applied in this respect. For instance, with customized AI, a recommendation for wellness or some type of preliminary diagnosis may give a patient the proactive wherewithal about being healthy. Routine queries in banking will be attended to by AI chatbots, and more complex algorithms can give one-to-one recommendations for planning finances. The same goes for the retail industry in terms of creating a virtual shopping assistant, developing an efficient inventory management system, or enhancing customer support in times of high demand. Industry-specific AI customization hence increases customer satisfaction and provides strength to brand identity in that it signifies a great understanding of specific challenges as well as expectations in particular sectors. Future work should be to figure out how such detailed AI applications affect customer perception, trust, and loyalty and encompass all industries to paint a better landscape of the role AI plays within the modern customer experience.

5. CONCLUSION

With AI embedded in brand management, today's digital space is quite different from when companies really transformed the ways they related to their customers and brought individualized experiences. Now, online access has exposed customers to greater varieties of products, services, and information than ever before; thus, seamless interaction expectations at every point of touch are higher than ever before. This has placed immense pressures on the brands to make good on the demands from the consumers, that the needs and expectations of those individuals are met or beaten. Such requirements have perhaps turned out to be amongst the biggest challenges to undertake: the complexity and reach of the data regarding their customers. However, AI was born as an inspiring answer to help brands realize this. It will be possible in real-time, and with AI, businesses will receive the power to scan an enormous volume of customer data that are aggregated into profound insights of customer behavior and preferences. More advanced algorithms will be able to predict what the future behavior is, personalise content and when interaction should be maximised in order to reach a constant level of consistency across digital channels. Personal connection, nowadays is increasingly becoming the critical determinant of brand loyalty. AI powered personalization is emerging vital for strategic brand management in making trust, customer satisfaction and eventually loyalty.

AI brings out transformative operational efficiencies to a business while it also perfects relationships with the customer. For instance, such tools as customer service chatbots and recommendation engines come in handy in streamlining time, cost, and resources required to support quality high personalized experiences. This is an evolution away from the conventional ways of marketing towards a new paradigm in which firms can respond to individual customer needs with unprecedented precision. Besides, natural language processing and machine learning together, contributing significantly to the realization of making AI-based personalization accessible and inherent to brand management strategies. Thus, for example, artificial intelligence helps brands understand a buyer's preference at micro and granular levels without basing themselves on demographic data and psychographics of past behaviour alone but are provided with real-time knowledge insights. In this context, the brands will be capable of identifying and segmenting a customer with greater clarity of accuracy, thereby fore-seeing his needs well before they do. Lastly, AI content personalization that has dynamic content configuration as well as recommendation engines helps to personalize product-related recommendations of specific customers, which in return promotes higher engagement and higher conversion rates.

Another arena in which AI is altering brand management is through an interaction with customer service. Since customer service is amongst the most direct touch points, it is what causes customer satisfaction and loyalty most. AI technologies, including chatbots and virtual assistants, enable customers to receive instant support from seamless experiences with rapid inquires response. The way AI tools can deal with routine service issues brings into sharp relief the salience value they provide in terms of combating customer frictions. However, this means of reliance on collecting highly extensive data raises a couple of key ethical questions that act as burdens on the shoulder of brands to handle. Such concerns related to issues of privacy and consent plus algorithmic bias continue to make being headachy problems when putting an AI driven personalization into any enterprise. Since increasingly more and more consumer data is found to become indispensable in support of assisting a business craft their strategic plan, issues of data use transparency take center stage when working towards building trusting relationships between a business enterprise and its customer base.

It's also the kind of danger that risks compromising the integrity of whatever experience AI-based services build - algorithms based on a particular prejudice lean toward producing certain results above others-even if just and equitable-and this results in less than equitable or even discriminatory effects where techniques of personalization may not work. Brands should be moving towards better data collection practices and ensuring constant monitoring of how their algorithms might be unfairly swaying the customer interaction. Such ethical considerations should thus stand at the core of what brands do, as building any trust with the consumer depends on this while adhering to the regulations provided in the GDPR, focusing on good, tight data protection measures. The landscape for customer experience is also getting shaped by other emerging technologies: the Internet of Things, augmented reality, virtual reality, and mixed reality; each improves interaction quality while making it more convenient. IoT connects different devices via sensors and the internet and, therefore, enables the business to collect real-time data from customers on usage patterns. This connectivity enables firms to optimize the performance of a product while trying to pre-feel a customer's demand by creating particular recommendation according to all the data collected. The smart fridge could, therefore, monitor the current quantities available in stock and prepare food products whose stock is almost exhausting soon. However, issues related to privacy and security arise in relation to mass volume data collection due to IoT integration.

There is the new dimension of customer experience through how customers engage with products with AR and VR. While AR enhances real-world interaction by overlaying digital information on top of physical environments to show customers what furniture will look like in their home before making a buying decision, VR creates totally immersive environments where users can walk around virtual settings, for example, hotel rooms or real estate properties, from anywhere. Mixed reality refers to a kind of technology that integrates both aspects of AR and VR, enabling users to interact with digital objects that appear as part of the real world. Several industries-including health and manufacturing-will find this technology useful. These immersive technologies enrich the engagement of customers by being able to give realistic experience that can make them engage in well-informed decisions. They also present their very own challenges: they have really high implementation costs and perhaps a potential user discomfort owing to the limitations of technology itself or inadequacy of design of user experience. Businesses must thus ensure that AR/VR/MR technologies are developed to provide high-quality intuitive and engaging user experiences in order to be successfully implemented.

The face of customer experience has changed with the digital transformation pertaining to e-commerce platforms, mobile commerce applications, and social media channels. E-commerce has revolutionized shopping in that customers can browse through large selections from the comfort of their homes while comparing prices and reading reviews before making a purchasing decision. This ease of access empowers consumers to make more-informed decisions while helping businesses reach more audiences than ever before. Mobile commerce enables customers to shop on the go via specially designed applications or responsive websites that are specifically made for a seamless shopping experience through smaller screens. Social media is the biggest playground between brands and customers, but now brands use it for marketing and direct communication with consumers through personalized content based on real-time insight from AI analytics. As brands evolve along with the complex context arising due to rapid advances in technology and changes in consumer behaviour, researching how artificial intelligence-driven personalization functions would be quite imperative toward keeping the methods adopted absolutely ethical while working to achieve maximum operational efficiency through the pathway of brand management policies.

Conclusion: artificial intelligence changes the way businesses treat its consumers by forming personalization in highly responsible communication lines, which helps customers show greater loyalty, meanwhile facing operations problems within the system as well. As such companies embracing these transformative technologies balance innovation with ethical responsibility, they will be better positioned to thrive in this increasingly competitive marketplace where technological advancements cause constant disruption to shifting consumer expectations. Brands can pledge transparency about the use of data while pledging fairness in algorithmic decisions across every touch point for every step along the journey of one's path through the whirlwind of today's digital landscape, wherein at least one of the most compelling reasons for powerful brand management has become personalization.

6.REFERENCES

Ameen, N., Hosany, S., & Tarhini, A. (2021). Consumer interaction with cutting-edge technologies: Implications for future research. *Computers in Human Behavior*, 120, 106761. DOI: 10.1016/j.chb.2021.106761

Cui, L., Huang, S., Wei, F., Tan, C., Duan, C., & Zhou, M. (2017). *SuperAgent: A Customer Service Chatbot for E-commerce Websites*. Microsoft Research Asia., DOI: 10.18653/v1/P17-4017

Daqar, M. a. A., & Smoudy, A. K. A. (2019). The role of artificial intelligence on enhancing customer experience

Daqar, M. A. M. A., & Smoudy, A. K. A. (2019, July 01). THE ROLE OF ARTIFICIAL INTELLIGENCE ON ENHANCING CUSTOMER EXPERIENCE. *International Review of Management and Marketing*, 9(4), 22–31. DOI: 10.32479/irmm.8166

Ghesh, N., Alexander, M., & Davis, A. (2023). The artificial intelligence-enabled customer experience in tourism: A systematic literature review. *Tourism Review*, 79(5), 1017–1037. DOI: 10.1108/TR-04-2023-0255

Hoyer, W. D. Mirja Kroschke, Bernd Schmitt, Karsten Kraume, & Venkatesh Shankar. (2020). Transforming the customer experience through new technologies. In Journal of Interactive Marketing (Vol. xx, p. xxx) [Journal-article]. https://doi.org/ DOI: 10.1016/j.intmar.2020.04.001

Kacar, M. (2023). Application of AI in Customer Experience Management. In Hannig, U., & Seebacher, U. (Eds.), *Marketing and Sales Automation. Management for Professionals*. Springer., DOI: 10.1007/978-3-031-20040-3_26

Kim, H. Y., Lee, J. Y., Choi, D., Wu, J., & Johnson, K. K. P. (2013). Perceived Benefits of Retail Loyalty Programs: Their Effects on Program Loyalty and Customer Loyalty. *Journal of Relationship Marketing*, 12(2), 95–113. DOI: 10.1080/15332667.2013.794100

Moore, S., Bulmer, S., & Elms, J. (2021). The social significance of AI in retail on customer experience and shopping practices. *Journal of Retailing and Consumer Services*, 64, 102755. DOI: 10.1016/j.jretconser.2021.102755

Nguyen, C., Tran, T., & Nguyen, T. (2024). Factors affecting users' brand awareness through social media marketing on TikTok. *Innovative Marketing*, 20(1), 122–131. DOI: 10.21511/im.20(1).2024.11

Shrestha, Y. R., Ben-Menahem, S. M., & Von Krogh, G. (2019). Organizational Decision-Making structures in the age of artificial Intelligence. *California Management Review*, 61(4), 66–83. DOI: 10.1177/0008125619862257

Sidaoui, K., Jaakkola, M., & Burton, J. (2020). AI feel you: Customer experience assessment via chatbot interviews. *Journal of Service Management*, 31(4), 745–766. DOI: 10.1108/JOSM-11-2019-0341

Trawnih, A., Al-Masaeed, S., Alsoud, M., & Alkufahy, A. M. Al-Ahliyya Amman University, & Jadara University. (2022). Understanding artificial intelligence experience: A customer perspective. In International Journal of Data and Network Science (Vol. 6, pp. 1471–1484) [Journal-article]. https://doi.org/DOI: 10.5267/j.ijdns.2022.5.004

Tula, S. T., Kess-Momoh, A. J., Omotoye, G. B., Bello, B. G., & Daraojimba, A. I.Sunday Tubokirifuruar TulaAzeez Jason Kess-MomohGaniyu Bolawale Omotoye-Binaebi Gloria BelloAndrew Ifesinachi Daraojimba. (2024). AI-enabled customer experience enhancement in business. *Computer Science & IT Research Journal*, 5(2), 365–389. DOI: 10.51594/csitrj.v5i2.789

Tulcanaza-Prieto, A. B., Cortez-Ordoñez, A., & Lee, C. W. (2023). Influence of customer perception factors on AI-Enabled customer experience in the Ecuadorian banking environment. *Sustainability (Basel)*, 15(16), 12441. DOI: 10.3390/su151612441

Zare, M., & Mahmoudi, R. (2021). CUSTOMER EXPERIENCE: BRANDING WITH EMOTIONAL TEXT MINING. *Journal of Management Information and Decision Sciences*, 24(1), 1–6. https://sdbindex.com/documents/00000161/00000-83428.pdf

Chapter 13
Integrating AI, Green Marketing, and Influencer Strategies:
Shaping Sustainable Consumer Behavior in the Digital Age

Ridhima Sharma
Vivekananda Institute of Professional Studies, India

Amrik Singh
https://orcid.org/0000-0003-3598-8787
Lovely Professional University, India

ABSTRACT

In the face of growing environmental concerns, such as global warming, climate change, and pollution, conscious consumerism and sustainable consumption have emerged as critical imperatives. These challenges have prompted businesses to adopt green marketing—an eco-friendly approach to the marketing mix that addresses both consumer concerns and environmental impact. Green marketing is increasingly recognized in developed countries, but it has recently gained traction in developing nations like India. This shift in focus has also sparked a trend in influencer marketing, where brands partner with prominent vloggers to promote green products on social media platforms like TikTok and Instagram. Such strategies have significant influence, especially on younger audiences who often lack the critical thinking skills to evaluate advertisements effectively.

DOI: 10.4018/979-8-3693-9461-8.ch013

INTRODUCTION

Businesses operate in a dynamic environment i.e an ever-changing environment where the needs and preferences of consumers keep changing from time to time. Keeping in mind the marketing philosophy, businesses need to ensure customer satisfaction by offering a product that the customers want. The launch of Eco mark scheme by the govt in 1991, led to the birth of Green Marketing practices in India. Its aim was to create awareness about eco-friendly products amongst the denizens. In recent times, businesses in India have had to switch to Green Marketing to meet the needs of customers who show a concern towards protecting the environment.

Environmental awareness has evolved into a worldwide concern and a significant topic in academic research. The concept of environmental sustainability has significantly influenced consumer behaviour since the 1970s. This alteration has caused a notable disturbance in the way consumers see things, with an increasing worry about safeguarding and preventing any additional harm to the environment. Green marketing is an initiative aimed at mitigating the negative effects on the environment by using a new approach that incorporates eco-friendly principles in the design, production, packaging, labelling, and consumption of products.

Companies frequently employ diverse strategies in various sectors of the market in order to get an edge over rivals by altering consumer perception through the introduction of innovative environmentally-friendly products (Qiu et al., 2023). Recently, there has been a focus on green marketing mostly in relation to product packaging, labelling, and incentive methods. A comprehensive evaluation should be conducted to ascertain the extent to which various organisations are engaging in environmentally-friendly initiatives.

The consumer's purchasing decision-making process typically comprises five stages: recognition of a perceived need for a particular benefit, doing a research search, evaluating several options, reaching the buy decision, and conducting an after the purchase review. During the customer purchase choice process, several aspects such as social, cultural, emotional, behavioural, marketing mix, and situational factors all have an impact to some extent.

Both the organisations and consumers have a shared duty for environmental matters and contribute to the cause by producing and buying eco-friendly items. It is important to acknowledge that ecological dedication and involvement in green initiatives are two distinct matters. Both organisations and consumers have significant roles to fulfil in this regard. However, the choice made by the customer is particularly crucial as it serves as a driving force for producers to offer environmentally friendly products (Mehraj et al., 2023). Consumers generally refrain from purchasing products that pose risks to the well-being of humans, the surroundings, animals, plants, and ecosystems (Sharma et al., 2023).

Gaining knowledge of these facts can have a significant impact on altering customer buying habits and fostering a favourable impression of ecologically sustainable items. Hence, research holds significance in specific geographical in nature social, contextual, and temporal contexts (Sharma, 2021).

Multiple studies have examined the shift in customer opinion, where individuals who are environmentally conscious express their worries through various actions, such as refraining from purchasing a product due to its potential harm (Nguyen et al., 2023).

The excessive consumption levels in the past, without keeping in mind their negative impact on the environment have led to environmental degradation. Marketers and customers have raised concerns towards increasing pollution, climate change, global warming etc. Measures have been adopted globally to protect the environment. Green marketing is one of the recent trends especially in developing countries like India. It has existed since a long time but has started gaining attention in the last few years due to increased awareness among customers. The word 'Green' has been associated with sustainable and eco-friendly activities. Green marketing is also referred to as sustainable marketing, environmental marketing and ecological marketing. According to the American Marketing Association, marketing of products that are presumed to be environmentally safe is called Green Marketing. This concept requires businesses to not only focus on the marketing concept, rather on societal marketing concept. Thus, businesses require to alter their production process, product, packaging and overall conduct in a manner that it is environmentally safe.

During the course of its development, Green Marketing has evolved over the past decades by several folds. The first era of Ecological Marketing, focussed more on the external environmental problems like air and water pollution. The Second era i.e. Green Environmental Marketing shifted its concentration to newer concepts of green products, clean technology and sustainability. This lauded the companies with a stronger customer base through competitive and first mover advantage. Third and the last era of Sustainable Green Marketing created a huge impact on the global economy. Several companies over the world are now certified with ISO-14000, which is a defined set of international standards, created to minimize the adverse impacts on the environment.

Famous people on social media, especially YouTube's vloggers, have become powerful figures in the shopping decisions of their young fans. People like these inspire others by sharing helpful information about the brands they use frequently and are enthusiastic about. In addition, they provide detailed instructions on what their followers should and should not utilize. Because of their large followings and apparent credibility, several companies have begun including young influencers—often children themselves—into their marketing campaigns. Some examples of such accounts include Stella and Blaise, The McClure Twins, AnnieLeblanc, and Evan-

TubeHD (Beichert et al., 2024). A few of these endorsers get hefty salaries while seeming like "ordinary" kids on the outside. As an example, Ryan's 2018 earnings were $22 million (Allal-Chérif et al., 2024). This is due to the fact that influencers are approached by firms that offer them free products or financial incentives in return for their endorsement of their products on various social media platforms. Because of their large online fan bases, their YouTube channels are able to earn money from advertisements. "Influencer marketing" is a common way to describe this phenomenon (Zheng et al., 2024). Advertising occurs when marketers pay influencers to promote their products or services and have editorial control over the material, such as final approval or broad post instructions (such "I want two posts about our product"). The standards offered by several advertising self-regulatory bodies include this definition of influencer marketing (Kim et al., 2024).

LITERATURE REVIEW

According to the research conducted by Homer &Kahle (1988), in specific circumstances, the effect is expected to originate from abstract values, then manifest in intermediate attitudes, and finally translate into specific behaviours. This sequence might be referred to as a hierarchical structure of values, attitudes, and behaviours. Values are the fundamental principles that might elucidate an individual's attitude and conduct. The attitude is defined as an outcome that arises from multiple circumstances, including an individual's own values. Van et al., 2023 argue that attitudes are seen to be less enduring in comparison to values. Attitudes are a crucial component to consider when assessing the advantages of buying environmentally friendly items, as stated (Zhuang et al., 2021). Values and attitudes directly influence a person's behaviour, leading to observable actions.

Green Marketing:

Green marketing is similar to traditional marketing. However, it differs in the sense that all the products, packaging, price, marketing mix are environmentally safe unlike in traditional marketing [Ansar, 2013]. It is also called sustainable marketing, environmental marketing or ecological marketing. The main aim is to practice marketing in a way that it is harmless to the environment and also motivate customers to protect the environment.[Stern and Ander, 2008]. Today, many companies have decided to adopt cleaner products and processes. They "Go Green" and are practicing green marketing. They feel in this way they can protect the environment and increase profits [Hart, 1997].

While various studies have provided diverse descriptions of green marketing through different viewpoints, the American Marketing Association (AMA) identifies three distinct approaches to define it, as outlined by Prakash (2002):

a) Retailing Meaning: The act of promoting and selling products that are believed to be ecologically friendly
b) Social Marketing Meaning: The process of creating and promoting products with the aim of enhancing the physical setting by preventing any more harm to it
c) Environmental Meaning: The organizational endeavour to create, endorse, package, and rehabilitate goods in a manner that aligns with ecological considerations

The idea of ecological marketing has evolved throughout time and may be categorised into distinct eras, each characterized by specific shifts in consumer demands based on considerations related to the environment.

The initial era, known as the ecologically green marketing age, extended until the beginning of the 1970s and mostly addressed external environmental issues such as pollution of the air and water. The second phase emerged in the late 1980s, specifically known to be the green environmental marketing era. It introduced a number of novel ideas to the previous area of focus, including the development of clean technology, ensuring environmental sustainability prioritizing consumer interests, and striving for competitive advantage (Raza & Khan, 2022).

The primary distinction between the first and second periods is in their respective focuses. The first era primarily emphasised the impact of industries on the environment, whereas the second era encompassed all of the manufacturing and service methods within the realm of environmental marketing (Raza & Khan 2022).

The third era, known as sustainable green marketing, focused on implementing stringent government regulations that the second era was unable to sustain. Subsequently, the implementation of sustainable development in the field of marketing has had a significant impact on the economy (Machová et al., 2022). Toyota's development of "environmental technology" was not solely driven by legal requirements, but additionally by consumer demand for a unified product line of future cars, such as electric-combustion hybrids (Machová et al., 2022).

The function of marketing is being debated due to the significant contribution of lifestyle and habits of consumption in the industrialised world to environmental degradation. Marketing has been criticised for exacerbating the degradation of the environment by promoting consumerism, hence fostering a throwaway culture and prioritising the immediate satisfaction of consumer desires. Alternatively, marketing can be regarded as a crucial tool for promoting new lifestyles and altering consumption patterns, not limited to environmentally conscious consumers. Hence, marketing ought to contribute towards the development of more environmentally friendly societal structures. Marketing has expanded its attention to include environmental problems in addition to the manufacturing process, transaction, and trade. Multiple definitions of green marketing exist. (Bhardwaj et al., 2023) identifies green marketing management as the comprehensive process of managing and meeting the needs of customers and society in a profitable and sustainable manner. Pancić et al., 2023 establishes it as marketing activities that acknowledge environmental stewardship as a responsibility for business development and growth. Both definitions encompass a broader eco-centric approach that extends beyond the marketing department, encompassing the overall strategy or philosophy.

Various tools are utilised for the objective of green marketing. Familiarity with these environmentally friendly advertising methods (such as eco-label, eco-brand, environmental advertisement) will facilitate a more effortless understanding of the traits and features of green products. Furthermore, it will assist consumers in recognising and acquiring environmentally friendly products. The utilisation of these regulatory mechanisms has an impact on how consumers perceive and behave when buying environmentally friendly items (Javed et al., 2023). Conducting an evaluation of consumers' understanding and acceptance of the green concept would be beneficial for marketers. This study specifically focuses on the public's view regarding environmentally friendly marketing.

Green Product:

Green product has been defined as an item that is produced keeping in mind that it has a minimum negative impact on the environment and is manufactured locally using natural resources [Diglel and Yazdanifard, 2014]. Consumers in today's time prefer green products as they are considered to be safer, organic and of better quality [Ottoman and Mallen, 2014].

According to Reinhardt, 1998, environmental product differentiation occurs when a company develops products that offer superior environmental advantages or carry lesser environmental burdens compared to similar products. This definition emphasises that green products encompass not just those with reduced environmental impact, but also those that offer superior environmental advantages in comparison to traditional products.

Ottman et al., 2006 argue that while no consumer product can have absolutely no impact on the environment, in the business context, the terms "green products" or "environmental products" are commonly used to refer to those that make an effort to safeguard or improve the natural environment by conserving energy and resources, and by minimising or eliminating the use of toxic substances, pollution, and waste. This concept emphasises the primary environmental concerns addressed in the development of green products, which include energy, resources, pollution, and waste.

Sustainability

Environment Sustainability is that approach of management which deals with development of strategies such that it produces profits for the company and sustains the environment at the same time. It is a difficult social target yet many companies have adopted it and are taking crucial actions to protect the environment from further deterioration.[Armstrong and Kotler, 2007].Sustainability Marketing has been defined as the means by which sustainable relationships are built and maintained with the customers, social environment and the natural environment [Charter and Polonsky, 1999].

Consumer Behaviour

According to The Gauge Study of Roper Organization [Crispell, 2001], the consumers have been segmented into True blue Greens and Sprouts on the basis of their association with green consumerism. A True blue green is a consumer who is more inclined to buy green products whereas Sprouts are the ones who can buy green products however they don't because they are not involved in the environment protection related activities. Due to the growing environmental consciousness among the consumers, it is believed that studies and researches on green consumerism will gain much more importance over the years as it will act as a lead in identifying the consumer altitudes, behaviors and intention.[Antonio et al, 2009]

Ecological Understanding

Environmental knowledge assesses consumers' understanding of environmental elements or outcomes and the shared responsibilities associated with sustainable development [Neves et al., 2022]. Empirical evidence demonstrates a direct correlation between individuals' understanding of the environment with their patterns of consumption [Neves et al., 2022]. Environmental information has a direct impact on ecological attitude, which in turn drives consumer behaviour [Moslehpour et al., 2023]. Consumer purchasing behaviour is frequently associated with individuals' environmental consciousness and commitment to sustainability [Jamil et al., 2022]. Environmental knowledge is an essential element of green consumer behaviour. According to Patwary et al., 2022, customer environmental understanding has an impact on their pro-environmental behaviour. According to Tamar et al., 2021, there is a strong correlation between environmental knowledge and the intention to make green purchases.

Environmental knowledge encompasses an individual's beliefs and comprehension of environmental matters, with the assumption that a higher level of environmental knowledge is linked to a greater inclination to engage in environmentally friendly purchases [Mohsin et al., 2022]. Consumer understanding of environmental problems is a crucial factor that influences consumer attitudes towards being more ecologically conscious, as indicated by a study conducted in Egypt [Paul &Bhukya, 2021]. Insufficient awareness among individuals may present a psychological obstacle to the acceptance of environmentally friendly products [Kumari et al., 2023]. Environmental awareness refers to the capacity to recognise and evaluate human consumption patterns and behaviours that might have a positive or negative impact on purchasing decisions. According to the study conducted by (Mohseniet al., 2022), individuals with a higher level of environmental knowledge are more likely to adopt ecologically friendly behaviours. These behaviours include consuming protein-rich meals that are healthful, using public transportation more often, and buying products with little disposable packaging (Hamann,et al., 2023)

Influencer Marketing

The power of personal recommendations and word-of-mouth has been amplified by the proliferation of social media platforms, which allow users to easily share content with a wide audience. Here we are in the modern day, where kids are not just media consumers but also creators. Children may easily produce electronic word of mouth (eWOM), which can increase a brand's visibility and awareness (Nazlan et al., 2024). The sales of children's goods are positively affected by this phenomena. As an example, kids these days can do things like post reviews (like on Amazon, where they're labeled as “A kid's review”), engage with brands on social media (even though Facebook and Instagram have an age restriction of 13, kids can easily make fake accounts), and even make and share videos showing their product ownership and experiences (like on YouTube Kids, where kids under 13 can have their own account). Because they are not in it for the money, peers consider them to be honest and reliable sources of information. As a result, the company's recommendations may be more readily accepted by both kids and their guardians than those from other sources or marketing communications (Le, 2024). Thus, brands work hard to encourage and reward electronic word-of-mouth, turning (perhaps insignificant) consumers into ad producers rather than passive consumers (e.g., by giving free stuff in return for reviews or involvement in online registrations, like and share competitions). But their huge reputation and impact might be undermined by the unpredictability of these real-life endorsers (Mulyati et al., 2024).

Companies have started a strategy called influencer marketing, where they engage with social media influencers (i.e., popular users who have built a large following or subscriber base) and encourage them to create and share relevant, authentic brand-content, in response to the impact of electronic word-of-mouth (eWOM) on customer perceptions and decisions (Tiwari et al., 2024). Brands and influencers can formally agree upon terms that allow corporations to leverage word-of-mouth while simultaneously recovering power. Since influencers want to keep their devotion towards the firms who pay them, it's likely that they'll act positively (Arora et al., 2024).

Social media influencers' promotional tactics blur the lines between entertainment and commercial content. These results imply that the younger audience may have trouble distinguishing sponsored content, such unboxing videos, as advertising, leading to unintentional bias (Hermawan et al., 2024). There are a number of interesting areas where future research on influencers and youth may go, given the originality of this persuasive method.Prior studies have determined that environmental knowledge is a crucial factor that has a beneficial impact on customers' intention to revisit. According to several experts, possessing knowledge about environmental friendliness is regarded as one of the most desirable behaviours and attitudes (Ogiemwonyi et al., 2023). Consumers' buying intention is greatly influenced by their level of environmental understanding. Individuals with a limited understanding of the environment will not comprehend the health-related aspects of environmental protection.

Artificial Intelligence & Consumer Buying Behaviour

Artificial intelligence is assisting online enterprises in interacting with customers. Modern AI and platforms for digital businesses may utilize comprehensive data on client behavior and usage patterns. Online shoppers may appreciate personalized shopping experiences facilitated by artificial reasoning and self-learning algorithms. Characteristics of AI-driven online shopping encompass immediate focus, visual search, voice-activated queries, selection intelligence tools, and conversational commerce.Associations and sponsors will benefit by understanding all data and acknowledging the influence of AI on clients to remain sufficiently prepared. Increased contemplation of your clientele and their actions may enhance the refinement of your business processes and advertising strategies to more effectively meet their wants.Amazon, the foremost online retailer in the USA, shows the seamless use of AI into e-commerce. A more tailored purchasing experience may be created through a diverse selection, rapid delivery, and competitive pricing. As a result, Amazon's clientele employs location-based pricing, receives destination-specific communications, and conducts transactions in local currencies. The utilization of artificial intelligence in digital contexts. Shopping enables customer-focused search and improved customization, leading to a more effective sales process. Emerging technologies, particularly AI systems, have catalyzed the development of creative marketing tactics to successfully engage target audiences and enhance user experiences.

Online merchants want a thorough understanding of customer attitudes and the degree of faith they have in the use of artificial intelligence by platforms for e-commerce.Considering the rising significance of temporal and economic effectiveness in purchasing, it is crucial to understand how to leverage AI effectively to improve online spending and purchase frequency. Online shopping is, in this context, a practical way for consumers to obtain the necessary goods. Research on consumer confidence and the implementation of AI in online purchasing has been limited to far. Artificial Intelligence may enhance the understanding of client online information gathering and purchase behaviors to provide a more tailored purchasing experience. E-commerce platforms possess a significant opportunity to evaluate the traits of both current and potential consumers, therefore offering marketing strategies that are meticulously customized for them. AI amplifies the regularity and involvement of interactions with customers and employees, hence enhancing customer happiness and engagement. The benefits can be encapsulated as follows: AI systems function autonomously, analyze extensive datasets instantaneously, and interpret and influence consumer behavior to provide individualized products and services, hence improving the purchasing experience.

Results

Descriptive analysis in this study illustrates the answers of 100 consumers by distributing questionnaires directly.

H1- Environmental Knowledge has a significant effect on Attitude towards green product.

Consumer attitudes refer to a person's positive or negative views of people, events, objects, or behaviors, which reflect preferences for these people, events, objects, or behaviors, resulting in positive or negative intentions towards buying behavior

Table 1. Effect of environmental knowledge on attitude towards green product

Environmental Knowledge --- Attitude towards Green Product	Direct Effect	0.308	0.056	5.486	Significant

H2- Environmental Knowledge has a positive effect on consumers' Green Purchase Intention.

Knowledge and awareness to protect the environment has become a major influence on consumer attitudes towards green products. A study in Egypt also concluded that consumer knowledge about environmental problems is an important factor that influences consumer attitudes to be more environmentally friendly.

Table 2. Effect of environmental knowledge on green purchase intention

Environmental Knowledge --- Attitude towards Green Product --- Green Purchase Intention	Indirect Effect	0.189	0.037	5.037	Significant

H3- Influencer marketing has a positive effect on consumers Purchase Intention.

The goal of influencer marketing on the internet is to blend in with the content they're promoting, whether it's an advertorial or an instructional video. There are a number of complicated elements that have come together to cause the present upsurge in influencer marketing. First, people's media consumption patterns have shifted from print to online media. Secondly, regardless of whether they use the internet or not, people react strongly to ads. Many people who shop online have a strong dislike for intrusive advertisements since they are goal-oriented. Less intrusive, more real, and covert advertising tactics have been required due to the difficulties of online environments.Thirdly, most people spend a considerable amount of time on social media, which isn't just a millennial thing.

Table 3. Marketing effect on purchase intention

Environmental Knowledge --- Attitude towards Green Product	Direct Effect	0.318	0.066	6.486	Significant

It shows that there is a direct relationship between variables that have a significant effect. Therefore, supporting H1, H2 & H3.

CONCLUSION:

Given India's population and GDP growth rate, the negative impact on environment is constantly increasing and needs to be controlled. This paper highlights that there is an increasing awareness about green product or green marketing. It suggests that the environmental knowledge has a direct effect on consumers attitude towards green products. The study concludes that the consumer behaviour could be influenced by spreading awareness about the environmental degradation among consumers that can influence their attitudes to be more environmental friendly. In the coming years, influencer marketing also is predicted to grow in popularity. Convergence culture is characterized by the general consensus that the advertising industry must adapt to the changing landscape of interactive content, emerging media, and consumer and production habits. Even skeptics will have a hard time ignoring the marketing plan given the massive growth of the influencer sector and the effectiveness of influencers. Executives in charge of marketing should be prepared to evaluate how this emerging marketing trend may improve their entire brand strategy and to include influencers within their most comprehensive campaigns. Undoubtedly, AI has improved customers' online experiences in a variety of ways. Customer satisfaction may be increased by swiftly responding to all questions and shortening the time it takes an agent to resolve a caller's issue. Furthermore, the research explores how artificial intelligence (AI) is revolutionizing green marketing. AI's predictive analytics and data-driven insights enable brands to enhance their resource efficiency and precision targeting, resulting in marketing operations that are both sustainable and economically viable. AI-enhanced products, such as robots capable of addressing environmental challenges—like removing pollutants and tracking invasive species—demonstrate how autonomous interactions can improve environmental performance. Finally, the study delves into the metaverse, a digital realm that mirrors the physical world, and examines its implications for sustainable business practices. The immersive, interactive experience offered by the metaverse presents transformative opportunities for green marketing, allowing brands to engage with consumers in environmentally friendly ways without depleting physical resources. By integrating AI, influencer marketing, and the metaverse, businesses can create innovative, sustainable marketing strategies that resonate with today's eco-conscious consumers. To provide genuinely exceptional customer service, a company must foresee and fix any difficulties before consumers contact them. AI-powered systems can quickly evaluate large datasets. By analyzing previous and present customer data, one may easily learn more about them and anticipate their future behavior.

REFERENCES:

Allal-Chérif, O., Puertas, R., & Carracedo, P. (2024). Intelligent influencer marketing: How AI-powered virtual influencers outperform human influencers. *Technological Forecasting and Social Change*, 200, 123113. DOI: 10.1016/j.techfore.2023.123113

Ansar, N. (2013). Impact of Green Marketing on Consumer Purchase Intention [online]. *Mediterranean Journal of Social Sciences*, 4(11), 650–655. DOI: 10.5901/mjss.2013.v4n11p650

Antonio, C., Sergio, R., & Francisco, M. J. (2009). Characteristics of Research on Green Marketing. *Business Strategy and the Environment*, 18(4), 223–239. DOI: 10.1002/bse.571

Arora, M., Mishra, K. K., Singh, M., Singh, P., & Tripathi, R. (2024). Deepfake Technology and Its Implications for Influencer Marketing. In *Navigating the World of Deepfake Technology* (pp. 66–90). IGI Global. DOI: 10.4018/979-8-3693-5298-4.ch005

Beichert, M., Bayerl, A., Goldenberg, J., & Lanz, A. (2024). Revenue generation through influencer marketing. *Journal of Marketing*, •••, 00222429231217471.

Bhardwaj, S., Nair, K., Tariq, M. U., Ahmad, A., & Chitnis, A. (2023). The State of Research in Green Marketing: A Bibliometric Review from 2005 to 2022. *Sustainability (Basel)*, 15(4), 2988. DOI: 10.3390/su15042988

Crispell, D. (2001). Going Green(ish). Public Perspective, September/October 2001, pp. 28-30

Diglel, A., & Yazdanifard, R. (2014). Green marketing and its Influence on Buying Behavior and the Attitudes of Purchasers towards Eco-friendly products [online]. *Global Journal of Management and Business Research*, 7(11), 11–18.

Hamann, K. R., Wullenkord, M. C., Reese, G., & van Zomeren, M. (2023). Believing that we can change our world for the better: A Triple-A (Agent-Action-Aim) Framework of self-efficacy beliefs in the context of collective social and ecological aims. *Personality and Social Psychology Review*, •••, 10888683231178056. PMID: 37386819

Hermawan, H., Hersona, S., &Suyaman, D. J. (2024). The Effect Of Influencer Marketing, Content Marketing, And Price Perceptions On Consumer Purchase Intention (An Investigation Of Luxcrime Cosmetic Consumers In Karawang). *At-Tadbir: jurnalilmiahmanajemen, 8*(2), 189-205.

Homer, P. M., & Kahle, L. R. (1988). A structural equation test of the value-attitude-behavior hierarchy. *Journal of Personality and Social Psychology*, 54(4), 638.

Jamil, K., Dunnan, L., Gul, R. F., Shehzad, M. U., Gillani, S. H. M., & Awan, F. H. (2022). Role of social media marketing activities in influencing customer intentions: A perspective of a new emerging era. *Frontiers in Psychology*, 12, 808525. DOI: 10.3389/fpsyg.2021.808525 PMID: 35111111

Javed, U., Rashid, M. A., Hussain, G., & Shafique, S. (2023). Consumers' perception of green brand attributes and its outcomes: A sustainable perspective. *Journal of Environmental Planning and Management*, •••, 1–23.

Kim, I., Ki, C. W., Lee, H., & Kim, Y. K. (2024). Virtual influencer marketing: Evaluating the influence of virtual influencers' form realism and behavioral realism on consumer ambivalence and marketing performance. *Journal of Business Research*, 176, 114611. DOI: 10.1016/j.jbusres.2024.114611

Kumari, R., Verma, R., Debata, B. R., & Ting, H. (2022). A systematic literature review on the enablers of green marketing adoption: Consumer perspective. *Journal of Cleaner Production*, 366, 132852. DOI: 10.1016/j.jclepro.2022.132852

Le, M. T. (2024). How does influencer marketing build up the engagement between brand and followers? *International Journal of Internet Marketing and Advertising*, 21(1-2), 3–25. DOI: 10.1504/IJIMA.2024.140447

Machová, R., Ambrus, R., Zsigmond, T., & Bakó, F. (2022). The impact of green marketing on consumer behavior in the market of palm oil products. *Sustainability (Basel)*, 14(3), 1364. DOI: 10.3390/su14031364

Martin Charter. (1999) Greener Marketing: A Global Perspective on Greener Marketing Practice https://www.worldcat.org/title/greener-marketing-a-global-perspective-on-greenermarketing-practice/oclc/247076134

Mehraj, D., Qureshi, I. H., Singh, G., Nazir, N. A., Basheer, S., & Nissa, V. U. (2023). Green marketing practices and green consumer behavior: Demographic differences among young consumers. *Business Strategy & Development*, 6(4), 571–585. DOI: 10.1002/bsd2.263

Mohseni, S., Brent, A. C., Kelly, S., & Browne, W. N. (2022). Demand response-integrated investment and operational planning of renewable and sustainable energy systems considering forecast uncertainties: A systematic review. *Renewable & Sustainable Energy Reviews*, 158, 112095. DOI: 10.1016/j.rser.2022.112095

Mohsin, M., Jamil, K., Naseem, S., Sarfraz, M., & Ivascu, L. (2022). Elongating nexus between workplace factors and knowledge hiding behavior: Mediating role of job anxiety. *Psychology Research and Behavior Management*, 15, 441–457. DOI: 10.2147/PRBM.S348467 PMID: 35250318

Moslehpour, M., Yin Chau, K., Du, L., Qiu, R., Lin, C. Y., &Batbayar, B. (2023). Predictors of green purchase intention toward eco-innovation and green products: Evidence from Taiwan. *Economic research-Ekonomskaistraživanja, 36*(2).

Mulyati, S., Putriani, R. D., Goestjahjanti, F. S., Marusaha, T. J., Farhan, A., Mendrofa, Y., & Purno, M. (2024). Analysis of The Influencer Marketing, Ratings and Customer Reviews on Purchasing Decisions. *Journal of E-business and Management Science*, 2(1), 230–239.

Nazlan, N. H., Zhang, H., Sun, J., & Chang, W. (2024). Navigating the online reputation maze: Impact of review availability and heuristic cues on restaurant influencer marketing effectiveness. *Journal of Hospitality Marketing & Management*, 33(3), 288–307. DOI: 10.1080/19368623.2023.2246471

Neves, C., Oliveira, T., & Santini, F. (2022). Sustainable technologies adoption research: A weight and meta-analysis. *Renewable & Sustainable Energy Reviews*, 165, 112627. DOI: 10.1016/j.rser.2022.112627

Nguyen, P. H., Nguyen, D. N., & Nguyen, L. A. T. (2023). Quantitative insights into green purchase intentions: The interplay of health consciousness, altruism, and sustainability. *Cogent Business & Management*, 10(3), 2253616. DOI: 10.1080/23311975.2023.2253616

Ogiemwonyi, O., Alam, M. N., Alshareef, R., Alsolamy, M., Azizan, N. A., & Mat, N. (2023). Environmental factors affecting green purchase behaviors of the consumers: Mediating role of environmental attitude. *Cleaner Environmental Systems*, 10, 100130. DOI: 10.1016/j.cesys.2023.100130

Ottman, J.A., Stafford, E.R., Hartman, C.L., (2006). Green marketing myopia. Environment 48 (5), 22e36.

Ottoman, J., & Mallen, D. (2014). 5 *Green Marketing strategies to earn consumer trust*. Available at:https://www.greenbiz.com/blog/2014/01/14/five-strategies-avoid-taint-greenwash-your-business

Pancić, M., Serdarušić, H., & Ćućić, D. (2023). Green Marketing and Repurchase Intention: Stewardship of Green Advertisement, Brand Awareness, Brand Equity, Green Innovativeness, and Brand Innovativeness. *Sustainability (Basel)*, 15(16), 12534. DOI: 10.3390/su151612534

Patwary, A. K., Rasoolimanesh, S. M., Rabiul, M. K., Aziz, R. C., & Hanafiah, M. H. (2022). Linking environmental knowledge, environmental responsibility, altruism, and intention toward green hotels through ecocentric and anthropocentric attitudes. *International Journal of Contemporary Hospitality Management*, 34(12), 4653–4673. DOI: 10.1108/IJCHM-01-2022-0039

Paul, J., & Bhukya, R. (2021). Forty-five years of International Journal of Consumer Studies: A bibliometric review and directions for future research. *International Journal of Consumer Studies*, 45(5), 937–963. DOI: 10.1111/ijcs.12727

Polonsky(1994): An Introduction To Green Marketing. Available at: https://escholarship.org/uc/item/49n325b7

Prakash, A. (2002). Green Marketing, Public Policy And Managerial Strategies. *Business Strategy and the Environment*, 11(5), 285–297. DOI: 10.1002/bse.338

Qiu, H., Wang, X., Wu, M. Y., Wei, W., Morrison, A. M., & Kelly, C. (2023). The effect of destination source credibility on tourist environmentally responsible behavior: An application of stimulus-organism-response theory. *Journal of Sustainable Tourism*, 31(8), 1797–1817. DOI: 10.1080/09669582.2022.2067167

Raza, S. A., & Khan, K. A. (2022). Impact of green human resource practices on hotel environmental performance: The moderating effect of environmental knowledge and individual green values. *International Journal of Contemporary Hospitality Management*, 34(6), 2154–2175. DOI: 10.1108/IJCHM-05-2021-0553

Reinhardt, F.L., (1998). Environmental product differentiation: implications for corporate strategy. California Management Review 40 (4), 43e73.

Sharma, A. P. (2021). Consumers' purchase behaviour and green marketing: A synthesis, review and agenda. *International Journal of Consumer Studies*, 45(6), 1217–1238. DOI: 10.1111/ijcs.12722

Sharma, K., Aswal, C., & Paul, J. (2023). Factors affecting green purchase behavior: A systematic literature review. *Business Strategy and the Environment*, 32(4), 2078–2092. DOI: 10.1002/bse.3237

Stern, N. Z., & Ander, W. N. (2008). *Greentailing and other revolutions in retail: hot ideas that are grabbing customers' attention and raising profits*. John Wiley & Sons.

Tamar, M., Wirawan, H., Arfah, T., & Putri, R. P. S. (2021). Predicting pro-environmental behaviours: The role of environmental values, attitudes and knowledge. *Management of Environmental Quality*, 32(2), 328–343. DOI: 10.1108/MEQ-12-2019-0264

Tiwari, A., Kumar, A., Kant, R., & Jaiswal, D. (2024). Impact of fashion influencers on consumers' purchase intentions: Theory of planned behaviour and mediation of attitude. *Journal of Fashion Marketing and Management*, 28(2), 209–225. DOI: 10.1108/JFMM-11-2022-0253

Van Tonder, E., Fullerton, S., De Beer, L. T., & Saunders, S. G. (2023). Social and personal factors influencing green customer citizenship behaviours: The role of subjective norm, internal values and attitudes. *Journal of Retailing and Consumer Services*, 71, 103190. DOI: 10.1016/j.jretconser.2022.103190

Zheng, L., Huang, B., Qiu, H., & Bai, H. (2024). The role of social media followers' agency in influencer marketing: A study based on the heuristic–systematic model of information processing. *International Journal of Advertising*, 43(3), 554–579. DOI: 10.1080/02650487.2023.2229148

Zhuang, W., Luo, X., & Riaz, M. U. (2021). On the factors influencing green purchase intention: A meta-analysis approach. *Frontiers in Psychology*, 12, 644020. DOI: 10.3389/fpsyg.2021.644020 PMID: 33897545

Chapter 14
Shaping the Future of Brand Management by AI-Powered Predictions

Mohamed Badouch
https://orcid.org/0000-0003-0495-3784
Ibn Zohr University, Morocco

Hasna Mahmoud
https://orcid.org/0009-0006-5457-3594
Ibn Zohr University, Morocco

Mehdi Boutaounte
https://orcid.org/0009-0001-0459-7532
National School of Commerce and Management, Morocco

ABSTRACT

This chapter explores the transformative potential of recommender systems for predictive analytics in brand management, emphasizing the crucial role of data-driven insights in shaping strategic decisions and driving sustainable growth. We analyze how AI-powered recommender systems can be leveraged to forecast consumer demand, identify emerging market trends, and proactively opportunities in a dynamic business environment. We will delve into the mathematical underpinnings of predictive analytics, exploring time series modeling and machine learning algorithms used in recommender systems. We will also discuss the role of big data and data visualization in informing strategic brand decisions, showcasing how these techniques can reveal hidden patterns, identify customer segments, and optimize resource allocation. Finally, this chapter will address the ethical considerations of predictive analytics, examining the potential for algorithmic bias and the erosion of

DOI: 10.4018/979-8-3693-9461-8.ch014

consumer trust, and proposing strategies for ensuring fairness and accountability in AI-driven brand management.

1. INTRODUCTION

The contemporary landscape of brand management is irrevocably intertwined with the digital age, a realm characterized by an unprecedented deluge of data. This data, a rich tapestry woven from consumer interactions, online behavior, and market fluctuations (Zuo et al., 2019), offers a treasure trove of insights for brands seeking to understand and anticipate consumer preferences. However, this data-driven landscape presents a unique challenge: how to navigate the intricate complexities of this information deluge and leverage it to inform strategic decision-making. Enter the recommender system, a powerful tool for predictive analytics that can illuminate the future of brand performance and propel growth in a dynamic and ever-changing market.

This chapter delves into the intricate relationship between predictive analytics and strategic brand management (Elliott et al., 2015), highlighting the profound impact of recommender systems on the trajectory of brands in the digital age. We examine how these systems, powered by the cutting-edge algorithms of machine learning and artificial intelligence (Bansal et al., 2022), can decipher the hidden patterns within vast datasets, enabling brands to forecast consumer demand with unprecedented accuracy, identify emerging market trends, and proactively manage risks and opportunities for growth.

The era of data-driven decision-making is upon us, and recommender systems (Badouch, M., and Boutaounte, M., 2025) are at the forefront of this revolution. They enable brands to move beyond reactive strategies, embracing a proactive approach to shaping their destinies in the face of continuous disruption. This chapter will explore the mathematical underpinnings of predictive analytics, the algorithmic techniques employed in recommender systems, and the ethical considerations surrounding the use of these powerful tools. We will examine the potential for algorithmic bias, data privacy violations, and the erosion of consumer trust, and propose strategies for ensuring fairness, transparency, and accountability in AI-driven brand management. This exploration will provide a comprehensive understanding of how recommender systems are transforming brand management, paving the way for a more informed and sustainable future in the dynamic digital landscape.

2. THE DATA DELUGE AND THE RISE OF PREDICTIVE ANALYTICS:

The digital age has ushered in a new era of data abundance, with businesses collecting vast amounts of information on consumer behavior, online activity, and market trends (Rosário, A., and Raimundo, R., 2021). This data deluge, characterized by an exponential growth in the volume, variety, and velocity of data, presents a unique challenge and opportunity for brands. Consider the sheer scale of data being generated daily:

- Online Shopping: Globally, e-commerce sales reached 4.2 trillion dollars in 2021, with billions of transactions and customer interactions generating a vast amount of data on purchase history, product preferences, and browsing behavior (Statista.com). This data can be analyzed by recommender systems to provide personalized recommendations, predict future purchases, and optimize marketing campaigns (Koehn et al., 2020).
- Social media: Platforms like Facebook, Instagram, and Twitter generate an unimaginable amount of user-generated content, including text, images, videos, and interactions (Chawla, Y., and Chodak, G., 2021). This data, rich with insights into consumer sentiment, cultural trends, and online behavior, can be analyzed by AI algorithms to identify emerging trends, understand audience preferences, and tailor marketing messages. For example, Natural Language Processing (NLP) algorithms can analyze social media posts to identify key topics, understand customer sentiment, and track the effectiveness of brand campaigns (Hodorog et al., 2022).
- Mobile Devices: The proliferation of smartphones and mobile devices has further accelerated the generation of massive amounts of data. This data encompasses location data, app usage patterns, and online searches, providing valuable insights into consumer behavior and preferences (Stachl et al., 2020). Recommender systems can leverage this data to offer personalized location-based recommendations, suggest relevant apps, and tailor online experiences.

This data deluge is not merely a collection of numbers; it is a complex and dynamic system that can be analyzed to uncover hidden patterns and predict future outcomes. The challenge lies in harnessing this data richness to extract valuable insights and inform strategic brand decisions. Recommender systems, with their sophisticated algorithms and machine learning capabilities, are playing a crucial role in this data-driven revolution.

Beyond the "Why" to the "What If": Recommender systems are not simply tools for suggesting products or content; they are powerful engines of prediction, capable of revealing the unseen forces shaping consumer behavior and market dynamics. By going beyond simple descriptive analytics and exploring causal relationships within data, these systems can provide valuable insights into the future of brand performance, enabling brands to anticipate trends, manage risks, and capitalize on opportunities with greater precision. This shift from descriptive to predictive analytics allows brands to make more informed strategic decisions, optimize resources, and proactively adapt to the ever-changing demands of the marketplace.

- **A retail store**: Could use time series analysis to analyze historical sales data for a specific product category, identifying seasonal patterns, day-of-week trends, and the impact of marketing campaigns (Bellini et al., 2023). This analysis can help them optimize stock levels, plan promotions, and anticipate demand for different product lines.
- **A social media platform**: Could utilize machine learning algorithms to analyze user engagement data, identifying users with similar preferences and behaviors. This information can then be used to personalize content recommendations, create targeted advertising campaigns, and improve user experience.
- **A financial institution**: Could use predictive modeling to forecast customer churn and identify potential risks of fraud. By analyzing customer behavior, transaction history, and demographic data, the institution can develop models that predict the likelihood of customers leaving and identify suspicious activity (de Lima Lemos et al., 2022). This information can be used to implement targeted retention strategies and proactively prevent fraud.

3. THE MATHEMATICAL FOUNDATIONS OF PREDICTIVE ANALYTICS

Predictive analytics relies on a foundation of mathematical modeling and statistical analysis. Recommender systems employ various techniques to forecast consumer behavior and identify market trends. These techniques often involve:

- **Time Series Modeling:** This approach analyzes historical data points over time to identify patterns and predict future values. Recommender systems can utilize time series analysis to forecast consumer demand, predict seasonal fluctuations, and optimize inventory management. For instance, a brand might use a moving average model to predict future sales based on historical data, or a ARIMA model (Autoregressive Integrated Moving Average) to incorporate trends and seasonality (Khan, S., and Alghulaiakh, H., 2020).

Figure 1. Example of Time Series Plot of Daily Sales Data for a Brand's Product.

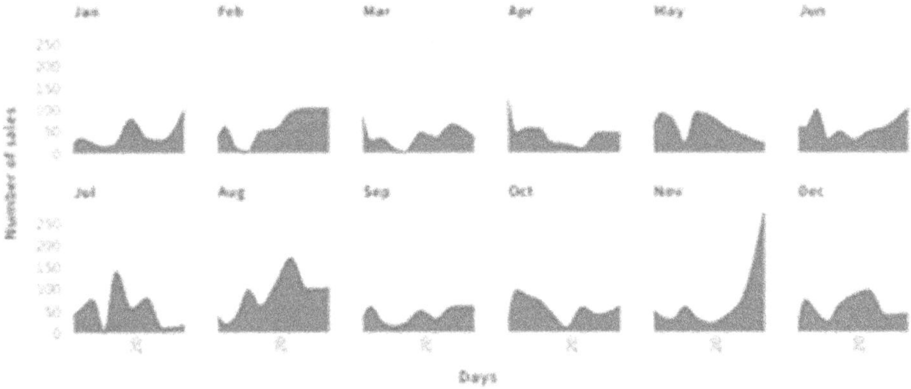

- **Regression Analysis:** This statistical technique models the relationship between a dependent variable (e.g., sales, customer engagement) and one or more independent variables (e.g., marketing spend, product features, seasonal factors). Recommender systems (Singh et al., 2021) can use regression analysis to predict future customer behavior based on various factors. For example, a brand might use linear regression to model the relationship between advertising expenditure and sales (Atulkar, 2020), or multiple regression to incorporate multiple predictors, such as price, promotions, and competitor activity.

Figure 2. Scatter Plot of Advertising Expenditure vs. Sales for a Brand.

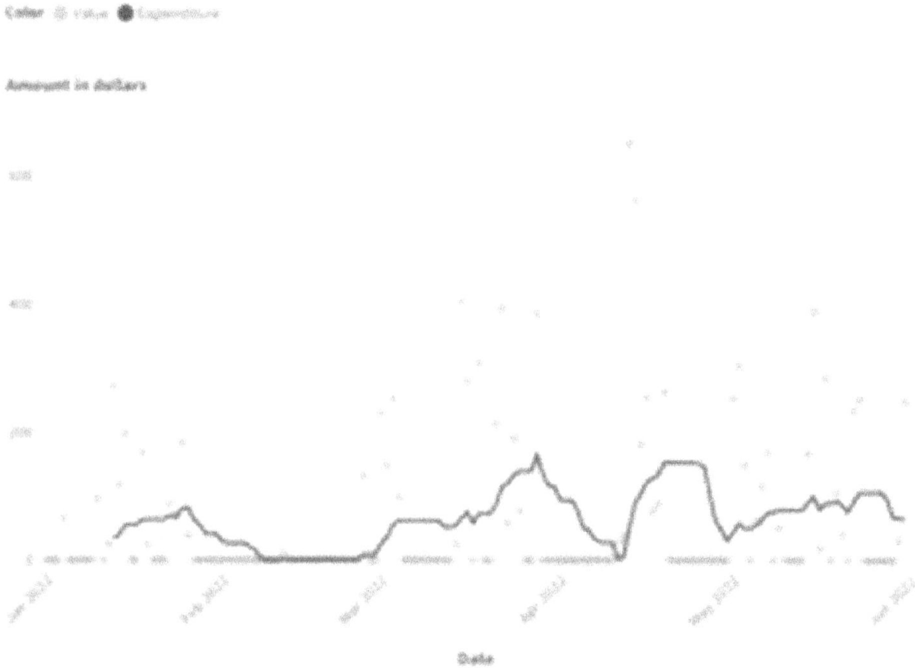

- **Machine Learning Algorithms:** A wide range of machine learning algorithms are employed in recommender systems to analyze complex data patterns and make predictions (Badouch, M., and Boutaounte, M., 2024). These algorithms often involve supervised learning, where the model is trained on labeled data, and unsupervised learning, where the model discovers patterns in unlabeled data. Popular machine learning algorithms used in recommender systems include:
  - **Random Forest:** This ensemble learning method combines multiple decision trees to improve prediction accuracy and reduce overfitting (Palimkar et al. 2022).
  - **Gradient Boosting:** This technique builds a sequence of weak learners (e.g., decision trees) that are combined to create a strong predictive model (Singh et al., 2021).
  - **Neural Networks:** These algorithms are inspired by the structure of the human brain, allowing them to learn complex patterns and relationships in data (Gao et al. 2023). Neural networks are increasingly used

in recommender systems for tasks such as predicting customer churn, identifying fraudulent activity, and recommending products.

- o **Bayesian Networks:** These graphical models represent probabilistic relationships between variables, allowing for the prediction of future events based on uncertain or incomplete data (Kirubahari, R., and Amali, S. M. J., 2024). Bayesian networks are particularly useful for situations where there is uncertainty or variability in the data.
- o **Markov Chains:** These stochastic processes model sequences of events, allowing for the prediction of future states based on current conditions. Markov chains can be used to model customer behavior and predict future purchases (Wang et al., 2021).

4. DATA-DRIVEN INSIGHTS: UNVEILING THE POWER OF BIG DATA

The success of predictive analytics in brand management hinges on the ability to effectively analyze and interpret vast amounts of data. Big data, with its unprecedented volume, variety, and velocity, offers a wealth of insights into consumer behavior, market trends, and the potential for brand growth (Perera, A., and Iqbal, K., 2021). However, raw data can be overwhelming and difficult to comprehend. This is where data visualization tools come into play, providing a crucial bridge between the complex data and actionable insights. By transforming data into visual representations, brands can uncover hidden patterns, identify key trends, and make more informed strategic decisions.

4.1. Visualizing Consumer Behavior and Market Dynamics:

Data visualization techniques can be used to represent complex data in ways that are easily understood and interpreted. Here are some examples of how data visualization can be employed in brand management:

- **Customer Segmentation:** Heat maps can be used to visualize customer segments based on their purchase history and online behavior. By analyzing data on demographics, purchase frequency, and product preferences, brands can identify distinct groups of customers and tailor their strategies accordingly (Alves Gomes, M., and Meisen, T., 2023).

Figure 3. A Heat Map Visualizing Population Segmentation

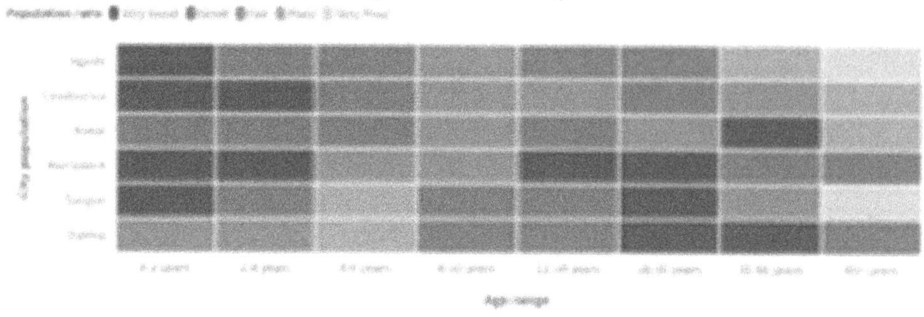

This heat map illustrates the population distribution by age group in five different Moroccan cities: Agadir, Casablanca, Rabat, Marrakech, Tangier, and Dakhla. It uses color-coded bars to represent the proportion of the population in each city that falls within different age ranges. Brands can use this visualization to identify key customer segments, understand their unique needs and preferences, and personalize their marketing messages.

- **Sentiment Analysis and Market Trends:** Trend line graphs can be used to visualize the correlation between social media sentiment and sales performance over time (Xu et al., 2022). By analyzing customer reviews, social media posts, and online forums, brands can track changes in consumer sentiment and identify potential risks or opportunities.

Figure 4. A Trend Line Graph Illustrating Correlation Between Social Media Sentiment and Interactions

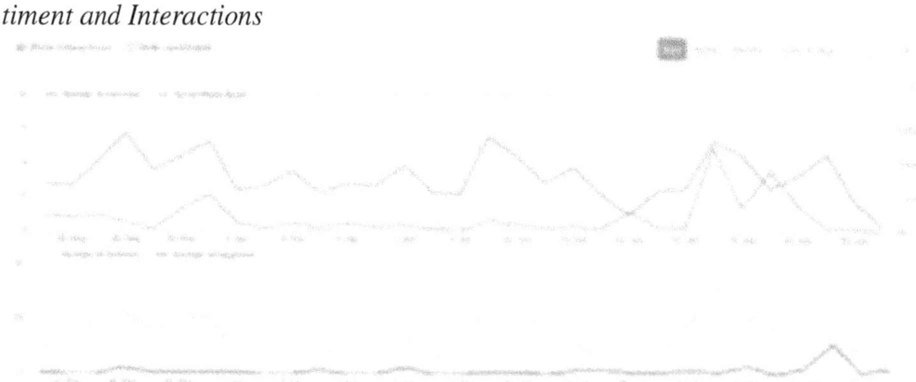

This graph shows how social media sentiment (measured by the frequency of positive and negative mentions) correlates with interactions (potential sales) performance over time. By analyzing this data, brands can identify trends, understand the impact of marketing campaigns, and proactively address potential challenges.

- **Predictive Modeling and Risk Management:** Data visualizations can be used to display the output of predictive models and visualize the factors that contribute to predictions. This can help brands understand the underlying drivers of customer behavior and manage risks more effectively.

Figure 5 provides a visual representation of the customer journey through a sales funnel, illustrating the flow of potential customers from awareness to purchase. By highlighting areas where customers drop off, it pinpoints bottlenecks and identifies factors contributing to customer acquisition. This visualization enables businesses to analyze their sales funnel, optimize marketing campaigns, and improve conversion rates by understanding customer behavior and identifying areas for improvement, such as a poor user experience, ineffective content, or pricing issues. The diagram's visual clarity facilitates data-driven decision-making, leading to continuous improvement in the sales funnel and ultimately, increased customer acquisition.

Figure 5. A Sankey Diagram Showing the Flow of Customers Through the Sales Funnel

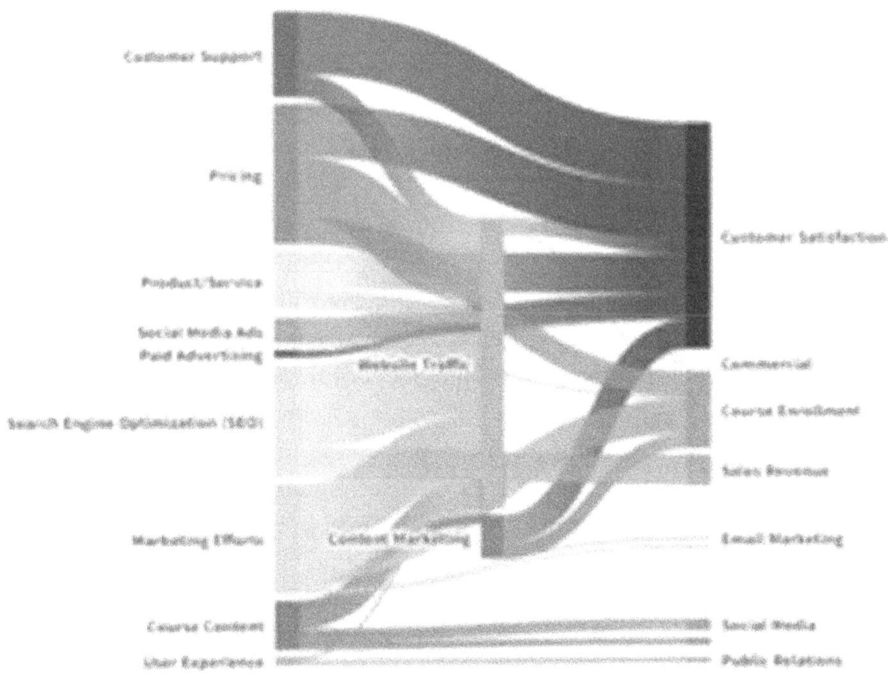

4.2. The Importance of Data Visualization in Brand Management:

Data visualization plays a crucial role in making sense of the data deluge and informing strategic decisions. By presenting complex information in a clear and accessible manner, visualization tools enable brands to:

- **Gain Deeper Insights:** Visualizations help to identify patterns, trends, and outliers that might not be apparent in raw data. This allows brands to understand the underlying dynamics of consumer behavior and market trends.
- **Improve Communication and Collaboration:** Visualizations facilitate effective communication of insights across teams and departments, enabling stakeholders to understand and interpret complex data in a shared and collaborative manner.
- **Drive Actionable Decisions** (Pearman, O., and Cravens, A. E., 2022): By providing a clear and concise view of data, visualization tools support informed decision-making and guide strategic initiatives. Brands can use visualizations to prioritize investments, optimize resource allocation, and develop effective marketing campaigns.
- **Enhance Trust and Transparency:** By showcasing data in a transparent and accessible manner, brands can build trust with their customers and stakeholders. Visualizations can help to communicate complex information in a way that is both informative and engaging.

5. ETHICAL CONSIDERATIONS AND THE FUTURE OF PREDICTIVE ANALYTICS

The use of predictive analytics in brand management raises important ethical considerations, particularly regarding data privacy, algorithmic bias, and the potential for manipulation. It is crucial for brands to prioritize fairness, transparency, and accountability in the development and deployment of these technologies:

- **Algorithmic Bias:** AI algorithms can perpetuate biases present in the data used to train them, leading to unfair or discriminatory outcomes. This bias can manifest in various forms, from gender bias in hiring recommendations to racial bias in loan applications. Brands must be vigilant in identifying and mitigating these biases to ensure that their predictive models are fair and equitable.

- **Data Privacy:** The use of personal data for predictive analytics raises concerns about privacy and the potential for misuse. Brands must comply with relevant regulations (e.g., GDPR, CCPA) and prioritize data security and privacy (Pantelic et al., 2022). This includes obtaining informed consent from consumers, implementing robust data anonymization techniques, and ensuring that data is used only for the intended purpose.
- **Transparency and Accountability:** Consumers need to understand how predictive analytics is being used to inform their experiences. Brands should be transparent about the data they are collecting (Krafft et al., 2021), the algorithms they are using, and the potential implications of these technologies. This transparency can help build trust with customers and mitigate concerns about manipulation.

6. CONCLUSION

Predictive analytics is a powerful tool for brand management that can help businesses anticipate market trends, identify opportunities, and drive sustainable growth. By leveraging the mathematical foundations of these technologies and analyzing big data, brands can gain a deeper understanding of consumer behavior and make informed decisions that will lead to greater success in the competitive landscape. However, it is essential to address the ethical considerations of predictive analytics, ensure fairness and transparency, and prioritize the protection of consumer privacy and trust. By embracing a responsible and ethical approach to predictive analytics, brands can harness the power of data and unlock new possibilities for growth in the age of AI.

7. FURTHER RESEARCH

Further research should delve into the intricate interplay between algorithmic fairness, data privacy, and the potential for manipulation in AI-driven brand management. Specifically, researchers should explore the development of fairness-aware recommender systems (Jin et al., 2023) that can mitigate bias in product recommendations based on demographic factors, past purchase history, and online behavior. For instance, examining how counterfactual analysis (e.g., using Shapley values to quantify the contribution of individual features to model predictions) can be used to identify and address biases in predictive models for customer churn, allowing brands to understand how different demographic groups are impacted by their algorithms. Furthermore, investigating the use of differential privacy techniques (e.g., applying

Laplacian noise to sensitive data) to anonymize user data and protect individual privacy while still enabling accurate predictive modeling (Zheng et al., 2022). This could involve developing privacy-preserving recommender systems that can generate personalized recommendations without compromising user data. Moreover, exploring explainable AI techniques (e.g., LIME, SHAP) to provide greater transparency into the decision-making processes of recommender systems (Roberts et al., 2022), allowing brands and consumers to understand how recommendations are generated and to identify potential areas of bias or unfairness. For example, developing visualizations and dashboards to illustrate how AI models are making predictions and the factors that are most influential in those predictions, while also employing interpretable machine learning models (e.g., decision trees, rule-based systems) to provide more accessible explanations of the underlying logic. This would facilitate a more informed understanding of how AI is shaping customer experiences and enable brands to make more ethical and responsible decisions. Finally, researchers should explore the impact of AI-driven prediction on consumer behavior and market dynamics, considering the potential for manipulation, information overload, and the erosion of consumer trust (Raji et al., 2024). Examining how AI algorithms are being used to influence consumer choices and the potential for these algorithms to create "filter bubbles" (Aridor et al., 2020) that limit exposure to diverse perspectives and information, while also exploring the ethical implications of AI-driven personalization and the potential for algorithmic manipulation of consumer preferences.

By incorporating these mathematical concepts, algorithms, and statistical techniques, researchers can further refine their studies on the ethical and societal implications of AI-driven prediction in brand management. This will allow them to develop more sophisticated methodologies for evaluating the fairness, transparency, and accountability of these systems, and to contribute to a more nuanced understanding of the complex relationship between AI, consumer behavior, and the future of marketing.

8. REFERENCES

Alves Gomes, M., & Meisen, T. (2023). A review on customer segmentation methods for personalized customer targeting in e-commerce use cases. *Information Systems and e-Business Management*, 21(3), 527–570. DOI: 10.1007/s10257-023-00640-4

Aridor, G., Goncalves, D., & Sikdar, S. (2020, September). Deconstructing the filter bubble: User decision-making and recommender systems. In *Proceedings of the 14th ACM conference on recommender systems* (pp. 82-91). DOI: 10.1145/3383313.3412246

Atulkar, S. (2020). Brand trust and brand loyalty in mall shoppers. *Marketing Intelligence & Planning*, 38(5), 559–572. DOI: 10.1108/MIP-02-2019-0095

Badouch, M., & Boutaounte, M. (2024). Design and Implementation of a Hotel Recommendation System Using Deep Learning. In *AI and Data Engineering Solutions for Effective Marketing* (pp. 388–408). IGI Global. DOI: 10.4018/979-8-3693-3172-9.ch019

Badouch, M., & Boutaounte, M. (2025). Smart E-commerce Recommendations with Semantic AI. Fusion. *Practice and Applications*, 17(1), 264–271. https://doi .org/10.54216/FPA.170120

Bansal, M., Goyal, A., & Choudhary, A. (2022). A comparative analysis of K-nearest neighbor, genetic, support vector machine, decision tree, and long short term memory algorithms in machine learning. *Decision Analytics Journal*, 3, 100071. DOI: 10.1016/j.dajour.2022.100071

Bellini, P., Palesi, L. A. I., Nesi, P., & Pantaleo, G. (2023). Multi clustering recommendation system for fashion retail. *Multimedia Tools and Applications*, 82(7), 9989–10016. DOI: 10.1007/s11042-021-11837-5 PMID: 35043044

Chawla, Y., & Chodak, G. (2021). Social media marketing for businesses: Organic promotions of web-links on Facebook. *Journal of Business Research*, 135, 49–65. DOI: 10.1016/j.jbusres.2021.06.020

Elliott, R. H., Rosenbaum-Elliott, R., Percy, L., & Pervan, S. (2015). *Strategic brand management.* Oxford University Press.

Hodorog, A., Petri, I., & Rezgui, Y. (2022). Machine learning and Natural Language Processing of social media data for event detection in smart cities. *Sustainable Cities and Society*, 85, 104026. DOI: 10.1016/j.scs.2022.104026

Kirubahari, R., & Amali, S. M. J. (2024). An improved restricted Boltzmann machine using Bayesian optimization for recommender systems. *Evolving Systems*, 15(3), 1099–1111. DOI: 10.1007/s12530-023-09520-1

Krafft, M., Kumar, V., Harmeling, C., Singh, S., Zhu, T., Chen, J., Duncan, T., Fortin, W., & Rosa, E. (2021). Insight is power: Understanding the terms of the consumer-firm data exchange. *Journal of Retailing*, 97(1), 133–149. DOI: 10.1016/j.jretai.2020.11.001

Palimkar, P., Shaw, R. N., & Ghosh, A. (2022). Machine learning technique to prognosis diabetes disease: Random forest classifier approach. In *Advanced computing and intelligent technologies: proceedings of ICACIT 2021* (pp. 219–244). Springer Singapore. DOI: 10.1007/978-981-16-2164-2_19

Pantelic, O., Jovic, K., & Krstovic, S. (2022). Cookies implementation analysis and the impact on user privacy regarding GDPR and CCPA regulations. *Sustainability (Basel)*, 14(9), 5015. DOI: 10.3390/su14095015

Pearman, O., & Cravens, A. E. (2022). Institutional barriers to actionable science: Perspectives from decision support tool creators. *Environmental Science & Policy*, 128, 317–325. DOI: 10.1016/j.envsci.2021.12.004

Raji, M. A., Olodo, H. B., Oke, T. T., Addy, W. A., Ofodile, O. C., & Oyewole, A. T. (2024). E-commerce and consumer behavior: A review of AI-powered personalization and market trends. GSC Advanced Research and Reviews, 18(3), 066-077.

Roberts, C. V., Elahi, E., & Chandrashekar, A. (2022). On the bias-variance characteristics of lime and shap in high sparsity movie recommendation explanation tasks. arXiv preprint arXiv:2206.04784.

Rosário, A., & Raimundo, R. (2021). Consumer marketing strategy and E-commerce in the last decade: A literature review. *Journal of Theoretical and Applied Electronic Commerce Research*, 16(7), 3003–3024. DOI: 10.3390/jtaer16070164

Singh, P. K., Pramanik, P. K. D., Dey, A. K., & Choudhury, P. (2021). Recommender systems: An overview, research trends, and future directions. *International Journal of Business and Systems Research*, 15(1), 14–52. DOI: 10.1504/IJBSR.2021.111753

Stachl, C., Au, Q., Schoedel, R., Gosling, S. D., Harari, G. M., Buschek, D., Völkel, S. T., Schuwerk, T., Oldemeier, M., Ullmann, T., Hussmann, H., Bischl, B., & Bühner, M. (2020). Predicting personality from patterns of behavior collected with smartphones. *Proceedings of the National Academy of Sciences of the United States of America*, 117(30), 17680–17687. DOI: 10.1073/pnas.1920484117 PMID: 32665436

Zuo, M., Liu, H., Zhu, H., & Gao, H. (2019). Dynamic property of consumer-based brand competitiveness (CBBC) in human interaction behavior. *Industrial Management & Data Systems*, 119(6), 1223–1241. DOI: 10.1108/IMDS-09-2018-0403

Chapter 15
Tourists' Winery Experiences in Portugal, New Zealand, and the United States:
A Review of User-Generated Content on TripAdvisor Using Business Intelligence and Orange Analytical

Eric Owusu Asamoah
https://orcid.org/0000-0003-0629-4778
Faculty of Economics, Universidade do Algarve, Portugal

Fatumata Ba
Faculty of Economics, Universidade do Algarve, Portugal

Ugbong Jessica Uwayin
Faculty of Economics, Universidade do Algarve, Portugal

Célia M.Q. Ramos
https://orcid.org/0000-0002-3413-4897
CinTurs, ESGHT, Universidade do Algarve, Portugal

ABSTRACT

User-generated content (UGC) is becoming common in wine tourism. People create texts, videos, and pictures to share online and inform others about their experiences

DOI: 10.4018/979-8-3693-9461-8.ch015

at wine destinations. UGC, coupled with managerial creativity and innovation, are essential to the growth of wineries as they offer insights into tourists' tastes and preferences, enhance brand awareness and reach and build trust between visitors and wine destinations. As popular wine tourism destinations, TripAdvisor comments published by tourists who visited Portugal, New Zealand, and the United States were copied and examined using Power BI and Orange. The wine industry commands a significant market value, while wine tourism is a substantial component of economic development in wine-producing countries. Also, the study revealed some tourists prefer to keep their identities hidden during online reviews. Seasonality is another issue that affects tourist destinations globally. The study concluded wine tourists will travel either domestically or abroad to wine destinations that offer the best services and experiences.

INTRODUCTION

Wine tourism is a recognizable niche within the tourism sector, attracting enthusiastic people seeking captivating experiences in wine-producing regions globally (Benoît et al., 2019; Garner & Kim, 2022). Wine tourism is traced to ancient times, although it became a structured sector in the 20th century (Kubát et al., 2024). Among the factors that affect tourists' decisions and experiences in wine destinations, user-generated content (UGC) on interactive media platforms such as TripAdvisor (Qin et al., 2024) is highly valuable. The information gleaned from these digital communication channels is deemed credible and greatly influences tourists' perceptions and purchase behaviors (Lim et al., 2017). This chapter investigates tourists' experiences in renowned wine destinations of Portugal, New Zealand and the United States, using Power BI and Orange data analytical tools to review UGC on TripAdvisor about vineyards in these areas. The specific objective is to evaluate tourists' sentiments, tastes, and preferences and their implications for tourism destinations.

The article has diverse sections. The next chapter is a literature review that shares insights about UGC, tourists' motivations to share their experiences on common online platforms used and the intended gap this study aims to fill. The third chapter discusses the methodology employed in the research. The results are presented and analyzed in the fourth section, with a conclusion, study limitations and possible future research scope as the last chapter of this work.

BACKGROUND

Definition of User-generated Content (UGC)

Many authors have defined UGC in several ways. Daugherty et al. (2008) posit that UGC is the online content created by the general public, other than paid third parties or influencers. In other words, UGC is the text, video, audio or image a tourist shares on Facebook, YouTube, TripAdvisor and Instagram at the point of consumption or after the experience to inform people about particular destinations (Garner & Kim, 2022; Saini et al., 2023). However, the definition of UGC as "content created by consumers that include social media posts, blogs and comments on online reviews of businesses" by Garner and Kim (2022, p. 414) fits the purpose of this study. The choice for the above description of UGC is the inclusion of most contemporary media consumers use to exchange information. Moreover, the data set for this research is from the TripAdvisor webpage.

UGC in Wine Tourism

Wine tourists visit destinations for the multisensory experience of wine tasting and learning about local communities' culture and the history of winemaking. Specifically, the scenery, sounds, smell, texture, social activities, co-creation and purchases enrich the sensory and overall wine tourism experience (Brochado et al., 2021; Thanh & Kirova, 2018). Technology has significantly improved communication and consumer engagement with tourism products and services. Digital communication media, including blogs, websites, vlogging and online reviews, are more popular. As stated differently, electronic word of mouth (eWOM) has become a more convenient and preferred choice among consumers than traditional word of mouth (WOM). As a common form of eWOM, UGC has made webpages such as TripAdvisor gain prominence and grow in scope and impact (Pezenka &Weismayer, 2020). While Garner and Kim (2022) argued that the surge in online media communication is attributable to the tech-savvy nature of modern tourists, Qiu et al. (2024) claimed that UGC is a strategic tourism destination marketing tool that creates awareness, promotion and branding to affect tourists' behaviors and purchase decisions.

UGC is particularly significant for smaller tourism businesses since consumers that create online content are intrinsically motivated to share their experiences to enable the general public to make informed decisions rather than for commercial gains and at no cost to the vineyards (Garner and Kim; 2022; Manap & Adzharudin, 2013). Destination Management Organizations (DMOs) integrate content created by tourists with their marketing strategies to promote destinations in ways that appeal to consumers (Daugherty et al., 2008; Hays et al., 2013). Most importantly, UGC "...

provides cost-effective communication and widespread demographic reach…compared to traditional communication mediums" (Saini et al., 2023, p.21). Meanwhile, consumers may have diverse motives for publishing their post-purchase experiences, making the authenticity of UGC debatable (Saini et al., 2023).

As shown in Figure 1, tourists' choice of a destination largely follows the five stages of the consumer decision-making model (Cox et al., 2009). When travelers identify the desire to undertake leisure activities, they seek relevant information and analyze their options to avoid poor destination choices. "… more consumers use UGC... for initial information search and ... recommendations during the buying process" (Ana & Istudor, 2019, cited by Garner & Kim, 2022, p. 416). Notably, tourists visit various online channels, including TripAdvisor, to search for information about the destination, gastronomy, attractions, cost and transportation (Pan & Fesenmaier, 2006), making UGC imperative to promote wineries. Cox et al. (2009) reported that UGC in the form of videos, pictures and written travel reviews customers share on websites after purchase experiences is essential for prospective tourists and destinations. "Travel-related user-generated content is a crucial resource for aspiring travelers to envision previous travelers' experiences with destinations, amenities and eateries and all travel-related decision-making" (Saini et al., 2023, p.1 21).

Figure 1. The Tourist Destination Selection Process.

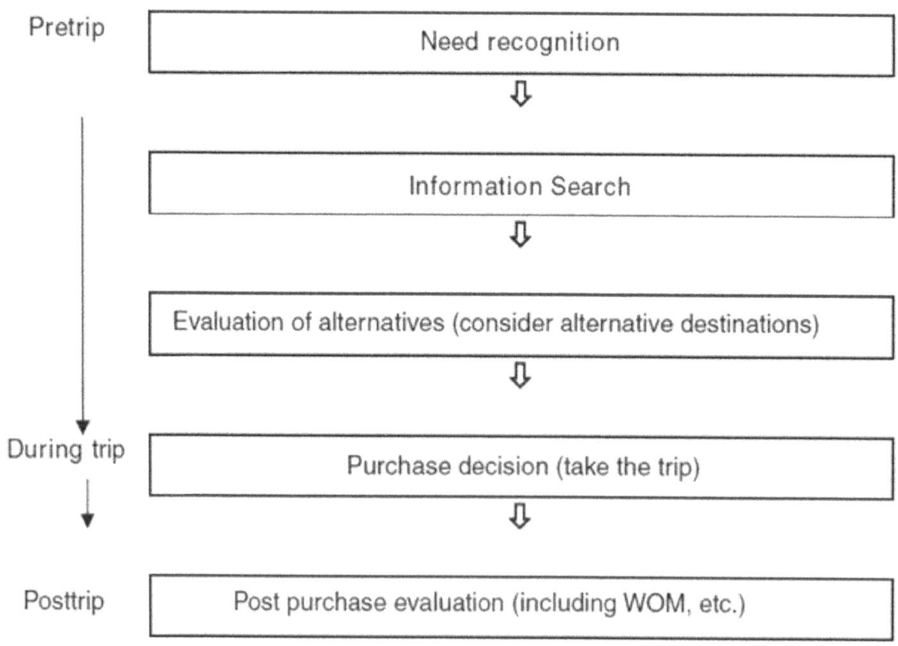

Source: Adapted from Cox et al. (2009, p. 745)

On the other hand, the authors Saini et al. (2023) argued that UGC is less significant compared to information provided by state tourism websites, accommodations providers and restaurants. They concluded that it is risky for destinations to overlook the usefulness of UGC. In other words, travelers have access to other sources of information. Therefore, wine destinations must explore the potential of these platforms/ channels to complement UGC rather than depending exclusively on it to maximize their reach, purchase and retention (Cox et al., 2009). In contrast, Dewantara et al. (2023) posit that UGC is a trusted source of information that tourists refer to for updates, trends and destinations before they purchase travel. Tourists perceive UGC as more accurate and valuable than information shared through traditional marketing media (Poulis et al., 2019). UGC potentially builds and sustains relationships between tourists and wineries, boosts sales and reinforces brand values (Kumar et al., 2016), although Bartoloni & Ancillai (2023) advised UGC may not rapidly increase sales. Wine-producing locations must strengthen their internal managerial resources and be creative and innovative to offer unique services or experiences to attract and retain clients. UGC "...from customers allows businesses to improve their product offerings" (Salem & Twining-Ward, 2018, p. 6).

To summarize, UGC has allowed wine tourists to become co-creators of value for the wineries they visit, using platforms like Booking.com, TripAdvisor, Expedia and Facebook to offer precious insights about consumers to enable brands to understand them better. Also, UGC, from these channels, helps destinations appraise customer satisfaction, review competitor offerings, and reflect on themselves to improve their products and services (Garner & Kim, 2022). UGC "provides extensive rich textual data and is a promising source ... to identify customer needs more efficiently,"(Timoshenko & Hauser, 2019, p. 2).

It is necessary to mention that a plethora of studies have examined the usefulness of UGC in the tourism sector (Albăstroiu & Felea, 2014; Ana & Istudor, 2019; Cox et al., 2009; Saini et al., 2023; Salem & Twining-Ward, 2018). Nevertheless, a gap remains regarding a comparative analysis of UGC selected from TripAdvisor about wineries in Portugal, New Zealand and the United States. This study fills this void by using Power B1 and Orange to evaluate comments published on TripAdvisor about selected vineyards to learn about wine tourism in these distinct places. Graham's Port Lodge, Porto, Portugal; Sculptureum Winery, Matakana, New Zealand; and 5-Hour Traverse City Winery, Michigan, United States, are chosen for this review. The focus is not on the above wineries per se but on the various comments published on TripAdvisor about them.

Wine Tourism

Wine tourism is "visitation to vineyards, wineries, wine festivals and wine shows for grape wine tasting and/or experiencing the attributes of a grape wine region" (Guzel & Gromova, 2016, p. 384). Wine tourism has witnessed significant growth in recent decades, leading to the development of many rural communities in wine-producing regions (Gu et al., 2020). It suffices to emphasize that wine and gastronomy are among the motivations for people to travel (World Food Travel Association, 2016). The tourists engage in wine-tasting and cellar door activities and show for the affective, sensorial and relational experiences offered (Gao et al., 2022). "In wine tourism, these experiences are considered hedonic in nature. That is, this is a type of tourism related to the search for pleasures ...," (Amaral et al., 2024, p.86). In sum, "a visit to a winery includes a complex set of value-creating aspects for tourists" (Gao et al., 2022, p. 2).

Characteristics of Wine Tourists

With the increasing popularity of wine tourism, it is appropriate to understand wine consumers and the factors that lend to their experiences. Usually, these tourists have higher expectations and incomes, may be domestic or out-of-state leisure seekers and prefer to travel alone than organized group tours. They demonstrate varying degrees of knowledge, engagement and involvement, which affects their purchase behaviors (Byrd et al., 2016; Garibaldi et al., 2017Tassiopoulos & Haydam, 2006). Wine tasting, education, savoring local cuisines, socialization with family and friends, getting to know the cultural heritage, history and art of winemaking and participating in wine-related activities and festivals are the common interests of wine tourists (Byrd et al., 2016; Charters & Ali-Knight, 2002). The higher the level of active participation in the wine tourism experiences, the more likely the consumer is wealthy and older. The younger tourists value the experiences offered, while elders place a premium on the actual wine product (Charters & Fountain, 2006; Nella & Christou, 2014).

In their study of wine tourism, Charters and Ali-Knight (2002) postulated four groups of wine tourists: wine lovers, wine interested, wine novices, and hangers-on. Wine lovers mainly have adequate knowledge about wines and travel to destinations to acquire further information about wineries and gastronomy. They tend to purchase wines during travels. Wine-interested tourists, compared to wine lovers, have a fair idea or education about wineries and are more motivated by wine-tasting experiences. On the other hand, wine novices are merely curious tourists without any education on wine tourism but are likely to visit vineyards to enjoy the taste of wines. The authors mentioned that hangers-ons are those wine tourists who visit wine tourism destinations as part of a group activity. In other words, hangers-ons have no interest in wine-related activities. They visit vineyards due to work commitments or necessity and are usually part of a larger group.

According to Thanh and Kirova's (2018) experiential model, wine tourists' attributes can be ascertained using the four parameters of education, entertainment, aesthetics, and escapist. Meanwhile, novelty, nostalgia and food are reasons wine tourists visit destinations (Crespi-Vallbona & Mascarilla-Miro, 2020). Both Alabaki and Iakovidou (2010) and Pratt (2014) proposed similar categorization of wine tourists like Charters and Ali-Knight (2002). Specifically, wine tourists fall among wine lovers, neophytes, occasional visitors and hangers-on (Alebaki & Iakovidou, 2010), while Pratt (2014) described wine tourists as wine lovers, wine interested, wine curious and wine disinterred.

Portugal, New Zealand and the United States as Wine Destinations

The total land area earmarked for wine production might have decreased, yet the demand for quality wines, sustainable wine production and the total volume of wines exported has grown exponentially (Jamali et al., 2020). To put it in perspective, a combination of ten countries of both the Old and New Wine Regions: France, Italy, Spain, United States, Australia and Portugal, to name but a few, produced 80% of the world's wine supply, which is about 35.1 billion bottles of wine (Guzel & Gromova, 2016). The Old Wine World, including Portugal, France, Italy and Spain, constituted 60% of wine consumption in 2014. The global wine industry has a mammoth market value of € 287 billion as of 2014. Worthy of reiterating is the significant role emerging wine regions are contributing to the global wine supply chain. For example, wine consumption in some parts of the emerging wine market rose from 6% in 2000 to 10% in 2014 (Benoît et al., 2019).

As a Mediterranean country, wine is ingrained in Portugal's culture, and wine production is one way the country expresses its visibility to the world (Guzel & Gromova, 2016). For instance, Portugal produced around 5,6 million hectoliters of wine in 2016. To a greater extent, wine is one of the main exports of the Iberian country. Additionally, wine tourism is among the rapidly growing sectors in Portugal and is crucial to boosting the country's economy. With its quality wine-making culture, Portuguese wines have become globally accepted brands, fetching the country several awards, notably a two–time UNESCO World Cultural and Natural Heritage plaque (do Nascimento Santos et al., 2020). To maintain the status of a top wine destination, stakeholders have invested heavily in research, technology, vineyard management, and production processes (Mendes, 2013). The beautiful landscapes, cuisine and weather add to her global appeal (Guzel & Gromova, 2016).

In the New World, the United States and New Zealand are the top wine exporters by volume in that area, with the United States leading in wine consumption (Benoît et al., 2019). New Zealand's wineries are a significant component of tourism in that region. Annually, 13% of visitors to New Zealand are wine tourists who tend to spend more and stay longer than regular travelers. Mouret et al. (2013) classified wine as a passion in New Zealand due to the locals' and visitors' deep appreciation of their vineyards and the immense role of the final product in their gastronomy and culture (Baird et al., 2018).

The United States is the only country from the New Wine World among the six highest wine-importing countries in the world, accounting for over 50% of imports valued at nearly € 4 billion. The United has emerged as a reputable wine destination, owing to its unique topography and climate. Approximately 90% of the United States wine is manufactured in California. Getz and Brown (2006) pointed out that the United States is a preferred wine destination for leisure seekers, with abundant agricultural regions and landscapes to support wine production.

METHODOLOGY

A mixed studies approach was employed (Grant & Booth, 2009), considering only academic works published between the early 2000s and 2024. For this study, the chosen journals were available in English on Web of Science, Google Scholar, Scopus and related databases using the keywords tourism, Portugal, New Zealand, United States, user-generated content, online reviews, electronic word of mouth, social media and associated topics to find articles. Following this was a rigorous thematic analysis of titles, abstracts and conclusions to identify common themes and papers fit for the study. Additionally, we searched the TripAdvisor website to identify wine destinations in Portugal, New Zealand and the United States, copying online reviews(texts) published about Portugal, New Zealand and the United States manually to Microsoft Excel, cleaned and used for analysis with the aid of Power BI and Orange.

The methodology considered in the present study aligns with the work of El-Masri et al. (2017) and Ramos (2022), where the data source considered was TripAdvisor.

As indicated earlier, many scholarly works abound about wines in the countries under consideration, and this study essentially seeks to see the type of views consumers express before, during, or after their post-purchase experience without particular emphasis on the wineries. The 5-star rated vineyards were selected and labeled 1, 2 and 3, with the comments from the TripAdvisor webpage published between 2021 and 2024.

RESULTS AND DISCUSSIONS

In terms of demographics, the study revealed many of the creators who published UGC did not mention their gender and nationalities. As shown in Figure 2 below, a colossal 92.71% of reviewers on TripAdvisor did not state their gender. These attributes were optional, although people prefer to remain anonymous online to hide themselves from those they know and "...disclose more online when the medium contains less information about real identity," (Kang et al., 2016).

Figure 2. Demographic characteristics of the UGC author's.

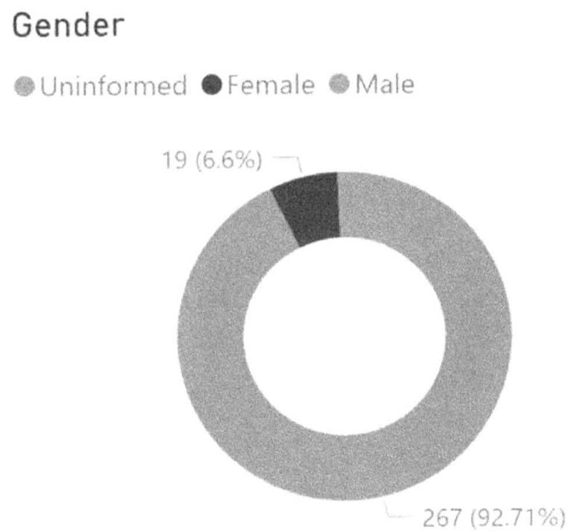

Source: Author's elaboration.

Kang et al. (2016) mentioned that tourists under disguise can express their positive and negative emotions. Wine tourists feel safe sharing their real experiences at vineyards when they do not have to reveal too much personal information. It is not always the case that UGC is online text. For example, some tourists share their experiences as videos, testimonials and product reviews via YouTube, Facebook and Instagram to influence online users (Alshuqaiqi & Omar, 2019). Saini et al. (2023) argued that the authenticity of UGC is debatable. Stated differently, tourists may decide only to share specific aspects of their travels when they are not anonymous, making the validity of their reviews questionable. People may create UGC for revenge. Some visitors blame wine destinations other than themselves for a bad experience, even when they are responsible for the negative outcome. Limba and Juozėnaitė (2024) used prospect and attribution theories to explain consumers' motives for negative reviews. They revealed that customers (visitors) would react differently based on whom they assume is responsible for bad outcomes. For example, when a tourist arrives at the winery on a wrong date and is turned away or made to reschedule the visit. As a result, they may publish poor comments about the destination without acknowledging their roles.

The reviews for the destination with Wine *ID 1*, see Figure 3, peaked in January, decreased to its lowest in October and rose again in November. Also, the reviews and/ or visitors declined slightly in December. Conversely, the reviews for Winery *ID 2* were minimal in the early months and peaked toward the end of the year, notably in September, as seen in Figure 4. And Winery *ID 3* is represented in Figure 5.

Figure 3. Winery ID 1 Review Ratings.

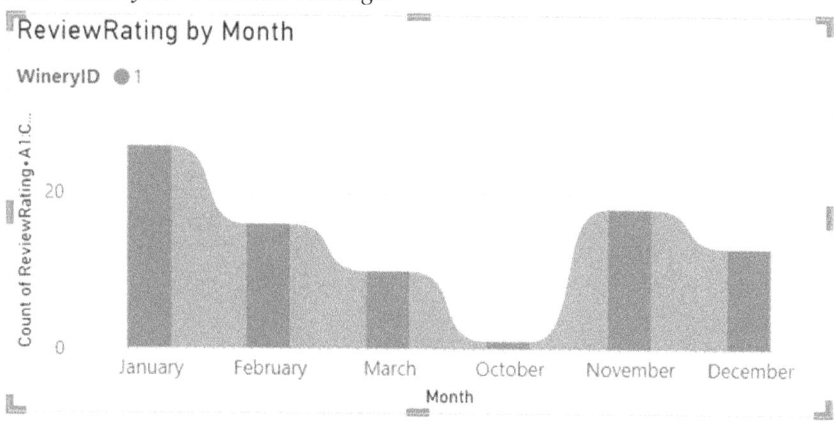

Source: Author's elaboration.

Figure 4. Winery ID 2 Review Ratings.

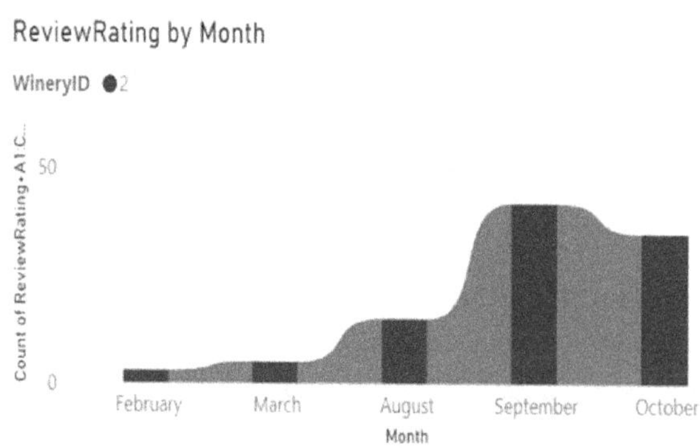

Source: Author's elaboration.

Figure 5. Winery ID 3 Review Ratings.

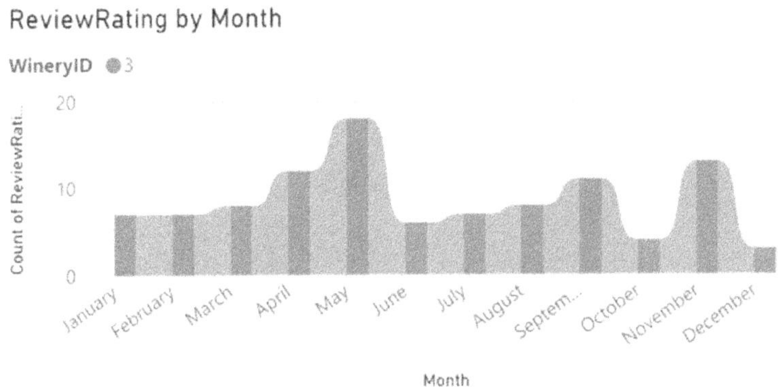

Source: Author's elaboration.

Winery with *ID 3* exhibited a steady rise in the early months, peaked in May, fell sharply in June, remained stable, fell again and heightened in November. One noticeable feature is that Winery *ID 3* received reviews (visitors) for all months of the year compared to the other two. It is imperative to stress that seasonality affects tourist destinations, which may explain the discrepancies in reviews or visitor numbers over the year at each destination. Corluka (2019) reported, "The majority of tourism destinations are characterized by fluctuations in tourism activities throughout the year.". Espinet et al. (2012) confirmed that seasonality is a permanent feature of tourism. Natural, institutional and human factors are some of the underlying causes of seasonality in tourism. For example, Spring and Fall alternate between the Northern and Southern Hemispheres, and a colder season in one place could lead to tourist exodus to substitute destinations. Tourists who like biking and the sun may visit warmer places during winter, which benefits the receiving locations at the expense of others. Wine destinations with more outdoor activities and facilities are prone to seasonality, even though there are activities which tourists may undertake, such as out-of-season displays, gastronomy events or competitions to attract visitors to address the visitor traffic fluctuations and seasonality altogether, keep businesses running and employees at work (Alshuqaiqi & Omar, 2019)

Figure 6. Ratings average by Country.

WineryID	1	2	3	4	5
1		1		7	76
2					100
3	1		3	11	89

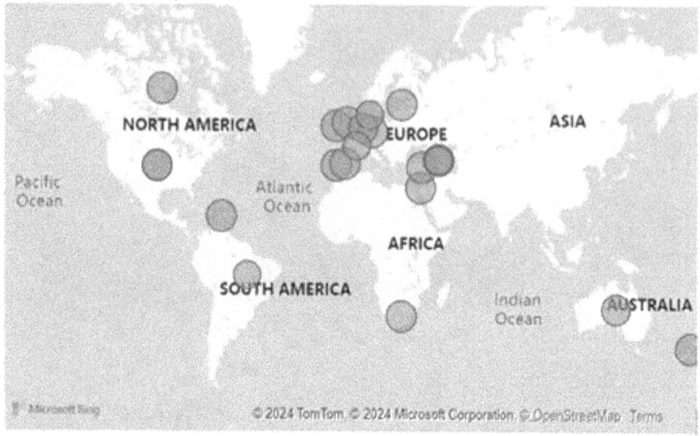

Source: Author's elaboration.

Figure 6, on the left, shows that most tourists rated all three wine destinations between one and five, with people from all corners of the world visiting owing to the quality services offered. Wine is a passion (Mouret et al., 2013), and wine destinations, notwithstanding their location, attract individuals from all walks of life, as seen in Figure 6 on the right. The study also revealed that wine tourists get value for their money at these destinations. The sentiments expressed online were positive and that of unique experiences. The comments in italics below are some excerpts of the online reviews extracted from the three regions:

"*The whole visit was a wonderful and inspirational experience. The staff were informative, friendly and welcoming. We will recommend a visit to our travelling friends.*" – Anonymous author

"*Excellent, so much more than we expected, something for all ages to enjoy. Will be back with the children and grandchildren for sure.*" – Unknown author.

"*Best art collectionI have ever seen, extremely well presented, varied and just amazing talent Thoroughly enjoyed our visit, gardens and displays are very well done and the operators/owners should be very proud. Staff were also very friendly and helpful and overall a most enjoyable experience. Highly recommended.*" – Anonymous writer.

Figure 7. Words Cloud.

Source: Author's elaboration.

From the excerpts of online reviews and the cloud of words generated above, it is possible to conclude that wine tourists are solely after unique experiences at the destinations they visit. Also, it clearly shows that vineyards are working hard to meet the demands of tourists. Most importantly, the study shows that wine tourists have common interests, tastes or preferences. As shown in Figure 9, exceptional, great, and excellent were some common sentiments. In essence, wine tourism "… is a type of tourism related to the search for pleasures…," (Zhang & Lee, 2022, cited by Amaral et al., 2024, p.86).

CONCLUSION

Wine and wine tourism have become part of human lives, dating back to ancient times. People from varied backgrounds travel far and near to visit vineyards in search of pleasures. Countries like Portugal, New Zealand and the United States have become common tourist destinations for wine lovers. Also, with the availability of technology, people can share their experiences at wine destinations. These days, consumers prefer to make videos or write texts online to share their opinions about places visited, otherwise termed UGC. They post UGC on YouTube, Facebook, TripAdvisor and Booking.com, to name but a few, enabling consumers to make informed choices before purchasing travel. The UGC copied and analyzed from TripAdvisor about wineries in the countries revealed that tourists desire unique experiences, making it imperative for DMOs, businesses and stakeholders involved in wine tourism to continually monitor UGC to provide the appropriate services for their customers. Yet, a destination's internal management, creativity and innovation are all relevant to meeting leisure seekers' demands.

The study had some limitations. Only a few wineries were selected, without much emphasis on the wineries but the comments about them. Nonetheless, the findings would allow managers to make the appropriate decisions for their business. Similarly, the study adds to the growing literature on tourism, data analytics and consumer behavior. Also, only a few scholars have done similar cross-regional exercises. Future studies could investigate more wineries in different areas.

ACKNOWLEDGMENT

This paper is financed by National Funds provided by FCT- Foundation for Science and Tech-nology through project UIDB/04020/2020 (CinTurs) and with DOI 10.54499/UIDB/04020/2020 (https://doi.org/10.54499/UIDB/04020/2020).

REFERENCES

Albăstroiu, I., & Felea, M. (2014). The implications of user-generated content websites for tourism marketing. *International Journal of Economic Practices and Theories*, 4(2), 222–229.

Alebaki, M., & Iakovidou, O. (2010). Segmenting the Greek wine tourism market using a motivational approach. *New Medit: Mediterranean Journal of Economics, Agriculture and Environment= Revue Méditerranéenne d Economie. Agriculture et Environment*, 9(4), 31.

Alshuqaiqi, A., & Omar, S. I. (2019). Causes and implication of seasonality in tourism. *Journal of Advanced Research in Dynamical and Control Systems*, 11(4), 1480–1486.

Amaral, M. M., Kuhn, V. R., dos Anjos, S. J. G., & Flores, L. C. D. S. (2024). Experiences in a wine tourism destination from the visitors' perspective. *International Journal of Wine Business Research*, 36(1), 85–102. DOI: 10.1108/IJWBR-05-2023-0028

Ana, M. I., & Istudor, L. G. (2019). The role of social media and user-generated-content in millennials' travel behavior. *Management Dynamics in the Knowledge Economy*, 7(1), 87–104. DOI: 10.25019/mdke/7.1.05

Baird, T., Hall, C. M., & Castka, P. (2018). New Zealand winegrowers attitudes and behaviours towards wine tourism and sustainable winegrowing. *Sustainability (Basel)*, 10(3), 797. DOI: 10.3390/su10030797

Bartoloni, S., & Ancillai, C. (2023). Twenty years of social media marketing: A systematic review, integrative framework, and future research agenda. *International Journal of Management Reviews*, 26(3), 435–457. DOI: 10.1111/ijmr.12360

Benoît, L., William, A., Lindsey, H., Adrienne, L. F., & Marianne, M. W. (2019). Wine sector: Definitions and nuances from global to country analysis—A comparison between Old World, New World, and emerging wine countries from 2005 to current. In *Case Studies in the Wine Industry* (pp. 7–32). Woodhead Publishing. DOI: 10.1016/B978-0-08-100944-4.00002-1

Brochado, A., Stoleriu, O., & Lupu, C. (2021). Wine tourism: A multisensory experience. *Current Issues in Tourism*, 24(5), 597–615. DOI: 10.1080/13683500.2019.1649373

Byrd, E. T., Canziani, B., Hsieh, Y. C. J., Debbage, K., & Sonmez, S. (2016). Wine tourism: Motivating visitors through core and supplementary services. *Tourism Management*, 52, 19–29. DOI: 10.1016/j.tourman.2015.06.009

Charters, S., & Ali-Knight, J. (2002). Who is the wine tourist? *Tourism Management*, 23(3), 311–319. DOI: 10.1016/S0261-5177(01)00079-6

Charters, S., & Fountain, J. (2006). Younger Wine Tourists: A study of generational differences in the cellar door experience. In *Global wine tourism: Research, management and marketing* (pp. 153–160). Cabi. DOI: 10.1079/9781845931704.0153

Corluka, G. (2019). Tourism seasonality–an overview. *Journal of Business Paradigms*, 4(1), 21–43.

Cox, C., Burgess, S., Sellitto, C., & Buultjens, J. (2009). The Role of User-Generated Content in Tourists' Travel Planning Behavior. *Journal of Hospitality Marketing & Management*, 18(8), 743–764. DOI: 10.1080/19368620903235753

Crespi-Vallbona, M., & Mascarilla-Miró, O. (2020). Wine lovers: Their interests in tourist experiences. *International Journal of Culture, Tourism and Hospitality Research*, 14(2), 239–258. DOI: 10.1108/IJCTHR-05-2019-0095

Daugherty, T., Eastin, M. S., & Bright, L. (2008). Exploring consumer motivations for creating user-generated content. *Journal of Interactive Advertising*, 8(2), 16–25. DOI: 10.1080/15252019.2008.10722139

Dewantara, M. H., Gardiner, S., & Jin, X. (2023). Travel vlog ecosystem in tourism digital marketing evolution: A narrative literature review. *Current Issues in Tourism*, 26(19), 3125–3139. DOI: 10.1080/13683500.2022.2136568

do Nascimento Santos, F. A., Vavdinos, N., & Martinez, L. F. (2020). Progress and prospects for research of Wine Tourism in Portugal. *Pasos (El Sauzal)*, 18(1), 159–170.

El-Masri, M., Altrabsheh, N., & Mansour, H. (2017). Successes and challenges of Arabic sentiment analysis research: A literature review. *Social Network Analysis and Mining*, 7(1), 1–22. DOI: 10.1007/s13278-017-0474-x

Espinet, J. M., Fluvià, M., Rigall-I-Torrent, R., & Saló, A. (2012). Hotel characteristics and seasonality in prices: An analysis using Spanish tour operators' brochures. *Tourism Economics*, 18(4), 749–767. DOI: 10.5367/te.2012.0145

Gao, D., Xia, H., Deng, W., Muskat, B., Li, G., & Law, R. (2022). Value creation in wine tourism–an exploration through deep neural networks. *Journal of Vacation Marketing*, 13567667221140605. Advance online publication. DOI: 10.1177/13567667221140605

Garibaldi, R., Stone, M. J., Wolf, E., & Pozzi, A. (2017). Wine travel in the United States: A profile of wine travellers and wine tours. *Tourism Management Perspectives*, 23, 53–57. DOI: 10.1016/j.tmp.2017.04.004

Garner, B., & Kim, D. (2022). Analyzing user-generated content to improve customer satisfaction at local wine tourism destinations: An analysis of Yelp and TripAdvisor reviews. *Consumer Behavior in Tourism and Hospitality*, 17(4), 413–435. DOI: 10.1108/CBTH-03-2022-0077

Getz, D., & Brown, G. (2006). Critical success factors for wine tourism regions: A demand analysis. *Tourism Management*, 27(1), 146–158. DOI: 10.1016/j.tourman.2004.08.002

Grant, M. J., & Booth, A. (2009). A typology of reviews: An analysis of 14 review types and associated methodologies. *Health Information and Libraries Journal*, 26(2), 91–108. DOI: 10.1111/j.1471-1842.2009.00848.x PMID: 19490148

Gu, Q., Qiu, H., King, B. E., & Huang, S. (2020). Understanding the wine tourism experience: The roles of facilitators, constraints, and involvement. *Journal of Vacation Marketing*, 26(2), 211–229. DOI: 10.1177/1356766719880253

Guzel, O., & Gromova, E. (2016). Wine tourism. *Global Issues and Trends in Tourism*, 383.

Hays, S., Page, S. J., & Buhalis, D. (2013). Social media as a destination marketing tool: Its use by national tourism organisations. *Current Issues in Tourism*, 16(3), 211–239. DOI: 10.1080/13683500.2012.662215

Jamali, H. R., Steel, C. C., & Mohammadi, E. (2020). Wine research and its relationship with wine production: A scientometric analysis of global trends. *Australian Journal of Grape and Wine Research*, 26(2), 130–138. DOI: 10.1111/ajgw.12422

Kang, R., Dabbish, L., & Sutton, K. (2016, February). Strangers on your phone: Why people use anonymous communication applications. In *Proceedings of the 19th ACM conference on computer-supported cooperative work & social computing* (pp. 359-370). DOI: 10.1145/2818048.2820081

Kubát, P., Králiková, A., & Ryglová, K. (2024). Shifting the Focus from mere Wine (and) Tourism to the Wine Destination and Winescape Concept. *Deturope-The Central European Journal of Regional Development and Tourism*, 15(3), 78–92. DOI: 10.32725/det.2023.018

Kumar, A., Bezawada, R., Rishika, R., Janakiraman, R., & Kannan, P. K. (2016). From Social to Sale: The Effects of Firm-Generated Content in Social Media on Customer Behavior. *Journal of Marketing*, 80(1), 7–25. DOI: 10.1509/jm.14.0249

Lim, X. J., Radzol, A. M., Cheah, J., & Wong, M. W. (2017). The impact of social media influencers on purchase intention and the mediation effect of customer attitude. *Asian Journal f Business Research*, 7(2), 19–36. DOI: 10.14707/ajbr.170035

Limba, T., & Juozėnaitė, E. (2024). Opportunities for Public Relations Specialists to Enhance their Knowledge in Managing Negative UGC. In *INTED2024 Proceedings* (pp. 1874-1883). IATED. DOI: 10.21125/inted.2024.0530

Manap, K. A., & Adzharudin, N. A. (2013, January). The role of user generated content (UGC) in social media for tourism sector. In *The 2013 WEI international academic conference proceedings* (Vol. 7, No. 1, pp. 52-58).

Mendes, A. R., Duarte, A. P., & Simões, M. C. (2013). The Portuguese wine sector: an export-led success story. In *Agriculture in Serbia and Portugal* (pp. 287–318). Recent Developments and Economic Policy Implications.

Mouret, M., Monaco, G. L., Urdapilleta, I., & Parr, W. V. (2013). Social representations of wine and culture: A comparison between France and New Zealand. *Food Quality and Preference*, 30(2), 102–107. DOI: 10.1016/j.foodqual.2013.04.014

Nella, A., & Christou, E. (2014). Segmenting wine tourists on the basis of involvement with wine. *Journal of Travel & Tourism Marketing*, 31(7), 783–798. DOI: 10.1080/10548408.2014.889639

Pan, B., & Fesenmaier, D. R. (2006). Online information search: Vacation planning process. *Annals of Tourism Research*, 33(3), 809–832. DOI: 10.1016/j.annals.2006.03.006

Pezenka, I., & Weismayer, C. (2020). Which factors influence locals' and visitors' overall restaurant evaluations? *International Journal of Contemporary Hospitality Management*, 32(9), 2793–2812. DOI: 10.1108/IJCHM-09-2019-0796

Poulis, A., Rizomyliotis, I., & Konstantoulaki, K. (2019). Do firms still need to be social? Firm generated content in social media. *Information Technology & People*, 32(2), 387–404. DOI: 10.1108/ITP-03-2018-0134

Qin, M., Qiu, S., Zhao, Y., Zhu, W., & Li, S. (2024). Graphic or short video? The influence mechanism of UGC types on consumers' purchase intention—Take Xiaohongshu as an example. *Electronic Commerce Research and Applications*, 65, 101402. DOI: 10.1016/j.elerap.2024.101402

Ramos, C. M. (2022). Business Intelligence Approach and Sentiment Analysis as a Management Strategy Applied to Study Customer Satisfaction in the Hospitality Sector. In *Advances in Tourism, Technology and Systems: Selected Papers from ICOTTS 2021* (Vol. 2, pp. 537–547). Springer Nature Singapore. DOI: 10.1007/978-981-16-9701-2_44

Saini, H., Kumar, P., & Oberoi, S. (2023). Welcome to the destination! Social media influencers as cogent determinant of travel decision: A systematic literature review and conceptual framework. *Cogent Social Sciences*, 9(1), 2240055. DOI: 10.1080/23311886.2023.2240055

Salem, T., & Twining-Ward, L. (2018). *The voice of travelers: leveraging user-generated content for tourism development*. World Bank., Available at https://openknowledge. worldbank.org/handle/10986/30451License:CCBY3.0IGO DOI: 10.1596/30451

Tassiopoulos, D., & Haydam, N. (2006). Wine tourists in South Africa: a demand-side study. In *Global wine tourism: Research, management and marketing* (pp. 141–152). Cabi. DOI: 10.1079/9781845931704.0141

Thanh, T. V., & Kirova, V. (2018). Wine tourism experience: A netnography study. *Journal of Business Research*, 83, 30–37. DOI: 10.1016/j.jbusres.2017.10.008

Timoshenko, A., & Hauser, J. R. (2019). Identifying customer needs from user-generated content. *Marketing Science*, 38(1), 1–20. DOI: 10.1287/mksc.2018.1123

World Food Travel Association. (2016). *The American Culinary Traveler: Profiles, Behaviors, and Attitudes*. World Food Travel Association.

KEY TERMS AND DEFINITIONS

Artificial intelligence: is the simulation of human intelligence processes, especially by computer systems. It presents many business potentialities, such as sales forecasting, customer segmentation, fraud detection, and quality control.

Business Intelligence: This results from information systems that combine data with analytical tools to provide information relevant to decision-making while seeking to improve the quality and availability of this information to decision-makers.

Data mining: The process of looking through big data sets to find trends, patterns, and important information. It entails applying methods from database systems, statistics, and machine learning to glean valuable insights from massive volumes of data. Through this process, businesses can find new possibilities, make data-driven decisions, and enhance many areas of their operations.

Online Review: Comments made by visitors about a service or tourist product, shared on social networks or travel websites, that convey a testimony of the experience lived during the visit.

Tourism: One of the largest industries in the world. It emerged to satisfy the human need to travel to and see different places as part of the service sector, including hospitality (e.g., accommodation, restaurants), transportation (e.g., airlines, car rental), travel facilitation and information (e.g., tour operators, tourist information centres), and attractions and entertainment (e.g., heritage sites and traditional and cultural events).

Tourism Experience: This is a set of activities in which individuals engage on their personal terms, such as pleasant and memorable places, allowing each tourist to build his or her own travel experiences so that these satisfy a wide range of personal needs, from pleasure to a search for meaning.

User-Generated Content (UGC): Shared content on social media that conveys an opinion about a product, which becomes a recommendation for future users looking for testimonials about the same product to support them in the decision-making process.

Wine tourism: Also referred to as enotourism or vinitourism, this travel industry segment includes visiting wineries, vineyards, wine-producing regions, and tasting rooms to sample, experience, and learn about wine. Wine tastings, vineyard and winery tours, and occasionally even harvesting are among the usual activities.

Chapter 16
The Influence of AI-driven Personalization on Customer Experiences:
A Case Study of Instagram

Waseem Hussain
https://orcid.org/0009-0003-4832-889X
National University of Modern Languages, Pakistan

ABSTRACT

The beginning of the digital revolution has significantly changed advertising and different management activities, mainly caused by easy access to enormous quantities of digitally transformed data and the incorporation of artificial intelligence (AI). The objective of this research is to investigate the effect of artificial intelligence-driven personalization (ADP) on customer Experience (CX) within the backdrop of Instagram, an influential social networking forum identified because of its novel implementation of AI. Instagram uses AI to evaluate user actions and choices, providing customized content that improves users enjoyment and fulfillment.

1. INTRODUCTION

Using technology that is now available to understand and interact with marketplaces has always been the goal of marketing. The arrival of the information age has brought about significant changes in advertising and other business operations (Xu et al., 2024). The availability of large databases of digital data represents a significant change (Abinesh et al., 2024). Technological advances has been instrumental in analyzing information, enhancing, and supporting decision-making by individuals.

DOI: 10.4018/979-8-3693-9461-8.ch016

As of right now, a multitude of algorithms are available that may analyze enormous volumes of data, gain knowledge via it, and use that information to make extremely intelligent decisions.Through work simplification, processing acceleration, and the use of data at levels exceeding individual's capabilities, this transforms job descriptions. AI, which includes machines' capacity to mimic intelligent human actions like acquiring knowledge and solving issues, is fundamental to this fundamental change (Thandayuthapani et al., 2024). The real difficulty for programmers is to create AI that can logic, acquire knowledge, and feel emotions on its own without assistance from humans (Ara et al., 2025). With real intelligence, this automated AI could be capable to take choices on its own (Mutyala et al., 2022). Modern social media networks include a strong AI integration, enabling robots to take part in interpersonal activities.In the background, AI-driven algorithms independently assess client feedback and conduct to discover their likes and dislikes (Whig et al., 2024). This makes it possible for the methods to choose customized material for every user. AI also improves producing material with capabilities like intelligent sound editing instruments and face-detecting filtration. Suggestions driven by AI help users grow their online communities even more (Thirupathi et al., 2024). Consequently, the use of AI technologies influences how customers engage and use social networks sites. Providing material on social networks that is customized to a the client's preferences and hobbies is known as customization (Akhtar et al., 2024). Personalization is essential in social business space because it creates value by making specific suggestions to each unique customer, which in turn encourages buying (Mutyala et al., 2022). However, according to Potla et al., (2024), personalization is the ability of a business to recognize every client as a person and handle them that way via specific interactions, like specific advertisements, customized provides, or customized actions, with the goal of improving the client's generally brand encounter and fostering loyalty. However, Gupta et al., (2022) suggests that personalization can come from businesses providing customized products or utilizing brand names in thanks, Alternatively, it could come from clients who customize the material of web pages.It is anticipated that AI has an enormous effect on personalization in advertising contexts (Potla et al., 2024). Akhtar et al., (2024) examined the relationship between personalization and AI, finding the usage and adoption of AI depend heavily on personalization. Personalization is now a core component of businesses globally, with a significant increase in importance following the incorporation of AI (Potla et al., 2024). Therefore, it is now easier for businesses to provide excellent Personalized services because to ADP abilities (Xu et al., 2024). The well-known social networking site Instagram uses AI in its activities, content distribution, and client relationships (Gujar et al., 2024). Instagram has been extremely common from its launch, and in 2022 it was the most downloaded app worldwide. Instagram, created by (Banik et al., 2024), rose to prominence in the social networks sphere by enticing users with its distinctive and fascinating user-generated material. The platform's algorithm is a crucial component. It acts as a search engine by selecting material for the For You page (FYP) based on users' browsing habits (Xu et al., 2024). This method allows CX to present a variety of material via the FYP, with the choice of content changing periodically in response to user behavior trends.Numerous studies were undertaken on ADP; nevertheless, the study by Xu et al., (2024) focused on web content distribution even though they discovered that ADP may provide tailored CX. Mutyala et al., (2022) claim that the introduction of ADP by AI has revolutionized the experiential advertising experiences of consumers. However, Gujar et al., (2024) also emphasizes the demand for more studies be conducted in order to fully understand the idea and implementation of ADP. After examining ADP in online shopping marketing, Bozkurt et al., (2025) point out that more studies may be needed to determine how much of an impact ADP has on buying habits. Singh et al., (2023) examine the various impacts of ADP, including how it influences consumer choice, how it builds confidence via open and honest business conduct, how it can gather comments and adjust to customized encounters, and how it helps to maintain loyal customers in the e-commerce industry. They assert that by providing relevant and tailored encounters, ADP is a key player that impacts consumer choices (Kannan et al., 2024). Whether ADP on web pages delivery or buyer habits on e-commerce is the focus of the prior studies. There wasn't any research done on the use of ADP and how it affects CX. Consequently, there's an investigation void in this field. Therefore, it is evident that there is not enough evidence on the impact of ADP on CX in overall, particularly when it comes to social networking sites. A single the top social media platforms, Instagram, is renowned for integrating analytics to draw users in and provide customized connections. To deliver provides, including information, suggestions, discounts, and so forth, tailored to the requirements and choices of consumers.Instagram affects client loyalty and CX through the use of ADP (Xu et al., 2024). Furthermore, argue that the capabilities of Instagram for customizing material turn the network into a digital playground that conflates social networking with artistic resources. With the wide range of lenses available, users may add flair to their clips and mimic the looks of superstars (Banik et al., 2024). Moreover, Instagram's method, which gives priority to client choices, has more influence than other networking sites' independently network-driven suggestion methods. Instagram is therefore a perfect place to obtain the relationship among CX and AI's analytical effect (Dai et al., 2024). Bhuiyan et al., (2024) found that AI has a good impact on CX and personalisation. They also conclude that the influence of AI on CX is significantly (42%) enhanced when Personalization serves as a middleman. Nevertheless, the impact of ADP on CX isn't investigated and evaluated in more detail through its incorporation of a particular company, like Instagram. Thus, the relationship among ADP and CX whenever Instagram incorporates AI was an issue the paper attempts to solve. More precisely, how ADP affects CX within the framework of Instagram.

1.2 Purpose

Examining ADP's effect on CX in the setting of perspective is the aim of this research. This study examines how Instagram uses AI to deliver ADP and examines the relationship within the CX and the ADP that Instagram provides. The Instagram CX as a whole becomes the main topic of this research.

2. LITERATURE REVIEW

These days, the field of AI is growing quickly, and academics are becoming more interested in examining how AI affects the marketing sector. The goal of study is to determine that AI and ADF may improve CX, which is going to end in greater client retention and more revenue. This segment will explore previous studies on AI, customization, customer experience, and their linkages. Coelho et al., (2025), "Marketing in Multimedia Electronic Circumstances intellectual basis," provides an important foundation for understanding how customization affects CX. The article is selected because it highlights the importance of personalization in such novel contexts and offers novel insights into way online surroundings change advertising tactics. Dai et al., (2024) is extremely pertinent to our research since it offers a comprehensive theoretical structure that emphasizes the significance of customized and collaborative advertising in multimedia settings—a feature that's increasingly essential to modern online advertising strategies. Gupta et al., (2022) explored the special qualities of multimedia electronic ecosystems (CMEs), emphasizing how they might promote an extremely customized and participatory CX. They contended that CMEs give advertisers the ability to produce customized knowledge and experiences that instantly adjust to the unique tastes and actions of each customer.Furthermore, the idea of the "motion" encountered in digital spaces constitutes one of the major theoretical developments of they proposed that personalized information that speaks to the individual's hobbies and requirements can lead to an experience of circulation, which is defined by complete participation and concentration (Bashyska et al., 2023). The resulting encounter demonstrates the substantial effect of customisation in CX by increasing customer pleasure and commitment. Singh et al., (2023) looked into how AI may improve customer experience in a variety of Pakistani businesses, such as finance and telecoms. This investigation emphasizes the life-changing effect of ADP in increasing CX, which makes it especially pertinent when conducting investigation into the benefits of personalization on CX. Hussain et al., (2023) used conversations and organized surveys as their primary means for gathering data. Representatives at two carefully chosen firms were interviewed to learn more about the possible advantages of implementing AI (Ara et al., 2025). Using both quantitative and qualitative evaluations, a closed-ended survey was used to gauge users' opinions toward AI.While the research recognized its drawbacks, including the limited sample size resulting from a small number of participants among the organizations chosen in Pakistan, its findings indicated a positive and substantial connection among CX and AI. Additionally, the data depended on predictions and assumptions because the organizations were still in the preparation stages of implementing AI (Asthana et al., 2024) notwithstanding these drawbacks, the results offer insightful information about the potential benefits of AI in customizing CX giving this research an important resource for investigating the wider effects of customization on CX. Heinemann et al., (2023) investigated the connection among AI and customized engagement advertising, offering information for this ADP study.The researchers emphasized how AI tools enable marketers to provide personalized and pertinent encounters to specific clients, hence improving connection and generating company outcomes (Ara et al., 2025). Organizations may deliver tailored information, suggestions, and conversations over various channels by utilizing AI-driven analysis and machine-learning algorithms to unlock useful knowledge about consumer needs and behaviors (Mukherjee et al., 2023). This involves harnessing massive volumes of data. Though the theoretical approach provides insightful understanding of the basic concepts of ADP advertising, the breadth of the examination and practicality of the conclusions are constrained by the lack of actual data. Ara et al., (2025) examined the effects of hedonistic inspiration and motivations on commitment and CX in multichannel retail environments. Despite having various fields of expertise, their study is especially pertinent to our investigation of how personalization affects CX. The investigators performed surveys amongst patrons of multichannel grocery stores in Pakistan by utilizing a mixed-methods technique (Ara et al., 2025). The investigation's sample included a wide variety of clients with different demographic experiences, guaranteeing a thorough comprehension of the investigation's phenomena. A comprehensive investigation of consumer thoughts and observations was made possible by the use of both quantitative questionnaires and qualitative conversations in the data gathering process.After doing a thorough examination, the investigators found a strong positive relationship among CX, hedonistic reasons, and personalization. The investigation recognized sample size and dependence on questionnaire responses restrictions, notwithstanding its substantial achievements. However, it highlights how important personalization tactics are to improving CX and building loyalty in the context of omnichannel sales (Khan et al., 2024). Paripati et al., (2024) provided insightful information about AI-user cooperation on Instagram for this research by examining the nature of human-AI engagements on the platform and their impact on Customer Participation. Using a mixed-methods strategy to acquire comprehensive data, the study concentrated on Instagram users who regularly interacted with AI-driven functionalities. Qualitative interviews with a selected group of those involved provided more information into their experiences and opinions toward human-AI interactions, incorporating complicated viewpoints to the research. The results showed that Instagram users are open to customized encounters facilitated by AI, emphasizing the complicated nature of human-AI conversations and their significant consequences for user participation and content usage (Hussain et al., 2021). Quantitative data was gathered through structured questionnaires to evaluate consumer opinions of AI versus human decision-making upon the platform and their content choices.This research highlights how important the ADP is to the formation of CX, which makes it a useful resource when analyzing the wider impact of personalization on customer pleasure and engagement (Babatunde et al., 2024). Gupta et al., (2022) investigated how personalization might improve lighthearted CX in retail environments; this research is closely related to our investigation into how personalization affects CX. The investigation used subjective as well as statistical methodologies to investigate the effect of customization on fun CX via a lab experiment (Ifekanandu et al., 2023). Quantitative information on consumer views on customized encounters and their influence on fun in retail settings was gathered through the use of structured questionnaires (Ara et al., 2025). Furthermore, qualitative interviews yielded more profound understandings of consumers' subjective encounters and attitudes regarding tailored encounters. Through the integration of both quantitative and qualitative studies, the study provides a comprehensive comprehension of the correlation among personalization and entertaining CX (Mishra et al., 2024). The results show that entertaining CX is greatly enhanced by both apparent and real personalization, which raises the level of client happiness and engagement in retail settings (Mutyala et al., 2022). Additionally, even though users are spending the same amount of time on the site, tailored information encourages users to pay closer attention to their favorite products (Oanh et al., 2024). The study adds to the body of knowledge on managing customer experiences by highlighting the importance of personalization in creating delightful and memorable encounters. It also offers marketers helpful advice on how to achieve this goal (Isidore et al., 2023). In conclusion, the literature review offers insightful information about how CX is changing and how AI and personalization are influencing it. Hussain et al., (2023) give a fundamental viewpoint on the revolutionary role that customization plays in online marketing by showing how hypermedia settings may produce highly rewarding and profoundly engaged CX through customized experiences and content. Paripati et al., (2024) illuminate the link between the application of AI and improved CX, while pointing out drawbacks like sample size and dependence on predictions. Rathore et al., (2020) show how AI and customized engagement marketing work together harmoniously, highlighting how AI-driven analytics can provide customized experiences and influence corporate results. Semwal et al., (2024) explore the role that hedonic incentive and personalization play in promoting CX and loyalty in omnichannel retail situations, even in the face of sample size and data collection restrictions. Kaperonis et al., (2024) provide information about the connections between humans and AI on Instagram, demonstrating users' susceptibility to customized experiences made possible by machine activity. In conclusion, the effect of personalization on fun CX in retail context (Hussain et al., 2021), which illustrates the usefulness of personalization in raising client satisfaction and engagement. All things considered, the studies under consideration underscore the significance of CX in modern business environments and stress the critical role that ADP plays in augmenting CX across a range of channels and sectors (Hussain et al., 2023). Organizations may create individualized experiences that connect with consumers and produce great results by utilizing AI technologies to obtain deep understanding into consumer wants and habits (Nalla et al., 2024). The research does, however, also highlight certain drawbacks, such as the necessity for empirical data to support theoretical Guidelines and limited sample sizes. By using quantitative approaches to expand on ADP and its impact on CX in the setting of Instagram while expanding on previous studies to give more thorough and reliable empirical proof, this investigation aims to close these gaps.

3. THEORETICAL FRAMEWORK

3.1 AI-driven Personalization

The definition of ADP is "the application of sophisticated algorithms and ML methods to customize content, product suggestions, and customer experience to Personal interests" (Shree et al., 2023). As per the source, ADP is the procedure that employs AI to customize information, experiences, and suggestions for each users by taking into account their distinct interests, behavior, and data (Bhattarai et al., 2024). Similarly, Ifekanandu et al., (2023) characterize ADP as the application of AI tools to tailor advertising, offerings, and products to each unique clients tastes and experience.The primary aspects of ADP are content customization (Khan et al., 2023), messaging customization (Hussain et al., 2023), location-based personalization (Ara et al., 2025), and recommendation systems (RS) (Bozkurt et al., 2025), which are based on prior research and Instagram's implementation of ADP.

3.2 Content Personalization

Delivering particular material to clients depending on their choices is known as content personalization (Kwong et al., 2024). Because personalized content is updated continuously in actual time to deliver customized user encounters, it is sometimes referred to as fluid content (Nimbalkar et al., 2021). ADP involves evaluating large-scale datasets that include user usage, choices, and past conversations in order to extract insights that allow sites to anticipate and provide incredibly relevant material (Saxena et al., 2024). This strategy calls for constant learning and modification. AI Algorithms gather information when users interact with the website, improve their understanding of users' choices, and continuously improve suggestions (Moghadd-asnian et al., 2024). Personalization stays relevant as time passes via this continuous procedure, adapting to changes in user habits and preferences (Instagram's algorithm distinguishes it from other social networks sites by emphasizing user engagement and content over following accounts (Hussain et al., 2023). Favorite voices, videos, and tags are among the factors that determine the content displayed on the "For You" tab, as is the watching history of subscribers. To choose the consumer's next piece of content, the algorithm considers information including whether a user watching a video through to the end, how often they watched it, if they interacted with it, and the type of engagement (Palumbo et al., 2023). Additionally, Instagram's algorithm examines videos into text, audio, and visual elements, leveraging Actual computer technology to recognize visual elements. The program can assess a video's entirety and show it to viewers who might find it fascinating thanks to this thorough examination (Sekar et al., 2024).

3.3 Message Personalization

Message personalization entails personalizing marketing communications for specific clients, taking into consideration their particular requirements, passions, habits, and choices (Sharma et al., 2024). The idea behind message personalization is that communications that are more in line with clients' personality characteristics and demographics would have a more persuasive impact (Thandayuthapani et al., 2024). The subject of automatic tailored marketing message production gains momentum through useful suggestions and scientific initiatives (Semwal et al., 2024). Isidore et al., (2023) introduced a system that can create individualized marketing material. The method effortlessly adjusts promotional material to each clients unique needs. By taking demographics, past purchases, and surfing habits into account, ADP provides customized marketing content, supports visual-linguistic inquiry responding, and activates automated photo captioning (Kwong et al., 2024). When Personalized communications are instantaneously pertinent consumers are more inclined to peruse, retain, and interpret them (Kaperonis et al., 2024). Click-through rates for personalized marketing messages are often higher (Nalla et al., 2024). Instagram might provide tailored messages based on a client's brand interests and demographics by using ADP (Senyapar et al., 2024).

3.4 Location-based Personalization

Analyzing client preferences and behavior to suggest relevant goods and services according to their priorities and location is known as location-based personalization (Ifekanandu et al., 2023). Making use of a clients wireless data, which includes time, place, and changing seasons, can improve the development of a more customized online experience (Dai et al., 2024). An Instagram user's Location preferences determine what material they see (Hussain et al., 2023). Instagram uses location data to show viewers the most popular material that is nearby and, when appropriate, to show them ads that seem more appropriate to their preferences (Asthana et al., 2024).

3.5 Recommender System (RS)

The recommender system (RS) is a widely recognized and often referenced example of ADP. An RS is a system engineered to grant consumers availability of preferred products and accessibility, recommending them based on their similarities to already-used items or ratings from analogous users (Isidore et al., 2023). The primary function of the recommender system is to provide customized product recommendations to satisfy consumer requirements (Bashyska et al., 2023). The FYP is a critical component that differentiates Instagram and its user interface from other online networks (Ara et al., 2025). The algorithm driving content suggestions on the FYP is fundamental to Instagram's growth. Instagram primarily encourages users to engage with content that appears on the FYP, leading many users to rarely explore beyond this section, even though the app offers a variety of other tools and sites (Heinemann et al., 2023). Asthana et al., (2024) examine the notion of an Instagram user's current emotional flow and the app's objective to augment this experience. Instagram utilizes many design concepts to maintain this sense of flow, emphasizing perceived suggestion accuracy, perceived suggestion serendipity, and perceived smoothness (Hussain et al., 2021). We refer to these elements as "technology advantages," indicating the potential of an action that an innovative device enables (Gupta et al., 2022). Perceived suggestion accuracy evaluates the extent to which users believe Instagram's algorithm aligns with their interests (Isidore et al., 2023). Instagram's algorithmic suggestions employ complex elements such as past usage statistics and ancillary data to deliver personalized content (Kannan et al., 2024). Users favor content aligned with their tastes because of time limitations; hence, it fosters a good flow experience (Kwong et al., 2024). Nonetheless, overly precise algorithms may result in a "data wrap," rendering content deterministic and obstructing the user's flowing state (Bhuiyan et al., 2024). This is where the significance of apparent recommended serendipity emerges. Perceived suggestion serendipity assesses the degree to which suggested videos surpass client expectations, eliciting emotions of pleasure and excitement that enrich the flow experience (Abinesh et al., 2024). Unanticipated suggestions positively affect user engagement, especially when they diverge from their preferences (Kwong et al., 2024). Users eventually become passive recipients of information, with the perceived suggestion of serendipity strongly linked with participation on short-video sites such as Instagram (Hussain et al., 2021). Perceived simplicity measures the ease of utilizing the platform, with less cognitive effort indicating an improved CX (Nulla et al., 2024). The FYP on Instagram provides users with a novel alternative to traditional social networking sites by reducing the cognitive load required for browsing, enabling users to seamlessly engage with content less requiring active searching (Bozkurt et al., 2025). In contrast to conventional sites where users rapidly browse material or scroll quickly to locate desired videos, Instagram eliminates these obstacles, facilitating a fluid viewing experience (Mukherjee et al., 2023). Nonetheless, video length diminishes the association among perceived simpleness and user flow behavior on Instagram, since short-form videos necessitate frequent scrolling and cognitive exertion (Isidore et al., 2023). Nevertheless, Instagram's FYP streamlines navigation by presenting suggested videos without the need for cognitive choice, thus improving the CX, particularly for novice users (Bhuiyan et al., 2024).

3.6 Customer Experience

The importance of CX has increased significantly in recent years. Industry executives and academics have acknowledged the substantial and strategic influence of CX on the progression of modern enterprises (Ara et al., 2025). Currently, attaining a competitive edge in the industry frequently depends on providing an outstanding CX (Khan et al., 2024). Customer satisfaction, loyalty, and expectations may correlate with an exemplary CX (Hussain et al., 2023). Ifekanandu et al., (2023) posited that individuals seek not merely products but rather enriching experiences. This concept established the foundation for subsequent talks on customer experience. They enhanced this concept, setting it apart from traditional goods and services (Dai et al., 2024). They characterized CX as a sequence of significant experiences curated by a corporation for its clientele. Later scientists regarded the client experience as a comprehensive phenomenon encompassing all interactions among consumers and vendors of services (Isidore et al., 2021). Likewise, CX comprises the aggregate attitude consumers have regarding a specific company, shaped by their experiences across diverse touchpoints (Heinemann et al., 2023). Consumers desire tailored encounters, and corporations are eager to fulfill this demand. Businesses particularly seek to elicit favorable opinions from clients, referred to as CX, by personalizing touchpoints (Kannan et al., 2024). Customization is a process that caters to individual interests and needs. Generally, CX results from multiple variables. We propose a complete conceptual structure to enhance our understanding of CX, which encompasses numerous aspects such as intellectual, affective, social, behavioral, and physical components (Paripati et al., 2024). Likewise, it was underscored that CX is a complex construct that includes mental procedures, consumer feelings, social reactions, customer behaviors, and sensations of the business's products (Heinemann et al., 2023). Additionally, Gujar et al., (2024) identified six components of the CX: psychological, cognitive, pragmatic, sensorial, interpersonal, and lifestyle. Furthermore, the fundamental rationale for these elements lies in consumers' comprehension of online store stimuli, where they assess both emotional and cognitive dimensions to define their overall CX. The analysis of diverse views on CX reveals that it is a highly individualized term that varies between contacts, collectively influencing the customer's journey (Hussain et al., 2021).

3.7 Emotions

Emotions significantly influence the customer experience. Emotions are defined as an emotional situation arising from the cognitive assessment of occurrences or ideas, possessing a subjective quality, and associated with physiological reactions (Banik et al., 2024). Experience design emphasizes the creation of personal relationships with clients through the purposeful arrangement of intangible and tangible components in physical and interpersonal contexts (Babatunde et al., 2024). CX substantial gratification when their emotions are involved, leading organizations to utilize diverse inventive strategies to elicit and satisfy consumers' emotional requirements (Gupta et al., 2022). Emotions stem from a person's distinct evaluation of their experiences, shaped by the appraisal and analysis of acts and their surroundings (Mishra et al., 2024). This indicates that emotions are intrinsically subjective, resulting in diverse emotional reactions from people to a single action under identical conditions (Dai et al., 2024). Moreover, emotions display variety and can manifest in various forms. Similar to the customer experience, social elements influence emotions, making them highly transmissible and attracting people through their interactions (Mukherjee et al., 2023). Creating a comfortable, engaging, pleasurable, and comprehensive atmosphere, together with designing a customer path that elicits emotions, enhances the overall CX (Heinemann et al., 2023).

3.8 Cognitive Processes

In addition to emotions, cognition is another essential element of CX. Cognitive procedures denote sophisticated mental operations including memories, perception, conceptual solving issues, and information application (Kwong et al., 2024). CX research analyzes cognitive procedures from two unique perspectives: achieving objectives and validating or refuting previous expectations (Mishra et al., 2024). The initial viewpoint is based on the assumption that customers exhibit goal-oriented behavior. Consumers set goals, either intentionally or unintentionally, within certain circumstances and employ consumption as a method to attain them (Gujar et al., 2024). In marketing literature, target-directed conduct is considered a cognitive process, with achieving objectives as the result. Consequently, the achievement of objectives constitutes a component of the customer experience, and assessing the achievement of objectives is essential in identifying the cognitive aspect of the customer experience (Kannan et al., 2024). The second viewpoint posits that clients possess expectations prior to choosing a service. The study has investigated whether the real client experience aligns with or diverges from past expectations, hence influencing pleasure or discontent (Singh et al., 2023).

3.9 Social Dimension

The social milieu also influences customer experience. The social aspect of CX pertains to the impact of staff, fellow consumers, and wider social networks on customer interactions (Shree et al., 2023). Prior research has primarily focused on the interactions between the business or its employees and the consumer, but it's important for researchers to recognize that consumer exchanges can significantly impact the CX. Similar to consumer interactions in a physical environment, individuals can engage in "communication" online by posting comments across different websites, posts, or forums (Rathore et al., 2020). Palumbo et al., (2023) indicates that this kind of knowledge is significantly influential and functions as a contemporary variant of traditional referrals. Moreover, physical and sensory characteristics are critical components of the customer experience; however, they are often assessed using experimental methodologies. Consequently, this article excludes them from the evaluation criteria (Heinemann et al., 2023).

4. CONCEPTUAL MODEL

The integration of AI tools, including sentiment evaluation, emotion recognition, digital assistants, chatbots, and content collection, augments customization, elevates service quality, and optimizes client interactions, thereby improving the entire CX. Good encounters cultivate contentment and establish trust in the brand, determined by the degree of client interaction and the perceived worth of the brand (Hussain et al., 2023). Customers that receive personalized, frictionless, and excellent service are more inclined to demonstrate brand loyalty, promote the business, and offer helpful suggestions regarding additional enhancements (Bozkurt et al., 2025). Mukherjee et al., (2023) indicates that AI substantially improves consumer experience, loyalty, and personalization. Furthermore, the influence of AI on customer experience and loyalty is facilitated by adaptive decision-making processes. Rathore et al., (2020) suggests ADP can augment the personalization and humanizing of experiences throughout diverse interactions and phases throughout the consumer journey, hence changing advertising approaches and enhancing CX. ADP has been extensively utilized by numerous corporations. Many B2C companies, such Amazon and Microsoft Premier, have developed advanced iterations of suggestion systems to offer series to consumers according on their monitored activities (Kwong et al., 2024). Prominently incorporated within major social media platforms such as Instagram, Twitter, and Facebook, the recommender feature provides video and content suggestions customized to users' attributes and habits (Bozkurt et al., 2025). Users are addressed by their register names, and content is recommended depending on their prior watching experience (Mukherjee et al., 2023). Furthermore, Coelho et al., (2025) assessed the application of AI in marketing and sales functions. It demonstrated that AI significantly contributes to lead generation by enabling the provision of tailored and highly customized advertising materials to people. Additionally, the incorporation of robo-advisers into the sales cycle was examined, revealing that these experts may examine consumers' communications records to tailor their conversations to each clients unique needs (Bhattarani et al., (2023). Instagram differentiates itself from the remainder of the major social media networks, including Twitter, by an important distinction: its content dissemination approach is solely dependent on algorithms, whereas other networks are strongly influenced by user connections in their content dissemination (Coelho et al., 2025). The popularity of Instagram is primarily attributed to its extensive customisation facilitated by suggestion algorithms. Instagram applies its AI algorithms mostly to identify consumers with a greater likelihood of engaging with video content (Hussain et al., 2021). Instagram curates material for users' FYP by assessing their prior conversations, hence providing an extremely personalized viewing experience (Bhuiyan et al., 2024). This method allows consumers to find Instagram videos that match their tastes, giving in a distinctive and customized watching experience (Hussain et al., 2021). Consequently, it is essential to perform a thorough analysis of the relationship among ADP and CX in the context of Instagram. In light of the above conversations, the subsequent hypothesis is proposed.

H1: ADP has a positive impact on CX in the Context of Instagram.

Based on the above discussion, the conceptual model of the hypothesis testing is Exhibited in Figure 1.

Figure 1. Conceptual model of hypothesis testing

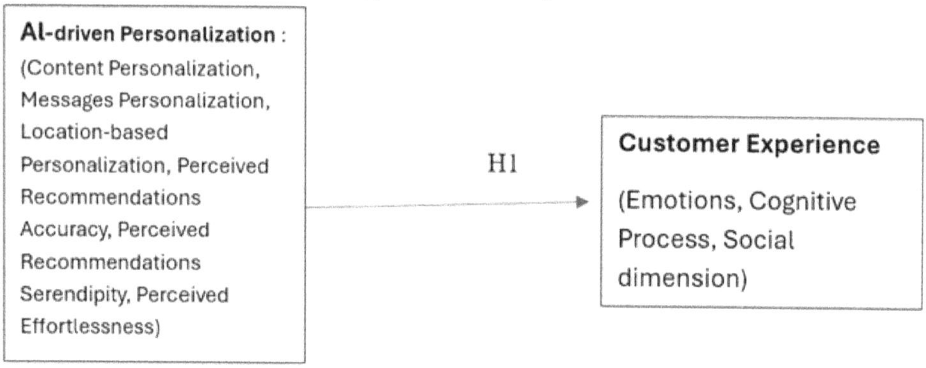

5. METHODOLOGY

This research use a deductive technique to evaluate and enhance current assumptions. The study regards the deductive technique as the most suitable, as previous investigations have employed the same approach. The data was gathered from 365 participants in Pakistan. This study employs quantitative study, regarded as an excellent method for gathering significant information via data. Utilizing these data, correlations among various factors are analyzed and hypotheses are evaluated to assess the outcomes. This study aims to adapt established theory to a novel context and to validate or refute it by developing a hypothesis.A self-administered questionnaire was selected for gathering data throughout the investigation. The item questionnaires pertaining to ADP are used from (Isidore et al., 2023) for measuring and CX from (Kwong et al., 2024). The surveys were administered online to enhance cost-effectiveness and efficiency in the study procedure. A seven-point Likert scale, as suggested by Khan et al., (2024), was employed in this investigation. Data gathering was conducted using websites like Google Forms.The population comprises all Instagram users, and individuals are chosen via convenience sampling for their immediate availability. The formula N > 50 + 8m was employed to calculate the sample size, wherein "m" denotes the amount of distinct factors. The present investigation comprised a minimum of 58 individuals due to the presence of one independent factor. The SPSS software, extensively utilized for quantitative data evaluation, was employed for the statistical evaluation of data. Before evaluation, the data was coded, inputted, and sanitized to guarantee proper entry into the software. Descriptive data, including mean, standard deviation, and skewness, were employed to characterize the outcomes. Mean, median, and mode were employed to represent a central trend. Furthermore, Measurements of Variation were employed to examine the data distribution.In the concluding phase, Bivariate Regression was employed to examine the connection among the independent factor ADP and the dependent factor CX. This approach comprises two fundamental tests: Pearson's correlation coefficient and R-squared, which indicate variations in the dependent factor.

6. DATA ANALYSIS

6.1 Demographic Backgrounds

Table 1. Demographics of Respondents

Category	Frequency	Percentage
Gender		
Male	180	49.32
Female	185	50.68
Age		
18-25 years	110	30.14
26-35 years	145	39.73
36-45 years	80	21.92
Age 46+	30	8.22
Occupation		
Student	100	27.30
Professional	150	41.10
Unemployed	60	16.44
Other	55	15.07
Education		
High School	75	20.55

continued on following page

Table 1. Continued

Category	Frequency	Percentage
Bachelors	150	41.10
Masters	100	27.40
PhD	40	10.96
Time spent on Instagram		
1 hour	60	16.44
1-3 hours	160	43.84
3-5 hours	100	27.40
5+ hours	45	12.33

The participants were well-balanced gender distribute, with females 50.68% and male 49.32%. Majority of participants age are 18-25 years old (69.87%). Through Educational background, majority of participants have bachelors degree (41.10%). Through data, 43.44% respondents spend 1-3 hours on Instagram.

6.1.1 Descriptive Analysis

Following the analysis of demographics, it is essential to discover any anomalies in the data. To accomplish this, we perform an descriptive examination of the data illustrated in Table 4. The study indicates that every component contains an aggregate of 355 participants, signifying the absence of missing values. Additionally, except the demographic characteristics, all items offer replies from 1 to 5. This corresponds with our 6-point Likert scale, wherein 1 signifies 'Strongly Disagree' and 5 denotes 'Strongly Agree'. Survey items 1-5 pertain to the independent factor "ADP." The mean for item 1 (ADP-1) is 5.46, indicating that participants exceeded the median value of 4. This signifies that the majority of participants concurred with the claim. The averages of the remaining inquiries exceed the median of 4, indicating consensus among a significant number of participants regarding the items. Items CX-1 to CX-3 pertain to the dependent factor "CX". The items possess the following means: 5.28, 5.38, and 5.01, which are numerical values. The values exceed the median of 4, indicating that more than half of responses demonstrate agreement with the claims. The standard deviation is approximately 1.5. This indicates that, on average, the answers diverge from the average by 1.5 degrees on the 5-demonstrate scale. A standard deviation of 1.5 on an index of 1 to 5 signifies a substantial dispersion in the replies. Responses from respondents exhibit considerable variability above the mean.

Table 2. Descriptive statistics

Items	Valid N	Min	Max	Mean	Std deviation	Skewness		Kurtosis	
						Statistic	Std.Error	Statistic	Std.Error
ADP-1	355	1	5	5.46	1.429	-0.678	0.126	-0.105	0.248
ADP-2	355	1	5	5.06	1.604	-0.604	0.126	-0.276	0.248
ADP-3	355	1	5	4.86	1.714	-0.488	0.126	-0.669	0.248
ADP-4	355	1	5	5.21	1.458	-0.562	0.126	-0.349	0.248
ADP-5	355	1	5	5.14	1.488	-0.409	0.126	-0.578	0.248
ADP-6	355	1	5	5.13	1.439	-0.438	0.126	-0.679	0.248
CX-1	355	1	5	5.28	1.459	-0.589	0.126	-0.304	0.248
CX-2	355	1	5	5.38	1.358	-0.538	0.126	-0.288	0.248
CX-3	355	1	5	5.03	1.563	-0.319	0.126	-0.718	0.248

6.1.2 Correlation Assessment

Correlation coefficients quantify the degree of the association among factors. The correlation values vary from -1 to 1. A value of 0 signifies minimal to no effect or connection among the elements, whereas scores of 1 and -1 denote a perfect correlation, either beneficial or detrimental, accordingly. The proximity of the outcome to 1 or -1 indicates a greater correlation among the parameters. An outcome within 0 and -1 signifies a negative correlation, when a rise in one variable reflects a decrease in another. Conversely, a value from 0 to 1 signifies a positive correlation, when a rise in one factor correlates to a rise in the other. This evaluation in SPSS investigates the correlation among factor pairs, necessitating the establishment of an appropriate factor for every element. A novel variable is calculated by aggregating every element within the component. The parameter "ADP" is determined by the average of its six sections: ADP-1, ADP-2, ADP-3, ADP-4, ADP-5, and ADP-6. The "CX" factor represents the average of three sections: CX-1, CX-2, and CX-3. The mean approach is employed for calculation due to the involvement of Likert scale data in the research. The freshly calculated factors are utilized for both correlations and later regression analyses. Table 3 illustrates the associations among the parameters "ADP" and "CX". Based on (), a prescribed metric exists for understanding the r value in correlation analyses. An r value ranging from 0.90 to 1.00 denotes an extremely significant relationship, 0.70 to 0.87 shows an elevated connection, 0.50 to 0.67 reflects a moderate connection, 0.30 to 0.47 implies a weak connection, and 0.10 to 0.27 signifies an insignificant correlation. The investigation of the link among ADP (IV) and CX (DV) revealed a two-tailed Pearson correlation value of r=0.788, with a threshold for significance of p=0.000. The robust a beneficial relationship signifies that a rise in ADP levels leads to a substantial enhancement in CX. The association is significantly different, evidenced by a p-value of 0.000. This indicates that we possess substantial proof to imply that the observed association is not attributable to unpredictability.

Table 3. Correlation Matrix

		ADP	**CX**
ADP	Pearson Correlation	1	0.788**
	Sig. (2-tailed)	0.000	
	N	355	355
CX	Pearson Correlation	0.788**	1
	Sig.(2-tailed)	0.000	
	N	355	355

Note. ** signifies correlation being statistically significant at 0.01 significance level.

6.1.3 Reliability

Dependability testing is performed to evaluate the uniformity of replies uniformity the dependability of the survey. This investigation employed a Likert scale to collect participants' thoughts and opinions about particular issues. Study utilizing the Likert scale may have inherent mistakes, as participants frequently find it challenging to connect with the questions, resulting in inconsistency and misunderstanding among notions. Consequently, reliability checks assesses and guarantees the accuracy of the assessment items inside the study. Cronbach's Alpha is a prevalent technique for assessing consistency across academics. This method bifurcates the criterion and juxtaposes the two segments to assess association and coherence. The resultant coefficient varies from 0 to 1, where 0 signifies the absence of uniformity or connection, and 1 denotes complete consistency. A reliability coefficient exceeding 0.6 is deemed favorable for the factors to be legitimate for research. Table 4 demonstrates that every factor possess a Cronbach's alpha value exceeding 0.6, signifying their reliability and appropriateness for study.

Table 4. Reliability Testing

	Reliability	
Factor	**Cronbach's Aloha**	**N of items**
ADP	0.906	5
CX	0.849	4

6.1.4 Validity

The findings of the KMO and Bartlett's Test are essential for evaluating the data's validity. The KMO statistic, which ranges from 0 to 1, signifies the appropriateness of the dataset. A score approaching 1 indicates improved productivity, while a value of 0 denotes inadequacy.The KMO index should surpass 0.6 for the dataset to be deemed adequate. Furthermore, the significance level in Bartlett's test of spherical must not exceed 0.05 to be deemed appropriate for subsequent research. The KMO index shouldn't be below 0.6 to guarantee the database's suitability for evaluation. Table 7 indicates that the KMO Level of adequacy is 0.928, which is remarkably high, signifying that the sample is greater than sufficient. Values approaching 1 indicate that the relationship networks are fairly compact and, therefore, dependable for investigation. Furthermore, Bartlett's Test of Sphericity yields an significance level (Sig.) of 0.000, which is below the acceptable level of 0.05, thereby validating the data set for further analytical procedures.

Table 5. KMO and Bartlett's Test

KMO and Bartlett's Test		
Kaiser-Meyer-Olkin Measure of sampling adequacy	**0.928**	
Bartlett's test of sphericity	**Approx.Chi-Square**	**2259.648**
	Df	34
	Sig.	0

6.1.5 Regression Analysis

Linear regression, as previously stated, is employed to ascertain the association among factors. The calculation of linear regression was conducted using SPSS software, and the results are presented in Tables 8 and 9 below. R-value denotes the relationship coefficient among the independent and dependent variables. An R-value of 0.796 signifies a robust positive correlation among the independent and dependent variables. Furthermore, the R-squared value signifies the extent of variation in the dependent factor that may be elucidated by the IV. An R^2 of 0.633 indicates that 63.3% of the variation in the DV is explained by the independent factor, signifying robust explanatory power of the framework. This indicates that 63.3% of the variability in CX is linked to ADP. The standardized regression coefficient, or Beta coefficient, quantifies the magnitude and trajectory of the IV effect on the DV (). A bigger Beta coefficient indicates a more substantial influence. The Beta coefficient is 0.796, signifying that the IV exerts a substantial beneficial effect on the DV. When the amount of ADP rises by one standard deviation, the CX can improve by 0.796 standard deviations. The t-value is employed to assess the importance of the regression coefficient, with a higher value signifying a more substantial influence of the IV on the DV. The t-value is 25.014, indicating a highly significant regression coefficient. The significance, shown as Sig., assesses the simulation's or factor's efficacy in predicting the variance in the DV. Given that the importance value is 0, which is below the conventional threshold of 0.05, the Beta coefficient is deemed extremely significant. The interpretation indicates that the simple linear regression findings demonstrate a considerable positive effect of the IV (ADP) on the DV (CX), with this effect being analytically significant.

Table 6. Model Summary

		Model Summary		
Model	**R**	**R-square**	**Adjusted R-square**	**Std.error of the estimate**
1	0.788a	0.629	0.628	0.781

a. Predictors: (Constant), ADP
b. DV: CX

Table 7. Linear Regression Coefficients

	Coefficients[a]						
	Unstandardized Coefficients		**Standardized Coefficients**			**95.0% Confidence Interval for B**	
Model	**B**	**Std.Error**	**Beta**	**t**	**Sig.**	**Lower Bound**	**Upper bound**
1 (Constant)	1.128	1.168	0.788	6.678	0.000	0.801	1.368
ADP	0.788	0.028		24.008	0.000	0.728	0.858

a. DV: CX

Findings

The findings indicated that H1 was validated, signifying that Instagram's Incorporating ADF can substantially enhance CX, demonstrating a direct correlation among the two factors. This result corresponds with the studies undertaken by Hussain et al., (2023), which asserted that ADF influences client satisfaction via the consumer process and enhances CX by delivering individualized offers. It additionally shows the way AI and ADF significantly improve the CX. The study conducted by Isidore et al., (2023) emphasizes AI, ADF client service, and client experience in the banking and telecoms sectors, excluding social networking sites. Content customization on Instagram is governed by algorithms that assess user behavior, including viewing patterns, engagement metrics, and the characteristics of their interactions with content. The website's FYP exemplifies this, as the system suggests movies based on historical user actions and choices, encompassing watching time, popular material, and input from users. This constantly iterative procedure guarantees that the material stays pertinent and captivating, matching with people' changing interests. The ADF utilized by Instagram provides tailored knowledge and suggestions determined by consumer habits and activities. This aligns with Gujar et al., (2024) along with substantiates their defenses in the context of Instagram. Such tailored material is more inclined to align with client interests and connect with them. This also conserves significant time for users in locating their preferred material. By promptly providing tailored content, clients may enjoy psychological ease, so fostering personalized encounters and enhancing CX. This is corroborated by (Kumar et al., 2024, Hussain et al., 2022). CX significantly enhances happiness when emotions are appropriately engaged. AI-driven tailored content This research reveals that resonating with clients emotionally fosters robust emotional relationships, hence contributing to its conclusions. AI enables the development of tailored advertisements, hence improving consumer engagement and happiness. Instagram employs ADF to provide customized adverts and messaging that engage more profoundly with clients, thereby enhancing the efficacy of those interactions. Similarly, Instagram utilizes location data to enhance the customer experience by displaying information and adverts pertinent to the user geographical location. This method not merely augments content relevancy but also boosts engagement by harmonizing with users' regional patterns and preferences. It demonstrates that Instagram's capacity to provide material that connects personally amplifies consumer emotional involvement. Consumers get an overwhelming feeling of connectedness and happiness when the content they encounter corresponds with their tastes and passions. This corroborates the research's results and supports the assertion that fostering a relaxed, stimulating, pleasurable, and comprehensive environment, coupled with a consumer experience meant to evoke emotions, boosts the whole CX. Furthermore, this study substantiates the claim that personalization favorably influences both CX and loyalty, despite the research's concentration on the retail setting. Consequently, by delivering personalized content, tailored messages, and location-specific suggestions, Instagram's ADF elicits profound emotional reactions from users, customizes the online experience, and consequently fosters a complete CX, resulting in a favorable CX. The recommendation mechanism of Instagram is fundamental to its customisation strategy. Through the analysis of customer interactions and choices, the algorithm recommends material that corresponds with individual preferences, thereby markedly improving user involvement and pleasure. The notion of flow, characterized by consumers' total immersion in the information, is essential here. Instagram's design seeks to maintain a sense of flow by combining suggestion precision with serendipity, thereby assuring users remain interested without becoming ensnared in a "data bubble." Perceived suggestion accuracy assesses consumers' beliefs regarding the alignment of Instagram's Method with their choices. Consumers choose material that aligns with their choices owing to time limitations, hence improving their flow encounter. Content that is inappropriate or unengaging leads to a detrimental CX. Conversely, pertinent and/or engaging content fosters good experiences. Moreover, the efficacy of Instagram's suggestion system is evidenced by the elevated viewership and its ability to maintain their interest. Users frequently experience an incessant stream of content that appears exceptionally pertinent and engaging, underscoring the efficacy of ADF in influencing CX. Furthermore, perceived suggestion serendipity assesses the extent to which suggested clips exceed consumer expectations, provoking sentiments of delight and awe that improve the CX. Unanticipated suggestions enhance client engagement, even if they deviate from their preferences. This is closely linked to the social aspect of CX, which encompasses user interaction and the impact of networking sites. Instagram's AI-powered suggestions enhance social connections by linking users to material that is trending across their social networks. It also promotes user-generated content and conversations, so augmenting the online experience. Furthermore, perceived simplicity assesses the system's use, where less cognitive exertion signifies an enhanced CX. The capacity of Instagram to provide pertinent material and communications Minimizes cognitive work necessary to discover engaging content, demonstrating that Instagram's AI-powered suggestions facilitate users in achieving their goals. This seamless browsing encounter improves client happiness and fosters a favorable general impression. This is substantiated by the cognitive dimension of CX, which encompasses the cognitive steps that users engage in when communicating on Instagram.The accomplishment of objectives is a fundamental element of CX, rendering the evaluation of achieving objectives crucial for assessing the cognitive aspect of CX. Consequently, Instagram's suggestion algorithm significantly enhances CX. In conclusion, content, message, and location-based customization, along with the suggestion system as the key elements and a connecting element, indicate that ADF utilized by Instagram and CX are intricately associated. This elucidates the conclusion that ADF exerts an important beneficial impact on CX within the framework of Instagram. Nonetheless, the manner in which various Elements of ADF individually affect the CX Its results can't be disclosed. Furthermore, it fails to elucidate the specific dimension(s) of CX via which ADF has attained a positive influence.

CONCLUSION

This research aimed to investigate the influence of ADF on CX in the setting of Instagram. The study study (H1) posited that ADF positively influences CX within the framework of Instagram. The results of empirical studies validated this idea, indicating a substantial positive correlation among ADF and CX. The findings indicated that ADF significantly improves the customer experience on Instagram via methods including content suggestion, message customization, and location-based customization. These elements jointly enhance a personalized enjoyable encounters, closely correlating with specific customer needs and habits. Content recommendations driven by AI guarantee that users receive videos and materials aligned with their preferences, hence enhancing the probability of sustained engagement with the application. Customized messaging enhances the bond among customers and the system by providing pertinent and timely messages. Furthermore, location-based customization increases relevance by delivering contextually suitable material according to the user's geographic position. The incorporation of ADF on Instagram markedly enhances CX by rendering conversations more pertinent, captivating, and pleasurable. A favorable user-friendly is essential for cultivating robust user loyalty and fostering ongoing involvement with the site. The results derived from the study offer significant recommendations for companies and advertising agencies aiming to utilize AI technologies to improve consumer engagement and happiness. Subsequent research may build upon these results by investigating the long-term impacts of ADF on CX and loyalty, as well as its possible implementation across additional digital channels.

Theoretical Contributions

These results contribute theoretically to the prior research on ADP and CX, especially in the context of social media sites like Instagram. This study empirically explores the impact of ADF on CX, so enhancing previous understanding while offering an extensive structure for comprehending the changing landscape of personalized online advertising. Our results substantiate the theoretical theories indicating that ADF is essential for improving CX and actually demonstrate that ADP positively influences CX. Secondly, this study adds to the academic discussion by elucidating the unique processes by which ADF promotes CX. This research analyzes the unique aspects of personalization—content personalization, message customization, service location-based, perceived suggestion accuracy, perceived suggestion randomness, and alleged effortlessness—to elucidate how every aspect affects customer engagement. This thorough examination provides a more refined understanding of the complex nature of ADF, building upon earlier research that has mostly concentrated on overarching trends. Furthermore, the research's focus on Instagram, a swiftly expanding social media site, introduces a modern aspect to the literature about AI and online advertising. By placing the study's within this framework, the investigation tackles the distinct challenges and prospects posed by social media sites that depend significantly on user-generated content and participatory functionalities. This contextual uniqueness increases the relevance of the results to other analogous systems, thereby expanding the range of ADF study.

Managerial Implications

This research's findings highlight ADF's considerable potential to improve CX on Instagram. This signifies an important chance for marketers and brand managers to utilize AI technologies to enhance customer interaction and pleasure. By using AI technologies that customize messages and information to specific user needs, managers could foster more interesting and useful conversations among users. This customization may enhance client satisfaction and promote increased loyalty and retention. Consequently, marketers ought to invest in sophisticated algorithms and ML techniques that can precisely assess user habits and preferences in order to provide personalized material and suggestions. The report emphasizes the significance of particular personalization features, including content and message customisation, location-based personalization, and recommendation algorithms. Managers ought to rank these elements to optimize their effect. For example, content and messaging customisation can enhance CX, making them more significant and stimulating, while location-based services may deliver spatially appropriate products and data. Efficient recommendations that provide perceived precision and serendipity can improve customer happiness by proposing pertinent and unforeseen information that users might find enjoyable. This comprehensive method for customisation guarantees an overall enhancement of the CX.

Limitations and Directions for Further Research

This research is subject to the fundamental limitations of quantitative analysis. The data for this investigation was gathered via an online survey questionnaire, serving as the foundation for subsequent evaluations and outcomes; nevertheless, this approach, albeit effective, presents several limitations. A notable constraint is the adaptability of the results. The survey addressed Instagram users irrespective of their geographical areas; yet, the limited sample size of 365 participants renders it challenging to generalize the findings worldwide. Furthermore, the predominant age range among respondents was 18 to 34, thus failing to encapsulate the encounters and perspectives of other age demographics. This age bias could possibly distort the findings, since younger viewers may exhibit distinct behaviors with ADF. In comparison to older consumers. A significant disadvantage of this investigation is the possible sampling bias resulting from the data collection approach. Employing Google Forms to collect questionnaires replies might not be an adequate sampling of the entire Instagram user demographic. This issue is especially evident due to the substantial disparities among Instagram and its foreign version. These websites appeal to diverse demographics, and cultural factors and legal disparities among Pakistan and Western nations might result in differing CX and impressions. Consequently, the data may substantially represent the encounters of specific user groups, resulting in biased outcomes. This constraint underscores the necessity for meticulous evaluation of sample techniques and demographic makeup in forthcoming research to guarantee a more equitable and precise depiction of customer experience across various locations. Furthermore, the dependence on closed-ended questions in the survey constrains the profundity of observations that might be obtained. Although quantitative data offers a comprehensive overview, it may fail to encapsulate the complex thoughts and CX concerning ADF on Instagram. A mixed-method technique, integrating qualitative components such as interviews or open-ended questions, could yield more comprehensive data and enhance the comprehension of CX. This work has considerable obstacles due to ethical considerations and issues regarding privacy. The implementation of AI for content personalization prompts inquiries regarding data protection and the ethical ramifications of user data. ADF depends significantly on the collection and evaluation of extensive user data, encompassing browsing histories, choices, and interactions. This comprehensive data collecting may result in possible breaches of user confidentiality, particularly if the data is insufficiently safeguarded or if users aren't thoroughly informed regarding the utilization of their personal information. The alteration of user data to enhance interaction may elicit issues over the openness and equity of such methods. Consequently, when investigating this subject, it is essential to take into account the aspects that may adversely affect CX.In conclusion, future research should expand the demographic breadth, augment sample sizes from different communities, and utilize mixed-method techniques to encompass a broader spectrum of experiences and perspectives. The influence of ethical and privacy limitations must be thoroughly evaluated. By addressing these limitations, additional studies can expand upon the results to provide more comprehensive insights and more broadly applicable conclusions regarding the examined topic.

REFERENCES

Abinesh, R. C., & Dulloo, R. (2024). The Impact of AI-Driven Personalization on Customer Satisfaction in E-Commerce: Balancing Technology, Transparency, and Control. [JoCAAA]. *Journal of Computational Analysis and Applications*, 33(2), 649–655.

Akhtar, P., Ghouri, A. M., Ashraf, A., Lim, J. J., Khan, N. R., & Ma, S. (2024). Smart product platforming powered by AI and Generative AI: Personalization for the circular economy. *International Journal of Production Economics*, 273, 109283. DOI: 10.1016/j.ijpe.2024.109283

Ara, A., & Thomas, A. (2025). Exploring Consumer Perceptions and Ethical Considerations in AI-Powered E-Commerce. In *Data Visualization Tools for Business Applications* (pp. 347–368). IGI Global.

Asthana, S., Im, J., Chen, Z., & Banovic, N. (2024, May). " I know even if you don't tell me": Understanding Users' Privacy Preferences Regarding AI-based Inferences of Sensitive Information for Personalization. *InProceedings of the CHI Conference on Human Factors in Computing Systems(pp.1-21).*

Babatunde, S. O., Odejide, O. A., Edunjobi, T. E., & Ogundipe, D. O.Sodiq Odetunde BabatundeOpeyemi Abayomi OdejideTolulope Esther EdunjobiDamilola Oluwaseun Ogundipe. (2024). The role of AI in marketing personalization: A theoretical exploration of consumer engagement strategies. *International Journal of Management & Entrepreneurship Research*, 6(3), 936–949. DOI: 10.51594/ijmer.v6i3.964

Banik, B., Banik, S., & Annee, R. R. (2024). AI-Driven Strategies for Enhancing Customer Loyalty and Engagement Through Personalization and Predictive Analytics. *International Journal of Machine Learning Research in Cybersecurity and Artificial Intelligence*, 15(1), 416–447.

Bashynska, I. (2023). AI-Driven Personalization in Advertising: Transforming Consumer Engagement through Sustainability and Circular Economy. *Scientific Journal of Bielsko-Biala School of Finance and Law*, 27(4), 106–112.

Bhattarai, A. (2023). Exploring Customer Engagement through Generative AI Innovative Strategies in Digital Marketing Campaigns. *Quarterly Journal of Emerging Technologies and Innovations*, 8(12), 1–9.

Bhuiyan, M. S. (2024). The role of AI-Enhanced personalization in customer experiences. *Journal of Computer Science and Technology Studies*, 6(1), 162–169. DOI: 10.32996/jcsts.2024.6.1.17

Bozkurt, S., Uğursoy, A. S., & Meral, S. P. (2025). The Impact of Personalized Messages and Designs on Consumer Experiences and Marketing Communications in Technology: Hyper-Personalization. In *Impact of Contemporary Technology on Art and Design* (pp. 135–164). IGI Global.

Coelho, M. C. C. D., & Imamović, I. (2025). AI-driven personalization in beauty retail: exploring how AI-based applications influence customer satisfaction and brand loyalty. In *Leveraging AI for Effective Digital Relationship Marketing* (pp. 131–162). IGI Global.

Dai, X., & Liu, Q. (2024). Impact of artificial intelligence on consumer buying behaviors: Study about the online retail purchase. *Journal of Infrastructure. Policy and Development*, 8(9), 7700. DOI: 10.24294/jipd.v8i9.7700

Gujar, V. (2024). New Age Marketing: AI Personalization Strategies In Digital World. *IARJSET International Advanced Research Journal in Science, Engineering and Technology, 11(3).*

Gupta, S., & Joshi, S. (2022, November). Predictive analytic techniques for enhancing marketing performance and personalized customer experience. In 2022 *International Interdisciplinary Humanitarian Conference for Sustainability (IIHC) (pp. 16-22). IEEE*. DOI: 10.1109/IIHC55949.2022.10060286

Heinemann, G., Sonntag, K., & Groß, M. (2023). Best Practices for AI in Retail: Also for Multisensory? In *Multisensory in Stationary Retail: Principles and Practice of Customer-Centered Store Design* (pp. 167–181). Springer Fachmedien Wiesbaden. DOI: 10.1007/978-3-658-38227-8_12

Hussain, Z., Mari, I. H., & Rind, A. A. (2022). Exploring The Barriers of Artificial Intelligence Adoption in Digital Marketing Landscape. *ULIL ALBAB: Jurnal Ilmiah Multidisiplin*, 1(4), 824–835.

Hussain, Z., & Saad, N. M. (2023). Investigating the Efficacy of Artification in the Context of Digital Marketing for Corporate Social Responsibility: Examining the Moderating Influence of Brand Authenticity. [IJCBE]. *International Journal of Contemporary Business and Economics*, 1(1), 57–68. DOI: 10.61338/ijcbe.v1i1.1

Hussain, Z., Sultan, R., Asadullah, A., Arif, M., & Ali, A. (2022). The Impact of Zakat Literacy, Trust, and the Accessibility of Digital Payments on Generation Z and Y's Intention to Pay Zakat to Central Zakat Fund, the State Bank of Pakistan. *International Journal of Zakat*, 7(2), 105–114.

Ifekanandu, C. C., Anene, J. N., Iloka, C. B., & Ewuzie, C. O. (2023). Influence of artificial intelligence (AI) on customer experience and loyalty: Mediating role of personalization. *Journal of Data Acquisition and Processing*, 38(3), 1936.

Isidore, R., & Arun, C. J. (2021). An enquiry into the purchase intention of AI–based virtual personal voice assistants in India. [IJBE]. *International Journal of Business & Economics*, 6(2), 52–63.

Isidore, R., & Arun, C. J. (2023). Dimensions of indian consumers' beliefs about AI: An orthogonal linear transformation approach. *Revista Gestão & Tecnologia*, 23(1), 10–28.

Isidore, R., & Arun, C. J. (2023). Are Indian Consumers willing to share personal data to avail personalized recommendations?-Indian Artificial Intelligence Market Perspective. [Formerly known as Iranian Journal of Management Studies]. *Interdisciplinary Journal of Management Studies*, 17(1), 277–293.

Kannan, R. (2024). Revolutionizing the Tourism Industry through Artificial Intelligence: A Comprehensive Review of AI Integration, Impact on Customer Experience, Operational Efficiency, and Future Trends. *International Journal for Multidimensional Research Perspectives, 2(2), 01-14.*

Kaperonis, S. (2024). How artificial intelligence (AI) is transforming the user experience in digital marketing. In *The use of artificial intelligence in digital marketing: Competitive strategies and tactics* (pp. 117–141). IGI Global.

Khan, A., Hamid, A. B. A., Saad, N. M., Hussain, Z., & Arif, A. R. (2023). Effectiveness of artificial intelligence in building customer loyalty: Investigating the mediating role of chatbot in the tourism sector of Pakistan. *International Journal of Academic Research in Business & Social Sciences*, 13(9), 657–671. DOI: 10.6007/IJARBSS/v13-i9/18895

Khan, A. W., & Mishra, A. (2024). AI credibility and consumer-AI experiences: A conceptual framework. *Journal of Service Theory and Practice*, 34(1), 66–97. DOI: 10.1108/JSTP-03-2023-0108

Kumar, G., Seshasai, S. J., & Shriya, K. (2024). Tailored to Perfection: How AI-Driven Service Customization Is Revolutionizing Emerging Markets. In *Integrating AI-Driven Technologies Into Service Marketing* (pp. 575–594). IGI Global. DOI: 10.4018/979-8-3693-7122-0.ch028

Kwong, A. T. M., Omar, S. I., & Aliah, M. N. (2024). The Ethical Implications of AI-Powered Personalization in Hospitality and Tourism. In *Impact of AI and Tech-Driven Solutions in Hospitality and Tourism* (pp. 103–122). IGI Global. DOI: 10.4018/979-8-3693-6755-1.ch006

Mishra, D., Das, S., & Patnaik, R. (2024). Application of AI Technology for the Development of Destination Tourism towards an Intelligent Information System. *Economic Affairs*, 69(2), 1083–1095.

Moghaddasnian, A. H. (2024). Artificial Intelligence and the Great Transformation in the Tourism Industry Revolutionizing Travel Services. *Journal of Business Data Science Research*, 3(01), 36–47.

Mukherjee, S. (2023). Understanding the Role of Data in Artificial Intelligence-Based Personalization. In *Artificial Intelligence in Customer Service: The Next Frontier for Personalized Engagement* (pp. 155–177). Springer International Publishing. DOI: 10.1007/978-3-031-33898-4_7

Mutyala, V., Anaparthi, V., Mundru, Y., & Yogi, M. K. (2022). Frontiers of AI beyond 2030: Novel Perspectives. *Journal of Artificial Intelligence*, 4(4), 246–262.

Nalla, L. N., & Reddy, V. M. (2024). AI-Driven Big Data Analytics for Enhanced Customer Journeys: A New Paradigm in E-Commerce. *International Journal of Advanced Engineering Technologies and Innovations*, 1(2), 719–740.

Nimbalkar, A. A., & Berad, A. T. (2021). The increasing importance of AI applications in e-commerce. *Vidyabharati International Interdisciplinary Research Journal*, 13(1), 388–391.

Oanh, V. T. K. (2024). Revolutionizing Engagement: How AI is Transforming the Digital Marketing Landscape. *Journal of Electrical Systems*, 20(4s), 2504–2514. DOI: 10.52783/jes.2914

Palumbo, S., & Edelman, D. (2023). What smart companies know about integrating AI. *Harvard Business Review*, 101(7–8), 116–125.

Paripati, L., Hajari, V. R., Narukulla, N., Prasad, N., Shah, J., & Agarwal, A. (2024). AI Algorithms for Personalization: Recommender Systems, Predictive Analytics, and Beyond. *Darpan International Research Analysis*, 12(2), 51–63.

Potla, R. T., & Pottla, V. K. (2024). AI-Powered Personalization in Salesforce: Enhancing Customer Engagement through Machine Learning Models. *Valley International Journal Digital Library, 1388-1420.*

Rathore, B. (2020). Personalization and profits: The impact of ai on targeted digital marketing. *International Journal of Transcontinental Discoveries*, 7(1), 1–14.

Saxena, S. K., Gupta, V., & Kumar, S. (2024). Enhancing Guest Loyalty in the Hotel Industry Through Artificial Intelligence-Drive Personalization. In *New Technologies in Virtual and Hybrid Events* (pp. 335–350). IGI Global. DOI: 10.4018/979-8-3693-2272-7.ch017

Sekar, S., Dutta, C., Spoorthi, R., Mohammed, N. Q., Al-Khuzaie, M. Y., & Almulla, A. A. (2024, May). A Well Design of Customer Centric Based Financing Service through Biometric Based Veritable System using Personalized AI Integrated System. *In 2024 4th International Conference on Advance Computing and Innovative Technologies in Engineering (ICACITE) (pp. 1109-1113). IEEE.*

Semwal, R., Tripathi, N., Rana, A., Dafouti, B. S., Bairwa, M. K., & Mathur, V. (2024, May). AI-Powered Personalization and Emotional Intelligence Integration for Enhanced Service Marketing in Transformative Tourism Experiences. *In 2024 International Conference on Communication, Computer Sciences and Engineering (IC3SE) (pp. 1851-1856). IEEE.*

Şenyapar, H. N. D. (2024). The Future of Marketing: The Transformative Power of Artificial Intelligence. *International Journal of Management and Administration*, 8(15), 1–19. DOI: 10.29064/ijma.1412272

Sharma, V., & Bose, I. (2024). Unlocking AI's Potential in Customer Service Marketing. In *AI Innovations in Service and Tourism Marketing* (pp. 80–103). IGI Global. DOI: 10.4018/979-8-3693-7909-7.ch005

Shree, S. (2023). Revolutionizing Ecommerce: Harnessing the Power of ChatGPT and Generative AI for Personalized Customer Engagement and Enhanced Shopping Experiences. *International Journal of Innovations in Science, Engineering And Management, 72-75.*

Singh, P. (2023). AI-Driven Personalization in Telecom Customer Support: Enhancing User Experience and Loyalty. *Distributed Learning and Broad Applications in Scientific Research*, 9, 325–363.

Thandayuthapani, S., Thirumoorthi, P., Elantheraiyan, P., Jenefa, L., & Selvakumar, M. (2024). An Exploration of Consumer Engagement Strategies Through the Lens of Artificial Intelligence in Marketing Personalization. In *Integrating AI-Driven Technologies Into Service Marketing* (pp. 135–152). IGI Global. DOI: 10.4018/979-8-3693-7122-0.ch008

Thirupathi, L., Sunkara, S. H., Boodala, I. R., & Vempati, V. S. (2024). Personalization and Customization Strategies With AI in Service Marketing. In *Integrating AI-Driven Technologies Into Service Marketing* (pp. 499–524). IGI Global. DOI: 10.4018/979-8-3693-7122-0.ch024

Whig, P., Bhatia, A. B., & Yathiraju, N. (2024). AI-Driven Innovations in Service Marketing Transforming Customer Engagement and Experience. In *AI Innovations in Service and Tourism Marketing* (pp. 17–34). IGI Global. DOI: 10.4018/979-8-3693-7909-7.ch002

Xu, S. (2024). Exploring the Impact of Personalization in Artificial Intelligence on Digital Marketing: Performance Evaluation. *Journal of Innovation and Development*, 8(1), 41–44. DOI: 10.54097/tht8d457

Chapter 17
Incorporating Artificial Intelligence in Branding:
Revolutionizing Strategies and Addressing Challenges in the Indian Market

Utsav Krishan Murari
https://orcid.org/0009-0007-1606-6775
Sharda University, India

Hemlata Parmar
https://orcid.org/0009-0009-1438-5427
Manipal University Jaipur, India

Rashid Hashmi
https://orcid.org/0009-0006-3232-0705
Sharda University, India

ABSTRACT

This chapter explores the incorporation of Artificial Intelligence (AI) in branding, particularly within the Indian market. It analyzes the impact of AI technology on branding strategies, improving consumer engagement, and addressing the problems encountered by Indian firms in embracing these breakthroughs. The study offers practical insights into AI applications in many sectors, identifying obstacles to effective implementation and providing strategic recommendations for brands aiming to optimize AI's potential. The findings indicate that, although AI presents substantial prospects to enhance brand equity, its effective implementation requires a strategic strategy that meticulously addresses technological, ethical, and consumer-related concerns.

DOI: 10.4018/979-8-3693-9461-8.ch017

1. INTRODUCTION

1.1 Background of Artificial Intelligence

In the recent past, Artificial Intelligence (AI) has become the determining factor for future advancement of technology that plays an active role in the operation of companies and the economy of various countries. This technology comprises many technologies intended to achieve tasks that necessitate human intellect, such as learning, reasoning and problem-solving. It is a cardinal metric conceived as the "science and engineering of intelligent action". This definition is considered one of the most important definitions concerning Artificial Intelligence. The central notion of artificial intelligence is the ability to implement basic thinking skills in machines to an extent or even more significant than the human mind. Artificial intelligence can be dated back to the mid-twentieth century when Alan Turing defined a critical question, "Can machines think?" in 1950, according to Turing. Since then, there have been a few waves of technological advancements in the artificial intelligence field. Symbolic AI, or the AI that combines logical reasoning and intelligence, was first conceived in 1950/1960. Expert systems subgrouped into rule-based expert systems, and machine learning evolved as a new area in the mid-eighties and early nineties. That was, instead, a significant improvement. By contrast, the twenty-first century is a delightful epoch for artificial intelligence, mainly due to significant progress in deep learning. Artificial neurons involved in deep learning are algorithms that copy the brain's structure to solve complex issues such as image understanding, natural language analysis, and decision-making.

A new wave of deployment of artificial intelligence has been marked due to the new social media, e-commerce, and big data platforms. This has enabled brands to receive real-time information from massive databases and change their communication strategy. Perhaps one of the most critical factors is the massive value artificial intelligence can place on customer behaviour. Questionnaires and face-to-face interviews are examples of traditional market research techniques that provide little information on the citizens' choices. There are numerous opportunities for gathering consumer sentiment information, starting from social networks and passing through reviews, e-shopping platforms, etc. All this information can be analysed with the help of AI. Businesses get an opportunity to design customer experiences that help fans especially engage with them, thus making them loyal to brands. This ability to extract business intelligence from big data enables the construction of these experiences.

Table 1. AI Adoption in Various Industries

Industry	Ai Application	Adoption Level	Key Benefits
Healthcare	Diagnostics, predictive analytics	High	Improved diagnostics, lower costs
Finance	Fraud detection, trading algorithms	Very high	Efficient transactions reduce fraud
Retail	Personalisation, supply chain optimisation	Moderate	Better customer engagement, optimised stock
Branding	Consumer insights, automation	High	Enhanced personalisation, operational efficiency

Due to advanced artificial intelligence automation techniques, several operational branding elements are less operational on the customer interface or supply chain management. Thus, companies' strategic objectives have been realised to enhance the effectiveness of internal activities and introduce more effective methods for resource allocation. In today's highly competitive world, it is imperative to be capable of fulfilling requests with high speed and quality where the customers' expectations are always and always on the rise. Besides reducing operating costs, AI tools such as chatbots, virtual assistants, and predictive analysis allow organisations to offer customers an experience that is as close to inspiring as possible (Bansal, 2020).

1.2 The Indian Market Landscape

On this topic, AI is one of the few unmissable opportunities for marketers in the world market, or at least in the Indian market. Indeed, India is among the three largest consumer markets, comprising over 1.4 billion people, but it is one of the most diverse. The country's population remains one of the most challenging markets for brands since it has a significant economic division, education, language, and cultural diversity. However, India's increasing computerisation has enabled companies to interact with customers in various ways, creating opportunities. India has undergone a digital transformation in the last ten years, due to which Internet connections and smartphones have become readily available. To connect more and more people and reduce the digital divide, the government of India launched a program known as Digital India in 2015. As a result, internet use in a new social segment has also increased. IAMAI believes that in 2025, the total Internet users in India will be over 900 million (IAMAI, 2022). With increased internet usage, information, communication, and even shopping are some aspects that Indians have benefited from. Out of them, one of the most noticeable shifts is the invasion of the online shopping space in India. A record number of the Indian population is now participating in online purchases mainly because of the improving affordability of cell phones and Internet connections. Increased digital payment systems, the emergence of online retail platforms, and changes in consumer behaviour will help the growth of the Indian e-commerce market. They may reach a figure of $ 200 billion by the year 2026, as depicted in Statista (2023). This is another primary e-commerce strategy taken by Amazon, Flipkart, Snapdeal, and several other more prominent and small e-commerce companies since they always display various products and services readily available from the marketplace and at more affordable prices. One of the biggest challenges facing brands is the problem of capturing and retaining consumers' attention in light of the rapidly evolving digital environment. Several information types are within their reach, resulting in increased consciousness and demand for quality among Indian customers. Generation Y expects to receive quality products and services from businesses and, simultaneously, expects to be offered personalised services or products based on their individualistic nature. To sum up, artificial intelligence has become one of the most important assets to brands seeking to stand out from competitors in this environment and develop relationships with consumers.

Personalisation is the process of making a product for a specific individual, and it is one of the trendiest factors in the Indian industry. Any message that has to be communicated to all the consumers in India cannot be acceptable now. Brands expect them to understand their personal preferences and create unique experiences. At the same time, marketing professionals can now use consumer data to design personal marketing approaches, products to offer, and methods to engage potential customers through AI (Jha, 2022). Traditional recommendation systems used by online stores like AMAZON and FLIPKART are intelligent recommendation engines that recommend products to users based on their earlier purchases, browsing and overall preferences.

Figure 1. Line graph showing the growth of internet penetration in India (from 2015 to 2025 projections)

Two line graphs show how internet usage has grown in India over the year 2015-2025 and the growth of e-commerce during the same period. This visualisation will help compare the value of the leading digital domains in accessing markets in India. IAMAI. (2022). Furthermore, AI enables Indian firms to deal with the factors of a heterogeneously constructed consumer base. One of the most significant challenges of communicating with consumers is the language; there are over 22 official languages and several dialects across the country. That is where brands can leverage AI-driven NLP solutions to overcome this challenge by helping them generate multilingually relevant content relevant to the consumers' language (Mehta & Jain, 2023). This is particularly relevant in the so-called 'emerging' markets, such as rural areas, where internet connection is growing, and the audience prefers to communicate with brands in their first language.

1.3 Importance of AI in Branding

The use of AI in branding may be categorised into five critical domains, each capable of profoundly influencing brand-consumer engagement and market differentiation.

1.3.1 Enhanced Personalization

Branding has become personalised, and AI is the epitome of personalisation in the modern world. Today, the consumer is continuously bombarded with several forms of marketing communications from different brands in the digital environment. As such, consumers have become more selective with whom they transact and what brands they patronise. Brands operating in this environment must find unique selling propositions to create a sense of relevance with selected target consumers. AI helps firms analyse vast amounts of information, including a client's buying profile, website visits, and interactions, to create relevant marketing communications and recommended products (Mehta & Jain, 2023). The value and impact of AI-based personalisation solutions are generally best illustrated by market leaders within e-commerce, such as Amazon or Netflix. These organisations use AI algorithms to examine user data and give personalised product marketing and content suggestions. Such a high level of customisation has illustrated the possibility of boosting consumer engagement and sales. Although Amazon's recommendation program is one of its most critical components, contributing to 35% of the company's revenue, AI-driven personalisation significantly impacts a business (Kumar & Singh, 2022). These are more than fleeting benefits of producing customised products. In other cases, consumers feel that a business understands their needs and gets it right; they will likely build long-term relationships with such a brand. This may lead to more excellent client loyalty and retention, which are crucial factors in the present intense market. Literature review shows that a one-on-one marketing approach can increase revenue returns by 20%, proving how important personalisation is in business growth (Kumar & Singh, 2022).

1.3.2 Improved Customer Insights

One of the first benefits here is the ability of AI to provide a deep and comprehensive analysis of brand-related consumer behaviours. Traditionally, companies have relied on processes such as polls and group discussions to gain insight into their target audience. While these methods can provide unique approaches, it is often the case that these methods are limited in their range, and results may take a while to yield themselves. On the other hand, with adequate data feeding, AI analyses vast amounts of data in record time, supplying brands with information on consumer trends or usage and other relevant data in real-time (Nair, 2023). Social media OPINION mining also allows a brand to review the result of its performance by examining the posts it receives on social media and other forms of consumer opinions like the reviews received by various brands. Understanding consumer attitudes towards their brand allows organisations to make sound decisions about product development, promotional activities and effective means of improving customer relations. A brand that identifies a negative attitude towards a particular product attribute can quickly address a problem before it escalates into a significant image crisis.

Figure 2. AI's Impact on Consumer Behavior across areas like personalised recommendations and automation.

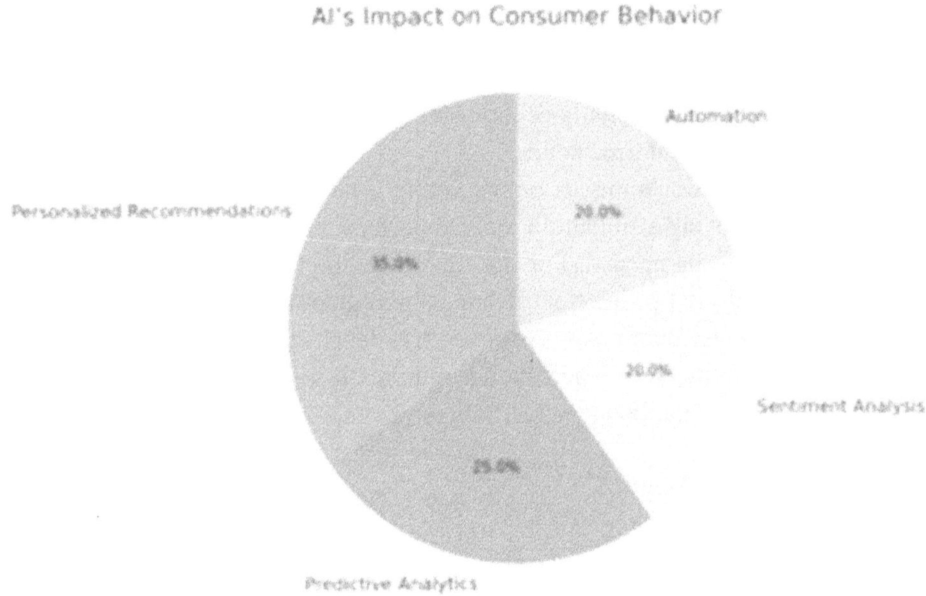

Predictive Analysis is one of the powerful AI tools that help brand owners foresee customers' actions shortly. The future behaviour of customers may be predicted by AI algorithms if there is historical data that the AI will analyse. Most branding concerns can be informed by such information, particularly on new product development and marketing activities. A fashion brand might use this analytical tool to forecast which clothing types and colours will likely gain popularity in the upcoming season. Hence, with this information, the brand can adapt its stock and strategy to promote goods to match consumers' behaviour (Rani, 2020).

1.3.3 Automation and Efficiency

It has impacted branding in several crucial aspects, including automation. AI manages core tasks, which helps the brands focus on other high-priority activities and cuts across processes. Consumers today expect brands to adapt and be quick in the digital economy, as Bansal (2020) has noted. This is of considerable significance consequently.

Among the solutions that help brands enhance their customer service function, AI chatbots have become indispensable. Indeed, chatbots can handle a wide range of consumer queries, from answering general and common questions to guiding the customer to a particular product or product type. This improves the customer experience since most questions are answered instantaneously, and humans assume more complex queries. In addition, the ability of the automated chatbot to stay online permanently means that customers will always be able to get the help they need at any time. This is exceptionally economical when used in a world market where buyers can be in different time zones.

However, automation's impact on marketing is becoming enormously influential. It also allows using efficient AI tools to perform real-time analysis and tweak the campaign result as needed. For instance, AI can change bidding approaches employed in the digital promotion of brands and guarantee the optimal value of undertaking advertisement costs. However, this level of efficacy is beneficial in today's competitive markets, where brands require the highest return on investment (ROI) on their marketing budgets.

1.3.4 Predictive Analytics

The assumed and virtual model powered by AI has emerged as a valuable instrument for guessing the likely behaviour of customers and the future course in terms of market trends. Forecasting is simply an extrapolation of trends analysed from past purchases or trends to tell us about how and what people will be more likely to want to buy in the future of the product. This helps the brands make decisions beforehand, like introducing new products, developing marketing strategies, and managing their supplies(Rani, 2020). For instance, in the retail segment of the economy, predictive analytics can be used to build a capability to predict how much of a given product will be required and to adjust the stock to such a level. When a brand makes correct assumptions about which products customers will desire, it can also minimise the times when there are no products to sell or when there are too many products, elevating profits over time. Marketing strategies can also be supported by the use of statistics about customers to show when and how to market to various classes of customers. This ensures that brands communicate the right message to the right audience at the right time, thus making their campaigns more pleasing.

1.4 Challenges in AI Adoption

1.4.1 Data Privacy Concerns

First, relying on consumer data focuses on privacy and security issues, while AI has numerous benefits in branding. Privacy concerns have now shifted to branding because consumers are now alert to the gathering of their personal information. Data privacy has been at the centre stage of public debate in recent years due to several data breaches and scandals, such as the Cambridge Analytica scandal (Sen & Roy, 2020). Hence, consumers are much more reluctant to share their personal information with brands, while any data misuse can be financially costly and damaging to the brand. These problems, therefore, call for the insurance of ethical and transparent approaches to company practices, primarily in the data processing areas. This touches on the necessity of compliance with data protection laws such as the GDPR of the European Union and India's Personal Data Protection Bill, which has yet to be released into the market. Then, there is the simple act of informing the users of the purpose for collecting, using and protecting the data collected. It is imperative to obtain consumer's trust in the modern world, which is why brands that focus on data protection can do so.

1.4.2 Technological Barriers

While AI offers a range of benefits to brands, some technological challenges may hinder the use of the technology. For instance, many small and medium-scale enterprises (SMEs) in India lack the correct physical infrastructure, financial capital, and training to implement AI solutions effectively. Despite the higher cost of AI-powered technologies and the relative shortage of skilled professionals, it becomes an issue for brands when they cannot fully leverage AI to its full potential (Rani, 2020). To overcome these challenges, brands must build staff competencies and partner with technology vendors. When engaging outside partners for AI solutions, organisations acquire the necessary tools and professional advice for applying AI solutions. In addition, governments and industry associations should help small and medium-sized businesses acquire the funds, education, and tools needed to adopt AI.

1.4.3 Ethical Considerations

The ethical implications of artificial intelligence in branding raise some pertinent questions regarding the proper use of those technologies. Issues such as algorithm bias, information manipulation, and influencing consumer behaviour must be carefully scrutinised to ensure AI's proper and clean use (Dhingra, 2021). However, if

AI algorithms are not built very carefully, they tend to repeat existing biases, which would be unjust or discriminating in marketing campaigns.

In order to solve these ethical problems, it is necessary to develop clear guidelines for AI use in organisations' marketing campaigns. This means ensuring that AI algorithms are seen to be open, unbiased and aligned to the customers' requirements. In addition, organisations should engage consumers in discussions on how their data will be used to make AI decisions and their role in making these decisions. This way, people will trust organisational ethical practices and ensure that AI is used to help enterprises and society.

1.5 Strategic Implications for Indian Brands

1.5.1 Consumer-Centric Strategies

Hence, the trending AI domain in the branding context implies that the relevancy of branding strategies is based on consumer preferences and demands for Indian brands. This means marketers seek to create valuable consumer interactions and enhance more targeted AI marketing. Finally, brands will serve customers' needs the best to encourage them to connect with the branded products, and by using artificial intelligence, companies will make sure that consumers feel some appeal towards brands. Besides, AI can help brands build communities around their products and services. When engaging in conversations and interacting with their fans on social media, brands are bound to have improved ways of interacting with consumers and gathering data on their choices. For instance, Nykaa beauty brands use AI tools to create a loyal customer base through meaningful engagement tools for virtual try-on services and product suggestions.

1.5.2 Collaborative Ecosystems

The second strategy crucial to Indian firms that want to adopt AI properly is partnership. Through partnering with technology firms, industry coalitions, and AI solution providers, brands need to get the enablers and guidance needed to implement AI solutions properly. In addition, there is an opportunity for cooperation with industries that help brands stay competitive in the increasing popularity of AI-based facilities and share knowledge. Indian retail brands could, for instance, enhance their inventory management and logistics by partnering with AI-enabled logistics and supply chain management companies. This partnership would help brands enhance their flow and the satisfaction of consumers through available stock and timely delivery.

1.5.3 Continuous Learning and Adaptation

Brands' challenge is to be committed to continuous education and improvement against the constantly evolving AI environment. One requirement is getting information regarding the current technological developments, consumer demands, and legislation policies that influence AI use. As WFA noted, for brands to maintain sustainable long-term success in today's rapidly evolving digital environment, there is a need to build an organisational culture of adaptability and innovation. Paying more on research is also necessary for brands that may want to explore new opportunities in the application of AI. Different technologies are ways brands can assemble competitive advantage and determine fresh growth alternatives. For instance, in the fashion industry, firms can incorporate AI to forecast trends and trends consumer inclinations, and thus, the competition will be kept off.

Thus, AI will gradually take a much more important place in branding as India is gradually becoming digital. Thus, leveraging AI technologies will put brands in a better position to build consumer loyalty and engagement and optimise their operations. To fully leverage the AI benefits, though, there are challenges that Indian brands will need to face, including ethics, technology, and data privacy.

However, the future of branding in India will depend more on the consumer-oriented strategic approach a brand chooses to employ when integrating it with AI. When these brands promote transparency and ethical practice, besides working together, they can become leaders in the market, and consumers will trust them. I do not doubt that in India and at the global level, AI will play a significant role in defining the future of branding as it unfolds.

2. AI AND ITS ROLE IN MODERN BRANDING

AI has turned into a critical component of approaches throughout many markets, making branding one of them. This has transformed from a mere theory to a powerful tool that brands use to boost effectiveness for internal audiences and customers and create new experiences. The article's next section is dedicated to applying AI to branding, its development, and examples of successful branding utilising AI by major brands.

2.1 Evolution of Artificial Intelligence in Business

AI's transformation from an immature idea to a usable tool in commerce has epitomised technical advancement and innovation. Cognitive science is the foundation of Artificial Intelligence. As such, thought processing and rule-based systems were developed to mimic human brain work. AI of yesteryears was designed to solve problems as it was programmed to conclude, like how humans follow set logical patterns to arrive at decisions. However, these systems were limited in the level of what they could get through because they relied extensively on human intervention and coding (Russell & Norvig, 2021).

The development of machine learning systems at the end of the twentieth century marked significant progress in artificial intelligence. Unlike symbolic reasoning, machine learning involves computers giving them some data, learning and making decisions by themselves with no need for instructions tailored for specific cases. This advancement opened new horizons for AI, especially for fields that require data analysis on large portions of the data available, such as finance, healthcare and marketing. There are numerous types of applications for machine learning, ranging from image recognition to NLP and even self-employing decision-making due to the development of high-quality computational systems.

To augment the first, the appearance of deep learning as a kind of machine learning bolstered AI's prospects. This has features such as deep learning models, which mimic the structure of the human brain but can learn and adapt on their own based on the data they scan. These models have shown explicit effectiveness in voice recognition, image categorisation, and predictive modelling. Therefore, AI gradually became not only an idea but also a tool that has become reasonably practical and a necessity for most business processes (Russell & Norvig, 2021). We currently use artificial intelligence in various areas of the business world, including prediction, automation, and customer relations. Artificial intelligence enables organisations to improve how they function and execute business processes, make enhanced decisions, and serve their clients better. AI incorporated into branding is not an isolated case: Generally, firms use AI tools to gain insights into consumers' behaviour, enhance their marketing strategy, and provide better experiences. Several technologies, including big data analytics, cloud computing, and IoT, have enabled AI to process large datasets in real-time.

2.2 AI's Strategic Role in Branding

Branding has now stepped beyond customer connectedness and inspired customer stories or concepts. Branding efforts in the current business society are centred on information technology, especially artificial intelligence. Due to such characteristics, brands can obtain new knowledge about customers, their preferences and attitudes with a very high level of accuracy thanks to the use of AI to work with big data. Through AI-powered branding campaigns, data collected in these three areas is used to launch unique marketing promotions, improve communication with consumers, and improve recommendations of specific products — all of which deepen the relationship between brands and their consumers.

Personalisation through AI

Personalisation is one of the most impactful areas where AI has changed branding. In the present day, the client expects the marketer to personalise the communication message the product recommended or even the customer care service offered. Based on consumer information, including web history, purchasing behaviour, and social media presence, AI helps brands understand what consumers want and need next (Kumar & Singh, 2022). As such, brands can offer these personalised experiences. For instance, for entertainment, Netflix uses artificial intelligence to recommend programs to watch given past performances. The platform's recommendation engine is an artificial intelligence that can progress through separate levels of machine learning to propose the movies and Television Shows that the particular user will probably enjoy. Such a level of customisation enhances the use of products and services, keeps the customers engaged and builds brand identity. Similarly, Amazon uses AI to suggest products a consumer has been browsing or related to his previous purchases, thus enhancing consumer sales by offering items they are likely to purchase (Mamoon et al., 2020).

The rise of AI-powered personalised marketing campaigns prohibits categorised media assumptions of universal everyday campaigns. AI can differentiate consumers by their interests and activity level, which ensures that the brand delivers the right message to the right consumer at the right time.

Enhancing Operational Efficiency

Likewise, the execution of branding is another domain advantageously supported by AI. For example, most companies have adopted chatbots driven by artificial intelligence. To be able to understand the consumer's message and switch to responding in real time, the use of natural language processing is incorporated into these chatbots. The following benefits are realised through outsourcing customer service: Brands can also adopt customer service automation to help them provide timely service to consumers. This also enhances the quality of experience that the customers are offered while at the same time sparing human labour resources, thus enabling brands to focus on more core strategic responsibilities.

AI can also perform repetitive tasks in marketing and consumer relations. For example, by analysing consumer data, AI can find the most suitable position to place advertisements so that brands can best target potential consumers. Also, AI solutions can promote social media messages, analyse the best time for sending emails, and adjust marketing budgets during the campaigns. The level of automation obtained with this type of solution will allow brands to maximise the ROI of their marketing campaigns, improve performance, and cut expenses.

Predictive Analytics and Consumer Insights

The last strategic use of AI in branding is that it can provide consumer insights and predictive analytics. AI can also analyse data related to past events and mitigate Brands to future trends in consumer demand. AI can predict which products will gain popularity from consumer behaviour and trends. This way, brands can adapt their inventory, marketing strategies, or product portfolio (Mehta & Jain, 2023). Also, using predictive analytics enables the various brands to forecast consumers' needs even before they are expressed. AI can help brands, in particular, remain competitive and innovative by revealing opportunities for new goods or services through the study of specific consumer patterns. Furthermore, with the help of AI and sentiment analysis, consumers' sentiments towards a particular brand or product can be identified simultaneously, taking into account blog posts, comments, and posts on social media platforms. In this manner, brands can fix existing consumer issues, regulate their reputation, and adapt branding strategies based on consumers' current reactions (Bansal, 2020).

Table 2. The role of AI in consumer-centric branding Kumar, A., & Singh, R. (2022)

Strategy	Consumer Engagement	Efficiency	Personalisation Level	Cost Efficiency	Return On Investment (ROI)
Traditional Marketing	Low	Moderate	Low	Moderate	Moderate
Ai-Driven Marketing	High	Very high	High	High	Very high

2.3 Case Studies: AI in Global Branding

AI has changed how international brands communicate with the consumer via branding with the help of AI. Through personalisation, improvement of customer experiences, and driving business growth, various organisations have applied AI. As we examine some of the brands that have utilised AI to transform their branding exercises, some of them are explained below.

Coca-Cola: Artificial Intelligence-Driven Consumer Sentiment Analysis

Coca-Cola has been a pioneer of branding for a long time, and to stay ahead in digital marketing, the firm has integrated artificial intelligence (AI). Coca-Cola's most significant use of AI is in consumer sentiment analysis. The company uses A. I programmed to discover consumer social media discussions about the company's products and its promotional strategies on various social sites, customer ratings, and reviews. Consumer expectations and perceptions can be met by Coca-Cola when the company adapts branding strategies by getting real-time data about consumer opinions. For instance, to establish which flavours its consumers liked when the company released new products, Coca-Cola used artificial intelligence (AI) to analyse the social media buzz of the new products. On the other hand, honest customer feedback helped the company to fine-tune its various marketing campaigns and products in the production line. Moreover, artificial intelligence is also used by Coca-Cola to produce various content for its customers, which will specifically depend on the individual's choices.

Starbucks: AI-Powered Personalization and Loyalty Programs

AI is also employed in Starbucks' branding, especially its loyalty platform. The Starbucks' mobile application uses artificial intelligence (AI) to enable the company to offer customers unique and customised rewards and suggestions based on the customers' purchase behaviour. The app's new features may include a feature for the next order to be made by a customer by analysing the data from customer interactions, which will make the targeted promotion timely and suitable (Mehta & Jain, 2023). Indeed, Starbucks has incorporated artificial intelligence into supply chain management. The company's consumer demand patterns are analysed through AI to ensure adequate inventory is ordered and stocked in stores without overstocking. Besides, this optimisation has an overall consumer advantage in ensuring that their frequently purchased products are constantly restocked and an operational benefit.

Amazon's AI-Powered Product Recommendations

It is accepted that Amazon has been one of the most successful enterprises in applying artificial intelligence to enhance customers' involvement and customisation. The recommendation engine powered by machine learning algorithms is one of the most potent branding weapons in the company's toolbox. It suggests buyers choose certain products by studying their browsing and purchasing behaviour. Through extensive consumer data analysis, Amazon has the potential to improve the general purchasing experience; therefore, the chances of making a purchase are likely to improve. The AI at Amazon extends far beyond the company's suggestions, which are just based on purchases and searches. Thus, AI is utilised by the organisation as a method of adapting the supply chain, predicting the clients' needs and automating its marketing campaigns. For example, Amazon uses AI in advertisements where brand owners can now sell advertisement slots besides targeting specific customers with adverts that are likely to capture their attention and appeal to them. Such targeting increases the efficiency of advertising messages and helps brands receive a better return on investment.

3. REVOLUTIONIZING BRANDING STRATEGIES WITH AI IN THE INDIAN MARKET

3.1 The Digital Transformation of India

India is standing at the precipice of a significant digital transformation as there is widespread smartphone penetration, increased internet connection, and the growth of e-business. With a more than 1.4 billion population, the nation represents one of the biggest and most involved consumer markets worldwide. Internet access is the key driver of this digital economy, and it is projected that the number of Internet users in India will reach 900 million by 2025 (IAMAI, 2022). This wave of technology is precipitating changes in consumer user profiles; consumers are more connected, informed, and demanding. Since there is a surge in digital media usage, organisations must respond to new consumer expectations and be equipped with information and choices that contrast the past. The fast-growing development of e-stores, web payment systems, and social media interfaces has drastically shifted the paradigm of brand-customer relations. It has become mandatory for every firm to create awareness and make a name for itself in the technological world. In this context, Artificial Intelligence (AI) has become revolutionary for brands to operate complex territories of digital platforms. AI helps brand players understand consumer trends and improve operational activities in the strategic application of campaigns. The AI-related findings help brands obtain the tools necessary to understand the likes and actions of distinct consumer segments, thereby adapting their communication and products. The capability to make an experience unique to many consumers is a prerogative for businesses operating in India, where consumer demand and expectation vary significantly across multiple categories, including urban/rural regions (Kumar & Singh, 2022).

3.2 AI in Personalization and Consumer Engagement

The use of personalisation is one of the key areas through which AI is transforming branding in India. The customers of today's world are already not just waiting but demanding more than just simple promotional techniques. They expect brands to break the mould and know what they want in order to provide them with the experience they need. AI brings this personalisation to life using consumer data, including web usage, purchase patterns and social media interactions, to deliver tailored marketing messages, product recommendations and customer experiences (Jha, 2022). This is because, through AI, brands can understand consumer data at an immense level and, therefore, develop more unique and personal content, improving customer engagement. For instance, Flipkart, one of India's leading e-tailing portals, uses Artificial intelligence algorithms to provide product recommendations based on customers' shopping activity. When Flipkart recommends products to buy, it can bring a good impression to the customer and boost the chance of purchase since buyers would prefer to get an item that suits their interest. Likewise, fashion e-tail seller Myntra uses AI to assist its clients in finding what they seek in an online shop. The site also employs an artificial intelligence system to assess consumer information and provide optimal product recommendations to guarantee that each client has the identical purchasing experience they perceive as appropriate for their individuality. In addition to enhancing consumers' satisfaction, Myntra provides them with a convenient shopping experience, increasing the chances of consumers shopping with the company due to loyalty. AI is not restricted to personalisation in e-commerce, although it plays a significant role in personalised recommendation systems. It is also changing how consumers are reached on popular social media platforms. Social media has become the platform where brands can interact with the consumer, and AI helps brands extract insights from social media conversations. This real-time engagement creates a feeling of togetherness with a brand, which is imperative in creating loyal customers in the marketplace (Kumar & Singh, 2022). However, brands can better use AI to understand customer interactions across social media sites, fueling effective marketing strategies targeting the particular target market. Consolidated communication and delivering the right message at the right time and on the right channel are big pluses for Indian brands targeting increasingly connected consumers. Thus, apart from increasing customer interactions, brand deployment as an AI solution offers an opportunity for a brand to have a qualitatively different and more profound interaction with an audience.

3.3 AI-Driven Marketing Automation

Marketing is another application for AI in India, as well as the augmentation of personalisation and enhancement of consumer engagements. Marketing automation uses artificial intelligence (AI) technologies to perform routine tasks such as marketing advertisements, scheduling social media posts and sending emails. At the same time, it ensures that their marketing campaigns will be even more efficient and effective. Brands can save time and money by automating these things. Applying marketing automation through artificial intelligence and machine learning means that brands use these tools to implement better marketing approaches that promote personalised and unique marketing communication. This level of automation helps brands enhance the effectiveness of their digital advertising campaigns without having to engage the services of the workforce all the time. AI marketing automation technology is now making a breakthrough in how different brands approach their marketing strategies, which are applied in India. AI increases brand efficiency, delivering higher consumer engagement by transforming marketing campaigns to optimise marketing efforts and eliminating routine tasks. Marketing automation by AI technologies will remain an ongoing process, and new possibilities in marketing performance optimisation will continue to appear in the future for brands with the development of AI.

3.4 Challenges and Opportunities for AI Adoption in Branding

While AI aids the branding process in many ways in India, there are still numerous challenges that brands must overcome to harness the power of AI fully. The limitations are still the lack of such fundamental infrastructure and skilled labour force to embrace AI technologies as they are. Many are inadequately equipped with human resources and technology for AI-assisted branding endeavours (Rani, 2020). Even today, the cost of implementing AI tools and, more importantly, access to AI talent is a significant challenge in India for lesser brands that do not have deep pockets. The other issue that needs to be addressed is safety, considering data security and privacy. AI heavily relies on consumer data to deliver customised experiences, but the extraction and usage of these data are privacy and security issues. Indian consumers are slowly gaining a better appreciation of their data and are beginning to be wary of how brands use them.

Figure 3. Primary challenges in adopting AI in branding Rani, A. (2020)

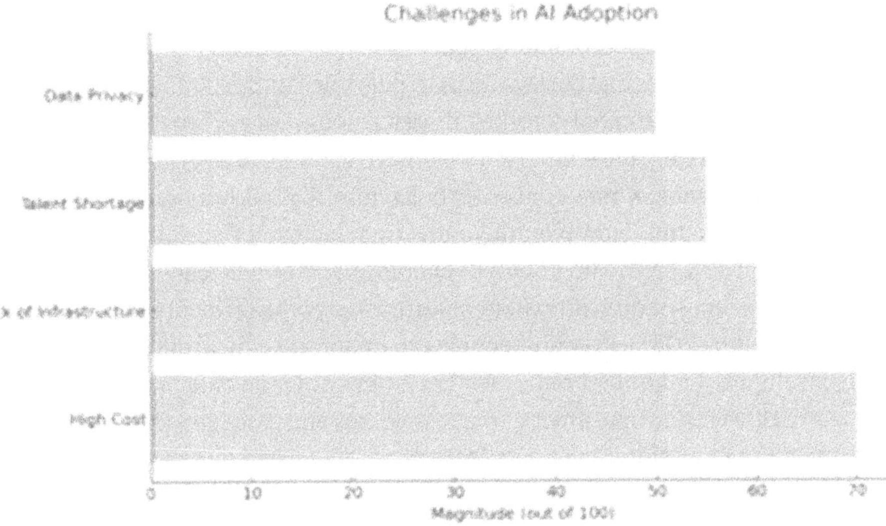

An illustrative bar chart showing the main challenges to AI use in branding is shown below: Every bar will represent a challenge; the bar height corresponds to the challenge level as assessed according to surveys or reports. In conclusion, it can be said that despite the significant number of threats accompanying AI integration into branding, the future opportunities outweigh all these threats. Technologies continue to develop, and businesses integrating AI will benefit from increased competitiveness, enabling them to interact with customers more effectively, offer personal interactions, and develop closer, longer-lasting relationships with consumers.

4. ETHICAL CONSIDERATIONS IN AI-DRIVEN BRANDING

With AI increasingly utilised in branding strategies, moral issues arise with opportunities for branding tactics. AI is changing brand-consumer connections by leveraging data to enhance marketing techniques and automate client relations. This reliance on AI regularly raises many dilemmas in the sphere of ethicality, starting with privacy and transparency alongside bias and regulation. Ethical branding execution utilising AI is critical to leveraging its possibilities, upholding clients' trust, and avoiding perpetuating inequity. In this chapter, related topics will be the relevance of ethical AI practices, problems with algorithmic bias and the common need for regulation to apply AI in branding properly.

4.1 The Importance of Ethical AI Practices

Integrating AI into the branding process makes branding more important by raising ethical questions that come with its expansion. Automated systems integrated into the usage of AI commonly work with vast amounts of personal and behavioural data in data processing, presenting personalised material, or decision-making. Used correctly, it is a window into consumer behaviour that allows brands to engage in narrow-cast marketing. However, the collection and use of such information raise definite ethical concerns. The improper handling of this data leads to privacy violations, the worsening of discriminatory algorithms and the influencing of customers' conduct (Dhingra, 2021). Privacy becomes an important ethical question to consider when developing branding through AI. Lack of trust in the data held by brands can lead to a backlash from consumers, financial losses and damage to brand reputation, as many of the most significant data leaks in recent years have shown (Sen & Roy, 2020). The main issue that has been identified is transparency.

Customers have a right to know how collected data is used and algorithms that stand behind AI-driven decisions such as recommendations or adverts. Transparency is of even greater importance for the Indian industry because several consumers may be unfamiliar with AI and its use in branding. A lack of transparency may cause confusion and mistrust in the relationship between the intended audience and the brand, especially detrimental to consumer trust. As a result, marketers must provide clear and easy-to-understand information about how their AI systems work and how customer data is used. While personalisation enables a better consumer experience, its negative aspects may be tricky because marketers may use AI to exploit people's weaknesses. Most AI systems can track the emotional conditions of consumers and apply them to situations where consumers are vulnerable to impulsive buying (Dhingra, 2021).

4.2 Addressing Algorithmic Bias

Algorithmic bias is one of the most essential ethical problems in branding based on artificial intelligence. Artificial prejudice in AI stems from the data set upon which the algorithms are based: this data may well express current social inequalities and discriminative practices. AI systems are built with and on past information; if these are biased, the sociopolitical biases inherited in the algorithms will also prove so. Automated decision-making in branding, such as recommendations on products or individualised marketing, may have significant consequences, thus is likely to have unfair or discriminative effects (Sen & Roy, 2020Algorithms can exacerbate existing disparities as seen in India where their different language preferences, regions, and culture make this possible, (Mehta & Jain, 2023). To somewhat reduce the preconceptions, organisations must ensure that their AI systems are trained on extensive datasets that encompass every kind of consumer trait and preference. This involves sourcing data from as many demographics as possible, always conducting assessments for bias in the systems, and fixing these as necessary. The brands must be aware of the biases inside the AI systems they use, and ways to deal with them must be developed beforehand. This is one way of reducing algorithmic bias; algorithmic auditing can be done. Algorithmic auditing is about recognising and eradicating bias from artificial intelligence while shrinking and examining it. While it is faster to analyse data than a human, AI does not inherently possess the judgment or moral scope necessary to understand the ethical implications of its judgments. By integrating human decision-makers into the process, firms can be sure that an ethical evaluator runs AI decisions before implementation. Algorithmic fairness is an emerging subfield that studies how it is possible to design machine-learning models that are fair to different groups of people. Scientists are working on preventing AI models from being prejudiced toward one type, gender, race, etc. One approach is to modify the learning process used in the training of AI algorithms in a way that the empirical error rates are balanced across the relevant categories (Kumar & Singh, 2022).

4.3 The Role of Regulation in Ensuring Ethical AI Use

Since branding has become dependent upon artificial intelligence, protocols are set that guard the usage of AI with the highest standards of ethicality. Many governments and regulatory authorities are adopting measures to protect consumer data privacy, restrict the use of data, and increase the accountability of AI-made decisions. India is on the verge of passing the Personal Data Protection Bill to establish the benchmark for collecting, using, and protecting personal data. This ensures that the consumer is fully aware of how data about him/ her is being processed, and it also enhances consumer confidence between the business entities and consumers.

It is helpful to address the phenomena identified by Dhingra (2021) as AI-facilitated influence, manipulation of the customers, and algorithmic bias. While brands have to follow stated regulatory requirements, they also have to go the extra mile to prevent improper usage of AI systems. This means creating internal policies of ethical AI practices for the organisation and engaging customers to increase brand trust and build trust in AI branding strategies. Brands are expected to adopt guidelines on data management that determine how brands collect, use and protect consumer data. This must meet the legal requirements that are also cultural in the matter. Brands should invest in the ethical training of AI personnel, especially those involved in analysis and AI creation.

This requires giving out time-to-time consumer feedback surveys to assess the overall perception regarding the use of AI by the brand and applying changes whenever they see fit. Consumer participation in AI branding strategy development and implementation is vital for the development of brand trust and for proving the firm's commitment to ethical practices. Branding based on AI utilisation needs careful regulation to prioritise consumers' rights and promote transparency. As we proceed with the regulation, all kinds of brands must adopt ethical policies and legal requirements, which Kim discussed.

5. EMERGING AI TECHNOLOGIES IN BRANDING

As artificial intelligence advances, various emergent technologies are poised to transform branding strategy. These technologies will enhance brand-consumer engagement and equip brands with tools to maintain competitiveness in a swiftly evolving industry. The two most significant developments in this field are conversational AI and predictive branding.

5.1 Conversational AI: Enhancing Brand-Consumer Interactions

Conversational AI based on Natural Language Processing is considered a highly potent technology in branding; as such, it opens up the possibility for more complex and personalised interactions between firms and buyers. Automated conversing interfaces fall into this category, including virtual voice companions, AI-controlled chatbots, and voice and speech detection technology, all designed to imitate human conversational interfaces (Bansal, 2020). This technology has been adopted by many organisations, mainly in customer care, where chatbots provide consumers with a solution to their questions and complaints on the go. The future of conversational AI seems to be ever more personal and effective in responding to users. Over time, as the NLP function enhances, the chatbot will begin to understand the finer emotions of the customer and, in turn, be able to respond in progressively more appropriate ways. This is done entirely using conversational AI as a new medium between brands and audiences – voice assistants like Amazon's Alexa or Apple's Siri. Such voice assistants allow the consumer to engage with the brands without touching something, which is convenient. That means that as speech technology evolves, companies must integrate new approaches that allow them to be optimised for voice search and voice-driven interaction.

5.2 Predictive Branding: Anticipating Consumer Needs

One innovation is predictive branding, which applies artificial intelligence. Predictive branding uses artificial intelligence to analyse broad consumer data, such as the history of clicks, purchases, shares in social networks, and trends, to predict future customer behaviour. By using predictive analytics, brands can predict the needs and wants of consumers before they skip the competition and hence can counteract it and change their products accordingly. This means that through an AI model of predictive branding, societies can identify items and services that will have high traffic shortly. When these patterns are identified early enough, firms can change marketing strategies, inventory levels and product development to meet the consumers' wants. In this context, such a precautionary approach can increase a brand's potential to gain market share and significantly develop customer loyalty. A good example of predictive branding is Netflix; the firm uses artificial intelligence to recommend serials and films to users based on programs they have watched at some point. The recommendation engine forms a significant portion of the company's viewing, illustrating that analytics can improve consumer loyalty (Mehta & Jain, 2023). Predictive analytics is used in retail firms, particularly in supply chains, to ensure that stocks are appropriate at the right time, with overhauling costs accruing to profit improvements. In addition, predictive branding helps firms market their brands more effectively by providing the right branding campaigns. Promoting content with messages expected to resonate primarily with a given consumer enables the marketer to tailor campaign variation to the consumer's inclination.

5.3 AI-Driven Personalization: Beyond Demographics

Therefore, while personalisation has been instrumental in making branding strategic for a long time, AI is taking personalisation to the next level beyond regular demographically based targeting. While this approach to using AI-driven personalisation could essentially be seen as a one-size-fits-all fix, personalisation utilises machine learning to disintegrate the customers further and offer them multiple data points that allow recognition of customer behaviours, preferences and overall relationships with the brand at any given time. In the future, brands will use AI more frequently to deliver first-level experiences at every stage of the path consumers take. This could include but is not limited to target email marketing and a firm's product suggestions based on a particular customer's interests and inclinations. For example, beauty companies such as Sephora are adopting AI to provide product recommendations based on the description of skin type, beauty type and even past purchase records by the customer (Kumar & Singh, 2022). Compelled purchases, more customer loyalty, and repeated purchasing are likely to emanate from these tailored experiences, which the consumer will appreciate

6. THE ROLE OF AI IN SUSTAINABLE BRANDING

Consumers increasingly prioritise sustainability in their purchasing decisions, so businesses are pressured to adopt eco-friendly practices and improve their environmental and social impacts. Artificial Intelligence (AI) has emerged as a transformative tool for sustainable branding, enabling brands to integrate sustainability into their operations, optimise supply chains, and engage with eco-conscious consumers. This section explores AI's pivotal role in reshaping branding strategies to align with sustainability and environmental responsibility values.

6.1 AI-Driven Supply Chain Optimization

Among all the supply chain components is a critical area where AI can significantly improve sustainable branding. They include activities like sourcing raw materials, production, movement of goods and delivery, all of which are accompanied by high environmental impacts. Therefore, brands use AI tools to ascertain where to make green changes that would help cut down the ecological footprint and positively impact business efficiency.

Several technological tools can provide insights into various aspects of SCM and hour-long, convoluted processes to suggest areas where resources are being utilised inefficiently or where waste can be reduced. For example, through the supply chain, logistics through a means of transport, means of assembling and distributing shipments, AI can suggest the means that have minimal environmental impact. Some of these optimisations reduce cost and decrease carbon footprint and other negative externalities, according to Nair (2023).

Only a few companies, such as Patagonia and Unilever, are among the pioneers using artificial intelligence to track their supply chains in real time. This helps them conform to an ethical supply chain and reduce waste.

6.2 AI-Enhanced Sustainable Product Development

Since AI implies the analysis of consumers' preferences and the trends in the market, it is inestimable value in developing sustainable products. Soon, consumers expect the brands to develop products that are kind to the planet as sustainability is becoming trendy. AI helps to achieve this by pinning down specific characteristics that consumers respond to positively, allowing brands to offer products that are both sustainable and can be quickly brought to market.

For Instance: AI trend analysis can identify new trends, such as customer preference for biodegradable packing or packing with recycled materials. Equipped with these tips, brands can modify their manufacturing processes to include eco materiel, minimising wastage and lowering impact on sustainability. Furthermore, AI evaluates consumers' feedback on existing products and can help improve such products to make them better and longer lasting (Rani, 2020).

In fashion, AI has emerged as a major revolution and has caused a paradigm shift in the industry. Today, large corporations like H&M or Zara apply AI to predict the demand for particular styles and work to minimise the number of clothes too many like. The styles and materials will be popular among consumers, thereby successfully utilising the resources.

6.3 Communicating Sustainability Efforts with AI

Sustainability is not only the act of going green but also the ability to convey this to consumers. AI allows brands to improve how their communications resonate with target consumers, all in a bid to improve the environment. Based on consumer opinion and feedback, AI gets brands the proper and penetrative sustainability stories to flow in the market.

Advanced tools such as those based on AI allow for determining consumers' attitudes towards a brand's sustainable activities in its supply chain based on consumer feedback, comments on social media, and other feedback. These insights will help the brands understand any strengths or weaknesses in the messaging intended by the brands to the appropriate audiences. For more illustration, a brand may realise customers are interested in their fight against plastic pollution. It may help the brand focus more on these strategies during their advertising campaigns (Mehta & Jain, 2023).

6.4 AI and the Circular Economy

AI is also used to improve the circular economy, a business model that seeks to reuse or recycle products rather than dispose of them. This strategy is consistent with the third principle of sustainable branding: minimising waste produced.

For instance, AI can calculate data on product usage and wear conditions to determine when a product is no longer helpful. This information aids brands in taking back schemes, whereby consumers can return products after use for recycling or remanufacturing. Further, AI can help plan products that may be easier to disassemble and recycle rather than being discarded, with most of their valuable elements ending up in the dump.

Circular economy projects are being facilitated by artificial intelligence in firms like IKEA. The post pointed out that the furniture retailer applies this to determine which products will most likely be returned for refurnishing or recycled. This role will increase as the brands adopt more innovative AI technology for circular business, meeting consumers' sustainable expectations and being environmentally friendly(Rani, 2020).

The Indian Context and Future Opportunities

During the branding process in India, the advancements of AI provide numerous possibilities for evolving the ways consumer relations are created and sustainable steps are taken. Due to the increasing consumer traffic and complexity in India, brands using AI tools can understand consumer interests and trends and target local consumers ideally.

However, using AI in branding strategies in India also has issues every company faces. These are the requirements for stimulating technology support, issues related to data privacy, and the compliance of contributing to ethical AI usage. These are the hurdles and tasks brands and companies have to face while managing their marketing strategies and ensuring that they follow the culture and preferences of India's populace.

CONCLUSION

AI offers unique possibilities for implementing sustainable branding on a higher level. From smart SCM and supporting sustainable product design to improving customer relations and advocating circular economy strategies, AI presents brands with a clear set of tools for integrating sustainability into business. Adopting AI erratic innovations is a way to the future by succeeding companies in the Indian B2C sector that confront a competitive and volatile environment. In this regard, the most significant potential that is constantly connected with technological development and increased focus on sustainability is that modern brands can affect the outcome and meet the expectations of consumers of the 21st century, participating in the fight for the planet's sustainable development.

REFERENCES

Bansal, S. (2020). AI and its impact on modern business practices. *Business Horizons*, 63(2), 197–205.

Bansal, S. (2020). AI and its impact on modern business practices. *Business Horizons*, 63(2), 197–205.

Dhingra, P. (2021). Ethics in AI: Navigating the complexities of algorithmic decision-making. *Journal of Ethics in Technology*, 15(3), 89–104.

IAMAI. (2022). *India's Internet revolution: Growth projections and market insights*. Internet and Mobile Association of India.

IAMAI. (2022). *India's Internet revolution: Growth projections and market insights*. Internet and Mobile Association of India.

Jha, P. (2022). Personalisation in branding: How AI is transforming consumer engagement in India. *International Journal of Marketing*, 40(4), 312–327.

Kumar, A., & Singh, R. (2022). The role of AI in consumer-centric branding. *Journal of Marketing Analytics*, 25(1), 45–58.

Kumar, A., & Singh, R. (2022). The role of AI in consumer-centric branding. *Journal of Marketing Analytics*, 25(1), 45–58.

Mehta, R., & Jain, S. (2023). AI-driven marketing strategies: Personalization and automation in the digital age. *Digital Marketing Quarterly*, 11(1), 55–74.

Nair, V. (2023). AI's impact on consumer insights and brand decision-making. *The Journal of Consumer Research*, 48(2), 224–239.

Rani, A. (2020). Algorithmic fairness and its implications for AI-driven marketing. *Marketing Analytics Journal*, 36(5), 67–78.

Rani, A. (2020). Predictive analytics and the future of marketing. *Marketing Analytics Journal*, 36(5), 67–78.

Rani, A. (2020). Predictive analytics and the future of marketing. *Marketing Analytics Journal*, 36(5), 67–78.

Russell, S., & Norvig, P. (2021). *Artificial Intelligence: A modern approach* (4th ed.). Prentice Hall.

Sen, A., & Roy, K. (2020). Data privacy in the AI era: Challenges and regulatory frameworks. *Indian Journal of Cyber Law*, 8(2), 113–129.

. Statista. (2023). *E-commerce market in India: Projections and growth drivers.*

Chapter 18
Revolutionizing Customer Experience With AI-Powered Personalization

Nitesh Behare
https://orcid.org/0000-0002-9338-8563
Balaji Institute of International Business, Sri Balaji University, Pune, India

Supriya Bhagat
MIT ADT University, India

Praful Sarangdhar
https://orcid.org/0009-0004-7079-8094
MM's Institute of Management Education, Research, and Training, India

ABSTRACT

The integration of AI into customer experience strategies is revolutionizing the way businesses engage with their customers. This chapter explores how AI-powered personalization is transforming customer journeys by delivering tailored, real-time interactions that resonate with individual preferences and behaviors. From recommendation engines and predictive analytics to natural language processing and dynamic content, AI technologies are enabling companies to offer highly relevant experiences at every stage of the customer lifecycle. By examining key AI concepts, real-world case studies and current trends, this chapter highlights critical role of AI in shaping the future of customer experience. Additionally, the ethical considerations, including data privacy and algorithmic bias, will be addressed, providing a balanced perspective on the opportunities and challenges of AI-driven personalization. This chapter will equip business leaders, marketers, and customer experience professionals with insights into how AI can drive engagement, foster

DOI: 10.4018/979-8-3693-9461-8.ch018

customer loyalty, and deliver business growth

1. INTRODUCTION

In the digital age, where competition is intense and customer expectations are high, personalization has emerged as a defining element in delivering exceptional customer experiences. Traditionally, businesses personalized customer interactions through segment-based approaches, basic demographic insights, and general trends. However, these methods often lacked the depth and precision to meet individual needs at scale. Today, artificial intelligence (AI) is enabling a seismic shift in how businesses approach personalization, moving beyond one-size-fits-all strategies to deliver highly tailored experiences that adapt in real-time to individual behaviors, preferences, and contexts (Venkateswaran, 2023).

As customer expectations evolve, they increasingly expect brands to understand them not as part of a larger segment, but as unique individuals with specific preferences, values, and needs. In response, personalization has advanced from using basic attributes—such as age, gender, and location—to a multi-dimensional approach where AI algorithms analyze a vast array of data points. These include browsing patterns, past purchases, time spent on content, responses to marketing campaigns, and even social media behaviors (Alghizzawi, Ezmigna, Jado, Alzeaideen, & Kanan, 2024). By harnessing this data, AI can dynamically predict and fulfill customer needs with unparalleled accuracy, creating a seamless, engaging, and valuable customer journey that aligns with each customer's unique profile.

The journey to achieving this level of personalization has seen a rapid evolution. In the early days, businesses utilized demographic-based segmentation, enabling companies to tailor offerings based on broad, general characteristics. As technology progressed, data-driven segmentation became more refined, incorporating behavioral and psychographic insights to build more targeted profiles. However, these approaches had limitations; they often lacked real-time adaptability, were constrained by static data, and, at times, were perceived as intrusive or disconnected from the customer's actual needs (Sinha, Sinha, & Dalmia, 2024).

At the core of AI-powered personalization is the capability to process enormous amounts of data in real-time, uncovering actionable insights with speed and accuracy that were previously unattainable. Machine learning algorithms, a subset of AI, can detect patterns, make predictions, and adjust strategies based on real-time information, allowing businesses to anticipate customer desires before they are even voiced. For instance, through recommendation engines, AI helps brands to suggest relevant products or content, thus increasing engagement and enhancing the overall customer experience. This proactive approach not only adds value for customers but also cultivates brand loyalty and drives repeat interactions, making AI an indispensable asset for forward-thinking organizations.

Moreover, AI-driven personalization goes beyond simply optimizing customer experience; it redefines customer journeys as interactive, dynamic, and highly intuitive. By implementing natural language processing (NLP) and sentiment analysis, businesses can gain a deeper understanding of customer emotions and preferences expressed through reviews, social media, and customer service interactions. This insight empowers brands to respond empathetically and tailor messages and offers that resonate with individual customers on a personal level. For instance, chatbots and virtual assistants equipped with NLP can interact conversationally, delivering consistent, personalized responses at any time, which fosters stronger customer relationships and builds trust (Tran, 2024).

The transformative potential of AI in personalization also extends to operational efficiency and scalability. Where traditional personalization approaches were labor-intensive and limited in reach, AI enables businesses to execute large-scale personalization strategies with minimal human intervention. AI-powered personalization platforms can seamlessly integrate across various customer touchpoints—email, social media, websites, and physical stores—ensuring a cohesive and unified brand experience that maintains continuity regardless of the platform or channel (Priya, Rudra, Kandula, Teja, & K., 2023). This scalability not only benefits large enterprises but also offers smaller businesses the opportunity to compete in personalization, leveling the playing field in the digital marketplace. AI is not merely a tool for enhancing customer experience; it is reshaping the very fabric of how businesses engage with their audiences, unlocking unprecedented opportunities for connection, loyalty, and growth. In the age of AI, personalized customer experiences are not just possible—they are inevitable (Whig, Bhatia, & Yathiraju, 2024).

2. AI IN PERSONALIZATION: KEY CONCEPTS AND TECHNOLOGIES

AI-powered personalization transforms customer engagement by delivering highly tailored experiences, made possible by a suite of advanced technologies. This overview covers the foundational elements—Machine Learning (ML), Natural Language Processing (NLP), Recommendation Systems, Predictive Analytics, and Customer Data Platforms (CDPs)—each integral in creating responsive, data-driven, and deeply individualized customer journeys.

2.1. Machine Learning (ML)

ML which is a core component of AI, enables systems to learn from data, adapt over time, and make data-driven decisions with minimal human intervention. Leveraging algorithms like decision trees, neural networks, and support vector machines, ML performs tasks such as classification, regression, and clustering to enhance personalization. It can accurately segment audiences, predict preferences, and analyze behavioral data for dynamic, scalable customer engagement (Deepika & Kalaiselvi, 2021). Techniques like supervised and unsupervised learning empower brands to develop targeted marketing strategies, anticipate real-time needs, and foster loyalty. ML's evolving nature ensures relevance, optimizing experiences, driving retention, and transforming customer engagement in an ever-competitive digital landscape.

2.2. Natural Language Processing (NLP)

Natural Language Processing (NLP), a vital field of AI, revolutionizes customer engagement by enabling computers to comprehend and generate human language naturally. By leveraging advanced techniques such as recurrent neural networks (RNNs) and transformers, NLP powers tasks like sentiment analysis, text summarization, and question answering. Sentiment analysis, for instance, allows businesses to assess emotions expressed in social media posts, reviews, and service interactions, enabling more empathetic and timely responses (Juglan, et al., 2023). NLP's ability to interpret nuanced feedback provides deeper insights into customer needs and preferences, helping brands tailor their strategies effectively.

Moreover, conversational AI solutions like chatbots and virtual assistants utilize NLP to offer personalized assistance, recommend products, and resolve queries seamlessly. These tools create intuitive, human-like interactions that enhance customer support and foster meaningful connections. By bridging the communication gap between humans and machines, NLP transforms customer engagement, improving satisfaction, building trust, and enabling brands to maintain relevance in dynamic, competitive markets (Jansen, Aldous, Salminen, Almerekhi, & Jung, 2024).

2.3. Recommendation Systems

Recommendation systems are crucial in AI-driven personalization, responsible for delivering product, content, or service suggestions based on user data. Techniques like collaborative filtering, content-based filtering, and hybrid methods work together to provide these recommendations. Collaborative filtering, which suggests items based on user similarities, and content-based filtering, which recommends based on item attributes, are foundational approaches. Hybrid systems combine both methods to overcome challenges like data sparsity and cold-start problems, where new users or items lack sufficient data for accurate recommendations. For instance, e-commerce platforms can leverage recommendation systems to suggest relevant products based on a customer's browsing and purchase history, leading to increased engagement and satisfaction.

Figure 1: Foundational Technologies (Source: Scopus AI Generated)

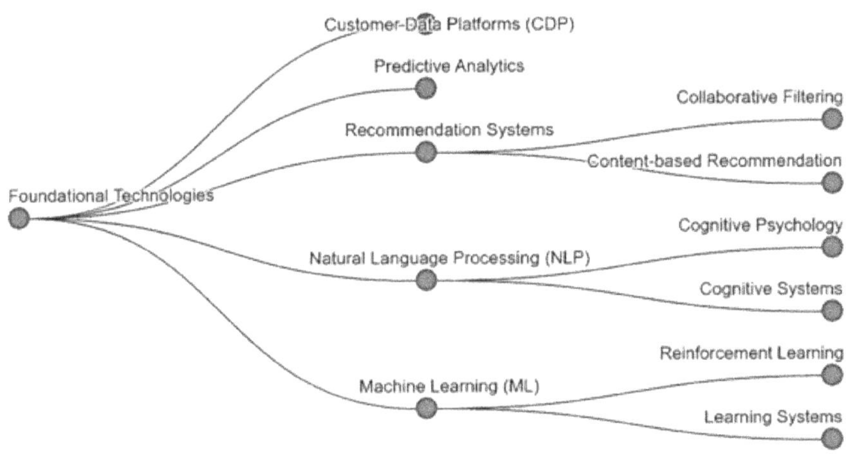

2.4. Predictive Analytics

Predictive Analytics involves using statistical algorithms and ML techniques to forecast future outcomes based on historical data, making it invaluable for personalized marketing and customer engagement. Widely applied in industries like healthcare and marketing, predictive analytics can anticipate a customer's likely behavior, helping brands tailor offers, promotions, and messaging effectively. For example, predictive models can identify customers likely to repurchase certain products, enabling businesses to send personalized reminders or offer targeted discounts. By transforming raw data into actionable insights, predictive analytics enables brands to stay one step ahead of customer expectations, thereby creating proactive and value-driven engagement.

2.5. Customer Data Platforms (CDP)

A Customer Data Platform is a centralized system that collects and unifies customer data from various sources, providing brands with a comprehensive, single view of each customer. This data, gathered from touchpoints like websites, apps, and CRM systems, fuels personalized marketing and engagement strategies. CDPs ensure that customer interactions across channels are informed by a unified dataset, allowing for seamless, consistent experiences (Boldt Sousa, 2022). They enable precise segmentation, ensuring messages are relevant and contextual to each customer. By consolidating and organizing data, CDPs provide a holistic understanding of customers' behaviors and preferences, forming a solid foundation for tailored communication.

3. PERSONALIZATION ACROSS CUSTOMER TOUCHPOINTS

AI-powered personalization has transformed how brands engage with customers at each stage of the customer journey, from initial discovery to long-term loyalty. By using data to understand individual behaviors and preferences, AI enables brands to offer relevant, contextually tailored experiences that enhance customer satisfaction and engagement. This approach improves the entire customer journey across touchpoints, creating a seamless, personalized path from pre-purchase interest through post-purchase retention. Here, we explore how AI personalizes interactions at three key stages: pre-purchase, purchase, and post-purchase.

3.1. Pre-Purchase: Tailored Recommendations, AI-Driven Marketing Campaigns, and Personalized Content

In the pre-purchase phase, customers are in the exploratory phase of their journey, researching options and forming impressions. AI plays a significant role in guiding customers through this phase by delivering relevant recommendations, targeted marketing campaigns, and personalized content that aligns with their preferences and interests.

Tailored Recommendations: Recommendation engines, driven by machine learning algorithms, analyze a customer's past behaviors, such as browsing history, search patterns, and even demographic data, to suggest products or services. For example, an online retailer might recommend items that complement products the customer has previously viewed or items that other customers with similar preferences have purchased. These recommendations, shown at the right moments, increase the likelihood of conversion by presenting customers with options that align with their interests.

AI-Driven Marketing Campaigns: AI enhances marketing efforts by enabling brands to design campaigns that reach customers with personalized messages at optimal times. Machine learning models segment audiences based on behavior, preferences, and previous interactions, allowing brands to tailor messaging to fit specific customer needs. For instance, AI-driven email marketing campaigns can include personalized subject lines, product recommendations, and timely promotions that are most likely to engage individual customers. Furthermore, AI can adapt messaging over time based on how customers respond, continually optimizing campaign effectiveness.

Personalized Content: Content personalization is crucial in creating meaningful engagement in the pre-purchase stage. AI enables dynamic content delivery across various platforms, whether through social media ads, websites, or apps. For example, a customer visiting a website might see a homepage tailored to their past interactions or a custom landing page created specifically for their demographic. AI also enhances content recommendation for articles, videos, or product descriptions that align with the user's preferences, boosting engagement and establishing an emotional connection early in the customer journey (Kompella, 2017).

3.2. Purchase Stage: Dynamic Pricing, Real-Time Support Using AI Chatbots, and Product Suggestions Based on Real-Time Behavior

The purchase stage is where customers make final decisions, and personalized assistance can ensure a smooth, positive experience. Here, AI-driven personalization strategies like dynamic pricing, real-time support, and contextual product suggestions play a significant role in supporting customers through the transaction process.

Dynamic Pricing: AI-driven dynamic pricing algorithms analyze factors such as demand, competitor pricing, customer behavior, and purchasing history to offer optimized prices to each customer. For example, an e-commerce platform might adjust pricing for specific customers based on their purchasing intent, offering them a small discount to encourage conversion or pricing certain products based on regional demand. By personalizing prices, businesses not only improve their chances of conversion but also remain competitive in the market (Hung, Kim, & Calugcug, 2010).

Real-Time Support Using AI Chatbots: AI chatbots provide instant, personalized assistance during the purchase process, addressing customer questions, handling inquiries, and even assisting in product selection. Chatbots, powered by natural language processing (NLP), can interpret customer queries, provide relevant responses, and deliver customized product suggestions in real-time. For instance, a customer uncertain about which product to purchase can chat with a virtual assistant that recommends items based on their responses. This level of support enhances the customer's confidence, reduces friction, and provides a more human-like interaction that ultimately contributes to a better shopping experience.

Product Suggestions Based on Real-Time Behavior: In the purchase stage, AI analyzes customers' real-time actions on websites or apps—like items viewed, added to carts, or removed—to make immediate, personalized product suggestions. These recommendations are particularly effective in driving cross-selling or upselling by suggesting complementary products at the checkout stage. For example, a customer buying a smartphone might see suggestions for compatible accessories, such as cases or headphones. These real-time recommendations help customers discover relevant items, improving their overall satisfaction with the purchase experience.

3.3. Post-Purchase: Personalized Feedback Loops, Loyalty Programs, and Retention Strategies Through Predictive Insights

Once a purchase is completed, the customer relationship enters the post-purchase phase, where retention and loyalty are the primary objectives. AI-driven personalization enhances post-purchase engagement through tailored feedback loops, loyalty programs, and predictive retention strategies.

Personalized Feedback Loops: AI helps businesses collect and act on feedback in ways that feel personalized and relevant to the customer. For instance, after a purchase, customers might receive an email with a personalized survey that asks specific questions about their experience with the product. NLP can be used to analyze responses and classify feedback into categories, helping brands understand and address pain points quickly. This proactive approach allows customers to feel heard and valued, reinforcing brand trust and encouraging repeat interactions.

Loyalty Programs: AI-driven personalization can transform loyalty programs by creating individualized rewards based on a customer's purchase history and preferences. For example, a customer who frequently buys eco-friendly products might receive rewards on sustainable brands, while a customer who makes regular, high-value purchases might gain access to exclusive offers or early access to sales. Personalized loyalty programs encourage ongoing engagement by aligning rewards with what the customer values most, thereby enhancing their overall brand experience.

Retention Strategies Through Predictive Insights: AI-based predictive analytics play a crucial role in identifying customers who may be at risk of churning. By analyzing purchase frequency, engagement patterns, and support interactions, AI can flag customers who display signs of declining interest (Mandák, 2017). Brands can then initiate retention efforts, such as personalized re-engagement campaigns, targeted discounts, or check-in emails, to re-establish connections. This targeted approach to retention ensures that brands can proactively address customer needs and preferences, increasing the likelihood of retaining them in the long run.

4. CASE STUDIES: SUCCESS STORIES OF AI-DRIVEN PERSONALIZATION

In today's digital age, personalization has emerged as a cornerstone of customer experience, reshaping how businesses connect with their audiences across industries. By leveraging advanced algorithms and data analytics, companies can now craft tailored interactions that not only meet customer expectations but anticipate their desires. This chapter delves into the transformative impact of AI-driven personalization, showcasing detailed case studies of industry leaders such as Amazon, Netflix, Spotify, and prominent retailers. These success stories highlight how strategic AI implementation enhances customer satisfaction, loyalty, and engagement, offering invaluable lessons for businesses aspiring to redefine their customer journeys.

4.1. Amazon's Recommendation Engine

Amazon's recommendation engine is one of the most notable examples of AI-driven personalization in action. The platform's success lies in its sophisticated machine learning algorithms, which analyze vast amounts of customer data to provide tailored recommendations that meet individual preferences. The recommendation engine, responsible for nearly 35% of Amazon's total sales, suggests products based on a customer's browsing and purchasing history, as well as related products other customers have bought (Biswas, Vineeth, Jain, & Mohana, 2020).

1. **Collaborative Filtering and Deep Learning**: Amazon's recommendation engine uses collaborative filtering, where customer behavior is analyzed to identify patterns. By looking at customers who bought similar items, Amazon is able to recommend products that align with a user's interests. Additionally, Amazon leverages deep learning to improve the accuracy and relevance of recommendations. This allows the system to identify subtle relationships between products, resulting in a more refined personalization experience.
2. **Personalized Homepages and Targeted Emails**: Amazon personalizes not only the product recommendations but also the customer's homepage and marketing emails. Based on past interactions, Amazon curates the homepage to feature items of interest, ongoing deals, and reminders to reorder previously bought

products. Similarly, its email campaigns contain customized recommendations, enticing customers to engage further. This highly personalized approach is a significant factor in Amazon's impressive customer retention rates and growth.

4.2. Netflix's Content Personalization

Netflix is another industry leader in AI-driven personalization, particularly in the entertainment sector. With more than 238 million subscribers worldwide, Netflix relies on personalization to provide tailored content recommendations that keep users engaged, reduce churn, and improve customer satisfaction. Netflix's recommendation engine is responsible for 80% of the content its users watch, underscoring the impact of its AI-driven strategy (Arkadiusz, 2024).

1. **Predictive Algorithms for Content Suggestions**: Netflix's personalization engine uses a variety of algorithms to analyze viewing patterns, including factors like watch history, viewing time, and content ratings. By combining collaborative filtering with deep learning, Netflix makes precise recommendations that align with a user's viewing habits. For instance, if a user enjoys documentaries, the platform will prioritize suggesting similar content while periodically introducing new genres to broaden the user's interests.
2. **Thumbnail Personalization**: Netflix customizes the artwork or thumbnail that users see for each title. By using machine learning, Netflix tests and presents the artwork most likely to engage a specific user. For example, a user who enjoys action movies may see a more intense, high-action thumbnail for a film than someone who prefers comedies. This subtle personalization technique has been shown to boost engagement significantly, as users are more likely to click on content that aligns with their preferences visually.
3. **Content Localization**: To cater to a global audience, Netflix personalizes its content offerings based on regional preferences and viewing trends. This localization is driven by AI algorithms that monitor regional demand and tailor recommendations accordingly, ensuring that users receive content that resonates with their cultural background and tastes. This approach has contributed to Netflix's rapid global expansion and high subscriber retention rates.

4.3. Spotify's AI-Powered Playlists

Spotify's success in the streaming music industry can be largely attributed to its AI-driven personalization features, particularly its customized playlists like "Discover Weekly" and "Daily Mix." These playlists leverage AI to recommend music based on a user's listening habits and preferences, creating a highly personalized music experience (Nina, 2024).

1. **Discover Weekly**: Spotify's "Discover Weekly" playlist, generated every Monday, is tailored to each user's taste in music. The playlist combines collaborative filtering, natural language processing (NLP), and audio analysis to deliver a mix of tracks that are new to the listener but align with their past preferences. Spotify uses machine learning models to analyze what similar users are listening to and recommend songs accordingly. This feature has been widely successful, with millions of users returning to the platform each week to explore new music.
2. **Real-Time Personalization with Daily Mixes**: Spotify's "Daily Mix" playlists are generated in real-time, offering users several mixes based on their listening history. These playlists adapt as users' tastes change, which keeps the content fresh and relevant. Real-time personalization ensures that each playlist reflects the user's current interests, whether they are exploring a new genre or revisiting familiar tracks.
3. **Customized Curated Content**: Beyond individual playlists, Spotify also uses AI to curate editorial playlists based on general user interests and seasonal trends. For example, Spotify might create playlists for specific moods, activities, or holidays and personalize them by placing songs that a user is likely to enjoy higher up in the order. This curated approach keeps users engaged and encourages them to explore new content that fits seamlessly into their tastes and preferences.

4.4. Retailers and Hyper-Personalized Shopping Experiences

Retailers around the world are also embracing AI to offer hyper-personalized shopping experiences that cater to individual needs. Many retail brands, both online and offline, use AI to enhance various aspects of the shopping experience, from product discovery to in-store personalization.

1. **AI-Driven Product Recommendations and Visual Search**: Retailers like Sephora and Walmart have integrated AI-powered recommendation engines and visual search tools to improve the shopping experience. Visual search allows customers to upload an image of a product they like, and the AI system then finds similar items available in the store. This technology helps customers discover products in a way that feels seamless and personalized, thereby increasing engagement and satisfaction.

2. **Dynamic Pricing and Personalized Offers**: Many retailers use AI-driven dynamic pricing models to adjust prices based on demand, customer behavior, and competitor pricing. For example, Walmart and Target employ dynamic pricing strategies that allow them to offer personalized discounts to customers based on their shopping behavior. By offering targeted discounts and promotions, retailers can encourage repeat purchases and foster brand loyalty (Kopalle, Pauwels, Akella, & Gangwar, 2023).
3. **In-Store Personalization with AI-Powered Kiosks and Mobile Apps**: Physical retailers are also using AI to personalize the in-store experience. Brands like Nike and Macy's have introduced AI-powered kiosks and mobile apps that provide product recommendations, inventory information, and even virtual try-ons based on the customer's preferences. These tools make the shopping experience more interactive and engaging, helping customers find exactly what they're looking for and encouraging them to make purchases.
4. **Hyper-Personalized Emails and Push Notifications**: Retailers are leveraging AI to send hyper-personalized emails and push notifications that recommend products based on browsing history, wishlists, and past purchases. For example, when a user leaves items in their cart, an AI-driven system might send a reminder email with a personalized message or a discount code to encourage them to complete the purchase. This approach boosts conversion rates by targeting customers with relevant, timely communications that are aligned with their preferences.

5. CHALLENGES AND ETHICAL CONSIDERATIONS

AI-driven personalization has transformed the way businesses interact with their customers by delivering tailored experiences that cater to individual preferences. However, implementing AI for personalization is not without its challenges and ethical concerns. Issues such as data privacy, over-reliance on algorithms, biases in AI models, and regulatory compliance present significant obstacles that require careful consideration. This discussion explores these challenges and highlights the ethical implications and regulatory frameworks that shape the responsible use of AI-driven personalization.

5.1 Data Privacy Concerns and the Balance Between Personalization and Privacy

One of the most significant challenges in AI-driven personalization is maintaining a balance between delivering personalized experiences and protecting user privacy. Personalization relies heavily on collecting, processing, and analyzing vast amounts of personal data to understand customer preferences, behaviors, and needs (Asthana, Im, Chen, & Banovic, 2024). However, this data collection raises privacy concerns as customers become increasingly aware of how their data is used and shared.

1. **Data Collection and Consent**: The extensive data collection needed for effective personalization can intrude on personal privacy if not handled with transparency and consent. Users may feel uncomfortable or even violated when they perceive that companies know too much about them or track their behaviors without permission. Organizations must therefore adopt practices that ensure customers are aware of the data collected and how it will be used, empowering them to control their data privacy.
2. **Data Security Risks**: Data security is paramount, as any breach or misuse of customer data can lead to severe reputational and financial damage for companies. AI systems store and analyze data that can include highly sensitive information, such as purchase history, location, and even biometric data. A data breach not only exposes customers to potential identity theft or fraud but also erodes trust, making customers hesitant to engage with brands that are unable to secure their information effectively.
3. **Transparency and the Right to Privacy**: Customers often question the transparency of AI algorithms, as personalization can feel invasive when they do not understand how or why certain recommendations are made. This lack of transparency can lead to customer dissatisfaction, especially when personalization encroaches upon personal privacy. Ensuring transparency in data handling practices and the decision-making processes of algorithms is critical to address privacy concerns and build trust.

5.2 Over-Reliance on Algorithms and Loss of Human Touch

AI-driven personalization, while highly efficient, can sometimes result in an over-reliance on algorithms, leading to a depersonalized experience that lacks the warmth and empathy of human interactions. Although AI can make highly accurate recommendations, it cannot fully replicate the nuanced understanding and emotional connection that human agents can provide (Venkateswaran, 2023).

1. **Automated Interactions vs. Human Empathy**: For many customers, automated interactions such as AI-driven chatbots may seem impersonal, especially when dealing with complex issues that require empathy and understanding. While chatbots can handle routine queries efficiently, the loss of human touch in customer interactions can negatively impact customer satisfaction and brand loyalty, particularly in service-driven industries where empathy is critical.
2. **Algorithmic Inflexibility**: Algorithms rely on historical data to predict customer needs, but they can sometimes lack the flexibility to adapt to unforeseen customer behavior or contextual nuances. For instance, during times of emotional distress, customers may prefer human contact over algorithmic recommendations, and rigid AI systems may fail to recognize these unique contexts, causing dissatisfaction.
3. **Need for a Hybrid Approach**: To overcome the limitations of over-reliance on algorithms, companies must develop hybrid approaches that combine AI with human agents. This hybrid approach can retain the efficiency of AI-driven personalization while reintroducing the human element that customers value, especially in more sensitive interactions. By offering a blend of human and automated interactions, companies can ensure that personalization is both effective and emotionally resonant.

5.3 Bias in AI Models Affecting Personalization Quality

AI systems used in personalization are only as good as the data they are trained on. When AI models are fed biased data, they can inadvertently reproduce and even amplify these biases, resulting in personalization that favors certain demographics over others. Such biases not only reduce the quality of personalization but can also lead to unfair treatment of certain groups, raising ethical concerns (Bamboat & Yu, 2023).

1. **Data Bias and Unintentional Discrimination**: AI models can inadvertently incorporate biases from historical data, such as gender, race, or age biases. For instance, if an AI model is trained on data that primarily includes purchasing patterns of a specific demographic, it may create recommendations that disproportionately favor that group, thereby alienating others. This unintentional discrimination can make customers feel marginalized or stereotyped.
2. **Algorithmic Fairness and Inclusive Personalization**: Addressing bias in AI models requires a commitment to algorithmic fairness, where companies actively work to minimize biases by diversifying training data and conducting regular audits of AI systems. Inclusive personalization involves ensuring that AI-driven recommendations are fair, accurate, and relevant to all customers,

regardless of their background. By prioritizing fairness, brands can build trust and avoid the reputational damage associated with biased AI models.

3. **Ethical AI Development**: Developing ethical AI systems means fostering an environment where fairness, accountability, and transparency are prioritized throughout the model development process. This includes conducting fairness tests, validating datasets for diversity, and implementing bias mitigation techniques. By embedding ethical principles in AI design, companies can mitigate bias and enhance personalization quality.

5.4 Regulatory Frameworks and Ethical Implications of AI-Based Customer Insights

With the rise of AI-driven personalization, governments and regulatory bodies are increasingly enacting laws to protect consumer rights and data privacy. Frameworks such as the General Data Protection Regulation (GDPR) have set new standards for data protection, requiring companies to handle customer data responsibly and ethically (Fehr & French, 2022).

1. **GDPR and Data Protection Standards**: The GDPR, enacted in the European Union, mandates strict guidelines for collecting, storing, and processing personal data. Under GDPR, companies must obtain explicit consent for data collection, and customers have the right to access, delete, or correct their data. Failure to comply with these standards can result in substantial fines and reputational damage, making GDPR compliance essential for any company implementing AI-driven personalization in Europe.
2. **Privacy by Design**: GDPR emphasizes "privacy by design," meaning that privacy considerations must be integrated into the development of AI-driven systems from the outset. Companies are encouraged to adopt privacy-focused AI practices, such as data minimization and anonymization, to limit the amount of personal data collected and ensure that data used in personalization is secure and unidentifiable.
3. **Ethical Implications of AI-Based Customer Insights**: As companies gain more customer insights through AI, the ethical implications of using this information become critical. AI can reveal highly sensitive information about customer preferences, behaviors, and even vulnerabilities. Ethical AI practices involve safeguarding this information and using it responsibly to avoid exploitation. For example, using AI insights to push manipulative marketing tactics, such as exploiting customer insecurities, is considered unethical and can lead to consumer backlash.

4. **Global Variability in Regulations**: Regulations around AI and data privacy vary globally, with different regions having distinct guidelines on data usage and consent. Companies with global operations must navigate this regulatory landscape carefully to ensure compliance across jurisdictions, as failing to adhere to local regulations can hinder operations and damage customer trust.

6. FUTURE TRENDS AND THE WAY FORWARD

The rapid evolution of artificial intelligence (AI) continues to transform customer personalization, pushing boundaries and reshaping expectations in customer experience. As AI capabilities expand, businesses have a unique opportunity to deliver more nuanced, real-time, and contextually aware interactions. This section explores emerging trends in AI-driven personalization, including contextual and real-time personalization, the rise of voice AI, omnichannel experiences, and collaborative AI models that adapt over time. Additionally, we discuss strategies for businesses to future-proof their AI investments to stay ahead in a competitive landscape.

6.1. Contextual and Real-Time Personalization

Contextual and real-time personalization represents a significant shift from traditional data-driven marketing to more dynamic, situational engagement. Rather than relying on static customer data, contextual personalization leverages real-time information, including a customer's location, time of day, and device usage, to tailor interactions at the moment they occur.

1. **Hyper-Targeted Experiences**: By using real-time data, businesses can deliver hyper-targeted content and offers that align with a customer's current needs. For instance, a retail app may recommend specific products based on a customer's browsing patterns or suggest complementary items when they enter a physical store. Real-time personalization also enables companies to optimize pricing dynamically, adjusting rates based on factors like demand, customer loyalty, and competition (Valdez & Flores-Cuautle, 2022).
2. **Adaptive AI Models**: Real-time personalization requires AI models that can adapt to changing data instantaneously. Traditional data analysis might focus on long-term trends, but AI-driven personalization requires a flexible approach that factors in both historical and real-time data, allowing brands to respond immediately to customer behavior changes and evolving preferences.

3. **Enhanced Customer Satisfaction**: Providing customers with relevant, timely content or product recommendations can increase satisfaction and engagement, creating a sense of responsiveness that aligns with their immediate context. For businesses, the ability to address customer needs as they arise can lead to higher conversion rates and greater brand loyalty.

6.2. The Rise of Voice AI in Customer Engagement

Voice AI, powered by advancements in natural language processing (NLP) and speech recognition, is becoming a cornerstone of AI-driven personalization. With the growing adoption of smart speakers and virtual assistants like Amazon's Alexa and Google Assistant, customers are becoming more comfortable with voice interactions, especially in customer service and e-commerce settings.

1. **Seamless and Intuitive Interactions**: Voice AI offers a hands-free, conversational way for customers to interact with brands, making it a convenient option for tasks such as placing orders, checking account information, or receiving recommendations. This trend reflects the demand for seamless experiences, especially in scenarios where visual or manual engagement is less practical, such as when customers are driving or multitasking (Devisivasankari & Vijayakumar, 2023).
2. **Voice-Based Personalization**: Voice AI also enables companies to personalize interactions based on individual speech patterns, preferences, and past interactions. For example, voice assistants can adjust tone, language, and even conversational style based on the user, creating a more personalized and human-like experience.
3. **Enhanced Engagement and Retention**: Integrating voice AI into customer engagement strategies allows businesses to build stronger connections with users, as it creates a more personal and engaging experience. Brands that embrace voice AI are likely to see higher levels of user engagement and retention due to the convenience and intimacy of voice interactions.

6.3. AI-Driven Omnichannel Experiences

The rise of omnichannel personalization reflects the growing need for a cohesive customer experience across various platforms and devices. AI is instrumental in creating these unified experiences, ensuring that personalization strategies are consistent across websites, mobile apps, social media, and physical stores.

1. **Consistent Customer Journey**: By leveraging AI, brands can synchronize their personalization efforts across channels, making it possible for a customer who browses products on a mobile app to see relevant recommendations when they visit the brand's website or physical store. This creates a seamless customer journey, where each interaction builds upon the previous ones (Nguyen & Mogaji, 2023).
2. **Unified Data and Personalization Efforts**: AI-driven omnichannel personalization requires the integration of data from multiple sources. Customer data platforms (CDPs) play a crucial role in consolidating information from diverse channels, allowing AI systems to access a comprehensive view of each customer. This data integration enables more effective personalization, ensuring that customers receive relevant experiences regardless of their chosen channel (Wetzlinger, Auinger, Kindermann, & Schönberger, 2017).
3. **Enhanced Customer Loyalty**: Omnichannel personalization strengthens customer loyalty by delivering consistent and satisfying experiences across all touchpoints. Brands that excel in omnichannel personalization often see higher customer retention rates, as customers appreciate the effort to provide a cohesive and responsive experience.

6.4. Collaborative AI Models that Evolve with Customer Behavior

Collaborative AI models represent a cutting-edge approach to personalization by continuously learning and evolving in response to customer behavior. Unlike traditional AI models that require periodic retraining, collaborative AI adapts in real-time, making it more responsive to subtle changes in customer preferences and market trends.

1. **Proactive Personalization**: Collaborative AI enables brands to move from reactive to proactive personalization, anticipating customer needs before they are explicitly expressed. By analyzing ongoing interactions, collaborative AI models can make recommendations or offer support based on predictive insights, enhancing the customer experience (Tran, Unlocking the AI-powered customer experience: Personalized service, enhanced engagement, and data-driven strategies for E-commerce applications, 2024).
2. **Self-Learning Algorithms**: Collaborative AI systems are typically self-learning, meaning they improve over time with each new interaction. As they gather more data, these models refine their understanding of customer preferences and can adjust personalization strategies accordingly, ensuring that the experience remains relevant.

3. **Enhanced Scalability**: Collaborative AI models are highly scalable, allowing companies to offer personalized experiences to a larger audience without compromising quality. This scalability is crucial for businesses looking to extend their reach while maintaining a high level of customer engagement.

6.5. Future-Proofing AI Strategies for Customer Personalization

To stay competitive, businesses must adopt strategies that future-proof their AI personalization initiatives. As AI technology and customer expectations continue to evolve, brands must remain agile and forward-thinking to leverage the full potential of AI.

1. **Investing in Robust Data Infrastructure**: Future-proofing requires a strong foundation in data management. Companies must ensure that their data infrastructure is capable of collecting, processing, and securing large volumes of data, which is essential for real-time and context-driven personalization. Implementing a reliable CDP and prioritizing data security and privacy are key components of a robust AI strategy (Hemadharshini, Kanchana Devi, Rajakumari, & Adline, 2024).
2. **Prioritizing Ethical AI Practices**: As personalization becomes more sophisticated, ethical considerations must be front and center. Companies should adopt transparency, fairness, and accountability principles in their AI practices, ensuring that personalization efforts respect customer privacy and mitigate potential biases. Ethical AI practices can also build customer trust and foster long-term loyalty.
3. **Embracing Continuous Learning and Innovation**: Future-proofing AI personalization strategies involves a commitment to innovation and flexibility. Companies should remain open to new developments in AI technology, such as advancements in NLP, reinforcement learning, and edge computing, to ensure that their personalization capabilities keep pace with emerging trends.
4. **Building Cross-Functional Teams**: Implementing successful AI-driven personalization requires collaboration between data scientists, marketers, designers, and customer service teams. Building cross-functional teams that can integrate AI insights into broader business strategies is essential for maximizing the value of AI personalization (Zalpuri & Hamlin, 2020).
5. **Testing and Iterating**: Finally, businesses must adopt a test-and-learn approach, using customer feedback and performance metrics to refine their AI personalization strategies. Regular testing ensures that AI systems remain effective and aligned with customer expectations, enabling businesses to respond to changes in customer behavior and market dynamics swiftly.

7. CONCLUSION

AI-driven personalization is revolutionizing customer experience by enabling businesses to deliver meaningful, responsive, and contextually relevant interactions. As explored in this chapter, the impact of AI on personalization spans all stages of the customer journey, from tailored recommendations and real-time support to proactive post-purchase engagement. Emerging trends like contextual personalization, voice AI, and omnichannel strategies demonstrate the vast potential of AI in enhancing customer engagement. However, implementing effective AI personalization requires overcoming challenges, from data privacy concerns to ethical implications. Future-proofing AI personalization involves investing in robust data infrastructures, adhering to ethical standards, and maintaining flexibility to adapt to evolving technologies and customer expectations. Ultimately, companies that embrace these trends and strategies can foster deeper customer relationships, build lasting brand loyalty, and achieve a competitive advantage by delivering experiences that resonate with customers on an individual level.

REFERENCES

Alghizzawi, M., Ezmigna, I., Jado, K., Alzeaideen, K., & Kanan, M. (2024). Theoretical Perspective of Artificial Intelligence in Digital Marketing for Business Organizations. In *Studies in Computational Intelligence* (pp. 167–177). Springer Science and Business Media Deutschland GmbH., DOI: 10.1007/978-3-031-56015-6_13

Arkadiusz, K. (2024, Jun 14). *Netflix Algorithm: How Netflix Uses AI to Improve Personalization*. Retrieved Nov 15, 2024, from https://stratoflow.com/: https://stratoflow.com/how-netflix-recommendation-algorithm-work/

Asthana, S., Im, J., Chen, Z., & Banovic, N. (2024). "I know even if you don't tell me": Understanding Users' Privacy Preferences Regarding AI-based Inferences of Sensitive Information for Personalization. *CHI Conference on Human Factors in Computing Sytems, CHI 2024*. Hybrid, Honolulu: Association for Computing Machinery. DOI: 10.1145/3613904.3642180

Bamboat, Q., & Yu, H. Q. (2023). Literature Study on Bias and Fairness in Machine Learning Systems. *22nd IEEE International Conference on Trust, Security and Privacy in Computing and Communications, TrustCom 2023* (pp. 1960-1965). Exeter: Institute of Electrical and Electronics Engineers Inc. DOI: 10.1109/TrustCom60117.2023.00267

Biswas, A., Vineeth, K. S., & Jain, A., & Mohana. (2020). Development of Product Recommendation Engine by Collaborative Filtering and Association Rule Mining Using Machine Learning Algorithms. *4th International Conference on Inventive Systems and Control, ICISC 2020* (pp. 272-277). Coimbatore: Institute of Electrical and Electronics Engineers Inc. DOI: 10.1109/ICISC47916.2020.9171210

Boldt Sousa, T. (2022). Customer Data Platforms: A Pattern Language for Digital Marketing Optimization with First-Party Data. *7th European Conference on Pattern Languages of Programs, EuroPLoP 2022*. Irsee: Association for Computing Machinery. DOI: 10.1145/3551902.3551984

Deepika, M., & Kalaiselvi, K. (2021). Machine learning-based data analysis. In *Machine Learning Approach for Cloud Data Analytics in IoT* (pp. 01-24). wiley. DOI: 10.1002/9781119785873.ch1

Devisivasankari, P., & Vijayakumar, R. (2023). Conversational AI Annotation System. *14th International Conference on Advances in Computing, Control, and Telecommunication Technologies, ACT 2023. 2023-June*, pp. 2788-2793. Hyderabad: Grenze Scientific Society. Retrieved Nov 26, 2024, from https://www.scopus.com/record/display.uri?eid=2-s2.0-85174395593&origin=scopusAI

Fehr, J. G., & French, A. M. (2022). Exploring the Characteristics and Needs of the Chief Privacy Officer in Organizations. *28th Americas Conference on Information Systems, AMCIS 2022.* Minneapolis: Association for Information Systems. Retrieved Nov 26, 2024, from https://www.scopus.com/record/display.uri?eid=2-s2.0-85180263632&origin=scopusAI

Hemadharshini, S., Kanchana Devi, R., Rajakumari, S., & Adline, F. R. (2024). E-commerce Customer Segmentation by Unsupervised Learning. *6th International Conference on Soft Computing and Signal Processing, ICSCSP 2023.* 864, pp. 285-296. Hyderabad: Springer Science and Business Media Deutschland GmbH. DOI: 10.1007/978-981-99-8628-6_25

Hung, H.-C., Kim, J.-K., & Calugcug, C. C. (2010). Dynamical pricing strategy for one-manufacturer and two-retailer supply chain model. *International Journal of Mathematical Models and Methods in Applied Sciences*, 04(03), 195–202. Retrieved November 14, 2024, from https://www.scopus.com/record/display.uri?eid=2-s2.0-78649336844&origin=scopusAI

Jansen, B. J., Aldous, K. K., Salminen, J., Almerekhi, H., & Jung, S.-g. (2024). Social Media Analytics. In *Synthesis Lectures on Information Concepts, Retrieval, and Services* (Vol. F1359, pp. 79-93). Springer Nature. DOI: 10.1007/978-3-031-41933-1_7

Juglan, K. C., Sharma, B., Gehlot, A., Singh, S. P., Hussein, A., & Alazzam, M. B. (2023). Exploring the Effectiveness of Natural Language Processing in Customer Service. *3rd International Conference on Advance Computing and Innovative Technologies in Engineering, ICACITE 2023* (pp. 814-818). Greater Noida: Institute of Electrical and Electronics Engineers Inc. DOI: 10.1109/ICACITE57410.2023.10183107

Kompella, K. (2017, September-October). How to achieve personalization on a global scale. *EContent (Wilton, Conn.)*, 40(05), 36–38. Retrieved November 11, 2024, from https://www.scopus.com/record/display.uri?eid=2-s2.0-85028673728&origin=scopusAI

Kopalle, P. K., Pauwels, K., Akella, L. Y., & Gangwar, M. (2023, December). Dynamic pricing: Definition, implications for managers, and future research directions. *Journal of Retailing*, 99(04), 580–593. DOI: 10.1016/j.jretai.2023.11.003

Mandák, J. (2017). Comparison of logistic regression and decision tree for customer churn prediction in Telecommunications. *12th International Conference on Strategic Management and its Support by Information Systems 2017, SMSIS 2017* (pp. 282-292). Ostrava: VSB-Technical University of Ostrava. Retrieved Nov 13, 2024, from https://www.scopus.com/record/display.uri?eid=2-s2.0-85026304194&origin=scopusAI

Nguyen, N. P., & Mogaji, E. (2023). Artificial Intelligence for Seamless Experience Across Channels. In *Artificial Intelligence in Customer Service: The Next Frontier to Personalized Engagement* (pp. 181-203). Springer International Publishing. DOI: 10.1007/978-3-031-33898-4_8

Nina, S. (2024). https://www.latterly.org/. Retrieved Nov 25, 2024, from Spotify Marketing Strategy 2024: A Case Study: https://www.latterly.org/spotify-marketing-strategy/

Priya, P. K., Rudra, K., Kandula, D. S., Teja, G. C., & K., V. K. (2023). An innovative analysis of AI-powered automation techniques for business management. In *Toward Artificial General Intelligence: Deep Learning, Neural Networks, Generative AI* (pp. 269-286). De Gruyter. DOI: 10.1515/9783111323749-013

Sinha, S., Sinha, D., & Dalmia, T. (2024). Role of AI in Enhancing Customer Experience in Online Shopping. *11th International Conference on Reliability, Infocom Technologies and Optimization, ICRITO 2024.* Hybrid, Noida: Institute of Electrical and Electronics Engineers Inc. DOI: 10.1109/ICRITO61523.2024.10522285

Tran, M. T. (2024). Unlocking the AI-powered customer experience: Personalized service, enhanced engagement, and data-driven strategies for e-commerce applications. *Journal of Infrastructure. Advances in Marketing, Customer Relationship Management, and E-Services*, 08(07), 375–382. Advance online publication. DOI: 10.4018/979-8-3693-4453-8.ch019

Tran, M. T. (2024). Unlocking the AI-powered customer experience: Personalized service, enhanced engagement, and data-driven strategies for E-commerce applications. In *Enhancing and Predicting Digital Consumer Behavior with AI* (pp. 375–382). IGI Global., DOI: 10.4018/979-8-3693-4453-8.ch019

Valdez, M. J., & Flores-Cuautle, J. (2022). Toward customer hyper-personalization experience — A data-driven approach. *Cogent Business and Management*, 09(01), 2041384. Advance online publication. DOI: 10.1080/23311975.2022.2041384

Venkateswaran, N. (2023, September 30). AI-DRIVEN PERSONALIZATION IN CUSTOMER RELATIONSHIP MANAGEMENT: CHALLENGES AND OPPORTUNITIES. *Journal of Theoretical and Applied Information Technology*, 101(18), 7392–7399. Retrieved November 05, 2024, from https://www.scopus.com/record/display.uri?eid=2-s2.0-85175453312&origin=scopusAI

Wetzlinger, W., Auinger, A., Kindermann, H., & Schönberger, W. (2017). Acceptance of personalization in omnichannel retailing. *14th International Conference on Logic Programming and Nonmonotonic Reasoning, LPNMR 2017. 10294 LNCS*, pp. 114-129. Espoo: Springer Verlag. doi:DOI: 978-331958483-6

Whig, P., Bhatia, A. B., & Yathiraju, N. (2024). AI-driven innovations in service marketing transforming customer engagement and experience. In *AI Innovations in Service and Tourism Marketing* (pp. 17–34). IGI Global., DOI: 10.4018/979-8-3693-7909-7.ch002

Zalpuri, M., & Hamlin, A. M. (2020). Building and leading successful cross-functional teams. In *ACS Symposium Series* (Vol. 1367, pp. 07-15). American Chemical Society. DOI: 10.1021/bk-2020-1367.ch002

Chapter 19
Predictive Analytics: Utilizing Machine Learning and Big Data for Forecasting Future Trends in Business and Consumer Behavior

P. S. Venkateswaran
https://orcid.org/0000-0001-8958-103X
PSNA College of Engineering and Technology, India

Sriramkumar Mm
https://orcid.org/0009-0006-5553-1142
PSNA College of Engineering and Technology, India

ABSTRACT

Predictive analytics, leveraging machine learning and big data, has emerged as a transformative tool in business and consumer behavior forecasting. This study explores the application of predictive models to anticipate market trends, optimize decision-making, and enhance customer engagement. Integrating machine learning algorithms with big data enables businesses to analyze vast amounts of structured and unstructured data, uncovering patterns that drive actionable insights. Results highlight the synergistic relationships among capabilities, such as real-time data availability and data source utilization, while emphasizing the foundational role of robust technical infrastructure. Managerial implications underscore the need for a balanced development of capabilities and strategic integration of predictive systems into decision-making processes. This study contributes to the understanding of how organizations can effectively deploy predictive analytics to anticipate trends, optimize decision-making, and achieve competitive advantage.

DOI: 10.4018/979-8-3693-9461-8.ch019

1. INTRODUCTION

Predictive analytics has emerged as a vital tool for organizations aiming to anticipate future trends and make informed decisions. The rise of machine learning and big data has significantly enhanced the ability to predict business outcomes, consumer behaviors, and market trends. At its core, predictive analytics involves using historical data, advanced algorithms, and statistical models to forecast future events. This technique is instrumental in a variety of fields, including finance, marketing, healthcare, and supply chain management, helping organizations to gain a competitive edge.

Predictive analytics refers to the branch of data analytics that focuses on making predictions about future outcomes based on historical data. It utilizes various statistical techniques, including data mining, machine learning, and artificial intelligence (AI), to identify patterns and relationships within data that can be leveraged for forecasting. Predictive models work by identifying correlations between variables and extrapolating those relationships into the future.

Predictive analytics, powered by machine learning (ML) and big data, is transforming the way businesses understand and forecast future trends in both business and consumer behaviors. (Agu, 2024) By leveraging vast datasets and advanced algorithms, companies can gain valuable insights into consumer preferences, market dynamics, and operational processes. (Tolulope, 2024) This ability to predict future outcomes enables businesses to make informed decisions, optimize resources, mitigate risks, and ultimately achieve sustainable growth. Big data refers to the massive volume of structured and unstructured data generated by businesses and consumers. (Ved, 2019) This data encompasses a wide range of sources, including customer transactions, social media interactions, website activity, and sensor readings. (Babadoan, 2024) Machine learning algorithms, on the other hand, are designed to analyze these vast datasets, identify patterns, and make predictions about future trends. (Ajiga, 2024)

Machine learning is a subset of AI that allows systems to automatically learn and improve from experience without explicit programming. It focuses on developing algorithms that can process large amounts of data, recognize patterns, and make decisions. Machine learning algorithms in predictive analytics continuously refine models based on new data to enhance prediction accuracy. Big data refers to the massive volumes of structured, semi-structured, and unstructured data generated by organizations daily. The term refers to not only the amount of data, but also its complexity, speed of generation, and variability. Big data is typically characterized by the "3 Vs": volume, velocity, and variety. Leveraging big data for predictive analytics allows organizations to consider a broader range of variables, making the predictions more reliable and comprehensive.

The increasing volume of data generated by digital platforms, combined with the growth of machine learning capabilities, has made predictive analytics more accessible and effective than ever. Organizations are increasingly recognizing the need to predict future trends to stay competitive in a rapidly evolving market. Predictive analytics enables companies to make data-driven decisions, optimize resources, and mitigate risks. For example, in marketing, predictive analytics can forecast consumer purchasing behaviors, helping businesses tailor their marketing strategies. Finance uses predictive analytics to forecast stock market trends and evaluate credit risks. In healthcare, predictive models can anticipate patient outcomes, enabling preventative care and reducing costs.

The use of machine learning algorithms in predictive analytics makes it possible to handle the massive datasets typical of big data environments. These algorithms can detect patterns that are too complex for humans or traditional statistical methods to uncover, thereby increasing the predictive power of the models. Additionally, machine learning models can adapt over time, refining their accuracy as more data becomes available. A variety of machine learning techniques are employed in predictive analytics, each tailored to specific tasks and data types. (Nishat, 2024) Some commonly used algorithms include:

Decision Trees: These algorithms create a hierarchical structure of rules, where each branch represents a decision based on specific features in the data (Kumari, 2022). Decision trees are particularly useful for classification tasks, such as predicting customer churn or identifying high-risk transactions. (Madani, 2021),

Regression Analysis: Regression models use statistical techniques to establish relationships between variables, allowing for predictions of continuous outcomes. They are often used to forecast sales, predict stock prices, or estimate customer lifetime value. (Khandelwal, 2020), (Myint, 2023)

Neural Networks: Inspired by the structure of the human brain, neural networks are complex algorithms that can learn intricate patterns from large datasets. They excel at tasks involving image recognition, natural language processing, and complex prediction tasks. (Babadoan, 2024)

Support Vector Machines (SVMs): SVMs are powerful algorithms that map data points into a high-dimensional space, enabling efficient classification and regression tasks. They are often used for tasks like sentiment analysis and fraud detection. (Chowdhury, 2024)

Random Forests: This ensemble learning method combines multiple decision trees to improve prediction accuracy and reduce overfitting. Random forests are particularly effective in handling complex datasets with high dimensionality. (Khandelwal, 2020)

While machine learning algorithms are essential for extracting insights from big data, data visualization plays a crucial role in making these insights comprehensible and actionable. (Lu, 2017) Visualizing data allows analysts to identify trends, patterns, and outliers that might be missed through purely numerical analysis. (Sahare, 2024) Moreover, data visualization can help communicate complex findings to stakeholders, facilitating informed decision-making. (Myint, 2023).

The success of predictive analytics depends on the accuracy of the model used. Accuracy is how well model predictions match actual outcomes. We can assess accuracy using a variety of methods, such as comparing predicted outcomes to actual historical results. Regular refinement and validation of the model against new data are important to maintain and improve accuracy over time. Many users use several evaluation metrics to assess the performance of predictive models. Common metrics include mean absolute error (MAE), mean squared error (MSE), root mean squared error (RMSE), and accuracy score. These metrics help analysts understand how well the model is performing and whether adjustments are necessary.

1.1 Marketing and Consumer Behavior:

In marketing, predictive analytics helps organizations understand consumer behavior and preferences, allowing for more personalized marketing strategies. By analyzing past purchases, website interactions, and social media engagement, predictive models can identify which customers are most likely to buy certain products, engage with promotions, or churn. This allows businesses to target the right customers with the right message at the right time, ultimately leading to increased sales and customer loyalty. Businesses use predictive analytics to predict future trends in consumer behavior. By analyzing market trends and external factors such as economic conditions, predictive models can help businesses anticipate shifts in consumer preferences and adapt their strategies accordingly.

Predictive analytics powers recommendation engines used by e-commerce platforms, streaming services, and social media platforms. These engines analyze a user's past behavior, preferences, and interactions to suggest products or content they are likely to be interested in. This personalized approach not only improves the user experience but also increases sales and engagement.

The integration of machine learning (ML) within predictive analytics has revolutionized how businesses approach marketing and consumer behavior. By leveraging ML algorithms, companies can analyze vast amounts of data to uncover complex patterns and predict future consumer actions with remarkable accuracy. For marketing and consumer behavior, predictive analytics, powered by machine learning, enables businesses to not only understand current customer preferences but also anticipate their needs, creating opportunities for more personalized and targeted interactions.

This approach helps companies build more strategic and customer-centric marketing campaigns, enhancing engagement, loyalty, and ultimately, profitability.

Machine learning models used in predictive analytics can adapt and learn from new data over time, making them particularly valuable in the dynamic and often unpredictable domain of consumer behavior. These models include techniques such as clustering, decision trees, and neural networks, each of which offers unique advantages in identifying consumer patterns and trends. For instance, clustering algorithms can segment consumers based on shared characteristics, allowing marketers to tailor campaigns to specific audience segments with increased precision. This approach moves beyond traditional demographics by incorporating behavioral data, such as purchase history, browsing patterns, and even social media activity, to reveal deeper insights into consumer motivations.

In the realm of consumer behavior, predictive analytics powered by machine learning helps marketers forecast purchasing tendencies, identify at-risk customers, and uncover emerging trends. For instance, recommendation engines, which are often driven by collaborative filtering or content-based filtering algorithms, are a popular application of machine learning in predictive analytics. These systems analyze past purchase behavior and product interactions to recommend products or services that align with the consumer's preferences, creating a highly personalized shopping experience. Amazon, Netflix, and Spotify are notable examples of companies that use machine learning-based recommendation systems to drive consumer engagement and satisfaction. These algorithms continuously refine recommendations as they receive more data, leading to a deeper and more personalized connection between the consumer and the brand.

Furthermore, predictive analytics can play a critical role in customer retention strategies by identifying consumers who may be at risk of disengagement or churn. Machine learning algorithms, such as logistic regression and support vector machines, can be trained on historical customer data to detect patterns indicative of churn, such as a decline in purchase frequency or engagement. By identifying these signals early, businesses can proactively implement retention strategies, such as personalized offers or targeted messaging, to re-engage customers and reduce attrition rates. This proactive approach helps not only in maintaining revenue but also in fostering customer loyalty, as consumers increasingly expect brands to understand and respond to their unique needs.

Sentiment analysis, an application of natural language processing (NLP) within machine learning, also offers valuable insights for marketing by analyzing text data from social media, reviews, and customer feedback. Sentiment analysis algorithms evaluate the emotional tone behind consumer opinions, allowing brands to gauge public perception and adjust their strategies accordingly. For instance, a company can monitor social media discussions around a new product launch to assess customer reactions in real-time and make adjustments if necessary. Such immediate insights enable marketers to refine their messaging, address customer concerns, and highlight aspects of the product that resonate with the audience, making sentiment analysis a powerful tool for enhancing consumer engagement.

1.2 Challenges in Predictive Analytics

Despite its many advantages, predictive analytics is not without its challenges. The effectiveness of a predictive model is determined by a number of factors, including the quality of the data, the selection of features, and the appropriateness of the algorithms used.

The quality of predictive models hinges on the quality of the data they rely on. Poor-quality data, such as incomplete, outdated, or biased data, can lead to inaccurate predictions. Additionally, the challenge of integrating multiple sources of data, especially when dealing with both structured and unstructured data, can affect the quality of the model.

The growing need for real-time data analytics also adds complexity, as organizations must continuously process and analyze incoming data. Machine learning algorithms, especially those used in predictive analytics, can be complex and require significant computational power. While more complex models can provide more accurate predictions, they can also be difficult to interpret, especially for non-technical stakeholders. Organizations that need to justify decisions based on these models face a challenge due to the emergence of black-box models in machine learning, which complicate the explanation of prediction generation. Businesses increasingly want accurate, interpretable, and transparent models.

As predictive analytics becomes more prevalent, ethical concerns related to privacy and data usage have emerged. We must collect and analyze consumer data in a way that respects individual privacy and complies with relevant regulations like GDPR and CCPA. Additionally, the potential for algorithmic bias poses ethical risks. Machine learning models trained on biased or unrepresentative data may reinforce existing inequalities or make unfair predictions, especially in sensitive areas like hiring, credit scoring, or healthcare. Ensuring fairness and transparency in predictive analytics is critical, and organizations must carefully audit their models for potential biases. Transparency in the generation of predictions is crucial for fostering trust, especially in industries such as healthcare and finance, where decisions can carry substantial ramifications. Organizations must ensure that their predictive models are not only accurate but also explainable and justifiable to stakeholders and consumers alike.

Big data serves as a foundational element in predictive analytics, providing the expansive, diverse, and dynamic datasets required for generating accurate and actionable insights into business trends and consumer behavior. The effective use of big data in predictive analytics enables companies to gain a nuanced understanding of their markets, optimize operations, and improve customer engagement through timely and well-informed decisions. However, leveraging big data for predictive analytics also brings a set of challenges, including data quality issues, computational demands, privacy concerns, and the complexity of data integration.

1.3 Effective Strategies for Using Big Data in Predictive Analytics

Data Collection and Integration: The first step in effectively using big data is gathering data from multiple sources and integrating it into a single framework that enables holistic analysis. Big data can be derived from a wide variety of sources, such as social media interactions, online transactions, sensor data, and customer relationship management (CRM) systems. By integrating these diverse data sources, businesses can build a more comprehensive view of customer behavior and market dynamics. Effective data integration, often facilitated by data warehouses or data lakes, ensures that companies are using all available data to create a fuller picture, allowing predictive models to be more accurate and reliable.

1.3.1 Data Cleaning and Preprocessing:

Big data is often characterized by variability, with unstructured, semi-structured, and structured data types that require cleaning and preprocessing before use in predictive analytics. Data cleaning involves removing inconsistencies, filling in missing values, and standardizing formats, while preprocessing includes transformations to make data compatible with machine learning algorithms. This step is crucial because poor-quality data can lead to inaccurate predictions and flawed insights. Using data cleaning tools and techniques like data wrangling and ETL (extract, transform, load) pipelines helps organizations ensure that their data is accurate and ready for analysis.

1.3.2 Applying Advanced Analytical Models:

Once the data is cleaned and prepared, organizations can apply predictive algorithms to identify patterns and forecast future behaviors. The effectiveness of predictive analytics often depends on the sophistication of the models applied, such as regression models, time-series analysis, and neural networks. By choosing the appropriate models and continuously optimizing them, businesses can derive more accurate and relevant predictions. The predictive insights can then be used to drive various outcomes, such as identifying emerging trends, optimizing pricing, or improving inventory management.

1.3.3 Real-Time Data Analysis and Decision-Making:

A significant advantage of big data is the ability to analyze data in real-time, providing insights that allow businesses to make prompt decisions. For instance, in retail, real-time data can help predict spikes in demand, enabling companies to adjust supply chain logistics accordingly. Predictive analytics powered by real-time big data is also widely used in financial services, where transaction data can be analyzed instantly to detect fraudulent activity. Incorporating real-time data into predictive models enhances responsiveness and agility, making companies better equipped to address changes in consumer behavior and market conditions.

1.3.4 Leveraging Cloud and Distributed Computing:

Due to the large volume and high velocity of big data, cloud and distributed computing have become essential for handling the storage and processing demands of predictive analytics. Platforms like Hadoop, Spark, and cloud-based services (AWS, Google Cloud, Microsoft Azure) provide the infrastructure to store and process large datasets efficiently. By leveraging these platforms, organizations can scale their predictive analytics efforts, running multiple complex algorithms simultaneously across large data sets, which ultimately improves the accuracy and utility of predictive insights.

1.4 CHALLENGES IN USING BIG DATA FOR PREDICTIVE ANALYTICS

1.4.1 Data Quality and Consistency:

One of the primary challenges in predictive analytics is ensuring the quality and consistency of big data. Inconsistent, incomplete, or inaccurate data can lead to misleading predictions. Data collected from multiple sources can vary greatly in format and relevance, which makes data cleaning and preprocessing challenging and time-consuming. Without reliable data quality, predictive models may produce inaccurate insights, leading to suboptimal business decisions. While the potential benefits of predictive analytics are undeniable, it is essential to acknowledge the challenges and ethical considerations associated with its implementation. (Nishat, 2024). As predictive models become increasingly complex, understanding how they arrive at their predictions can be challenging. This lack of interpretability can hinder trust in the models and make it difficult to identify and address potential biases.

Research is ongoing to develop techniques that improve the explainability of predictive models, making them more transparent and accountable. (Chowdhury, 2024)

As predictive analytics relies on vast amounts of personal data, concerns about privacy and security are paramount. Businesses must implement robust data protection measures to safeguard sensitive information and comply with relevant regulations. Transparency and user consent are essential for building trust and maintaining ethical data practices (Babadoan, 2024).

The accuracy of predictive analytics relies heavily on the quality and integrity of the data used to train the models. Inaccurate, incomplete, or biased data can lead to flawed predictions and poor decision-making. Ensuring data quality and integrity is crucial for building reliable predictive models. (Adebiyi, 2023).

Predictive models can perpetuate existing biases present in the training data, leading to unfair or discriminatory outcomes. This is a critical ethical concern, as biased algorithms can reinforce social inequalities and lead to unfair treatment of individuals. Addressing algorithmic bias requires careful selection of training data, rigorous model evaluation, and ongoing monitoring to ensure fairness and equity. (Mhlhoff, 2021). Visual analytics systems are evolving to support more complex models and provide richer insights. Interactive visualizations, immersive experiences, and AI-powered insights will enhance the ability to understand and communicate predictive findings. (Lu, 2017)

1.4.2 Data Privacy and Compliance:

The use of big data often involves sensitive and personal information, raising concerns about privacy and data security. With strict regulations such as GDPR in the European Union and CCPA in California, companies must ensure that they handle and store data in a way that complies with legal requirements. This involves establishing robust data governance practices, such as anonymizing data, securing storage systems, and obtaining user consent for data collection. The challenge is balancing data-driven insights with the ethical and legal obligations of privacy, especially in predictive analytics where insights are generated from sensitive customer information.

1.4.3 Complexity in Data Integration:

Integrating data from various sources can be challenging due to differences in formats, structures, and storage methods. Big data often includes unstructured data from social media, emails, and video content, which can be difficult to combine with structured data like transaction records. Overcoming this complexity requires advanced data management tools and practices, such as using data lakes or employing data integration platforms, to bring disparate data into a unified environment. Without effective integration, data silos can form, limiting the scope and accuracy of predictive analytics.

1.4.4 High Computational and Storage Demands:

The volume and complexity of big data require substantial computational power and storage. Running predictive models on large datasets often demands significant processing capabilities, which can strain an organization's infrastructure. While cloud computing and distributed computing technologies have mitigated some of these issues, the cost and resource demands associated with big data analytics remain a challenge. Businesses need to carefully consider the scalability of their infrastructure and choose solutions that can efficiently handle large-scale predictive analytics without compromising performance or cost-efficiency.

1.4.5 Interpreting and Communicating Insights:

Predictive analytics generates vast amounts of data, and translating these data into actionable insights can be difficult. Advanced predictive models, particularly those involving machine learning, can act as "black boxes," where it is challenging to interpret how certain predictions were made. This lack of transparency can make it difficult to trust the insights or to communicate findings effectively to non-technical stakeholders. To address this, businesses must invest in visualization tools and data interpretation skills, ensuring that insights from predictive analytics are both understandable and actionable.

2. REVIEW OF LITERATURE

Predictive analytics, leveraging machine learning and big data, has emerged as a transformative force in various sectors, including business and consumer behavior forecasting. This analytical approach utilizes historical data to identify patterns and trends that can inform future decisions, thereby enhancing strategic planning and operational efficiency. The integration of predictive analytics into business practices allows organizations to anticipate market shifts, optimize resource allocation, and improve customer engagement, ultimately leading to increased profitability and competitive advantage.

The use of machine learning algorithms enhances the accuracy of these predictions, as they can process vast amounts of data and uncover complex relationships that traditional statistical methods might overlook. By adopting a proactive approach to data analysis, businesses can not only anticipate market trends but also innovate their offerings and improve customer satisfaction (Joel, 2024). The ongoing evolution of predictive analytics will likely lead to more sophisticated models that can integrate diverse data sources and provide deeper insights into consumer behavior and market dynamics (Farayola, 2024). Ensuring that predictive models are transparent and fair is essential for maintaining consumer trust and compliance with regulatory frameworks. This personalized approach not only increases the likelihood of conversion but also fosters customer loyalty by creating a more relevant shopping experience (Adesina, 2024).

The application of predictive analytics extends beyond marketing and sales; it is also pivotal in enhancing operational efficiencies within supply chains. As highlighted by, the transition from intuition-based decision-making to data-driven strategies has revolutionized supply chain management (Adewusi, 2024). Predictive analytics enables organizations to forecast demand more accurately, optimize inventory levels, and streamline logistics operations. This capability is particularly beneficial in industries where demand is volatile and supply chain disruptions can have significant financial repercussions (Oyewole, 2024).

Moreover, the integration of predictive analytics with emerging technologies such as the Internet of Things (IoT) further amplifies its impact. IoT devices generate vast amounts of data that, when analyzed through predictive models, can provide real-time insights into operational performance and consumer behavior (Rozhdestvenskiy, 2024). For example, in smart manufacturing, predictive analytics can monitor equipment performance and predict maintenance needs, reducing downtime and operational costs (Ochuba, 2024).

In the realm of consumer behavior, predictive analytics provides insights into purchasing patterns and preferences, allowing businesses to tailor their marketing efforts effectively. By analyzing data from various sources, including social media, transaction histories, and customer feedback, organizations can segment their customer base and develop targeted marketing campaigns that resonate with specific demographics (Habel et al., 2023). The role of predictive analytics in business is multifaceted, encompassing various applications such as sales forecasting, customer relationship management, and supply chain optimization. For instance, predictive models can analyze past sales data to forecast future sales trends, enabling businesses to adjust their inventory and marketing strategies accordingly (Jangam, 2023). By leveraging predictive models, companies can anticipate potential disruptions and develop contingency plans, thereby enhancing resilience and responsiveness (Suwignjo, 2023).

Similarly, in retail, IoT-enabled analytics can track customer movements within stores, allowing businesses to optimize store layouts and improve customer experiences (Kshirsagar, 2023). Additionally, organizations must invest in robust data governance frameworks to ensure the integrity and security of the data used in predictive analytics (Alotaibi, 2023).

Financial institutions utilize predictive models to evaluate credit risk, detect fraudulent activities, and forecast market trends. By analyzing vast amounts of transactional data, these institutions can identify anomalies and patterns that may indicate fraudulent behavior, thereby enhancing their security measures (Kshirsagar, 2023). Despite the numerous benefits of predictive analytics, organizations face several challenges in its implementation. One significant hurdle is data quality; the accuracy of predictive models heavily relies on the quality of the data used. Incomplete or inaccurate data can lead to erroneous predictions, undermining the effectiveness of the analytics (Nugroho, 2023).

Machine learning algorithms are instrumental in predicting consumer behavior by analyzing patterns in purchasing data. For instance, Yan, (2023) emphasizes that understanding consumer purchase characteristics allows enterprises to tailor their marketing strategies effectively, thereby enhancing brand image and commercial value. Similarly, Zhang (2023) discusses how deep analysis of consumer psychological activities and purchasing behaviors can lead to continuous optimization of marketing models, particularly through neural network technologies. The application of these technologies not only aids in predicting consumer preferences but also in adjusting marketing strategies dynamically to capture greater market share.

Big data analytics further enriches this predictive capability by providing insights derived from diverse data sources, including social media and e-commerce interactions. Li (2023) highlights that big data analytics can optimize various operational aspects of e-commerce platforms, such as pricing and inventory management, by analyzing consumer shopping habits and preferences. This sentiment is echoed by Vasilopoulou et al., (2023) that big data enables businesses to gain insights into consumer behavior, thereby optimizing the customer journey and creating personalized experiences. The ability to process large volumes of structured and unstructured data allows organizations to extract actionable intelligence that can significantly enhance marketing effectiveness (Putra, 2023).

Moreover, the role of big data in understanding consumer behavior extends to the analysis of online reviews and social media interactions. Huang et al. illustrate how insights from online consumer behaviors can inform real-time marketing actions, thereby enhancing user-centric optimization (Cavaliere et al., 2021; Huang et al., 2019). The predictive analysis of consumer behavior also involves the use of advanced machine learning models that can handle complex datasets. For example, Chaudhary et al., (2021) present a model that utilizes machine learning to predict consumer behavior on social media platforms, demonstrating the effectiveness of such approaches in capturing the nuances of consumer preferences. This capability is crucial for businesses looking to refine their marketing strategies based on real-time consumer data.

However, the implementation of predictive analytics is not without challenges. Organizations must grapple with issues related to data quality, privacy, and ethical considerations. As noted by, the ethical implications of predictive analytics, particularly in terms of data privacy and the potential for bias in algorithmic decision-making, are critical concerns that must be addressed (Mühlhoff, 2021). Moreover, predictive analytics aids in investment decision-making by providing insights into market trends and potential returns, enabling investors to make more informed choices (Souza et al., 2020). This capability is particularly crucial in the fast-paced retail environment, where consumer preferences can shift rapidly. By employing predictive analytics, companies can not only react to changes but also proactively shape their offerings to meet anticipated demand (Morsi, 2020).

The application of predictive analytics spans various domains, including marketing, finance, supply chain management, and customer relationship management. In marketing, for instance, predictive analytics enables businesses to segment their customer base more effectively and tailor their marketing strategies to meet the specific needs of different consumer groups. By analyzing past purchasing behaviors and preferences, companies can anticipate future buying patterns and optimize their promotional efforts accordingly Shah et al. (2018). Moreover, predictive analytics can identify potential churn risks, enabling companies to implement retention strategies before losing valuable customers (Shah et al., 2017).

The future of predictive analytics in business is promising, with advancements in machine learning and artificial intelligence poised to enhance its capabilities further. As organizations continue to harness the power of big data, the potential for predictive analytics to drive strategic decision-making will only grow.

3. RESEARCH METHODOLOGY

3.1. Research Design

The research will adopt a mixed-methods approach that combines qualitative insights with quantitative data to explore the application and effectiveness of predictive analytics in various industries. The primary focus will be on understanding how businesses utilize machine learning algorithms and big data to make predictions and how these forecasts impact decision-making in real-time.

3.2. Research Questions and Objectives:

The primary objectives of this study are:

1. To explore how predictive analytics is being used in business operations and consumer behavior forecasting.
2. To identify the challenges and limitations associated with integrating machine learning and big data in predictive analytics.

Key Research Questions:

- How are businesses leveraging machine learning and big data to improve predictions in consumer behavior?
- What are the most effective machine learning algorithms for predictive analytics?
- What challenges do businesses face when integrating predictive analytics into their decision-making processes?
- How can the accuracy of predictive models be improved for better forecasting of business and consumer trends?

3.3 Sample Size:

A sample size of 279 respondents will be targeted. This includes professionals from multiple industries who are directly involved in using predictive analytics, machine learning, and big data. A balance of respondents from small, medium, and large organizations will be sought to ensure diversity in data. For the qualitative interviews, purposive sampling will be employed. This non-probability sampling method is ideal for selecting participants who have specific knowledge and experience with predictive analytics in their industries. Initially 10 IT industries in Chennai was identified and 500 questionnaires (50 questionnaires per firm) were mailed. The responses rate was poor and researcher was received responses only from106 respondents. Then researcher approached manually to the IT firms and distributed the questionnaire and conducted interview to the respondents when respondents are available. Finally, researcher collected a sample of 279, which is a respective number to proceed further analysis.

3.4 Limitations of the Study

Some limitations that may affect the outcomes of this research include:

- While secondary data will be used, access to proprietary big data from companies might be limited. This could restrict the analysis of certain business use cases.
- Machine learning and predictive analytics are fast-evolving fields, meaning new models and techniques may emerge that could outperform those evaluated in this study. Therefore, the research may not capture the very latest advancements in the field.
- The findings from specific industries or organizations may not be directly applicable to all businesses, particularly those that have different data infrastructures or operate in distinct market environments.

4. ANALYSIS AND INTERPRETATION

Table 1. Factor analysis

Predictive analysis variables	**Factor loadings**
Machine Learning Algorithms	
The machine learning algorithms we use effectively analyze historical data for predicting future trends.	.972
Our predictive models leverage advanced machine learning techniques to improve forecast accuracy.	.958
Machine learning algorithms enable our organization to identify complex patterns in consumer behavior data.	.944
We regularly update and refine machine learning algorithms to adapt to changes in business and consumer data.	.940
Our team has the necessary skills to implement machine learning algorithms for predictive analytics.	.929
Machine learning models in our organization deliver reliable insights for decision-making.	.908
Our organization considers algorithm performance metrics (e.g., accuracy, precision) to evaluate predictive analytics effectiveness.	.860
Big Data Characteristics	
Our organization collects a high volume of data relevant to predicting business and consumer behaviors.	.955
The speed at which our data is generated is adequate for real-time predictive analytics.	.946
We integrate various data types (structured, semi-structured, unstructured) to enhance prediction accuracy.	.923
Our data management system effectively handles the large volume and complexity of data.	.919
The diversity of data sources in our organization provides a comprehensive view of trends.	.897

continued on following page

Table 1. Continued

Predictive analysis variables	Factor loadings
Machine Learning Algorithms	
We have effective tools in place to manage the velocity and variability of our data.	.883
Our big data processes are aligned with our predictive analytics goals for future trend forecasting.	.841
Data Quality and Preprocessing	
We ensure that data is cleaned and preprocessed before it is used in predictive models.	.965
Our data quality is high, with minimal inconsistencies, missing values, or inaccuracies.	.948
Our data validation processes are effective in maintaining the reliability of our predictive analytics.	.932
The preprocessing methods used (e.g., normalization, transformation) enhance the performance of predictive models.	.876
We address any data quality issues promptly to ensure accurate predictions.	.857
Our data quality protocols are consistently applied to all sources of data.	.813
The quality of our data directly impacts the effectiveness of our predictive analytics.	.743
Data Source Utilization	
We integrate social media data to enrich our predictive models for consumer behavior.	.959
Our organization uses transactional data to improve the accuracy of trend forecasting.	.948
We utilize CRM data to capture customer interactions for predictive purposes.	.934
Sensor data (if applicable) is a valuable component of our predictive analytics strategy.	.908
We incorporate external market data to broaden the scope of our trend forecasting.	.879
Multiple data sources provide a well-rounded view of both current and future trends.	.862
The diversity of our data sources strengthens our predictive analytics capabilities.	.858
Real-Time Data Availability	
Our organization has access to real-time data, which supports timely decision-making.	942
We use real-time data to predict short-term consumer behavior changes accurately.	. .936
Real-time data enables our organization to respond quickly to emerging market trends.	.931
The ability to analyze real-time data enhances the reliability of our forecasts.	.914
We regularly monitor real-time data for actionable insights into business trends.	.848
Real-time data analytics have improved our organization's agility in market response.	.768
Delays in data availability hinder our predictive analytics accuracy and timeliness.	.756
Infrastructure and Computational Power	
Our organization's infrastructure is equipped to process large datasets quickly.	.946
We utilize cloud or distributed computing for scalable data storage and processing.	.904
Computational limitations do not affect our ability to run complex predictive models.	.868
Our predictive analytics system can handle a high volume of concurrent data streams.	.866

continued on following page

Table 1. Continued

Predictive analysis variables	Factor loadings
Machine Learning Algorithms	
We have the necessary resources (hardware, software) for effective data analytics.	.838
The computational power available allows for real-time processing of big data.	.829
Infrastructure investments have improved our predictive analytics performance.	.813
Future Trends in Business and Consumer Behaviors (Dependent Variable)	
Our predictive analytics accurately forecasts consumer purchasing behaviors.	.928
We are able to anticipate market demand trends based on our analytics outputs.	.923
Predictive analytics helps us stay ahead of consumer preferences and shifts.	.864
We leverage insights from predictive analytics to enhance customer engagement strategies.	.856
Predictive analytics allows us to make informed adjustments to product offerings.	.852
Our organization relies on predictive insights to proactively respond to market changes.	.817
Future trends identified through analytics align closely with actual outcomes in our business.	.738
Extraction Method: Principal Component Analysis. *Rotation Method: Varimax with Kaiser Normalization.* *Rotation converged in 7 iterations.*	

Machine Learning Algorithms emerged as the strongest, with loadings ranging from .860 to .972. The highest loading item (.972) addressed historical data analysis capabilities, while the lowest (.860) concerned algorithm performance metrics. The consistently high loadings suggest a well-integrated machine learning infrastructure. Big Data Characteristics demonstrated strong loadings ranging from .841 to .955, indicating robust big data capabilities.

The factor structure suggests a comprehensive understanding of big data's volume, velocity, and variety. Data Quality and Preprocessing showed a wider range of loadings (.743 to .965), suggesting varying levels of data quality management maturity. Data Source Utilization Loadings ranged from .858 to .959, indicating strong data integration capabilities across various sources. Real-Time Data Availability showed strong initial loadings but declined in later items (.756 to .942), suggesting potential challenges in real-time data utilization. Infrastructure and Computational Power Loadings ranged from .813 to .946, indicating robust technical infrastructure with some variation in capability maturity. Future Trends showed moderate to strong loadings (.738 to .928), with declining strength in long-term prediction items.

The factor analysis provides strong empirical support for a seven-factor model of predictive analytics capabilities. The results suggest that organizations should take a structured approach to developing these capabilities, focusing on foundational elements while addressing gaps in real-time processing and long-term prediction accuracy.

A multiple regression analysis was conducted to examine the relationship between organizations' predictive analytics capabilities and their ability to forecast future business and consumer trends. The predictive model included six independent variables: Infrastructure and Computational Power, Machine Learning Algorithms, Data Quality and Preprocessing, Real-Time Data Availability, Big Data Characteristics, and Data Sources Utilization.

The results indicate that the model explained a significant proportion of variance in future trend prediction capabilities, $R^2 = .467$, $F(6, 272) = 7.831$, $p < .001$. The adjusted R^2 of .428 indicates that approximately 42.8% of the variability in an organization's ability to predict future trends is accounted for by the combined effect of the six predictors in the model. Table 2 presents the complete model summary statistics.

Table 2. Multiple Regression Model Summary for Predicting Future Business and Consumer Trends

Model Summary[b]									
					Change Statistics				
Model	R	R Square	Adjusted R Square	SE	R Square Change	F Change	df1	df2	Sig. F Change
1	.684[a]	.467	.428	.942	.467	7.831	6	272	.000

a. Predictors: (Constant), Infrastructure and Computational Power, Machine Learning Algorithms, Data Quality and Preprocessing, Real-Time Data Availability, Big Data Characteristics, Data Sources utilization

b. Dependent Variable: Future Trends in Business and Consumer Behaviors

Note. SE = Standard Error of the Estimate; df = degrees of freedom; Sig. = Significance.

The regression model demonstrates a moderately strong relationship between the predictor variables and future trend prediction capabilities ($R = .684$). The standard error of the estimate (SEE = .942) indicates the average deviation of predictions from observed values, suggesting moderate prediction accuracy given the measurement scale. The significant F-change ($p < .001$) provides strong evidence against the null hypothesis, indicating that the combination of predictive analytics capabilities significantly improves the ability to forecast future business and consumer trends beyond what would be expected by chance.

The model explains 46.7% of the total variance in future trend prediction capabilities ($R^2 = .467$). The relatively small difference between R^2 (.467) and adjusted R^2 (.428) suggests good model stability and generalizability. However, the presence of unexplained variance (53.3%) indicates that additional factors not included in the current model may also influence an organization's predictive capabilities.

The results demonstrate that organizational predictive analytics capabilities collectively explain a substantial portion of the variance in future trend prediction ability. The significant model fit suggests that investments in these six areas of predictive analytics capability can meaningfully improve an organization's ability to forecast future business and consumer trends.

Analysis of Variance

To assess the statistical significance of the predictive analytics model, a one-way analysis of variance was conducted. The ANOVA results confirm that the regression model significantly predicts the organization's ability to forecast future business and consumer trends, $F(6, 272) = 7.831$, $p < .001$. Table 3 presents the complete ANOVA results.

Table 3. Analysis of Variance Results for Predictive Analytics Capabilities Model

ANOVA[a]						
Model		Sum of Squares	df	Mean Square	F	Sig.
1	Regression	41.702	6	6.950	7.831	.000[b]
	Residual	241.402	272	.888		
	Total	283.104	278			

a. Dependent Variable: Future Trends in Business and Consumer Behaviors

b. Predictors: (Constant), Infrastructure and Computational Power, Machine Learning Algorithms, Data Quality and Preprocessing, Real-Time Data Availability, Big Data Characteristics, Data Sources utilization

Note. SS = Sum of Squares; df = degrees of freedom; MS = Mean Square.

Multiple regression analysis was conducted to examine the predictive relationship between organizations' analytics capabilities and their ability to forecast future business and consumer trends. The model included six predictors: Infrastructure and Computational Power, Machine Learning Algorithms, Data Quality and Preprocessing, Real-Time Data Availability, Big Data Characteristics, and Data Sources Utilization. The results indicated that the regression model significantly predicted Future Trends in Business and Consumer Behaviors, $F(6, 272) = 7.831$, $p < .001$, accounting for 46.7% of the variance ($R^2 = .467$, Adjusted $R^2 = .428$). The model demonstrated a moderately strong relationship between the predictor variables and future trend prediction capabilities ($R = .684$), with a standard error of estimate of .942.

Analysis of variance decomposed the total sum of squares (283.104) into explained variance (SS_regression = 41.702) and unexplained variance (SS_residual = 241.402), with a mean square error of 0.888. The significant F-statistic and moderate R^2 value suggest that while the six predictive analytics capabilities collectively explain a substantial portion of variance in future trend prediction ability, additional factors not included in the current model may also influence an organization's predictive capabilities. The relatively small difference between R^2 and adjusted R^2 indicates good model stability and generalizability, though the presence of unexplained variance suggests opportunities for model enhancement through the inclusion of additional predictors or examination of interaction effects.

Table 4. Regression analysis

Coefficients[a]						
		Unstandardized Coefficients		Standardized Coefficients		
Model		B	Std. Error	Beta	t	Sig.
1	(Constant)	1.856	.304		6.110	.000
	Machine Learning Algorithms	.219	.088	.228	2.486	.014
	Big Data Characteristics	-.025	.093	-.025	-.272	.786
	Data Quality and Preprocessing	.090	.061	.089	1.479	.140
	Data Sources utilization	-.078	.112	-.079	-.700	.485
	Real-Time Data Availability	.049	.076	.051	.640	.523
	Infrastructure and Computational Power	.248	.121	.257	2.046	.042

a. Dependent Variable: Future Trends in Business and Consumer Behaviors

The regression analysis revealed varying levels of influence among the predictive analytics capabilities on future trend forecasting ability. Infrastructure and Computational Power emerged as the strongest significant predictor ($\beta = .257$, $t = 2.046$, $p = .042$), followed by Machine Learning Algorithms ($\beta = .228$, $t = 2.486$, $p = .014$), both demonstrating significant positive relationships with future trend prediction capabilities. The remaining predictors showed non-significant relationships: Data Quality and Preprocessing ($\beta = .089$, $t = 1.479$, $p = .140$), Real-Time Data Availability ($\beta = .051$, $t = .640$, $p = .523$), Data Sources Utilization ($\beta = -.079$, $t = -.700$, $p = .485$), and Big Data Characteristics ($\beta = -.025$, $t = -.272$, $p = .786$).

The model's constant term was significant ($B = 1.856$, $SE = .304$, $t = 6.110$, $p < .001$), indicating a baseline level of trend prediction capability independent of the measured predictors. These findings suggest that while all six capabilities contribute to the model's overall significance, organizations' investments in infrastructure, computational power, and machine learning algorithms may yield the most substantial improvements in their ability to predict future business and consumer trends. Notably, the negative coefficients for Data Sources Utilization and Big Data Characteristics, though not statistically significant, warrant further investigation into potential suppression effects or complex interactions among predictors.

Table 5. Correlation analysis among all the predictive analytics variables

	Machine Learning Algorithms	Big Data Characteristics	Data Quality and Preprocessing	Data Sources utilization	Real-Time Data Availability	Infrastructure and Computational Power	Future Trends in Business and Consumer Behaviors
Machine Learning Algorithms	1						
Big Data Characteristics	.788**	1					
Data Quality and Preprocessing	.252**	.243**	1				
Data Sources utilization	.242**	.294**	.213**	1			
Real-Time Data Availability	.177**	.163**	.289**	.612**	1		
Infrastructure and Computational Power	.243**	.278**	.274**	.866**	.705**	1	
Future Trends in Business and Consumer Behaviors	.283**	.233**	.209**	.241**	.246**	.298**	1

Pearson correlation analysis revealed significant bivariate relationships among all predictive analytics capabilities and future trend forecasting ability. Infrastructure and Computational Power demonstrated the strongest correlation with Future Trends in Business and Consumer Behaviors ($r = .298$, $p < .01$), followed by Machine Learning Algorithms ($r = .283$, $p < .01$), Real-Time Data Availability ($r = .246$, $p < .01$), Data Sources Utilization ($r = .241$, $p < .01$), Big Data Characteristics ($r = .233$, $p < .01$), and Data Quality and Preprocessing ($r = .209$, $p < .01$). Notable inter-correlations among predictors were observed, particularly strong relationships between Infrastructure and Computational Power with Data Sources Utilization ($r = .866$, $p < .01$) and Real-Time Data Availability ($r = .705$, $p < .01$).

Machine Learning Algorithms and Big Data Characteristics also showed a strong positive correlation ($r = .788$, $p < .01$). Moderate correlations were found between Real-Time Data Availability and Data Sources Utilization ($r = .612$, $p < .01$). The remaining inter-correlations were relatively modest, ranging from $r = .163$ to $r = .289$ (all $p < .01$), suggesting generally distinct constructs while maintaining significant relationships. These correlation patterns indicate a complex interplay among predictive analytics capabilities, with infrastructure and machine learning capabilities showing the strongest associations with future trend prediction ability.

5. FINDINGS

The findings highlight three key patterns in organizational predictive analytics capabilities. First, the significant but moderate R^2 value (.467) indicates that while the identified capabilities are important, additional factors likely influence an organization's predictive success. Second, the emergence of Infrastructure and Computational Power as the strongest predictor ($\beta = .257$) emphasizes the fundamental importance of robust technical infrastructure in enabling effective predictive analytics. Third, the strong correlations among technical capabilities (infrastructure, data sources, and real-time availability) suggest that organizations tend to develop these capabilities in tandem rather than in isolation. Interestingly, while Data Quality and Preprocessing,

Real-Time Data Availability, and Data Sources Utilization showed significant bivariate correlations with future trend prediction (r ranging from .209 to .246, $p < .01$), their non-significant regression coefficients suggest their effects may be mediated through other capabilities, particularly infrastructure and machine learning algorithms.

These results have important implications for organizations investing in predictive analytics capabilities. The significant role of infrastructure and machine learning algorithms suggests these should be priority areas for investment. However, the strong inter-correlations among capabilities indicate that a balanced approach to capability development may be necessary, as these systems appear to work synergistically rather than independently. The relatively moderate overall model fit ($R^2 = .467$) also suggests that organizations should consider factors beyond technical capabilities, such as organizational culture, human capital, and strategic alignment, in developing their predictive analytics capabilities.

6. SUGGESTIONS

- Organizations should prioritize developing robust infrastructure and computational power as these form the backbone of predictive analytics. Investments in high-performance computing systems, cloud-based platforms, and scalable data storage solutions are critical to support the demands of predictive modeling and big data analytics.
- Machine learning algorithms are essential for extracting actionable insights from large datasets. Businesses should invest in advanced machine learning models, ensure access to skilled data scientists, and adopt continuous training and fine-tuning of algorithms to enhance accuracy and reliability in forecasting.

- Given the strong inter-correlations among technical capabilities such as data sources utilization, real-time data availability, and infrastructure, organizations should aim for an integrated strategy. Coordinated development of these capabilities can amplify their effectiveness through synergistic interactions, improving overall predictive analytics outcomes.
- While data quality and preprocessing did not show direct predictive power in regression models, their strong correlations with other predictors underscore their foundational role. Organizations must implement rigorous data cleaning, integration, and standardization processes to ensure data readiness for machine learning applications.
- The moderate R^2 value (46.7%) indicates that non-technical factors significantly influence predictive analytics outcomes. Organizations should also consider enhancing their organizational culture, fostering cross-functional collaboration, and aligning predictive analytics efforts with strategic goals to improve implementation success.
- The complementary relationship between machine learning algorithms and big data characteristics suggests that leveraging the unique attributes of big data—such as volume, velocity, and variety—can enhance forecasting accuracy. Additionally, integrating real-time analytics capabilities can improve responsiveness to dynamic market and consumer trends.
- Advanced predictive analytics requires skilled personnel who understand both technical methods and domain-specific contexts. Training programs and cross-functional teams can bridge the gap between technical and business expertise, ensuring analytics outputs are both relevant and actionable.
- To ensure the insights generated from predictive analytics are effectively communicated and actionable, organizations should use advanced data visualization tools and dashboards. These tools can help decision-makers quickly understand complex predictions and respond proactively to emerging trends.
- Organizations should regularly evaluate the effectiveness of their predictive analytics systems and adapt their strategies based on emerging technologies and business needs. Continuous improvement cycles can help maintain competitiveness in forecasting future trends.
- Future research should explore mediating effects (e.g., organizational alignment, leadership support) and moderating factors (e.g., industry type, market volatility) to better understand their roles in enhancing the predictive capabilities of machine learning and big data analytics.

7. MANAGERIAL IMPLICATIONS

- Managers should allocate resources strategically to enhance infrastructure, computational power, and machine learning capabilities, as these are pivotal for accurate trend forecasting. Prioritizing investments in scalable technology solutions will ensure organizations are equipped to handle large datasets and complex predictive models.
- Predictive analytics should not function in isolation. Managers need to integrate these capabilities into organizational strategy, aligning forecasting outputs with decision-making processes. This alignment will improve the relevance of predictions to business goals and facilitate informed decision-making.
- Predictive analytics spans multiple domains, including IT, marketing, operations, and strategy. Managers should foster collaboration across departments to ensure insights are actionable and that technical teams work closely with business units to address organizational priorities.
- Organizations should prioritize recruiting and retaining skilled data scientists, analysts, and domain experts who can interpret complex predictions and translate them into strategic actions. Managers must invest in training and upskilling programs to develop a workforce proficient in big data and machine learning applications.
- Given the strong interdependencies among predictive analytics capabilities (e.g., infrastructure, real-time data availability, and data sources), managers should ensure balanced development rather than overemphasizing any single area. A holistic approach will maximize synergies and improve overall system effectiveness.
- Real-time data processing enables organizations to respond swiftly to market changes. Managers should emphasize implementing systems that can handle real-time data streams, ensuring timely insights for proactive decision-making in dynamic business environments.
- High-quality data is essential for reliable predictions. Managers need to enforce strict data governance policies, ensuring accuracy, completeness, and consistency in datasets. Investments in automated data preprocessing tools can further streamline this process.
- Predictive analytics fosters agility by enabling organizations to anticipate and adapt to future trends. Managers should create an environment that supports innovation and experimentation, using analytics insights to explore new market opportunities and drive innovation.
- Managers must establish systems for regular performance evaluation of predictive analytics. By analyzing the accuracy and relevance of predictions,

organizations can iteratively improve their models, ensuring they remain competitive in forecasting future trends.

- Managers play a critical role in cultivating a culture that values data-driven decision-making. Leadership should champion predictive analytics initiatives, encouraging buy-in across all levels of the organization and ensuring alignment with the organization's vision and objectives.

8. CONCLUSION

Predictive analytics, powered by machine learning and big data, has emerged as a transformative tool for organizations aiming to forecast future trends in business and consumer behaviors. This study highlights the critical role of technical capabilities, particularly infrastructure and computational power, alongside machine learning algorithms, in enhancing predictive accuracy. However, the findings also emphasize the importance of adopting a holistic approach, recognizing the synergistic interplay among capabilities like real-time data availability and data source utilization.

While the regression analysis demonstrates significant predictive power, it also highlights the influence of non-technical factors, such as organizational culture, strategic alignment, and human expertise. These findings suggest that organizations should not only invest in advanced technologies but also focus on fostering a culture of collaboration, continuous learning, and agility.

By strategically integrating technical capabilities with organizational priorities, managers can harness the full potential of predictive analytics. This integration will enable organizations to anticipate market shifts, address consumer needs proactively, and maintain a competitive edge in an increasingly data-driven business landscape. Future research should delve deeper into the role of mediating and moderating factors to provide a more comprehensive understanding of predictive analytics' effectiveness in diverse organizational contexts.

9. REFERENCES

Adebiyi, O. O. (2023). Exploring the Impact of Predictive Analytics on Accounting and Auditing Expertise: A Regression Analysis of LinkedIn Survey Data. Asian Journal of Economics Business and Accounting. DOI: 10.9734/ajeba/2023/v23i221153

Adesina, A. A., Iyelolu, T. V., & Paul, P. O.Abayomi Abraham AdesinaToluwalase Vanessa IyeloluPatience Okpeke Paul. (2024). Leveraging predictive analytics for strategic decision-making: Enhancing business performance through data-driven insights. *World Journal of Advanced Research and Reviews*, 22(3), 1927–1934. DOI: 10.30574/wjarr.2024.22.3.1961

Adewusi, A. O., Komolafe, A. M., Ejairu, E., Aderotoye, I. A., Abiona, O. O., & Oyeniran, O. C. (2024). The role of predictive analytics in optimizing supply chain resilience: A review of techniques and case studies. International Journal of Management &Amp. *Entrepreneurship Research*, 6(3), 815–837. DOI: 10.51594/ijmer.v6i3.938

. Agu, E. E. et al. (2024). Building sustainable business models with predictive analytics: Case studies from various industries. International journal of advanced economics. DOI: 10.51594/ijae.v6i8.1436

. Ajiga, D. et al. (2024). Predictive analytics for market trends using AI: A study in consumer behavior. International Journal of Engineering Research Updates. DOI: 10.53430/ijeru.2024.7.1.0032

Alotaibi, E. (2023). Risk assessment using predictive analytics. *International Journal of Professional Business Review*, 8(5), e01723. DOI: 10.26668/businessreview/2023.v8i5.1723

Babadoan, B. (2024). *Harnessing AI and Predictive Analytics to Revolutionize Customer Retention Strategies*. None., DOI: 10.62802/k2a4gf39

Babadoan, B. (2024). *Unveiling the Power of AI-Driven Personalization: Transforming Consumer Behavior in the Age of Digital Marketing*. None., DOI: 10.62802/fj43xy18

Cavaliere, L. P. L., Mangalasserri, K., Venkateswaran, P. S., Byloppilly, R., & Effendy, F. (2021). The impact of brand counterfeiting on consumer behavior in the fashion sector. *Turkish Journal of Physiotherapy and Rehabilitation*, 32(3), 19831–19847. DOI: 10.5606/tjpr.2021.13842

Chaudhary, K., Alam, M., Al-Rakhami, M. S., & Gumaei, A. (2021). Machine learning-based mathematical modelling for prediction of social media consumer behavior using big data analytics. *Journal of Big Data*, 8(1), 73. Advance online publication. DOI: 10.1186/s40537-021-00466-2

Chowdhury, R. H.. (2024). *The impact of predictive analytics on financial risk management in businesses*. World Journal of Advanced Research and Reviews., DOI: 10.30574/wjarr.2024.23.3.2807

Farayola, O. A., Adaga, E. M., Egieya, Z. E., Ewuga, S. K., Abdul, A. A., & Abrahams, T. O.Oluwatoyin Ajoke FarayolaEjuma Martha AdagaZainab Efe EgieyaSarah Kuzankah EwugaAdekunle Abiola AbdulTemitayo Oluwaseun Abrahams. (2024). Advancements in predictive analytics: A philosophical and practical overview. *World Journal of Advanced Research and Reviews*, 21(3), 240–252. DOI: 10.30574/wjarr.2024.21.3.2706

Habel, J., Alavi, S., & Heinitz, N. (2023). A theory of predictive sales analytics adoption. *AMS Review*, 13(1-2), 34–54. DOI: 10.1007/s13162-022-00252-0

Huang, Y., Liu, H., Li, W., Wang, Z., Hu, X., & Wang, W. (2019). Lifestyles in amazon: Evidence from online reviews enhanced recommender system. *International Journal of Market Research*, 62(6), 689–706. DOI: 10.1177/1470785319844146

Igorevich Rozhdestvenskiy, O., & Poornima, E. (2024). Enabling sustainable urban transportation with predictive analytics and iot. MATEC Web of Conferences, 392, 01179. DOI: 10.1051/matecconf/202439201179

Jangam, D. S., & Deshpande, A. R. (2023). Business analytics using predictive algorithms. *International Journal on Recent and Innovation Trends in Computing and Communication*, 11(8s), 595–609. DOI: 10.17762/ijritcc.v11i8s.7242

Khandelwal, R.. (2020). *Comparative Analysis of Machine Learning Techniques Using Predictive Modeling*. Recent Advances in Computer Science and Communications., DOI: 10.2174/2666255813999200904164539

Kshirsagar, P. S., & Pawar, A. M. (2023). Predictive analytics for cyber threats to enhance security in the cyber supply chain. *Research Journal of Computer Systems and Engineering*, 4(1), 102–109. DOI: 10.52710/rjcse.68

Kumari, L., & Aggrawal, D. R. (2022). An Insight into Predictive Analytics Techniques. *International Journal for Research in Applied Science and Engineering Technology*, 10(12), 984–987. Advance online publication. DOI: 10.22214/ijraset.2022.48071

Li, Y. (2023). Big data analysis in consumer behavior: Evidence from social media and mobile payment. Advances in Economics. *Management and Political Sciences*, 64(1), 269–275. DOI: 10.54254/2754-1169/64/20231548

Madani, B.. (2021). *Predicting Consumer Purchasing Decision in The Online Food Delivery Industry*. ArXiv. DOI: 10.5121/csit.2021.111510

. Mhlhoff, R. (2021). Predictive privacy: towards an applied ethics of data analytics. Springer Science+Business Media. DOI: 10.1007/s10676-021-09606-x

. Morsi, S. (2020). A predictive analytics model for e-commerce sales transactions to support decision making: a case study. International Journal of Computer and Information Technology (2279-0764), 9(1). DOI: 10.24203/ijcit.v9i1.3

Mühlhoff, R. (2021). Predictive privacy: Towards an applied ethics of data analytics. *Ethics and Information Technology*, 23(4), 675–690. DOI: 10.1007/s10676-021-09606-x

Myint, K., ... (2023). Predictive Analytics System for Stock Data: methodology, data pre-processing and case studies. International Conferences on Computing Advancements. DOI: 10.1109/ICCA51723.2023.10182047

Nishat, N.. (2024). Predictive Analytics for Business Decision-Making: Unleashing the Power of Data-driven Insights. *International Conference on Computing Communication and Networking Technologies*. DOI: 10.1109/ICCCNT61001.2024.10724574

Nugroho, H. (2023). A review: Data quality problem in predictive analytics. [International Journal of Applied Information Technology]. *IJAIT*, 7(02), 79. DOI: 10.25124/ijait.v7i02.5980

Ochuba, N. A., Usman, F. O., Okafor, E. S., Akinrinola, O., & Amoo, O. O. (2024). Predictive analytics in the maintenance and reliability of satellite telecommunications infrastructure: A conceptual review of strategies and technological advancements. Engineering Science &Amp. *Technology Journal*, 5(3), 704–715. DOI: 10.51594/estj.v5i3.866

. Oloruntosin Tolulope Joel and Vincent Ugochukwu Oguanobi (2024). Data-driven strategies for business expansion: utilizing predictive analytics for enhanced profitability and opportunity identification. International Journal of Frontiers in Engineering and Technology Research, 6(2), 071-081. DOI: 10.53294/ijfetr.2024.6.2.0035

Putra, A. H. P. K., Rivera, K. M., & Pramukti, A. (2023). Optimizing marketing management strategies through it innovation: Big data integration for better consumer understanding. *Golden Ratio of Mapping Idea and Literature Format*, 3(1), 71–91. DOI: 10.52970/grmilf.v3i1.398

Sahare, P. R. (2024). *Sales Data Analysis Using BI and WEKA*. INTERANTIONAL JOURNAL OF SCIENTIFIC RESEARCH IN ENGINEERING AND MANAGEMENT., DOI: 10.55041/IJSREM30123

Shah, N. D., Steyerberg, E. W., & Kent, D. M. (2018). Big data and predictive analytics. *Journal of the American Medical Association*, 320(1), 27. DOI: 10.1001/jama.2018.5602 PMID: 29813156

Shah, R. M., Butt, M. A., & Baba, M. Z. (2017). Predictive analytic modeling: A walkthrough. *International Journal of Advanced Research in Computer Science and Software Engineering*, 7(6), 421–426. DOI: 10.23956/ijarcsse/V7I6/0305

. Souza, J., Leung, C. K., & Cuzzocrea, A. (2020). An innovative big data predictive analytics framework over hybrid big data sources with an application for disease analytics. Advanced Information Networking and Applications, 669-680. https://doi.org/DOI: 10.1007/978-3-030-44041-1_59

. Suwignjo, P., Panjaitan, L., Baihaqy, A. R., & Rusdiansyah, A. (2023). Predictive analytics to improve inventory performance: a case study of an fmcg company. Operations and Supply Chain Management: An International Journal, 293-310. https://doi.org/.DOI: 10.31387/oscm0530390

. Tolulope, O. et al. (2024). Data-driven strategies for business expansion: Utilizing predictive analytics for enhanced profitability and opportunity identification. International Journal of Frontiers in Engineering and Technology Research. DOI: 10.53294/ijfetr.2024.6.2.0035

Vasilopoulou, C., Theodorakopoulos, L., & Γιαννούκου, I. (2023). Big data and consumer behavior: The power and pitfalls of analytics in the digital age. *Technium Social Sciences Journal*, 45, 469–480. DOI: 10.47577/tssj.v45i1.9135

Ved, M.. (2019). Big Data Analytics in Telecommunication using State-of-the-art Big Data Framework in a Distributed Computing Environment: A Case Study. *Annual International Computer Software and Applications Conference*. DOI: 10.1109/COMPSAC.2019.00066

Yan, J. (2023). Prediction of consumer behavior based on machine learning algorithm. Proceedings of the 2nd International Conference on Mathematical Statistics and Economic Analysis, MSEA 2023, May 26–28, 2023, N. https://doi.org/DOI: 10.4108/eai.26-5-2023.2334304

Zhang, Z. (2023). Consumer behavior prediction and marketing strategy optimization based on big data analysis. *Applied Mathematics and Nonlinear Sciences*, 9(1). Advance online publication. DOI: 10.1142/13173

Chapter 20
Metaverse Branding:
A Review and Future Directions

Belem Barbosa
https://orcid.org/0000-0002-4057-360X
University of Porto, Portugal

ABSTRACT

The main aims of this chapter were to explore metaverse branding by identifying the main trends and contributions in extant literature. Through a bibliometry and the critical analysis of the main contributions in the literature, the chapter proposes a metaverse branding conceptualization, which shows how immersive metaverse experiences that provide multi-dimensional value enhance brand engagement, which leads to increased brand awareness, brand love, satisfaction, trust, and brand equity. These factors ultimately drive online and offline purchases and strengthen brand loyalty. Overall, this chapter and the proposed framework provide relevant insights for both managers defining metaverse branding strategies, and researchers interested in these topics.

INTRODUCTION

In a world marked by a continuous technological revolution and the growing digitalization of the economy, the metaverse stands out as one of the most promising innovations for managers and marketers, given the challenges and opportunities it presents for businesses and brands.

Constantin et al. (2023) define the metaverse broadly as "the next evolution of the internet—a collective space where physical and digital worlds converge to deliver more immersive, interactive virtual or augmented reality (VR/AR) user experiences, often referred to together as extended reality (XR)". The applications

DOI: 10.4018/979-8-3693-9461-8.ch020

of the metaverse are unlimited, as it can be "a gaming platform, a virtual retail destination, a training tool, an advertising channel, a digital classroom, a new gateway to digital experiences. The metaverse seems to be whatever people's imaginations dream it to be" (McKinsey and Company, 2022, p. 10).

Overall, the metaverse is viewed as having the potential to revolutionize several industries (Bruni et al., 2024; Dwivedi et al., 2023), such as tourism (Ampountolas et al., 2024; de Almeida, 2023; Gursoy et al., 2023; Natarajan et al., 2024; Rather, 2023; Sanchez-Amboage et al., 2024; Shin & Kang, 2024; Zhu et al., 2024), fashion (Blazquez, 2024; Kniazeva et al., 2024; Murtas et al., 2024; Park & Lim, 2023; Prashar & Prashar, 2024; Profumo et al., 2024; Sanmiguel et al., 2024; Venturini & Columbano, 2024), and luxury products (Jiang et al., 2023; Joy et al., 2022; Sung et al., 2023). Marr (2024) anticipates that, in a decade, the metaverse will change the typical features of the internet and the way we use it by increasingly integrating immersive experiences into our physical experiences through a diversity of devices and data management, including in areas such as healthcare, digital goods, and services, fostering the digital economy. Correspondingly, the literature highlights its anticipated impacts on marketing and branding (e.g., Ahn et al., 2023; Cheah & Shimul, 2023; Crespo-Pereira et al., 2023; Dwivedi et al., 2023; Kaur et al., 2024; Kshetri, 2022, 2023; Lee et al., 2023; Park & Lim, 2023; Ramadan, 2023; Yadav et al., 2024), challenging brands to leverage metaverse opportunities while staying relevant to their target audiences (Bilgihan et al., 2024).

Early adopters are using the metaverse for marketing, events, product design, and creating digital twins. This includes fashion luxury brands (e.g., Gucci, Balenciaga), luxury cars (e.g., Lamborghini), fast food brands (e.g., Burger King), sports apparel brands (e.g., Nike), technology brands (e.g., Samsung), and tourist destinations such as Saudi Arabia's UNESCO World Heritage Site Hegra.

McKinsey and Company (2022) estimates that, by 2030, the metaverse could reach a value of 5 trillion US dollars, as the majority of consumers seem excited about this new technology and are willing to shift some daily activities to this platform, particularly for socializing, entertainment, gaming, travel, and shopping. Kotler et al. (2023) and Bruni et al. (2024) emphasize that metaverse marketing could replace omnichannel marketing due to the ideal combination of digital and real-world elements and the ability to offer immersive experiences to consumers. Overall, the metaverse is seen as essential for brands that want to remain relevant to younger generations (Cheah & Shimul, 2023; Joy et al., 2022; Kotler et al., 2023), particularly Generation Z (Bogicevic et al., 2024; Crespo-Pereira et al., 2023; Payal et al., 2024), as these consumers expect brands to offer valuable immersive experiences. The expected positive impacts of metaverse branding include customer loyalty (e.g., Bilgihan et al., 2024; Natarajan et al., 2024; Payal et al., 2024; Yadav et al., 2024), consumer-brand engagement (Ahn et al., 2022; Arya et al., 2024; Bilgihan et al., 2024, pp. e.g., ; Mogaji et al., 2024; Payal et al., 2024; Yadav et al., 2024), and even offline sales (e.g., Payal et al., 2024; Sung et al., 2023).

As stressed by Malter et al. (2020) and Yoo et al. (2023), social and technological trends have significant implications for consumer decision-making, as they strongly impact the customer journey, make consumers more sophisticated, and affect brand touchpoints. Consequently, there is an urgent need to investigate and understand the impacts of technological advancements, such as the metaverse, on brands. Being an emergent technology, metaverse impacts on brands and businesses are not fully understood and need further attention from researchers (Ahn et al., 2022; Bruni et al., 2024; Cheah & Shimul, 2023; Dwivedi et al., 2022; Payal et al., 2024). While the literature on the topic is growing, its contributions are particularly scattered and fragmented. This chapter addresses a research gap by providing an overview of the literature on using the metaverse as a branding strategy. A bibliometric analysis of the literature identified the main topics being researched and highlighted the key trends in this emerging field. The main contributions to the literature are also discussed. Based on the findings, the chapter provides suggestions for future research and the main implications for managers considering including the metaverse in their branding initiatives.

BACKGROUND

For brands, the metaverse offers relevant opportunities for value creation, capture, and delivery. Payal et al. (2024) note that brands create and capture value by providing relevant immersive experiences for their target audiences, who can be involved in events, get access to exclusive information, or acquire exclusive digital assets. Park and Lim (2023) describe branding strategies on the metaverse as encompassing digital brand assets, particularly non-fungible tokens (NFTs), and immersive brand experiences used to fostering brand engagement. As such, brands can get involved in the metaverse through diverse initiatives, including virtual events, digital products, or virtual e-commerce stores. While the metaverse is still emerging as a marketing and branding platform, brands are starting to explore their unique features. However, the immersion and interaction that characterizes the metaverse has a great potential to foster customer engagement through richer brand experiences (Ahn et al., 2022; Arya et al., 2024; Barrera & Shah, 2023; Buhalis et al., 2023; Kniazeva et al., 2024; Kshetri, 2023; Mogaji et al., 2024; Park & Lim, 2023) and thus to create value to both brands and customers. The metaverse can also be adopted by brands that want to pursue brand awareness objectives, as well as a platform to get insights from customers and better understand their audiences (Bilgihan et al., 2024). Kniazeva et al. (2024) compared the motivations behind metaverse strategies implemented by luxury and fast-fashion brands. They found that, while fostering consumer-brand relationships and exploring omnichannel strategies were common motivations, fast-fashion brands were driven by sustainability and sales promotions, whereas luxury fashion brands were motivated by competitive advantage and brand identity.

Kshetri (2023) categorizes strategies in the metaverse into product and branding strategies:

- From a product strategy perspective, the metaverse enables brands to manipulate the product mix, test new products, contribute to product quality enhancement, reduce sales costs, enhance customer confidence in products, and increase the success of new product launches.
- From a branding perspective, the metaverse can be used for brand enhancement by offering rich, immersive experiences and facilitating customer-brand interactions.

In line with these contributions, Yadav et al. (2024) stress that the literature highlights both consumer level outcomes (e.g., trust, loyalty, attitude, satisfaction, purchase intention) and firm-level outcomes, including cost reduction, disintermediation, brand reputation, innovation in product development, and fostering social dynamics in marketing strategies.

Overall, the literature indicates that, in these early stages of metaverse adoption by brands, the two most common strategies are the development of immersive brand experiences and of digital assets. These are covered in more detail in the next two sections.

Brand Experience through the Metaverse

The concept of experience is rooted in the seminal contribution by Pine and Gilmore (2011), who define the experience economy as an evolution from selling products and services to offering memorable and impactful experiences for customers. These authors propose the "four realms of experience," comprising entertainment, education, escapism, and aesthetic dimensions. They emphasize that customers may engage passively (as spectators) or actively (as participants) in these experiences. Moreover, Pine and Gilmore (2011) highlight that some experiences are inherently immersive. Businesses that successfully design and implement memorable experiences for their target customers can create value, foster brand loyalty, and gain a competitive advantage. In line with this view, Schmitt (1999) argues that consumers are emotional beings who seek enjoyable experiences. Consequently, holistic brand experiences should include sensory, affective, cognitive, physical, and social components, integrated into branding and communication initiatives.

The experiential branding perspective (Pine & Gilmore, 2011; Schmitt, 1999) is particularly adapted to the metaverse and reflected by extant literature, as several authors stress the importance to research the immersive brand experiences and their impacts on consumers (e.g., Barrera & Shah, 2023; Buhalis et al., 2023; Dwivedi et al., 2022; Dwivedi et al., 2023; Payal et al., 2024).

Future trends for metaverse experiences include online shopping in the metaverse. As noted by Payal et al. (2024), the immersive nature of the metaverse will help combine online and offline shopping, providing more personalized, relevant, and rich experiences to customers.

Non-Fungible Tokens as a Branding Strategy

Non-fungible tokens (NFTs) are "digital certificates of ownership that can be attached to virtual or physical assets" (Deventer et al., 2024, p. 33), which may represent either a digitalized version of a physical asset or an independent digital asset (e.g., image, video, sound) (Bilgihan et al., 2024; Hofstetter et al., 2022). Alkhudary et al. (2023, p. 322) define NFTs as "a certificate of authenticity or ownership that is immutably registered on a public blockchain network as a piece of data managed by a smart contract, a pre-defined code agreement with clear conditions, to denote a unique digital or physical asset". NFTs were originally associated with art assets but quickly expanded to various industries, including healthcare (Alshater et al., 2024) and luxury products (Sung et al., 2023). The growing popularity of NFTs in the metaverse has been fueled by branding initiatives motivated by diverse goals, from generating new revenue streams to fostering customer engagement and positioning the brand as innovative (Deventer et al., 2024). Overall, NFTs are expected to offer relevant opportunities for marketing and branding in the metaverse (Alshater et al., 2024; Bilgihan et al., 2024; Colicev, 2023; Deventer et al., 2024; Hofstetter et al., 2022; Sung et al., 2023), as they can be used to provide exclusive services and value to customers.

Lee et al. (2023) summarized the attributes of NFTs from a branding perspective, and suggested that they encompass six main characteristics that provide value and appeal to metaverse users:

- **Scarcity:** As NFTs are often created in limited quantities and associated with special time-limited releases, generating a sense of scarcity and exclusivity.
- **Financial value:** NFTs are seen as financial investments, as they can be bought and traded, attracting consumers looking for potential returns on investment.

- **Uniqueness**: NFTs are unique and exclusive digital assets, as their ownership and identity can be certified using blockchain and digital ledger technology.
- **Prestige**: The exclusiveness and scarcity of NFTs can convey social status to their owners, particularly when associated with limited editions and exclusive access to services or information, as is often the case of NFTs issued by luxury or other high-involvement brands.
- **Originality**: NFTs are marked by their novelty, creativity, and innovativeness, which create value for customers and also help position brands and enhance brand image.

Nevertheless, Lee et al. (2023) stress the need for a clear consistency between metaverse initiatives and the overall communication of the brand, as NFTs should be used to reinforce brand values and image coherently.

Overall, NFTs may have an important role in building brand awareness and customer engagement (Colicev, 2023; Deventer et al., 2024), particularly through their ability to showcase brands' products, logos, and images. In terms of financial potential, recent research highlights that revenue streams are highly volatile and unpredictable (Chalmers et al., 2022), and many NFTs are difficult to trade and do not generate revenue for their owners.

From a customer journey perspective, interaction with NFTs occurs in four distinct stages: liking, purchasing, holding, and selling (Yilmaz et al., 2023), each associated with different motivations and value perceptions. All stages of NFT interaction appear to create monetary, functional, emotional, and social value for customers (Yilmaz et al., 2023), however, emotional value is most prominent in the liking stage, while monetary value is more prominent in the others.

METAVERSE BRANDING: STATE OF THE ART

Adopted Methodology

This chapter adopts a bibliometric analysis approach to provide an overview of the state of the art in metaverse branding. Data was gathered on August 22nd, 2024, using the Web of Science platform. The search query combined two topics, "metaverse" AND "brand," and was restricted to the document type "Article." The platform listed 102 results. After analyzing the titles, keywords, and abstracts, 52 articles were excluded from the analysis for not focusing on branding and being beyond the scope of this study. Consequently, 50 articles were retained for analysis. The bibliometric analysis was performed using the R-Studio Bibliometrix package and Biblioshiny, an open-source application for comprehensive science mapping analysis (Aria & Cuccurullo, 2017). A summary of the articles considered for this review is presented in Table 1.

Table 1. Summary of the articles considered for the bibliometric analysis

Main Information	
Timespan	**2022:2024**
Sources (Journals, Books, etc)	35
Documents	50
Document Average Age	0.5
Average citations per doc	7.6
References	3669
Authors	
Authors	150
Authors of single-authored docs	5
Single-authored docs	6
Co-Authors per Doc	3.1
International co-authorships %	38
Documents	
article	34
article; early access	16

Source: Own elaboration using Biblioshiny

As detailed in Table 1, the sample of articles considered for this study was published between 2022 and 2024, with 16 of them being articles in press (i.e., early access). The number of authors involved in this field of research and the number of journals that published the 50 articles indicate a high degree of fragmentation in the literature. Additionally, this is an emerging topic, as evidenced by the recent timespan and the average age of the articles being less than one year. The average number of authors per article is three, and more than one-third of the articles involve international collaboration.

Overview of the Literature on Metaverse Branding

The literature on metaverse branding is relatively recent but is growing rapidly. In 2022, five articles were published. The annual growth rate was 300% in 2023 and 100% in the first eight months of 2024, demonstrating the high level of interest the topic is generating among researchers. Moreover, the literature has garnered a considerable number of citations, particularly the initial articles published in 2022, which have an average of over 26 citations each. Additionally, the articles published in 2023 and early 2024 have an average of four citations per year, further attesting to the ongoing interest in the topic. This information is summarized in Table 2.

Table 2. Number of publications and citations per year

Year	Number of articles	Average number of citations (ANC)	Citable Years	ANC per citable years
2022	5	26.4	3	8.8
2023	15	8.67	2	4.34
2024 (until August)	30	3.93	1	3.93

Source: Own elaboration using Biblioshiny

The fragmented nature of this research field is evident from the total number of journals (35) and authors (150) involved in the 50 articles on metaverse branding. As shown in Table 3, only five authors have more than one article on the topic. However, the journal with the highest number of articles (10% of the total) focuses on the fashion industry, indicating an important focus of the research.

Table 3. Main contributors (journals and authors)

Most Frequent Journals	**Articles**	**Most Cited Journals**	**Citations**
Journal of Global Fashion Marketing	5	Journal of Business Research	205
Asia Pacific Journal of Marketing and Logistics	3	Journal of Retail Consumer Services	117
Journal of Consumer Behaviour	3	Psychology & Marketing	95
Journal of Islamic Marketing	3	Computers In Human Behavior	88
Psychology & Marketing	3	Journal of Consumer Research	81
		Journal of Marketing	66
Most Frequent Countries - Corresponding Author	**Articles**	**Most Prolific Authors**	**Articles**
Korea	6	Dwivedi YK	2
Spain	6	Kim KH	2
USA	6	Kshetri N	2
India	5	Prashar A	2
China	4	Ramadan Z	2
Italy	4		

Source: Own elaboration using Biblioshiny

The dozen most cited articles (Table 4) comprise a mix of editorial, conceptual, review, and empirical studies. Overall, these articles build on common ideas of the potential of the metaverse to foster brand engagement by providing immersive brand experiences.

In his editorial article, Kshetri (2022) argues that the metaverse will transform brand strategies, namely through non-fungible tokens and experiences within virtual environments. The focus is on creating immersive, memorable, and engaging, experiences to foster brand activation, brand reach, and brand loyalty.

The two conceptual articles focus on the fashion industry (Joy et al., 2022; Mogaji et al., 2024). Joy et al. (2022) highlight the growing importance of non-fungible tokens (NFTs) for fashion brands, offering opportunities for brand extension and enhancing consumer experiences, particularly for luxury brands. Similarly, Mogaji et al. (2024) explore the potential of the metaverse for brand extension and brand experience, emphasizing its capacity to foster consumer-brand engagement. Beyond the potential for the marketing mix (e.g., digital products), they recommend that fashion brands create experiences and relevant content for their target audiences on the metaverse to enhance engagement. These authors propose that a key performance indicator for metaverse branding would be the time consumers spend engaging in immersive activities provided by the brand's metaverse platform, such as events and fashion shows.

Table 4. Most cited articles

Title	Authors (Year)	Type	Total Citations	Citations per Year
"Digital future of luxury brands: Metaverse, digital fashion, and non-fungible tokens"	Joy et al. (2022)	Conceptual	65	21. 7
"Metaverse meets branding: Examining consumer responses to immersive brand experiences"	Wongkitrungrueng and Suprawan (2024)	Empirical (quantitative)	40	40
"An innovative e-commerce platform incorporating metaverse to live commerce"	Jeong et al. (2022)	Review	35	11.7
"Fashion and the metaverse: Clarifying the domain and establishing a research agenda"	Park and Lim (2023)	Review	30	15
"Brands are calling your AVATAR in Metaverse-A study to explore XR-based gamification marketing activities & consumer-based brand equity in virtual world"	Arya et al. (2024)	Empirical (quantitative)	27	27
NFT luxury brand marketing in the metaverse: Leveraging blockchain-certified NFTs to drive consumer behavior"	Sung et al. (2023)	Empirical (Quantitative)	25	12.5
"Web 3.0 and the metaverse shaping organizations' brand and product strategies"	Kshetri (2022)	Editorial	24	8
"Building brand engagement in metaverse commerce: The role of branded non-fungible tokens (BNFTs)"	Lee et al. (2023)	Empirical (Mixed methods)	23	11.5

continued on following page

Table 4. Continued

Title	Authors (Year)	Type	Total Citations	Citations per Year
"Telepresence in live-stream shopping: An experimental study comparing Instagram and the metaverse"	Barta et al. (2023)	Empirical (Experiment)	18	9
"The metaverse experience in luxury brands"	Jiang et al. (2023)	Empirical (quantitative)	13	6.5
"Fashion marketing in the metaverse"	Mogaji et al. (2024)	Conceptual	9	9
"'Fashioning' the metaverse: A qualitative study on consumers' value and perceptions of digital fashion in virtual worlds"	Venturini and Columbano (2024)	Empirical (qualitative)	9	9

Source: Own elaboration using Biblioshiny

The two reviews included in the most cited literature on metaverse branding explore particular contexts, live commerce (Jeong et al., 2022) and fashion (Park & Lim, 2023). Park and Lim (2023) identified three brand strategies related to the metaverse: releasing brand assets (e.g., non-fungible tokens), creating unique brand experiences with immersive technologies, and engaging with customers through games and virtual branded worlds, suggesting that metaverse-associated innovation can create brand equity. Jeong et al. (2022) suggest the combination of live commerce with the metaverse, as the use of a digital twin can improve customer engagement and improve brand awareness and customer loyalty. In line with this, Barta et al. (2023) conducted an experiment demonstrating that, compared to social media such as Instagram, the metaverse has a high perceived telepresence which increases the experiential value of live-stream shopping, leading to higher satisfaction and loyalty.

The qualitative study included in the most cited articles explores consumers' perceptions related to fashion brands in the metaverse. Venturini and Columbano (2024) found that metaverse branding is associated with consumer value perceptions of "utilitarianism, social identity, personification, hedonism, and personal beliefs" (p. 6), which leads fashion consumers to adopt the metaverse to interact with brands.

Of the twelve most cited articles, four include empirical studies using quantitative methodology. Wongkitrungrueng and Suprawan (2024) explore consumers' behavioral responses (consumer-brand engagement, brand image, and virtual purchase intention) as influenced by the experiential value of the metaverse. In examining the impacts of three dimensions of brand value, they found significant effects of symbolic and utilitarian value, while the impact of hedonic value on consumer responses was non-significant. Arya et al. (2024) analyzed metaverse experiences from a gamification perspective, exploring their impact on consumer-based brand equity. Their findings indicate that brand engagement and brand love mediate the relationship between gamification and consumer-brand equity in the metaverse. Furthermore, they found that consumer-brand equity led to purchase intentions in the metaverse and resistance to negative information about the brand. Sung et al. (2023) explored the psychological mechanisms of purchasing luxury brands' NFTs in the metaverse and found that desire, perceived economic value, perceived social value, perceived authenticity, and scarcity are essential variables in determining consumer behavior. These authors also found that the results generally apply to both individualistic and collectivist cultures, although differences emerged in the perception of opportunity loss (when not buying NFTs) and perceived economic value. Jiang et al. (2023) developed a measurement scale for assessing the metaverse experience with luxury brands. Their scale comprises three dimensions: fantasy, feeling, and fun. Their findings indicate that the metaverse experience has a strong and significant impact on user happiness.

Finally, one of the most cited studies on metaverse branding, conducted by Lee et al. (2023), adopted mixed methods to further understand behaviors associated with branded NFTs. They identified scarcity, financial value, prestige, uniqueness, originality, and communication consistency as the NFT attributes that determine brand attitudes, which in turn influence brand commitment, active engagement with NFTs, and purchase intentions of NFTs.

Overall, three themes are recurrent in the most cited literature on metaverse branding. First, there is a strong focus on luxury branding in the metaverse, highlighting this platform's potential to enhance brand engagement and stimulate virtual purchase intentions. The use of NFTs emerges as the most explored strategy, serving as a tool to create unique brand experiences, drive engagement, and support virtual sales. Additionally, the literature examines drivers of brand engagement, including various value dimensions and attributes like authenticity and scarcity.

Complementarily, the word cloud presented in Figure 1 indicates that much of the literature on metaverse branding is dedicated to the impacts of this strategy on consumers.

Figure 1. Word cloud

Source: Own elaboration using Biblioshiny

Hence, the literature particularly explores consumer engagement, purchase intentions, perceived value, acceptance, and consumption. Other key focus areas include virtual reality, augmented reality, social media, and future challenges. In terms of applications, the fashion and tourism industries appear to be the primary areas of research thus far. Additionally, in terms of strategy, most research published so far explores the use of NFTs by brands. While some articles mention other branding strategies, such as events and advertising, these are only scantily addressed.

Main Topics on Metaverse Branding Explored by Extant Literature

Extant literature on metaverse branding is mainly focused on its outcomes, namely regarding consumer behavior. In fact, the bibliometric analysis conducted for this chapter highlights that the main themes covered in the literature on metaverse branding are experience, perceived value, engagement, loyalty, purchase intentions, and brand equity. These themes are explored in detail in the following sections.

Brand Experiences in the Metaverse

The metaverse expands the horizons of experiential marketing (Bogicevic et al., 2024; Joy et al., 2022; Park & Lim, 2023). The immersive nature of the metaverse enables the creation of experiences that engage multiple consumer senses and evoke strong and holistic emotional responses (Bogicevic et al., 2024; Jiang et al., 2023; Kshetri, 2022; Murtas et al., 2024; Park & Lim, 2023; Rauschnabel et al., 2024; Yu et al., 2024). Moreover, its vivid virtual reality and the integration of participants' avatars foster escapism and fantasy (Jiang et al., 2023). Jiang et al. (2023) suggest that, in the context of luxury brands, the metaverse experience should be seen as a combination of fantasies, fun, and feelings, a combination that should also be valid to other industries. According to Arya et al. (2024) and Natarajan et al. (2024), the metaverse experience comprises entertainment, interaction, trendiness, intimacy, and novelty.

Wongkitrungrueng and Suprawan (2024) add that the ability of the metaverse to connect physical and digital realms should be viewed as a way to enhance consumer experiences. In line with this, Natarajan et al. (2024) conceptualize the metaverse is inherently associated with the immersive experiences:

"metaverse is considered as the environment and the various elements of the customer experiences in the metaverse could be viewed as a set of parts coordinated to have an impact on the spatial presence quality and perceived augmentation which are all various dimensions having an impact on brand equity leading the user to achieve a goal like intention to visit the destination physically after using metaverse" (p. 3).

For example, in the context of tourism, the metaverse enables tourists to reimagine destination discovery and enhance travel experiences (Buhalis et al., 2023; Natarajan et al., 2024). de Almeida (2023) studied the case of Seoul, the first "metaverse global city", and concluded that metaverse initiatives can be effective marketing tools to position brands as innovative, while they also contribute to enhance brand reputation and awareness. In the case of territorial brands, metaverse initiatives can also contribute to urban revitalization and serve as an immersive field laboratory for immersive reality (de Almeida, 2023)

Overall, the logic of integrating the metaverse in brand experiences is to enhance them, however potential drawbacks need also to be considered (Bilgihan et al., 2024), such as physical discomfort, mental fatigue, and privacy concerns. However, extant literature mostly highlights the expected positive impacts of the metaverse for brands, suggesting that unique and relevant brand experiences in the metaverse can contribute to brand equity (Park & Lim, 2023), customer engagement (Arya et al., 2024; Bogicevic et al., 2024; Chohan & Schmidt-Devlin, 2024; Farah et al., 2024; Ferraro et al., 2024; Park & Lim, 2023), and brand loyalty (Bogicevic et al., 2024; Park & Lim, 2023).

Perceived Value of Metaverse Branding

Holbrook (1999, p. 9) conceptualized consumer value by emphasizing that it "resides not in the product purchased, not in the brand chosen, not in the object possessed, but rather in the consumption experience(s)". To this end, extrinsic value can include elements such as efficiency, excellence, status, and esteem, while intrinsic value encompasses aesthetics, ethics, spirituality, and play. Furthermore, Hirschman and Holbrook (1982) and Holbrook and Hirschman (1982) have offered relevant contributions to consumer behavior literature by highlighting that consumption decisions are guided by both utilitarian and hedonic values, stressing the importance of emotional and symbolic dimensions of consumption.

These perspectives apply to diverse contexts, including the metaverse. Wongkitrungrueng and Suprawan (2024) suggest that metaverse experience creates utilitarian, hedonic, and symbolic value to users, have substantial effects on brand image and contribute both directly and indirectly (through brand image enhancement) to brand engagement, besides increasing purchase intentions.

In the realm of fashion brands, Venturini and Columbano (2024, pp. 11-12) identified five dimensions of value in metaverse consumption, including "utilitarianism, social identity, personification, hedonism, and personal beliefs". However, findings by Zaman et al. (2024) suggest that the perceived costs and benefits of metaverse experiences depend on the stakeholder, given the consistency gaps found between the views of customers and managers.

A similar perspective of multidimensional value is suggested for NFTs. Deventer et al. (2024) and Hofstetter et al. (2022) stress that the value delivered by NFTs to consumers is beyond financial value, as brands often use them to foster brand loyalty and brand engagement. As such, the value created by NFTs is, according to Deventer et al. (2024), better described through an experiential perspective, as NFTs can provide, for example, functional value, status, contemplation, or community belonging, besides being seen as an investment.

Hence, the overall literature highlights the multidimensional value the metaverse provides to consumers through both brand experiences and NFT purchases. Consequently, value creation is expected to strengthen consumer-brand relationships and positively impact satisfaction (Barta et al., 2023), brand engagement (Aysan & Syarif, 2024; Deventer et al., 2024), purchase intention (Prashar & Prashar, 2024; Sung et al., 2023; Yang et al., 2024), and loyalty (Deventer et al., 2024; Yang et al., 2024).

Brand Engagement in the Metaverse

As noted in the previous sections, brand engagement is a central element of metaverse branding. It has guided the initiatives of early adopters, especially the ones investing in immersive experiences such as events, and is one of the most consensual expected outcomes of metaverse experiences. Payal et al. (2024, p. 3) define brand engagement in the metaverse as "customers passionately participating in the virtual events, visiting the experiences created by the brands in the metaverse, participating in the gamified experiences, wining rewards, contributing to the experiences by co-creation and giving feedback". Based on the engagement literature, Bilgihan et al. (2024) conceptualized brand engagement in the metaverse as interactive, social, experiential, economic, and emotional.

The expected outcomes of brand engagement in the metaverse include brand awareness (Bilgihan et al., 2024), brand equity (Arya et al., 2024), brand loyalty (Bilgihan et al., 2024; Chakraborty & Biswal, 2024), and purchase intentions (Payal et al., 2024). Bilgihan et al. (2024) emphasize that, given the diverse nature of immersive branded experiences, from virtual events to games and interactive discussions, the choice must be aligned not only with the particular features of the metaverse platform but also with the strategic objectives of the brand.

The positive impacts on brand engagement are also suggested for NFTs strategies. Lee et al. (2023) suggest that the attributes of NFTs, such as originality, prestige, financial value, uniqueness, and scarcity, have a positive impact on brand attitudes, which, in turn, increase brand engagement.

Brand Loyalty and Purchase Intentions

It is generally accepted that the metaverse can play an important role in enhancing customer loyalty (Bilgihan et al., 2024; Chakraborty & Biswal, 2024) and may also contribute to increase not only online (Aris et al., 2023; Arya et al., 2024; Joy et al., 2022; Prashar & Prashar, 2024; Sung et al., 2023) but also offline purchases (Bruni et al., 2024; Colicev, 2023; Jeong et al., 2022; Kim & Bae, 2023; Mansoor et al., 2024; Park & Kim, 2024; Payal et al., 2024; Sung et al., 2023; Wongkitrungrueng & Suprawan, 2024).

Regarding the tourism industry, several studies suggest that young adults' experiences in the metaverse may result in intentions to visit physical tourism destinations (Buhalis et al., 2023; Natarajan et al., 2024; Shin & Kang, 2024), acting as a catalyst for travel decisions. Payal et al. (2024) found that brand engagement in the metaverse, namely associated with holistic brand experiences, affects consumer emotions (e.g., trust, attitudes) and contributes to brand knowledge, which increase offline purchase intentions regarding the products and services experienced in the metaverse. The retail industry is also expected to be revolutionized by the metaverse, as this technology enables the development of what Bruni et al. (2024, p. 969) describe as "an alternative channel of distribution that integrates elements of both physical and digital channels".

Additionally, the attributes of the metaverse also contribute to purchasing intention of virtual assets, such as NFTs (Alkhudary et al., 2023; Chalmers et al., 2022; Colicev, 2023; Deventer et al., 2024; Lee et al., 2023; Mogaji et al., 2024; Sung et al., 2023; Yilmaz et al., 2023).

Brand Equity

The metaverse is expected to increase brand equity. Without surprise, brand equity is a recurrent theme in the literature on metaverse branding, including studies on gamification strategies by luxury brands using NFTs (Arya et al., 2024) and regarding tourism destinations (Natarajan et al., 2024).

An important contribution is provided by Park and Lim (2023), who developed a framework summarizing how immersive brand experiences in the metaverse can help build brand equity, particularly in the realm of fashion brands. Park and Lim (2023) suggest four complementary mechanisms:

- **Brand Awareness:** Brands can significantly enhance visibility and recognition and attract new customers by releasing branded NFT assets or creating exclusive brand experiences in virtual worlds and games. The immersive nature of the metaverse also aids in capturing consumer attention and boosting brand awareness.
- **Brand Associations:** Offering unique and memorable experiences in the metaverse allows brands to provide a distinctive brand experience that reinforces positive brand memories and feelings. This is particularly effective in creating associations with innovation, exclusivity, and luxury, which are key for many fashion brands.
- **Perceived Quality:** Immersive technologies enable consumers to interact with products in more realistic and engaging ways, enhancing a brand's perceived quality. The scarcity and exclusivity associated with some metaverse assets and experiences also contribute to higher perceived quality.
- **Brand Loyalty:** The immersive experiences provided by the metaverse can deepen emotional connections with the brand, leading to stronger brand loyalty. Additionally, the metaverse facilitates community engagement, allowing access to exclusive content and assets, which fosters a sense of belonging and loyalty.

According to Natarajan et al. (2024), brand equity in the metaverse is a result of the perceived augmentation and the spatial presence quality, which result from the metaverse experience. Jiang et al. (2023) stress that it is the positive emotional experience that triggers value creation. According to Arya et al. (2024), brand equity is a result of brand love and brand engagement in the metaverse, as gamified experiences offered by brands foster emotional connections that boost brand equity. Additionally, the unique virtual experiences encourage consumers to invest more time and money in the brand in both virtual and real-world settings, including purchase intentions (Arya et al., 2024). In the case of tourism destinations, metaverse experiences foster the intention to visit the physical location (Natarajan et al., 2024). However, Arya et al. (2024) stress the importance of authenticity, namely for its role in fostering brand love in the metaverse. Furthermore, Natarajan et al. (2024) highlight the potential role of the fear of missing out (FOMO), suggesting that it moderates the impact of destination brand equity on visiting intentions.

SOLUTIONS AND RECOMMENDATIONS

The metaverse is rapidly evolving and is expected to transform not only online experiences in general but also the consumer decision-making process and e-commerce. This study provides valuable insights for marketers and brand managers, demonstrating that the metaverse is a powerful platform for innovative and consumer-centered branding.

Overall, the literature emphasizes the potential advantages of metaverse branding, particularly because immersive experiences and the resulting value perceptions have positive effects on brand engagement, loyalty, purchase intentions, and brand equity. Findings from existing literature confirm these positive impacts. However, success in metaverse branding requires a clear definition of objectives (e.g., brand awareness, customer engagement, loyalty, revenue) aligned with a comprehensive understanding of metaverse features.

Different brands may benefit from varied branding strategies in the metaverse, from immersive brand experiences to selling NFTs and hybrid retail models. The best choice of strategies depends on the brand's objectives, available resources, and optimal allocation, as well as the preferences and perceived value generation of target audiences. Overall, brands need to explore the current potential of the metaverse and identify strategies that best align with their goals and budgets. The potential for differentiation in value propositions (Bruni et al., 2024) needs to be evaluated in terms of efficiency (Cheah & Shimul, 2023), as the current costs associated with metaverse branding may be inadequate for smaller businesses.

That said, the essential aspects of metaverse branding highlighted by the literature are the focus on immersive experiences and the creation of multidimensional value for customers. The metaverse enables the creation of rich, multi-sensory experiences that foster strong emotional connections with target audiences, especially younger generations. These should be seen as tools to foster brand engagement, which, in turn, is expected to positively impact attitudinal and behavioral responses, such as satisfaction, brand equity, brand loyalty, and purchase intentions and behaviors.

Another implication for managers is the urgency to prepare for the future hybrid retail. The metaverse will soon offer immersive marketplaces projected to redefine the overall shopping experience for both digital and physical goods and services

(Bilgihan et al., 2024; Payal et al., 2024). With the expected growth of hybrid shopping experiences, managers should explore synergies between online and offline retail through metaverse platforms. This integration can help brands reach customers across multiple touchpoints, enhancing both the digital and physical shopping experience. Additionally, consumer expectations for immersive experiences in the metaverse are also expected to evolve, which may require continuous investments in experience quality, value, and differentiation.

Finally, the privacy and ethical concerns associated with immersive experiences need to be addressed to enable future innovations like hybrid retail. Data privacy, transparency, and security need to be aligned with current regulations on personal data, with careful consideration of new regulatory trends. Overall, brands should engage in metaverse branding by prioritizing responsibility, well-being, sustainability, and ethical considerations, so that the potential competitive advantages of metaverse branding are maximized.

FUTURE RESEARCH DIRECTIONS

This study identified several avenues for future research, particularly: (i) expanding metaverse branding studies across industries, (ii) further exploring the different strategies and their implications, (iii) understanding advertising effectiveness, and (iv) further explore hybrid retail and metaverse commerce models.

First, it is necessary to broaden studies on the metaverse to encompass diverse contexts and industries, as the current literature is dominated by fashion, luxury, and tourism, meaning its insights may not be generalized to other contexts. More research is needed to understand how metaverse branding could be applied in diverse industries and what unique challenges or outcomes may be derived from metaverse branding. These include fast moving consumer goods, the comparison between high and low involvement goods and services, and particular industries that are expected to be strongly impacted by the metaverse such as healthcare, bank and finance, education, events, or real estate. Other specific contexts that are worth exploring include non-profit organizations, social marketing, collaborative consumption, and sustainability.

It is also worth noting that even popular communication tools on metaverse platforms, such as events, despite being frequently mentioned in the literature, have not yet been studied in detail. Therefore, it is necessary that future research explores context-specific branding strategies and the determinants of their success. Potential differences in perceived value and impacts of metaverse branding strategies across industries and target audiences can also provide substantial contributions to the literature and help brand managers in strategy definition.

Additionally, there is a clear gap in literature regarding advertising in the metaverse. As a critical brand communication strategy, studies are needed to test the effectiveness of various types of advertising in immersive contexts. This absence of studies can be partially explained by the still underdeveloped advertising mechanisms on metaverse platforms. However, more research is essential to guide managers on effective communication strategies within these platforms (Cheah & Shimul, 2023). As a gradual shift toward advertising on metaverse platforms is expected (Ahn et al., 2022, 2023), it is important to understand the factors that may impact the effectiveness of immersive advertising, which should create value for both customers and brands. Hence, future research should explore advertising in the metaverse and provide empirical data on the effectiveness of various ad formats (e.g., immersive ads, interactive product placements). Future research should also assess which types of metaverse advertising resonate most with consumers and lead to behavioral outcomes, such as purchase and engagement. Ad intrusiveness and avoidance within metaverse experiences are other aspects that would benefit from further research.

Also, there is an urgent need for studies on metaverse retail, specifically exploring the synergies between online and offline sales and between digital and physical products. Alongside advertising, this is one of the significant strategic potentials of the metaverse, which is anticipated to experience substantial growth in the near future, driven by the increasing connectivity between virtual and real worlds (Ahn et al., 2022). This growth is expected to play an essential role in retail's competitive advantages (Bruni et al., 2024; Yoo et al., 2023). Conducting empirical studies on metaverse retail is crucial to support managers in their decision-making. Future studies could explore the effectiveness of metaverse-driven strategies in creating hybrid shopping experiences and promoting both digital and real-world products.

Finally, it is worth noting that, despite the expected positive impacts on brand loyalty and purchase behavior, much of the literature explores attitudes and intentions. The literature would benefit form longitudinal studies on brand loyalty that assess how metaverse interactions translate into sustainable customer relationships, brand preference, and purchase. Moreover, assessing and explaining the impact of metaverse branding on purchases, both online and offline, would also provide valuable contributions to researchers and managers.

CONCLUSION

The main objectives of this chapter were to explore metaverse branding by identifying the main trends and contributions in extant literature. Through a bibliometry and the critical analysis of the main contributions in the literature, the chapter conceptualized metaverse branding, provided practical implications for managers, and highlighted the current research gaps and directions for future research. Despite the novelty of the topic, literature on metaverse branding has grown significantly since 2022. Research has predominantly focused on tourism, fashion, and luxury branding, alongside the role of NFTs as a central branding strategy within the metaverse. The literature stresses the importance of brand experience, brand engagement, brand equity, and consumer attitudinal and behavioral responses to brand experience and engagement in the metaverse as essential perspectives to analyze the effectiveness of metaverse branding initiatives. Figure 1 summarizes the main findings and highlights the main variables involved in the brand-consumer interactions in the metaverse.

Figure 2. Metaverse Branding Framework

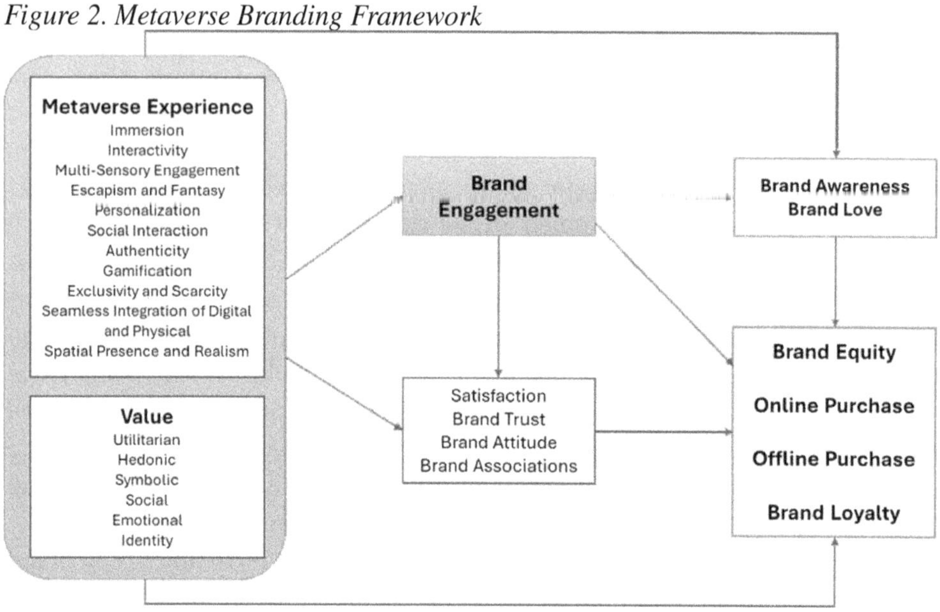

Source: Developed by the Author based on the findings

The metaverse, with its immersive, interactive, and personalized features, has the potential to transform customer decision-making, shopping experiences, and brand interactions, hence introducing a new era of experiential marketing and branding. Brand engagement is a central feature of the metaverse experience. It is driven by the experiential features of the metaverse, as well as the ability of brands to create value to customers within these platforms.

Brand experiences in the metaverse are characterized as immersive, multi-sensory, often associated with escapism and fantasy. The relevance of brand experiences in the metaverse may result in brand engagement, as well as several positive brand impacts, from satisfaction, trust, positive attitudes and associations to brand awareness, brand love, brand loyalty, and brand equity. Both online and offline purchases of real and virtual goods and services are additional outcomes of metaverse experiences.

In such a context, it is essential to provide value to rclevant audiences, considering its multidimensional nature. Indeed, the metaverse can be used to create different types of consumer value, including hedonic, utilitarian (e.g., financial), and symbolic value.

Overall, this chapter and the proposed framework provide relevant insights for both managers defining metaverse branding strategies, and researchers interested in these topics.

REFERENCES

Ahn, S. J., Kim, J., & Kim, J. (2022). The Bifold Triadic Relationships Framework: A Theoretical Primer for Advertising Research in the Metaverse. *Journal of Advertising*, 51(5), 592–607. DOI: 10.1080/00913367.2022.2111729

Ahn, S. J., Kim, J., & Kim, J. (2023). The future of advertising research in virtual, augmented, and extended realities. *International Journal of Advertising*, 42(1), 162–170. DOI: 10.1080/02650487.2022.2137316

Alkhudary, R., Belvaux, B., & Guibert, N. (2023). Understanding non-fungible tokens (NFTs): Insights on consumption practices and a research agenda. *Marketing Letters*, 34(2), 321–336. DOI: 10.1007/s11002-022-09655-2

Alshater, M. M., Nasrallah, N., Khoury, R., & Joshipura, M. (2024). Deciphering the world of NFTs: A scholarly review of trends, challenges, and opportunities. *Electronic Commerce Research*. Advance online publication. DOI: 10.1007/s10660-024-09881-y

Ampountolas, A., Menconi, G., & Shaw, G. (2024). Metaverse research propositions: Online intermediaries. *Tourism Economics*, 30(1), 255–261. DOI: 10.1177/13548166231159520

Aria, M., & Cuccurullo, C. (2017). Bibliometrix: An R-tool for comprehensive science mapping analysis. *Journal of Informetrics*, 11(4), 959–975. DOI: 10.1016/j.joi.2017.08.007

Aris, S., Sarfi, T., Akhavan, M., & Sabbar, S. (2023). Motivations for consuming avatar-specific virtual items on the Zepeto gaming platform. *Cadernos Educacao Tecnologia E Sociedade, 16*(4), 1248-1258. https://doi.org/DOI: 10.14571/brajets.v16.n4.1248-1258

Arya, V., Sambyal, R., Sharma, A., & Dwivedi, Y. K. (2024). Brands are calling your AVATAR in Metaverse-A study to explore XR-based gamification marketing activities & consumer-based brand equity in virtual world. *Journal of Consumer Behaviour*, 23(2), 556–585. DOI: 10.1002/cb.2214

Aysan, A. F., & Syarif, M. F. (2024). Shaping the halal tourism industry landscape through NFT and metaverse: New horizons for halal brand and halal booking hotel. *Journal of Islamic Marketing*. Advance online publication. DOI: 10.1108/JIMA-07-2023-0206

Barrera, K. G., & Shah, D. (2023). Marketing in the Metaverse: Conceptual understanding, framework, and research agenda. *Journal of Business Research*, 155, 113420. Advance online publication. DOI: 10.1016/j.jbusres.2022.113420

Barta, S., Gurrea, R., & Flavián, C. (2023). Telepresence in live-stream shopping: An experimental study comparing Instagram and the metaverse. *Electronic Markets*, 33(1), 29. Advance online publication. DOI: 10.1007/s12525-023-00643-6

Bilgihan, A., Leong, A. M. W., Okumus, F., & Bai, J. Y. (2024). Proposing a metaverse engagement model for brand development. *Journal of Retailing and Consumer Services*, 78, 103781. Advance online publication. DOI: 10.1016/j.jretconser.2024.103781

Blazquez, M. (2024). The Metaverse and its potential for digital sustainability in fashion. *Journal of Global Fashion Marketing*, 15(3), 303–319. DOI: 10.1080/20932685.2024.2339236

Bogicevic, V., Liu, S. Q., Kandampully, J. A., Seo, S., & Rudd, N. A. (2024). Experiential marketing to Gen Z: Fine-tuning brand experience through virtual reality. *Journal of Hospitality & Tourism Research (Washington, D.C.)*, 48(8), 1424–1438. Advance online publication. DOI: 10.1177/10963480241256564

Bruni, R., Colamatteo, A., & Mladenovic, D. (2024). How the metaverse influences marketing and competitive advantage of retailers: Predictions and key marketing research priorities. *Electronic Commerce Research*, 24(2), 965–982. DOI: 10.1007/s10660-023-09779-1

Buhalis, D., Leung, D., & Lin, M. C. (2023). Metaverse as a disruptive technology revolutionising tourism management and marketing. *Tourism Management*, 97, 104724. Advance online publication. DOI: 10.1016/j.tourman.2023.104724

Chakraborty, U., & Biswal, S. K. (2024). Diffusion of innovation in direct-to-avatar (D2A): A study of immersive communication and branding in the metaverse. *Computers in Human Behavior*, 158, 108318. Advance online publication. DOI: 10.1016/j.chb.2024.108318

Chalmers, D., Fisch, C., Matthews, R., Quinn, W., & Recker, J. (2022). Beyond the bubble: Will NFTs and digital proof of ownership empower creative industry entrepreneurs? *Journal of Business Venturing Insights*, 17, e00309. DOI: 10.1016/j.jbvi.2022.e00309

Cheah, I., & Shimul, A. S. (2023). Marketing in the metaverse: Moving forward - What's next? *Journal of Global Scholars of Marketing Science*, 33(1), 1–10. DOI: 10.1080/21639159.2022.2163908

Chohan, R., & Schmidt-Devlin, E. (2024). Sports fandom in the metaverse: Marketing implications and research agenda. *Marketing Letters*, 35(1), 1–14. DOI: 10.1007/s11002-023-09702-6

Colicev, A. (2023). How can non-fungible tokens bring value to brands. *International Journal of Research in Marketing*, 40(1), 30–37. DOI: 10.1016/j.ijresmar.2022.07.003

Constantin, M., Genovese, G., Munawar, K., & Stone, R. (2023). *Tourism in the metaverse: Can travel go virtual?* McKinsey & Company. https://www.mckinsey.com/industries/travel-logistics-and-infrastructure/our-insights/tourism-in-the-metaverse-can-travel-go-virtual

Crespo-Pereira, V., Sánchez-Amboage, E., & Membiela-Pollán, M. (2023). Facing the challenges of metaverse: A systematic literature review from Social Sciences and Marketing and Communication. *El Profesional de la Información*, 32(1), e320102. Advance online publication. DOI: 10.3145/epi.2023.ene.02

de Almeida, G. G. F. (2023). Cities and territorial brand in the metaverse: The metaverse Seoul case. *Sustainability (Basel)*, 15(13), 10116. Advance online publication. DOI: 10.3390/su151310116

Deventer, C., de Sousa, V. A., & Pirnay, L. (2024). NFTByBrands: Value Identification Framework for Analysis and Design of NFT Initiatives. *International Journal of Electronic Commerce*, 28(1), 33–62. DOI: 10.1080/10864415.2023.2295070

Dwivedi, Y. K., Hughes, L., Baabdullah, A. M., Ribeiro-Navarrete, S., Giannakis, M., Al-Debei, M. M., Dennehy, D., Metri, B., Buhalis, D., Cheung, C. M. K., Conboy, K., Doyle, R., Dubey, R., Dutot, V., Felix, R., Goyal, D. P., Gustafsson, A., Hinsch, C., Jebabli, I., & Wamba, S. F. (2022). Metaverse beyond the hype: Multidisciplinary perspectives on emerging challenges, opportunities, and agenda for research, practice and policy. *International Journal of Information Management*, 66, 102542. Advance online publication. DOI: 10.1016/j.ijinfomgt.2022.102542

Dwivedi, Y. K., Hughes, L., Wang, Y. C., Alalwan, A. A., Ahn, S. J., Balakrishnan, J., Barta, S., Belk, R., Buhalis, D., Dutot, V., Felix, R., Filieri, R., Flavián, C., Gustafsson, A., Hinsch, C., Hollensen, S., Jain, V., Kim, J., Krishen, A. S., & Wirtz, J. (2023). Metaverse marketing: How the metaverse will shape the future of consumer research and practice. *Psychology and Marketing*, 40(4), 750–776. DOI: 10.1002/mar.21767

Farah, M. F., Ramadan, Z., & Nassereddine, Y. (2024). When digital spaces matter: The influence of uniqueness and place attachment on self-identity expression with brands using generative AI on the metaverse. *Psychology and Marketing*, 41(12), 2965–2976. Advance online publication. DOI: 10.1002/mar.22097

Ferraro, C., Sands, S., Demsar, V., & Cohen, J. (2024). Diversity Representation in Virtual Environments: How Brand Motives Mediate Consumer Perceptions. *Australasian Marketing Journal*, 32(3), 239–249. Advance online publication. DOI: 10.1177/14413582241244535

Gursoy, I. T., Aktas, E., Tecim, V., & Kurgun, O. A. (2023). Beta tourist world: A conceptual framework for organizing an event in the metaverse. *Information Technology & Tourism*, 25(4), 529–548. DOI: 10.1007/s40558-023-00266-9

Hirschman, E. C., & Holbrook, M. B. (1982). Hedonic consumption: Emerging concepts, methods and propositions. *Journal of Marketing*, 46(3), 92–101. DOI: 10.1177/002224298204600314

Hofstetter, R., de Bellis, E., Brandes, L., Clegg, M., Lamberton, C., Reibstein, D., Rohlfsen, F., Schmitt, B., & Zhang, J. Z. (2022). Crypto-marketing: How non-fungible tokens (NFTs) challenge traditional marketing. *Marketing Letters*, 33(4), 705–711. DOI: 10.1007/s11002-022-09639-2

Holbrook, M. B. (1999). *Consumer Value: A Framework for Analysis and Research*. Routledge.

Holbrook, M. B., & Hirschman, E. C. (1982). The experiential aspects of consumption: Consumer fantasies, feelings, and fun. *The Journal of Consumer Research*, 9(2), 132–140. DOI: 10.1086/208906

Jeong, H., Yi, Y., & Kim, D. (2022). An innovative e-commerce platform incorporating metaverse to live commerce. *International Journal of Innovative Computing, Information, & Control*, 18(1), 221–229. DOI: 10.24507/ijicic.18.01.221

Jiang, Q., Kim, M., Ko, E. J., & Kim, K. H. (2023). The metaverse experience in luxury brands. *Asia Pacific Journal of Marketing and Logistics*, 35(10), 2501–2520. DOI: 10.1108/APJML-09-2022-0752

Joy, A., Zhu, Y., Peña, C., & Brouard, M. (2022). Digital future of luxury brands: Metaverse, digital fashion, and non-fungible tokens. *Strategic Change*, 31(3), 337–343. DOI: 10.1002/jsc.2502

Kaur, J., Mogaji, E., Paliwal, M., Jha, S., Agarwal, S., & Mogaji, S. A. (2024). Consumer behavior in the metaverse. *Journal of Consumer Behaviour*, 23(4), 1720–1738. DOI: 10.1002/cb.2298

Kim, J., & Bae, J. (2023). Influences of persona self on luxury brand attachment in the Metaverse context. *Asia Pacific Journal of Marketing and Logistics*. Advance online publication. DOI: 10.1108/APJML-05-2022-0390

Kniazeva, M., Aiello, G., Dasmi, C., Mazzoli, V., Nechaeva, O., & Syed, F. U. (2024). Why fashion brands enter the metaverse: Exploring the motivations of fast fashion and luxury fashion brands. *Journal of Global Fashion Marketing, 15*(1), 62-89. *Article*, 2269952. Advance online publication. DOI: 10.1080/20932685.2023.2269952

Kotler, P., Kartajaya, H., & Setiawan, I. (2023). *Marketing 6.0: The Future is Immersive*. John Wiley & Sons.

Kshetri, N. (2022). Web 3.0 and the metaverse shaping organizations' brand and product strategies. *IT Professional*, 24(2), 11–15. DOI: 10.1109/MITP.2022.3157206

Kshetri, N. (2023). Metaverse technologies in product management, branding and communications: Virtual and augmented reality, artificial intelligence, non-fungible tokens and brain-computer interface. *Central European Management Journal*, 31(4), 511–521. DOI: 10.1108/CEMJ-08-2023-0336

Lee, C. T., Ho, T. Y., & Xie, H. H. (2023). Building brand engagement in metaverse commerce: The role of branded non-fungible tokens (BNFTs). *Electronic Commerce Research and Applications*, 58, 101248. Advance online publication. DOI: 10.1016/j.elerap.2023.101248

Malter, M. S., Holbrook, M. B., Kahn, B. E., Parker, J. R., & Lehmann, D. R. (2020). The past, present, and future of consumer research. *Marketing Letters*, 31(2-3), 137–149. DOI: 10.1007/s11002-020-09526-8 PMID: 32836799

Mansoor, S., Rahman, S. M., & Bowden, J. L. H. (2024). Purchase spillovers from the metaverse to the real world: The roles of social presence, trialability, and customer experience. *Journal of Consumer Behaviour*, 23(5), 2501–2552. Advance online publication. DOI: 10.1002/cb.2353

Marr, B. (2024). Forbes. Retrieved November 5, 2024 from https://www.forbes.com/sites/bernardmarr/2024/07/26/beyond-the-metaverse-top-immersive-internet-trends-for-the-next-decade/

McKinsey and Company. (2022). *Value Creation in the Metaverse*. McKinsey. https://www.mckinsey.com/capabilities/growth-marketing-and-sales/our-insights/value-creation-in-the-metaverse

Mogaji, E., Dwivedi, Y. K., & Raman, R. (2024). Fashion marketing in the metaverse. *Journal of Global Fashion Marketing*, 15(1), 115–130. DOI: 10.1080/20932685.2023.2249483

Murtas, G., Pedeliento, G., & Mangio, F. (2024). Luxury fashion brands at the gates of the Web 3.0: An analysis of early experimentations with NFTs and the metaverse. *Journal of Global Fashion Marketing*, 15(1), 90–114. DOI: 10.1080/20932685.2023.2249476

Natarajan, T., Pragha, P., Dhalmahapatra, K., & Raghavan, D. R. V. (2024). Exploring tourist's metaverse experience using destination spatial presence quality & perceived augmentation: Metaverse exploration, physical expedition (MEPE). *Current Issues in Tourism*, 1–23. Advance online publication. DOI: 10.1080/13683500.2024.2372652

Park, H., & Lim, R. E. (2023). Fashion and the metaverse: Clarifying the domain and establishing a research agenda. *Journal of Retailing and Consumer Services*, 74, 103413. Advance online publication. DOI: 10.1016/j.jretconser.2023.103413

Park, J., & Kim, N. (2024). Examining self-congruence between user and avatar in purchasing behavior from the metaverse to the real world. *Journal of Global Fashion Marketing*, 15(1), 23–38. DOI: 10.1080/20932685.2023.2180768

Payal, R., Sharma, N., & Dwivedi, Y. K. (2024). Unlocking the impact of brand engagement in the metaverse on Real-World purchase intentions: Analyzing Pre-Adoption behavior in a futuristic technology platform. *Electronic Commerce Research and Applications*, 65, 101381. Advance online publication. DOI: 10.1016/j.elerap.2024.101381

Pine, B. J., & Gilmore, J. H. (2011). *The Experience Economy*. Harvard Business Press.

Prashar, A., & Prashar, A. (2024). Digital fashion and metaverse platforms: Do platform attributes drive shopper's purchase intention? *Australian Journal of Management*, 03128962241246696. Advance online publication. DOI: 10.1177/03128962241246696

Profumo, G., Testa, G., Viassone, M., & Ben Youssef, K. (2024). Metaverse and the fashion industry: A systematic literature review. *Journal of Global Fashion Marketing*, 15(1), 131–154. DOI: 10.1080/20932685.2023.2270587

Ramadan, Z. (2023). Marketing in the metaverse era: Toward an integrative channel approach. *Virtual Reality (Waltham Cross)*, 27(3), 1905–1918. DOI: 10.1007/s10055-023-00783-2 PMID: 37360809

Rather, R. A. (2023). Metaverse marketing and consumer research: Theoretical framework and future research agenda in tourism and hospitality industry. *Tourism Recreation Research*, 1–9. Advance online publication. DOI: 10.1080/02508281.2023.2216525

Rauschnabel, P. A., Hüttl-Maack, V., Ahuvia, A. C., & Schein, K. E. (2024). Augmented reality marketing and consumer-brand relationships: How closeness drives brand love. *Psychology and Marketing*, 41(4), 819–837. DOI: 10.1002/mar.21953

Sanchez-Amboage, E., Crespo-Pereira, V., Membiela-Pollan, M., & Faustino, J. P. J. (2024). Tourism marketing in the metaverse: A systematic literature review, building blocks, and future research directions. *PLoS One*, 19(5), e0300599. Advance online publication. DOI: 10.1371/journal.pone.0300599 PMID: 38728243

Sanmiguel, P., Sádaba, T., & Sayeed, N. (2024). Fashion brands in the metaverse: Achievements from a marketing perspective. *Journal of Global Fashion Marketing*, 15(3), 320–340. DOI: 10.1080/20932685.2024.2331518

Schmitt, B. (1999). Experiential marketing. *Journal of Marketing Management*, 15(1-3), 53–67. DOI: 10.1362/026725799784870496

Shin, H., & Kang, J. (2024). How does the metaverse travel experience influence virtual and actual travel behaviors? Focusing on the role of telepresence and avatar identification. *Journal of Hospitality and Tourism Management*, 58, 171–183. DOI: 10.1016/j.jhtm.2023.12.009

Sung, E., Kwon, O., & Sohn, K. (2023). NFT luxury brand marketing in the metaverse: Leveraging blockchain-certified NFTs to drive consumer behavior. *Psychology and Marketing*, 40(11), 2306–2325. DOI: 10.1002/mar.21854

Venturini, A., & Columbano, M. (2024). 'Fashioning' the metaverse: A qualitative study on consumers' value and perceptions of digital fashion in virtual worlds. *Journal of Global Fashion Marketing*, 15(1), 6–22. DOI: 10.1080/20932685.2023.2234918

Wongkitrungrueng, A., & Suprawan, L. (2024). Metaverse meets branding: Examining consumer responses to immersive brand experiences. *International Journal of Human-Computer Interaction*, 40(11), 2905–2924. DOI: 10.1080/10447318.2023.2175162

Yadav, S., Pandey, S. K., & Sharma, D. (2024). Marketing beyond reality: A systematic literature review on metaverse. *Management Research Review*, 47(7), 1029–1051. DOI: 10.1108/MRR-06-2023-0456

Yang, H. T., Cho, Y. R., & Han, S. Y. (2024). Understanding user perceptions toward marketing in the metaverse. *Kybernetes*. Advance online publication. DOI: 10.1108/K-08-2023-1524

Yilmaz, T., Sagfossen, S., & Velasco, C. (2023). What makes NFTs valuable to consumers? Perceived value drivers associated with NFTs liking, purchasing, and holding. *Journal of Business Research*, 165, 114056. Advance online publication. DOI: 10.1016/j.jbusres.2023.114056

Yoo, K., Welden, R., Hewett, K., & Haenlein, M. (2023). The merchants of meta: A research agenda to understand the future of retailing in the metaverse. *Journal of Retailing*, 99(2), 173–192. DOI: 10.1016/j.jretai.2023.02.002

Yu, X. L., Cheng, X. X., Kim, K. H., & Wang, H. Z. (2024). Exploring the brand experience in the metaverse under the perspective of technology acceptance model. *Asia Pacific Journal of Marketing and Logistics*, 36(12), 3410–3426. Advance online publication. DOI: 10.1108/APJML-10-2023-0952

Zaman, M., Hasan, R., Vo-Thanh, T., Shams, R., Rahman, M., & Jasim, K. M. (2024). Adopting the metaverse in the luxury hotel business: A cost-benefit perspective. *International Journal of Contemporary Hospitality Management*. Advance online publication. DOI: 10.1108/IJCHM-08-2023-1265

Zhu, C. S., Io, M. U., Hall, C. M., Ngan, H. F. B., & Peralta, R. L. (2024). How to use augmented reality to promote a destination? The mediating role of augmented reality attachment. *International Journal of Tourism Research*, 26(1), e2603. Advance online publication. DOI: 10.1002/jtr.2603

Compilation of References

Agu, E. E. et al. (2024). Building sustainable business models with predictive analytics: Case studies from various industries. International journal of advanced economics. DOI: 10.51594/ijae.v6i8.1436

Ajiga, D. et al. (2024). Predictive analytics for market trends using AI: A study in consumer behavior. International Journal of Engineering Research Updates. DOI: 10.53430/ijeru.2024.7.1.0032

Forbes. (2017). How chatbots are changing customer service. *Forbes.*

Mhlhoff, R. (2021). Predictive privacy: towards an applied ethics of data analytics. Springer Science+Business Media. DOI: 10.1007/s10676-021-09606-x

Morsi, S. (2020). A predictive analytics model for e-commerce sales transactions to support decision making: a case study. International Journal of Computer and Information Technology (2279-0764), 9(1). DOI: 10.24203/ijcit.v9i1.3

Oloruntosin Tolulope Joel and Vincent Ugochukwu Oguanobi (2024). Data-driven strategies for business expansion: utilizing predictive analytics for enhanced profitability and opportunity identification. International Journal of Frontiers in Engineering and Technology Research, 6(2), 071-081. DOI: 10.53294/ijfetr.2024.6.2.0035

Souza, J., Leung, C. K., & Cuzzocrea, A. (2020). An innovative big data predictive analytics framework over hybrid big data sources with an application for disease analytics. Advanced Information Networking and Applications, 669-680. https://doi.org/DOI: 10.1007/978-3-030-44041-1_59

Statista. (2023). *E-commerce market in India: Projections and growth drivers.*

Suwignjo, P., Panjaitan, L., Baihaqy, A. R., & Rusdiansyah, A. (2023). Predictive analytics to improve inventory performance: a case study of an fmcg company. Operations and Supply Chain Management: An International Journal, 293-310. https://doi.org/.DOI: 10.31387/oscm0530390

Aaker, D. A. (1991). *Managing Brand Equity: Capitalizing on the value of a Brand Name*. Free Press.

Aaker, D. A. (2020). *Managing brand equity*. Simon and Schuster.

Abdelkader, A. A., Hassan, H., Mohamed, M. A., & Khashaba, I. O. (2024). Advances in Brand Management Strategies: Conceptualising the Interrelationships among Emerging Brand Concepts. *Kurdish Studies*, 12(2), 5278–5300.

ABIDAR, L., ZAIDOUNI, D., Ikram, E. L., & ENNOUAARY, A. (2023). Predicting Customer Segment Changes to Enhance Customer Retention: A Case Study for Online Retail using Machine Learning. *International Journal of Advanced Computer Science and Applications*, 14(7).

Abinesh, R. C., & Dulloo, R. (2024). The Impact of AI-Driven Personalization on Customer Satisfaction in E-Commerce: Balancing Technology, Transparency, and Control. [JoCAAA]. *Journal of Computational Analysis and Applications*, 33(2), 649–655.

Adami, C. (2015). Artificial intelligence: Robots with instincts. *Nature*, 521(7553), 426–427. DOI: 10.1038/521426a PMID: 26017437

Adami, M. (2015). Artificial Intelligence in Marketing and Consumer Behavior Analysis. *Marketing Science Journal*, 15(4), 23–45.

Adebiyi, O. O. (2023). Exploring the Impact of Predictive Analytics on Accounting and Auditing Expertise: A Regression Analysis of LinkedIn Survey Data. Asian Journal of Economics Business and Accounting. DOI: 10.9734/ajeba/2023/v23i221153

Adegbola, O., Smith, P., & Harrison, T. (2024). Consumer Analytics and Digital Marketing Transformation. *Journal of Digital Marketing*, 12(3), 112–128.

Adesina, A. A., Iyelolu, T. V., & Paul, P. O.Abayomi Abraham AdesinaToluwalase Vanessa IyeloluPatience Okpeke Paul. (2024). Leveraging predictive analytics for strategic decision-making: Enhancing business performance through data-driven insights. *World Journal of Advanced Research and Reviews*, 22(3), 1927–1934. DOI: 10.30574/wjarr.2024.22.3.1961

Adewusi, A. O., Komolafe, A. M., Ejairu, E., Aderotoye, I. A., Abiona, O. O., & Oyeniran, O. C. (2024). The role of predictive analytics in optimizing supply chain resilience: A review of techniques and case studies. International Journal of Management &Amp. *Entrepreneurship Research*, 6(3), 815–837. DOI: 10.51594/ijmer.v6i3.938

Adner, R. (2017). *The wide lens: A new strategy for innovation*. Penguin.

Adula, M., & Kant, S. (2025). Impact of Smart Entrepreneurship and Territorial Marketing on Regional Branding: Case of Ethiopia. In *Sustainable and Intelligent Territorial Marketing and Entrepreneurship* (pp. 229–256). IGI Global., DOI: 10.4018/979-8-3693-9775-6.ch008

Afoudi, Y., Lazaar, M., & Al Achhab, M. (2021). Hybrid recommendation system combined content-based filtering and collaborative prediction using artificial neural network. *Simulation Modelling Practice and Theory*, 113, 102375. DOI: 10.1016/j.simpat.2021.102375

Afsar, M. M., Crump, T., & Far, B. (2022). Reinforcement learning based recommender systems: A survey. *ACM Computing Surveys*, 55(7), 1–38. DOI: 10.1145/3543846

Agersborg, C., Månsson, I., & Roth, E. (2020). Brand Management and Artificial Intelligence-A World of Man Plus Machine-A qualitative study exploring how Artificial Intelligence can contribute to Brand Management in the B2C sector.

Agrawal, A., Gans, J. S., & Goldfarb, A. (2018). *Prediction machines: The simple economics of artificial l intelligence*. Harvard Business School Press.

Aguirre, E., Mahr, D., Grewal, D., de Ruyter, K., & Wetzels, M. (2015). Unraveling the personalization paradox: The effect of information collection and trust-building strategies on online advertisement effectiveness. *Journal of Retailing*, 91(1), 34–49. DOI: 10.1016/j.jretai.2014.09.005

Agustina, S. (2023). Ethical Business Practices And AI-Driven Marketing For Product Branding In MSMEs. *Maeswara: Jurnal Riset Ilmu Manajemen dan Kewirausahaan, 1*(2), 01-10.

Ahmed, A., Saleem, K., Khalid, O., & Rashid, U. (2021). On deep neural network for trust aware cross domain recommendations in E-commerce. *Expert Systems with Applications*, 174, 114757. DOI: 10.1016/j.eswa.2021.114757

Ahn, S. J., Kim, J., & Kim, J. (2022). The Bifold Triadic Relationships Framework: A Theoretical Primer for Advertising Research in the Metaverse. *Journal of Advertising*, 51(5), 592–607. DOI: 10.1080/00913367.2022.2111729

Ahn, S. J., Kim, J., & Kim, J. (2023). The future of advertising research in virtual, augmented, and extended realities. *International Journal of Advertising*, 42(1), 162–170. DOI: 10.1080/02650487.2022.2137316

Ahuvia, A. C. (2005). Beyond the extended self: Loved objects and consumers' identity narratives. *The Journal of Consumer Research*, 32(1), 171–184. DOI: 10.1086/429607

Akbulut, O., Çelik, T., Ekin, Y., & Yetim, A. Ç. (2024). A research on Fethiye Babadag commercial tandem paragliding participants within the scope of experiential tourism. *Journal of Outdoor Recreation and Tourism*, 47, 100806.

Akhtar, P., Ghouri, A. M., Ashraf, A., Lim, J. J., Khan, N. R., & Ma, S. (2024). Smart product platforming powered by AI and Generative AI: Personalization for the circular economy. *International Journal of Production Economics*, 273, 109283. DOI: 10.1016/j.ijpe.2024.109283

Akter, S., Sultana, S., Mariani, M., Wamba, S. F., Spanaki, K., & Dwivedi, Y. K. (2023). Advancing algorithmic bias management capabilities in AI-driven marketing analytics research. *Industrial Marketing Management*, 114, 243–261. DOI: 10.1016/j.indmarman.2023.08.013

Alamdari, P. M., Navimipour, N. J., Hosseinzadeh, M., Safaei, A. A., & Darwesh, A. (2020). A systematic study on the recommender systems in the E-commerce. *IEEE Access : Practical Innovations, Open Solutions*, 8, 115694–115716. DOI: 10.1109/ACCESS.2020.3002803

Alawamleh, M., Shammas, N., Alawamleh, K., & Ismail, L. B. (2024). Examining the limitations of AI in business and the need for human insights using Interpretive Structural Modelling. *Journal of Open Innovation*, 10(3), 100338. DOI: 10.1016/j.joitmc.2024.100338

Albăstroiu, I., & Felea, M. (2014). The implications of user-generated content websites for tourism marketing. *International Journal of Economic Practices and Theories*, 4(2), 222–229.

Alberti, A. M., Pivoto, D. G., Rezende, T. T., Leal, A. V., Both, C. B., Facina, M. S., Moreira, R., & de Oliveira Silva, F. (2024). Disruptive 6G architecture: Software-centric, AI-driven, and digital market place-based mobile networks. *Computer Networks*, 252, 110682. DOI: 10.1016/j.comnet.2024.110682

Albert, N., & Merunka, D. (2013). The role of brand love in consumer. *Journal of Consumer Marketing*, 30(3), 258–266. DOI: 10.1108/07363761311328928

Alebaki, M., & Iakovidou, O. (2010). Segmenting the Greek wine tourism market using a motivational approach. *New Medit: Mediterranean Journal of Economics, Agriculture and Environment= Revue Méditerranéenne d Economie. Agriculture et Environment*, 9(4), 31.

Alexandruand, C., & Maher, K. (2019). Matching the future capabilities of an artificial intelligence-based software for social media marketing with potential users' expectations. *Technological Forecasting and Social Change*, 151(119794), 10–15.

Alghizzawi, M., Ezmigna, I., Jado, K., Alzeaideen, K., & Kanan, M. (2024). Theoretical Perspective of Artificial Intelligence in Digital Marketing for Business Organizations. In *Studies in Computational Intelligence* (pp. 167–177). Springer Science and Business Media Deutschland GmbH., DOI: 10.1007/978-3-031-56015-6_13

Ali, S. (2023). *Impact of Artificial Intelligence and Advertisement on Project Customer Engagement and Project Success in Project based Firm with Mediating Role of Brand Image*. Capital University of Science and Technology.

Alkhudary, R., Belvaux, B., & Guibert, N. (2023). Understanding non-fungible tokens (NFTs): Insights on consumption practices and a research agenda. *Marketing Letters*, 34(2), 321–336. DOI: 10.1007/s11002-022-09655-2

Allahverdiyeva, M., Aghayeva, K., & Tavakkulova, S. (2024). The importance of advertising in global trade. *Науковий журнал «Економіка і регіон»*, (1 (92)), 20-25.

Allal-Chérif, O., Puertas, R., & Carracedo, P. (2024). Intelligent influencer marketing: How AI-powered virtual influencers outperform human influencers. *Technological Forecasting and Social Change*, 200, 123113. DOI: 10.1016/j.techfore.2023.123113

Alnawas, I., & Altarifi, S. (2016). Exploring the role of brand identification and brand love in generating higher levels of brand loyalty. *Journal of Vacation Marketing*, 22(2), 111–128. DOI: 10.1177/1356766715604663

Alnoor, A., & Bayram, G. E. XinYing, C., & Shah, S. H. A. (Eds.). (2024). The Role of Artificial Intelligence in Regenerative Tourism and Green Destinations.

Alotaibi, E. (2023). Risk assessment using predictive analytics. *International Journal of Professional Business Review*, 8(5), e01723. DOI: 10.26668/businessreview/2023.v8i5.1723

Alratemi. Mohammed Ali,(2012). "Artificial Intelligence and Expert Systems," Libyan Academy of Graduate Studies.First edition. Eygpt.

Alruwaili, M. M., Abuadas, F. H., Alsadi, M., Alruwaili, A. N., Elsayed Ramadan, O. M., Shaban, M., & El Arab, R. A. (2024). Exploring nurses' awareness and attitudes toward artificial intelligence: Implications for nursing practice. *Digital Health*, 10, 20552076241271803.

Alshater, M. M., Nasrallah, N., Khoury, R., & Joshipura, M. (2024). Deciphering the world of NFTs: A scholarly review of trends, challenges, and opportunities. *Electronic Commerce Research*. Advance online publication. DOI: 10.1007/s10660-024-09881-y

Alshuqaiqi, A., & Omar, S. I. (2019). Causes and implication of seasonality in tourism. *Journal of Advanced Research in Dynamical and Control Systems*, 11(4), 1480–1486.

Alves Gomes, M., & Meisen, T. (2023). A review on customer segmentation methods for personalized customer targeting in e-commerce use cases. *Information Systems and e-Business Management*, 21(3), 527–570. DOI: 10.1007/s10257-023-00640-4

Amankwah-Amoah, J., Abdalla, S., Mogaji, E., Elbanna, A., & Dwivedi, Y. K. (2024). The impending disruption of creative industries by generative AI: Opportunities, challenges, and investigation agenda. *International Journal of Information Management*, 79, 102759. DOI: 10.1016/j.ijinfomgt.2024.102759

Amaral, M. M., Kuhn, V. R., dos Anjos, S. J. G., & Flores, L. C. D. S. (2024). Experiences in a wine tourism destination from the visitors' perspective. *International Journal of Wine Business Research*, 36(1), 85–102. DOI: 10.1108/IJWBR-05-2023-0028

Ambrosini, V., & Bowman, C. (2009). What are dynamic capabilities and are they a useful construct in strategic management? *International Journal of Management Reviews*, 11(1), 29–49. DOI: 10.1111/j.1468-2370.2008.00251.x

Ameen, N., Hosany, S., & Tarhini, A. (2021). Consumer interaction with cutting-edge technologies: Implications for future research. *Computers in Human Behavior*, 120, 106761. DOI: 10.1016/j.chb.2021.106761

Ameen, N., Sharma, G. D., Tarba, S., Rao, A., & Chopra, R. (2022). Toward advancing theory on creativity in marketing and artificial intelligence. *Psychology and Marketing*, 39(9), 1802–1825. DOI: 10.1002/mar.21699

Ampountolas, A., Menconi, G., & Shaw, G. (2024). Metaverse research propositions: Online intermediaries. *Tourism Economics*, 30(1), 255–261. DOI: 10.1177/13548166231159520

Ana, M. I., & Istudor, L. G. (2019). The role of social media and user-generated-content in millennials' travel behavior. *Management Dynamics in the Knowledge Economy*, 7(1), 87–104. DOI: 10.25019/mdke/7.1.05

Andrii, K. (2023). MODERN PERSPECTIVES AND PROBLEMS OF MARKETING IN EUROPE. *Нейромаркетинг, штучний інтелект та цифровий маркетинг*, 112.

Angela, E., & Alexandru, C. (2018, September). Exploring Artificial Intelligence Techniques' Applicability in Social Media Marketing. *Journal of Emerging Trends in Marketing and Management*, 1(1), 156–164.

Anjorin, O., Raji, A., & Olodo, S. (2024). Elaboration likelihood model and consumer persuasion. *Journal of Marketing and Digital Media*, 12(3), 45–60.

Ansar, N. (2013). Impact of Green Marketing on Consumer Purchase Intention [online]. *Mediterranean Journal of Social Sciences*, 4(11), 650–655. DOI: 10.5901/mjss.2013.v4n11p650

Antonio, C., Sergio, R., & Francisco, M. J. (2009). Characteristics of Research on Green Marketing. *Business Strategy and the Environment*, 18(4), 223–239. DOI: 10.1002/bse.571

Appel, G., Grewal, L., Hadi, R., & Stephen, A. T. (2020). The future of social media in marketing. *Journal of the Academy of Marketing Science*, 48(1), 79–95. DOI: 10.1007/s11747-019-00695-1 PMID: 32431463

Ara, A., & Thomas, A. (2025). Exploring Consumer Perceptions and Ethical Considerations in AI-Powered E-Commerce. In *Data Visualization Tools for Business Applications* (pp. 347–368). IGI Global.

Ardito, L., Scuotto, V., Del Giudice, M., & Petruzzelli, A. M. (2019). A bibliometric analysis of research on Big Data analytics for business and management. *Management Decision*, 57(8), 1993–2009. DOI: 10.1108/MD-07-2018-0754

Aria, M., & Cuccurullo, C. (2017). Bibliometrix: An R-tool for comprehensive science mapping analysis. *Journal of Informetrics*, 11(4), 959–975. DOI: 10.1016/j.joi.2017.08.007

Aridor, G., Goncalves, D., & Sikdar, S. (2020, September). Deconstructing the filter bubble: User decision-making and recommender systems. In *Proceedings of the 14th ACM conference on recommender systems* (pp. 82-91). DOI: 10.1145/3383313.3412246

Aris, S., Sarfi, T., Akhavan, M., & Sabbar, S. (2023). Motivations for consuming avatar-specific virtual items on the Zepeto gaming platform. *Cadernos Educacao Tecnologia E Sociedade, 16*(4), 1248-1258. https://doi.org/DOI: 10.14571/brajets.v16.n4.1248-1258

Arkadiusz, K. (2024, Jun 14). *Netflix Algorithm: How Netflix Uses AI to Improve Personalization*. Retrieved Nov 15, 2024, from https://stratoflow.com/: https://stratoflow.com/how-netflix-recommendation-algorithm-work/

Arora, M., Mishra, K. K., Singh, M., Singh, P., & Tripathi, R. (2024). Deepfake Technology and Its Implications for Influencer Marketing. In *Navigating the World of Deepfake Technology* (pp. 66–90). IGI Global. DOI: 10.4018/979-8-3693-5298-4.ch005

Arya, V., Sambyal, R., Sharma, A., & Dwivedi, Y. K. (2024). Brands are calling your AVATAR in Metaverse-A study to explore XR-based gamification marketing activities & consumer-based brand equity in virtual world. *Journal of Consumer Behaviour*, 23(2), 556–585. DOI: 10.1002/cb.2214

Asthana, S., Im, J., Chen, Z., & Banovic, N. (2024). "I know even if you don't tell me": Understanding Users' Privacy Preferences Regarding AI-based Inferences of Sensitive Information for Personalization. *CHI Conference on Human Factors in Computing Sytems, CHI 2024*. Hybrid, Honolulu: Association for Computing Machinery. DOI: 10.1145/3613904.3642180

Asthana, S., Im, J., Chen, Z., & Banovic, N. (2024, May). " I know even if you don't tell me": Understanding Users' Privacy Preferences Regarding AI-based Inferences of Sensitive Information for Personalization. *InProceedings of the CHI Conference on Human Factors in Computing Systems(pp.1-21).*

Atulkar, S. (2020). Brand trust and brand loyalty in mall shoppers. *Marketing Intelligence & Planning*, 38(5), 559–572. DOI: 10.1108/MIP-02-2019-0095

Avdimiotis, S. (2019). Emotional intelligence and tacit knowledge management in hospitality. *Journal ofTourism* [JTHSM]. *Heritage & Services Marketing*, 5(2), 3–10.

Aydin, B., & Sirkeci, I. (2024). Navigating the Frontier: Addressing Artificial Intelligence Challenges in Tourism and Hospitality Education. *Transnational Education Review*, 2(1), 49–53.

Aysan, A. F., & Syarif, M. F. (2024). Shaping the halal tourism industry landscape through NFT and metaverse: New horizons for halal brand and halal booking hotel. *Journal of Islamic Marketing*. Advance online publication. DOI: 10.1108/JIMA-07-2023-0206

Aziz, A., Lita, R. P., & Yeni, Y. H. (2023). Performance of Fighting Brands in Maintaining Market Share in Cement Trading during Oversupply. *Inovbiz: Jurnal Inovasi Bisnis Seri Manajemen, Investasi dan Kewirausahaan, 3*(1), 43-53.

Babadoan, B. (2024). *Harnessing AI and Predictive Analytics to Revolutionize Customer Retention Strategies*. None., DOI: 10.62802/k2a4gf39

Babadoan, B. (2024). *Unveiling the Power of AI-Driven Personalization: Transforming Consumer Behavior in the Age of Digital Marketing*. None., DOI: 10.62802/fj43xy18

Babatunde, S. O., Odejide, O. A., Edunjobi, T. E., & Ogundipe, D. O.Sodiq Odetunde BabatundeOpeyemi Abayomi OdejideTolulope Esther EdunjobiDamilola Oluwaseun Ogundipe. (2024). The role of AI in marketing personalization: A theoretical exploration of consumer engagement strategies. *International Journal of Management & Entrepreneurship Research*, 6(3), 936–949. DOI: 10.51594/ijmer.v6i3.964

Backhaus, K., Becker, J., Beverungen, D., Frohs, M., Müller, O., Weddeling, M., Knackstedt, R., & Steiner, M. (2010). Enabling individualized recommendations and dynamic pricing of value-added services through willingness-to-pay data. *Electronic Markets*, 20(2), 131–146. DOI: 10.1007/s12525-010-0032-0

Badouch, M., & Boutaounte, M. (2024). Design and Implementation of a Hotel Recommendation System Using Deep Learning. In *AI and Data Engineering Solutions for Effective Marketing* (pp. 388–408). IGI Global. DOI: 10.4018/979-8-3693-3172-9.ch019

Badouch, M., & Boutaounte, M. (2025). Smart E-commerce Recommendations with Semantic AI. Fusion. *Practice and Applications*, 17(1), 264–271.

Bae, B. R., & Kim, S. E. (2023). Effect of brand experiences on brand loyalty mediated by brand love: The moderated mediation role of brand trust. *Asia Pacific Journal of Marketing and Logistics*, 35(10), 2412–2430. Advance online publication. DOI: 10.1108/APJML-03-2022-0203

Bahrami, M., Bozkaya, B., & Balcisoy, S. (2020). Using Behavioral Analytics to Predict Customer Invoice Payment. *Big Data*, 8(1), 25–37. DOI: 10.1089/big.2018.0116 PMID: 31976741

Baird, T., Hall, C. M., & Castka, P. (2018). New Zealand winegrowers attitudes and behaviours towards wine tourism and sustainable winegrowing. *Sustainability (Basel)*, 10(3), 797. DOI: 10.3390/su10030797

Bairrada, C. M., Coelho, F., & Coelho, A. (2018). Antecedents and outcomes of brand love: Utilitarian and symbolic brand qualities. *European Journal of Marketing*, 52(3/4), 656–682. DOI: 10.1108/EJM-02-2016-0081

Bakopoulos, V., Baranello, A., & Briggs, A. (2017). Mobile marketing: The next frontier of advertising research. *Journal of Interactive Advertising*, 17(1), 41–52. DOI: 10.1080/15252019.2017.1367880

Balog, K., & Radlinski, F. (2020, July). Measuring recommendation explanation quality: The conflicting goals of explanations. In *Proceedings of the 43rd international ACM SIGIR conference on research and development in information retrieval* (pp. 329-338). DOI: 10.1145/3397271.3401032

Bamboat, Q., & Yu, H. Q. (2023). Literature Study on Bias and Fairness in Machine Learning Systems. *22nd IEEE International Conference on Trust, Security and Privacy in Computing and Communications, TrustCom 2023* (pp. 1960-1965). Exeter: Institute of Electrical and Electronics Engineers Inc. DOI: 10.1109/TrustCom60117.2023.00267

Banik, B., Banik, S., & Annee, R. R. (2024). AI-Driven Strategies for Enhancing Customer Loyalty and Engagement Through Personalization and Predictive Analytics. *International Journal of Machine Learning Research in Cybersecurity and Artificial Intelligence*, 15(1), 416–447.

Bansal, M., Goyal, A., & Choudhary, A. (2022). A comparative analysis of K-nearest neighbor, genetic, support vector machine, decision tree, and long short term memory algorithms in machine learning. *Decision Analytics Journal*, 3, 100071. DOI: 10.1016/j.dajour.2022.100071

Bansal, S. (2020). AI and its impact on modern business practices. *Business Horizons*, 63(2), 197–205.

Barney, J. B. (2011). *Gaining and sustaining competitive advantage* (4th ed.). Pearson.

Barrera, K. G., & Shah, D. (2023). Marketing in the Metaverse: Conceptual understanding, framework, and research agenda. *Journal of Business Research*, 155, 113420. Advance online publication. DOI: 10.1016/j.jbusres.2022.113420

Barta, S., Gurrea, R., & Flavián, C. (2023). Telepresence in live-stream shopping: An experimental study comparing Instagram and the metaverse. *Electronic Markets*, 33(1), 29. Advance online publication. DOI: 10.1007/s12525-023-00643-6

Bartoloni, S., & Ancillai, C. (2023). Twenty years of social media marketing: A systematic review, integrative framework, and future research agenda. *International Journal of Management Reviews*, 26(3), 435–457. DOI: 10.1111/ijmr.12360

Barua, P. D., Vicnesh, J., Gururajan, R., Oh, S. L., Palmer, E., Azizan, M. M., Kadri, N. A., & Acharya, U. R. (2022). Artificial intelligence enabled personalized assistive tools to enhance education of children with neurodevelopmental disorders—A review. *International Journal of Environmental Research and Public Health*, 19(3), 1192. DOI: 10.3390/ijerph19031192 PMID: 35162220

Bashynska, I. (2023). AI-Driven Personalization in Advertising: Transforming Consumer Engagement through Sustainability and Circular Economy. *Scientific Journal of Bielsko-Biala School of Finance and Law*, 27(4), 106–112.

Batra, R., Ahuvia, A., & Bagozzi, R. P. (2012). Brand love. *Journal of Marketing*, 76(2), 1–16. DOI: 10.1509/jm.09.0339

Batra, R., Ahuvia, A., & Bagozzi, R. P. (2022). Brand love: Development and implications for brand and consumer behavior. *Journal of Marketing*, 86(1), 1–20.

Bauer, H., Heinrich, D., & Albrecht, C. M. (2009). All you need is love: Assessing consumers' brand love. In *Proceedings of the American Marketing Association summer educators conference* (Vol. 15, No. 2, pp. 252-253). Chicago: American Marketing Association.

Bayighomog Likoum, S. W., Shamout, M. D., Harazneh, I., & Abubakar, A. M. (2020). Market-sensing capability, innovativeness, brand management systems, market dynamism, competitive intensity, and performance: An integrative review. *Journal of the Knowledge Economy*, 11(2), 593–613. DOI: 10.1007/s13132-018-0561-x

Bayuk, A., & Demir, S. (2021). Artificial intelligence in marketing: Emergence, development, and applications. *Journal of Business Research*, 128, 378–389.

Beichert, M., Bayerl, A., Goldenberg, J., & Lanz, A. (2024). Revenue generation through influencer marketing. *Journal of Marketing*, •••, 00222429231217471.

Belhadi, A., Mani, V., Kamble, S. S., Khan, S. A. R., & Verma, S. (2024). Artificial intelligence-driven innovation for enhancing supply chain resilience and performance under the effect of supply chain dynamism: An empirical investigation. *Annals of Operations Research*, 333(2), 627–652. DOI: 10.1007/s10479-021-03956-x

Belk, R. (2021). Technophilia and its impact on branding. *The Journal of Consumer Research*, 48(3), 412–431.

Bellini, P., Palesi, L. A. I., Nesi, P., & Pantaleo, G. (2023). Multi clustering recommendation system for fashion retail. *Multimedia Tools and Applications*, 82(7), 9989–10016. DOI: 10.1007/s11042-021-11837-5 PMID: 35043044

Benoît, L., William, A., Lindsey, H., Adrienne, L. F., & Marianne, M. W. (2019). Wine sector: Definitions and nuances from global to country analysis—A comparison between Old World, New World, and emerging wine countries from 2005 to current. In *Case Studies in the Wine Industry* (pp. 7–32). Woodhead Publishing. DOI: 10.1016/B978-0-08-100944-4.00002-1

Berger, J., Humphreys, A., Ludwig, S., Moe, W. W., Netzer, O., & Schweidel, D. A. (2020). Uniting the tribes: Using text for marketing insight. *Journal of Marketing*, 84(1), 1–25. DOI: 10.1177/0022242919873106

Bernarto, I., Berlianto, M. P., Meilani, Y. F. C. P., Masman, R. R., & Suryawan, I. N. (2020). The influence of brand awareness, brand image, and brand trust on brand loyalty. *Jurnal Manajemen*, 24(3), 412–426. DOI: 10.24912/jm.v24i3.676

Berry, L. L. (1983). Customer relationship management in the service sector. *Journal of Retailing*, 59(2), 25–48.

Bettman, J. (1973). Perceived risk and its components: A model and empirical test. *Journal of Marketing*, 10(2), 184–190.

Beverland, M., Napoli, J., & Farrelly, F. (2015). Brands as cultural resources: Organizational and brand identity co-creation in a sport context. *Journal of the Academy of Marketing Science*, 43(4), 453–470. DOI: 10.1007/s11747-015-0431-3

Beverland, M., Napoli, J., & Farrelly, F. (2015). Can all brands innovate in the same way? A typology of brand position and innovation effort. *Journal of Product Innovation Management*, 32(1), 109–120. DOI: 10.1111/jpim.12250

Bhardwaj, S., Nair, K., Tariq, M. U., Ahmad, A., & Chitnis, A. (2023). The State of Research in Green Marketing: A Bibliometric Review from 2005 to 2022. *Sustainability (Basel)*, 15(4), 2988. DOI: 10.3390/su15042988

Bhattarai, A. (2023). Exploring Customer Engagement through Generative AI Innovative Strategies in Digital Marketing Campaigns. *Quarterly Journal of Emerging Technologies and Innovations*, 8(12), 1–9.

Bhowmik, O., Chowdhury, S., Ashik, J. H., Mahmud, G. I., Khan, M. M., & Hossain, N. U. I. (2024). Application of Artificial Intelligence in Reverse Logistics: A Bibliometric and Network Analysis. *Supply Chain Analytics*, 100076.

Bhuiyan, M. S. (2024). The role of AI-Enhanced personalization in customer experiences. *Journal of Computer Science and Technology Studies*, 6(1), 162–169. DOI: 10.32996/jcsts.2024.6.1.17

Bıçakcıoğlu, N., İpek, İ., & Bayraktaroğlu, G. (2018). Antecedents and outcomes of brand love: The mediating role of brand loyalty. *Journal of Marketing Communications*, 24(8), 863–877. DOI: 10.1080/13527266.2016.1244108

Bilgihan, A., Leong, A. M. W., Okumus, F., & Bai, J. Y. (2024). Proposing a metaverse engagement model for brand development. *Journal of Retailing and Consumer Services*, 78, 103781. Advance online publication. DOI: 10.1016/j.jretconser.2024.103781

Biswas, A., Vineeth, K. S., & Jain, A., & Mohana. (2020). Development of Product Recommendation Engine by Collaborative Filtering and Association Rule Mining Using Machine Learning Algorithms. *4th International Conference on Inventive Systems and Control, ICISC 2020* (pp. 272-277). Coimbatore: Institute of Electrical and Electronics Engineers Inc. DOI: 10.1109/ICISC47916.2020.9171210

Biswas, A., Bhowmick, S., Guha, A., & Grewal, D. (2013). Consumer evaluations of sale prices: Role of the subtraction principle. *Journal of Marketing*, 77(4), 49–66. DOI: 10.1509/jm.12.0052

Blau, P. M. (1964). *Exchange and power in social life*. Wiley.

Blazquez, M. (2024). The Metaverse and its potential for digital sustainability in fashion. *Journal of Global Fashion Marketing*, 15(3), 303–319. DOI: 10.1080/20932685.2024.2339236

Bogicevic, V., Liu, S. Q., Kandampully, J. A., Seo, S., & Rudd, N. A. (2024). Experiential marketing to Gen Z: Fine-tuning brand experience through virtual reality. *Journal of Hospitality & Tourism Research (Washington, D.C.)*, 48(8), 1424–1438. Advance online publication. DOI: 10.1177/10963480241256564

Boldt Sousa, T. (2022). Customer Data Platforms: A Pattern Language for Digital Marketing Optimization with First-Party Data. *7th European Conference on Pattern Languages of Programs, EuroPLoP 2022*. Irsee: Association for Computing Machinery. DOI: 10.1145/3551902.3551984

Borges, A. F., Laurindo, F. J. B., Spínola, M. M., Gonçalves, R. F., & Mattos, C. A. (2021). The strategic use of artificial intelligence in the digital era: Systematic literature review and future research directions. *International Journal of Information Management*, 57, 102225. Advance online publication. DOI: 10.1016/j.ijinfomgt.2020.102225

Borić, J., Simmons, L., & Chandra, K. (2024). The Impact of Digital Transformation on Consumer Behavior. *Journal of Digital Economy*, 10(2), 45–67.

Boyd, R., & Holton, R. J. (2018). Technology, innovation, employment and power: Does robotics and artificial intelligence really mean social transformation? *Journal of Sociology (Melbourne, Vic.)*, 54(3), 331–345. DOI: 10.1177/1440783317726591

Bozkurt, S., Uğursoy, A. S., & Meral, S. P. (2025). The Impact of Personalized Messages and Designs on Consumer Experiences and Marketing Communications in Technology: Hyper-Personalization. In *Impact of Contemporary Technology on Art and Design* (pp. 135–164). IGI Global.

Brandtzaeg, P. B., & Følstad, A. (2017). Why people use chatbots. *Proceedings of the 2017 CHI Conference on Human Factors in Computing Systems*, 4847–4857.

Brochadó, A., Stoleriu, O., & Lupu, C. (2021). Wine tourism: A multisensory experience. *Current Issues in Tourism*, 24(5), 597–615. DOI: 10.1080/13683500.2019.1649373

Broekhuizen, T., Dekker, H., de Faria, P., Firk, S., Nguyen, D. K., & Sofka, W. (2023). AI for managing open innovation: Opportunities, challenges, and a research agenda. *Journal of Business Research*, 167, 114196. DOI: 10.1016/j.jbusres.2023.114196

Bruni, R., Colamatteo, A., & Mladenovic, D. (2024). How the metaverse influences marketing and competitive advantage of retailers: Predictions and key marketing research priorities. *Electronic Commerce Research*, 24(2), 965–982. DOI: 10.1007/s10660-023-09779-1

Brynjolfsson, E., & McAfee, A. N. (2017). What's driving the Machine Learning explosion? *Harvard Business Review*, •••, 18.

Buhalis, D., Leung, D., & Lin, M. C. (2023). Metaverse as a disruptive technology revolutionising tourism management and marketing. *Tourism Management*, 97, 104724. Advance online publication. DOI: 10.1016/j.tourman.2023.104724

Buhalis, D., & Park, S. (2021). Brand management and cocreation lessons from tourism and hospitality: Introduction to the special issue. *Journal of Product and Brand Management*, 30(1), 1–11. DOI: 10.1108/JPBM-10-2020-3158

Bulchand-Gidumal, J., William Secin, E., O'Connor, P., & Buhalis, D. (2024). Artificial intelligence's impact on hospitality and tourism market placing: Exploring key themes and addressing challenges. *Current Issues in Tourism*, 27(14), 2345–2362. DOI: 10.1080/13683500.2023.2229480

Burnasheva, R., Suh, Y. G., & Villalobos-Moron, K. (2019). Sense of community and social identity effect on brand love: Based on the online communities of a luxury fashion brands. *Journal of Global Fashion Marketing*, 10(1), 50–65. DOI: 10.1080/20932685.2018.1558087

Byrd, E. T., Canziani, B., Hsieh, Y. C. J., Debbage, K., & Sonmez, S. (2016). Wine tourism: Motivating visitors through core and supplementary services. *Tourism Management*, 52, 19–29. DOI: 10.1016/j.tourman.2015.06.009

Campbell, C., & Farrell, J. (2020). Influencer Marketing and Its Impact on Brand Management. *Journal of Advertising Research*, 22(1), 87–102.

Campbell, C., & Price, L. (2021). Predictive modeling and AI in marketing. *Marketing Science*, 40(2), 123–135.

Cantallops, A. S., & Salvi, F. (2014). Understanding AI-driven brand interactions: A TAM perspective. *Computers in Human Behavior*, 31, 19–25.

Carroll, B. A., & Ahuvia, A. C. (2006). Some antecedents and outcomes of brand love. *Marketing Letters*, 17(2), 79–89. DOI: 10.1007/s11002-006-4219-2

Castelo, N., Bos, M., & Lehman, D. (2018). Consumer adoption of algorithms that blur the line between human and machine. Graduate School of Business: Columbia University Working Paper. (Castelo et al., 2018)

Castelo, N., & Ward, A. (2016). Political affiliation moderates attitudes towards artificial intelligence. In Moreau, P., & Puntoni, S. (Eds.), *NA - advances in consumer research* (pp. 723–723). Association for Consumer Research.

Castillo, D., Canhoto, A. I., & Said, E. (2021). The dark side of AI-powered service interactions: Exploring the process of co-destruction from the customer perspective. *Service Industries Journal*, 41(13-14), 900–925. DOI: 10.1080/02642069.2020.1787993

Cavaliere, L. P. L., Mangalasserri, K., Venkateswaran, P. S., Byloppilly, R., & Effendy, F. (2021). The impact of brand counterfeiting on consumer behavior in the fashion sector. *Turkish Journal of Physiotherapy and Rehabilitation*, 32(3), 19831–19847. DOI: 10.5606/tjpr.2021.13842

Çelik, Z. (2022). The moderating role of influencer attractiveness in the effect of brand love, brand trust, brand awareness and brand image on brand loyalty. *İstanbul Ticaret Üniversitesi Sosyal Bilimler Dergisi, 21*(43), 148-167. https://doi.org/DOI: 10.46928/iticusbe.1050122

Chae, B.. (2014). Big Data and Marketing Analytics: Insights into Consumer Behavior. *International Journal of Business Analytics*, 2(3), 33–47.

Chakraborty, U., & Biswal, S. K. (2024). Diffusion of innovation in direct-to-avatar (D2A): A study of immersive communication and branding in the metaverse. *Computers in Human Behavior*, 158, 108318. Advance online publication. DOI: 10.1016/j.chb.2024.108318

Chalmers, D., Fisch, C., Matthews, R., Quinn, W., & Recker, J. (2022). Beyond the bubble: Will NFTs and digital proof of ownership empower creative industry entrepreneurs? *Journal of Business Venturing Insights*, 17, e00309. DOI: 10.1016/j.jbvi.2022.e00309

Chan, H. K., Lacka, E., Yee, R. W., & Lim, M. K. (2017). The role of social media data in operations and production management. *International Journal of Production Research*, 55(17), 5027–5036. DOI: 10.1080/00207543.2015.1053998

Chanthati, S. R. (2024). Website Visitor Analysis & Branding Quality Measurement Using. *Artificial Intelligence*.

Charters, S., & Ali-Knight, J. (2002). Who is the wine tourist? *Tourism Management*, 23(3), 311–319. DOI: 10.1016/S0261-5177(01)00079-6

Charters, S., & Fountain, J. (2006). Younger Wine Tourists: A study of generational differences in the cellar door experience. In *Global wine tourism: Research, management and marketing* (pp. 153–160). Cabi. DOI: 10.1079/9781845931704.0153

Chaturvedi, R., & Verma, S. (2023). Opportunities and challenges of AI-driven customer service. *Artificial Intelligence in customer service: The next frontier for personalized engagement*, 33-71.

Chaudhary, K., Alam, M., Al-Rakhami, M. S., & Gumaei, A. (2021). Machine learning-based mathematical modelling for prediction of social media consumer behavior using big data analytics. *Journal of Big Data*, 8(1), 73. Advance online publication. DOI: 10.1186/s40537-021-00466-2

Chawla, Y., & Chodak, G. (2021). Social media marketing for businesses: Organic promotions of web-links on Facebook. *Journal of Business Research*, 135, 49–65. DOI: 10.1016/j.jbusres.2021.06.020

Cheah, I., & Shimul, A. S. (2023). Marketing in the metaverse: Moving forward - What's next? *Journal of Global Scholars of Marketing Science*, 33(1), 1–10. DOI: 10.1080/21639159.2022.2163908

Cheng, S. H., & Park, J. (2023). The role of AI in sentiment analysis for enhancing customer-brand relationships. *Computers in Human Behavior*, 142, 107812.

Cheng, X., & Jiang, Z. (2020a). Impact of artificial intelligence on customer-brand relationship. *Journal of Business Research*, 109, 112–120.

Cheng, X., & Jiang, Z. (2020b). AI in digital marketing: A case study on chatbot-powered branding. *Journal of Marketing Science*, 10(4), 159–171.

Cheng, Y., & Jiang, H. (2022). Customer–brand relationship in the era of artificial intelligence: Understanding the role of chatbot marketing efforts. *Journal of Product and Brand Management*, 31(2), 252–264. DOI: 10.1108/JPBM-05-2020-2907

Chen, L., Li, X., & Xu, Y. (2023). How AI is transforming marketing: Leveraging artificial intelligence in the AIDA model. *Journal of Marketing Technology*, 41(3), 56–72.

Chen, R., Zhou, Z., Zhan, G., & Zhou, N. (2020). The impact of destination brand authenticity and destination brand self-congruence on tourist loyalty: The mediating role of destination brand engagement. *Journal of Destination Marketing & Management*, 15, 100402. DOI: 10.1016/j.jdmm.2019.100402

Chen, Y., Zhang, X., & Liu, Y. (2023). Artificial intelligence and its impact on brand engagement: A consumer-focused perspective. *Journal of Marketing Management*, 39(2), 123–140.

Chen, Z. F., & Cheng, Y. (2020). Consumer response to fake news about brands on social media: The effects of self-efficacy, media trust, and persuasion knowledge on brand trust. *Journal of Product and Brand Management*, 29(2), 188–198. DOI: 10.1108/JPBM-12-2018-2145

Chintalapati, A., & Pandey, R. (2022). The Influence of Artificial Intelligence on Marketing Strategy. *AI in Business Journal*, 9(1), 98–110.

Chintalapati, R., & Pandey, N. (2022). Impact of AI-based recommendations on customer engagement in e-commerce. *Journal of Retail and Digital Marketing*, 18(4), 250–267.

Cho, C. H., & Cheon, H. J. (2004). Why do people avoid advertising on the internet? *Journal of Advertising*, 33(4), 89–97. DOI: 10.1080/00913367.2004.10639175

Chohan, R., & Schmidt-Devlin, E. (2024). Sports fandom in the metaverse: Marketing implications and research agenda. *Marketing Letters*, 35(1), 1–14. DOI: 10.1007/s11002-023-09702-6

Choi, J., Lee, H., & Kim, S. (2023). Enhancing brand loyalty through AI-driven personalization and sentiment analysis. *Journal of Brand Management*, 30(1), 18–32.

Chowdhury, R. H.. (2024). *The impact of predictive analytics on financial risk management in businesses.* World Journal of Advanced Research and Reviews., DOI: 10.30574/wjarr.2024.23.3.2807

Chung, K., Thaichon, P., & Quach, S. (2022). Types of artificial intelligence (AI) in marketing management. In *Artificial intelligence for marketing management* (pp. 29–40). Routledge. DOI: 10.4324/9781003280392-4

Chung, M., & Park, J. (2022). The impact of AI on brand management. *Journal of Brand Management*, 29(1), 1–15.

Chung, Y., Park, Y., & Kim, S. (2018). Understanding consumer attitudes toward AI-powered chatbots in digital marketing. *Journal of Business Research*, 92, 11–20.

Coelho, M. C. C. D., & Imamović, I. (2025). AI-driven personalization in beauty retail: exploring how AI-based applications influence customer satisfaction and brand loyalty. In *Leveraging AI for Effective Digital Relationship Marketing* (pp. 131–162). IGI Global.

Colicev, A. (2023). How can non-fungible tokens bring value to brands. *International Journal of Research in Marketing*, 40(1), 30–37. DOI: 10.1016/j.ijresmar.2022.07.003

Constantin, M., Genovese, G., Munawar, K., & Stone, R. (2023). *Tourism in the metaverse: Can travel go virtual?* McKinsey & Company. https://www.mckinsey.com/industries/travel-logistics-and-infrastructure/our-insights/tourism-in-the-metaverse-can-travel-go-virtual

Corluka, G. (2019). Tourism seasonality–an overview. *Journal of Business Paradigms*, 4(1), 21–43.

Corrales, D. C., Ledezma, A., & Corrales, J. C. (2020). A case-based reasoning system for recommendation of data cleaning algorithms in classification and regression tasks. *Applied Soft Computing*, 90, 106180. DOI: 10.1016/j.asoc.2020.106180

Cox, C., Burgess, S., Sellitto, C., & Buultjens, J. (2009). The Role of User-Generated Content in Tourists' Travel Planning Behavior. *Journal of Hospitality Marketing & Management*, 18(8), 743–764. DOI: 10.1080/19368620903235753

Crane, A., & Matten, D. (2016). *Business ethics: Managing corporate citizenship and sustainability in the age of globalization*. Oxford University Press.

Crespi-Vallbona, M., & Mascarilla-Miró, O. (2020). Wine lovers: Their interests in tourist experiences. *International Journal of Culture, Tourism and Hospitality Research*, 14(2), 239–258. DOI: 10.1108/IJCTHR-05-2019-0095

Crespo-Pereira, V., Sánchez-Amboage, E., & Membiela-Pollán, M. (2023). Facing the challenges of metaverse: A systematic literature review from Social Sciences and Marketing and Communication. *El Profesional de la Información*, 32(1), e320102. Advance online publication. DOI: 10.3145/epi.2023.ene.02

Creswell, J. W., & Creswell, J. D. (2022). *Research Design: Quantitative, qualitative, and mixed methods* (6th ed.). Sage.

Crispell, D. (2001). Going Green(ish). Public Perspective, September/October 2001, pp. 28-30

Cui, L., Huang, S., Wei, F., Tan, C., Duan, C., & Zhou, M. (2017). *SuperAgent: A Customer Service Chatbot for E-commerce Websites*. Microsoft Research Asia., DOI: 10.18653/v1/P17-4017

Cunha, C. R., Gomes, J. P., & Mendonça, V. (2024). The Role of Artificial Intelligence to Empower and Leverage Brands. In *AI Innovation in Services Marketing* (pp. 27–47). IGI Global. DOI: 10.4018/979-8-3693-2153-9.ch002

Dai, X., & Liu, Q. (2024). Impact of artificial intelligence on consumer buying behaviors: Study about the online retail purchase. *Journal of Infrastructure. Policy and Development*, 8(9), 7700. DOI: 10.24294/jipd.v8i9.7700

Danaher, P. J., & Mullarkey, G. W. (2003). Factors affecting online advertising recall: A study of students. *Journal of Advertising Research*, 43(3), 252–267. DOI: 10.2501/JAR-43-3-252-267

Danciu, V. (2021). Adapting and Modernizing the Post-Covid Market placing Policy Under the Impact of Consumption Challenges. *Romanian Economic Journal*, (79).

Daqar, M. a. A., & Smoudy, A. K. A. (2019). The role of artificial intelligence on enhancing customer experience

Daqar, M. A. M. A., & Smoudy, A. K. A. (2019, July 01). THE ROLE OF ARTIFICIAL INTELLIGENCE ON ENHANCING CUSTOMER EXPERIENCE. *International Review of Management and Marketing*, 9(4), 22–31. DOI: 10.32479/irmm.8166

Daugherty, T., Eastin, M. S., & Bright, L. (2008). Exploring consumer motivations for creating user-generated content. *Journal of Interactive Advertising*, 8(2), 16–25. DOI: 10.1080/15252019.2008.10722139

Davenport, T. (2019). Artificial Intelligence in Marketing: Present and Future Applications. *Marketing Intelligence Journal*, 15(5), 110–125.

Davenport, T. H. (2018). *The AI advantage: How to put the artificial intelligence revolution to work*. MIT Press. DOI: 10.7551/mitpress/11781.001.0001

Davenport, T. H., Dalle Mule, L., & Lucker, J. (2011). Know what your customers want before they do. *Harvard Business Review*, 89(12), 84–92.

Davenport, T., Guha, A., Grewal, D., & Bressgott, T. (2020). How artificial intelligence will change the future of marketing. *Journal of the Academy of Marketing Science*, 48(1), 24–42. DOI: 10.1007/s11747-019-00696-0

Davenport, T., & Ronanki, R. (2018). Artificial intelligence for the real world. *Harvard Business Review*, 96(1), 108–116.

Davenport, T., & Ronanki, R. (2018). Artificial Intelligence for the Real World. *Harvard Business Review*, 96(1), 108–116.

Davis, F. D. (1989). Perceived ease of use and perceived usefulness: A test of the technology acceptance model. *Journal of Management Information Systems*, 13(3), 319–340.

de Almeida, G. G. F. (2023). Cities and territorial brand in the metaverse: The metaverse Seoul case. *Sustainability (Basel)*, 15(13), 10116. Advance online publication. DOI: 10.3390/su151310116

De Cremer, D., Nguyen, B., & Simkin, L. (2017). Blockchain technology: What is it good for? *California Management Review*, 60(1), 64–87. DOI: 10.1177/0008125617741344

Deepika, M., & Kalaiselvi, K. (2021). Machine learning-based data analysis. In *Machine Learning Approach for Cloud Data Analytics in IoT* (pp. 01-24). wiley. DOI: 10.1002/9781119785873.ch1

Deryl, M. D., Verma, S., & Srivastava, V. (2023). How does AI drive branding? Towards an integrated theoretical framework for AI-driven branding. *International Journal of Information Management Data Insights*, 3(2), 100205. DOI: 10.1016/j.jjimei.2023.100205

Deventer, C., de Sousa, V. A., & Pirnay, L. (2024). NFTByBrands: Value Identification Framework for Analysis and Design of NFT Initiatives. *International Journal of Electronic Commerce*, 28(1), 33–62. DOI: 10.1080/10864415.2023.2295070

Devisivasankari, P., & Vijayakumar, R. (2023). Conversational AI Annotation System. *14th International Conference on Advances in Computing, Control, and Telecommunication Technologies, ACT 2023. 2023-June*, pp. 2788-2793. Hyderabad: Grenze Scientific Society. Retrieved Nov 26, 2024, from https://www.scopus.com/record/display.uri?eid=2-s2.0-85174395593&origin=scopusAI

Dewantara, M. H., Gardiner, S., & Jin, X. (2023). Travel vlog ecosystem in tourism digital marketing evolution: A narrative literature review. *Current Issues in Tourism*, 26(19), 3125–3139. DOI: 10.1080/13683500.2022.2136568

Dhingra, P. (2021). Ethics in AI: Navigating the complexities of algorithmic decision-making. *Journal of Ethics in Technology*, 15(3), 89–104.

Dias, P., & Cavalheiro, R. (2021). The role of storytelling in the creation of brand love: The PANDORA case. *Journal of Brand Management*, 29(1), 58–71. DOI: 10.1057/s41262-021-00254-6

Dias, P., & Duarte, A. (2022). How Portuguese adolescents relate to influencers and brands on TikTok. *Journal of Digital & Social Media Marketing*, 10(1), 82–95. DOI: 10.69554/VSHW2788

Dias, P., & Duarte, A. (2023). *Social Brand Management in a Post Covid-19 Era*. Taylor & Francis. DOI: 10.4324/9781003382331

Diglel, A., & Yazdanifard, R. (2014). Green marketing and its Influence on Buying Behavior and the Attitudes of Purchasers towards Eco-friendly products [online]. *Global Journal of Management and Business Research*, 7(11), 11–18.

Dikow, H., Hasan, O., Kosch, H., Brunie, L., & Sornin, R. (2015). Improving the accuracy of Business-to-Business (B2B) reputation systems through rater expertise prediction. *Computing*, 97(1), 29–49. DOI: 10.1007/s00607-013-0345-x

do Nascimento Santos, F. A., Vavdinos, N., & Martinez, L. F. (2020). Progress and prospects for research of Wine Tourism in Portugal. *Pasos (El Sauzal)*, 18(1), 159–170.

Dogan, S., Mistry, T. G., & Nanu, L. (2024). Revolutionizing getaways: Automation and artificial intelligence's transformative journey in tourism and hospitality. *Worldwide Hospitality and Tourism Themes*, 16(2), 248–251.

Dogru, T., Line, N., Mody, M., Hanks, L., Abbott, J. A., Acikgoz, F., & Zhang, T. (2023). Generative artificial intelligence in the hospitality and tourism industry: Developing a framework for future research. *Journal of Hospitality & Tourism Research (Washington, D.C.)*, •••, 10963480231188663.

Dong, Y., Huang, X., Sinha, K. K., & Xu, K. (2014). Collaborative demand forecasting:toward the design of an exception-based forecasting mechanism. *Journal of Management Information Systems*, 31(2), 245–284. DOI: 10.2753/MIS0742-1222310209

Duan, Y., Edwards, J. S., & Dwivedi, Y. K. (2019). Artificial intelligence for decision making in the era of Big Data–evolution, challenges and research agenda. *International Journal of Information Management*, 48, 63–71. DOI: 10.1016/j.ijinfomgt.2019.01.021

Duarte, A. (2023). *The relationship between brands and consumers*, in Social Brand Management in a Post Covid-19 Era, 3-16. Routledge. https://doi.org/DOI: 10.4324/9781003382331-2

Duarte, A., & Gregório, M. S. M. (2022). Empathic Brands: Proposing a Model for Its Measure and Evaluation. In Navigating Digital Communication and Challenges for Organizations (pp. 168-185). IGI Global. https://doi.org/[REMOVED HYPERLINK FIELD]9790-3.ch010DOI: 10.4018/978-1-7998

Duarte, A., & Dias, P. (2022). Post-Pandemic Changes in the Consumption Habits of the Portuguese. In *G. Sange & E.E. Basar (orgs.), Pandemics and Consumer Behavior* (pp. 189–207). Nova Science Publishers.

Durmaz, Y., & Baser, M. Y. (2023). A Systematic Literature Review on Artificial Intelligence Applications in Tourism Marketing. *International Journal of Research in Business Studies and Management*, 10(1), 21–30.

Dwivedi, A. (2015). A higher-order model of consumer brand engagement and its impact on loyalty intentions. *Journal of Retailing and Consumer Services*, 24, 100–109. DOI: 10.1016/j.jretconser.2015.02.007

Dwivedi, Y. K., Hughes, L., Baabdullah, A. M., Ribeiro-Navarrete, S., Giannakis, M., Al-Debei, M. M., Dennehy, D., Metri, B., Buhalis, D., Cheung, C. M. K., Conboy, K., Doyle, R., Dubey, R., Dutot, V., Felix, R., Goyal, D. P., Gustafsson, A., Hinsch, C., Jebabli, I., & Wamba, S. F. (2022). Metaverse beyond the hype: Multidisciplinary perspectives on emerging challenges, opportunities, and agenda for research, practice and policy. *International Journal of Information Management*, 66, 102542. Advance online publication. DOI: 10.1016/j.ijinfomgt.2022.102542

Dwivedi, Y. K., Hughes, L., Wang, Y. C., Alalwan, A. A., Ahn, S. J., Balakrishnan, J., Barta, S., Belk, R., Buhalis, D., Dutot, V., Felix, R., Filieri, R., Flavián, C., Gustafsson, A., Hinsch, C., Hollensen, S., Jain, V., Kim, J., Krishen, A. S., & Wirtz, J. (2023). Metaverse marketing: How the metaverse will shape the future of consumer research and practice. *Psychology and Marketing*, 40(4), 750–776. DOI: 10.1002/mar.21767

Dwivedi, Y. K., & Wang, Y. (2022). Guest editorial: Artificial intelligence for B2B marketing: Challenges and opportunities. *Industrial Marketing Management*, 105, 109–113. DOI: 10.1016/j.indmarman.2022.06.001

Dwivedi, Y.. (2021). The role of subjective norms in AI branding. *Journal of Marketing Theory and Practice*, 29(1), 45–67.

Ebrahim, R. S. (2020). The role of trust in understanding the impact of social media marketing on brand equity and brand loyalty. *Journal of Relationship Marketing*, 19(4), 287–308. DOI: 10.1080/15332667.2019.1705742

El Fawal, A., Mawlawi, A., Zakhem, N. B., Baydoun, H., Yassine, D., & Kassably, C. (2024). The impact of AI marketing activities on consumer-based brand equity: The mediating role of brand experience. *Journal of Infrastructure. Policy and Development*, 8(7), 3851. DOI: 10.24294/jipd.v8i7.3851

Elliott, R. H., Rosenbaum-Elliott, R., Percy, L., & Pervan, S. (2015). *Strategic brand management*. Oxford University Press.

El-Masri, M., Altrabsheh, N., & Mansour, H. (2017). Successes and challenges of Arabic sentiment analysis research: A literature review. *Social Network Analysis and Mining*, 7(1), 1–22. DOI: 10.1007/s13278-017-0474-x

Elsharnouby, M. H., Mohsen, J., Saeed, O. T., & Mahrous, A. A. (2021). Enhancing resilience to negative information in consumer-brand interaction: The mediating role of brand knowledge and involvement. *Journal of Research in Interactive Marketing*, 15(4), 571–591. DOI: 10.1108/JRIM-05-2020-0107

Erkollar, A., & Oberer, B. (2016). Multidimensional dashboards for evaluating strategic brand management processes for multi-brand companies. *Procedia: Social and Behavioral Sciences*, 235, 505–513. DOI: 10.1016/j.sbspro.2016.11.062

Espinet, J. M., Fluvià, M., Rigall-I-Torrent, R., & Saló, A. (2012). Hotel characteristics and seasonality in prices: An analysis using Spanish tour operators' brochures. *Tourism Economics*, 18(4), 749–767. DOI: 10.5367/te.2012.0145

Familoni, O., & Onyebuchi, A. (2024). Influence of peer recommendations on consumer behavior in digital spaces. *African Journal of Business and Consumer Studies*, 8(4), 89–101.

Farah, M. F., Ramadan, Z., & Nassereddine, Y. (2024). When digital spaces matter: The influence of uniqueness and place attachment on self-identity expression with brands using generative AI on the metaverse. *Psychology and Marketing*, 41(12), 2965–2976. Advance online publication. DOI: 10.1002/mar.22097

Farayola, O. A., Adaga, E. M., Egieya, Z. E., Ewuga, S. K., Abdul, A. A., & Abrahams, T. O.Oluwatoyin Ajoke FarayolaEjuma Martha AdagaZainab Efe EgieyaSarah Kuzankah EwugaAdekunle Abiola AbdulTemitayo Oluwaseun Abrahams. (2024). Advancements in predictive analytics: A philosophical and practical overview. *World Journal of Advanced Research and Reviews*, 21(3), 240–252. DOI: 10.30574/wjarr.2024.21.3.2706

Farooq, M., Ramzan, M., & Yen, Y. Y. (2024). Exploring the Impact of Artificial Intelligence on Brand Management: A Multi-Dimensional Analysis. *Transformative Impacts of AI in Management*, 157.

Farrell, C., Campbell, C., & Sands, S. (2022). Virtual Influencers in Branding and Consumer Engagement. *Journal of Interactive Marketing*, 20(2), 57–73.

Fehr, J. G., & French, A. M. (2022). Exploring the Characteristics and Needs of the Chief Privacy Officer in Organizations. *28th Americas Conference on Information Systems, AMCIS 2022*. Minneapolis: Association for Information Systems. Retrieved Nov 26, 2024, from https://www.scopus.com/record/display.uri?eid=2-s2.0-85180263632&origin=scopusAI

Fernandez, L. M. V., Nicolas, C., & Merigó, J. M. (2019). Industrial marketing research: A bibliometric analysis (1990-2015). *Journal of Business and Industrial Marketing*, 34(3), 550–560. DOI: 10.1108/JBIM-07-2017-0167

Ferraro, C., Hemsley, A., & Sands, S. (2023). Embracing diversity, equity, and inclusion (DEI): Considerations and opportunities for brand managers. *Business Horizons*, 66(4), 463–479. DOI: 10.1016/j.bushor.2022.09.005

Ferraro, C., Sands, S., Demsar, V., & Cohen, J. (2024). Diversity Representation in Virtual Environments: How Brand Motives Mediate Consumer Perceptions. *Australasian Marketing Journal*, 32(3), 239–249. Advance online publication. DOI: 10.1177/14413582241244535

Ferraro, C., Sands, S., & Tziati, N. (2022). Virtual influencers in social media: A branding perspective. *Journal of Brand Management*, 29(1), 24–38. DOI: 10.1057/s41262-021-00258-5

Fischer, M., Völckner, F., & Sattler, H. (2010). How important are brands? A cross-category, cross-country study. *JMR, Journal of Marketing Research*, 47(5), 823–839. DOI: 10.1509/jmkr.47.5.823

Fournier, S. (1998). Consumers and their brands: Developing relationship theory in consumer research. *The Journal of Consumer Research*, 24(4), 343–373. DOI: 10.1086/209515

French, K. (2018). Your new best friend: AI chatbot. Retrieved February 13, 2019 from https://futurism.com/ai-chatbot-meaningful-conversation

Galanakis, C. M., Rizou, M., Aldawoud, T. M., Ucak, I., & Rowan, N. J. (2021). Innovations and technology disruptions in the food sector within the COVID-19 pandemic and post-lockdown era. *Trends in Food Science & Technology*, 110, 193–200. DOI: 10.1016/j.tifs.2021.02.002 PMID: 36567851

Ganapathi, R., Rangarajan, A., & Mukherjee, A. (2022). Artificial intelligence and its impact on consumer-based brand equity. *Marketing Intelligence & Planning*, 40(1), 45–60.

Ganapathi, S., Subramanian, R., & Narayan, S. (2022). Personalization in branding: The influence of AI-driven experiences on consumer loyalty. *International Journal of Marketing Studies*, 14(3), 45–61.

Gans, J., Agrawal, A., & Goldfarb, A. (2017). How AI will change strategy: A thought experiment. Harvard Business Review online. Retrieved February 11, 2019 from https://hbr.org/product/how-ai-will-change-strategy-a-thought-experiment/H03XDI-PDF-ENG

Gao, B., Wang, Y., Xie, H., Hu, Y., & Hu, Y. (2023). Artificial intelligence in advertising: Advancements, challenges, and ethical considerations in targeting, personalization, content creation, and ad optimization. *SAGE Open*, 13(4), 21582440231210759. DOI: 10.1177/21582440231210759

Gao, D., Xia, H., Deng, W., Muskat, B., Li, G., & Law, R. (2022). Value creation in wine tourism–an exploration through deep neural networks. *Journal of Vacation Marketing*, 13567667221140605. Advance online publication. DOI: 10.1177/13567667221140605

Garibaldi, R., Stone, M. J., Wolf, E., & Pozzi, A. (2017). Wine travel in the United States: A profile of wine travellers and wine tours. *Tourism Management Perspectives*, 23, 53–57. DOI: 10.1016/j.tmp.2017.04.004

Garner, B., & Kim, D. (2022). Analyzing user-generated content to improve customer satisfaction at local wine tourism destinations: An analysis of Yelp and TripAdvisor reviews. *Consumer Behavior in Tourism and Hospitality*, 17(4), 413–435. DOI: 10.1108/CBTH-03-2022-0077

Gaudin, S. (2016). At Stitch Fix, data scientists and A.I. become personal stylists. Retrieved February 11, 2019 from https://www.computerworld.com/article/3067264/artificial-intelligence/at-stitch-fix-data-scientists-and-ai-become-personal-stylists.html

Gazi, M. S., Hasan, M. R., Gurung, N., & Mitra, A. (2024). Ethical Considerations in AI-driven Dynamic Pricing in the USA: Balancing Profit Maximization with Consumer Fairness and Transparency. *Journal of Economics. Finance and Accounting Studies*, 6(2), 100–111.

Gentner, D., Stelzer, B., Ramosaj, B., & Brecht, L. (2018). Strategic Foresight of Future B2B Customer Opportunities through Machine Learning. *Technology Innovation Management Review*, 8(10), 5–17. DOI: 10.22215/timreview/1189

Getz, D., & Brown, G. (2006). Critical success factors for wine tourism regions: A demand analysis. *Tourism Management*, 27(1), 146–158. DOI: 10.1016/j.tourman.2004.08.002

Ghani, N. H. B., & Tuhin, M. K. W. (2016). Consumer brand relationships. *International Review of Management and Marketing*, 6(4), 950–957. DOI: 10.2139/ssrn.3497812

Ghesh, N., Alexander, M., & Davis, A. (2023). The artificial intelligence-enabled customer experience in tourism: A systematic literature review. *Tourism Review*, 79(5), 1017–1037. DOI: 10.1108/TR-04-2023-0255

Godey, B., Manthiou, A., Pederzoli, D., Rokka, J., Aiello, G., Donvito, R., & Singh, R. (2016). Social media marketing efforts of luxury brands: Influence on Brand equity and customer behavior. *Journal of Business Research*, 69(12), 5833–5841. DOI: 10.1016/j.jbusres.2016.04.181

Gökerik, M., & Aktaş, Ö. Digital Marketing Trends Reshaped by Artificial Intelligence: A Bibliometric Approach. *JOEEP: Journal of Emerging Economies and Policy, 9*(1), 75-90.

Gołąb-Andrzejak, E. (2023). AI-powered digital transformation: Tools, benefits and challenges for marketers–case study of LPP. *Procedia Computer Science*, 219, 397–404. DOI: 10.1016/j.procs.2023.01.305

Gołąb-Andrzejak, E. (2024). AI-enhanced digital communication in marketing: Impact and future trends. *Journal of Digital Marketing*, 42(3), 215–230.

Grant, M. J., & Booth, A. (2009). A typology of reviews: An analysis of 14 review types and associated methodologies. *Health Information and Libraries Journal*, 26(2), 91–108. DOI: 10.1111/j.1471-1842.2009.00848.x PMID: 19490148

Greco, F., & Polli, A. (2020). Emotional Text Mining: Customer profiling in brand management. *International Journal of Information Management*, 51, 101934. DOI: 10.1016/j.ijinfomgt.2019.04.007

Guest, G., Bunce, A., & Johnson, L. (2006). How many interviews are enough? An experiment with data saturation and variability. *Field Methods*, 18(1), 59–82. DOI: 10.1177/1525822X05279903

Gujar, V. (2024). New Age Marketing: AI Personalization Strategies In Digital World. *IARJSET International Advanced Research Journal in Science, Engineering and Technology, 11(3).*

Gumparthi, V. P., & Patra, S. (2020). The phenomenon of brand love: A systematic literature review. *Journal of Relationship Marketing*, 19(2), 93–132. DOI: 10.1080/15332667.2019.1664871

Gupta, A., Raj, A., Puri, M., & Gangrade, J. Ethical Considerations in the Deployment of AI. *Tuijin Jishu/Journal of Propulsion Technology, 45*(2), 2024.

Gupta, S., & Joshi, S. (2022, November). Predictive analytic techniques for enhancing marketing performance and personalized customer experience. In 2022 *International Interdisciplinary Humanitarian Conference for Sustainability (IIHC) (pp. 16-22). IEEE*. DOI: 10.1109/IIHC55949.2022.10060286

Gupta, M., Sharma, R., & Verma, S. (2020). E-commerce and consumer behavior: How AI influences personalized shopping experiences. *International Journal of Marketing and E-commerce*, 22(3), 145–160.

Gupta, S., Gallear, D., Rudd, J., & Foroudi, P. (2020). The impact of brand value on brand competitiveness. *Journal of Business Research*, 112, 210–222. DOI: 10.1016/j.jbusres.2020.02.033

Gupta, Y., & Khan, F. M. (2024). Role of artificial intelligence in customer engagement: A systematic review and future research directions. *Journal of Modelling in Management*.

Gu, Q., Qiu, H., King, B. E., & Huang, S. (2020). Understanding the wine tourism experience: The roles of facilitators, constraints, and involvement. *Journal of Vacation Marketing*, 26(2), 211–229. DOI: 10.1177/1356766719880253

Gursoy, I. T., Aktas, E., Tecim, V., & Kurgun, O. A. (2023). Beta tourist world: A conceptual framework for organizing an event in the metaverse. *Information Technology & Tourism*, 25(4), 529–548. DOI: 10.1007/s40558-023-00266-9

Guzel, O., & Gromova, E. (2016). Wine tourism. *Global Issues and Trends in Tourism*, 383.

Habel, J., Alavi, S., & Heinitz, N. (2023). A theory of predictive sales analytics adoption. *AMS Review*, 13(1-2), 34–54. DOI: 10.1007/s13162-022-00252-0

Haenlein, M., & Kaplan, A. M. (2019). A brief history of artificial intelligence: On the past, present, and future of artificial intelligence. *California Management Review*, 61(4), 5–14. DOI: 10.1177/0008125619864925

Hajahmadi, S., Calvi, I., Stacchiotti, E., Cascarano, P., & Marfia, G. (2024). Heritage elements and Artificial Intelligence as storytelling tools for virtual retail environments. *Digital Applications in Archaeology and Cultural Heritage*, 34, e00368.

Haleem, A., Javaid, M., Qadri, M. A., Singh, R. P., & Suman, R. (2022). Artificial intelligence (AI) applications for marketing: A literature-based study. *International Journal of Intelligent Networks*, 3, 119–132. DOI: 10.1016/j.ijin.2022.08.005

Hallikainen, H., Luongo, M., Dhir, A., & Laukkanen, T. (2022). Consequences of personalized product recommendations and price promotions in online grocery shopping. *Journal of Retailing and Consumer Services*, 69, 103088. DOI: 10.1016/j.jretconser.2022.103088

Hamann, K. R., Wullenkord, M. C., Reese, G., & van Zomeren, M. (2023). Believing that we can change our world for the better: A Triple-A (Agent-Action-Aim) Framework of self-efficacy beliefs in the context of collective social and ecological aims. *Personality and Social Psychology Review*, •••, 10888683231178056. PMID: 37386819

Hamichi, S., Mangalagiu, D., & Guessoum, Z. (2013). A Multi-Agent System for production networks simulation: Toward a pheromone-based model for agents' coordination. In Supply Chain Management: Concepts, Methodologies, Tools, and Applications (pp. 1666-1682). IGI Global.

Han, J., Ma, Y., Mei, Q., & Liu, X. (2021, April). DeepRec: On-device deep learning for privacy-preserving sequential recommendation in mobile commerce. In *Proceedings of the Web Conference 2021* (pp. 900-911). DOI: 10.1145/3442381.3449942

Han, Y., Li, H., & Zhang, W. (2022). Generative adversarial networks in AI-driven product design: Implications for branding. *Journal of Business Research*, 131, 1–13.

Han, Y., Wu, L., & Zhao, T. (2022). AI-driven predictive analytics in fashion retail: Enhancing consumer engagement. *Fashion and Textile Research Journal*, 10(4), 256–270.

Hashem, T. N. (2021). Environmental legitimacy through adopting green products and its effect on the brand equity: Moderating role of management awareness. *Review of World Economics*, 12(2), 197–210.

Hashem, T. N. (2023). The Influence of Rebranding on Brand Value Within Cosmetic Industry Sector: Mediating Role of Value Engineering. *Journal of Law and Sustainable Development*, 11(11), e1701–e1701. DOI: 10.55908/sdgs.v11i11.1701

Hashem, T. N., Al-Qeed, M., & Qtaish, R. M. (2024). Brand Linguistics: The Influence of Using Local Terminology Through Social Media in Marketing Products on Customers' Purchase Behavior. *Journal of System and Management Sciences*, 14(2), 291–309.

Hashem, T. N., & Al-Zyoud, M. F. (2020). Influence Of Decoy Marketing On Impulsive Purchasing Behavior Among Adult Customers Of Tech Market In Jordan, Mediating Role Of Brand Equity. *Image*, 7(15), 2020.

Hays, S., Page, S. J., & Buhalis, D. (2013). Social media as a destination marketing tool: Its use by national tourism organisations. *Current Issues in Tourism*, 16(3), 211–239. DOI: 10.1080/13683500.2012.662215

Heaven, W. D. (2019). The humans teaching AI to understand feelings. MIT Technology Review. Retrieved February 11, 2019 from https://www.technologyreview.com/2019/02/12/103694/the-humans-teaching-ai-to-understand-feelings/

Heding, T., Knudtzen, C. F., & Bjerre, M. (2020). *Brand management: Mastering research, theory and practice*. Routledge. DOI: 10.4324/9780367172596

He, G. S., Tran, T. T. H., & Leonidou, L. C. (2024). It's here to stay: Lessons, reflections, and visions on digital transformation amid public crisis. *Technological Forecasting and Social Change*, 206, 123557.

Heinemann, G., Sonntag, K., & Groß, M. (2023). Best Practices for AI in Retail: Also for Multisensory? In *Multisensory in Stationary Retail: Principles and Practice of Customer-Centered Store Design* (pp. 167–181). Springer Fachmedien Wiesbaden. DOI: 10.1007/978-3-658-38227-8_12

Heinrich, D., Albrecht, C. M., & Bauer, H. H. (2012). *Love actually? Measuring and exploring consumers' brand love. Consumer-Brand Relationships–Theory and Practice*. Routledge.

Hemadharshini, S., Kanchana Devi, R., Rajakumari, S., & Adline, F. R. (2024). E-commerce Customer Segmentation by Unsupervised Learning. *6th International Conference on Soft Computing and Signal Processing, ICSCSP 2023*. 864, pp. 285-296. Hyderabad: Springer Science and Business Media Deutschland GmbH. DOI: 10.1007/978-981-99-8628-6_25

Hermann, E. (2022). Leveraging artificial intelligence in marketing for social good—An ethical perspective. *Journal of Business Ethics*, 179(1), 43–61. DOI: 10.1007/s10551-021-04843-y PMID: 34054170

Hermawan, H., Hersona, S., &Suyaman, D. J. (2024). The Effect Of Influencer Marketing, Content Marketing, And Price Perceptions On Consumer Purchase Intention (An Investigation Of Luxcrime Cosmetic Consumers In Karawang). *At-Tadbir: jurnalilmiahmanajemen, 8*(2), 189-205.

Hirschman, E. C., & Holbrook, M. B. (1982). Hedonic consumption: Emerging concepts, methods and propositions. *Journal of Marketing*, 46(3), 92–101. DOI: 10.1177/002224298204600314

Hodorog, A., Petri, I., & Rezgui, Y. (2022). Machine learning and Natural Language Processing of social media data for event detection in smart cities. *Sustainable Cities and Society*, 85, 104026. DOI: 10.1016/j.scs.2022.104026

Hofer, K. M., & Grohs, R. (2018). The role of internal branding in the workplace culture of brand management. *Journal of Brand Management*, 25(4), 341–354. DOI: 10.1057/s41262-018-0098-3

Hofstetter, R., de Bellis, E., Brandes, L., Clegg, M., Lamberton, C., Reibstein, D., Rohlfsen, F., Schmitt, B., & Zhang, J. Z. (2022). Crypto-marketing: How non-fungible tokens (NFTs) challenge traditional marketing. *Marketing Letters*, 33(4), 705–711. DOI: 10.1007/s11002-022-09639-2

Högberg, K., & Willermark, S. (2023). Strategic responses to digital disruption in incumbent firms–a strategy-as-practice perspective. *Journal of Computer Information Systems*, 63(2), 281–292. DOI: 10.1080/08874417.2022.2057373

Holbrook, M. B. (1999). *Consumer Value: A Framework for Analysis and Research*. Routledge.

Holbrook, M. B., & Hirschman, E. C. (1982). The experiential aspects of consumption: Consumer fantasies, feelings, and fun. *The Journal of Consumer Research*, 9(2), 132–140. DOI: 10.1086/208906

Hollebeek, L. D., Glynn, M. S., & Brodie, R. J. (2014). Consumer brand engagement in social media: Conceptualization, scale development and validation. *Journal of Interactive Marketing*, 28(2), 149–165. DOI: 10.1016/j.intmar.2013.12.002

Homburg, C., Krohmer, H., & Workman, J. P.Jr. (2004). A strategy implementation perspective of market orientation. *Journal of Business Research*, 57(12), 1331–1340. DOI: 10.1016/S0148-2963(03)00069-9

Homer, P. M., & Kahle, L. R. (1988). A structural equation test of the value-attitude-behavior hierarchy. *Journal of Personality and Social Psychology*, 54(4), 638.

Ho, S. P. S., & Chow, M. Y. C. (2024). The role of artificial intelligence in consumers' brand preference for retail banks in Hong Kong. *Journal of Financial Services Marketing*, 29(2), 292–305. DOI: 10.1057/s41264-022-00207-3

Hoyer, W. D. Mirja Kroschke, Bernd Schmitt, Karsten Kraume, & Venkatesh Shankar. (2020). Transforming the customer experience through new technologies. In Journal of Interactive Marketing (Vol. xx, p. xxx) [Journal-article]. https://doi.org/ DOI: 10.1016/j.intmar.2020.04.001

Hoyer, W. D., MacInnis, D. J., & Pieters, R. (2020). *Consumer behavior* (7th ed.). Cengage Learning.

Huang, M. H., & Rust, R. T. (2018). Artificial intelligence in service. *Journal of Service Research*, 21(2), 155–172. DOI: 10.1177/1094670517752459

Huang, M. H., & Rust, R. T. (2021). A strategic framework for artificial intelligence in marketing. *Journal of the Academy of Marketing Science*, 49(1), 30–50. DOI: 10.1007/s11747-020-00749-9

Huang, M. H., & Rust, R. T. (2021). Artificial intelligence in service: Implications for service research and branding. *Journal of Service Research*, 24(1), 8–29.

Huang, M.-H., & Rust, R. T. (2021). Engaged to a robot? The role of AI in service branding. *Journal of Service Research*, 24(1), 30–41. DOI: 10.1177/1094670520902266

Huang, Y., Liu, H., Li, W., Wang, Z., Hu, X., & Wang, W. (2019). Lifestyles in amazon: Evidence from online reviews enhanced recommender system. *International Journal of Market Research*, 62(6), 689–706. DOI: 10.1177/1470785319844146

Hung, H.-C., Kim, J.-K., & Calugcug, C. C. (2010). Dynamical pricing strategy for one-manufacturer and two-retailer supply chain model. *International Journal of Mathematical Models and Methods in Applied Sciences*, 04(03), 195–202. Retrieved November 14, 2024, from https://www.scopus.com/record/display.uri?eid=2-s2.0-78649336844&origin=scopusAI

Hussain, Z., Mari, I. H., & Rind, A. A. (2022). Exploring The Barriers of Artificial Intelligence Adoption in Digital Marketing Landscape. *ULIL ALBAB: Jurnal Ilmiah Multidisiplin*, 1(4), 824–835.

Hussain, Z., & Saad, N. M. (2023). Investigating the Efficacy of Artification in the Context of Digital Marketing for Corporate Social Responsibility: Examining the Moderating Influence of Brand Authenticity. [IJCBE]. *International Journal of Contemporary Business and Economics*, 1(1), 57–68. DOI: 10.61338/ijcbe.v1i1.1

Hussain, Z., Sultan, R., Asadullah, A., Arif, M., & Ali, A. (2022). The Impact of Zakat Literacy, Trust, and the Accessibility of Digital Payments on Generation Z and Y's Intention to Pay Zakat to Central Zakat Fund, the State Bank of Pakistan. *International Journal of Zakat*, 7(2), 105–114.

IAMAI. (2022). *India's Internet revolution: Growth projections and market insights*. Internet and Mobile Association of India.

Iansiti, M., & Lakhani, K. R. (2020). *Competing in the age of AI: Strategy and leadership when algorithms and networks run the world*. Harvard Business Press.

İbrahim Halil Efendioğlu, "The Change of Digital Marketing with Artificial Intelligence"

Ifekanandu, C. C., Anene, J. N., Iloka, C. B., & Ewuzie, C. O. (2023). Influence of artificial intelligence (AI) on customer experience and loyalty: Mediating role of personalization. *Journal of Data Acquisition and Processing*, 38(3), 1936.

Igbinenikaro, O., & Adewusi, K. (2024). Influence of social media interactions on consumer behavior: A comprehensive review. *Journal of Digital Marketing*, 15(5), 223–245.

Iglesias, O., & Ind, N. (2020). Towards a theory of conscientious corporate brand co-creation: The next key challenge in brand management. *Journal of Brand Management*, 27(6), 710–720. DOI: 10.1057/s41262-020-00205-7

Igorevich Rozhdestvenskiy, O., & Poornima, E. (2024). Enabling sustainable urban transportation with predictive analytics and iot. MATEC Web of Conferences, 392, 01179. DOI: 10.1051/matecconf/202439201179

Ihzaturrahma, N., & Kusumawati, N. (2021). Influence of Integrated Marketing Communication To Brand Awareness and Brand Image Toward Purchase Intention of Local Fashion Product. *International Journal of Entrepreneurship and Management Practices*, 4(15), 23–41. DOI: 10.35631/IJEMP.415002

Indrawan, D., Yorman, Y., Stiadi, M., Hendayani, N., & Al-Amin, A. A. (2023). Revolutionizing social media marketing through AI and automation: An in-depth analysis of strategies, ethics, and future trends. *International Journal of Humanities* [INJOSS]. *Social Sciences and Business*, 3(1), 22–45.

Isidore, R., & Arun, C. J. (2021). An enquiry into the purchase intention of AI–based virtual personal voice assistants in India. [IJBE]. *International Journal of Business & Economics*, 6(2), 52–63.

Isidore, R., & Arun, C. J. (2023). Are Indian Consumers willing to share personal data to avail personalized recommendations?-Indian Artificial Intelligence Market Perspective. [Formerly known as Iranian Journal of Management Studies]. *Interdisciplinary Journal of Management Studies*, 17(1), 277–293.

Isidore, R., & Arun, C. J. (2023). Dimensions of indian consumers' beliefs about AI: An orthogonal linear transformation approach. *Revista Gestão & Tecnologia*, 23(1), 10–28.

Iyer, P., Davari, A., & Paswan, A. K. (2019). Market orientation, brand management processes, and brand performance. *Journal of Business Research*, 119, 464–472. DOI: 10.1016/j.jbusres.2019.08.020

Jabo, D., Kant, S., & Borji, B. (2025). Customer Orientation and Ethiopian Bank Performance With Mediation of Competitive Advantage. In Leveraging AI for Effective Digital Relationship Marketing (pp. 459-482). IGI Global. DOI: 10.4018/979-8-3693-5340-0.ch015

Jamali, H. R., Steel, C. C., & Mohammadi, E. (2020). Wine research and its relationship with wine production: A scientometric analysis of global trends. *Australian Journal of Grape and Wine Research*, 26(2), 130–138. DOI: 10.1111/ajgw.12422

Jamil, K., Dunnan, L., Gul, R. F., Shehzad, M. U., Gillani, S. H. M., & Awan, F. H. (2022). Role of social media marketing activities in influencing customer intentions: A perspective of a new emerging era. *Frontiers in Psychology*, 12, 808525. DOI: 10.3389/fpsyg.2021.808525 PMID: 35111111

Jangam, D. S., & Deshpande, A. R. (2023). Business analytics using predictive algorithms. *International Journal on Recent and Innovation Trends in Computing and Communication*, 11(8s), 595–609. DOI: 10.17762/ijritcc.v11i8s.7242

Jankovic, S., & Curovic, T. (2023). Ensuring fairness in AI models: Addressing algorithmic bias in digital brand management. *Journal of Ethical AI in Branding*, 15(2), 95–108.

Jansen, B. J., Aldous, K. K., Salminen, J., Almerekhi, H., & Jung, S.-g. (2024). Social Media Analytics. In *Synthesis Lectures on Information Concepts, Retrieval, and Services* (Vol. F1359, pp. 79-93). Springer Nature. DOI: 10.1007/978-3-031-41933-1_7

Javed, U., Rashid, M. A., Hussain, G., & Shafique, S. (2023). Consumers' perception of green brand attributes and its outcomes: A sustainable perspective. *Journal of Environmental Planning and Management*, •••, 1–23.

Jelonek, D., Kumar, N., & Pawełoszek, I. (2024). Artificial Intelligence Applications In Brand Management. *Scientific Papers of Silesian University of Technology. Organization & Management/Zeszyty Naukowe Politechniki Slaskiej. Seria Organizacji i Zarzadzanie*, (202).

Jeong, H., Yi, Y., & Kim, D. (2022). An innovative e-commerce platform incorporating metaverse to live commerce. *International Journal of Innovative Computing, Information, & Control*, 18(1), 221–229. DOI: 10.24507/ijicic.18.01.221

Jeong, I., Jean, R. J. B., Kim, D., & Samiee, S. (2023). Managing disruptive external forces in international market placing. *International Market placing. RE:view*, 40(5), 936–956.

Jha, P. (2022). Personalisation in branding: How AI is transforming consumer engagement in India. *International Journal of Marketing*, 40(4), 312–327.

Jiang, Q., Kim, M., Ko, E. J., & Kim, K. H. (2023). The metaverse experience in luxury brands. *Asia Pacific Journal of Marketing and Logistics*, 35(10), 2501–2520. DOI: 10.1108/APJML-09-2022-0752

Jiang, Z. (2018). Data-driven design: How AI is changing the way we create. *IEEE Computer Graphics and Applications*, 38(4), 75–79.

Jin, H., & Lowry, P. B. (2021). Using sentiment analysis to analyze brand emotions in social media. *Management Information Systems Quarterly*, 45(2), 571–599.

Johnson, H. (2018). The age of AI: How artificial intelligence is changing our lives. Retrieved February 11, 2019 from https://www.theatlantic.com/technology/archive/2018/11/ai-and-the-age-of-the-internet-of-things/575992/

Jooste, J. L., & Vlok, P. J. (2015). A decision support model to determine the critical success factors of asset management services. *South African Journal of Industrial Engineering*, 26(1), 27–43. DOI: 10.7166/26-1-1043

Jorge, B., & Ross, A. (2019) "Artificial Intelligence Ethics: Governance through Social Media," Conference Paper, IEEE International Symposium on Technologies for Homeland Security.vol.10,no.1109,November,pp 1-4.

Jorzik, P., Antonio, J. L., Kanbach, D. K., Kallmuenzer, A., & Kraus, S. (2024). Sowing the seeds for sustainability: A business model innovation perspective on artificial intelligence in green technology startups. *Technological Forecasting and Social Change*, 208, 123653.

Joy, A., Zhu, Y., Peña, C., & Brouard, M. (2022). Digital future of luxury brands: Metaverse, digital fashion, and non-fungible tokens. *Strategic Change*, 31(3), 337–343. DOI: 10.1002/jsc.2502

Juglan, K. C., Sharma, B., Gehlot, A., Singh, S. P., Hussein, A., & Alazzam, M. B. (2023). Exploring the Effectiveness of Natural Language Processing in Customer Service. *3rd International Conference on Advance Computing and Innovative Technologies in Engineering, ICACITE 2023* (pp. 814-818). Greater Noida: Institute of Electrical and Electronics Engineers Inc. DOI: 10.1109/ICACITE57410.2023.10183107

Jun, S., & Yi, J. (2020). What makes followers loyal? The role of influencer interactivity in building influencer brand equity. *Journal of Product and Brand Management*, 29(6), 803–814. DOI: 10.1108/JPBM-02-2019-2280

Kacar, M. (2023). Application of AI in Customer Experience Management. In Hannig, U., & Seebacher, U. (Eds.), *Marketing and Sales Automation. Management for Professionals*. Springer., DOI: 10.1007/978-3-031-20040-3_26

Kang, R., Dabbish, L., & Sutton, K. (2016, February). Strangers on your phone: Why people use anonymous communication applications. In *Proceedings of the 19th ACM conference on computer-supported cooperative work & social computing* (pp. 359-370). DOI: 10.1145/2818048.2820081

Kang, Y., Cai, Z., Tan, C. W., Huang, Q., & Liu, H. (2020). Natural language processing (NLP) in management research: A literature review. *Journal of Management Analytics*, 7(2), 139–172. DOI: 10.1080/23270012.2020.1756939

Kannan, R. (2024). Revolutionizing the Tourism Industry through Artificial Intelligence: A Comprehensive Review of AI Integration, Impact on Customer Experience, Operational Efficiency, and Future Trends. *International Journal for Multidimensional Research Perspectives, 2(2), 01-14.*

Kant, S., & Adula, M. (2024). Mediated by AI-Based Generative Re-Enforcement Learning and Work Attitude: Are Intrinsic Rewards Transforming Employee Perceived Organizational Support? In Gomathi Sankar, J., & David, A. (Eds.), *Generative AI for Transformational Management* (pp. 83–108). IGI Global., DOI: 10.4018/979-8-3693-5578-7.ch004

Kaperonis, S. (2024). How artificial intelligence (AI) is transforming the user experience in digital marketing. In *The use of artificial intelligence in digital marketing: Competitive strategies and tactics* (pp. 117–141). IGI Global.

Kapferer, J. N. (2008). *The new strategic brand management: Creating and sustaining brand equity long term*. Kogan Page Publishers.

Kaplan, J. (2016). The age of AI: How artificial intelligence is changing our world. Forbes, March 15. Retrieved February 11, 2019 from https://www.forbes.com/sites/joshkaplan/2016/03/15/the-age-of-ai-how-artificial-intelligence-is-changing-our-world/

Karim, S., Saxena, S., Singh, D. A., Deshmukh, P., Lokare, A. B., Gour, O. G., ... & Ranjan, M. K. (2023). Revolutionising Marketing: Leveraging Blockchain and AI for Impactful Management.

Katragadda, V. (2024). Ethical AI in Customer Interactions: Implementing Safeguards and Governance Frameworks. *Iconic Research And Engineering Journals*, 7(12), 394–397.

Kattel, S. (2023). *Implementation of an AI-based Content Creation Strategy in the Wine Tourism Organization: The case study at Winalist*. University of Bordeaux.

Katz, D., Kahn, R. L., & Adams, J. S. (1973). *The social psychology of organizations* (2nd ed.). Wiley.

Katz, E., Blumler, J. G., & Gurevitch, M. (1973). Uses and gratifications research. *Public Opinion Quarterly*, 37(4), 509–523. DOI: 10.1086/268109

Katz, E., & Lazarsfeld, P. F. (2017). *Social influence and the mass media*. Free Press.

Kaur, J., Mogaji, E., Paliwal, M., Jha, S., Agarwal, S., & Mogaji, S. A. (2024). Consumer behavior in the metaverse. *Journal of Consumer Behaviour*, 23(4), 1720–1738. DOI: 10.1002/cb.2298

Keller, K. L. (1993). Conceptualizing, measuring, and managing customer-based brand equity. *Journal of Marketing*, 57(1), 1–22. DOI: 10.1177/002224299305700101

Keller, K. L. (2003). *Strategic brand management: Building, measuring, and managing brand equity* (2nd ed.). Pearson.

Kelley, L. D., Sheehan, K. B., Dobias, L., Koranda, D. E., & Jugenheimer, D. W. (2022). *Advertising media planning: a brand management approach*. Routledge. DOI: 10.4324/9781003258162

Kerkkanen, A., Huiskonen, J., Korpela, J., & Pirttila, T. (2012). How do managers perceive the needs of sales forecasting process improvement in a B2B environment. *International Journal of Management Practice*, 5(2), 107–124. DOI: 10.1504/IJMP.2012.047580

Khaled, W. (2024). Securing brand trust and reputation in an era of political polarisation and AI-driven disinformation. *Journal of Brand Strategy*, 13(1), 6–14. DOI: 10.69554/PJFE5856

Khan, A. W., & Mishra, A. (2024). AI credibility and consumer-AI experiences: A conceptual framework. *Journal of Service Theory and Practice*, 34(1), 66–97. DOI: 10.1108/JSTP-03-2023-0108

Khan, A., Abu Bakar, A. H., Saad, N. M., Hussain, Z., & Arif, A. R. (2023). *Effectiveness of Artificial Intelligence in Building Customer Loyalty: Investigating the Mediating Role of Chatbot in the Tourism Sector of Pakistan*. Human Resource Management Academic Research Society.

Khan, A., Hamid, A. B. A., Saad, N. M., Hussain, Z., & Arif, A. R. (2023). Effectiveness of artificial intelligence in building customer loyalty: Investigating the mediating role of chatbot in the tourism sector of Pakistan. *International Journal of Academic Research in Business & Social Sciences*, 13(9), 657–671. DOI: 10.6007/IJARBSS/v13-i9/18895

Khandelwal, R.. (2020). *Comparative Analysis of Machine Learning Techniques Using Predictive Modeling*. Recent Advances in Computer Science and Communications., DOI: 10.2174/2666255813999200904164539

Khan, S. A. R., Ponce, P., Tanveer, M., Aguirre-Padilla, N., Mahmood, H., & Shah, S. A. A. (2021). Technological innovation and circular economy practices: Business strategies to mitigate the effects of COVID-19. *Sustainability (Basel)*, 13(15), 8479. DOI: 10.3390/su13158479

Khan, S. I. (2022). Impact of artificial intelligence on consumer buying behaviors: Study about the online retail purchase. *International Journal of Health Sciences*, (II), 8121–8129.

Kharfan, M., LeBlanc, A., & Miller, R. (2021). Predictive analytics in brand management: AI's role in inventory and pricing strategies. *Journal of Business Analytics and Marketing Strategies*, 13(1), 58–74.

Kietzmann, J. H., Hermkens, K., McCarthy, I. P., & Silvestre, B. S. (2018). Social media? Get serious! Understanding the functional building blocks of social media. *Business Horizons*, 54(3), 241–251. DOI: 10.1016/j.bushor.2011.01.005

Kim, A. J., & Ko, E. (2012). Do social media marketing activities enhance customer equity? An empirical study of luxury fashion brand. *Journal of Business Research*, 65(10), 1480–1486. DOI: 10.1016/j.jbusres.2011.10.014

Kim, D., Lee, J., & Cho, S. (2022). Virtual assistants and chatbots: Enhancing customer satisfaction in branding. *Journal of Interactive Marketing*, 55, 1–16.

Kim, H. Y., Lee, J. Y., Choi, D., Wu, J., & Johnson, K. K. P. (2013). Perceived Benefits of Retail Loyalty Programs: Their Effects on Program Loyalty and Customer Loyalty. *Journal of Relationship Marketing*, 12(2), 95–113. DOI: 10.1080/15332667.2013.794100

Kim, I., Ki, C. W., Lee, H., & Kim, Y. K. (2024). Virtual influencer marketing: Evaluating the influence of virtual influencers' form realism and behavioral realism on consumer ambivalence and marketing performance. *Journal of Business Research*, 176, 114611. DOI: 10.1016/j.jbusres.2024.114611

Kim, J., & Bae, J. (2023). Influences of persona self on luxury brand attachment in the Metaverse context. *Asia Pacific Journal of Marketing and Logistics*. Advance online publication. DOI: 10.1108/APJML-05-2022-0390

Kim, J., Giroux, M., & Lee, J. C. (2021). When do you trust AI? The effect of number presentation detail on consumer trust and acceptance of AI recommendations. *Psychology and Marketing*, 38(7), 1140–1155. DOI: 10.1002/mar.21498

Kim, S., & Wang, D. (Eds.). (2021). *Future of Tourism Marketing*. Routledge.

Kim, Y., Lee, H., & Park, J. (2022). AI-powered ecosystems and their impact on consumer experiences in e-commerce. *Electronic Commerce Research and Applications*, 52, 101141.

King, C., & Grace, D. (2012). Examining the antecedents of positive employee brand-related attitudes and behaviours. *European Journal of Marketing*, 46(3/4), 469–488. DOI: 10.1108/03090561211202567

Kiradoo, G. (2023). Unlocking the potential of ai in business: Challenges and ethical considerations. *Recent Progress in Science and Technology*, 6, 205–220. DOI: 10.9734/bpi/rpst/v6/18935D

Kirubahari, R., & Amali, S. M. J. (2024). An improved restricted Boltzmann machine using Bayesian optimization for recommender systems. *Evolving Systems*, 15(3), 1099–1111. DOI: 10.1007/s12530-023-09520-1

Klaus, P., & Zaichkowsky, J. (2020). AI voice bots: A services marketing research agenda. *Journal of Services Marketing*, 34(3), 389–398. DOI: 10.1108/JSM-01-2019-0043

Klimanov, D., & Tretyak, O. (2019). Linking business model research and marketing: New network-based approach to business model analysis. *Journal of Business and Industrial Marketing*, 34(1), 117–136. DOI: 10.1108/JBIM-12-2017-0330

Kniazeva, M., Aiello, G., Dasmi, C., Mazzoli, V., Nechaeva, O., & Syed, F. U. (2024). Why fashion brands enter the metaverse: Exploring the motivations of fast fashion and luxury fashion brands. *Journal of Global Fashion Marketing, 15*(1), 62-89. *Article*, 2269952. Advance online publication. DOI: 10.1080/20932685.2023.2269952

Kompella, K. (2017, September-October). How to achieve personalization on a global scale. *EContent (Wilton, Conn.)*, 40(05), 36–38. Retrieved November 11, 2024, from https://www.scopus.com/record/display.uri?eid=2-s2.0-85028673728&origin=scopusAI

Kopalle, P. K., Pauwels, K., Akella, L. Y., & Gangwar, M. (2023, December). Dynamic pricing: Definition, implications for managers, and future research directions. *Journal of Retailing*, 99(04), 580–593. DOI: 10.1016/j.jretai.2023.11.003

Koponen, J. P., & Rytsy, S. (2020). Social presence and e-commerce B2B chat functions. *European Journal of Marketing*, 54(6), 1205–1224. DOI: 10.1108/EJM-01-2019-0061

Kotler, K. (2016). Koshy and Jha. *Marketing Management*, 13, 2015–2016.

Kotler, P., Kartajaya, H., & Setiawan, I. (2023). *Marketing 6.0: The Future is Immersive*. John Wiley & Sons.

Kot, M. T., & Leszczyński, G. (2020). The concept of intelligent agent in business interactions: Is virtual assistant an actor or a boundary object? *Journal of Business and Industrial Marketing*, 35(7), 1155–1164. DOI: 10.1108/JBIM-10-2018-0291

Krafft, M., Kumar, V., Harmeling, C., Singh, S., Zhu, T., Chen, J., Duncan, T., Fortin, W., & Rosa, E. (2021). Insight is power: Understanding the terms of the consumer-firm data exchange. *Journal of Retailing*, 97(1), 133–149. DOI: 10.1016/j.jretai.2020.11.001

Kshetri, N. (2022). Web 3.0 and the metaverse shaping organizations' brand and product strategies. *IT Professional*, 24(2), 11–15. DOI: 10.1109/MITP.2022.3157206

Kshetri, N. (2023). Metaverse technologies in product management, branding and communications: Virtual and augmented reality, artificial intelligence, non-fungible tokens and brain-computer interface. *Central European Management Journal*, 31(4), 511–521. DOI: 10.1108/CEMJ-08-2023-0336

Kshirsagar, P. S., & Pawar, A. M. (2023). Predictive analytics for cyber threats to enhance security in the cyber supply chain. *Research Journal of Computer Systems and Engineering*, 4(1), 102–109. DOI: 10.52710/rjcse.68

Kubát, P., Králiková, A., & Ryglová, K. (2024). Shifting the Focus from mere Wine (and) Tourism to the Wine Destination and Winescape Concept. *Deturope-The Central European Journal of Regional Development and Tourism*, 15(3), 78–92. DOI: 10.32725/det.2023.018

Kumar, A.; Gupta, N.; Bapat, G. Who is making the decisions? How retail managers can use the power of ChatGPT. J. Bus. Strategy 2023. ahead-of-Print

Kumar, A., Bezawada, R., Rishika, R., Janakiraman, R., & Kannan, P. K. (2016). From Social to Sale: The Effects of Firm-Generated Content in Social Media on Customer Behavior. *Journal of Marketing*, 80(1), 7–25. DOI: 10.1509/jm.14.0249

Kumar, A., & Singh, R. (2019). Impact of artificial intelligence on the marketing strategies of Indian firms. International Journal of Research in Commerce. *IT & Management*, 9(4), 25–30.

Kumar, A., & Singh, R. (2022). The role of AI in consumer-centric branding. *Journal of Marketing Analytics*, 25(1), 45–58.

Kumar, D., & Suthar, N. (2024). Ethical and legal challenges of AI in marketing: An exploration of solutions. *Journal of Information. Communication and Ethics in Society*, 22(1), 124–144. DOI: 10.1108/JICES-05-2023-0068

Kumar, G., Seshasai, S. J., & Shriya, K. (2024). Tailored to Perfection: How AI-Driven Service Customization Is Revolutionizing Emerging Markets. In *Integrating AI-Driven Technologies Into Service Marketing* (pp. 575–594). IGI Global. DOI: 10.4018/979-8-3693-7122-0.ch028

Kumari, L., & Aggrawal, D. R. (2022). An Insight into Predictive Analytics Techniques. *International Journal for Research in Applied Science and Engineering Technology*, 10(12), 984–987. Advance online publication. DOI: 10.22214/ijraset.2022.48071

Kumari, R., Verma, R., Debata, B. R., & Ting, H. (2022). A systematic literature review on the enablers of green marketing adoption: Consumer perspective. *Journal of Cleaner Production*, 366, 132852. DOI: 10.1016/j.jclepro.2022.132852

Kumar, V., Ashraf, A. R., & Nadeem, W. (2024). AI-powered marketing: What, where, and how? *International Journal of Information Management*, 77, 102783. DOI: 10.1016/j.ijinfomgt.2024.102783

Kumar, V., & Dey, D. (2020). AI and consumer engagement in marketing: A framework for MSMEs. *JMR, Journal of Marketing Research*, 57(3), 95–113.

Kumar, V., Shah, D., & Gupta, S. (2024). AI-powered personalization in brand marketing: Trends and strategies. *JMR, Journal of Marketing Research*, 61(2), 101–117.

Kumar, V., Shah, D., & Rajan, B. (2016). Digital Communication in a Modern Business Framework. *Marketing Communications*, 7(2), 151–168.

Labib, E. (2024). Artificial intelligence in marketing: Exploring current and future trends. *Cogent Business & Management*, 11(1), 2348728. DOI: 10.1080/23311975.2024.2348728

Lee, C. T., Ho, T. Y., & Xie, H. H. (2023). Building brand engagement in metaverse commerce: The role of branded non-fungible tokens (BNFTs). *Electronic Commerce Research and Applications*, 58, 101248. Advance online publication. DOI: 10.1016/j.elerap.2023.101248

Lee, C. T., Pan, L. Y., & Hsieh, S. H. (2022). Artificial intelligent chatbots as brand promoters: A two-stage structural equation modeling-artificial neural network approach. *Internet Research*, 32(4), 1329–1356. DOI: 10.1108/INTR-01-2021-0030

Lee, M., Lee, S., & Lee, H. (2021). The impact of AI transparency on consumer trust: The moderating role of brand reputation. *The Journal of Consumer Research*, 48(3), 431–450.

Lee, S., Kim, Y., & Oh, H. (2021). The impact of transparency on trust in AI-driven branding: Evidence from the technology acceptance model. *Journal of Business Ethics*, 169(2), 383–400.

Le, M. T. (2024). How does influencer marketing build up the engagement between brand and followers? *International Journal of Internet Marketing and Advertising*, 21(1-2), 3–25. DOI: 10.1504/IJIMA.2024.140447

Lemos, M., Cardoso, P. J., & Rodrigues, J. M. (2024). Harnessing AI and NLP Tools for Innovating Brand Name Generation and Evaluation: A Comprehensive Review. *Multimodal Technologies and Interaction*, 8(7), 56. DOI: 10.3390/mti8070056

Liao, M., & Sundar, S. S. (2022). When e-commerce personalization systems show and tell: Investigating the relative persuasive appeal of content-based versus collaborative filtering. *Journal of Advertising*, 51(2), 256–267. DOI: 10.1080/00913367.2021.1887013

Liao, X., Zhao, Z., Barth, M. J., Abdelraouf, A., Gupta, R., Han, K., Ma, J., & Wu, G. (2024). A review of personalization in driving behavior: Dataset, modeling, and validation. *IEEE Transactions on Intelligent Vehicles*, 1–22. DOI: 10.1109/TIV.2024.3425647

Li, H., & Vargo, S. L. (2019). A service-dominant logic perspective on artificial intelligence in marketing. *Journal of Marketing Theory and Practice*, 27(1), 1–19.

Limba, T., & Juozėnaitė, E. (2024). Opportunities for Public Relations Specialists to Enhance their Knowledge in Managing Negative UGC. In *INTED2024 Proceedings* (pp. 1874-1883). IATED. DOI: 10.21125/inted.2024.0530

Lim, W. M., Jee, T. W., & De Run, E. C. (2020). Strategic brand management for higher education institutions with graduate degree programs: Empirical insights from the higher education marketing mix. *Journal of Strategic Marketing*, 28(3), 225–245. DOI: 10.1080/0965254X.2018.1496131

Lim, X. J., Radzol, A. M., Cheah, J., & Wong, M. W. (2017). The impact of social media influencers on purchase intention and the mediation effect of customer attitude. *Asian Journal f Business Research*, 7(2), 19–36. DOI: 10.14707/ajbr.170035

Lindgreen, A., & Swaen, V. (2010). Corporate social responsibility: An ethical approach to business strategy. *Business and Society Review*, 115(3), 365–384.

Ling, G. Y., Yuang, G., Zhicheng, G., Xuan, G. T. X., Maharani, C. D., Genira, C. F., & Saidhanyakumar, M. (2023). Analysis of factors affecting brand loyalty: A study of Coca-Cola. [APJME]. *Asia Pacific Journal of Management and Education*, 6(3), 16–29. DOI: 10.32535/apjme.v6i3.2635

Lissah, S. Y., Ayanore, M. A., Krugu, J. K., Aberese-Ako, M., & Ruiter, R. A. (2021). Managing urban solid waste in Ghana: Perspectives and experiences of municipal waste company managers and supervisors in an urban municipality. *PLoS One*, 16(3), e0248392. DOI: 10.1371/journal.pone.0248392 PMID: 33705483

Liu, H., Wang, F., & Zhang, P. (2024). AI applications in dynamic branding strategies: Insights and implications. *Strategic Marketing Journal*, 32(1), 77–98.

Liu, X., & Shin, K. (2018). The impact of artificial intelligence on human decision-making in business environments. *Technological Forecasting and Social Change*, 136, 130–139.

Liu, Y., & Chen, W. (2021). Optimization of brand marketing strategy of intelligent technology under the background of artificial intelligence. *Mobile Information Systems*, 2021(1), 9507917. DOI: 10.1155/2021/9507917

Liu, Y., Zhang, X., & Xie, Y. (2024). Leveraging predictive analytics in branding: Dynamic capabilities for competitive advantage. *Journal of Strategic Marketing*, 32(1), 45–58.

Li, Y. (2023). Big data analysis in consumer behavior: Evidence from social media and mobile payment. Advances in Economics. *Management and Political Sciences*, 64(1), 269–275. DOI: 10.54254/2754-1169/64/20231548

Li, Y., Wang, S., & Li, Z. (2024). Animating arousal and engagement: Empirical insights into AI-enhanced robotic performances and consumer reactions. *Journal of Hospitality and Tourism Technology*, 15(5), 737–768.

Ljepava, N. (2022). AI-enabled marketing solutions in Marketing Decision making: AI application in different stages of marketing process. *TEM Journal*, 11(3), 1308–1315. DOI: 10.18421/TEM113-40

Loufek, B., Vidal, D., McClintock, D. S., Lifson, M., Williamson, E., Overgaard, S., & Pardi, D. S. (2024). Embedding Internal Accountability into Healthcare Institutions for Safe, Effective, and Ethical Implementation of Artificial Intelligence into Medical Practice: A Mayo Clinic Case Study. *Mayo Clinic Proceedings. Digital Health.*

Loureiro, S. M. C. (2011, November). Consumers love and willingness to sacrifice for a brand. In Conference book Proceedings of ANZMAC conference-Marketing in the Age of Consumerism: Jekyll or Hyde (pp. 28-30).

Loureiro, S. M. C., & Bilro, R. G. (2022). AI in brands and consumer relationships: Where we are and where we are heading. *Journal of Business Research*, 139, 1063–1073. DOI: 10.1016/j.jbusres.2021.10.014

Loureiro, S. M. C., Ruediger, K. H., & Demetris, V. (2012). Brand emotional connection and loyalty. *Journal of Brand Management*, 20(1), 13–27. DOI: 10.1057/bm.2012.3

Luo, S., & Hamlin, R. (2022). A cross cultural comparison of brand love in consumer brand relationships: Is 'transmissive brand love' a potential platform for developing brand equity? *Journal of Brand Management*, 29(5), 484–497. DOI: 10.1057/s41262-022-00286-6

Machová, R., Ambrus, R., Zsigmond, T., & Bakó, F. (2022). The impact of green marketing on consumer behavior in the market of palm oil products. *Sustainability (Basel)*, 14(3), 1364. DOI: 10.3390/su14031364

Madadi, R., Torres, I. M., & Zúñiga, M. Á. (2021). Hierarchical relationships among brand equity dimensions: The mediating effects of brand trust and brand love. *Services Marketing Quarterly*, 42(1-2), 74–92. DOI: 10.1080/15332969.2021.1947086

Madani, B.. (2021). *Predicting Consumer Purchasing Decision in The Online Food Delivery Industry*. ArXiv. DOI: 10.5121/csit.2021.111510

Madeleine, S., & Sihombing, S. O. (2019). The impacts of brand experiences on brand love, brand trust, and brand loyalty: an empirical study. *Jurnal Bisnis dan Manajemen, 20*(2), 91-107. https://doi.org/DOI: 10.24198/jbm.v20i2.241

Mahadev Madgule, N. (2023). Vinayaka, Yeshwant M. Sonkhaskar, Dhiren Ramanbhai Patel, R. Karthikeyan, P. Selvakumar,(2023). Mechanical properties and microstructure of activated TIG welded similar joints of Inconel alloys by desirability approaches. *Materials Today: Proceedings*, 77, 528–533. DOI: 10.1016/j.matpr.2022.12.250

Mahmood, N. Z., Ahmed, S. R., Al-Hayaly, A. F., Algburi, S., & Rasheed, J. (2023, October). The Evolution of Administrative Information Systems: Assessing the Revolutionary Impact of Artificial Intelligence. In *2023 7th International Symposium on Multidisciplinary Studies and Innovative Technologies (ISMSIT)* (pp. 1-7). IEEE.

Makosa, S. (2024). Brand Management Driven by Artificial Intelligence.

Malhotra, N., & Malhotra, K. (2017). Artificial intelligence and its impact on marketing strategies. *Journal of Business Research*, 82, 159–168.

Malik, S. (2020). Artificial Intelligence for Social Media safety and security. *International Engineering Journal*, 5, 5–7.

Malter, M. S., Holbrook, M. B., Kahn, B. E., Parker, J. R., & Lehmann, D. R. (2020). The past, present, and future of consumer research. *Marketing Letters*, 31(2-3), 137–149. DOI: 10.1007/s11002-020-09526-8 PMID: 32836799

Manap, K. A., & Adzharudin, N. A. (2013, January). The role of user generated content (UGC) in social media for tourism sector. In *The 2013 WEI international academic conference proceedings* (Vol. 7, No. 1, pp. 52-58).

Mandák, J. (2017). Comparison of logistic regression and decision tree for customer churn prediction in Telecommunications. *12th International Conference on Strategic Management and its Support by Information Systems 2017, SMSIS 2017* (pp. 282-292). Ostrava: VSB-Technical University of Ostrava. Retrieved Nov 13, 2024, from https://www.scopus.com/record/display.uri?eid=2-s2.0-85026304194&origin=scopusAI

Mansoor, S., Rahman, S. M., & Bowden, J. L. H. (2024). Purchase spillovers from the metaverse to the real world: The roles of social presence, trialability, and customer experience. *Journal of Consumer Behaviour*, 23(5), 2501–2552. Advance online publication. DOI: 10.1002/cb.2353

Manthiou, A., Kang, J., Hyun, S. S., & Fu, X. X. (2018). The impact of brand authenticity on building brand love: An investigation of impression in memory and lifestyle-congruence. *International Journal of Hospitality Management*, 75, 38–47. DOI: 10.1016/j.ijhm.2018.03.005

Mariani, M. M., Perez-Vega, R., & Wirtz, J. (2022). AI in marketing, consumer research and psychology: A systematic literature review and research agenda. *Psychology and Marketing*, 39(4), 755–776. DOI: 10.1002/mar.21619

Marinchak, C., Forrest, E., & Hoanca, B. (2018). AI and personalization in marketing. *Journal of Research in Interactive Marketing*, 12(4), 516–534.

Marius, G., & Angela, E. (2018, December). "Using Artificial Intelligence on Social Media's User Generated Content for Disruptive Marketing Strategies in ecommerce." Annals of "Dunarea de Jos" University of Galati Fascicle I. *Economics and Applied Informatics*, 10(3), 5–11.

Marr, B. (2018). The 10 best examples of how companies use AI in marketing. Forbes, July 19. Retrieved February 11, 2019 from https://www.forbes.com/sites/bernardmarr/2018/07/19/the-10-best-examples-of-how-companies-use-ai-in-marketing/

Marr, B. (2024). Forbes. Retrieved November 5, 2024 from https://www.forbes.com/sites/bernardmarr/2024/07/26/beyond-the-metaverse-top-immersive-internet-trends-for-the-next-decade/

Marr, B. (2020). How Artificial Intelligence is Transforming Digital Marketing. *Journal of AI in Marketing*, 8(4), 67–92.

Martin Charter. (1999) Greener Marketing: A Global Perspective on Greener Marketing Practice https://www.worldcat.org/title/greener-marketing-a-global-perspective-on-greenermarketing-practice/oclc/247076134

Martin, K., Shilton, K., & Smith, J. E. (2022). Business and the ethical implications of technology: Introduction to the symposium. In *Business and the ethical implications of technology* (pp. 1–11). Springer Nature Switzerland. DOI: 10.1007/978-3-031-18794-0_1

Masnita, Y., Ali, J. K., Zahra, A., Wilson, N., & Murwonugroho, W. (2024). Artificial intelligence in marketing: Literature review and future research agenda. *Journal of System and Management Sciences*, 14(1), 120–140.

Matz, S. C., & Netzer, O. (2017). Using big data as a window into consumers' psychology. *Current Opinion in Behavioral Sciences*, 18, 7–12. DOI: 10.1016/j.cobeha.2017.05.009

McKinsey and Company. (2022). *Value Creation in the Metaverse*. McKinsey. https://www.mckinsey.com/capabilities/growth-marketing-and-sales/our-insights/value-creation-in-the-metaverse

Mehraj, D., Qureshi, I. H., Singh, G., Nazir, N. A., Basheer, S., & Nissa, V. U. (2023). Green marketing practices and green consumer behavior: Demographic differences among young consumers. *Business Strategy & Development*, 6(4), 571–585. DOI: 10.1002/bsd2.263

Mehta, A., Singh, R., & Kaur, P. (2023). Ethical AI and its role in branding: Balancing innovation with responsibility. *Journal of Business Research*, 150, 46–59.

Mehta, R., & Jain, S. (2023). AI-driven marketing strategies: Personalization and automation in the digital age. *Digital Marketing Quarterly*, 11(1), 55–74.

Mehta, S., Sharma, P., & Joshi, A. (2023). AI-driven loyalty programs: Leveraging data analytics for customer retention. *Journal of Consumer Marketing*, 40(2), 125–137.

Mell, S., & Alexander, L. (2024). *Hornung, Catherine Yuh, Dino Samartzis*. Virtual Clinical Trials - Implications of Computer Simulations and Artificial Intelligence for Musculoskeletal Research.

Mendes, A. R., Duarte, A. P., & Simões, M. C. (2013). The Portuguese wine sector: an export-led success story. In *Agriculture in Serbia and Portugal* (pp. 287–318). Recent Developments and Economic Policy Implications.

Milano, S., Taddeo, M., & Floridi, L. (2020). Recommender systems and their ethical challenges. *AI & Society*, 35(4), 957–967. DOI: 10.1007/s00146-020-00950-y

Miles, S. J., & Mangold, G. (2004). A conceptualization of the employee branding process. *Journal of Relationship Marketing*, 3(2-3), 65–87. DOI: 10.1300/J366v03n02_05

Mills, A. J., & Robson, K. (2020). Brand management in the era of fake news: Narrative response as a strategy to insulate brand value. *Journal of Product and Brand Management*, 29(2), 159–167. DOI: 10.1108/JPBM-12-2018-2150

Minsky, L., & Kotler, P. (2024). Sustainable Practices and Demarketing: An Interview with Philip Kotler. *Advertising & Society Quarterly, 25*(1).

Mishra, A., Singh, J., & Kumar, P. (2020). Adoption of artificial intelligence in retail marketing: A study on consumer trust and perceptions. *International Journal of Retail & Distribution Management*, 48(3), 258–276.

Mishra, D., Das, S., & Patnaik, R. (2024). Application of AI Technology for the Development of Destination Tourism towards an Intelligent Information System. *Economic Affairs*, 69(2), 1083–1095.

Mogaji, E., Dwivedi, Y. K., & Raman, R. (2024). Fashion marketing in the metaverse. *Journal of Global Fashion Marketing*, 15(1), 115–130. DOI: 10.1080/20932685.2023.2249483

Moghaddasnian, A. H. (2024). Artificial Intelligence and the Great Transformation in the Tourism Industry Revolutionizing Travel Services. *Journal of Business Data Science Research*, 3(01), 36–47.

Mohseni, S., Brent, A. C., Kelly, S., & Browne, W. N. (2022). Demand response-integrated investment and operational planning of renewable and sustainable energy systems considering forecast uncertainties: A systematic review. *Renewable & Sustainable Energy Reviews*, 158, 112095. DOI: 10.1016/j.rser.2022.112095

Mohsin, M., Jamil, K., Naseem, S., Sarfraz, M., & Ivascu, L. (2022). Elongating nexus between workplace factors and knowledge hiding behavior: Mediating role of job anxiety. *Psychology Research and Behavior Management*, 15, 441–457. DOI: 10.2147/PRBM.S348467 PMID: 35250318

Moore, S., Bulmer, S., & Elms, J. (2021). The social significance of AI in retail on customer experience and shopping practices. *Journal of Retailing and Consumer Services*, 64, 102755. DOI: 10.1016/j.jretconser.2021.102755

Morgan, R. M., & Hunt, S. D. (1994). The commitment-trust theory of relationship marketing. *Journal of Marketing*, 58(3), 20–38. DOI: 10.1177/002224299405800302

Moslehpour, M., Yin Chau, K., Du, L., Qiu, R., Lin, C. Y., &Batbayar, B. (2023). Predictors of green purchase intention toward eco-innovation and green products: Evidence from Taiwan. *Economic research-Ekonomskaistraživanja, 36*(2).

Mouret, M., Monaco, G. L., Urdapilleta, I., & Parr, W. V. (2013). Social representations of wine and culture: A comparison between France and New Zealand. *Food Quality and Preference*, 30(2), 102–107. DOI: 10.1016/j.foodqual.2013.04.014

Muchenje, C., Mtengwa, E., & Kabote, F. (2023). Building a strong brand: Future strategies and insights. In *Sustainable Marketing, Branding, and Reputation Management: Strategies for a Greener Future* (pp. 238-257). IGI Global.

Mukherjee, S. (2023). Understanding the Role of Data in Artificial Intelligence-Based Personalization. In *Artificial Intelligence in Customer Service: The Next Frontier for Personalized Engagement* (pp. 155–177). Springer International Publishing. DOI: 10.1007/978-3-031-33898-4_7

Mukherjee, S., & Jha, S. (2022). Artificial intelligence in branding: Transforming customer experiences in e-commerce. *Marketing Intelligence & Planning*, 40(3), 350–364.

Mulyati, S., Putriani, R. D., Goestjahjanti, F. S., Marusaha, T. J., Farhan, A., Mendrofa, Y., & Purno, M. (2024). Analysis of The Influencer Marketing, Ratings and Customer Reviews on Purchasing Decisions. *Journal of E-business and Management Science*, 2(1), 230–239.

Murphey, Y. L., Kolmanovsky, I., & Watta, P. (2022). Advances, Opportunities and Challenges in AI-enabled Technologies for Autonomous and Connected Vehicles. *AI-enabled Technologies for Autonomous and Connected Vehicles*, 1-16.

Murtas, G., Pedeliento, G., & Mangio, F. (2024). Luxury fashion brands at the gates of the Web 3.0: An analysis of early experimentations with NFTs and the metaverse. *Journal of Global Fashion Marketing*, 15(1), 90–114. DOI: 10.1080/20932685.2023.2249476

Musa, H. G., Garad, A., & Mussa, M. (2024). Trends and Innovations in Tourism Marketing Within Government Policy. *JIAN-Jurnal Ilmiah Administrasi Negara*, 8(2), 28–48.

Musaiqer, H. H., & Hamdan, A. (2023). The Role of Artificial Intelligence in Brand Building: A Review. *Emerging Trends and Innovation in Business and Finance*, 307-318.

Mustak, M.. (2021). Toward a unified theory of AI-driven branding. *Journal of Business Research*, 135, 335–346.

Mustak, M., Salminen, J., Plé, L., & Wirtz, J. (2021). Artificial intelligence in marketing: Topic modeling, scientometric analysis, and research agenda. *Journal of Business Research*, 124, 389–404. DOI: 10.1016/j.jbusres.2020.10.044

Mutyala, V., Anaparthi, V., Mundru, Y., & Yogi, M. K. (2022). Frontiers of AI beyond 2030: Novel Perspectives. *Journal of Artificial Intelligence*, 4(4), 246–262.

Myint, K., ... (2023). Predictive Analytics System for Stock Data: methodology, data pre-processing and case studies. International Conferences on Computing Advancements. DOI: 10.1109/ICCA51723.2023.10182047

Nadarajah, D., & Bakar, A. (2019). Marketing in the age of AI: Challenges and opportunities. *Journal of Marketing Management*, 35(3-4), 238–261.

Naeem, M., & Khawaja, H. (2019). The impact of artificial intelligence on consumer behavior. International Journal of Business and Management, 14(6), 36-48. (Naeem & Khawaja, 2019)

Naga Srinivasu, P., Ijaz, M. F., & Woźniak, M. (2024). XAI-driven model for crop recommender system for use in precision agriculture. *Computational Intelligence*, 40(1), e12629. DOI: 10.1111/coin.12629

Nair, V. (2023). AI's impact on consumer insights and brand decision-making. *The Journal of Consumer Research*, 48(2), 224–239.

Nalbant, K. G., & Aydın, S. (2023). Development and transformation in digital marketing and branding with artificial intelligence and digital technologies dynamics in the Metaverse universe. *Journal of Metaverse*, 3(1), 9–18. DOI: 10.57019/jmv.1148015

Nalla, L. N., & Reddy, V. M. (2024). AI-Driven Big Data Analytics for Enhanced Customer Journeys: A New Paradigm in E-Commerce. *International Journal of Advanced Engineering Technologies and Innovations*, 1(2), 719–740.

Natarajan, T., Pragha, P., Dhalmahapatra, K., & Raghavan, D. R. V. (2024). Exploring tourist's metaverse experience using destination spatial presence quality & perceived augmentation: Metaverse exploration, physical expedition (MEPE). *Current Issues in Tourism*, 1–23. Advance online publication. DOI: 10.1080/13683500.2024.2372652

Nazlan, N. H., Zhang, H., Sun, J., & Chang, W. (2024). Navigating the online reputation maze: Impact of review availability and heuristic cues on restaurant influencer marketing effectiveness. *Journal of Hospitality Marketing & Management*, 33(3), 288–307. DOI: 10.1080/19368623.2023.2246471

Necula, S. C., & Păvăloaia, V. D. (2023). AI-Driven Recommendations: A Systematic review of the state of the art in E-Commerce. *Applied Sciences (Basel, Switzerland)*, 13(9), 5531. DOI: 10.3390/app13095531

Nella, A., & Christou, E. (2014). Segmenting wine tourists on the basis of involvement with wine. *Journal of Travel & Tourism Marketing*, 31(7), 783–798. DOI: 10.1080/10548408.2014.889639

Neves, C., Oliveira, T., & Santini, F. (2022). Sustainable technologies adoption research: A weight and meta-analysis. *Renewable & Sustainable Energy Reviews*, 165, 112627. DOI: 10.1016/j.rser.2022.112627

Ngai, E. W. T. (2005). Customer Relationship Management in the Digital Age. *International Journal of CRM*, 9(3), 203–216.

Nguyen, N. P., & Mogaji, E. (2023). Artificial Intelligence for Seamless Experience Across Channels. In *Artificial Intelligence in Customer Service: The Next Frontier to Personalized Engagement* (pp. 181-203). Springer International Publishing. DOI: 10.1007/978-3-031-33898-4_8

Nguyen, C., Tran, T., & Nguyen, T. (2024). Factors affecting users' brand awareness through social media marketing on TikTok. *Innovative Marketing*, 20(1), 122–131. DOI: 10.21511/im.20(1).2024.11

Nguyen, P. H., Nguyen, D. N., & Nguyen, L. A. T. (2023). Quantitative insights into green purchase intentions: The interplay of health consciousness, altruism, and sustainability. *Cogent Business & Management*, 10(3), 2253616. DOI: 10.1080/23311975.2023.2253616

Nguyen, T. (2023). Exploring the Effectiveness of Virtual Influencers in Brand Promotion. *Journal of Social Media Research*, 17(2), 89–107.

Nguyen, T. D. (2024). *New Technologies in Travelling and Tourism*. Brno University of Technology.

Nia, N. B. (2023). Brand Management Internationalization: Case Study of Nike. *Journal of International Trade. Logistics and Law*, 9(2), 181–187.

Nichifor, E., Trifan, A., & Nechifor, E. M. (2021). Artificial intelligence in electronic commerce: Basic chatbots and the consumer journey. *Amfiteatru Economic*, 23(56), 87–101. DOI: 10.24818/EA/2021/56/87

Niguse, T., Kant, S., & Adula, M. (2025). Mediation Effect of Customer Loyalty in Relationship between Market Orientation, Entrepreneurial Orientation, and Firm Performance in Ethiopia. In Leveraging AI for Effective Digital Relationship Marketing (pp. 419-458). IGI Global. DOI: 10.4018/979-8-3693-5340-0.ch014

Niininen, O. (2022). *Contemporary Issues in Digital Marketing*. Routledge.

Nimbalkar, A. A., & Berad, A. T. (2021). The increasing importance of AI applications in e-commerce. *Vidyabharati International Interdisciplinary Research Journal*, 13(1), 388–391.

Nina, S. (2024). https://www.latterly.org/. Retrieved Nov 25, 2024, from Spotify Marketing Strategy 2024: A Case Study: https://www.latterly.org/spotify-marketing-strategy/

Nishat, N.. (2024). Predictive Analytics for Business Decision-Making: Unleashing the Power of Data-driven Insights. *International Conference on Computing Communication and Networking Technologies*. DOI: 10.1109/ICCCNT61001.2024.10724574

Nufer, G., & Muth, M. (2022). Artificial intelligence in marketing analytics: The application of artificial neural networks for brand image measurement. *Journal of Marketing Development and Competitiveness*, 16(1), 55–63.

Nugroho, H. (2023). A review: Data quality problem in predictive analytics. [International Journal of Applied Information Technology]. *IJAIT*, 7(02), 79. DOI: 10.25124/ijait.v7i02.5980

Oanh, V. T. K. (2024). Revolutionizing Engagement: How AI is Transforming the Digital Marketing Landscape. *Journal of Electrical Systems*, 20(4s), 2504–2514. DOI: 10.52783/jes.2914

Ochuba, N. A., Usman, F. O., Okafor, E. S., Akinrinola, O., & Amoo, O. O. (2024). Predictive analytics in the maintenance and reliability of satellite telecommunications infrastructure: A conceptual review of strategies and technological advancements. Engineering Science &Amp. *Technology Journal*, 5(3), 704–715. DOI: 10.51594/estj.v5i3.866

Odonkor, A., Agyei, D., & Asante, J. (2024). Data Analytics in Digital Marketing. *Marketing Research and Insights*, 14(2), 33–45.

Ogiemwonyi, O., Alam, M. N., Alshareef, R., Alsolamy, M., Azizan, N. A., & Mat, N. (2023). Environmental factors affecting green purchase behaviors of the consumers: Mediating role of environmental attitude. *Cleaner Environmental Systems*, 10, 100130. DOI: 10.1016/j.cesys.2023.100130

Oh, L. B., & Teo, H. H. (2020). Consumer value co-creation in a multi-channel environment: Analyzing the role of information technology. *International Journal of Information Management*, 52, 102067.

Olusegun, J. (2024). The Role of AI in Enhancing Sentiment Analysis for Brand Management.

Ottman, J.A., Stafford, E.R., Hartman, C.L., (2006). Green marketing myopia. Environment 48 (5), 22e36.

Ottoman, J., & Mallen, D. (2014). 5 *Green Marketing strategies to earn consumer trust*. Available at:https://www.greenbiz.com/blog/2014/01/14/five-strategies-avoid-taint-greenwash-your-business

Oyekunle, D., Boohene, D., & Preston, D. (2024). Ethical Considerations in AI-Powered Work Environments: A Literature Review and Theoretical Framework for Ensuring Human Dignity and Fairness. *Valley International Journal Digital Library*, 6166-6178.

Palimkar, P., Shaw, R. N., & Ghosh, A. (2022). Machine learning technique to prognosis diabetes disease: Random forest classifier approach. In *Advanced computing and intelligent technologies: proceedings of ICACIT 2021* (pp. 219–244). Springer Singapore. DOI: 10.1007/978-981-16-2164-2_19

Palumbo, S., & Edelman, D. (2023). What smart companies know about integrating AI. *Harvard Business Review*, 101(7–8), 116–125.

Palusuk, N., Koles, B., & Hasan, R. (2019). 'All you need is brand love': A critical review and comprehensive conceptual framework for brand love. *Journal of Marketing Management*, 35(1-2), 97–129. DOI: 10.1080/0267257X.2019.1572025

Pan, B., & Fesenmaier, D. R. (2006). Online information search: Vacation planning process. *Annals of Tourism Research*, 33(3), 809–832. DOI: 10.1016/j.annals.2006.03.006

Pancić, M., Serdarušić, H., & Ćućić, D. (2023). Green Marketing and Repurchase Intention: Stewardship of Green Advertisement, Brand Awareness, Brand Equity, Green Innovativeness, and Brand Innovativeness. *Sustainability (Basel)*, 15(16), 12534. DOI: 10.3390/su151612534

Pangburn, D. (2018). AI is learning how to read human emotions. The Verge. Retrieved February 11, 2019 from https://www.theverge.com/2018/10/16/17982392/emotional-ai-human-feelings-research-2018

Pantelic, O., Jovic, K., & Krstovic, S. (2022). Cookies implementation analysis and the impact on user privacy regarding GDPR and CCPA regulations. *Sustainability (Basel)*, 14(9), 5015. DOI: 10.3390/su14095015

Paraschi, E. P., Panagopoulos, A., & Fragkogianni, M. (2024). COVID-19 crisis management in Greek airlines. *Journal of the Air Transport Research Society*, 3, 100032.

Paripati, L., Hajari, V. R., Narukulla, N., Prasad, N., Shah, J., & Agarwal, A. (2024). AI Algorithms for Personalization: Recommender Systems, Predictive Analytics, and Beyond. *Darpan International Research Analysis*, 12(2), 51–63.

Park, C. W., Eisingerich, A. B., & Park, J. W. (2013). Attachment-aversion (AA) model of customer-brand relationships. *Journal of Consumer Psychology*, 23(2), 229–248. DOI: 10.1016/j.jcps.2013.01.002

Park, C. W., MacInnis, D. J., Priester, J., Eisingerich, A. B., & Iacobucci, D. (2010). Brand attachment and brand attitude strength: Conceptual and empirical differentiation of two critical brand equity drivers. *Journal of Marketing*, 74(6), 1–17. DOI: 10.1509/jmkg.74.6.1

Park, H., & Lim, R. E. (2023). Fashion and the metaverse: Clarifying the domain and establishing a research agenda. *Journal of Retailing and Consumer Services*, 74, 103413. Advance online publication. DOI: 10.1016/j.jretconser.2023.103413

Park, J., & Kim, N. (2024). Examining self-congruence between user and avatar in purchasing behavior from the metaverse to the real world. *Journal of Global Fashion Marketing*, 15(1), 23–38. DOI: 10.1080/20932685.2023.2180768

Paschen, J. (2020). Investigating the emotional appeal of fake news using artificial intelligence and human contributions. *Journal of Product and Brand Management*, 29(2), 223–233. DOI: 10.1108/JPBM-12-2018-2179

Pasupulati, R., Mahendran, J., & Majumdar, A. (2024). Predictive Analysis of Digital Consumer Behaviour: Key to Understanding Success and Failure of a Brand. In *Enhancing and Predicting Digital Consumer Behavior with AI* (pp. 238-267). IGI Global.

Patil, D., Rane, N. L., & Rane, J. (2024). The future of customer loyalty: How ChatGPT and generative artificial intelligence are transforming customer engagement, personalization, and satisfaction. *The Future Impact of ChatGPT on Several Business Sectors*, 48-106. Khan, S., & Iqbal, M. (2020, June). AI-Powered Customer Service: Does it optimize customer experience? In *2020 8th International Conference on Reliability, Infocom Technologies and Optimization (Trends and Future Directions) (ICRITO)* (pp. 590-594). IEEE.

Patricia, M., Roberts, T., & Allen, D. (2022). Ethical dilemmas in AI-driven marketing strategies. *Journal of Business Ethics*, 40(2), 91–104.

Patrizi, M., Šerić, M., & Vernuccio, M. (2024). Hey Google, I trust you! The consequences of brand anthropomorphism in voice-based artificial intelligence contexts. *Journal of Retailing and Consumer Services*, 77, 103659. DOI: 10.1016/j.jretconser.2023.103659

Patwary, A. K., Rasoolimanesh, S. M., Rabiul, M. K., Aziz, R. C., & Hanafiah, M. H. (2022). Linking environmental knowledge, environmental responsibility, altruism, and intention toward green hotels through ecocentric and anthropocentric attitudes. *International Journal of Contemporary Hospitality Management*, 34(12), 4653–4673. DOI: 10.1108/IJCHM-01-2022-0039

Paul, J., & Bhukya, R. (2021). Forty-five years of International Journal of Consumer Studies: A bibliometric review and directions for future research. *International Journal of Consumer Studies*, 45(5), 937–963. DOI: 10.1111/ijcs.12727

Payal, R., Sharma, N., & Dwivedi, Y. K. (2024). Unlocking the impact of brand engagement in the metaverse on Real-World purchase intentions: Analyzing Pre-Adoption behavior in a futuristic technology platform. *Electronic Commerce Research and Applications*, 65, 101381. Advance online publication. DOI: 10.1016/j.elerap.2024.101381

Payne, A., & Frow, P. (2005). A Strategic Framework for Customer Relationship Management. *Journal of Marketing*, 69(4), 167–176. DOI: 10.1509/jmkg.2005.69.4.167

Pearman, O., & Cravens, A. E. (2022). Institutional barriers to actionable science: Perspectives from decision support tool creators. *Environmental Science & Policy*, 128, 317–325. DOI: 10.1016/j.envsci.2021.12.004

Peñarroya-Farell, M., & Miralles, F. (2022). Business model adaptation to the COVID-19 crisis: Strategic response of the Spanish cultural and creative firms. *Journal of Open Innovation: Technology, Market place, and Complexity, 8*(1), 39.

Perakakis.E and Mastorakis.G,(2019)."Social Media Monitoring: An Innovative Intelligent Approach," Mdpi journal designs,vol.3, no.2,pp.1-12.

Pezenka, I., & Weismayer, C. (2020). Which factors influence locals' and visitors' overall restaurant evaluations? *International Journal of Contemporary Hospitality Management*, 32(9), 2793–2812. DOI: 10.1108/IJCHM-09-2019-0796

Piehler, R., King, C., Burmann, C., & Xiong, L. (2015). The importance of employee brand understanding, brand identification, and brand commitment in realizing brand citizenship behavior. *European Journal of Marketing*, 50(9/10), 1575–1601. DOI: 10.1108/EJM-11-2014-0725

Pillai, R., Sivathanu, B., & Dwivedi, Y. K. (2020). Shopping intention at AI-powered automated retail stores (AIPARS). *Journal of Retailing and Consumer Services*, 57, 102207. DOI: 10.1016/j.jretconser.2020.102207

Pine, B. J., & Gilmore, J. H. (2011). *The Experience Economy*. Harvard Business Press.

Polonsky(1994): An Introduction To Green Marketing. Available at: https://escholarship.org/uc/item/49n325b7

Potla, R. T., & Pottla, V. K. (2024). AI-Powered Personalization in Salesforce: Enhancing Customer Engagement through Machine Learning Models. *Valley International Journal Digital Library, 1388-1420.*

Poulis, A., Rizomyliotis, I., & Konstantoulaki, K. (2019). Do firms still need to be social? Firm generated content in social media. *Information Technology & People*, 32(2), 387–404. DOI: 10.1108/ITP-03-2018-0134

Prahalad, C. K., & Ramaswamy, V. (2004). Co-creation experiences: The next practice in value creation. *Journal of Interactive Marketing*, 18(3), 5–14. DOI: 10.1002/dir.20015

Prakash, A. (2002). Green Marketing, Public Policy And Managerial Strategies. *Business Strategy and the Environment*, 11(5), 285–297. DOI: 10.1002/bse.338

Prashar, A., & Prashar, A. (2024). Digital fashion and metaverse platforms: Do platform attributes drive shopper's purchase intention? *Australian Journal of Management*, 03128962241246696. Advance online publication. DOI: 10.1177/03128962241246696

Priya, P. K., Rudra, K., Kandula, D. S., Teja, G. C., & K., V. K. (2023). An innovative analysis of AI-powered automation techniques for business management. In *Toward Artificial General Intelligence: Deep Learning, Neural Networks, Generative AI* (pp. 269-286). De Gruyter. DOI: 10.1515/9783111323749-013

Profumo, G., Testa, G., Viassone, M., & Ben Youssef, K. (2024). Metaverse and the fashion industry: A systematic literature review. *Journal of Global Fashion Marketing*, 15(1), 131–154. DOI: 10.1080/20932685.2023.2270587

Punia, S. K., Kumar, M., Stephan, T., Deverajan, G. G., & Patan, R. (2021). Performance Analysis of Machine Learning Algorithms for Big Data Classification. *International Journal of E-Health and Medical Communications*, 12(4), 60–75. DOI: 10.4018/IJEHMC.20210701.oa4

Punjaisri, K., Wilson, A., & Evanschitzky, H. (2009). Internal branding to influence employees' brand promise delivery: A case study in Thailand. *Journal of Service Management*, 20(5), 561–579. DOI: 10.1108/09564230910995143

Putha, S. (2021). AI-Driven Personalization in E-Commerce: Enhancing Customer Experience and Sales through Advanced Data Analytics. *Journal of Bioinformatics and Artificial Intelligence*, 1(1), 225–271.

Putra, A. H. P. K., Rivera, K. M., & Pramukti, A. (2023). Optimizing marketing management strategies through it innovation: Big data integration for better consumer understanding. *Golden Ratio of Mapping Idea and Literature Format*, 3(1), 71–91. DOI: 10.52970/grmilf.v3i1.398

Qin, M., Qiu, S., Zhao, Y., Zhu, W., & Li, S. (2024). Graphic or short video? The influence mechanism of UGC types on consumers' purchase intention—Take Xiaohongshu as an example. *Electronic Commerce Research and Applications*, 65, 101402. DOI: 10.1016/j.elerap.2024.101402

Qiu, H., Wang, X., Wu, M. Y., Wei, W., Morrison, A. M., & Kelly, C. (2023). The effect of destination source credibility on tourist environmentally responsible behavior: An application of stimulus-organism-response theory. *Journal of Sustainable Tourism*, 31(8), 1797–1817. DOI: 10.1080/09669582.2022.2067167

Rahman, H., & Dekkati, A. (2022). Dynamic pricing with AI: Managing consumer behavior and competitiveness in e-commerce. *Journal of Pricing Strategy and Analytics*, 19(5), 105–121.

Raji, M. A., Olodo, H. B., Oke, T. T., Addy, W. A., Ofodile, O. C., & Oyewole, A. T. (2024). E-commerce and consumer behavior: A review of AI-powered personalization and market trends. *GSC Advanced Research and Reviews, 18*(3), 066-077.

Ramadan, Z. (2023). Marketing in the metaverse era: Toward an integrative channel approach. *Virtual Reality (Waltham Cross)*, 27(3), 1905–1918. DOI: 10.1007/s10055-023-00783-2 PMID: 37360809

Ramakrishnan, T., Mohan Gift, M. D., Chitradevi, S., Jegan, R., & Subha Hency Jose, P. Nagaraja, Rajneesh Sharma H.N., Selvakumar P., Sintayehu Mekuria Hailegiorgis, (2022). "Study of Numerous Resins Used in Polymer Matrix Composite Materials", Advances in Materials Science and Engineering, vol. 2022, Article ID 1088926, 8 pages, 2022. https://doi.org/DOI: 10.1155/2022/1088926

Ramanjaneyulu, R., & Khirbat, S. (2021). A Meta-Synthesis Review of AI in Marketing with special reference to Marketing Research, Branding and Supply Chain Management. *ZENITH International Journal of Multidisciplinary Research*, 11(12)

Ramos, C. M. (2022). Business Intelligence Approach and Sentiment Analysis as a Management Strategy Applied to Study Customer Satisfaction in the Hospitality Sector. In *Advances in Tourism, Technology and Systems: Selected Papers from ICOTTS 2021* (Vol. 2, pp. 537–547). Springer Nature Singapore. DOI: 10.1007/978-981-16-9701-2_44

Ramos-Rodriguez, A. R., & Ruiz-Navarro, J. (2004). Changes in the intellectual structure of strategic management research: A bibliometric study of the Strategic Management Journal, 1980–2000. *Strategic Management Journal*, 25(10), 981–1004. DOI: 10.1002/smj.397

Rana, J., Gaur, L., Singh, G., Awan, U., & Rasheed, M. I. (2022). Reinforcing customer journey through artificial intelligence: A review and research agenda. *International Journal of Emerging Markets*, 17(7), 1738–1758. DOI: 10.1108/IJOEM-08-2021-1214

Rani, A. (2020). Algorithmic fairness and its implications for AI-driven marketing. *Marketing Analytics Journal*, 36(5), 67–78.

Rani, A. (2020). Predictive analytics and the future of marketing. *Marketing Analytics Journal*, 36(5), 67–78.

Rantala, T., Apilo, T., Palomäki, K., & Valkokari, K. (2020). Selling Data-Based Value in Business-to-Business Markets. *Technology Innovation Management Review*, 10(1), 45–53. DOI: 10.22215/timreview/1313

Rather, R. A. (2023). Metaverse marketing and consumer research: Theoretical framework and future research agenda in tourism and hospitality industry. *Tourism Recreation Research*, 1–9. Advance online publication. DOI: 10.1080/02508281.2023.2216525

Rathore, B. (2020). Personalization and profits: The impact of ai on targeted digital marketing. *International Journal of Transcontinental Discoveries*, 7(1), 1–14.

Rauschnabel, P. A., Hüttl-Maack, V., Ahuvia, A. C., & Schein, K. E. (2024). Augmented reality marketing and consumer-brand relationships: How closeness drives brand love. *Psychology and Marketing*, 41(4), 819–837. DOI: 10.1002/mar.21953

Raza, S. A., & Khan, K. A. (2022). Impact of green human resource practices on hotel environmental performance: The moderating effect of environmental knowledge and individual green values. *International Journal of Contemporary Hospitality Management*, 34(6), 2154–2175. DOI: 10.1108/IJCHM-05-2021-0553

Rego, L., Brady, M., Leone, R., Roberts, J., Srivastava, C., & Srivastava, R. (2022). Brand response to environmental turbulence: A framework and propositions for resistance, recovery and reinvention. *International Journal of Investigation in Market placing, 39*(2), 583-602.

Reinhardt, F.L., (1998). Environmental product differentiation: implications for corporate strategy. California Management Review 40 (4), 43e73.

Ries, A., & Trout, J. (2001). Positioning: The battle for your mind (20th anniversary ed.). McGraw-Hill.

Ries, A., & Trout, J. (2001). *Positioning: The battle for your mind* (2nd ed.). McGraw-Hill.

Roberts, C. V., Elahi, E., & Chandrashekar, A. (2022). On the bias-variance characteristics of lime and shap in high sparsity movie recommendation explanation tasks. arXiv preprint arXiv:2206.04784.

Roberts, K. (2005). *Lovemarks: The future beyond brands*. Powerhouse books.

Roberts, H., Zhang, J., Bariach, B., Cowls, J., Gilburt, B., Juneja, P., Tsamados, A., Ziosi, M., Taddeo, M., & Floridi, L. (2024). Artificial intelligence in support of the circular economy: Ethical considerations and a path forward. *AI & Society*, 39(3), 1451–1464. DOI: 10.1007/s00146-022-01596-8

Rodrigues, P., Reis, R., & Cantista, I. (2015). Consumer behavior: How the "brand love" affects you. In Ideas in Marketing: Finding the New and Polishing the Old: Proceedings of the 2013 Academy of Marketing Science (AMS) Annual Conference (pp. 583-588). Springer International Publishing. https://doi.org/DOI: 10.1007/978-3-319-10951-0_212

Rodrigues, C., Brandão, A., Billore, S., & Oda, T. (2023). The mediating role of perceived brand authenticity between brand experience and brand love: A cross-cultural perspective. *Journal of Brand Management*, •••, 1–17. DOI: 10.1057/s41262-023-00342-9

Rogers, E. M. (1962). *Diffusion of innovations*. Free Press.

Rosário, A., & Raimundo, R. (2021). Consumer marketing strategy and E-commerce in the last decade: A literature review. *Journal of Theoretical and Applied Electronic Commerce Research*, 16(7), 3003–3024. DOI: 10.3390/jtaer16070164

Roy, P., Khandeparkar, K., & Motiani, M. (2016). A lovable personality: The effect of brand personality on brand love. *Journal of Brand Management*, 23(5), 97–113. DOI: 10.1057/s41262-016-0005-5

Russell, S. J., & Norvig, P. (2010). *Artificial intelligence: A modern approach. Nova Jersey, EUA*. Prentice Hall.

Russell, S., & Norvig, P. (2021). *Artificial Intelligence: A modern approach* (4th ed.). Prentice Hall.

Rust, R. T. (2020). The future of marketing. *International Journal of Research in Marketing*, 37(1), 15–26. DOI: 10.1016/j.ijresmar.2019.08.002

Rust, R. T., & Huang, M.-H. (2020). The service revolution and the transformation of marketing science. *Marketing Science*, 39(3), 357–380.

Sabbar, A., & Nygren Gustafsson, L. (2021). The impact of AI on branding elements: Opportunities and challenges as seen by branding and IT specialists.

Sahare, P. R. (2024). *Sales Data Analysis Using BI and WEKA*. INTERANTIONAL JOURNAL OF SCIENTIFIC RESEARCH IN ENGINEERING AND MANAGEMENT., DOI: 10.55041/IJSREM30123

Saini, H., Kumar, P., & Oberoi, S. (2023). Welcome to the destination! Social media influencers as cogent determinant of travel decision: A systematic literature review and conceptual framework. *Cogent Social Sciences*, 9(1), 2240055. DOI: 10.1080/23311886.2023.2240055

Salem, T., & Twining-Ward, L. (2018). *The voice of travelers: leveraging user-generated content for tourism development*. World Bank., Available at https:// openknowledge. worldbank.org/handle/10986/30451License:CCBY3.0IGO DOI: 10.1596/30451

Sanchez-Amboage, E., Crespo-Pereira, V., Membiela-Pollan, M., & Faustino, J. P. J. (2024). Tourism marketing in the metaverse: A systematic literature review, building blocks, and future research directions. *PLoS One*, 19(5), e0300599. Advance online publication. DOI: 10.1371/journal.pone.0300599 PMID: 38728243

Sands, S., Campbell, C., & Farrell, J. (2022). Virtual Influencers and Digital Engagement. *The Journal of Consumer Research*, 18(3), 67–92.

Sanmiguel, P., Sádaba, T., & Sayeed, N. (2024). Fashion brands in the metaverse: Achievements from a marketing perspective. *Journal of Global Fashion Marketing*, 15(3), 320–340. DOI: 10.1080/20932685.2024.2331518

Santoro, G., Jabeen, F., Kliestik, T., & Bresciani, S. (2024). AI-powered growth hacking: Benefits, challenges and pathways. *Management Decision*. Advance online publication. DOI: 10.1108/MD-10-2023-1964

Santos-Vijande, M. L., del Río-Lanza, A. B., Suárez-Álvarez, L., & Díaz-Martín, A. M. (2013). The brand management system and service firm competitiveness. *Journal of Business Research*, 66(2), 148–157. DOI: 10.1016/j.jbusres.2012.07.007

Sarkar, A. (2013). Romantic brand love: A conceptual analysis. *The Marketing Review*, 13(1), 23–37. DOI: 10.1362/146934713X13590250137709

Sawhney, M., & Lurie, N. H. (2004). The power of the product mix: How product variety impacts brand perceptions. *JMR, Journal of Marketing Research*, 41(3), 257–268.

Saxena, S. K., Gupta, V., & Kumar, S. (2024). Enhancing Guest Loyalty in the Hotel Industry Through Artificial Intelligence-Drive Personalization. In *New Technologies in Virtual and Hybrid Events* (pp. 335–350). IGI Global. DOI: 10.4018/979-8-3693-2272-7.ch017

Schmid, D. A., & Huber, F. (2019). Brand love: Emotionality and development of its elements across the relationship lifecycle. *Psychology and Marketing*, 36(4), 305–320. DOI: 10.1002/mar.21180

Schmitt, B. (1999). Experiential marketing. *Journal of Marketing Management*, 15(1-3), 53–67. DOI: 10.1362/026725799784870496

Schulterbraucks, L. (2017). The impact of artificial intelligence on the marketing landscape. *Journal of Marketing Trends*, 6(2), 45–50.

Sekar, S., Dutta, C., Spoorthi, R., Mohammed, N. Q., Al-Khuzaie, M. Y., & Almulla, A. A. (2024, May). A Well Design of Customer Centric Based Financing Service through Biometric Based Veritable System using Personalized AI Integrated System. *In 2024 4th International Conference on Advance Computing and Innovative Technologies in Engineering (ICACITE) (pp. 1109-1113). IEEE.*

Sekarini, S., & Selvabaskar, S. (2024). AI-Powered Branding: Enhancing Consumer Experience in Emerging Markets. In *Integrating AI-Driven Technologies Into Service Marketing* (pp. 19-48). IGI Global.

Selvakumar, P., Mariappan, P., Shunmugam, S., Paul, R., & Jabez, S. (2024). Removal of chemicals from effluent using photobioreactor technology to improve environmental and health impacts. *Zeitschrift für Physikalische Chemie*, 2024(7), 1295–1302. Advance online publication. DOI: 10.1515/zpch-2023-0450

Semwal, R., Tripathi, N., Rana, A., Dafouti, B. S., Bairwa, M. K., & Mathur, V. (2024, May). AI-Powered Personalization and Emotional Intelligence Integration for Enhanced Service Marketing in Transformative Tourism Experiences. *In 2024 International Conference on Communication, Computer Sciences and Engineering (IC3SE) (pp. 1851-1856). IEEE.*

Sen, A., & Roy, K. (2020). Data privacy in the AI era: Challenges and regulatory frameworks. *Indian Journal of Cyber Law*, 8(2), 113–129.

Şenyapar, H. N. D. (2024). The Future of Marketing: The Transformative Power of Artificial Intelligence. *International Journal of Management and Administration*, 8(15), 1–19. DOI: 10.29064/ijma.1412272

Setiawan, A. S., Widyartono, A., & Ony, J. G. (2021). Implementation of Business Strategy, Technology Usage, and Business Continuity During the Covid-19 Pandemic. *Jurnal Akuntansi*, 25(2), 186–200. DOI: 10.24912/ja.v25i2.805

Setyawan, A. A., Misidawati, D. N., Aryatama, S., Jaya, A. A. N. A., & Wiliana, E. (2024). Exploring Innovative Strategies for Sustainable Organizational Growth. *Global International Journal of Innovative Research*, 2(5), 861–872.

Shah, N. D., Steyerberg, E. W., & Kent, D. M. (2018). Big data and predictive analytics. *Journal of the American Medical Association*, 320(1), 27. DOI: 10.1001/jama.2018.5602 PMID: 29813156

Shah, R. M., Butt, M. A., & Baba, M. Z. (2017). Predictive analytic modeling: A walkthrough. *International Journal of Advanced Research in Computer Science and Software Engineering*, 7(6), 421–426. DOI: 10.23956/ijarcsse/V7I6/0305

Shankar, V., & Kannan, P. K. (2018). AI and data-driven marketing. *Journal of Marketing*, 82(4), 1–17.

Shan, L. (2024). Computing advertising intelligent computing and push based on artificial intelligence in the big data era. *Heliyon*, 10(17).

Sharma, A., Patel, N., & Gupta, R. (2022). Leveraging BERT and Sentiment Analysis Algorithms for Enhanced AI-Driven Brand Sentiment Monitoring. *European Advanced AI Journal, 11*(8).

Sharma, R., Kaur, A., Bajaj, K. B., Bindra, K., Rashmi, D. S. D., Yadav, V., ... & Singh, B. GURUGRAM UNIVERSITY BUSINESS REVIEW (GUBR).

Sharma, A. P. (2021). Consumers' purchase behaviour and green marketing: A synthesis, review and agenda. *International Journal of Consumer Studies*, 45(6), 1217–1238. DOI: 10.1111/ijcs.12722

Sharma, K., Aswal, C., & Paul, J. (2023). Factors affecting green purchase behavior: A systematic literature review. *Business Strategy and the Environment*, 32(4), 2078–2092. DOI: 10.1002/bse.3237

Sharma, M., Luthra, S., Joshi, S., & Kumar, A. (2021). Accelerating retail supply chain performance against pandemic disruption: Adopting resilient strategies to mitigate the long-term effects. *Journal of Enterprise Information Management*, 34(6), 1844–1873. DOI: 10.1108/JEIM-07-2020-0286

Sharma, M., Singh, A., & Rana, S. (2024). Empowering Hospitality Brands AI Strategies for Enhanced Customer Experiences in Emerging Market places. In *Integrating AI-Driven Technologies Into Service Market placing* (pp. 173–190). IGI Global. DOI: 10.4018/979-8-3693-7122-0.ch010

Sharma, R., Srivastva, S., & Fatima, S. (2023). E-Commerce and Digital Transformation: Trends, Challenges, and Implications. [IJFMR]. *International Journal for Multidisciplinary Research*, 5(5).

Sharma, V., & Bose, I. (2024). Unlocking AI's Potential in Customer Service Marketing. In *AI Innovations in Service and Tourism Marketing* (pp. 80–103). IGI Global. DOI: 10.4018/979-8-3693-7909-7.ch005

Shekhar, E. S., Goyal, D. S., & Jain, U. J. J. A. W. A. L. (2024). Enhancing customer engagement with AI and ML: Techniques and case studies. *International Journal of Computer Science and Publications, 14 (2), 1-15. IJCSP24B1346. Pdf.*

Sheykhan, S., & Boozary, P., GhorbanTanhaei, H., Pourmirza, M., & Rabiee, M. (2024). Evaluation of Sustainable Marketing Strategy Based on Product Perceived Value in Attracting Brand Loyalty Using FCM & Rough BWM Methods. *Power System Technology*, 48(1), 806–827.

Shin, H., & Kang, J. (2024). How does the metaverse travel experience influence virtual and actual travel behaviors? Focusing on the role of telepresence and avatar identification. *Journal of Hospitality and Tourism Management*, 58, 174–183. DOI: 10.1016/j.jhtm.2023.12.009

Shree, S. (2023). Revolutionizing Ecommerce: Harnessing the Power of ChatGPT and Generative AI for Personalized Customer Engagement and Enhanced Shopping Experiences. *International Journal of Innovations in Science, Engineering And Management, 72-75.*

Shrestha, Y. R., Ben-Menahem, S. M., & Von Krogh, G. (2019). Organizational Decision-Making structures in the age of artificial Intelligence. *California Management Review*, 61(4), 66–83. DOI: 10.1177/0008125619862257

Sidaoui, K., Jaakkola, M., & Burton, J. (2020). AI feel you: Customer experience assessment via chatbot interviews. *Journal of Service Management*, 31(4), 745–766. DOI: 10.1108/JOSM-11-2019-0341

Siebert, T., Jones, L., & McMillan, E. (2020). AI and automation in customer service: Chatbots as brand management tools. *Customer Experience and Technology Review*, 7(1), 33–42.

Sigala, M., Ooi, K. B., Tan, G. W. H., Aw, E. C. X., Buhalis, D., Cham, T. H., & Ye, I. H. (2024). Understanding the impact of ChatGPT on tourism and hospitality: Trends, prospects and research agenda. *Journal of Hospitality and Tourism Management*, 60, 384–390.

Singh, M. K., & Rishi, O. P. (2020). Event driven recommendation system for E-commerce using knowledge based collaborative filtering technique. Scalable Computing. *Practice and Experience*, 21(3), 369–378.

Singh, M., & Singh, S. (2020). The role of ethical business practices in small enterprises. *Journal of Small Business Management*, 34(1), 71–82.

Singh, P. (2023). AI-Driven Personalization in Telecom Customer Support: Enhancing User Experience and Loyalty. *Distributed Learning and Broad Applications in Scientific Research*, 9, 325–363.

Singh, P. K., Pramanik, P. K. D., Dey, A. K., & Choudhury, P. (2021). Recommender systems: An overview, research trends, and future directions. *International Journal of Business and Systems Research*, 15(1), 14–52. DOI: 10.1504/IJBSR.2021.111753

Sinha, S., Sinha, D., & Dalmia, T. (2024). Role of AI in Enhancing Customer Experience in Online Shopping. *11th International Conference on Reliability, Infocom Technologies and Optimization, ICRITO 2024*. Hybrid, Noida: Institute of Electrical and Electronics Engineers Inc. DOI: 10.1109/ICRITO61523.2024.10522285

Sohaib, M., Mlynarski, J., & Wu, R. (2022). Building brand equity: The impact of brand experience, brand love, and brand engagement—A case study of customers' perception of the Apple brand in China. *Sustainability (Basel)*, 15(1), 746. DOI: 10.3390/su15010746

Sonboli, N., Smith, J. J., Cabral Berenfus, F., Burke, R., & Fiesler, C. (2021, June). Fairness and transparency in recommendation: The users' perspective. In *Proceedings of the 29th ACM Conference on User Modeling, Adaptation and Personalization* (pp. 274-279). DOI: 10.1145/3450613.3456835

Srifi, M., Oussous, A., Ait Lahcen, A., & Mouline, S. (2020). Recommender systems based on collaborative filtering using review texts—A survey. *Information (Basel)*, 11(6), 317. DOI: 10.3390/info11060317

Srivastava, K. B., & Bhatnagar, J. (2008). Talent acquisition due diligence leading to high employee engagement: Case of Motorola India MDB. *Industrial and Commercial Training*, 40(5), 253–260. DOI: 10.1108/00197850810886496

Stachl, C., Au, Q., Schoedel, R., Gosling, S. D., Harari, G. M., Buschek, D., Völkel, S. T., Schuwerk, T., Oldemeier, M., Ullmann, T., Hussmann, H., Bischl, B., & Bühner, M. (2020). Predicting personality from patterns of behavior collected with smartphones. *Proceedings of the National Academy of Sciences of the United States of America*, 117(30), 17680–17687. DOI: 10.1073/pnas.1920484117 PMID: 32665436

Stahl, B. C., Antoniou, J., Ryan, M., Macnish, K., & Jiya, T. (2022). Organisational responses to the ethical issues of artificial intelligence. *AI & Society*, 37(1), 23–37. DOI: 10.1007/s00146-021-01148-6

Stehlík, V., & Ge, M. (2023). TOPSIS-based Recommender System for Big Data Visualizations. *Journal of Applied Interdisciplinary Research*, (1), 50–74.

Sternberg, R. J. (1986). A triangular theory of love. *Psychological Review*, 93(2), 119–135. DOI: 10.1037/0033-295X.93.2.119

Sterne, J. (2017). *Artificial intelligence for marketing: Practical applications*. Wiley. DOI: 10.1002/9781119406341

Stern, N. Z., & Ander, W. N. (2008). *Greentailing and other revolutions in retail: hot ideas that are grabbing customers' attention and raising profits*. John Wiley & Sons.

Sugumaran, K. M. D., Pandiyarajan V., Y. B S, Selvakumar P. and M. S, (2024). "Analysis of Electromyography Signals for Control of Mechanical Prosthesis using Machine Learning Techniques," 2024 2nd International Conference on Intelligent Data Communication Technologies and Internet of Things (IDCIoT), Bengaluru, India, 2024, pp. 1059-1067, DOI: 10.1109/IDCIoT59759.2024.10467707

Sung, E., Kwon, O., & Sohn, K. (2023). NFT luxury brand marketing in the metaverse: Leveraging blockchain-certified NFTs to drive consumer behavior. *Psychology and Marketing*, 40(11), 2306–2325. DOI: 10.1002/mar.21854

Sun, H., Zafar, M. Z., & Hasan, N. (2022). Employing natural language processing as artificial intelligence for analyzing consumer opinion toward advertisement. *Frontiers in Psychology*, 13, 856663. DOI: 10.3389/fpsyg.2022.856663 PMID: 35769737

Sweeney, J. C., & Soutar, G. N. (2001). Consumer perceived value: The development of a multiple item scale. *Journal of Retailing*, 77(2), 203–220. DOI: 10.1016/S0022-4359(01)00041-0

Swiatek, L., Galloway, C., Vujnovic, M., & Kruckeberg, D. (2024). Humanoid artificial intelligence, media conferences and natural responses to journalists' questions: The end of (human-to-human) public relations? *Public Relations Inquiry*, 13(1), 113–121. DOI: 10.1177/2046147X231221828

Taddeo, M., & Floridi, L. (2018). How AI can be a force for good: The role of responsible AI. *AI & Society*, 33(2), 291–297.

Talukder, M. B., Kumar, S., & Tyagi, P. K. (Eds.). (2024). *Impact of AI and Tech-Driven Solutions in Hospitality and Tourism*. IGI Global. DOI: 10.4018/979-8-3693-6755-1

Tamar, M., Wirawan, H., Arfah, T., & Putri, R. P. S. (2021). Predicting pro-environmental behaviours: The role of environmental values, attitudes and knowledge. *Management of Environmental Quality*, 32(2), 328–343. DOI: 10.1108/MEQ-12-2019-0264

Teece, D. J. (2007). Explicating dynamic capabilities: The nature and microfoundations of (sustainable) enterprise performance. *Strategic Management Journal*, 28(13), 1319–1350. DOI: 10.1002/smj.640

Teece, D. J., Pisano, G., & Shuen, A. (1997). Dynamic capabilities and strategic management. *Strategic Management Journal*, 18(7), 509–533. DOI: 10.1002/(SICI)1097-0266(199708)18:7<509::AID-SMJ882>3.0.CO;2-Z

Thakur, J., & Kushwaha, B. P. (2024). Artificial intelligence in marketing research and future research directions: Science mapping and research clustering using bibliometric analysis. *Global Business and Organizational Excellence*, 43(3), 139–155. DOI: 10.1002/joe.22233

Thanh, T. V., & Kirova, V. (2018). Wine tourism experience: A netnography study. *Journal of Business Research*, 83, 30–37. DOI: 10.1016/j.jbusres.2017.10.008

Thomas, B., & Fowler, J. (2020). Addressing data challenges in AI implementation. *Business Horizons*, 63(3), 321–330.

Tien, N. H., Thai, T. M., & Thao, N. P. (2020). Brand management in convenience store business comparative analysis between VinMart+ and FamilyMart in Vietnamese Market.

Timan, T., & Mann, Z. (2021). Data protection in the era of artificial intelligence: trends, existing solutions and recommendations for privacy-preserving technologies. In *The elements of big data value: Foundations of the research and innovation ecosystem* (pp. 153–175). Springer International Publishing. DOI: 10.1007/978-3-030-68176-0_7

Timoshenko, A., & Hauser, J. R. (2019). Identifying customer needs from user-generated content. *Marketing Science*, 38(1), 1–20. DOI: 10.1287/mksc.2018.1123

Tinston, R. (2023). Leveraging Behavioural Science Language and Artificial Intelligence in Tourism Marketing.

Tirunillai, S., & Tellis, G. J. (2019). Does AI enhance consumer engagement? Insights from the AI marketing industry. *JMR, Journal of Marketing Research*, 56(6), 1038–1051.

Tiwari, A., Kumar, A., Kant, R., & Jaiswal, D. (2024). Impact of fashion influencers on consumers' purchase intentions: Theory of planned behaviour and mediation of attitude. *Journal of Fashion Marketing and Management*, 28(2), 209–225. DOI: 10.1108/JFMM-11-2022-0253

Tran, M. T. (2024). Unlocking the AI-powered customer experience: Personalized service, enhanced engagement, and data-driven strategies for e-commerce applications. *Journal of Infrastructure. Advances in Marketing, Customer Relationship Management, and E-Services*, 08(07), 375–382. Advance online publication. DOI: 10.4018/979-8-3693-4453-8.ch019

Tran, T. P., van Solt, M., & Zemanek, J. E.Jr. (2020). How does personalization affect brand relationship in social commerce? A mediation perspective. *Journal of Consumer Marketing*, 37(5), 473–486. DOI: 10.1108/JCM-12-2017-2499

Trawnih, A., Al-Masaeed, S., Alsoud, M., & Alkufahy, A. M. Al-Ahliyya Amman University, & Jadara University. (2022). Understanding artificial intelligence experience: A customer perspective. In International Journal of Data and Network Science (Vol. 6, pp. 1471–1484) [Journal-article]. https://doi.org/DOI: 10.5267/j.ijdns.2022.5.004

Trivedi, J., & Sama, R. (2020). The effect of influencer marketing on consumers' brand admiration and online purchase intentions: An emerging market perspective. *Journal of Internet Commerce*, 19(1), 103–124. DOI: 10.1080/15332861.2019.1700741

Trudel, R. (2019). Sustainable consumer behavior. *Consumer Psychology Review*, 2(1), 85–96. DOI: 10.1002/arcp.1045

Tula, S. T., Kess-Momoh, A. J., Omotoye, G. B., Bello, B. G., & Daraojimba, A. I.Sunday Tubokirifuruar TulaAzeez Jason Kess-MomohGaniyu Bolawale OmotoyeBinaebi Gloria BelloAndrew Ifesinachi Daraojimba. (2024). AI-ENABLED CUSTOMER EXPERIENCE ENHANCEMENT IN BUSINESS. *Computer Science & IT Research Journal*, 5(2), 365–389. DOI: 10.51594/csitrj.v5i2.789

Tulcanaza-Prieto, A. B., Cortez-Ordoñez, A., & Lee, C. W. (2023). Influence of customer perception factors on AI-Enabled customer experience in the Ecuadorian banking environment. *Sustainability (Basel)*, 15(16), 12441. DOI: 10.3390/su151612441

Unal, S., & Aydın, H. (2013). An investigation on the evaluation of the factors affecting brand love. *Procedia: Social and Behavioral Sciences*, 92, 76–85. DOI: 10.1016/j.sbspro.2013.08.640

Urefe, O., Odonkor, A., & Agu, C. (2024). Data Analytics and CRM Tools in Marketing Transformation. *Journal of Marketing Technology*, 19(1), 33–54.

Vaio, A. D.. (2020). Sustainable business models through AI in branding. *Journal of Cleaner Production*, 256, 120–135.

Valdez, M. J., & Flores-Cuautle, J. (2022). Toward customer hyper-personalization experience — A data-driven approach. *Cogent Business and Management*, 09(01), 2041384. Advance online publication. DOI: 10.1080/23311975.2022.2041384

Van der Waa, J., Nieuwburg, E., Cremers, A., & Neerincx, M. (2021). Evaluating XAI: A comparison of rule-based and example-based explanations. *Artificial Intelligence*, 291, 103404. DOI: 10.1016/j.artint.2020.103404

van Esch, P. (2024). Disruptive AI: the response depends on the buyer's political ideology. *Journal of Business & Industrial Market placing, 39*(4), 673-691.

Van Tonder, E., Fullerton, S., De Beer, L. T., & Saunders, S. G. (2023). Social and personal factors influencing green customer citizenship behaviours: The role of subjective norm, internal values and attitudes. *Journal of Retailing and Consumer Services*, 71, 103190. DOI: 10.1016/j.jretconser.2022.103190

Varsha, P. S., Akter, S., Kumar, A., Gochhait, S., & Patagundi, B. (2021). The impact of artificial intelligence on branding: A bibliometric analysis (1982-2019). [JGIM]. *Journal of Global Information Management*, 29(4), 221–246. DOI: 10.4018/JGIM.20210701.oa10

Vasilopoulou, C., Theodorakopoulos, L., & Γιαννούκου, I. (2023). Big data and consumer behavior: The power and pitfalls of analytics in the digital age. *Technium Social Sciences Journal*, 45, 469–480. DOI: 10.47577/tssj.v45i1.9135

Ved, M.. (2019). Big Data Analytics in Telecommunication using State-of-the-art Big Data Framework in a Distributed Computing Environment: A Case Study. *Annual International Computer Software and Applications Conference*. DOI: 10.1109/COMPSAC.2019.00066

Veloutsou, C., & Guzman, F. (2017). Brand management and the role of consumer insights. *Journal of Brand Management*, 24(3), 219–233.

Venkateswaran, N. (2023, September 30). AI-DRIVEN PERSONALIZATION IN CUSTOMER RELATIONSHIP MANAGEMENT: CHALLENGES AND OPPORTUNITIES. *Journal of Theoretical and Applied Information Technology*, 101(18), 7392–7399. Retrieved November 05, 2024, from https://www.scopus.com/record/display.uri?eid=2-s2.0-85175453312&origin=scopusAI

Venturini, A., & Columbano, M. (2024). 'Fashioning' the metaverse: A qualitative study on consumers' value and perceptions of digital fashion in virtual worlds. *Journal of Global Fashion Marketing*, 15(1), 6–22. DOI: 10.1080/20932685.2023.2234918

Verhoef, P. C., Kannan, P. K., & Inman, J. J. (2021). From multi-channel retailing to omni-channel retailing: Introduction to the special issue on multi-channel retailing. *Journal of Retailing*, 97(1), 63–68. DOI: 10.1016/j.jretai.2020.10.004

Verma, P. (2021). The effect of brand engagement and brand love upon overall brand equity and purchase intention: A moderated–mediated model. *Journal of Promotion Management*, 27(1), 103–132. DOI: 10.1080/10496491.2020.1809591

Verma, S.. (2021). The disruptive impact of AI on marketing. *International Journal of Technology Marketing*, 16(4), 385–399.

Vij, M., Vij, A., Kumar, P., & Shameem, B. (2024, February). Impact of AI-Driven Customer Insights on Brand Engagement and Loyalty in Tourism Marketing. In *2024 2nd International Conference on Cyber Resilience (ICCR)* (pp. 1-6). IEEE.

Vijayakumar, G., Rajkumar, M., Rajiv Chandar, N., Selvakumar, P., & Duraisamy, R. (2024). Muniyandi Rajkumar, Rajiv Chandar N, Selvakumar P and Ramesh Duraisamy, (2024). Environmentally friendly TDS removal from waste water by electrochemical ion exchange batch-type recirculation (EIR) technique. *Environmental Science. Water Research & Technology*, 10(4), 826–835. DOI: 10.1039/D3EW00793F

Vinoth, S., Vemula, H. L., Haralayya, B., Mamgain, P., Hasan, M. F., & Naved, M. (2022). Application of cloud computing in banking and e-commerce and related security threats. *Materials Today: Proceedings*, 51, 2172–2175. DOI: 10.1016/j.matpr.2021.11.121

Vishnoi, R., Shah, P., & Chauhan, K. (2019). Deep learning and one-shot learning in AI. *International Journal of Computational Intelligence*, 15(3), 154–162.

Vitaveska, L. (2017). "Machine Learning and Social Media in Crisis Management: Agility vs.Ethics," *Proceedings of the 14th ISCRAM Conference*, vol.13,no. May,pp.256-260.

Vivek, S. D., Beatty, S. E., & Morgan, R. M. (2012). Customer engagement: Exploring customer relationships beyond purchase. *Journal of Marketing Theory and Practice*, 20(2), 122–146. DOI: 10.2753/MTP1069-6679200201

VLASCEANU, C. F., Valentin, T. A., & Gabriela, . I. G. U. (2023). The Fusion of Advanced Technology: Artificial Intelligence and Virtual Reality in the Cruise Industry and Global Hospitality Organizations. Review of International Comparative Management/Revista de Management Comparat International, 24(4).

Vorhies, D. W., & Morgan, N. A. (2005). Benchmarking marketing capabilities for sustainable competitive advantage. *Journal of Marketing*, 69(1), 80–94. DOI: 10.1509/jmkg.69.1.80.55505

Walek, B., & Fajmon, P. (2023). A hybrid recommender system for an online store using a fuzzy expert system. *Expert Systems with Applications*, 212, 118565. DOI: 10.1016/j.eswa.2022.118565

Wamba, S. F., Gunasekaran, A., & Akter, S. (2017). Big Data Analytics in E-Commerce: A Systematic Review and Agenda for Future Research. *Journal of Business Research*, 70, 263–273.

Wang, L., Xiao, J., Luo, Z., & Guo, Y. (2024). The Impact of Default Options on Tourist Intention Post Tourism Chatbot Failure: The Role of Service Recovery and Emoticon. *Tourism Management Perspectives*, 53, 101299.

Wang, T., & Liu, Z. (2023). AI and consumer behavior in branding: A systematic review. *The Journal of Consumer Research*, 45(5), 609–624.

Wang, X., Li, Y., & Zhang, J. (2021). Consumer trust in AI-powered virtual assistants: The role of transparency and brand reputation. *Journal of Business Research*, 126, 84–94.

Wang, Y., & Benbasat, I. (2016). Artificial intelligence in e-commerce: The role of intelligent agents. *International Journal of Electronic Commerce*, 21(3), 5–9.

Wedel, M., & Kannan, P. K. (2016). Marketing analytics for data-rich environments. *Journal of Marketing*, 80(6), 97–121. DOI: 10.1509/jm.15.0413

Werner, A. (2020). Organizing music, organizing gender: Algorithmic culture and Spotify recommendations. *Popular Communication*, 18(1), 78–90. DOI: 10.1080/15405702.2020.1715980

West, D. M. (2018). *The future of work: Robots, AI, and automation*. Brookings Institution Press.

Wetzlinger, W., Auinger, A., Kindermann, H., & Schönberger, W. (2017). Acceptance of personalization in omnichannel retailing. *14th International Conference on Logic Programming and Nonmonotonic Reasoning, LPNMR 2017. 10294 LNCS*, pp. 114-129. Espoo: Springer Verlag. doi:DOI: 978-331958483-6

Wiestner, D., & Spiller, R. (2025). Brand Management in the Digital Era. In *Digital Transformation Initiatives for Agile Marketing* (pp. 403–434). IGI Global.

Wojewoda, M. (2023). ARTIFICIAL INTELLIGENCE AS A SOCIAL UTOPIA. *Ethos (0860-8024), 36*(143).

Wongkitrungrueng, A., & Suprawan, L. (2024). Metaverse meets branding: Examining consumer responses to immersive brand experiences. *International Journal of Human-Computer Interaction*, 40(11), 2905–2924. DOI: 10.1080/10447318.2023.2175162

World Food Travel Association. (2016). *The American Culinary Traveler: Profiles, Behaviors, and Attitudes*. World Food Travel Association.

Wu, S., Sun, F., Zhang, W., Xie, X., & Cui, B. (2022). Graph neural networks in recommender systems: A survey. *ACM Computing Surveys*, 55(5), 1–37. DOI: 10.1145/3535101

Xu, S. (2024). Exploring the Impact of Personalization in Artificial Intelligence on Digital Marketing: Performance Evaluation. *Journal of Innovation and Development*, 8(1), 41–44. DOI: 10.54097/tht8d457

Xu, S. X., & Huang, G. Q. (2017). Efficient Multi- Attribute Multi- Unit Auctions for B2B E- Commerce Logistics. *Production and Operations Management*, 26(2), 292–304. DOI: 10.1111/poms.12638

Xu, X., Chen, X., Jia, F., Brown, S., Gong, Y., & Xu, Y. (2018). Supply chain finance: A systematic literature review and bibliometric analysis. *International Journal of Production Economics*, 204, 160–173. DOI: 10.1016/j.ijpe.2018.08.003

Yadav, M. S., & Pavlou, P. A. (2021). Artificial intelligence in marketing. *Journal of the Academy of Marketing Science*, 49(1), 7–24.

Yadav, S., Pandey, S. K., & Sharma, D. (2024). Marketing beyond reality: A systematic literature review on metaverse. *Management Research Review*, 47(7), 1029–1051. DOI: 10.1108/MRR-06-2023-0456

Yagüe, M., Rodríguez, E., & Delgado, J. (2007). Verification algorithms for governed use of multimedia content. *Online Information Review*, 31(1), 38–58. DOI: 10.1108/14684520710731029

Yahelska, K., Vasylyshyna, L., & Shkurov, Y. (2023). Development Of Information And Communication Technologies To Study Consumer Behavior In The Process Of Brand Management. *Eastern-European Journal of Enterprise Technologies*, 123(13).

Yan, J. (2023). Prediction of consumer behavior based on machine learning algorithm. Proceedings of the 2nd International Conference on Mathematical Statistics and Economic Analysis, MSEA 2023, May 26–28, 2023, N. https://doi.org/DOI: 10.4108/eai.26-5-2023.2334304

Yang, H. T., Cho, Y. R., & Han, S. Y. (2024). Understanding user perceptions toward marketing in the metaverse. *Kybernetes*. Advance online publication. DOI: 10.1108/K-08-2023-1524

Yang, Z., Shang, C., Liu, Q., & Zhao, C. (2010). A dynamic web services composition algorithm based on the combination of ant colony algorithm and genetic algorithm. *Journal of Computer Information Systems*, 6(8), 2617–2622.

Ye, X., Yan, Y., Li, J., & Jiang, B. (2024). Privacy and personal data risk governance for generative artificial intelligence: A Chinese perspective. *Telecommunications Policy*, 48(10), 102851.

Yilmazdogan, O. C. (2024). Elevating workforce stability: Augmented reality and artificial intelligence solutions for overcoming employee turnover challenges in hospitality and tourism. *Worldwide Hospitality and Tourism Themes*, 16(5), 598–610.

Yilmaz, T., Sagfossen, S., & Velasco, C. (2023). What makes NFTs valuable to consumers? Perceived value drivers associated with NFTs liking, purchasing, and holding. *Journal of Business Research*, 165, 114056. Advance online publication. DOI: 10.1016/j.jbusres.2023.114056

Yin, J., Cao, B., Deng, S. and Wu, Z., (2012). Process Discovery from the Log of Business Rule Engine. International Journal of Innovative Computing Information and Control, 8(7 B), pp.5277-5293.

Yin, C., Shi, L., Sun, R., & Wang, J. (2020). Improved collaborative filtering recommendation algorithm based on differential privacy protection. *The Journal of Supercomputing*, 76(7), 5161–5174. DOI: 10.1007/s11227-019-02751-7

Yoo, K., Welden, R., Hewett, K., & Haenlein, M. (2023). The merchants of meta: A research agenda to understand the future of retailing in the metaverse. *Journal of Retailing*, 99(2), 173–192. DOI: 10.1016/j.jretai.2023.02.002

Yu, X. L., Cheng, X. X., Kim, K. H., & Wang, H. Z. (2024). Exploring the brand experience in the metaverse under the perspective of technology acceptance model. *Asia Pacific Journal of Marketing and Logistics*, 36(12), 3410–3426. Advance online publication. DOI: 10.1108/APJML-10-2023-0952

Zablah, A. R., & Bell, S. J. (2022). Consumer loyalty and AI-based personalization: The role of brand trust. *Journal of Marketing Theory and Practice*, 30(2), 202–218.

Zahay, D., & Griffin, A. (2004). Customer learning processes, strategy selection, and performance in business- to- business service firms. *Decision Sciences*, 35(2), 169–203. DOI: 10.1111/j.00117315.2004.02338.x

Zalpuri, M., & Hamlin, A. M. (2020). Building and leading successful cross-functional teams. In *ACS Symposium Series* (Vol. 1367, pp. 07-15). American Chemical Society. DOI: 10.1021/bk-2020-1367.ch002

Zaman, M., Hasan, R., Vo-Thanh, T., Shams, R., Rahman, M., & Jasim, K. M. (2024). Adopting the metaverse in the luxury hotel business: A cost-benefit perspective. *International Journal of Contemporary Hospitality Management*. Advance online publication. DOI: 10.1108/IJCHM-08-2023-1265

Zare, M., & Mahmoudi, R. (2021). CUSTOMER EXPERIENCE: BRANDING WITH EMOTIONAL TEXT MINING. *Journal of Management Information and Decision Sciences*, 24(1), 1–6. https://sdbindex.com/documents/00000161/00000-83428.pdf

Zha, D., Melewar, T. C., Foroudi, P., & Jin, Z. (2020). An assessment of brand experience knowledge literature: Using bibliometric data to identify future research direction. *International Journal of Management Reviews*, 22(3), 287–317. DOI: 10.1111/ijmr.12226

Zhang, Z. (2023). Consumer behavior prediction and marketing strategy optimization based on big data analysis. *Applied Mathematics and Nonlinear Sciences*, 9(1). Advance online publication. DOI: 10.1142/13173

Zhao, K., & Wu, Y. (2019). Consumer attitudes toward artificial intelligence: A cross-cultural study. *Journal of Global Marketing*, 32(5), 331–346.

Zhao, S., Wu, R., Tao, J., Qu, M., Zhao, M., Fan, C., & Zhao, H. (2023). perCLTV: A general system for personalized customer lifetime value prediction in online games. *ACM Transactions on Information Systems*, 41(1), 1–29. DOI: 10.1145/3530012

Zheng, L., Huang, B., Qiu, H., & Bai, H. (2024). The role of social media followers' agency in influencer marketing: A study based on the heuristic–systematic model of information processing. *International Journal of Advertising*, 43(3), 554–579. DOI: 10.1080/02650487.2023.2229148

Zhou, B., & Zou, T. (2023). Competing for recommendations: The strategic impact of personalized product recommendations in online marketplaces. *Marketing Science*, 42(2), 360–376. DOI: 10.1287/mksc.2022.1388

Zhuang, W., Luo, X., & Riaz, M. U. (2021). On the factors influencing green purchase intention: A meta-analysis approach. *Frontiers in Psychology*, 12, 644020. DOI: 10.3389/fpsyg.2021.644020 PMID: 33897545

Zhu, C. S., Io, M. U., Hall, C. M., Ngan, H. F. B., & Peralta, R. L. (2024). How to use augmented reality to promote a destination? The mediating role of augmented reality attachment. *International Journal of Tourism Research*, 26(1), e2603. Advance online publication. DOI: 10.1002/jtr.2603

Zhu, Y., & Wang, T. (2019). The effect of AI on customer satisfaction in e-commerce: A systematic review. *Journal of Retailing and Consumer Services*, 51, 51–64.

Zuo, M., Liu, H., Zhu, H., & Gao, H. (2019). Dynamic property of consumer-based brand competitiveness (CBBC) in human interaction behavior. *Industrial Management & Data Systems*, 119(6), 1223–1241. DOI: 10.1108/IMDS-09-2018-0403

Козак, К., Корсікова, Н., Морщавка, А., Шиленко, І., & Деревянко, О. (2023). МІСЦЕ ТЕХНОЛОГІЙ КАДРОВОГО МЕНЕДЖМЕНТУ В СИСТЕМІ АНТИКРИЗОВОГО УПРАВЛІННЯ ПІДПРИЄМСТВА THE ROLE OF HUMAN RESOURCE MANAGEMENT TECHNOLOGIES IN THE ENTERPRISE ANTI-CRISIS MANAGEMENT SYSTEM. *Technology*, 8(4), 93–98.

About the Contributors

Zahid Hussain currently in his postgraduate degree in Marketing from Khadim Hussain Shah Institute of Technology, Karachi, Pakistan (KASBIT). He has done several research publications, conference papers and book chapters related Marketing, Food Marketing, Metaverse Marketing, Customer Satisfaction and Artificial Intelligence in Marketing related fields in different impact factor journals at national and international level.

Mohamad-Noor Salehhudin Sharipudin is a Senior Lecturer at the Department of Communication, Faculty of Modern Languages and Communication, Universiti Putra Malaysia, Malaysia. He holds a PhD in Marketing from Victoria University of Wellington. His research interests include Marketing communication, sponsorship, generational marketing, non-profit marketing, marketing communication, consumer behavior, consumer culture and digital technology (e-WOM, Web 2.0, Immersive technology etc.). His research publications have appeared in Journal of Retailing and Consumer Services, Journal of Product and Brand Management, Journal of Hospitality and Tourism Research, Acta Polytechnica Hungaric, SEARCH: Journal of Media and Communication Research, Asian Journal of Business Research, Malaysian Journal of Communication, among others. He serves in the editorial board of scholarly journals. Dr Sharipudin has industry experience in banking and corporate branding before turning to academia.

Ahmad Albattat is an Associate Professor and Program Leader in School of Global Hospitality and Tourism, Asia Pacific University of Technology and Innovation, Kuala Lumpur, Malaysia. He is a Visiting Professor and External Examiner in Medan Academy of Tourism (Akpar Medan). He is a Doctoral Supervisor in European Global Institute of Innovation & Technology, Malta, and Rushford Business School, Switzerland. He received PhD in Hospitality Management "Disaster and Emergency Planning and Preparedness" from University Sains Malaysia (USM), Malaysia. He worked as an Associate Professor in Graduate

School of Management, Post Graduate Centre, Management and Science University, Shah Alam, Selangor, Malaysia. Assistant Professor, Ammon Applied University College, Amman, Jordan. Senior Lecturer and Research Coordinator in School of Hospitality & Creative Arts, Management and Science University, Shah Alam, Selangor, Malaysia, and Researcher at Sustainable Tourism Research Cluster (STRC), Pulau Pinang, Malaysia. He was working for the Jordanian hospitality industry for 17 years. His teaching and consultancy fields include hospitality management, events management, research methodology, strategic management and final research projects. His research areas include hospitality management, hotel, tourism, events, emergency planning, disaster management, sustainable development goals and human resource. He is an active member of several Scientific and Editorial Board of International journals, reviewer, author and editor for book projects with Emeralds, Routledge, and IGI Global. His latest works have been published in the refereed international journals, conference proceedings, books and book chapters.

Arman Khan an Assistant Professor affiliated with the "Department of Business Administration, at Shaheed Benazir Bhutto University, Nawabshah, Pakistan. His area of expertise lies in Artificial intelligence Marketing, Neuro-marketing, Digital marketing, and Customer behaviour. He is an active member of the scientific and editorial review board, this research has been presented and published in several international conferences, refereed journals, and research projects worldwide.

***

Mohamed Badouch is a PhD student in computer science at Faculty of Sciences, Ibn Zohr University, Agadir, Morocco. He received the master degree in information systems engineering from Cadi Ayyad University in 2017. His main research is in the areas of artificial intelligence, and machine learning.

Belem Barbosa received her PhD in Business and Management Studies – Specialisation in Marketing and Strategy from the University of Porto, Portugal. She is Assistant Professor at the School of Economics and Management of the University of Porto. She is full researcher at cef.up Center for Economics and Finance at the University of Porto. Her research interests lie primarily in the areas of digital marketing and consumer behavior.

Nitesh Behare is an accomplished author with a wealth of knowledge and 15 years of experience in the academic field. He currently holds the position of Associate Professor at the Balaji Institute of International Business (BIIB), Sri Balaji University Pune (SBUP). Throughout his career, Dr. Behare has made significant contributions to the academic world through the publication of numerous research papers and book chapters, establishing himself as a recognized authority in his field.

Supriya Bhagat is Ph.D. in Human Resource Management and has done her Graduation in Biotechnology; she is SET in Management and completed Masters in Human Resource Management from Savitribai Phule Pune University and PGDIMM from IGNOU .She has 10 years of academics and 1.5 years of Industry experience where she has worked as anHR & Admin executive. She has also assisted a couple of startups in framing their HR policies andfunctions.Dr. Supriya has published papers in various reputed and UGC indexed journals, ABDC and Scopus indexed journals. She has presented 20+ research papers at National and International conferences and FDP. She has also got a couple of appointments from Savitribai Phule Pune University for University exam related work.Dr. Supriya Bhagat has conducted various sessions on Personality Development, Soft Skill and Emerging concepts & trends in Human Resource Management for Undergraduate and Post graduate students from Management.Currently she is working with MIT ADT University as an Assistant Professor and has taught subjectslike Organizational Behavior, Human Resource Management, Employment Relations, and Soft Skills, personal selling, consumer behaviour, Principles of Marketing and Talent Management.

J.Bhargav,completed M.Tech in Compurt Science and Engineering. working as CSIT-HOD in Chalapathi Institute of engineering and Technology Lam,Guntur,andrapradesh,India.i am having almost 12 years of teaching experiences in different engineering colleges and an associate member of CSI and Life member of ISTE.published more then 12 international journals in different areas . i have published two books.

Gnanaprakasam D Completed graduation in M.E, Applied Electronics during May 2013. Working as Assistant Professor at Dr.Mahalingam College Of Engineering And Technology,Pollachi from June 2013.

Patrícia Dias is an associate professor at Universidade Católica Portuguesa. Her research interests focus on the use of digital media by children, and within organizational communication, marketing, and branding. As a researcher at the Research Centre for Communication and Culture and Católica Research Centre for Psychological, Family and Social Wellbeing, Dr Dias coordinates a project investigating the use of touchscreen devices by children up to the age of three; she also leads the Portuguese team for the Joint Research Centre–European Commission's investigation into the use of digital technologies by children and teenagers during the COVID-19 pandemic in Europe. She is the author of multiple publications on the use of smartphones and the social impact of digital media.

Alexandre Duarte, PhD in Communication Sciences (specialization in Organizational and Strategic communications) by the University of Minho, is a Professor at Universidade Nova de Lisboa, a researcher at ICNOVA/UNL, and an Invited Professor at the Catholic University of Portugal, where coordinates the Postgraduate Courses in Communication and Advertising Creativity, and Service Design. Having worked in several multinational advertising agencies for more than 20 years as a Senior Creative Copywriter, he was a Tutor of the Young Marketers Academy of the EUROBEST Festival, CEO of RESTART – Institute of Arts and Creativity, and advisor to SUPERBRANDS Portugal. Since 2021, is a member of the Research Committee of EDCOM - European Institute for Commercial Communications Education, and from 2024, assumed the Coordination of the Advertising Working Group of the Portuguese Association of Communication Sciences - SOPCOM.

Tareq Nael Hashem is a Full Professor of Marketing at Applied Science Private University, Amman, Jordan and holds PH.D. from Amman Arab University, Jordan. He is Permanent Member Senior Consultant For Development programs(EABAFF) in European Arab Business Fellowship Foundations.(2007-up to now), Member in EMBRI/EMAB &Emerald (EMAB Associate Fellow- AF-EMAB),Membership in American Association of International Researchers (AAIR),Member of European Marketing Academy (EMAC),Member in European Institute for Advanced Studies in Management (EIASM),Member in International Corporate and Marketing Communication Association (ICMCA),Member in European Retail Academy and Member of IGI Global Editorial Advisory Review Board

Rashid Hashmi is a seasoned senior journalist with a rich and diverse experience spanning over 22 years in Broadcast, Digital, and Print Media. Prior to joining Sharda University, he held the position of Executive Editor and Senior Anchor at the renowned national news channel, 'India News'. Throughout his illustrious journalistic career, Rashid Hashmi has served in various capacities across prominent media platforms including Dainik Jagran Newspaper, ETV, Total TV, FM News, and India News. His expertise encompasses anchoring, debating, and ground zero reporting of numerous parliamentary and assembly elections, providing insightful coverage of pivotal political events. Rashid Hashmi is renowned for his engaging interviews with prominent personalities from the worlds of politics, sports, and Bollywood. His interviews have featured distinguished celebrities, political leaders, and sports icons, offering unique perspectives and valuable insights to viewers and readers alike. With a keen eye for detail and a commitment to journalistic integrity, Rashid Hashmi has earned widespread acclaim for his contribution to media discourse in India. His dynamic approach to storytelling and extensive experience across multiple media formats underline his versatility and depth as a journalist. Rashid Hashmi's tenure in the media industry reflects a dedication to delivering compelling and informative content while upholding the values of responsible journalism. His role in shaping public discourse through impactful reporting and incisive interviews underscores his standing as a respected figure in Indian journalism.

Sujay Jayadeva, M.J. Ph.D, MBA(HRM), UGC NET (Management), and B.E (Computer science) currently working as Assistant Professor in the Dept. of Health System Management Studies (Faculty of Management Studies) at JSS Academy of Higher Education & Research, Mysuru. and have corporate experience of 06 years and more than 14 years of Teaching experience in Management field (both UG & PG).

Anuj Kumar works as Head of Research and Associate Professor, at Rushford Business School, Switzerland. His significant thrust areas are marketing, international business, and general management. He has completed an M.Sc. in International Business from University College Dublin, Michael Smurfit Graduate Business School, Ireland (Ranked among the top 200 colleges of the world – QS World ranking). He is pursuing an Executive-Ph. D in Management from Aligarh Muslim University (Central University). He has published research papers in reputed SCOPUS/Web of Science/SCI/ABDC/UGC Care Journals. Prof. Kumar has over seventy publications (Scopus- 40, ABDC- 23, Web of Science- 20, SCI-3). He also has three e-books and five book chapters to his credit (two are Scopus-indexed). He has published several cases in Emerald Emerging Case Studies (Scopus), International Social Science Journal (ABDC-B and Scopus), Small Enterprise Research (Scopus and Web of Science), Case Centre-UK, and other reputed Scopus, ABDC, and Web of Science journals. He has three internationally granted patents by South Africa and one patent granted by the Indian Government.

T.C. Manjunath is a distinguished academician and researcher serving as a Professor in the Department of Computer Science & Engineering at Rajarajeswari College of Engineering, Bangalore. He is an expert in areas like IoT Cybersecurity and Blockchain Technology. In addition to his teaching role, Dr. Manjunath is the Dean of Research & Development at the institution. His contributions in the field of technology and engineering have earned him recognition in both academic and industry circles. Located on Mysore Road, Ramohalli Cross, Kumbalgodu Post, Bangalore, Dr. Manjunath is an influential figure in the academic community, driving innovations in cutting-edge technologies.

Utsav Krishan Murari is a gifted writer, dedicated life coach, motivational speaker, passionate educator, and, above all, an exceptional mentor. He holds a doctorate in communication and media studies from the Central University of South Bihar. Graced with a vivid imagination, he is a genuine catalyst for ideas and is always open to trying new things. His one such initiative is Saarthi, which began as Saarthi Entertainment. Saarthi is a Delhi-based creative media production start-up that wants to leave a legacy of artistry in the production industry. Delivering content with a strong emotional connection and the potential to transform the world is what Team Saarthi is all about.

P. Selvakumar is currently an Associate Professor in the Department of Science and Humanities at Nehru Institute of Technology, Coimbatore, Tamil Nadu, India. Since 2023, he has served as the Department IQAC Coordinator at the institute. Prior to joining Nehru Institute of Technology, he held positions as an Assistant Professor in the Department of Science and Humanities various engineering colleges in Coimbatore, Tamil Nadu, India, spanning from 2011 to 2023. Dr.P. Selvakumar's academic and research interests lie primarily in the field of phytochemistry. He has made significant contributions to his field, with an impressive record that includes 30 journal publications, 12 patents, and 20 conference papers. Additionally, he has organized 5 seminars and conferences, further demonstrating his commitment to academic and scientific exchange. Throughout his career, Dr. P.Selvakumar has been recognized for his dedication and excellence in teaching, having been honored with several awards, including the Best Teacher Awards. He holds a prominent position in the academic community, contributing actively to research.

Hemlata Parmar, a luminary in the field of computer Science and Engineering. Her Journey is defined by a constellation of achievements from prolific publications and patents to enlightening guest lectures. Yet, her brilliance is matched only by her unwavering commitment to human ethics. With a heart as vast as her intellect, she champions women's empowerment, bridging the gap with empathy and insight. In every endeavor, she embodies the perfect fusion of academic process and compassionate advocacy, inspiring generations to come.

Célia M. Q. Ramos holds a PhD in Quantitative Methods Applied to Economics and Management from Faculty of Economics, University of Algarve, obtained her Master in Electrical and Computers Engineering from the Higher Technical Institute, Lisbon University, and is graduated in Computer Engineering from the University of Coimbra, Portugal. She is Coordinator Professor with Habilitation at School for Management, Hospitality and Tourism, also in the UALG, where she lectures mainly Information Systems. Current research interests includes, information systems, data analytics, electronic tourism, business intelligence, digital marketing, panel data models. Has published in the fields of information systems, marketing and tourism,

She is reviewer of several scientific journals. At the level of applied research, she has participated in several funded projects. Researcher at the Centre for Tourism, Sustainability and Well-being (CinTurs). Email: cmramos@ualg.pt. ORCID ID: 0000-0002-3413-4897

S.K. Manikandan, Working as Professor in the Department of Biomedical Engineering from Velalar College of Engineering and Technology, Erode, Tamilnadu. He has Completed his UG Degree in Electronics and Communication Engineering in Periyar University in the year 2003 and Obtained his Master of Technology in Embedded Systems at SASTRA University, Tanjore in the Year 2006. He has completed his Doctor of Philosophy in the year 2017 under Anna University. His Ph.D thesis was highly commented by both Indian and Foreign examiners. His research was Design a High Speed Vedic Multiplier for various applications. He has received 2 patents, one Indian patent another one Australian Patent, Published 15 papers in various International Journals and 13 papers in various International conferences, He has 3 copyrights and authored a book tiled as "Cryptography and Network Security".

Praful D. Sarangdhar is working as an Assistant Professor at MM's Institute of Management Education, Research and Training (IMERT). He has more than 14 years experience in Teaching and 4 years in Sales and Marketing Industry. His area of research is online buying behavior, e-commerce portals. Has publication in 3 Scopus/ International research journals and 8 National Journals. He has also worked with Indira Global Business School Pune and Indira Institute of Career Studies as an lecturer. Elite Certification by NPTEL for course in Integrated Marketing Communication. Completed several online courses through Coursera.

Amrik Singh is working as Professor in the School of Hotel Management and Tourism at Lovely Professional University, Punjab, India. He obtained his Ph.D. degree in Hotel Management from Kurukshetra University, Kurukshetra. He started his academic career at Lovely Professional University, Punjab, India in the year 2007. He has published more than 40 research papers in UGC and peer-reviewed and Scopus/Web of Science) journals. He has published 12 patents and 01 patent has been granted in the inter-disciplinary domain. Dr. Amrik Singh participated and acted as a resource person in various national and international conferences, seminars, research workshops, and industry talks. His area of research interest is accommodation management, ergonomics, green practices, human resource management in hospitality, waste management, AR VR in hospitality, etc. He is currently guiding 8Ph.D. scholars and 2 Ph.D. scholars have been awarded Ph.D.

P.S. Venkateswaran is currently working as a Professor in the Department of Management Studies, PSNA College of Engineering & Technology, Dindigul affiliated to Anna University, Chennai where he teaches courses in Advertising, marketing and Research Methods. He has served in various faculty positions from Assistant Professor to Professor in leading Arts & Colleges such as Cherran Arts and Science College, Kangeyam and Sree Saraswathi Thyagaraja College, Pollachi. He received MSc in Physics, an M.B.A., from Bharathiar University and MPhil from Alagappa University Karaikudi. He received his Ph.D in Business Administration from Madurai Kamaraj University, Madurai. He is having twenty two years of teaching and nine years of research & consultancy experience. His research activities include on Branding, Advertising and Digital marketing He conducted more than 90 Entrepreneurship Awareness Camps and trained around 8000 Engineering, Arts and Science College students and motivated them towards entrepreneurship. He also conducted 10 Faculty Development programmes, 10 EDP/WEDP programmes and 7 TEDP programmes. He trained more the 200 women entrepreneurs in Dindigul District.

Index

A

B

C

D

E

N

O

P

R

S

T

U

W

www.ingramcontent.com/pod-product-compliance
Lightning Source LLC
LaVergne TN
LVHW080355011026
849161LV00009B/2311